GOVERNMENT
FINANCE

GOVERNMENT FINANCE
National, State, and Local

Wayland D. Gardner

Western Michigan University

Prentice-Hall, Inc., Englewood Cliffs, New Jersey 07632

Library of Congress Cataloging in Publication Data

GARDNER, WAYLAND DOWNING (DATE)
Government finance.

Includes bibliographies and index.
1. Finance, Public—United States. 2. Finance,
Public—United States. 3. Local finance—
United States. I. Title.
HJ257.2.G37   336.73   77-3572
ISBN 0-13-360743-7

Printed in the United States of America

10   9   8   7   6   5   4   3   2   1

Prentice-Hall International, Inc., *London*
Prentice-Hall of Australia Pty. Limited, *Sydney*
Prentice-Hall of Canada, Ltd., *Toronto*
Prentice-Hall of India Private Limited, *New Delhi*
Prentice-Hall of Japan, Inc., *Tokyo*
Prentice-Hall of Southeast Asia Pte. Ltd., *Singapore*
Whitehall Books Limited, *Wellington, New Zealand*

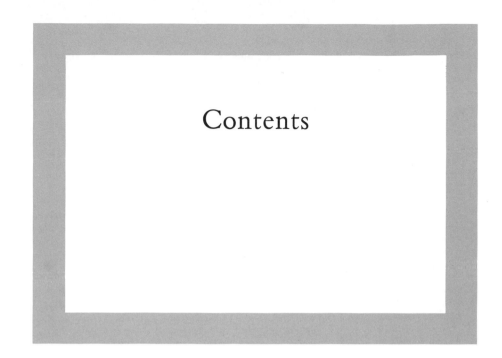

Contents

Chapter 2

Collective Goods and Services / 14

PRIVATE AND COLLECTIVE CONSUMPTION. Private Consumption. Collective Consumption. Efficient Allocation. Measuring Demand. PURE AND NONPURE COLLECTIVE GOODS. Joint Products and the Marginal Rule. EXTERNALITIES. APPLYING THE MODEL TO A POLICY QUESTION. SUMMARY. SUGGESTED READINGS.

Chapter 3

Revenue Systems and Voting / 26

DIFFERENTIAL BENEFITS AND DIFFERENTIAL TAXES. The Wicksellian Decision Procedure. DECISION CRITERIA AND VOTING. Costs of Decision Making. Analysis of Voting Results. Efficiency and Equity. THE GENERAL REVENUE SYSTEM. The Constitutional Nature of the General Revenue System. Amending the Fiscal Constitution. VOTE TRADING. Three Voters and Two Issues. Increasing the Number of Voters. Increasing the Number of Issues. Changing Tax Shares. Other Variables. SUMMARY. SUGGESTED READINGS.

Chapter 4

Ability to Pay / 47

INCOME DISTRIBUTION AND COLLECTIVE DEMAND. EQUITY AND FAIRNESS. The Equity Principle. Measuring Ability: The Tax Base. Vertical Equity: Tax Rates. MODELS FOR VERTICAL EQUITY. The Sacrifice Approach. Sacrifice Models. Critique of the Sacrifice Approach. REDISTRIBUTION AS A COLLECTIVE GOOD. SUMMARY. SUGGESTED READINGS.

Part II

The National Government / 59

Chapter 5

The Budget of the National Government / 61

THE BUDGET REQUEST STAGE. The Budget Document. The Planning Programming Budget System (PPBS). THE CONGRESSIONAL ACTION STAGE. The

FISCAL APPROACH TO STABILIZATION. The Taxation Multiplier. The Balanced Budget Multiplier. A MONETARY APPROACH TO STABILIZATION. The Linkage of Money and Aggregate Demand. The Monetary Approach and Budget Imbalances. Coordinating Fiscal and Monetary Approaches. STABILIZATION POLICY. The Unemployment-Inflation Dilemma. The Phillips Curve. Shifting the Phillips Curve. Cost-Push Inflation. Price Controls and Incomes Policy. SUMMARY. SUGGESTED READINGS.

Part III

State Governments / 271

Chapter 20

State Individual Income Taxes / 316

PROS AND CONS OF STATE INCOME TAXATION. Merit Considerations. Revenue Considerations. Coexistance with the Federal Income Tax. CHARACTERISTICS OF STATE INCOME TAXES. Jurisdiction. Deductability of Federal Income Tax. Property and Sales Tax Credits. INCREASED UTILIZATION OF INCOME TAXATION. SUMMARY. SUGGESTED READINGS.

Chapter 21

State Inheritance, Estate, and Gift Taxes / 326

ESTATE AND INHERITANCE TAXES. FEDERAL CREDIT FOR STATE DEATH TRANSFER TAXES. The Pickup Tax. PROBLEMS AND PROPOSALS. SUMMARY. SUGGESTED READINGS.

Chapter 22

State Corporation Income Taxation / 332

ALLOCATING INTERSTATE INCOME. Overapportionment. Origin of Production Formula. ENFORCEMENT AND COMPLIANCE. INTERSTATE COMPETITION. SUMMARY. SUGGESTED READINGS.

Chapter 23

Financing Highways / 337

USER AND NONUSER FINANCING. The Nonuser Share. Nonuser Payments for Specific Roads. PRICING SERVICES TO HIGHWAY USERS. Toll Roads. The Motor Fuel Tax. THE COSTS OF HIGHWAY SERVICES. Allocating Basic Costs. Incremental Costs: Size, Weight. Incremental Costs: Peak Load Users. DIVERSIONS OF HIGHWAY USER FUNDS. Paying All the Costs. Highway Congestion and Rationing. Highway User Funds for Mass Transit. SUMMARY. SUGGESTED READINGS.

Part IV

Local Governments / 351

Preface

This is a text on the economics of government finance designed for under-graduate courses that include not only students majoring or minoring in eco-nomics, but also students specializing in other areas, such as political science, public administration, and business. Many introductory government finance courses enroll students with diverse backgrounds and interests because the sub-ject has applications in many areas. Government finance is interesting to stu-dents of economics because many economic concepts and principles yield important insights about government decisions and about the consequences of these decisions on the private sector of the economy. Government finance is interesting to students of political science because it lies in an overlap zone between these two disciplines. The economist's perspective can be useful to the political scientist, just as the political scientist's perspective can be useful to the economist. The rapidly growing field of public administration, which has be-come a profession in its own right, encourages many students to study the economics of government finance because this knowledge is helpful in fulfilling the responsibilities of the public administrator. Students of business are inter-ested because government expenditures support a significant portion of the total demand for goods and services, because taxes claim a significant share of the earnings of corporations and individuals, and because government-guided stabilization programs have an important impact on the level of economic activity, prices, and unemployment.

Both the content and the organization of this book are designed for stu-dents with diverse backgrounds and interests. Since this is a book on the *eco-nomics* of government finance, those who use it should have completed basic courses in the principles of economics, but the content does not presume training beyond that ordinarily acquired in the basic course. The book is organized somewhat differently than most other books on government finance. After Part I, which presents basic concepts about the responsibilities of government, collective consumption, social choice, benefits-received taxation, and ability to pay, the subject matter is arranged according to levels of government rather than economic concepts or principles. Part II examines the national government, Part III deals with state governments, and Part IV considers local governments.

There are two reasons for arranging the subject matter this way. First, from a pedagogical point of view, there is an advantage in organizing the presentation in a format already familiar to beginning students. This is particularly helpful in connection with the economics of state and local government finance, since a separate treatment of these levels of government permits students to draw upon the identifications they have with their own state and local governments. This arrangement is also helpful to public administration and political science students, who are likely to be aiming at careers in state or local government. The second reason for organizing the subject by level of government is to reflect the idea that a federal system recognizes distinctive characteristics, opportunities, and responsibilities at different levels of government. Economic reasoning suggests that a federal or multilevel system of governments can respond more precisely to the desires of citizens and can offer more options than a single, unitary government. Separate treatment of each level of government underlines the idea of federalism in government finance.

The development of this book has extended over several years and many classroom experiences with the subject. I owe an expression of gratitude and appreciation to the many students who put up with photocopied developmental versions of most of the chapters and who, both knowingly and unknowingly, provided many suggestions for improvement. It is a pleasure to have an opportunity to thank Professor Stewart Nelson, of Doane College, who started me in economics, and the late Professor Harold Groves, of the University of Wisconsin, whose teaching excellence and interest in state and local government provide continuing inspiration. I am also indebted to Susan Anderson, Bob Hall, and Paul McKenney of Prentice-Hall for their encouragement in the enormous task of writing and preparing the manuscript for publication and to the several anonymous reviewers of earlier versions who provided valuable suggestions. Their suggestions led to many improvements in both content and organization. The errors that remain, of course, are my own responsibility. Very special appreciation is due my wife, Suzanne, who typed and retyped many sections of the manuscript, who called my attention to statements and presentations that were unclear or confusing, and who, along with our children, Janet, Elaine, Edward, and James, endured the consequences of a husband and father preoccupied with book writing.

WAYLAND D. GARDNER

Kalamazoo, Michigan

A Note
to the Instructor

Courses that focus specifically on state and local government finance may skip Part II (The National Government) and go directly from Chapter 4 (or even from Chapter 3) to Chapter 17. Chapter 17, which presents an economic model for fiscal federalism and multilevel governments, is an especially important chapter and provides an introduction to the economics of state and local government finance.

The suggested readings listed at the end of each chapter can be used for library assignments and for written student reports. Only a few of these readings will be too technical for beginning students in public finance. A library search at the start of the course for more recent issues of public finance periodicals (such as the *National Tax Journal*, *Public Finance*, and *Public Finance Quarterly*) can keep the reading list up to date and stimulate student interest in the subject.

Statistical data presented in this book have been selected from sources which are readily available in college libraries. Therefore, it is relatively easy to keep this information up to date. At the start of the course, the instructor may wish to obtain a copy of the most recent issue of *The Economic Report of the President* and the Census Bureau publications *Governmental Finances* and *State Tax Collections*.

GOVERNMENT
FINANCE

I

Collective Services
and
Taxation

Governments are expected to fulfill certain economic responsibilities. The general nature of these responsibilities is outlined in Chapters 1 and 2. In a democratic political system, the responsibilities of government are determined by the citizenry as they express themselves through the political process. Chapter 3 explores how the voting process and the institutional arrangements for taxation and expenditures operate to guide the government in meeting its responsibilities. The analysis reveals that the tax system is an important link in the process through which citizens communicate with government and transmit their instructions about what government is expected to do. Government is expected to treat citizens in a fair and equitable manner, and this includes a responsibility to recognize and perhaps alter the distribution of income in the society. Chapter 4 discusses how the ability to pay philosophy of taxation incorporates these responsibilities for fairness, equity, and income distribution.

I

Economic Responsibilities of Government

In undertaking a study of government finance, it is helpful to begin by attempting to define the subject, that is, to identify those activities or responsibilities which belong to government. One way of doing this is to use the *positive* approach, which accepts the fact that governments exist and undertakes to identify the activities governments actually attempt to carry out. It attempts to explain why governments do what they do and tries to develop models that help in predicting how governments will respond to different events and various circumstances. The positive approach calls for a mingling of economics, anthropology, politics, history, sociology, business, and many other sciences. The descriptive and predictive models are complicated, because the real world itself is complicated. Thus far, efforts to develop positive models of government have met with very little success. Voter profile analyses and public opinion polls can be used to make some predictions in democratic societies, but their results must be expressed in general terms and allow for a wide margin of error. In totalitarian systems, analysts can explore the personalities of leaders and predict how they may respond to circumstances, but these models also are far from satisfactory as comprehensive pictures of government responsibilities. The fact is there does not now exist a positive theory of government that is comprehensive enough and simple enough to provide the basis for an introductory study of government finance.

The second approach to a definition of the role of government is a *normative* one. It begins with some idea or image of how the activities of a society ought to be structured and organized and then develops a picture of the activities governments should carry out in this ideal or preferred set of circumstances.

3

The normative approach is the one used in most undergraduate textbooks on government finance, and it is the approach used in this book. For example, a guiding principle or value used in this book is that governments ought to be established on a democratic foundation and ought to pursue the objective of satisfying the wants of the individuals who are citizens or who reside under their jurisdiction. This approach has a strong individualistic flavor because it implies that individuals know what they want their government to do and that these individual judgments should be respected. Another value or guiding principle in the normative picture presented in this book is that an economic organization built around free markets and voluntary exchanges among individuals is a constructive and efficient way of satisfying individual wants. In fact, the model presumes that much of the economic activity of the society actually is carried out through the market system and that this system is functioning in a way which is generally satisfactory to most of the people in the society.

Starting with these values and assumptions, we may now proceed to outline a set of economic responsibilities. Three general responsibilities of government are recognized: (1) the responsibility to ensure a high level of utilization of the resources of the economy ("full employment") and a stable level of prices, (2) the responsibility to ensure that the distribution of income among the individuals who comprise the society is satisfactory or acceptable, and (3) the responsibility to ensure that the resources of the society are used efficiently for the satisfaction of the wants of the people in the society. These responsibilities are labeled, respectively, the *stabilization* function, the *distribution* function, and the *allocation* function. There are two steps in identifying and refining each of these basic government responsibilities. The first is the *market failure* step, which identifies a want which, for one reason or another, is not satisfied by the operation of the market system. The second is the *government instruments* step, which identifies instruments governments can use and procedures governments can follow that are capable of overcoming the market failure and satisfying the want. It is important to recognize that both steps are necessary in order to establish a government responsibility. Markets may fail to satisfy certain wants, but it does not necessarily follow that government can be equipped with the means for achieving satisfaction of these wants. For example, some government programs launched in the 1960s and early 1970s in connection with the "war on poverty," crime prevention, environmental quality, and the energy problem have not produced results satisfactory to many citizens or commensurate with the hopes and expectations that surrounded their inauguration. Simply throwing money at a problem does not appear to be an effective instrument for the correction of market failures. Better instruments, it seems, are needed, and it remains an open question in some cases whether, when and if discovered, they will be in the government's tool kit or in that of the market system.

THE STABILIZATION FUNCTION

The stabilization function relates to the maintenance of high levels of resource utilization and stable price levels. All persons actively seeking employment should be able to find positions, and the jobs held should match the talents and capabilities of the jobholders. Price stability means that the purchasing power of money should not change drastically over time. People should be able to hold wealth in forms involving fixed money denominations (such as bonds and insurance policies) without fear that the real value of these holdings will be eroded by inflation. There is little doubt that the objectives of full employment and price stability rank high for most people.

Reasons for Market Failure

The historical record provides considerable evidence that markets, operating without government stabilization efforts, sometimes fail to provide the degree of full employment and price stability desired by most people. The United States and most other developed economies built around the market system experienced business cycles of varying degrees of severity as industrialization proceeded and as exchange systems became more complicated. The Great Depression of the 1930s was an especially damaging episode in this long record of instability, for it was so severe as to threaten the collapse of the market system as a means of organizing economic activity.

The search for the causes of economic instability in market systems has gone on for hundreds of years and has generated a great volume of economic literature. Karl Marx found the cause to lie deep in the foundations of capitalism itself and predicted that business cycles and unemployment eventually would bring the downfall of that system. Other scholars have concluded that market systems experience instability because they are not sufficiently competitive and particularly because certain prices (such as interest rates) become so inflexible that the economy is not able to respond promptly to changes in conditions. Monopoly power vested in business or in labor or in both may refuse to permit prices or wages to fall when aggregate demand is less than aggregate supply and thus force the economy to accept conditions of unemployment. Conversely, economic power centers may increase wages and prices instead of increasing output when aggregate demand exceeds aggregate supply, thus forcing rising price levels on the economy.

Behind these explanations of unemployment and inflation lies the basic proposition that the aggregate levels of supply and demand will not be stable or maintain stable relationships with one another in market systems where decisions on output and expenditure are made by individuals each seeking his own self-interest and each responding to his own perceptions of what may lie ahead in the economy. Particular emphasis is placed on fluctuation in aggregate demand because individuals who are in possession of enough purchasing power to permit some discretion in the timing of their expenditures or who possess wealth which they can hold in various forms apparently do change their spending and wealth-holding behaviors from time to time. For example, if people, for some reason or other, lose confidence in the future prospects of the economy, they are likely to reduce current expenditures and purchases of investment securities and increase their holdings of cash. This increase in the desire for liquidity will shrink the flow of circulating money in the economy, reducing demand for goods and services and bringing unemployment.

The privately managed banking system will make this contraction even more severe by actually reducing the stock of money in the economy as notes and loans are retired and as poor economic conditions discourage the issuance of new bank money. The market economy enters a downward spiral of recession. The reverse situation arises when expectations about the future of the economy turn from pessimistic to optimistic. The desire to hold liquid cash balances will diminish, expenditures and security purchases will increase, and the banking system will add to the expansion of aggregate demand by increasing the money stock as the volume of new loans exceeds the volume of loan retirements. The expansion of economic activity can proceed, augmented by money supply increases and accelerator effects, until demand for goods and services can exceed output at current price levels and price levels are forced upward.

Markets fail to satisfy the demand for stable prices and consistently high levels of resource utilization because fluctuations do occur in economic expectations and in the demand for liquidity and because the market system's behavior in respect to the stock of money tends to exaggerate rather than moderate the impact of these fluctuations on the level of economic activity.

Government Stabilization Instruments

The classic work of John M. Keynes, *The General Theory of Employment Interest and Money*, which appeared in 1936, provided an analysis of the causes of instability in employment and prices and suggested that governments have the ability to correct or prevent these fluctuations. The modern study of macroeconomics has grown out of the work of Keynes, and the stabilization activity of government is an application of the principles developed through these studies. The basic idea is that effective demand is the chief regulator of aggregate economic activity in advanced economies and that prices and/or employment will adjust to match whatever level of aggregate demand exists.

The initial step in implementing government responsibility for stabilization is to determine the level of aggregate demand that will support the desired level of employment and price stability. If the size of the labor force is known and if the output per man-hour can be determined (incorporating the technology and capital expected to be available for the time period in question), estimates can be made about the level of aggregate demand required. The target level of demand can then be compared with the level of demand that would prevail in the absence of government intervention in order to determine whether the market would, if left to its own functioning, experience an excess or a deficiency of demand. If the expected level of demand exceeds the capacity of the economy (measured at current price levels), price inflation is forecast, that is, the expectation is that prices will be forced upward through competition among buyers. On the other hand, if the anticipated level of demand falls short of the capacity of the economy to produce, unemployment and/or falling prices are expected. Once these forecasts have been made, the stabilization responsibility requires that government take steps to increase aggregate demand if the economy is headed toward recession or to reduce aggregate demand or increase aggregate supply if the economy is headed toward inflation.

Two basic instruments available to government in carrying out the stabilization responsibility are (1) the ability to increase or decrease the stock of money, which can increase or decrease aggregate demand and influence the rate of interest; and (2) the ability to influence spending, saving, investment, and output decisions in the economy through alterations in the composition of the government expenditures budget or in the tax system, which enter into the decision processes of producers and consumers throughout the economy. The national government also has the ability to influence trading relationships with other nations through controls imposed directly on trade (tariffs, quotas, etc.) or through actions relating to the official exchange rate of the nation's currency in comparison with the currencies of other nations.

In the United States, the institutional arrangements for carrying out stabilization responsibilities are well established at the national government level. The Council of Economic Advisors makes forecasts of expected levels of aggregate supply and demand and recommends stabilization policy alternatives to the President. The budget recommended by the President and the actual spending and taxing measures adopted by Congress incorporate stabilization policy provisions both in the specific provisions of these enactments and in the surplus or deficit dimension of the total budget. Day to day responsibility for control of the stock of money in the economy is lodged with the Board of Governors of the Federal Reserve System (the central bank), which has the authority to regulate the money-creating activity of the private banking system and which can effectively determine whether the deficits or surpluses in the government's budget will be financed through the creation or destruction of money or through exchanges of existing money between the government and the private sector of the economy. The interaction of these various agencies of the national government determines the nature and effectiveness of the government's stabilization efforts. Policy choices are difficult and coordination among the agencies responsible for the implementation of stabilization policies is not always fully realized, but there is no doubt that the national government does possess instruments which can be effective in moving toward the objectives of high-level employment and price stability.

This brief examination of the stabilization instruments of government suggests that the federal government is better suited to meeting this responsibility than are state and local governments, which do not possess the powers necessary for effective performance in this area. State and local governments do not have the authority to create or destroy money, which is a crucial dimension of stabilization activity, nor can these governments effectively control the private banking system. Moreover, states and localities are *open* economies; they have no authority to shut themselves off from other states by regulating the flow of commerce and finance across their boundaries. As open economies, states and localities are subject to the consequences of national economic instability and to the efforts of the national government to stabilize the national economy, but they have little power to implement stabilization policies.

THE DISTRIBUTION FUNCTION

A society may wish to establish some distribution of incomes among its members different from the one that arises through the market processes. Since the economic system presumably is made to serve people, and not the other way around, it seems clear that society should not be denied either the opportunity to alter the distribution of incomes if it chooses to do so or the utilization of the instruments of government for that purpose. Stated in its bare-bones simplicity, the objective of government in carrying out a distribution responsibility should be to establish the distribution of incomes desired by the people in the society.

Distribution objectives cannot be stated with the degree of confidence and precision possible in expressing stabilization objectives, since less of a popular consensus prevails regarding distribution. Certainly notions about equity and justice are one stream of values that enter into the determination of distributional objectives. There is an ethical dimension to the question of how much inequality is acceptable or tolerable. But there also is a political dimension to the distribution question, since the stability of the system and the character of the social order itself may be related to the degree of income inequality that prevails within it. To what extent do extremes of income inquality strain the fabric of society and create unrest and dissension that can damage the welfare of all? Finally, there is an economic dimension to the distribution question. The quantity of goods and services that will be produced from a given resource base is not unrelated to the kind of incentive system used to motivate resource owners to engage in productive activities, and the quest for income (and perhaps the quest for income greater than that enjoyed by others) apparently is an important element in the incentive system. Thus, there may be a connection between how the economic pie is divided and the size of the pie itself. A question arises about the extent to which the society may be willing to accept a perhaps smaller pie in exchange for a division of the pie that is ethically or politically more acceptable.

Reasons for Market Failure

Markets may fail in the sense that they may not yield the type of distribution desired by the society. This use of the term "failure" is somewhat awkward, since there is no scientific way to determine the "correct" distribution of incomes. The distribution generated by market processes may be quite acceptable ethically, politically, and economically. Nevertheless, several characteristics of the market system can be expected to generate a significant degree of inequality in the distribution of incomes among people, and it is quite apparent from the actions taken by democratic governments over the past century or more that the inequalities so generated exceed acceptable magnitudes.

Probably the outstanding market characteristic that results in significant income inequality is that markets reward participants according to their productivity—that is, according to their contribution to the satisfaction of the wants expressed by those who have enough purchasing power to influence the allocation of resources in the economy. The market system results in a kind of meritocracy in which merit (and income) is accorded those who are endowed with or who acquire the ability to be productive according to the specifications of the system. Except for private charity and philanthropy, the market system makes no provision for the support or even the survival of those who lack the required abilities to be productive. This indifference or relative insensitivity to the fate of those who are "unproductive" is a failure of the market that people may wish to correct through government intervention.

Some inequalities of income may arise in the market system through the presence of monopoly power or through the broader dimensions of unequal economic opportunity revealed in patterns of discrimination. Low income even may be regarded as a *cause* of low productivity and unequal opportunity rather than as an *effect* of the absence of these hallmarks of merit if private financial and educational institutions are unable to provide avenues of escape from the vicious circle of poverty, low productivity, and low income. Certainly monopoly and the unearned incomes associated with it are dimensions of the market system that can result in inequalities which violate ethical, political, and economic criteria for income distribution. These can reasonably be regarded as market failures which invite government intervention within the frame of reference of the distribution responsibility and which also may invite intervention in terms of the allocation responsibility.

Finally, the institution of private property, which is regarded as a basic characteristic of market systems, may set in motion a stream of events that can produce a degree of income inequality not tolerable to the society. Market systems recognize that capital is productive, and the allocation of capital resources among alternative production activities is accomplished through the payment of interest to the private owners of those resources. Thus, those members of the society who find themselves possessed of wealth (either through their own saving efforts or through inheritance) enjoy a source of income not available to those who do not possess equivalent wealth. This extra stream of income, in turn, provides the opportunity to acquire further accumulations of wealth and a still greater stream of capital income. The long-term consequence of the private property system, especially when combined with the institution of inheritance, can be a progressive widening of the degree of inequality in the market system. Even if ethically and economically there is no objection to this progressively increasing inequality, political factors may call for some distribution adjustments.

Government Distribution Instruments

Once it has been determined that the public wishes to establish a distribution of incomes different from that arising through the market, certain government instruments or powers can be used to carry out this objective. Governments have the authority to compel individuals to engage in transactions in which they would not engage on a voluntary basis, and it is this power that enables government to take income or wealth from some individuals and to transfer it to others. In a pure or unadulterated exercise of the distribution responsibility, government would provide money transfers to those individuals whose wealth or income was to be increased and would obtain the funds to finance these transfers by imposing taxes on those whose wealth or income was to be diminished. Progressive income taxation based upon the ability to pay doctrine is a rather clear illustration of government implementation of a distributional responsibility. On the disbursements side of the budget, distributional objectives may be served either by the direct transfer of money or by the funding of expenditure programs designed to deliver benefits primarily to individuals who are to be aided by the distribution program. Nonfiscal instruments, such as minimum wage laws, may also be employed in the pursuit of distributional objectives, although these approaches often prove to be ineffective or actually perverse in terms of their expressed distributional goals.

Many of the traditional activities of state and local governments in the United States have been in the area of income redistribution, but with the increased mobility of persons, states and localities are experiencing great difficulty in sustaining redistributional efforts. If a given state or locality undertakes a more ambitious redistributional program than those carried out in other states, high-income persons will leave the state and low-income persons will move in. Those with high incomes leave in order to avoid being taxed to support the redistribution program and those with low incomes move in to participate in the benefits of the program. The result of these population movements is that the state undertaking the more ambitious program will find itself unable to finance it. Therefore, it is apparent that the primary responsibility for income distribution must rest with the national government and not with states and localities. Progressive taxation is associated with the national government rather than with state and local governments. Redistribution programs on the disbursement side of the budget may be carried out either directly by the national government or through grants to the states and localities. In these situations, the states and localities become the agents of the national government in promoting its distributional objectives.

Some of the consequences of income inequality manifest themselves most clearly at the state or local levels of government and generate demands that these governments "do something" in the area of income distribution. For example, low-quality housing and high crime rates may be associated with concentrations of low-income citizens in urban areas. These problems, which appear to call for changes in resource allocation, actually may be rooted in the distribution of income. State or local efforts to deal with them through allocating resources to housing or crime prevention may prove to be quite ineffective. Because local governments are not capable of carrying out substantial income redistribution programs, state and local officials find themselves facing demands they cannot satisfy.

THE ALLOCATION FUNCTION

The third major functional responsibility of government is to ensure that the resources of the society are used efficiently for the satisfaction of the wants of its members. This responsibility can readily be distinguished from the stabilization responsibility, which required only that the society's resources be fully employed, since allocation deals with the question of which specific goods and services ought to be provided through the employment of these resources. The root of the allocation question lies with the basic economic proposition that scarcity exists—that is, that wants exceed the means available to satisfy them, so that choices must be made about which wants will be satisfied and which wants must remain unsatisfied.

Reasons for Market Failure

Markets may fail to provide an efficient allocation of resources for a variety of reasons. Some of these inefficiencies arise from failure to ensure full employment or from failure to generate an acceptable distribution of income and therefore are not directly the concern of the allocation responsibility of government. For example, if income is improperly distributed, markets will produce an incorrect collection of goods and services, since these markets respond to the demands of consumers who have money to spend. Likewise, if unemployment prevails in the economy, resources are being allocated to involuntary idleness, which surely is an inefficient way to use them. But markets may fail to provide an efficient allocation of resources even if the correct distribution of income exists and even when full employment and price stability are secured. It is these failures that are the proper concern of the allocation responsibility.

One type of market failure, which is clearly in the resource allocation area, arises when imperfections exist in the functioning of the market system. Even in highly developed market systems, imperfections are likely to exist because of producers' and consumers' lack of information about alternative products and opportunities available to them. There may be limitations on the ability to move resources from one area of endeavor to another, or monopoly situations may send out distorted signals about relative costs of different goods and services. Economic theory indicates that, in each of these situations, some reallocation of resources could result in a more efficient satisfaction of wants.

A second type of market failure in the allocation of resources arises when the production or consumption of certain goods or services result in "external" effects that impose hardships on or deliver benefits to persons who do not have an effective voice in determining the quantity of such goods or services that will be produced. The presence of these external effects means that the supply and demand information used to determine prices and outputs in the market system will be incorrect—that is, markets will not accurately reflect benefits received or costs incurred in the provision of these goods. An inefficient allocation of resources will result.

Finally, markets may fail to provide an efficient supply of those goods and services consumed collectively or jointly by all members of the society. Since no person can be excluded from consuming these services once they have been produced, it will not be possible to charge a market price as a condition or prerequisite to consuming them and profit-motivated private producers will not be willing to use resources to produce them. The characteristics of these collectively consumed goods and services and the reasons why markets fail to provide them efficiently will be examined further in the next chapter.

Government Allocation Instruments

Governments possess several instruments that can influence the allocation of resources in the economy. The power to tax and the power to spend clearly are part of government's allocation tool kit, since expenditures can be used to increase the output of goods and services which otherwise would be underproduced and taxes can be used to discourage the production of goods and services which otherwise would be overproduced. These are the basic fiscal instruments of government and constitute the goods and services component of the budget. Government expenditures can be seen as subsidies for the production of certain goods and services just as taxes can be seen as penalties or additions to the cost of producing other goods and services. If the production or consumption of certain goods and services generate beneficial external effects, government expenditure can subsidize or augment the private demand for them so that a more efficient quantity can be achieved. When harmful external effects are present, taxes can be imposed to increase the money cost of providing the goods or services responsible for these effects, thus reducing supply and achieving a more efficient level of output. Taxation and expenditure are also instruments that can bring about the provision of goods and services which are consumed collectively and which the private markets will fail to provide. Taxes can be used to establish "prices" for these goods, thus correcting the market's failure to establish such prices, and the tax revenues can be expended to finance the actual provision of these goods and services. The application of taxes and expenditures in meeting government's allocation responsibility will be explored in more detail in Chapters 2 and 3.

Taxation and expenditure are not the only allocation instruments available to government. Government regulation, through what is termed the police power of government, can also be applied to improve allocation. Although these are nonfiscal instruments and do not appear in budget figures, their impact on resource allocation should not be overlooked. For example, the damaging external effects of automobile exhaust emissions and the misallocations that arise from this condition may be dealt with through regulations requiring that automobiles be equipped with certain emission control devices. Although budgeted expenditures and taxes are not used, resource allocation is changed because the regulations require private demanders and suppliers to include the external factors in their buying and selling behavior. The regulation approach can also be used to correct market failures arising from the presence of monopoly power or practices of discrimination in the market. The regulatory instruments are powerful and pervasive in performing allocation responsibilities and correcting for market failures; the choice between using them or using the alternative fiscal instruments depends on which can most effectively and efficiently accomplish the objective.

State and local governments also possess the ability to perform effectively in carrying out the allocation responsibilities of government. The factors that largely disqualify these governments from significant efforts in stabilization and distribution, such as their inability to control the money stock and to restrict commerce, do not prevent them from using the fiscal and regulatory instruments which influence the allocation of resources. In fact, the openness of state and local economies and the largely unrestricted flow of people and resources among these governments provide elements of choice and competition which suggest that a system of multilevel governments can do a better job than a single, unitary national government could do in meeting government's resourcc allocation responsibilities. The basis for this conclusion will be developed in Chapter 17.

SUMMARY

The study of public finance may be approached either from a *positive* point of view, which attempts to account for the activities actually undertaken by governments and to predict how governments will respond to various situations, or from a *normative* point of view, which specifies the conditions that would prevail in some ideal or preferred state of affairs and proceeds to outline the tasks that government ought to perform in order to achieve and perpetuate this ideal situation. The approach adopted in this text is normative, specifying a preference for democracy and asserting that governments should seek to establish those conditions and provide those goods and services desired by the people. It assumes the existence of a market system that is well developed and that performs in a manner generally acceptable to the people.

Three basic areas of government responsibility, *stabilization, distribution,* and *allocation,* have been identified by first establishing how markets may fail to satisfy the wants of people in these areas and then by examining the instruments governments possess to correct or compensate for these market failures. In the stabilization area, markets fail because of fluctuations in the levels of aggregate demand and supply and because markets alone are unable to adjust the stock of money in such a way as to avoid unemployment or price instability. Monetary and fiscal instruments enable governments to perform a stabilization function. The distribution of incomes that arises from market processes may be undesirable from various ethical, political, and economic points of view, and government may be called upon to establish a more acceptable distribution. Governments have the authority to collect taxes and to dispense transfer payments and thereby to alter the distribution of incomes in the society. In the allocation area, markets may fail to provide the collection of goods and services required for efficient satisfaction of wants in the society because of the presence of imperfections in the way markets operate or because external benefits and costs and the demand for goods and services consumed collectively are not accurately reflected in market demand and supply functions. Taxation, expenditures, and government regulation are instruments that can be used to improve the allocation of resources in the economy.

The national government is equipped to operate effectively in all three of these basic areas of responsibility. State and local governments are largely unable to perform effectively except in one. They are able to engage in resource allocation activities, and, in fact, the existence of a system of multilevel governments can increase the ability of government in general to improve the allocation of resources.

SUGGESTED READINGS

MUSGRAVE, R. A. *The Theory of Public Finance* (New York: McGraw-Hill, 1959), Chap. 1.

HAVEMAN, R.H., *The Economics of the Public Sector* (Santa Barbara, Cal.: Wiley, 1976), Chap. 3.

2

Collective Goods
and
Services

Goods and services consumed collectively by the people within the jurisdiction of a government merit especially careful consideration in an introductory examination of public finance. Ensuring efficient provision of these goods and services is the substance of the allocation responsibility of government.[1] The objective of this chapter is to enable students to identify those characteristics of collectively consumed goods and services that distinguish them from goods and services consumed privately. Analysis of collective consumption leads to an understanding of why markets cannot provide an efficient quantity of these services and suggests a basis for decisions about the tax and expenditure components of government budgets for goods and services.

PRIVATE AND COLLECTIVE CONSUMPTION

The first step in understanding the theory of public finance is to recognize the distinction between private and collective consumption. This distinction is important because the process of adding up individual demands for a service in order to determine the total demand for that service is carried out differently for services consumed collectively and for those consumed privately.

---

[1] More advanced analyses of the economics of public finance take into consideration the fact that it is not possible fully to separate allocation responsibilities from responsibilities for the distribution of income.

Private Consumption

Private consumption of a good or service is rival and divisible among different individuals. The rivalry of this consumption means that if I consume a particular unit of this good or service, you cannot also consume that same unit of it—that is, my consuming it prevents you from consuming it. For example, a hamburger is privately consumed because if I eat it, you cannot also eat it. The divisibility characteristic means that different individuals can consume different quantities of the good or service if they choose to do so. My decision to eat a hamburger does not require that you also eat a hamburger. You may decide to have two hamburgers or none at all; that is, we each may go our separate ways in our patterns of consumption.

Because private consumption is rival and divisible, total demand is the *horizontal* sum of the demand curves of individuals: the quantity of the good or service demanded at some given price consists of the amount I would buy at that price plus the amount you would buy at that price, plus the amount that all other persons would buy at that price. This is the way market demand curves for private goods are formulated in economic analysis. Markets operate like adding machines: they total the quantities of the good or service demanded by separate individuals.

Collective Consumption

Collective consumption is neither rival nor divisible among individuals. The consumption of a unit of the service by one individual does not prevent another individual from also consuming the same unit of that service. In fact, the essence of collective consumption is that all individuals consume the identical units of the service once it has been provided. If the service is provided to one consumer, it must be provided to all. Collective consumption is not divisible among individuals in the sense that one individual can consume a quantity of the service different from that consumed by other individuals. Each individual must consume ("accept") the same quantity and quality of service as is provided to all other individuals. Consider, for example, the defense system of a nation. Each citizen is a consumer of this service and each must accept or consume the same quantity and quality as is consumed by every other citizen of the nation. The citizens of the nation are consuming the protection service *collectively*. A parallel example is provided by the nation's monetary system. Each person must consume the same monetary system as is consumed by the other people in the system.

The demand curve for collectively consumed goods or services is derived differently from the demand curve for privately consumed goods or services. For privately consumed goods or services, the total demand was a *horizontal* sum of the quantities demanded by individuals at different prices, and the units being summed were units of output of the good or service. For collective goods, a *vertical* summation is required; that is, for each successive unit of output of a collectively consumed good or service, the demand is the sum of the willingness to pay for this unit by all the individuals who consume it. Figures 2.1 and 2.2

FIGURE 2.1   Demand for a Private Good

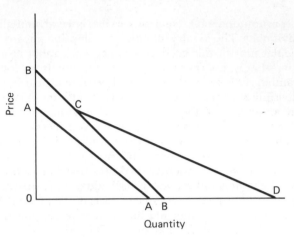

FIGURE 2.2   Demand for a Collective Good

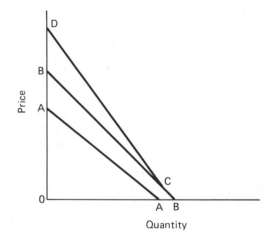

illustrate the difference in demand curve formulation between privately and collectively consumed goods. In both illustrations, the horizontal axis represents the quantity of the good or service and the vertical axis represents the willingness to pay for each successive unit of the good or service. In both illustrations there are two consumers, represented by individual demand curves labeled *AA* and *BB*, and a total demand curve labeled *BCD*. For the privately consumed good or service, the total demand is the horizontal sum of the individual demand curves, since a unit of the good consumed by one of these persons cannot also be consumed by the other person. For the collectively consumed good or service, the total demand is the vertical sum of the individual demand curves, since both persons simultaneously consume each unit of the good or service that is produced.

Efficient Allocation

In conventional economic analysis, the provision of a particular unit of a good or service is justified or efficient if the additional benefit derived from the provision of this unit (its *marginal benefit*) is equal to or greater than the additional cost that must be incurred in order to provide it (its *marginal cost*). The easiest way to grasp the meaning of this proposition is to consider situations in which it is not fulfilled. Note that in such situations, some reallocation of resources would increase the total amount of benefit or welfare that would be realized from the available stock of resources. If marginal cost is greater than marginal benefit, that is, if the benefits foregone (*opportunity cost*) when resources are devoted to the production of the marginal unit of the good or service are greater than the benefits realized from that marginal unit of the good or service, the output of the good or service is excessive and total benefits would be increased if the resources were released for utilization in alternative, more beneficial, applications. Conversely, if marginal benefits exceed marginal costs, the unit of output in question is a justified utilization of resources and decision makers should proceed to consider the next potential addition to output of the good or service. If marginal benefit exceeds marginal cost for this next unit, it should also be produced. The sequence of decisions at the margin and expansions of output should continue until a *breakeven* situation is encountered, that is, until marginal benefit equals marginal cost. At this level of output, expansion should cease because additional units of output would cost more than they are worth and thus would lower total welfare.

Figure 2.3 reproduces the demand curves from Figures 2.1 and 2.2 but adds, in each case, a marginal cost curve representing the addition to total cost required for the provision of each successive unit of output. These graphs show that an efficient allocation of resources to collective goods and services requires the same test as that for efficient allocation to privately consumed goods and

FIGURE 2.3   (a) Output of a Private Good   (b) Output of a Collective Good

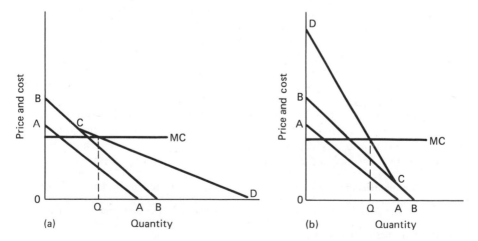

(a)   Quantity   (b)   Quantity

services. If we assume that demand or the price willingly paid by a consumer is a measure of the benefit he feels he will receive from that particular (marginal) unit of the service, the difference between the two graphs is simply that marginal benefit in the case of privately consumed services is an expression of the benefit received by one individual (the marginal consumer), whereas for collectively consumed services, marginal benefit is an expression of the sum of the benefits received by a number of individuals who consume that marginal unit of the service. The "adding machine" operation in markets for privately consumed services is a summation of quantities demanded at specified prices; the same operation for collectively consumed services is a summation of marginal benefits enjoyed by a number of consumers at specified outputs of the collective service.[2]

Measuring Demand

The models presented in the preceding section indicate that there are differences between collectively and privately consumed services in the way in which individual demand curves are added together in order to obtain a total demand curve. At a practical level, there are also differences in the mechanisms or procedures that can be used to identify the actual location of the individual demand curves themselves.

Consider first the task of obtaining an honest or reliable reporting of an individual's demand or willingness to pay for a privately consumed good or service. The reporting task is relatively simple because of the operation of the exclusion principle, which can be characterized rather crudely as "if you don't pay, you don't get." Since private goods are consumed separately by different individuals, the seller of the good can deny an individual the opportunity to enjoy it unless that individual pays the price asked. Since the individual cannot enjoy the benefits of consuming the good unless he purchases it and pays for it, the market mechanism provides a system for reporting information about demand for the good or service. The operation of the exclusion principle forces the individual to reveal his preference for the good and his willingness to pay for it.

For collectively consumed goods or services, the task of reporting information about the level of demand is complicated by the fact that each unit of the good or service is consumed by a number of individuals and by the fact that, once the good or service has been produced, each of these individuals may consume and enjoy the good or service without regard to whether or not he contributed to financing its production. The exclusion principle does not operate for collectively consumed goods or services and therefore does not exert pressure on individuals to reveal their perceived benefits from consuming the item. This is where government can help improve resource allocation. For collectively consumed goods and services, information about demand is generated through collective decision-making procedures (voting in democratic processes). The

---

[2] Marginal benefit is not the whole story about the price willingly paid or the demand for some unit of a commodity. Other matters, such as the amount of purchasing power the consumer commands and the prices of other commodities, also influence the demand for a particular commodity. However, it is convenient to focus on the concept of marginal benefit in illustrating the model of efficient allocation.

stimulus for the revelation of individual benefit perceptions is provided by the compulsory aspects of the revenue system, which is used to finance the provision of these goods and services. Given that a compulsory revenue system exists, each citizen is expected to recognize that an increase in the collective services provided will necessitate certain payments by him, and he is expected to vote "yes" or "no" on the proposed increase in services depending on whether he anticipates that his benefit from the increase will exceed or fall short of the payment that will be required. The compulsory aspects of the government revenue system provide the collective goods counterpart to the exclusion principle. Thus, the resource allocation responsibilities of government arise (1) because the voluntary transactions of the private market will fail to measure correctly the demand for services consumed collectively, and (2) because government possesses the power of coercion which, through a properly devised tax system, can generate a measurement of the demand for these collectively consumed services.

PURE AND NONPURE COLLECTIVE GOODS

If the entire output of a good or service is consumed collectively (that is, equally) by the members of the group and if additional members can be added without any cost, the good or service is termed a *pure* collective good. National defense is a pure collective good. There is no way that one citizen can consume a national defense service different from the one provided to all citizens (although some might wish to), and each new baby or naturalized citizen is an additional consumer whose presence does not diminish the consumption by any others (that is, marginal cost of the added consumption is zero).

There are few pure collective goods or services; the concept is useful primarily because it provides a convenient way to gain an understanding of the nature of collective consumption and of why government action is necessary to provide an efficient quantity of collectively consumed goods and services. Most goods and services involve a mixture of collective and private consumption. These are *nonpure* collective goods. It is important to recognize, however, that the government's responsibility for serving *collective* consumption demand remains the same whether the collective consumption accounts for all or for only a part of the benefit generated by the provision of the good or service.

Education is an example of a service consumed in part privately and separately and in part publicly or collectively. The collective portion includes, for example, the improved legislative processes possible in a society in which literacy is widespread. Literacy, civility, patriotism, common decency, and sensitivity are collective goods all members of the society consume equally and for which the marginal cost of adding another consumer (for example, a new immigrant) to the beneficiary group is zero. Private consumption of education exists along with the collective consumption. Reading is a private satisfaction enjoyed separately and privately. Writing and mathematics lend themselves to separate and private utilization and the furtherance of one's own well-being and thus can be and are privately consumed. In other words, education is a nonpure good, generating private and collective consumption simultaneously. The allocative responsibility of government is to determine the collective demand for the educational services as distinct from the private demand for it and to ensure that the collective demand is met.

Joint Products and the Marginal Rule

In the case of education, the resources used are in fact generating two consumption streams simultaneously. One of these streams is privately consumed and the other is collectively consumed, and the technology of production and consumption has bound these streams together in such a way as to make it impossible to distinguish the resources that generate the private services from those that generate the collective services. The private consumption could be conceived of as a by-product of the production of the collective service, or vice versa.

The *marginal rule* is a policy position which states that initial reliance should be placed on private consumers to finance the production of goods and services. According to this rule, the collectively consumed services that accompany the satisfaction of private demands are by-products. The collective consumer group enjoys benefits without contributing to the financing of production through taxation. The marginal rule states, therefore, that collective or government financing should be called for only if some collective demand remains unsatisfied at the margin of what is provided by private financing. In other words, government finance supplements private finance to the extent necessary to ensure the satisfaction of collective demand. Under the marginal rule, therefore, the mere existence of a collective consumption component is not a sufficient condition for government support for the service. Financial participation by government is required only to the extent that private finance fails to satisfy collective demand.

The marginal rule is not the only approach that could be taken in regard to the financing of nonpure (partly collective and partly private) goods and services. In a system in which market processes are well developed and operate in a way generally satisfactory to most citizens, this marginal rule provides a workable guideline for government involvement in the allocation of resources. In different circumstances, other approaches to financing nonpure goods may be preferred. For example, if markets are not developed or operate in ways that consistently and by wide margins fail to satisfy collective demand, the marginal rule might be reversed, placing initial responsibility on government and permitting individuals to supplement demand when they choose to do so. Health care for communicable diseases might be provided collectively, with individuals permitted to purchase additional care at their own expense.

EXTERNALITIES

A slightly different approach to government responsibility in the allocation of resources is provided by the concept of externalities. When resources are allocated through market processes, buyers and sellers each represent their own interests, and neither of these parties to conventional market transactions is expected to pay much attention to the effects his activities have on other persons.

But production and consumption activities do have effects on persons not represented in market decisions. These effects are called *externalities*. In some situations, the external effects are beneficial (positive), such as when one person's subscription to a garbage collection service conveys external benefits to neighbors downwind. In other situations, the external effects are harmful (negative), such as when a factory discharges pollutants into a river or the atmosphere and thus affects the welfare of people located downstream or downwind.

When externalities are present, the demand and supply curves that determine equilibrium prices and outputs for various goods and services fail to record all costs and/or benefits, and thus an efficient allocation of resources may not be realized. Figure 2.4 illustrates misallocations due to externalities. Figure 2.4(a) shows a situation of positive externalities. The market demand curve, D_m, fails to include all the benefits generated by the production and consumption of the good or service, and the market-determined quantity is less than would be indicated if full benefit reporting had been achieved. The demand curve D_t includes the external benefits and indicates a full benefit accounting price and quantity situation. Figure 2.4(b) illustrates a situation in which external effects are negative. The conventional market supply curve S_m fails to incorporate all costs associated with the production and consumption of the good, and the equilibrium output level is excessive compared to the output that would be indicated if all costs were included, as with supply curve S_t.

FIGURE 2.4 (a) Positive Externalities (b) Negative Externalities

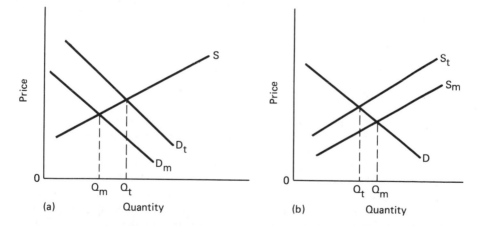

Since markets fail to result in an efficient allocation of resources when external effects are present, some government action may be able to improve the allocation of resources. Specifically, the task is to find ways through which the external benefits and costs can be given representation in allocative decision making. The function of government is to provide means through which persons experiencing external effects can have an appropriate voice in resource allocation. Government may carry out the responsibility in several ways. For example, if externalities are positive, so that the quantity of a service provided by the market is too small, the government may subsidize the provision of the service and finance the subsidy with taxes collected from the external beneficiary group. Conversely, if externalities are negative, so that markets provide an inefficiently large amount of the good or service, government may impose a tax on production or consumption of the service. The tax will reduce the quantity provided and result in a more efficient allocation of resources. Revenue collected may be used to compensate those who suffer the external effects or to overcome the external effects themselves. Government environmental protection programs, for example, operate in this way.

At this point, it is helpful to examine the relationship between the externalities and the collective consumption approaches to government responsibility in the allocation of resources. The two approaches arrive at the same conclusion, but approach the question from different directions. Once again, the education illustration can be applied. A person who privately finances education for his children is also financing the provision of external benefits that accrue to other members of the society. These external benefits from his consumption of education services are the same benefits as those identified from collective consumption in the collective goods construct of the responsibility of government. A government expenditure for education to recognize the external benefits of education is the same as the purchase of the collectively consumed component of education. A purely collective good or service is simply the extreme externalities situation. If a private person finances a submarine and uses it for protection against foreign attack, he would at the same time be providing defense services to his fellow citizens as a by-product or external effect of his private act. In the submarine case, however, essentially all of the beneficial consumption is external and only a minutely small portion can be enjoyed privately. This is why private provision of such services is not observed in practice and why the collective good construct is more comprehensible than the externality construct for this type of service.

APPLYING THE MODEL TO A POLICY QUESTION

Let us now bring together several aspects of collective consumption and externalities in an analysis of a public policy issue, namely, the question of how educational services should be financed and operated. As has been suggested, education services appear to fall in the category of partly collective and partly private consumption. If the marginal rule is applied to this situation, the implication is that private finance (tuition) should be relied upon to provide some amount of education service and that public funds (taxes) should be used only to the extent that collective demand is not satisfied at the margin of private provision. In relating this model to actual practice, we observe that the prescription of mixed public and private financing does appear at the college and university level, where tuition and government appropriations each play a prominent financing role, but that the mixed financing prescription is applied very modestly, if at all, to privately operated schools, whether at the college, the secondary, or elementary levels. Mixed financing does not apply to publicly operated elementary and secondary schools. These observations suggest that there are two dimensions to the question, one relating to the level of instruction (elementary and secondary schools or colleges and universities) and one relating to whether the educational institutions delivering the service are privately or publicly operated.

If we first examine the dimension relating to level of instruction, we find that the model of collective consumption and externalities invites the question of whether there are differences in the mix between private and collective benefits at different levels of education. To put it differently, are there differences in the importance the public attaches to the external benefits generated at different education levels? Application of the marginal rule raises the question of whether private markets can be relied upon more fully at one level than at another to serve collective demands as by-products. The observation that public funding pays a much larger portion of the bill for elementary and secondary education than it does for college education suggests that the perceived external or collective benefits are proportionately greater at the elementary and secondary levels than they are at the college level. Private benefits reflected in the willingness to pay tuition are relied upon to finance a substantial portion of higher education output, leaving relatively little need for public funding, whereas private tuition payments are not relied upon to finance the output of elementary and secondary education in publicly operated schools. So long as attention is focused only on publicly operated schools, the actual practice is not inconsistent with the implications of the collective consumption and externalities model operated through the marginal rule. Indeed, it is reasonable to suppose that the collective interest in the education provided at the elementary and secondary levels is great and to suppose that, for college and university education, private markets do provide opportunities for individuals to appropriate much of the benefits to themselves through higher earned incomes after graduation.

The observed distinction between privately and publicly operated educational institutions, that is, the second dimension of actual practice, is an especially sensitive area of public policy. The simple collective consumption and externalities model is not able to explain the distinction between public and private schools so long as it is assumed that the type of education being provided by private schools is the same as that being provided by public schools. If their products are the same, the model suggests that private schools should have the same financial opportunities as public schools. The distinction between private and public schools could be viewed as a peculiar application of the marginal rule permitting the private market to "do its thing" before public funding is called for, but this application appears inconsistent with the joint nature of the production of collective and private benefit streams from education. Thus, the collective consumption and externalities model directs attention to the characteristics of education output and to the question of whether the collective benefit is different for one type of output than for another. The distinction between public and private schools implies that some product differences may be perceived, and the validity of the funding distinctions may depend on the correctness of these perceived differences. The fact that many private schools are operated by religious organizations and include religious instruction in their curriculums may be relevant to the collective consumption argument without regard to the constitutional statements about the separation of church and state.

This line of reasoning from the collective consumption and externalities model focuses attention on the *joint product* aspect of partly collective goods and services. If it were possible to set up output criteria that could be applied through the regulatory instruments of government, public monies required to satisfy the demand for collective consumption could be made available to any institution (public or private) whose output satisfied these criteria, and there would be no need for government to undertake direct managerial responsibilities in education. The fact that schools are directly managed by governments implies that managerial control at the immediate point of service delivery is seen as the best way to secure satisfaction of the collective demand for educational service. Whether this is in fact the case is, of course, an empirical question. The point is that a distinction can be drawn between the financing of collective consumption and the technical question of the most efficient way to actually produce the service demanded by the collective consumers. The prevailing practice implies that publicly managed education producers are more efficient than privately managed education producers in providing the type of collective service demanded.

This application of government finance theory to a current policy issue illustrates that the model provides a way of identifying the empirical questions which must be resolved. The models do not resolve the empirical questions but, by identifying them, play an important role in the development of public policy.

SUMMARY

In this chapter we have examined the nature of collective consumption, distinguished collective from private consumption, and explained why private markets are unable to provide an efficient quantity of collectively consumed goods and services. Because private consumption is rival or divisible among individuals, demand curves are horizontal summations of quantities demanded. Output decisions can be reached in an efficient manner (equating marginal benefit with marginal cost), since transactions take place between producers and individual consumers who are obligated to reveal their willingness to pay for the service. The exclusion principle operates to prevent them from consuming the service if they do not pay for it. Collective consumption, on the other hand, means that many people consume each unit of the service provided and that consumption of the service by one person does not preclude other persons from also consuming it. Thus, the demand curve for collectively consumed services is the summation of the benefits realized by all consumers of the service. Markets are unable to provide an efficient quantity of collectively consumed services because the exclusion principle does not operate to compel consumers to reveal the amount of their benefit from the service and their willingness to help finance its production. Governments, however, have the authority to compel people to pay taxes, and this coercive capability can be applied to obtain some measure of the demand for collectively consumed services. Thus, governments can improve the allocation of resources if an accurate demand estimate can be developed through the use of a properly designed tax system.

Government responsibility for the provision of collectively consumed services includes responsibility for the collective component of services that are in part privately and in part collectively consumed. In respect to these partly collective services, the particular division of responsibility between government and private financing is a matter of public policy. The marginal rule expounds a policy position favoring private financing of these services and recommending government financing only to the extent that collective demands are not satisfied as by-products of the private provision. Education illustrates the partly collective, partly private (nonpure) type of service. The methods actually used to provide educational services show that public policy issues involve the identification of collectively demanded services, the measurement of that demand, and the technical question of the most efficient way that demand can be satisfied.

Government responsibility for resource allocation can also be approached from the externalities point of view. Markets will fail to provide an efficient resource allocation when persons who are not parties to a market transaction nevertheless are affected by the consequences of that transaction. In these situations, market demand and supply curves will fail to measure benefits and costs accurately, and government intervention may be able to improve resource allocation. The externalities approach and the collective consumption approach blend into one another when the external effects of transactions are dominant and private interests in transactions are insignificant.

SUGGESTED READINGS

SAMUELSON, PAUL A. "The Pure Theory of Public Expenditures," *Review of Economics and Statistics*, November 1954.

DAVIS, OTTO H., "On the Distinction Between Public and Private Goods," *American Economic Review*, May 1967.

BUCHANAN, JAMES, M. *The Demand and Supply of Public Goods* (Chicago: Rand McNally, 1968).

SHOUP, CARL S., and JOHN HEAD. "Public Goods, Private Goods, and Ambiguous Goods," *Economics Journal*, September 1969.

3

Revenue Systems
and
Voting

We have recognized that private markets cannot be expected to provide an efficient quantity of those goods and services consumed collectively. This market failure opens up the possibility that government action may be able to improve the allocation of resources. We have also recognized that governments have the power to compel people to pay taxes and that this power to tax can be used to obtain some expression from citizens about their preferences and willingness to pay for collective services. The next task is to explore more specifically the devices governments may use to accomplish this purpose. Clearly, the outcomes of the government decision-making process depend both on the demand and supply facts and also on the methods and procedures used to discover these facts and incorporate them into actual decisions. Institutions and available instruments do influence outcomes.

DIFFERENTIAL BENEFITS AND DIFFERENTIAL TAXES

Let us begin by recognizing a simple but very important fact about the demand for collectively consumed services, namely, that equality of consumption does *not* mean equality of benefit. All citizens may consume a service equally, but it is unlikely that all benefit equally from it. This is because benefit is a subjective matter. Different consumers of a collective good or service may perceive different amounts of benefit from a given unit of this service even though they all share equally in the consumption of it.

A revenue system which does not recognize that benefit perceptions differ will fail to provide an accurate measure of demand for a collective service. Consider, for example, a proposal that the defense capability of a nation should be increased by the addition of a new missile system, and suppose that the revenue system were such as to divide the cost of the addition equally among all citizens. Some citizens would place a considerable value on this increase in defense capability and would be willing to pay even more for it than they would be required to pay under the equal-share payment system. They would, of course, vote in favor of expansion of the defense service. Other citizens, however, might place less value on the increase in defense service, and if their valuation of the benefits of expansion is lower than the equal-share payment that would be required of them, they would vote against the expansion. A vote could be taken, of course, and a decision reached about whether or not to go ahead with the new missile system depending on whether the number of votes cast in favor of the project passed whatever test or criteria had been set up to govern collective decision making.

The point of interest, however, is that voting on the basis of the hypothetical equal-share payment system fails to provide an opportunity for a full recording of the marginal benefits from the proposed defense system. The marginal benefits perceived by many of those voting in favor of the expansion presumably were greater than their equal-share payment, but the collective process provided no means of recording these extra perceived marginal benefits. The marginal benefits to those who voted against the expansion were less than their equal-share payment, but it certainly seems unreasonable to suppose that the marginal benefit of the expansion was zero for these citizens. Thus, for this group also, the collective decision process utilizing the equal-share revenue system understated the demand for the proposed project.

Accurate determination of the demand for collectively consumed goods and services depends on the nature of the revenue system used to finance the provision of these services. Since each citizen does, and indeed must, consume collective services equally with all other citizens, accurate demand information requires that compulsory payments from these citizens be differentiated among them on some basis that reflects their different marginal benefit perceptions. The ideal revenue system must provide the same differentiation as differential amounts of consumption provide in the market for privately consumed goods. Uniform prices can serve the allocation function when individuals can make separate decisions on the amounts of a service to consume, but efficient allocation requires differential payments per unit (prices) when the service is consumed collectively.

Figure 3.1 illustrates an aggregate demand for a collective service which is a vertical summation of the demands of each of the members of the consumer group. The notion of an ideal distribution of tax payments among these citizens suggests that, for a given amount of the service, each citizen would pay an amount of tax equal to his marginal benefit multiplied by the number of units of the service provided. So long as such a taxing system were adhered to, a unanimous "yes" vote would be forthcoming for any level of output that might be proposed. That is, for each citizen, the price-quantity relationship would fall on his demand curve, meaning that the resulting allocation of his spending

FIGURE 3.1   Allocationally Efficient Taxation

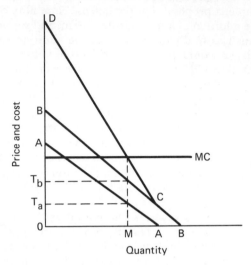

power would be at least as satisfactory to him as any alternative allocation. The demand for the collective service would be fully reported by the revenue potential of the tax system at each level of possible output of the service.

The efficient amount of the service that actually should be provided under this tax system would be determined by consulting information about the marginal cost of the service—that is, the addition to total cost arising from the provision of each successive unit. An increase in the amount of service is appropriate so long as the cost of this increase (marginal cost) is less than the revenue that would be generated by the "ideal" tax system for that increment of service. Expansion of output should cease as soon as it is recognized that the next unit of output would incur cost which would not be covered by revenue. At this equilibrium level of output, OM, citizen A would pay the tax represented by the area OT_a multiplied by OM, and citizen B would pay the amount of tax represented by the area OT_b multiplied by OM.

The constant or horizontal MC curve in Figure 3.1 means that a balanced budget would exist if each citizen paid tax equal to his marginal benefit multiplied by the quantity of the service. Decreasing or increasing marginal costs would mean that budget deficits or surpluses would arise. More complicated tax arrangements would be required under these circumstances. The objective would be to keep each person's marginal tax rate equal to his maginal benefits. Rebates or surcharges could be used to deal with surpluses or deficits.

The practical problem in the ideal model is that it requires some a priori information about each citizen's marginal benefit curve. Since this information is not available in actual practice, most tax allocations will not in fact match individual marginal benefits, tax revenues will involve some misstatement of collective demand, and votes on proposed collective services will not be unanimous. However, the model does provide information that can be used to improve future expenditure-tax proposals. Citizens who vote "no" on a proposal for collective service are revealing information about the relation between the taxes they would be required to pay and their perception of benefit from the service. They are saying that the marginal cost exceeds the marginal benefit from their point of view. It is then appropriate to consider whether or not the service could be modified to make it more beneficial to these citizens or whether the tax system could be modified to require these citizens to pay a smaller amount for the service. Those who vote "yes" on the proposal are providing some information about the relation between the taxes they would be required to pay and the benefits they expect to obtain from the service. Modifications might then be increases in the tax required of these voters or program changes which they might view as undesirable.

The Wicksellian Decision Procedure

One of the early attempts to provide a connection between revenues and expenditures was made by Professor Knut Wicksell, who devised a government decision procedure capable of producing outcomes consistent with the efficiency arguments of economic theory.[1] Figure 3.2 is a flow chart illustrating the essential features of Wicksell's proposal. The initial step requires the preparation of a package proposal that sets forth both the expenditures to be undertaken and the tax to be used to finance these expenditures. Both the details of expenditure and the details of taxation would be variables in developing these package proposals. The drafters of legislation would have complete freedom to adjust the distribution of benefits and taxes in the hope of discovering a combination that would be approved by the legislature itself. The package proposal would be viewed as a hypothesis about the benefit and cost perceptions of the public and would be tested by the votes cast in the legislature.

FIGURE 3.2 The Wicksellian Decision Procedure

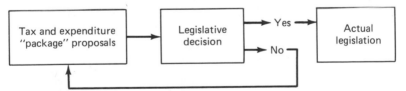

In the pure Wicksellian system, the test of the hypothesis would be very rigorous, since unanimous agreement would be required in order for the proposal to be enacted into law. If unanimous agreement were achieved, it would be clear that the welfare of no citizen would be harmed by the proposed action and that the action, therefore, would be optimizing. If the package failed to obtain unanimous agreement, the drafters of the legislation would have to modify either the expenditure provisions or the tax provisions or both. The revised package could then be resubmitted to the legislature and the process would repeat itself.

[1] Knut Wicksell, "A New Principle of Just Taxation," in R. A. Musgrave and A. T. Peacock (eds.), *Classics in the Theory of Public Finance* (London: Macmillan, 1958). Wicksell wrote in 1896.

The distinctive features about the pure Wicksellian system are (1) that unanimous agreement would be required before action could be taken and (2) that each expenditure would be tied to a specified distribution of tax responsibilities. This combination of features would ensure that each expenditure actually undertaken would be optimizing, since no citizen would suffer a welfare loss as a result. Although the Wicksellian model is an interesting benchmark or reference point for understanding the idea of efficiency in collective decision making, several considerations suggest that it must be modified in practical application.

DECISION CRITERIA AND VOTING

The first modification of Wicksell's model focuses on the requirement that unanimous agreement must be secured before expenditures can be made. Decision making itself is costly. If unanimous agreement is required, a great amount of time and effort would be needed to arrive at acceptable expenditure-tax packages. Valuable opportunities to undertake useful activities would slip by while the legislative debate continued. In the face of these arguments, Wicksell himself modified the decision criterion to one of substantial but not complete unanimity, that is, he conceded that something like 80 percent agreement would provide adequate protection against nonoptimizing expenditures. But the selection of an efficient decision rule or criterion itself requires an analysis of the costs of decision making.

Costs of Decision Making

Legislatures can be viewed as being in the "decision-making business." Their output consists of decisions, and one of the criteria governing the organization and operation of the business is the objective of minimizing the cost of producing those decisions. In Figure 3.3 the horizontal axis sets forth the various

FIGURE 3.3   Costs of Decision Making

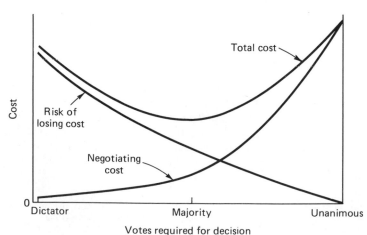

decision-making rules that may be employed. They range from unilateral decrees by a single decision maker at one extreme through increasingly higher requirements of agreement until the other extreme of unanimous agreement is reached. It is hypothesized that the costs of decision making are related, in part at least, to the extent of agreement required for affirmative action. The vertical axis of the graph records the various costs of decision making as they are related to the extent of agreement required for affirmative action. In this illustration, two types of decision-making costs are shown, *negotiating* costs and *risk of losing* costs.

From the point of view of an individual who contributes to the decision-making process and who is bound by its outcomes, the negotiating costs would be very low if decisions were made by one person, that is, if a dictator made all the decisions. The individual would incur no costs of informing himself about alternative actions or about the views of others on the questions to be decided. However, the risk of losing would be very great under the one-man rule criterion; that is, there would be a strong likelihood that the decisions actually made might not be the ones the individual would wish to be made.

Decision rules that require the agreement of increasingly larger fractions of the population impose larger negotiating costs, since effort must be expended in searching for terms and conditions acceptable to an increasingly large number of different individuals who presumably have differing preferences. Thus, the negotiating cost curve rises as the decision rules become more inclusive and becomes extremely high if unanimous agreement is required. The curve for the risk of losing, on the other hand, slopes downward as the decision criterion requires agreement from an increasingly larger fraction of the population. At the extreme of unanimous agreement, each person possesses what amounts to veto power in regard to any proposed action, and the risk of losing is zero.

The analysis of Figure 3.3 is completed by constructing a total cost curve by summing vertically the negotiating costs and the risk of losing costs. The lowest point on this total cost curve identifies an efficient decision rule. The graph suggests that this efficient decision criterion is unlikely to lie near either extreme of the range of criteria. Instead, the efficient rule in a democratic system is likely to lie with some intermediate or compromise decision criterion.

The efficient decision criterion, however, need not turn out to be that corresponding to majority rule. In fact, the implication is that the efficient decision rule will depend on the type of question being decided. For example, if the question relates to a matter people feel is very important, such as one relating to civil rights, great weight may be attached to the risk of losing. This curve in Figure 3.3 would rotate clockwise on its unanimous consent origin, and the efficient decision rule would move in the direction of a more demanding, or more nearly unanimous, criterion. Similarly, the negotiating cost curve may be steeper or flatter, depending on the nature of the question posed. If proposals are narrowly drawn and readily understood, the negotiating cost curve may be flatter, total costs will be lower, and a more demanding rule may be feasible, other things held constant. Finally, the character of the population itself will have an important influence on determining the appropriate decision rule and on the costs of decision making under any given rule. If the population is relatively homogeneous, both the negotiating costs and the risk of losing costs may be low enough that the total cost of decision making can be low under any given rule.

Analysis of Voting Results

Once adopted, a decision criterion, such as majority rule, opens the way to the analysis of the outcomes of the legislative process. We will continue the Wicksellian ideal of package legislation, which links certain expenditures with certain taxes, and examine how the decision-making rule contributes to an understanding and evaluation of the outcomes of the collective choice process.

The decision rule used helps to identify the "swing voter," that is, it helps to discover the voter whose position is crucial for the outcome. If majority rule is the criterion, the swing voter will be the median voter on each question tested at the ballot box. If the decision criterion is two-thirds approval, then the swing voter will be the one at the crucial two-thirds point along the spectrum of voter positions on the question.

The notion of a spectrum of voter positions is fundamental to the swing voter model and requires some elaboration. The key idea is that the issue placed before the voters is *one dimensional*, that is, that some common characteristic or thread of logic is generally recognized by the voters and provides the basis on which they select positions. For example, the question may be "How much of this collective service shall be provided?" The issue of how much provides the common theme. Voters will recognize this issue and will organize their own preferences on the basis of this question. Suppose that the choice is among a small, a medium, or large quantity of the specified service. The preference ordering of a person who feels himself to benefit greatly from the service will be (1) the large amount, (2) the medium amount, and (3) the small amount. Conversely, a person who is not benefited by the service will order his preferences (1) the small amount, (2) the medium amount, and (3) the large amount. A voter who is moderately benefited will give first preference to the medium amount and will award second and third preferences to the other options. If the questions posed are of this one-dimensional character and if most voters exhibit *single peaked* preference orderings so as to be more favorable to alternatives closer (along the spectrum) to their preferred positions, then the voting process will yield an unambiguous outcome that can be scientifically analyzed.

The analysis of collective decision making relies heavily on the assumptions that the questions posed are indeed perceived to be one dimensional and that voters actually do order their preferences in receding sequence along this dimension. If these assumptions are not accurate, the analysis is not applicable. If voters do not share a common perception of what the question actually is, the votes cast will not provide a resolution of any question. The analysis will also not be accurate if significant numbers of voters exhibit a nonsingle peaked preference ordering, such as that illustrated by the notion "anything worth doing is worth doing well" (so that the ordering is first for the large amount and second for the small amount rather than for the medium amount) or by the "demonstration strategy" (under which the first choice might be the small expenditure but the second choice might be the large expenditure rather than the medium expenditure in order to demonstrate the bad features of the proposal). It is, of course, a great oversimplification to suppose that voters actually perceive questions along a common dimension or that preference orderings always are of the straightforward single-peaked variety, but many public finance questions dealing with amounts of expenditure are rather clearly of the more vs. less character, so that one-dimension and single-peaked patterns may frequently occur. It is therefore useful to accept the one-dimension and single-peaked assumptions and to explore the implications of this method of analysis.

Figure 3.4 illustrates how, under these assumptions, a majority rule decision criterion develops decisions about the supply of a collective service. Suppose that the question before the voters is "How much street improvement shall be made?" In Figure 3.4, different quantities of street improvement are recorded on the horizontal axis. The vertical axis shows the costs of street improvement and the marginal benefit (expressed in dollar terms) voters expect to realize from the various possible amounts of street improvement. Assume that the voters who will decide on the amount of street improvement to be made are the three citizens whose homes are located along the street in question.

FIGURE 3.4   Analysis of Voting Outcomes (Equal Tax Shares)

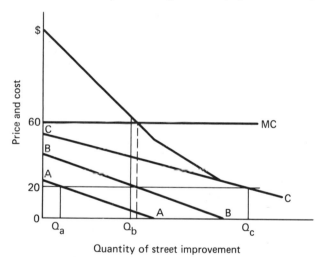

Quantity of street improvement

Citizen A owns one automobile but is able to walk or use public transportation (available within walking distance), and thus has a relatively small demand for street improvement, as illustrated by demand curve *AA*. Citizen B also owns one automobile but makes use of it regularly and thus has a demand for street improvement, *BB*, which is greater than that of citizen A. The third citizen, C, has three automobiles (one each for himself, his wife, and his teenage children) and thus has a significantly greater demand for street improvement, as illustrated by demand curve *CC*.

If we assume that the marginal cost of street improvement is $60 for each unit (constant over the range of street improvements under consideration) and if we assume that the revenue system would impose equal tax prices per unit of improvement on each citizen (perhaps through front footage assessments), then each citizen would face a tax price of $20 per unit of improvement. At this tax price, citizen A would prefer quantity Q_a, citizen B would prefer quantity Q_b, and citizen C would prefer quantity Q_c. Under a system of majority rule, quantity Q_b would be chosen, since citizen A would side with B to reject any alternative greater than Q_b and citizen C would side with B to reject any alternative smaller than Q_b.

Citizen A will be dissatisfied with this outcome, since he will be required to purchase more improvement than his preferred amount. Citizen C will be dissatisfied, since he is not able to obtain the amount of improvement he would be willing to pay for at that price. Moreover, it is apparent from Figure 3.4 that the choice of Q_b is not an efficient outcome in terms of resource allocation, since the sum total of benefits from an increase in street improvement beyond Q_b would exceed the costs of installing these improvements.

Since dissatisfaction with the outcome of the political process exists in this illustration, a campaign may be undertaken to replace the front footage revenue system (which resulted in equal tax payments among the three citizens) with a revenue system basing tax payments for street improvement on the number of automobiles garaged along the street. Since five automobiles are garaged along the street, this revenue system would impose a tax price per unit of street improvement of $12 per automobile, with citizens A and B each being liable for a tax price of $12 and citizen C being liable for a tax price of $36 per unit of street improvement. Figure 3.5 reproduces the demand and marginal cost curves shown in Figure 3.4 and illustrates the outcome of the majority rule voting process under this new revenue system. Citizen C becomes the median voter who determines the outcome of the voting process, and the quantity of street improvement actually enacted would be Q_c'. Citizen A is required to purchase more street improvement than he would prefer at the new price and citizen B is receiving less street improvement than he would be willing to pay for at the new tax price. Once again, however, the tax system has failed to result in a

FIGURE 3.5   Analysis of Voting Outcomes (Unequal Tax Shares)

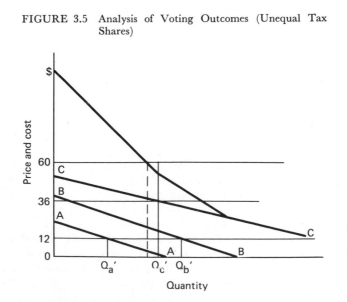

decision to provide the allocationally efficient quantity of street improvement, since the quantity now provided, Q_c', involves marginal costs in excess of the benefits from the marginal unit of street improvement.

Efficiency and Equity

The decision-making rule and the revenue system combine to determine the outcome of the decision-making process. In the case of the majority rule criterion, the revenue system determines which voter will be the median or swing voter on specific questions. Figures 3.4 and 3.5 showed that different amounts of street improvement would be approved under a system of front footage assessment and under a system which assessed financing responsibility according to the number of automobiles garaged along the street. Other illustrations include the question of whether different amounts of school expenditure would be adopted if these services were financed by income or sales taxation rather than by property taxation.

Neither of the revenue alternatives used in the illustration resulted in the allocationally efficient amount of street improvement. Under the front footage system (Figure 3.4), which applied equal tax prices to each voter, less than the efficient quantity of service was provided. Under the system of assessment on the basis of the number of automobiles (Figure 3.5), the amount supplied was greater than the efficient amount. The illustration suggests that whether or not the efficient amount is provided depends on both the revenue system used and the pattern of benefits perceived by the voters.

Figures 3.4 and 3.5 actually illustrated a double failure of the revenue system. Each system failed to provide the efficient amount of the service and each also failed to establish an equitable (that is, consistent with marginal benefit) distribution of tax liabilities for the services actually supplied. It is conceivable, however, that a revenue system could lead to efficient output decisions in spite of the fact that it might distribute the tax prices for these services inequitably. For example, if an equal tax price were applied to all voters and if the marginal benefits to the median voter happened to be also equal to the *average* of the marginal benefits of the other voters, then the majority rule system would yield an efficient level of output, even though inequities would exist among taxpayers. In theory, revenue systems that apply differential tax prices to different voters are capable of achieving both the efficient amount of output and an equitable distribution of taxes, but such a situation is rare. It seems reasonable to conclude, therefore, that decisions made regarding collective goods and services typically are both inefficient and inequitable to some degree and that these problems are inherent in collective consumption and in the use of decision rules requiring less than unanimous agreement.

THE GENERAL REVENUE SYSTEM

We may now examine the second way in which prevailing collective decision processes depart from the ideal model outlined by Wicksell. The procedures actually used by contemporary governments do not set up a separate tax instrument for each expenditure program. Instead, a general revenue system is established as a more or less permanent component of the decision process, and

expenditure proposals are expected to adapt themselves to the constraints of
the taxes prescribed by this system. Figure 3.6 presents a flow diagram for the
general revenue system procedure of government decision making. The drafting
of potential legislation concentrates only on the expenditure details of proposals,
taking the general revenue system as given. Expenditure proposals are submitted
to the legislature; if the proposal is rejected, adjustments are undertaken only
in respect to the details of the expenditure.[2]

The general revenue system does, of course, have an influence on the legislation actually adopted or rejected by the legislature. However, this revenue
system will not be modified to obtain the adoption of any single expenditure
proposal. A reexamination of the general revenue system takes place only in
a general way (that is, in a way not tied to specific expenditure actions) and only
after considerable information has been accumulated about the pattern of
expenditure legislation that emerges from the legislative process. In other words,
the task of restructuring this general revenue system (the dotted line in Figure
3.6) will not be undertaken unless and until it becomes apparent that an existing
pattern in expenditure enactments is both unsatisfactory to the citizens and

FIGURE 3.6   General Revenue System Decision Procedure

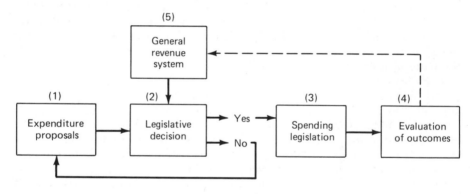

attributable to the influence of the revenue system in the decision process. As
long as the outcomes of the decision process are generally acceptable, the general
revenue system is not revised.

The Constitutional Nature of the General Revenue System

The reluctance to tamper with the general revenue system or to make
changes in it to facilitate the enactment of specific expenditure proposals is
readily understandable. Taxes affect people in the pocketbook, an extremely

---

[2] In practice, of course, there are instances in which spending and revenue provisions are
linked together in the legislative process. Trust fund expenditures and earmarked taxes illustrate
such instances. Most expenditures, however, are financed through the general fund.

sensitive portion of an individual's fiscal anatomy. On the other hand, government expenditure decisions involve a less direct impact on the day to day life of the individual (especially in a market-oriented society), and many citizens find themselves largely unconcerned and unaffected by many of the spending actions undertaken by government. Thus, the political (negotiating) costs of tax legislation can be expected to be considerably higher than the political costs of expenditure legislation. Proposals for change in taxation arouse the interest of a great many citizens and lead those citizens to scrutinize legislators looking for reelection. The high political costs of tax legislation relative to expenditure legislation suggest that tax legislation will be less frequently undertaken and that revenue systems, once established, will remain in effect for a considerable period of time.

Another way of understanding why general revenue systems tend to become institutionalized, fixed features of the fiscal landscape is to recognize that the distribution of tax liabilities is a kind of zero-sum game. What one individual may gain through a reduction in taxes imposed on him, another individual will lose through an increased tax liability, at least if it is assumed that most expenditures are embedded in ongoing programs so that the total budget is fixed. In this context, debate over relative tax shares is reduced to debate over the distribution of after-tax incomes, for which no scientifically verifiable guidelines are available. These debates are socially divisive and open the way for charges that majority coalitions may simply use their power to exploit minorities by forcing them to pay increased taxes for programs already in existence. Outcomes may be quite uncertain, and many citizens therefore may prefer that the question of revising tax shares not be brought up at all.

Finally, once a general revenue system has become established, vested interests develop to favor a continuation of this system. Many long-range plans and decisions, such as those relating to career choices, home ownership, and business investments, are made with tax considerations in mind. Once such plans and decisions have been made, proposals to change the general revenue system amount to proposals to change the rules in the middle of the game. Such changes would indeed impose genuine welfare losses on many people. Some assurance that the general revenue system will remain in effect for a long period of time is genuinely helpful to people because it reduces the uncertainties which inherently surround the making of long-term plans and decisions.

When people have some effective options or choices among governments with which to affiliate, as is the case for state and local governments, it can be argued that the character and assurance of permanence in the general revenue system constitute conditions and parts of the agreement to affiliate. An implicit contract can be said to exist under which the individual agrees to affiliate with a given government unit in exchange for the assurance that the rules of the game in connection with taxation will not be significantly altered after he has made his move and established fixed ties with the community.

Amending the Fiscal Constitution

During the 1960s, the demand for collective services increased significantly. Many of the new demands were directed at state and local governments. The fiscal constitutions for local governments specified almost exclusive reliance on property taxation for internal revenue and state governments relied primarily on sales and income taxes. These fiscal constitutions affected the legislation adopted by states and localities during the period, and the pattern of legislation actually adopted proved to be unsatisfactory to many people. Taxpayers resisted many expenditure proposals because the marginal tax costs to them exceeded their perceptions of marginal benefit. Because both taxpayers and proponents of increased expenditures were unhappy with the outcomes of the decision process, attempts were made to go to the root of the problem and amend the fiscal constitution. Revenue sharing, broadening of the tax bases to include local income and sales taxes, increases in intergovernment grants-in-aid, and the shifting of functional responsibilities among levels of government are examples of changes in the fiscal constitution that took place or were attempted during this period. The process was and continues to be an agonizing one. It has been accompanied by migrations of people among government units and by an increase in the amount of uncertainty faced by people in making long-term plans and decisions. The costs of change have been significant.

VOTE TRADING

The use of a general revenue system means that separate expenditure questions are not decided in isolation from one another, as was the case when a particular revenue source was tied to a particular expenditure proposal. With a general revenue system, the same group of voter-taxpayers must render decisions on several different expenditure programs, that is, a number of expenditure programs will be financed out of the same general fund revenue. This situation complicates the analysis of voting procedures. Specifically, it opens the way for vote trading which, in turn, offers further insight into the operation of collective choice processes.

Three Voters and Two Issues

Consider first the very simplified situation in which there are only two expenditure alternatives and three voters in the decision-making group. In Figure 3.7, the alternative expenditures are designated as recreation services and police services and the three voters, labeled A, B and C, are identified in terms of their own perceptions of the ideal combination or mix of these services, given their respective tax share contributions to the general fund. Individual A appears as a "law and order" buff because he favors a large expenditure for police services but is moderate in connection with expenditures for recreation services, at least so long as the existing tax share arrangements are in effect. Individual B is a moderate on the matter of police expenditure but does not wish to expend much on recreation services. Individual C is strong for recreation expenditure but would prefer little spending on police services. It is important to remember that these ideal combination points reflect the fact that the tax-sharing system is already determined and is known to each individual. If the tax-share system were different, these ideal combination points might have different locations.

If the two questions (police expenditures and recreation expenditures)

FIGURE 3.7   Vote Trading: Two Issues and Three Voters

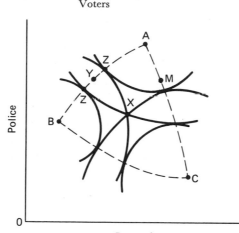

were decided in complete isolation from one another, the swing voter analysis suggests that A would determine the amount of recreation spending and that B would determine the amount of police spending. But when the questions are no longer decided in isolation from one another, the problem becomes "What combination or mixture of police and recreation service expenditures will be selected through the operation of majority voting?" Since two votes for a proposed combination are required if it is to be selected, it is immediately apparent that none of the voters will be able to have his ideal combination. Some concession will have to be made to at least one of the other voters, that is, each voter will have to recognize that he will have to settle for some combination which is less attractive than his ideal combination.

At this point, the analysis can be advanced by constructing a type of indifference curve (or actually a set of indifference curves) for each voter.[3] For individual A, a circle can be drawn around his ideal combination point such that points on this circle identify combinations of police and recreation expenditures which are less attractive than the ideal combination but which are equally attractive to individual A. In fact, a whole family of such circles can be constructed around A's ideal combination point. Each circle consists of combinations that are equally attractive to A, but circles farther removed from the ideal combination point identify combinations which are less attractive than those on circles closer to the ideal combination. In the same manner, circle or attractiveness contour lines can be constructed around the ideal combination point of the other voters. To help in grasping the idea being presented, we can visualize these attractiveness contour lines as comparable to the contour lines drawn on maps to show locations that have the same elevation above sea level. It is not necessary that these contours be circles, but it is helpful to the analysis to assume that all segments of each contour line are concave toward the ideal combination point and convex outward from it.

[3] See the appendix to Chapter 13 for a discussion of indifference curves.

The shape that has been assumed for the attractiveness contours for each of the voters leads to the recognition that points of tangency will exist between individual contour lines for each pair of voters, that is, tangency points will exist for contours of A and B, of B and C, and of A and C. In Figure 3.7, dashed lines have been drawn between A and B, between B and C, and between A and C connecting the tangency points of their respective indifference contours. These lines are *contract lines* in that they show the locus of points of various vote-trading deals which might be worked out between the different pairs of voters in this group. To illustrate this idea, suppose that A and B enter into negotiations in the hope of finding a combination of police and recreation spending on which they could agree and thereby establish under the majority rule system of collective decision making. Any proposed combination that did *not* fall on their contract line could be improved upon (from their points of view) by some combination that did fall on this line. To demonstrate this, select any point not on the *AB* contract line (point x, for example) and note that a movement to the *AB* contract line (to point y, for example) can be devised which would permit each of the negotiating parties (A and B) to reach an indifference contour more attractive than the one associated with the original position (point x). But, we are not saying that point y is the necessary outcome of negotiations between A and B. If the initial combination were at x, voluntary agreement could be reached between A and B and any point on the zz segment of their contract line, since any point in this segment would mean an improvement to one of the parties without harming the other. It is apparent also that other segments of the AB contract line would be relevant if the starting point was different from point x.

So far in our analysis, individual C has been left out of the bargaining. It is apparent, however, that C is a victim of an agreement between A and B and that C will attempt to engage in bargaining himself in order to avoid the adverse effects of a decision in favor of some combination along the *AB* contract line. For example, C might attempt to win the support of A for a combination at point m, which would be better for A than anything in the zz segment of the *AB* contract line and which would also be better for C than anything in the zz segment of this line. Alternatively, C might attempt to win the support of B through similar offers.

So long as the analysis is confined to the special case of three voters and two alternative expenditure programs, the vote-trading process leads to the conclusion that any decisions reached will be quite unstable (that is, subject to continuing renegotiations as alliances are altered) and that they will "cycle" between different points on the contract lines. Considerable importance will attach to the bargaining skill of the different voters. Most important, in any given decision, one voter will have been "frozen out" and exploited by the majority coalition. From the point of view of welfare economics, it can be observed that any point in the area bounded by the contract lines (or on these lines) must be accepted as Pareto optimal, since any move from any such point would harm at least one member of the group. But the judgment may be submitted that the cycling of outcomes and the exploitation of the minority voter are undesirable features in a democratic society.

Increasing the Number of Voters

The situation presented in Figure 3.7 was quite unrealistic in several respects. In the real world, there ordinarily will be more than two issues confronting voters and there will be more than three voters in the decision-making group. Let us extend the analysis first by increasing the number of voters in the decision-making group, while retaining the two-issue frame of reference. In Figure 3.8, there are five voters, so that agreement among three of them is required in order to determine an outcome under a majority rule system. Contract lines are drawn to illustrate the bargains that might be struck between each pair of voters, but the point to recognize is that the final outcome will not fall on the boundaries of the area described by the exterior contract lines. In order to be a member of a winning coalition, a voter will have to come to terms with two other voters. For example, an agreement between A and B along their contract line will no longer be sufficient to determine an outcome. Some concession to one of the other voters will be necessary if a majority coalition is to be formed. This concession to one of the other voters will move the final outcome into the interior portion of the area.

FIGURE 3.8   Vote Trading: Two Issues and
Five Voters

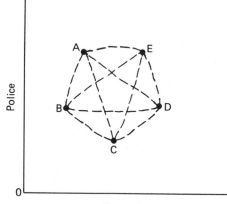

Several inferences can be drawn from the model in Figure 3.8. For example, since the final outcome will fall in the interior space of the contract line area, those voters who hold moderate positions on a particular issue are likely to be more satisfied with the outcome than are those voters whose positions are more extreme on that issue. Another way of expressing this is to observe that no voter is likely to be be so completely frozen out in the decision-making process as was possible in the three-voter case. All parties obtain some gains from trading. A second inference is that the bargaining in this political process will focus around those voters who hold "middle of the road" positions on the issues. Voters who hold more extreme positions will find it more advantageous to deal with the moderates than to attempt to deal with the voters on the opposite extreme. This brings the analysis back to the swing voter emphasis presented in the earlier analysis of majority voting systems and may help to explain why the working out of political party platforms seems to move the major parties to a more or less common ground. People with more extreme views sometimes complain that the major parties offer very little real choice to voters in general elections, and indeed this would appear to be a predictable outcome of majority rule procedures. But extremists who sought to abandon majority rule in favor of decisions by less than a majority face the risk that an opposing extreme might prevail and determine an outcome even less acceptable than that set by the majority rule system.

Still another inference suggests a useful role for a system of local governments. If a group of citizens finds itself rather regularly dissatisfied with the decisions reached by the central government, it may be appropriate to consider whether responsibility for the issues involved might be given to a system of local governments rather than to the single national government. If this were done (and it will be noted later that the appropriateness of such a transfer of responsibility depends on externality features of the matters being decided), those persons with a given set of views on a question might group themselves together and form one local government, while persons with a different set of views might form a separate local government. In this way, the system of local governments could accommodate differing viewpoints more effectively than could a single national government.

Increasing the Number of Issues

An additional degree of realism can be incorporated into the analysis by increasing the number of issues (programs financed out of the general fund) as well as the number of voters. In terms of Figure 3.7, this would require a third dimension to the graph (an axis labeled, for example, "expenditures for public health"). In this construct, each individual's ideal combination would be visualized as a point in three-dimensional space, and the Pareto optimal area of potential outcomes would be suspended in three-dimensional space. The indifference curve illustrations would be replaced by "surfaces" of equal attractiveness as different mixtures of the three different programs were evaluated by each voter. The possibilities of tradeoffs and contract lines would be considerably increased. As the number of issues and the number of voters increase, a complex web of tradeoffs among issues and among voters emerges that is in some degree descriptive of the environment within which practicing politicians must operate. Tradeoffs and compromises become the "tools of the trade" for the politician. When many such tools are available, deadlocks or standoffs can be averted and decisions actually reached without face to face and potentially destructive confrontation.

We may now think about a benefit-cost summing up of the system that uses a predetermined general revenue system to gather money into the general fund and majority voting techniques to allocate these funds among many competing possible programs. The benefit side of the summing up surely must recognize that there is value in a system which actually is capable of reaching decisions on complex matters and which can thus sustain itself as an agency for ensuring some level of satisfaction of collective wants. This is, perhaps, a requirement for collective action. But the cost side of the picture should not be overlooked. The actual outcomes of the process are likely to be fully acceptable only to that very rare individual who is a moderate on all things under the terms set down by the general revenue system in existence. Most voters will be dissatisfied to various degrees with each outcome, and a general frustration and undercurrent of dissatisfaction with politics will likely exist.

Changing Tax Shares

An attempt to move away from the nebulous world of compromise suggests a move back toward the Wicksell system and to a reexamination of the general revenue system itself. The middle of the road type of outcome that can be expected from the many-voter and many-issue model will be especially unsatisfactory to those voters who, under the existing general revenue system, find themselves holding relatively extreme positions on the particular issues being decided. Figure 3.9 presents, once again, the preferred positions of three different voters on two issues, police expenditures and recreation expenditures, but in this case it is assumed that there actually are many voters participating in the decision-making process and that the three voters whose positions are illustrated are merely representative of minority groups whose positions are somewhat extreme on one issue or the other.

FIGURE 3.9   Reduced Disagreement by Altered Tax Shares

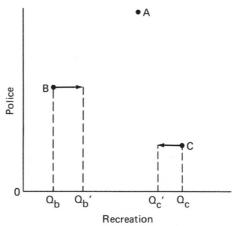

Because many voters participate in the decision, actual outcomes will be of the middle of the road variety, and the voters illustrated in Figure 3.9 will be dissatisfied with the outcome on one issue or the other or both. It is important to recall at this point that the positions taken by these voters arose from individual benefit-cost calculations which took into account the tax-sharing system established in the general revenue system. If a different tax-sharing system had been in effect, different preferred positions on expenditures would have been adopted. Recognition of this suggests that appropriate changes in the system used to collect the revenues to finance these services could reduce the extent of dissatisfaction with majority rule outcomes. Suppose, for example, that the preferred positions of these people in regard to recreation expenditures is found to be positively related to the frequency with which these individuals actually visit and directly utilize the recreational facilities provided. In this situation, some portion of the financing of recreational expenditures might be withdrawn from the general fund source and replaced with financing based on admissions charges collected when individuals actually use the facilities. This would increase the share of recreational service financing collected from individual C (who utilizes the service frequently) and would probably move his preferred total expenditure point to the left, as illustrated by the arrow on Figure 3.9.

On the other hand, the admission charge financing approach would reduce the share of recreational service financing collected from individual B (who utilizes the service infrequently) and move his preferred total expenditure position to the right, also illustrated by the arrow in Figure 3.9. The end result of this change in the financing system will reduce the extent of dissatisfaction with the outcome of the majority voting system. Individual B will be more content with the outcome, since he no longer is required to pay so large a share to finance a service on which he places little value. Of course, individual C has been denied the opportunity to enjoy as much of a free ride at the expense of other taxpayers (and he may not be overjoyed at this), but the reduced political opposition of individual B to recreation expenditures may result in some increase in the amount of spending actually decided upon, that is, in a movement toward an amount favored by C.

It is apparent that the key to reducing dissatisfaction through altered revenue-collecting systems lies in discovering taxable events or circumstances reliably associated with differing voter positions. The recreation admission fee illustration is only partly appropriate because it relied on a private or divisible component of a semicollective service and upon the applicability of an exclusion device for the collection of revenue. But it is possible that similar tax-share alterations may be discoverable for pure collective consumption. Suppose it were discovered, for example, that the direction of disagreement with voting outcomes on a particular issue was significantly associated with the size of the voter's income. If higher-income voters consistently favored larger expenditures than were actually agreed upon while lower-income voters consistently favored smaller expenditures than those actually agreed upon, the progressiveness of the tax system might be increased, thus increasing the tax share paid by higher-income groups and reducing that paid by lower-income groups. Through this procedure, the preferred output positions of the dissatisfied groups would be moved closer to the position of the median voter and the degree of dissatisfaction with the final outcome would be reduced. Conversely, if the directions of dissatisfaction were in the opposite direction, a reduction in the progressivity of the general revenue system would be indicated.

Other Variables

This introduction to revenue systems and voting only scratches the surface of the exceedingly complex matter of designing a political system capable of accurately discovering the preferences of citizens and able to apply these discoveries in government decision making. It should be recognized, for example, that the one person, one vote approach does not in itself provide a way to recognize differences in the intensity of the views held by individual citizens. Under a majority rule system, 51 voters who are only mildly concerned with the question under consideration can override 49 voters who feel very strongly about the matter. Vote trading provides some opportunity to incorporate the intensity variable because the terms of trade that will be acceptable to or insisted upon by the various voters will be influenced by intensities of view, but the underlying one person, one vote standard still operates as a constraint.

The role of political parties also merits examination as an instrument to discover voter preferences and apply this information to decisions. The package of positions set up in the party platform involves a vote-trading operation that can include consideration of the intensity of various wants as well as other factors, such as the contribution different groups can make in winning elections. Although majority rule imposes a strong force in the direction of middle of the road solutions, well-disciplined coalition parties may be able to push through legislation desired by groups holding relatively extreme positions. Political parties can also be analyzed in terms of their abilities to alter information costs and the costs of negotiating decisions in the legislative process.

SUMMARY

In this chapter, the proposition has been presented that the quantity of a collective service preferred by an individual depends upon the amount of benefit he expects to enjoy from the service and the price he will have to pay in order to obtain it. In other words, each citizen is seen as generating an individual demand curve for the collective service that relates the quantity he wishes to purchase to the tax price of that service to him. Because the services must be consumed collectively, the same level of output must be consumed by each individual and some group system of decision making must be utilized. If a democratic majority-rule system is utilized, actual quantities provided are likely to correspond with the wishes of the median voter or, through the operation of vote trading among numerous voters and issues, are likely to be moderate or middle of the road solutions that will leave some minority groups of voters dissatisfied. Some amount of toleration or acceptance of dissatisfaction is likely to exist in the interests of preserving a system of collective decision making in which all parties obtain at least some gains from the political processes and some degree of protection from excessive exploitation. But at some point, it may become desirable to attempt to reduce the strain on the social fabric by altering the revenue system in a way calculated to bring especially dissatisfied groups more nearly into agreement with the outcomes that will actually be determined by the voting processes.

SUGGESTED READINGS

ARROW, KENNETH. *Social Choice and Individual Values* (New York: Wiley, 1951).

DOWNS, ANTHONY. *An Economic Theory of Democracy* (New York: Harper & Row, 1957).

WICKSELL, KNUT, "A New Principle of Just Taxation," in R. A. MUSGRAVE and A. T. PEACOCK, *Classics in the Theory of Public Finance* (London: Macmillan, 1964), pp. 72-118.

BUCHANAN, JAMES M., and GORDON TULLOCK. *The Calculus of Consent* (Ann Arbor: The University of Michigan Press, 1965).

BUCHANAN, JAMES M. *Public Finance in Democratic Process* (Chapel Hill: University of North Carolina Press, 1967).

BRETON, ALBERT, *The Economic Theory of Representative Government* (Chicago: Aldine, 1974).

BUCHANAN, JAMES M. "A Contractarian Paradigm for Applying Economic Theory," *American Economic Review*, May 1975, pp. 225–31.

FEREJOHN, JOHN A., and MORRIS P. FIORINA, "Purposive Models of Legislative Behavior," *American Economic Review*, May 1975, pp. 407–15.

BUCHANAN, JAMES M., "Public Finance and Public Choice," *National Tax Journal*, Dec. 1975.

MUELLER, DENNIS C., "Public Choice: A Survey," *Journal of Economic Literature*, June 1976.

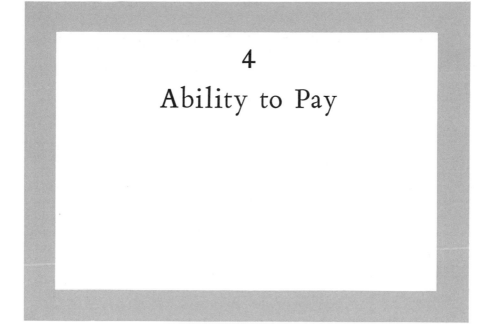

4
Ability to Pay

The model or guideline of taxation outlined in Chapters 2 and 3 is known as the *benefits-received* principle. It is an attractive model for taxation because it is consistent with the notion of fairness, which asserts that it is fair and proper that a person should pay for what he receives. The benefits-received model is also attractive because it provides a connection or link between government receipts and expenditures and therefore can be applied to develop a model for efficiency in the provision of collective goods and services. A closer examination of this approach, however, reveals that governments probably cannot and should not rely exclusively on benefits-received taxation. Instead, a different principle of taxation, the principle of *ability to pay*, provides the foundation or guideline for many of the taxes actually imposed.

INCOME DISTRIBUTION AND COLLECTIVE DEMAND

Elementary economics texts point out that an individual's demand for a good or service reflects not only his taste or preference for that service (the benefits received from it) but also his spending power or ability to pay. Even if two persons have identical taste or preference for a service and therefore would benefit equally from it, the person with a large amount of spending power will be able to mount a stronger or greater demand for it. This means that demand curves, such as those drawn to illustrate efficient taxation and expenditure under the benefits-received approach, reveal more than simply the benefits received by consumers. These demand curves reflect individual spending power as well.

When this insight is applied to the benefits-received model, it is immediately apparent that the pattern of collective wants which would be determined under one distribution of income might be quite different from the pattern determined under some different distribution. So long as different individuals have different sets of tastes and preferences, a redistribution of income will result in a restructuring of effective demand curves. It also means that the benefits-received approach to government finance is a willing servant of *any* distribution of income and that the efficiency characteristics of that approach are as valid under one distribution as under another. A truly efficient allocation of resources cannot be realized through the benefits-received approach until the correct or efficient distribution of income has been established. A satisfactory distribution of incomes must be secured *before* the allocational efficiency of benefits-received taxation can be accorded a genuinely legitimate status.

The task of securing the desired distribution of income is the responsibility of the federal government. Some of the difficulties in identifying this desired distribution will be discussed later; for the moment, the point is that taxation is an instrument of government which can be called upon to serve the distribution responsibility as well as the allocational responsibility. Ability to pay is the principle or guideline for taxation that asserts that the distribution of income should be recognized in the establishment of tax responsibilities. In fact, when the general fund revenue system is used so that any connection between tax payments and specific expenditure outlays is substantially eliminated, the ability to pay principle of taxation becomes the dominant criterion for the assessment of tax responsibilities. Some people pay a higher tax price than other people for the collection of services financed out of the general fund. The differential pricing of collective services becomes a device for income distribution rather than a device for determining the demand for collective services themselves. In other words, the ability to pay approach to taxation considers only the revenue side of the budget and provides little guidance to legislators either in setting the total amount of expenditures or in allocating expenditures among alternative collective services. Clearly, this absence of guidance for expenditure legislation is a weakness of the ability to pay approach.

This dual role required of taxation, that is, that it serve both to measure demand for collective services and also to redistribute income, greatly complicates the task of the elected official. In his efforts to understand the messages being sent by voters in elections, he must determine whether the message relates to an allocation question or to a distribution question. If voters in a particular income class consistently vote against expenditure proposals, it is not clear whether they are saying that the expenditure ought not to be made or that the distribution of tax responsibilities ought to be changed. Finding a way to separate or compartmentalize these two dimensions of taxation is a difficult task. The pure theory of government finance suggests that the distinction might be institutionalized by setting up a separate component of the budget which would deal only in distributive taxes and transfer payments. Revenues from distributive taxes or from the components of other taxes designated as the distributive component would be earmarked into this portion of the budget and legislators could make distributive decisions separately from allocational decisions. But this institutionalized separation does not exist in fact. Lacking it, legislators may attempt to carry out a mental discounting process when they interpret voting results. For example, this mental calculus might attach different weighting factors to votes from different income levels. These weighting factors would be used to remove the distributional element and leave a residual that might be interpreted as demand for collective services. The basic problem is that a single instrument (taxation) is used for two purposes (allocation of services and redistribution of income), so that a clear message for either purpose is impossible to discover.

EQUITY AND FAIRNESS

The notion that ability to pay taxation is a device for income redistribution probably is not the meaning attached to this principle by the typical citizen. Instead, the strong support that citizens give ability to pay taxation probably arises from the feeling that it is fair and equitable that people should contribute to the support of collective undertakings according to their individual abilities or capacities. This attitude can be observed in many situations other than taxation. For example, able-bodied persons are selected for military service while others are excused not only because the military service can operate more effectively in this way, but also because it is felt that able-bodied persons have a special obligation to perform this service by virtue of their native endowments. Churches solicit funds on an ability to pay basis and contend that it is an obligation of the well-to-do to support a greater share of the church budget.[1] Medical practitioners have been known to base fees on an ability to pay principle. Within the family, older children are expected to assist younger children and the able are expected to assist the infirm. In short, individuals are commonly reared in a cultural environment in which acceptance into the group (with the benefit that acceptance bestows) is conditional in some degree upon willingness to contribute according to ability. As the social "family" is more broadly conceived, it is not surprising that rules or guidelines which connect the ability to pay with an obligation to pay are supported.

The Equity Principle

The basic principle of equity is: "Treat equals equally and unequals unequally." Each portion of this principle is important. The first portion, which states that equals should be treated equally, is the principle of *horizontal* equity. It means that two persons who are equally capable of paying taxes or otherwise contributing to a common undertaking should in fact pay an equal amount of tax or perform an equal amount of service. The second part of the principle, which states that unequals should be treated unequally, is the principle of *vertical* equity. It means that if two persons differ from one another in some way relevant to their ability to support collective undertakings, this difference in abilities should be reflected in different tax payments or different contributions to collective undertakings. Both portions of the equity principle must be satisfied

---

[1] A benefits-received rationale might be suggested by the proposition that it is easier for a camel to pass through the eye of a needle than for a rich man to enter the Kingdom of Heaven!

in order for a tax or a tax system to be equitable. For example, it would be a simple matter to satisfy the first portion without satisfying the second. A poll or head tax which collected the same amount of money from every person would fulfill the requirement that equals be treated equally, since all persons who in fact were equal to one another would pay an equal amount of tax. But this poll tax would fail to fulfill the second portion of the equity principle, since no account would have been taken of differences considered relevant to supporting collective actions. A poll tax violates the generally recognized notion of vertical equity.

Measuring Ability: The Tax Base

The first step in establishing a tax in accordance with the equity principle is to define a tax *base* that can be used to compare the taxpaying ability of one citizen with the taxpaying ability of another. The tax base is the aspect of a person's affairs through which ability to pay is measured and on the basis of which actual tax liabilities are computed. Many possible tax bases can be proposed. Income is the most widely accepted base for taxation according to ability to pay. A broad definition of income measures the economic power of the individual and provides a counting system that can be readily used in assessing taxes. The definition of income is a complicated matter, since receipts may arise in many different forms and may come from many different sources, not all of which necessarily imply the same dollar for dollar ability to pay. Similarly, the ability to pay approach ordinarily suggests that a certain amount of income should be exempted entirely from tax because it is necessary for the basic living requirements of the individual. Various other deductions from income may be allowed if it is concluded that they improve the measure of ability to pay. The definition of income will be discussed further in connection with income taxation.

Although income is the most widely accepted measure of ability to pay, a case can be made for other tax bases or for measuring ability to pay by the combination of several different tax bases. For example, consumption expenditure could measure ability to pay under the rationale that the quantity of goods and services an individual withdraws from the social stockpile for his own personal enjoyment is a measure of that person's ability to contribute to the provision of collectively consumed services. A consumption expenditures tax might utilize an annual return summing total consumption expenditure, which would permit personal exemptions for subsistence consumption and employ graduated rates to meet the requirements of vertical equity.

Still another possible base for ability to pay measurement might be the amount of wealth or property owned by an individual. However, a wealth tax would make more sense in terms of ability to pay if it were a supplement to other taxes rather than the sole basis for ability to pay taxation. For example, if an income tax were the basic ability to pay instrument, a wealth tax might be proposed on the ground that income from property has a greater ability to pay, dollar for dollar, than income from labor services. The wealth tax would supplement the income tax in this situation. The income tax itself would not discriminate on the basis of source of income, but the supplementary wealth tax would provide such discrimination. The basic problem with a wealth tax is that the value of wealth is determined by the stream of income expected to flow from it, so that income taxation can accomplish much the same result as wealth taxation. But wealth taxation would give an incentive in favor of consumption rather than saving and introduce potential reductions in the rate of investment and economic growth.

Neither a genuine wealth tax nor a genuine consumption expenditures tax is used in the United States. The property tax, which is almost universally used by local governments, is not a genuine wealth tax because it imposes tax on the market value of certain types of property only (and not on the total wealth of an individual) and because the tax rates are not graduated according to the amount of wealth or property owned by an individual, as would be implied by an ability to pay concept of taxation. Sales taxes are widely used by both state and local governments, but these are not individualized consumption expenditures taxes. Only certain consumption expenditures are taxed, and no individual return is filed to permit graduation of rates on the basis of total consumption expenditures. Thus, income taxation is the primary vehicle for ability to pay taxation in the United States.

The legal or constitutional constraint on the selection of a tax base is that the base must provide a reasonable classification for the assessment of responsibilities. This requirement flows from the constitutional prohibition against taking property without "due process of law." If taxes were based on individual weight, height, or color, for example, they would be unconstitutional on the ground that the unreasonable classification took property without due process of law. Such taxes would violate the norm of horizontal equity, since unequal treatment would be accorded to people who were in fact equal in ability to pay.

Vertical Equity: Tax Rates

Vertical equity requires that differences in ability to pay, as revealed by the accepted measuring rod of the tax base, should be recognized in the assessment of actual tax liabilities. A person with a greater ability to pay should pay more dollars in tax than a person with lesser ability to pay. However, the principle of vertical equity does not answer the question of how much more tax should be paid by the person with greater ability; that is, the principle does not indicate which *rate structure* should be selected. For example, a tax may employ a flat or *proportional* rate structure, which means that the amount of tax liability is determined by multiplying the tax base by a rate (usually expressed as a percentage) which is the same for all taxpayers regardless of the size of their base. Under this proportional or flat rate structure, a person with a $20,000 income (assuming income to be the tax base) would pay twice as much tax as a person with a $10,000 income. The technical requirement of vertical equity would be satisfied, since the person with the greater ability would pay more than the person with the lesser ability.

But the technical requirement of vertical equity could also be satisfied by a different rate structure. For example, a tax could apply a pattern of tax rates graduated upward (that is, a *progressive* rate structure) so that the person with a higher income would pay a higher rate of tax than a person with a lower income. In this case, the person with a $20,000 income would pay more than twice as much tax as a person with a $10,000 income. The progressive rate structure would satisfy the technical requirement of vertical equity, but the equity principle itself would not indicate whether the progressive rate structure was a better or a worse recognition of the difference in ability to pay. Even a tax with a *regressive* rate structure could satisfy the technical requirements of vertical equity. A regressive rate structure applies a lower rate of tax to a larger tax base than to a smaller tax base (that is, the rate structure is graduated downward), but it is perfectly possible that such a tax also might collect more dollars from the high-income person than from the low-income person. For example, a person with income of $10,000 would pay a tax of $2,000 if his tax rate were 20 percent, but the person with income of $20,000 would pay $3,000 in tax even if his tax rate were only 15 percent. If the proportionate decrease in tax rates is smaller than the proportionate increase in the tax base, even the regressive rate structure is not inconsistent with the technical requirement of vertical equity.

The terms "proportional," "progressive," and "regressive" sometimes are used in a broader sense than simply as a reference to the relationship between the rate and the base of a particular tax. For example, sales taxes are often described as "regressive," even though the tax itself is a flat rate or proportional tax in terms of its own base, which is the price paid for a taxable commodity. The rate of the sales tax is the same whether the commodity has a high or a low price tag. The regressivity description is applied to sales taxes because it is alleged that the sales tax will claim a larger fraction of the income of the low-income person than of the higher-income person. Hence, the tax may be regressive in terms of income even though it is proportional in terms of its own base.

In ordinary conversation, it is customary to use income as the reference in describing various taxes or systems of taxes as progressive, regressive, or proportional. It is apparent, of course, that the characterization of sales taxes (or property taxes) as regressive requires some analysis of relationships between spending patterns (or property ownership patterns) and income levels. Moreover, these analyses are complicated by possibilities that taxes may be shifted so that the actual burden may fall on some person other than the one who pays the tax in the first instance. Errors can be made so that the labels may not fit the reality. For the moment, however, the point is that ability to pay and vertical equity tests may be applied even to taxes which do not themselves use bases broad enough or inclusive enough properly to measure ability to pay.

MODELS FOR VERTICAL EQUITY

We may now examine the question of whether there are any scientific or analytical models that can help in the selection of the rate structure for ability to pay taxation. The question is whether we can go beyond the basic notion that those with greater ability should pay more tax than those with lesser ability. Is there an answer to the question of how much more tax should be paid by those with greater ability?

The Sacrifice Approach

The sacrifice approach to taxation recognizes that the money an individual pays in taxes would have been used to acquire privately consumed goods and services if it had not been taken by government. Thus, the payment of taxes requires the individual to forego private goods and services, and this means that the individual must "sacrifice" some private enjoyments. The sacrifice approach ignores any benefits individuals may receive from the collective services financed by their tax dollars. These models focus only on the private satisfaction that must be given up when taxes are collected. Satisfaction, however, is a subjective phenomenon. For example, each of two people may be required to pay $100 in tax and each may therefore be forced to give up $100 worth of private goods and services, but it does not follow that these two people have incurred equal sacrifice as a result of their tax payment. If one of these persons attaches greater importance to the private goods that must be foregone, then he will make a greater sacrifice than the other person as a result of the tax payment. In fact, the main point about the sacrifice approach to taxation is that the sacrifice involved, dollar for dollar, in giving up private goods and services is not the same for all people. But the sacrifice approach asserts more than this. It contends that the amount of sacrifice imposed by the collection of a dollar in tax is related to the size of a person's income and that this relationship can provide a guideline for equitable taxation.

The principle of diminishing marginal utility is the key element in the sacrifice approach. According to this principle, as successive units of a commodity are consumed in some limited period of time, the satisfaction or enjoyment derived from each successive unit will, at least after some point, be less than the satisfaction derived from the preceding unit. In texts on the principles of economics, this principle is used to help explain why the demand curve for a commodity will slope downward to the right in the conventional graphic presentation. The consumer is said to be willing to purchase an additional unit of the commodity only if the price is lowered, because the satisfaction he expects to receive from this added unit is also lower. The sacrifice approach applies the principle of diminishing marginal utility to money itself and asserts that the last or marginal dollar of income of the wealthy person will be expended to purchase commodities which generate relatively lesser satisfaction than the expenditure of the last or marginal dollar of income by the low-income person. Thus, the payment of a dollar in tax will impose a smaller sacrifice on the high-income person than on the low-income person.

Sacrifice Models

Assuming the law of diminishing marginal utility to be applicable to income, several models are offered as guidelines for the establishment of a fair and equitable tax system. One such model suggests that *equal sacrifice* would be a fair way to distribute tax responsibilities. Equal sacrifice would require that more dollars of tax would be collected from high-income than from low-income persons. The different tax liabilities would be arranged so that the sacrifice experienced by one taxpayer would be equal to the sacrifice experienced by another. The actual rate structure needed to establish equal sacrifice would depend on the rate at which marginal utility diminishes as income advances. If the marginal utility of money diminishes at the same rate as income advances (for example, if a 10 percent increase in income brought a 10 percent reduction in the marginal utility of money), a proportional or flat rate structure would accomplish equal sacrifice. If marginal utility declines proportionately faster than income advances, progressive rates would be indicated, and regressive rates would be indicated if marginal utility declines more slowly than income advances.

Another view suggests that *proportional sacrifice* would be a fair way to distribute tax liabilities. Once again, the high-income taxpayer would pay more dollars of tax than the low-income taxpayer, but the difference in tax liability would be arranged so that each taxpayer sacrifices an equal portion or fraction of his total utility. All taxpayers would make some sacrifice, but in absolute terms, the amount of sacrifice asked from high-income persons would be greater than the amount asked from low-income persons. Proportional sacrifice is more likely to involve progressively graduated tax rates than would equal sacrifice, but the actual rate structure still requires information about the rate at which the utility of money declines as income advances.

A third sacrifice model, known as *minimum aggregate sacrifice*, is the simplest of the various sacrifice doctrines. Minimum aggregate sacrifice requires that taxes be collected *only* from the individual or individuals with the lowest marginal utility, and the assumption of diminishing marginal utility of income suggests that the dollars with the least utility will be found in the hands of the highest income person. As funds are required for financing government services, taxes will be collected only from the highest income person until that person's after-tax income has been reduced to the level of the second highest income person. If more funds were required, tax would be collected from these (now) top two income receivers until their after-tax incomes equaled that of the third highest income receiver, and so on. In this manner, the minimum aggregate sacrifice model involves a leveling of incomes, from the top down, to whatever extent necessary in order to generate needed government revenues. Although a sophisticated application of the minimum aggregate sacrifice model would also require information about individual marginal utilities, this model is the least ambiguous of the several models advanced under the sacrifice approach.

Critique of the Sacrifice Approach

The entire sacrifice approach to taxation is rejected by modern welfare economics on the ground that interpersonal comparison of utility cannot be scientifically verified. This means, for example, that even if two individuals have the same income, it cannot be established that they actually derive the same utility from that income. One person may attach little importance to money and the things that money can buy, so that he may suffer little sacrifice by yielding a dollar in tax to the government. But the other person may attach great importance to money and the things money can buy, so that he would suffer great sacrifice in yielding a dollar of tax to the government. High-income persons may attach more utility to their marginal dollar than do low-income persons (which may explain, in part, why they are wealthy and why others are less wealthy).

In short, modern welfare economics is unwilling to accept either the assumption that different individuals are equally "efficient" in deriving satisfaction from money or the assumption that the marginal utility of money declines as income advances. Marginal utility may diminish as successive units of a *given commodity* are consumed within some *limited time period*, but the utility of money is not restricted to expenditure on any specified commodity, the demand for which may be satiable. Thus, even the least demanding sacrifice model, that of minimum aggregate sacrifice, cannot be accepted in the frame of reference established by modern welfare economics. Tax dollars collected from the very rich may entail more sacrifice, in the introspective sense contemplated by the sacrifice approach, than tax dollars collected from persons with smaller incomes.

REDISTRIBUTION AS A COLLECTIVE GOOD

The inability to measure the sacrifice entailed in the payment of taxes or to describe how this sacrifice is related to income size does not mean that voters may not vote as if sacrifice could be measured and as if the marginal utility of money diminishes as income rises. Likewise, the inability to specify scientifically a "correct" income distribution does not mean that voters are indifferent to income distribution or that taxation may not be employed to redistribute incomes. In fact, income distribution and the progressivity of income taxation are political questions precisely because scientific investigation is not able to provide solutions that command the agreement of all reasonable people. Taxation according to ability to pay is public policy, and the meaning of ability to pay has not been defined outside the political process through which its directives are expressed. This is indeed a dilemma for those who seek "eternal verities" or guidelines to correct provisions for vertical equity that can be verified outside the system itself.

Progressive taxation was vigorously debated more than a century ago in England. The absence of any definable guideline to the correct degree of progression led to some apprehension. Some people contended that if taxation departed from the simple and firm rule of proportionality it would be "like a ship at sea without rudder or compass" or that progressive taxation combined with democratic processes would amount to a license for the numerous poor to expropriate the income of the rich and drain away the funds needed for investment and development. The classic argument in favor of progression was that "it is better to be roughly right (that is, equitable) than to be certainly wrong (that is, inequitable)." Each of these positions reveals a desire to discover some guideline for the correct provision of vertical equity in taxation. The more modern view is that vertical equity (or income distribution) itself is a collective service and that people may express their demand for this service when they cast their votes in the democratic process. This view, however, returns the analysis to the dilemma posed at the beginning of the chapter—namely, that the income distribution which actually prevails is an important influence on the collective demands themselves.

The fact is that a progressive rate structure is a firmly established characteristic of income taxation in the United States. Some modifications in this rate structure have been made in relatively recent years, both at the upper and lower income ends of the scale, but the basic structure of progressive rates and income redistribution has remained generally intact for a long time. This suggests that the tax has exhibited vertical and horizontal equity outcomes which have not been grossly out of line with the perceptions of fairness or the desires for redistribution of the majority of voters. But this record of stability is no guarantee that modifications may not be required at some future time. In spite of their relatively permanent or "constitutional" nature, adjustments are made in many taxes in every session of Congress. Major reforms are rare, but minor revisions are commonplace. Thus, changing notions of equity or ability to pay can be incorporated into the tax system. The whole process is a delicate one and of great significance for the stability and well-being of the society. Recent proposals for negative income taxation, for example, may reflect a broadening of the ability to pay notion and a more direct recognition of income redistribution as a collective service. Under a negative income tax system, persons with income below a specified level would receive money *from* the government just as persons with income above this level would be required to transmit money *to* the government.

SUMMARY

The demand for collective services expressed through democratic political processes reflects both the benefits received by citizens and the distribution of income among these citizens. The ability to pay principle of taxation is a recognition of the importance of the distribution of income, even though it is expressed indirectly through the notion of fairness or equity in taxation. The principle of ability to pay requires that both horizontal and vertical equity be achieved by the tax system, but particular interest attaches to the requirement of vertical equity, which is generally taken to mean that persons with greater ability to pay should pay more tax.

But the principle of vertical equity does not provide an answer to the question of how much more should be paid by those with greater ability. Sacrifice doctrines, which attempt to develop guidelines for tax rate structures based on the law of diminishing marginal utility, are rejected by modern welfare economics because the interpersonal comparisons of welfare or utility required by the sacrifice approach cannot be established. Thus, the guidelines for ability to pay and vertical equity become products of the collective decision-making process itself and the redistribution of income is a collective service for which voters express their demands much as they do for other collective services. Progressive rate structures are firmly established aspects of the tax system in the United States. The stability of these rate structures implies that they do not seriously violate prevailing majority views about vertical equity and the desire for income redistribution. If the democratic political process operates effectively, changing views about ability to pay will lead to different tax rate structures.

SUGGESTED READINGS

BLUM, WALTER J., and HARRY KALVIN, JR. *The Uneasy Case for Progressive Taxation* (Chicago: The University of Chicago Press, 1953).

HOCHMAN, HAROLD M., and JAMES D. RODGERS, "Pareto Optimal Redistribution," *American Economic Review*, Sept. 1969.

THUROW, LESTER C., "The Income Distribution as a Pure Public Good," *Quarterly Journal of Economics*, May 1971.

II

The National

Government

The national or federal government of the United States has responsibilities in each of the functions conventionally identified for government. Resource allocation, income distribution, and economic stabilization all are responsibilities of the national government. It is this "full service" characteristic of the national government that distinguishes it from state and local governments, which have relatively little capability to fulfill demands for income distribution and economic stabilization. The authority to create money and to regulate international migration and trade enables the national government to perform stabilization and distribution tasks. State and local governments do not have authority in these matters.

Chapter 5 surveys the budgetary, or fiscal, operations of the federal government and examines the procedures employed in establishing the budget. The allocation, distribution, and stabilization functions are examined in some detail in Chapters 6 through 10. The major components of the revenue system of the federal government are analyzed in Chapters 11 through 16.

5

The Budget
of the National Government

The budget of the national or federal government is a planning instrument, because the fiscal operations of the government for the coming fiscal year are planned and decided upon in the process of formulating the budget. It is also an administrative instrument because, once adopted, the budget guides the administration of fiscal operations during the period it covers. The budget also provides a record of the fiscal operations of past years. This chapter deals primarily with the budget as a planning instrument, that is, it examines the procedures followed in formulating the budget. The actual size and composition of the federal budget for fiscal 1967 and the fiscal 1977 are presented in the brief appendix to this chapter.

The budgetary process in the federal government does not correspond with the ideal picture painted by Wicksell, in which each expenditure is teamed with the taxes that finance it so that a direct confrontation of benefits and costs can be obtained in the decision-making process. Instead, the federal budgetary process utilizes the general revenue system, in which money is poured into a general fund through taxes that continue year after year in generally unchanged form and in which expenditures are financed with monies appropriated out of this general fund. Most of the action in the budgetary process, therefore, focuses on the expenditure side of the budget.

The budget of the federal government is developed through a rather long and complex deliberative process in which various agencies and departments of the government play important roles. There are two stages or basic sets of processes in the enactment of expenditure legislation. The first of these is the *budget request stage* in which the agencies of the executive branch initiate pro-

61

posals for expenditures. The second is the *congressional action stage* in which Congress takes official action on expenditure appropriations.

THE BUDGET REQUEST STAGE

In a formal or procedural sense, the initiative in securing budgetary support for a service lies with what can be termed the "action agencies" of the government, that is, with those agencies which already exist and which are actively engaged in delivering services approved by past legislative actions. These agencies are located in the executive branch of the government, since it is the responsibility of the executive to implement or carry out the programs prescribed by Congress. These agencies are expected to be aware of the services presently being rendered and to be knowledgeable about the demands of citizens (or at least of the agency client group) for changes, extensions, or reductions in the services being provided. In an indirect or informal sense, of course, the initiative lies with the demands of the citizenry as perceived by these agencies. These action agencies regularly engage in long-term planning in respect to program changes that may be desirable in the future.

In a political context, the action agencies play an "advocacy" role in respect to the programs for which they are responsible. The personnel and especially the leadership of these agencies firmly believe in the importance of the work they are doing and are convinced that an expansion of these programs would be desirable. Indeed, the agencies not only carry out programs already authorized but continually press for new programs or expansions of existing programs in their area of interest. Congress and the President may welcome and encourage the "advocate" posture of the agencies not only because this attitude stimulates the search for new or improved programs, but also because the advocates' requests for ever-increasing budget appropriations permit the executive and the legislature to grant less than has been requested and thereby to appear as "guardians of taxpayer interests."[1]

Let us now trace the step by step procedure that takes place between the time a proposed program is "a gleam in the eye" of an action agency until it finally is acted upon, either favorably or unfavorably, by Congress and the President. The procedure is a lengthy one and there are many participants. Therefore, it will be helpful to use a flow diagram to illustrate what happens. Figure 5.1 outlines the step by step process in the executive branch of the government and culminates with the submission of the budget message by the President to Congress.

The major players in this process are the agencies themselves and the Office of Management and Budget (OMB), which is a part of the Executive Office of the President and which works on behalf of the President in bringing together the requests of the various agencies into an acceptable budget package. The first box in Figure 5.1 indicates that the agencies are formulating their initial budget requests. Ordinarily, this will take place in the spring (April and May) of the calendar year preceding the one in which the fiscal year is scheduled to begin, that is, some eighteen months before the start of the fiscal year for

[1] Aaron Wildavsky, *The Politics of the Budgetary Process* (Boston: Little, Brown, 1964).

FIGURE 5.1 Executive Branch Preparation of Budget Requests

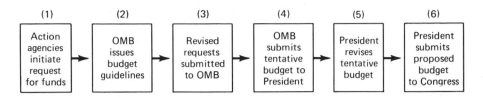

which the funds are requested. The second box indicates that the OMB develops general guidelines reflecting the priorities of the President, examines agency requests in the light of these guidelines, and returns the requests to the agencies so that they can revise their requests according to these guidelines. In the third box, the necessary revisions are made by the agencies and the revised agency requests are forwarded, once again, to the OMB.

By the end of the summer and into the early months of fall, the OMB is engaged in assembling the revised requests of the various agencies, developing estimates of revenues that can be expected for the fiscal year in question, and fitting all these together into a comprehensive budget document. Compromises must be made and recommendations developed in respect to both the revenue and expenditure sides of the budget. The tentative budget document that emerges in box 4 of Figure 5.1 is submitted to the President generally around November. In box 5, the President directs such changes in the budget document as appear to be appropriate in the light of his priorities and circumstances at that time. The final step in the executive branch development of the budget takes place in late January or early February when the President submits his budget proposals to Congress (box 6).

The Budget Document

The budget submitted by the President to Congress each year is the nearest thing that the federal government has to a comprehensive written plan for its fiscal operations for the forthcoming year. Congress will work from this budget as it proceeds to act upon the requests made by the President. Consequently, the form in which this budget is submitted is of considerable importance.

The format presently employed is referred to as the *unified budget* because it unifies or brings together all the various fiscal operations of the federal government into a single comprehensive statement. The importance of bringing together all the various fiscal operations into a single document is illustrated by the greatly increased importance of trust funds in these total operations. Prior to the latter part of the 1960s, trust fund receipts and outlays (such as those for the social security programs and the interstate highway program) were not included in the budget submitted by the President, which then was referred to as the *administrative budget*. The logic of this procedure lay in the fact that trust fund receipts and outlays generally were governed by legislation adopted by previous Congresses and constituted commitments which could not be significantly altered by actions of the present Congress. However, it became increasingly apparent that the number of dollars being received and expended through these trust funds did have important impacts on the operation of the economy and that the volume of these transactions had become so great that their omission from the administrative budget was no longer acceptable. The dollar volume of trust fund receipts and outlays estimated for fiscal 1978 was itself greater than the total nontrust fund operations of the federal government only ten years earlier, in fiscal 1968.[2]

The budget submitted to Congress actually is several separate budgets combined in the same package. The basic information about the plan for the fiscal operation of the federal government is presented in several different formats. This is done in order to facilitate the examination of proposals from several different perspectives or points of view. For example, in one presentation, the financial plan for the government appears in the format of the national income and product accounts so that the demands of the government on the productive capabilities of the economy can be evaluated along with the demands arising from private consumers and businesses. This formulation is helpful in judging the budget from a macroeconomic point of view. Another presentation organizes the financial plan according to the administrative agencies that will be responsible for the implementation of the plan once it is adopted. This is the traditional administrative format for the budget. Responsibilities must be clearly expressed both for effectiveness in implementation and in order to facilitate the audits and reviews needed to ensure that funds have been applied as directed by the appropriations measures.

The Planning Programming Budget System (PPBS)

The budget is also presented in a program format, that is, organized according to the objectives the government wishes to accomplish through the budgeted operations. Indeed, since 1960 there has been a great deal of innovation in the budgetary process based on the philosophy of program budgeting.

The essential idea of program budgeting is that decision making on expenditure programs ought to be focused on the goals or objectives the government hopes to accomplish. Certainly, the whole notion of comparing benefits and costs in determining the appropriateness of programs suggests that objectives must be given prominent attention at all stages of the budgetary process. The procedure begins with a consideration of objectives. Possible objectives in different areas are identified and consideration is given to the priorities attached to these programs. Specificity is important. Ideally, objectives should be formulated in ways that will facilitate quantification so that it will be possible to measure the degree of success attainable through alternative approaches. The development of alternatives is also important, since a given objective may be accomplished in ways that may involve cost differences or have different side effects, either positive or negative, on other programs of the government.

A particularly useful aspect of the programmatic organization is that this type of presentation forces decision makers to recognize that most program objectives cannot be accomplished in the span of one budget year, but will require support through a number of years. Thus, the PPBS requires estimates

[2] *Economic Report of the President, 1977* (Washington, D.C.: Government Printing Office, 1977), pp. 266–67.

of financing requirements extending beyond the budget period for which a request is being made. Of course, different programs will require different time spans for their accomplishment, but existing PPBS procedures require estimates extending at least five years into the future. Thus, when the PPBS process is effectively carried out, Congress is given some opportunity to determine the commitments that approval will impose on future budgets.

The modern impetus for the PPB system arose in the Department of Defense in the early 1960s. By executive order, the system was required of all government agencies starting in 1965. Since that time, experience with the procedure has been mixed, with some departments finding it more suitable to their programs than other departments. In general terms, agencies and departments that deal with people-oriented services (such as welfare and education) have encountered considerable difficulty with the quantification and specificity requirements of the system. Data required for specification and quantification may not exist, and the estimating procedures or proxy measures developed in these cases may be inaccurate or contain biases that may seriously detract from the validity of final decisions. Certainly the staffing requirements of the PPB system are great, both for the agencies themselves in preparation of budget requests and also for Congress in understanding and evaluating the resulting requests.

The programmatic organization reveals that important relationships exist between programs undertaken by one agency or department and those undertaken or requested by other agencies or departments. Sometimes the relationship is complementary, so that appropriate actions by one department cannot be determined until proposals from or authorizations to other departments are known. In other cases, programs of one agency may be found to compete with or work at cross purposes to programs of other agencies. These factors place considerable stress on coordination of agencies and point to the enormous complexity in the operations of large government.

The commonsense appeal of the planning-programmatic approach is great. Certainly it makes sense to attempt to identify objectives clearly, to quantify as much as possible the benefits and costs of realizing these objectives, to consider alternative ways of accomplishing them, to coordinate the programs of one agency with those of other agencies, and to recognize the commitments placed on future budgets by actions taken in the current time period. The resource costs of the procedure are also great, of course, since many hours of effort must be expended in developing and analyzing detailed proposals. Mountains of paperwork are generated. There are dangers in the implicit biases between quantifiable areas of endeavor and those other areas that may be equally or more important but that do not lend themselves to quantification. But there would seem to be little merit in supposing that government decision making is less complicated than it is. If the PPB system conveys a recognition of the complexity and difficulty of the process, then it at least lays the groundwork for improvements in the years to come.[3]

---

[3] A number of interesting and useful contributions to an understanding of the government expenditure process and the PPB system are contained in Robert H. Haveman and Julius Margolis (eds.), *Public Expenditures and Policy Analysis* (Chicago: Markham, 1970).

THE CONGRESSIONAL ACTION STAGE

After the President has submitted his budget proposals to Congress in late January or early February, the scene of action focuses on the legislature, and specifically on certain of its committees. Once again, it will be helpful to utilize a flow chart illustrating the successive stages of congressional consideration of budget requests (Figure 5.2). Under reform legislation enacted in 1974,

FIGURE 5.2   Legislative Branch Consideration of Budget Requests

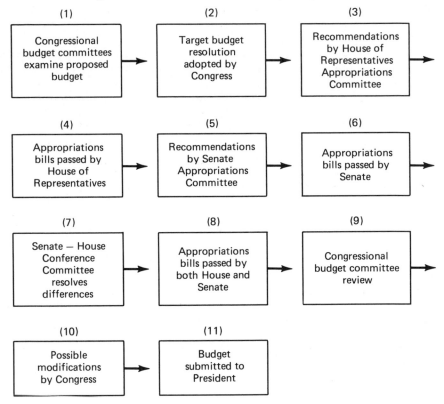

the first step in congressional consideration of the President's request is an examination of the entire package of presidential proposals by budget committees of the House of Representatives and of the Senate. These are new committees established under the 1974 reform legislation. Their job is to consider the budget in its aggregate totals and in its general functional subdivisions and to submit a resolution to Congress indicating "targets" both in the total figures and in the broad category subdivisions. These committee resolutions are to be submitted to Congress not later than April 15 and, in the month between April 15 and May 15, Congress is expected to consider these proposals, to make such amendments as appear appropriate, and finally to adopt a resolution establishing target levels for the forthcoming fiscal year, both in aggregate totals and in major budget functional subdivisions (box 2). This resolution is expected to provide guidance to the various committees of the Congress as they then proceed to consider budget proposals in specific functional areas.

Committee work in Congress on specific elements of the budget begins in the Appropriations Committee of the House of Representatives (box 3). The President's budgetary requests are broken down into some dozen or fifteen functional categories, each of which is assigned to a subcommittee of the Appropriations Committee. This breaking down of the budget into functional categories is important because the bills finally acted upon by Congress will maintain essentially this same breakdown.[4] The subcommittees of the House Appropriations Committee, after considering the requests in the functional areas assigned to them, report an appropriations bill for this function to the full committee, which then will report an appropriations bill for this function to the floor of the House of Representatives for consideration and ultimate adoption (box 4). After House action, a similar procedure is carried out in the Senate, starting with subcommittees of the Senate Appropriations Committee and proceeding through the full committee (box 5) to the Senate floor for consideration and adoption (box 6). If the bill enacted by the Senate differs from that adopted by the House, as will typically be the case, the matter will be taken up by a conference committee including members both from the House and the Senate (box 7). The compromise version worked out by the conference committee is then considered and acted upon by each of the houses of Congress (box 8).

In September, the congressional budget committees review the actual budget legislation that has been adopted, compare these results with the targets adopted earlier in the year, and report their findings to the Congress, along with any recommendations (box 9). This review is to be completed by September 15. Congress could then enact last-minute budget modifications based on the aggregate review provided by the committees (box 10). The final budget is submitted to the President for approval or veto (box 11).

The Budget Reform of 1974

The reform legislation of 1974 established the budget committees of the House and the Senate, which had no counterpart prior to this reform, and gave these new committees the responsibility of subjecting the President's proposed budget to an initial examination and of submitting resolutions to Congress in respect to these aggregate considerations (boxes 1 and 2 in Figure 5.2). The reform also directed Congress to adopt an aggregate budget target early in the budget process and directed the budget committees to make a review of the aggregate budget at the close of the appropriations process. The Congressional Budget Office was established to assist Congress in analysis of budget proposals and to keep Congress informed of its progress in adhering to targets established in the initial stages of the budget process.[5] In order to provide time for these

---

[4] Table 5.1, in the appendix to this chapter, shows the breakdown of budget outlays for fiscal year 1978.

[5] C. William Fischer, "The New Congressional Budget Establishment and Federal Spending: Choices for the Future," *National Tax Journal*, March 1976.

additional steps, the starting date of the fiscal year was set back by three months, from July 1 to October 1.

The point behind the reform of 1974 was to provide Congress with an opportunity to view the proposed budget in its aggregate dimension. Clearly Congress was sensitive to the complaint that it had "failed to recognize the forest because of the trees," that is, that preoccupation with the specific proposals had meant that adequate attention was not given to the total budget picture. In addition, the new procedure injected a clearer exercise of marginal analysis into the decision-making process. By reviewing the big picture, programs marginal in one functional area may be compared to marginal programs in other functional areas and the acceptability of these marginal programs may be determined in connection with the levels of taxation necessitated by the aggregate totals of appropriations from all functional areas.

It is too early to determine, of course, whether the reform procedures adopted in 1974 will be successful. Previous attempts to obtain congressional consideration of aggregate budget totals, such as the effort to utilize an omnibus appropriations bill in the early post-World War II period, were not successful. The enormity and complexity of the omnibus appropriations bill proved to be more than Congress could handle. The 1974 reform continued the traditional procedure of separate actions in different functional areas of the budget but grafted onto this procedure the initial establishment of guidelines and the later opportunity for review and revision. This adding of new procedures to old may have a greater chance of success than earlier attempts at aggregate consideration. The procedure, however, increased the lead time for the agencies by three months, which may increase the difficulty of anticipating demands for collective services.

Implementation and Auditing

The executive branch of the government is responsible for carrying out the decisions of Congress. Therefore, after appropriations have been signed into law, the scene of action returns to the agencies of the executive branch and to the Office of Management and Budget. The money appropriated by Congress does not go directly to the action agencies but instead is channeled through the OMB, which releases the funds in instalments, usually on a quarterly basis, as required by the programs authorized by Congress. This periodic release of funds by the OMB is a means by which the President through the OMB can exercise control over the action agencies. Periodic release prevents agencies from using up all their appropriations early in the fiscal year and then confronting the executive and Congress with the dilemma of either granting additional funds or seeing the functions of the agency seriously modified in the later portions of the fiscal year.

The procedure also enables the executive branch to respond to unanticipated events that alter the need for funds. Certainly emergencies can alter the need for funds within limits reasonably encompassed in the intent of Congress, and some need for executive authority in these situations cannot be denied. The issue of presidential "impoundment" of appropriated funds arises when the withholding or denying of funds to an action agency takes place not in consequence of unanticipated developments but because of policy differences between the President and Congress. Such impoundment is illegal, but it is apparent that the circumstances surrounding each particular instance of withholding funds must be examined in order to determine whether illegal impoundment has taken place.

The final step in the budgetary process involves auditing of agency expenditures by the General Accounting Office (GAO), which is responsible to Congress rather than to the President. The General Accounting Office serves a watchdog function: it identifies instances in which agencies may have expended funds in a manner contrary to the specifications set forth by Congress. Findings by the General Accounting Office may lead to legal action if criminal offenses are alleged.

EVALUATION OF THE BUDGETARY PROCESS

In a democratic system, the criterion for evaluating the budgetary process is the extent to which the outcomes of the process match up with the benefit and cost perceptions of the citizens. That is, the responsibility of government is to respond to the wishes of the people or "to do those things which the people wish to have done but cannot do as well for themselves." It is readily apparent, therefore, that any evaluation of the budgetary process encounters a difficult problem at the outset: If the budgetary process is to be evaluated in terms of how well its outcomes match up with the wishes of the people, then some separate or independent indicator of the people's wishes must be found against which to compare these outcomes. But no such separate or independent indicator is available in the sense of a "social welfare function" that exists apart from the political process itself. And the budget is a product of this very political process.

In the face of this dilemma, it will be helpful to refer back to the earlier discussion of decision systems and voting (Chapter 3). In Wicksell's ideal system, there would be no budgetary process and indeed no budget at all in the sense of a coordinated government plan for fiscal operations. There would be only separate expenditure and tax enactments, each considered on its own benefit-cost merits and each accepted or rejected by reference to the budget plans of the individual citizens themselves. The only budget for the collectivity would be the package of legislation actually enacted. In a sense, there would be no entity or separate being that could be identified as "government."

Trust fund operations (such as the social security system) do bear the stamp of Wicksell's inspiration and the earmarking of particular taxes for expenditure in specified programs is an approximation of the Wicksell approach, but for a great many activities actually carried on in the public sector, the Wicksellian or "no budget" approach has not been found to be satisfactory. Instead, the general revenue system has been adopted. Money is fed into a general fund through a variety of more or less permanent tax measures and expenditures are financed with funds drawn out of this fund. Budgeting and a budgetary process become useful instruments in the institutional setup known as government, and government thus becomes an entity or separate being in some degree.

It is now possible to return to the dilemma of finding a test or criterion for evaluating the budgetary process as it actually exists. The test must be the ballot box. As was outlined in the discussion of revenue systems and voting, a given budgetary system may generate or produce an identifiable pattern of outcomes. If this pattern is acceptable, that is, if the outcomes conform adequately to the wishes of the citizens, calls for significant reforms in the process will not be heard or will not gather great political strength. The budgetary process could be given good grades (at least a grade of "satisfactory") as an instrument for responding to the wishes of the people. If the pattern of outcomes is found not acceptable, calls for significant reform will be heard and will gather political force.

The budget reform legislation of 1974 provides an obvious example of the evaluation process in action. A pattern of budgetary outcomes was perceived and interpreted to suggest that the prevailing system gave insufficient attention to aggregate totals of expenditures and revenues. Changes designed to remedy this defect in the existing process were proposed and adopted. It remains to be seen whether this particular package of reform will succeed or whether further modifications will be sought. We will now examine certain other dimensions of the budgetary process that have generated controversy and have led to positions for or against reform.

Fragmentation and Dilution of Power

The general revenue system sets up a conflict situation within the institutional structure of the government. The amount of money available to the general fund is like a pie to be divided among the competing demands for collective services. The budgetary process provides the mechanism through which these conflicts are resolved. Thus, the budgetary process can be evaluated in terms of whether or not these conflicts are resolved in a manner satisfactory to the citizens.[6]

The fragmentation of the budget into a dozen or so separate appropriations bills has the effect of limiting or placing constraints on the exercise of power. Because the total budget is broken down into a number of separate bills, it is highly unlikely that a single coalition of voting strength could be mobilized and maintained in such a way as to work its will in all of them. Instead, different coalitions are likely to be required in different areas of appropriation. Each voting member is endowed with as many votes as there are measures to be voted upon. Therefore, by judiciously husbanding these voting resources, effective opposition to power domination can be focused at selected points in the total budget.

This horizontal fragmentation of the budget also sets up competing interest groups within the government agency structure. Each specific agency is interested primarily in the appropriations bill which provides funds for that agency. Thus, whatever political resources are at its disposal may be focused on

---

[6] The reform legislation of 1974 focused on the aggregate dimension of the budget, that is, on the size of the pie available for division among the competing claimants. If these reforms are effective in imposing more constraint upon the size of the pie, it will be less possible to resolve the microconflicts among competing demands for collective service with the response of "more for all." Thus, if the aggregative reform is effective, it will produce greater stress on the conflict resolution dimension of the budgetary process.

that particular piece of legislation and may have a significant effect on the outcomes of the legislative process in that particular area. In short, the fragmentation of the budget into a number of separate parts represents a classic strategy of reducing the threat of excessive power by diluting that power. That is, all the eggs are not in one basket.

Extra costs. The fragmentation of the budget also has its disadvantages. Some costs are incurred in exchange for the protection against an unbridled exercise of power. One of these arises in the legislative process, when the separate treatment of a dozen or so appropriations bills increases the difficulty of comparing marginal programs in one area with marginal programs in another area. Because of the fragmentation, programs in one area that offer a relatively high return per unit of input may be rejected while, in a different appropriation, a program with a lower relative return per unit of input may be accepted. If the two programs had been subject to comparison in a single appropriations bill, a more efficient allocation of resources might have been achieved. But with the fragmented budget some amount of inefficient resource allocation at the margins can be expected. Similarly, fragmentation probably leads to some duplication of activities among different agencies and to overhead costs that would not arise if a more unitary approach were taken.

Fixing responsibility. Difficulty in fixing responsibility, or assessing credit and blame, is another problem that is attributable to the fragmentation of the budget. The process of debate and compromise on twelve or fifteen different appropriations measures may result in waste, duplication, and lack of coordination among agencies and programs. It may be difficult or impossible to trace the steps taken in such a way as to determine responsibility for the final outcome. The legislation finally placed before the President may differ in important ways from the proposals submitted to Congress. Changes may have originated in subcommittees of either house, on the floor of either house, or in the conference committee directed to iron out differences between the enactments of the two houses. If the final outcome proves unsatisfactory, the President can blame Congress, or Congress can blame the President, or one house of Congress can blame the other.

Special interests. In the fragmented system, considerable power over certain sections of the budget may come to rest with a few congressmen or senators, specifically the members of the subcommittees of the House and Senate appropriations committees who deal year after year with particular items of expenditure. Many of the matters considered in the budget process require a great deal of experience and technical information if informed decisions are to be made. No senator or congressman has the capability of being well-informed on all the many expenditure programs on which he is expected to pass judgment. Therefore, members with expertise or interest in a specific area will seek appointment to the subcommittee that makes recommendations to the full appropriations committee on that aspect of expenditure proposals. Likewise, members who have served on these subcommittees for a number of years will develop a grasp of that particular aspect of the budget which is respected and relied upon by other members. The recommendations of the subcommittee are therefore likely to be accepted largely intact by the full committee, and the entire House or Senate, in turn, is likely to accept the recommendations of its appropriations committee.

The result of this system of expertise on the one hand and deference to this expertise by the larger bodies of Congress on the other gives these subcommittee members considerable responsibility and power. In order to have influence on the final legislation, it is necessary to gain the support of these few members. Success in gaining this support may in large measure be sufficient to obtain the desired outcomes in the final legislation. Although the entire process works to focus a high level of information and experience on particular segments of proposed legislation, it also opens the way for effective lobbying by interest groups that have much at stake in particular tax or expenditure positions of the government. Thus, the power of special interests and the critical role of lobbyists increase with the fragmentation of the budget. A tradeoff is imposed between the desirability of securing as much information and expertise as possible on segments of the budget and the danger that the budgetary process may be subverted to narrow or special interests through the power that comes to rest with subcommittee members.

Proposals for change. Citizen dissatisfaction with waste and duplication and frustration with the difficulty of fixing responsibility sometimes lead to proposals for changes in the budgetary process so that it would operate along the lines employed by parliamentary democracies. In the parliamentary system, the government is formed by the majority party of parliament (or by some coalition among parties in the parliament), and this government develops a proposed budget that must be acted upon as a unit by the parliament. If the budget is not adopted, that is, if the government is unable to develop a budget package acceptable to a majority of the legislators, this amounts to a vote of "no confidence." New elections are called, and a new government is formed. On the other hand, if the budget proposal is approved by the parliament, the responsibility for policy orientation and for effective coordination of government activity is clearly placed on the government party or coalition and particularly on its leadership.

These calls to replace the existing system with a parliamentary system have not succeeded in mobilizing sizable or sustained support. The fragmented system "muddles through," albeit with considerable inefficiency and frustration. Conflicts are resolved between relatively small interest groups and at a low level on a quantum scale of national political involvement. Major conflicts are avoided and the decision-making business of government is accomplished at a fairly even pace and without protracted stalemates.

Incrementalism

Decision making for the federal budget is carried out in an incremental frame of reference, which means that most existing expenditure programs are allowed to continue essentially intact with no concerted attempts to cut back or discontinue them. Instead of devoting time and energy to reconsideration of programs launched in previous Congresses, the limited resources of Congress are concentrated on proposals for new programs or for increases in existing programs. The logic of the incremental approach is readily apparent. Information is costly and negotiation costs are high. Not only have existing programs already been subjected to examination when they themselves were viewed as increments in the budgetary process, but political realities suggest that vested interests have already developed in connection with these programs, so that discontinuance or major contraction would spark heated controversy and politically difficult situations. Thus, the incremental approach to budget making is another device that limits or constrains the basic conflict situation in the budgetary process and permits the system to continue without major confrontations or protracted stalemates.

Incrementalism and the fragmentation of the budget into a number of separate pieces are effective ways of economizing on information, which is expensive, and of ensuring continuity in the budgetary process and in the operations of the government. One of the costs of proceeding in this manner is that programs tend to remain in force even when changed circumstances or priorities would suggest that they could be discontinued or contracted in favor of other uses for resources. The process may also operate to prevent a global reassessment of priorities; that is, there is little occasion in the budgetary process for a grand debate encompassing the whole range of government expenditure programs and aimed at restructuring expenditures in a major way.

Incrementalism does not mean that changed priorities are completely impossible. Neither does it mean that an agency can expect, each year, to receive a fixed or guaranteed increment (either in percentage or dollar amount terms) over its budget for the preceding year. Agencies whose programs are in areas of increased citizen demand will receive increments larger than those they received in the past and larger than those received by agencies whose programs are in areas of diminishing demand. The system is responsive to changes in the demands for collective services, but the response in any given year will be moderate. Several successive years of consistent demand pressure will be required to institute major changes in expenditure priorities.

Checks and Balances

An expenditure proposal must pass many tests before it can be enacted into law. A brief checklist will illustrate the rather impressive number of hurdles that must be successfully cleared. First, a proposal must be acceptable to the action agency and gain inclusion in its initial budgetary requests. Next, it must pass the tests specified by the OMB and the President as consistent with the general policy orientation of the executive branch. After this, it must survive examinations by a subcommittee of the Appropriations Committee of the House of Representatives, by the full committee, and by the House itself. Next it is subjected to similar scrutiny in the Senate, through a subcommittee of the Appropriations Committee, the full committee, and the Senate itself. Further tests may be imposed in a House-Senate conference committee. The President must sign the final appropriations bill and the OMB must actually release the funds needed to carry out the activity. This lengthy process constitutes a system of checks and balances in which the proposed expenditure faces critical examination by many different interest groups and from many different perspectives. Somewhere along the line, the proposal is likely to be subjected to examination by individuals or groups that possess significant technical expertise in the area of the proposed expenditure program.

In his analysis of the budgetary process, Aaron Wildavsky suggests that role playing by the various participants in the process has evolved through experience and that this role playing enhances the check and balance and critical examination aspects of the process. The action agencies play the role of "advocates" and regularly request appropriations that would expand the quantity and range of services they render. This enables the President and the House of Representatives to play the role of "guardians of the taxpayers' interests" by cutting back or denying some portions of the requests made by the agencies. It also provides an opportunity to be selective in choosing among proposed new programs, accepting some and rejecting others. After the House of Representatives has protected the taxpayers' interest by cutting back on agency requests, the Senate is in a position to play the role of a court of appeals in which the agency can seek a reinstatement of some of the programs deleted by the House. In like manner, the House of Representatives can serve as a spokesman for local interests, since its members are numerous, have relatively short terms of office, and represent constituencies that are fairly small or localized in nature. The Senate and the President, on the other hand, can adopt the more statesmanlike posture of "seeing the big picture" or viewing proposals from a national rather than a local point of view.

This extended or many-staged deliberative process (which can be termed a *longitudinal* fragmentation of the budgetary process to distinguish it from the horizontal fragmentation noted earlier) has its cost as well as its benefit aspects. It requires a great deal of time and imposes delay in the implementation of programs. It involves much duplication of activity. The lead time required for the implementation of new programs becomes a matter of years. Forecasting errors can be serious when agencies must attempt to anticipate demands and program needs years into the future. Opportunities may be missed because of the long lead time or programs may come into being after the need for them has passed or when a new set of priorities has arisen. Moreover, the necessity of passing the tests of various interest groups can dilute programs and weaken their effectiveness or burden them with peripheral requirements that can increase costs and complexity.

Against these obvious costs of the protracted budgetary process we can balance the advantage that the process provides protection against hasty or ill-considered undertakings. Once put into effect, government expenditure programs develop client groups or vested interests that can effectively argue for continuation of the program. Much experience supports the notion that government programs are nonreversible and that the level of expenditures is a one-way street which can be expanded as needs are recognized but which can be contracted only rarely and with great difficulty. Under the existing budgetary process, groups interested in securing new programs must be able to mobilize support that is broadly based and that can be sustained over at least the several years required to pilot the proposal through the budgetary process. Sudden inspirations are thus not likely to become fixed into the expenditure programs of the government.

Proposals for change in the budgetary process in the interest of obtaining speedier action on expenditure legislation have not advocated the removal of steps in the long process. Instead, these proposals have focused on increasing the staff capabilities of congressmen and senators in the hope that elapsed time might be reduced internally or within the existing series of steps. Other approaches to the problem have suggested that the President be authorized to exercise options and take actions without the necessity of advance approval from Congress. Some changes along each of these lines actually have taken place, which suggests that there is some perceived dissatisfaction with the time required to get action on budgetary matters. But the budget reform measure of 1974 moved in the opposite direction and actually increased the time span of budgetary operations by three months by moving the start of the new budget year from July 1 to October 1.

Logrolling and Inefficient Allocation

The general revenue system that sets up a conflict situation among competing demanders of public service also separates decisions on expenditures from decisions on tax shares. The rules governing the imposition of taxes are different from those governing the expenditures of funds. These differences give rise to the type of power alliances known as *logrolling*. Let us examine how logrolling operates and how it may lead to inefficiency in the allocation of resources.

One of the basic rules in taxation is that taxes must be uniform throughout the entire nation. This means that the federal government is not permitted to levy a tax on a certain section of the country (say, New England) unless the same tax is imposed, at the same rates, in all other sections of the country as well. If the national government restricts itself to the provision of genuinely national collective services, then there is no subnational or regional basis for differential taxation and the rule of geographical uniformity of taxation is reasonable. In this context of national collective services, any deviation from the geographic uniformity rule would open the way for a geographically oriented majority coalition to exploit other regions of the country through discriminatory taxation. The majority coalition would be able to lower its taxes and gain the advantages of the collective services at a lower price, whereas the regions in the minority would face higher taxes and higher prices for the collective services provided. Thus, the uniformity rule of taxation is designed to preclude the possibility of outright tax discrimination on a geographic basis.

But the national government does *not*, in fact, restrict itself to the provision of collective services that are national in their benefit boundaries[7]. There is no rule on the expenditure side of the budgetary process comparable to the geographic uniformity rule that applies on the taxation side. Expenditures that have a distinctly regional or even quite local benefit pattern may be proposed and there is nothing in the budgetary process which rules out consideration of these proposals. It might be supposed, however, that proposals of a purely

[7] See Chapter 17 for discussion of the geographic dimensions of collective goods.

regional or local character would be unable to achieve adoption in the majority rule system of Congress because the areas that do not benefit would vote against the proposal. But this overlooks the possibilities of vote trading and logrolling that exist in a budgetary process in which separate votes are taken on separate expenditure proposals and in which all expenditures are financed through general fund revenues derived from taxes that are uniform through the country.

Consider Figure 5.3, in which the nation is divided into three regions or areas represented by circles. Taxation uniformity requires equal payments from all regions to finance any national government project that may be undertaken.

FIGURE 5.3   Logrolling and Wasteful Expenditures

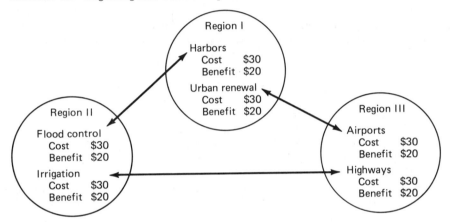

Suppose that each region has a certain pet project which it would like to have carried out, such as harbor improvements in region I, flood control in region II, and airport construction in region III. In each case, the pet project would cost $30 million, but the voters in the region are unwilling to finance it on their own, presumably because the aggregate marginal benefits from the project are less than $30 million. Let us assume that the aggregate marginal benefits actually amount to $20 million for the pet project and let us also assume that the same situation prevails in each of the other regions in respect to their pet projects. None of the projects is economically justified assuming, of course, that the voters accurately judge marginal benefits and that the benefits from each project are confined to its particular region.

But vote trading (logrolling) can result in the adoption of all three of these pet projects. Region I can enter into an agreement with region II in which region I agrees to vote in favor of the flood control project in exchange for the vote of region II in favor of the harbor project. Taxes to finance these projects will be divided evenly among all three regions (at $10 million from each region for each project), so that region I will pay $20 million in tax and obtain its $30 million project and region II will pay $20 million in tax and obtain its $30 million project. Each party to the coalition will be satisfied with the outcome, but region III will be quite unhappy, since it is paying $20 million in tax but is obtaining no benefit from the expenditures. By ganging up on region III, regions I and II have obtained tax prices lower than the actual cost of the projects and the adoption of inefficient expenditure programs.

But this does not end the logrolling process. Region III still wants its airport project, and with a little ingenuity and political entrepreneurship it will be able to obtain it. Region III may suggest to region I that a $30 million urban renewal project in region I might be worth at least $20 million to the voters in that region. If this argument is persuasive, as it probably would be, a coalition between region I and region III can be set up to obtain approval of both the airport project in region III and the urban renewal project in region I, with region II now being required to pay taxes to finance projects that generate no benefits for it. Again, economically unjustified projects have been legislated into effect through the process of logrolling.

The logrolling process comes full circle when region II realizes that it now is paying $40 million in taxes ($10 million each for the flood control project, the harbor project, the airport project, and the urban renewal project) but is receiving benefits only from the flood control project carried out in its own area. Region II now exercises political ingenuity and entrepreneurship and proposes a coalition with region III, perhaps for an irrigation project in region II in exchange for a highway project in region III. Once again the logrolling coalition should be successful, and two more economically unjustified projects will be undertaken. Through this process of "revolving majorities," economically unjustified projects totalling $180 million in expenditure have been undertaken (six projects at $30 million each). In each region, $60 million is being expended and taxes of $60 million are being collected ($10 million for each of the six projects), but voters are frustrated and unhappy with the inefficiency generated by the whole process because the marginal benefits in each region total only $40 million. At the limit, $60 million of waste and inefficiency has resulted from the process of logrolling and revolving majorities.

In economic language, the income effects of the logrolling process have canceled out, since each region is paying taxes equal to the amount of expenditure carried out in that region. No region is suffering a net exploitation at the hands of the other regions. But the price or substitution effects of the vote-trading process have not disappeared, and these price effects are responsible for the inefficient resource allocation that results from the vote-trading process. For each project, the majority coalition has compared the benefits from the projects against a price or cost which is lower than the actual cost or price in terms of real resource alternatives in the economy. More resources are channeled into the public sector through logrolling than would be channeled to that sector otherwise, and resources are wasted.

What sort of reform of the budgetary process might come to grips with the problem of allocational inefficiency because of logrolling? The problem is the nonparallel nature of the rules governing expenditure and those governing taxation. Relaxation of the geographic uniformity rule of taxation would open one route to the correction of logrolling, since regional or locally beneficial expenditures might then be financed with taxes that also were regional or local. Such an approach, however, would raise the specter of outright tax discrimination and would violate the commitment to federalism and local decision making in the government structure. An alternative strategy would be to seek agreement that the national government would abstain from expenditure legislation on matters in which benefit patterns were clearly local in nature. But there is an unrealistic sound to this alternative. Even if elected representatives were willing to forego the political advantages of regional or local legislation, the difficulty of measuring the geographic dimension of the benefits from expenditure programs would make implementation of such a posture extremely difficult. So the problem remains unresolved. Local citizens and constituent groups continue to vie for expenditure programs funded with "federal money" and continue to reward with reelection representatives who engage in logrolling on behalf of their constituents. All this continues in spite of some realization that the entire process increases the total of federal expenditures and that the "federal money" includes a good deal of local money routed through Washington. Each local group is confronted with the proposition that the money will be spent in some other district if it is not spent in their own, so that their decision not to play the game would lead not to a reduction in their taxes but to a loss of the benefits of the federal funding.

Controllability

The issue of controllability raises the question of whether the government budget is responsive to citizen demands for collective services or whether the institutions and processes of budgeting themselves determine the outcome. Putting the question in this way implies that the budget is neither completely controllable by the citizens nor completely determined by the process itself. Contentions that the budget is out of control overstate the situation, but it would be naive to suppose that the institutions of the budgetary process do not have an influence on the types of programs undertaken and on the total sum of government expenditures. If controllability is measured by the portion of the total budget that could be altered by action of Congress in a given year, roughly half the budget may be controllable and half not.[8] Extending the time frame to consider budgetary adjustments that could be made over a series of years would increase the portion of the budget in the controllable category. This is rather like the time period analysis of the elasticity of a supply curve, which suggests that responsiveness will be increased when more time is allowed during which adjustments can be implemented.

Several institutional devices in the budgetary process help to explain why sizable portions of the budget in any given year are not controllable by congressional action. For example, large amounts of money are expended each year on the authority of *permanent appropriations*; that is, on the authority of appropriations actions taken in previous Congresses which stated that the appropriation would continue through future fiscal years unless Congress in these future years specifically acted to alter these appropriations. Of course, a given Congress cannot impose a legally binding restraint on future Congresses, but

[8] See Murray L. Weidenbaum, "Institutional Obstacles to Reallocating Government Expenditures," in Haveman and Margolis, *op. cit.*

the nature of the expenditures provided through these permanent appropriations imposes powerful moral or political constraints. Permanent appropriations for the payment of interest on the national debt and for the payment of benefits provided under the social security system (financed through a trust fund) are leading examples. Statutes that set up programs of services to veterans or payments under public assistance programs impose severe limitations on congressional control of the budget, even though these may not be formalized into permanent appropriations. In addition to these more or less formally imposed commitments, a good many partially completed projects will be under way at any given time. In effect, these also cannot be cut off by the present Congress unless it is willing to subject itself to the criticism of voters who are sensitive to the waste in the termination of a partially completed project. Since logic suggests that the sunk costs themselves ought not to figure in decisions about future expenditures, an incremental benefit-cost analysis (that is "where do we go from here") may conclude that the project ought to be completed even though it may be a losing proposition in an aggregate analysis of benefits and costs that would include the sunk costs.

In recent years, the major areas of increase in the national government budget have been in the uncontrollable category, including debt interest, social security, and various welfare programs. Increases also have occurred in the controllable categories, of which the leading entry is defense spending, but these increases have been smaller and in some cases are nonexistent in real terms, that is, when price level changes are used to deflate current year expenditure figures. The greatly increased spending in the noncontrollable categories has led to the charge that the budget is out of control and that some major reappraisal of the budgetary process is needed. Important alterations in the process have been undertaken, including the PPB system instituted in the 1960s and the budget reform actions of 1974. The reforms of 1974 attacked the problem of controllability by directing Congress to set aggregate targets before considering specific expenditure proposals, but they did not deal with the specific institutional factors that enable one Congress to effectively commit future Congresses to certain expenditures. It remains to be seen whether further changes in the budget process itself will be demanded.

APPENDIX: FEDERAL BUDGET RECEIPTS AND OUTLAYS

Table 5.1 shows estimated federal government receipts and outlays for fiscal 1978. For comparison purposes, the table also shows budget receipts and outlays for fiscal 1968, one decade earlier. These data show the importance of various revenue sources and outlay categories and provide some initial impressions about changes that have taken place in one decade.[9]

Looking first at budget receipts, it is apparent that the federal government relies heavily on revenues generated by taxes based on individual incomes.

[9] The *Economic Report of the President,* which is published annually and is available in bookstores or directly from the Superintendent of Documents in Washington, provides a useful reference source on many economic subjects. Students may wish to consult the most recent economic report for up-to-date information on the national government budget.

TABLE 5.1   Federal Government Budget Receipts and Outlays, Fiscal Years 1968
            and 1978 (Millions of dollars)

DESCRIPTION	1968	1978*
Budget Receipts	153,671	393,017
Individual income taxes	68,726	171,217
Corporation income taxes	28,665	58,910
Social insurance taxes and contributions	34,622	126,068
Excise taxes	14,079	18,513
Estate and gift taxes	3,051	5,806
Customs duties	2,038	5,262
Miscellaneous receipts:		
Deposit of earnings by Federal Reserve System	2,091	6,400
All other	400	841
Budget Outlays	178,833	439,967
National defense	79,409	112,262
International affairs	4,612	7,281
General science, space, and technology	5,522	4,725
Natural resources, environment, and energy	4,010	19,747
Agriculture	4,541	2,333
Commerce and transportation	10,637	19,252
Community and regional development	1,891	7,868
Education, training, employment, and social services	7,004	19,358
Health	9,708	43,205
Income security	33,680	143,892
Veterans benefits and services	6,882	18,279
Law enforcement and justice	650	3,789
General government	1,684	3,930
Revenue sharing and general purpose fiscal assistance	311	8,089
Interest	13,751	39,735
Allowances		2,651
Undistributed offsetting receipts	−5,460	−16,429

* Estimate.

Source: Economic Report of the President, 1977 (*Washington, D.C.: Government Printing Office, 1977*), *Table B–68, pp. 266–67.*

Both the individual income tax, which is the largest revenue producer in the
federal system, and social security taxes and contributions, which is the second
largest revenue producer, are income-based taxes. The combination of individual income taxes and social security taxes (and contributions) amounted to
more than 75 percent of total estimated federal government receipts for fiscal
1978. Corporation income tax receipts ranked third among federal revenue
sources and provided some 15 percent of total federal receipts. All these income-
related receipts are quite sensitive to changes in the level of aggregate economic
activity, which is a factor of great importance in connection with the federal
government's responsibility for the stabilization function of government.

    Budget outlays are displayed in the table according to an agency classifica-
tion corresponding to the different separate appropriations measures considered
by the Congress. The largest outlay item, income security (including social

security benefits and various welfare transfer programs), accounts for nearly one-third of total budget outlays of the federal government in fiscal 1978. National defense, the second largest outlay category, accounts for over one-fourth of the total. Interest on the national debt is third largest and equal to almost 10 percent of the total. Income security outlays and debt interest are important elements in the noncontrollable portion of the total budget and have increased greatly in recent years, leading to the contention that the budget is out of control.

The total figures for budget receipts and outlays suggest, rather dramatically, that a vast increase in federal government fiscal operations took place over this decade. Total outlays were $178.8 billion in fiscal 1968 (equal to about $900 per capita) and $440.0 billion in fiscal 1978 (equal to about $2,000 per capita). However, several important adjustments must be made in these figures before a reasonable picture can be obtained of changes in the size of federal budget operations. An adjustment for the change in the general price level is particularly important, since record-breaking inflations occurred during this period. The implicit GNP price deflator was 82.57 in 1968 (1972 = 100), had risen to 133.79 in 1976, and was expected to be still higher in 1978. If the GNP price deflator should stand at, say, 145 in 1978, the "real" increase in federal government outlays between 1968 and 1978 would be in the neighborhood of 40 percent, considerably smaller than the approximately 150 percent increase suggested by the data before adjustment for price level changes.

Another way to examine the size of government budget operations is to compare budget size with total GNP. For example, fiscal 1968 federal budget outlays amounted to approximately 21 percent of 1968 GNP, and fiscal 1978 budget outlays may amount to about the same percentage. These figures suggest that the federal government budget has increased in absolute size but that the growth of federal outlays has been roughly in step with the rest of the economy. However, students should be very careful in making judgments about the changes in the size of federal budget operations relative to the total level of economic activity. For example, the greatest increases in budget outlays have occurred in the income security category, which consists largely of transfer payments that place purchasing power in the hands of private citizens who will expend these funds mainly in purchasing private rather than collective goods. Thus, an increase in total budget outlays does not necessarily mean an increase in government purchase of resources to provide collective services. Direct government command over resources may be decreasing in proportion to total GNP even while total budget outlays are increasing. It is also important to recognize that price inflation does not affect all goods and services in the same way. Over the past decade, the prices of goods and services purchased by governments have risen more rapidly than prices of most other goods and services. This means that government purchases of goods and services could increase as a percentage of dollar GNP even if, in real terms, the government share of resources is constant or even diminishing.[10]

[10] Morris Beck, "The Expanding Public Sector: Some Contrary Evidence," *National Tax Journal*, XXIX, 1 (March 1976), 15–21.

SUMMARY

The budget of the federal government is a planning instrument, it is a guideline for administration, and it is a record of fiscal activity. This chapter has emphasized the use of the budget as a planning instrument. The procedure used for developing a budget for a forthcoming fiscal year subjects expenditure proposals to critical analysis by many different agencies of the government and by several committees of Congress and extends over a lengthy period of time. Both the horizontal fragmentation of the budget into functional categories for separate examination by different committees and the longitudinal fragmentation through time protect against hasty or ill-considered actions. But, this fragmentation also imposes costs of duplication and delay and has led to difficulty in controlling the aggregate size of the budget and in fixing responsibility for the final outcome. The budget reform of 1974 was an attempt to increase congressional control over the aggregate size of the budget.

Taxes to support government outlays must be imposed at rates that are geographically uniform throughout the country, which prevents majority coalitions from engaging in outright tax discrimination on a geographic basis. However, government expenditures are not subject to an equivalent requirement for geographic uniformity. The opportunity to legislate expenditures that are not geographically uniform opens the way for the phenomenon known as logrolling and for a system of revolving majority coalitions that can result in excessive and wasteful expenditure.

The dollar amount of federal budget outlays grew substantially in the decade between 1968 and 1978. However, adjustments for price level changes and for growth in the total volume of economic activity reveal that federal government purchases, as a percentage of GNP, would be roughly the same or perhaps somewhat smaller in 1978 than in 1968.

SUGGESTED READINGS

WILDAVSKY, AARON. *The Politics of the Budgetary Process* (Boston: Little, Brown, 1964).

BURKHEAD, JESSE, and JERRY MINER. *Public Expenditure* (Chicago: Aldine-Atherton, 1971).

BECK, MORRIS. "The Expanding Public Sector: Some Contary Evidence," *National Tax Journal*, March 1976, pp 15–21.

FISCHER, C. WILLIAM. "The New Congressional Budget Establishment and Federal Spending: Choices for the Future," *National Tax Journal*, March 1976, pp. 9–14.

The Economic Report of the President (This appears annually, in January or February, and can be obtained from the Superintendent of Documents, Washington, D.C.).

6

The Allocation Function: Benefit-Cost Analysis

The fundamental fact of economic life is that wants exceed means, that is, that the resources available are not sufficient to permit the satisfaction of all wants. This means that choices must be made and that the satisfaction of some wants must be sacrificed in order to secure others. In other words, resources must be allocated among different possible uses. The allocation function of government is to ensure that resources are efficiently allocated to the provision of collectively consumed services. The budget process is the procedure used in making these decisions. This chapter examines the criteria for allocating resources from the private to the government sector and for choosing among alternatives inside the government sector.

Benefit-cost analysis is simply a systematic effort to identify and measure the benefits and the costs of possible undertakings and to render decisions on the basis of the findings. The systematic or orderly nature of this process is important because it provides some guarantee against the omission of significant benefit or cost considerations in the evaluation of proposals and because it helps to ensure that a consistent set of criteria will be applied in reaching final decisions. Thus, benefit-cost analysis is *internal* to the budgetary process and is capable of improving the results of this process, provided, of course, that the operation of the analysis does not in fact cause the systematic omission of important elements of benefit or cost.

There is nothing mysterious about the fundamental character of benefit-cost decision making. The net benefits of doing something are simply the total benefits derived from it minus the total costs that are incurred in order to do it. If the net benefits from a proposed undertaking are positive (that is, greater than zero), then welfare will be increased by going ahead with the project. If the net benefits are negative (less than zero), the proposal should be rejected. It is an eminently commonsense way to proceed, especially when it is remembered that the concept of cost employed in economics means opportunity cost or the benefits that could have been realized if resources had been devoted to the best alternative available. As long as the opportunity cost concept is kept in mind, benefit-cost decision making will allot resources to more beneficial employments and will withhold them from less beneficial uses.

Although the fundamental nature of benefit-cost decision making is simple and straightforward, complications arise in its implementation. Most of this chapter deals with problems that arise in the application of benefit-cost analysis to government decision making. The general procedure of benefit-cost decision making is outlined in the first section. The second section focuses on the selection of the correct discount rate to employ in benefit-cost analysis. The final section examines certain constraints or limitations applicable to benefit-cost decision making.

BENEFIT-COST PROCEDURE

The Preanalytical Stage

The initial questions in benefit-cost analysis are "What objectives shall be sought?" and "What proposals or alternatives shall be analyzed?" Since the range of possibilities is conceptually infinite, judgments must be made about which possible projects warrant the investment of the resources required by the benefit-cost procedure itself. This judgment is *preanalytical*, that is, it must be made before the alternatives can be fully explored with extensive analysis. Agency chiefs must possess some experience or intuition that enables them to direct the resources under their control into the analysis of alternatives consistent with the policy orientation of the executive and Congress and offering reasonable expectation that benefits will exceed costs. Proposals must be formulated with some degree of specificity about what will be undertaken, the methods that will be employed, and the scale or magnitude of the operation. Judgments about methods and about the scale of operations require considerable technical experience and expertise. If the method proposed offers important economies of scale, the findings of the benefit-cost analysis and perhaps the outcome of the legislative process itself can hinge on the judgments made in the preanalytical stage of the process.

Estimates of Benefit and Cost

The heart of the analytical process is the actual estimation of benefits and costs that would be realized if a proposed project were carried out. The aim is to include all real benefits and costs from the project, including those directly attributable to the project and those indirectly attributable to it as external or third-party benefits and costs.

Consumer goods projects. Because government projects provide collective services, market tests of benefits ordinarily will not be available, that is, consumers will not have an opportunity to reveal their benefit perceptions through voluntary purchases. Instead, ultimate financing will come from taxes, which are compulsory rather than voluntary payments. Therefore, proxy measures for benefits must be developed to indicate how much consumers would be willing to pay for the services if these services could have been provided through the utilization of exclusion devices in a competitive test against alternative services consumers might wish to enjoy.

Occasionally private markets provide services comparable to those provided by the public project, and inferences about the demand for the collective service may be gleaned from the observed price-quantity behavior of these comparable private services. However, if comparable private market services are not available to help in the estimation process, other approaches must be used. For example, estimates may be made of the number of people who would make use of the government service, and the value or benefit these people attach to the service may be estimated on the basis of the associated costs they would incur in order to use the service. If the proposal were for the construction of parks or recreation facilities, estimates may be made of the number of people who would utilize the facility and of the amounts that these users would spend for transportation to the facility and for equipment needed to use it. Transportation costs and equipment purchases become proxies for admission tickets and as such provide an estimate of the value consumers attach to using the facility.

It is apparent, of course, that these *associated costs* can provide only rough approximations of benefits from the proposed project. Also, care must be taken that estimates are made at the appropriate margins. Benefits of the proposed project are only the additions to total welfare over and above the welfare situation that would prevail in the absence of the proposed project. Thus, projects that merely divert activity from existing alternatives should not be given a benefit rating which fails to record the benefit *foregone* in the alternative, which is a cost insofar as evaluation of the proposed facility is concerned.

Intermediate goods projects. Projects that provide services which are intermediate inputs in the production of products for eventual market sale (such as irrigation projects) may be evaluated through estimates of the increased production which would result from the project, with the value of the increased production based on the market prices expected to prevail when these products are sold. Again, however, there are great difficulties in the estimation process, since there can be great uncertainty about the level of future market prices.

Moreover, if the project redistributes the market from one producer group to another, there may be little net benefit. For example, if an irrigation project relocates production from one region of the country to another, benefit-cost analysis must recognize the losses suffered in the one region as well as the benefits enjoyed in the other. The point here is that benefit-cost analysis must restrict itself to net real benefits (both direct and indirect) of the project and must not permit its calculations to be distorted by benefits that are of only a pecuniary nature. Because of the relocation of economic activity, land values may increase in an area benefiting from a project, but such pecuniary gains are offset by reductions in land values elsewhere, yielding no net real increase in wealth from the project.

Multiplier effects. The determination to stick with real rather than pecuniary increments of benefits and costs suggests that the *multiplier effects* of a proposed project should not be included in the benefit-cost evaluation of the proposal. Multiplier effects mean, for example, that the installation of a recreational facility will bring with it the location of restaurant, motel, and sporting goods businesses in the area. Irrigation projects will bring implement dealers and processing establishments, and so on. From the point of view of the region itself, these multiple effects can mean great increases in production and employment. But in the larger perspective of an entire economy operating at full employment, these same resources would have located elsewhere and would have been productive elsewhere if the project had not been undertaken. Therefore, these multiplier effects should not be counted as benefits associated with the project.

The full employment question is of crucial importance in the entire benefit-cost procedure. If full employment prevails, all resources used in a particular undertaking are drawn away from alternative activities and real opportunity costs are incurred. On the other hand, if the economy is suffering from unemployment, the real costs of any proposed undertaking that would make use of otherwise idle resources is zero and many projects that would not be attempted in a full employment situation might be undertaken. Benefit-cost analysis is useful, of course, even in a situation of unemployment, since differential benefits can provide a basis for choosing among alternative projects. In an unemployment situation, decision making on proposed projects becomes a blending of allocation and stabilization activity, and there is a basis for including multiplier consequences of alternative proposals. If unemployment has a regional rather than a national character, still further complexity enters the calculation of benefit and cost. Multiplier or second-round spending effects confined largely to the region experiencing unemployment may contribute to the net benefit valuation of the project.

The Time Factor

Each element of benefit and each element of cost estimated for a proposed project must be identified with the point in time at which that benefit or cost will be realized. The importance of this time identification of benefits and costs is easily illustrated by the arithmetic of interest rates. If the rate of interest is, say, 8 percent, $100 put into a savings account today will grow to $108 one year from today and will be able to purchase $108 worth of benefits at that time. Thus, the present value of a benefit valued at $108 to be realized one year from today is $100. The future value has been *discounted* at a rate of 8 percent per year, which is to say that the future value has been divided by 1.08 to determine the present value. If an estimated benefit were to be realized two years into the future, then the discounting process would have to be carried out twice, that is, once for each of the two years. In this case, a $108 benefit experienced after two years would be worth $100 after one year had elapsed, but worth only $92.59 before any time had elapsed. The benefit two years into the future has been discounted two years at the rate of 8 percent, that is, the estimated benefit has been divided by $(1.08)^2$. Likewise, a \$100 cost payment that will be due and payable one year from today will have a present value of \$92.59.

Net present value. The net present value of a project is simply the present value of the stream of anticipated benefits minus the present value of the stream of costs that will be required to acquire these benefits. The calculation of net present value is illustrated in the equation below, in which each benefit and each cost is identified with the year in which it will be experienced and in which the rate of discount is r.

$$\text{Net present value} = \frac{B_1 - C_1}{(1 + r)} + \frac{B_2 - C_2}{(1 + r)^2} + \frac{B_3 - C_3}{(1 + r)^3} + \ldots + \frac{B_n - C_n}{(1 + r)^n}$$

This equation can be summarized as follows, with each year represented by i and the estimates carried over a total of n years:

$$\text{NPV} = \sum_{i=1}^{n} \left[\frac{B_i - C_i}{(1 + r)^i} \right]$$

Net present value is one of the ways in which the findings of a benefit cost study can be expressed. If the selection of projects is not constrained by outside factors, such as a limited amount of total money that can be spent,[1] then any project with a net present value greater than zero would be accepted because the benefits derived from that use of resources will be greater than the benefits which would be derived from alternative uses of these resources. Projects with net present values of less than zero would not be justified on the basis of the benefit-cost analysis.

Benefit-cost ratios. The findings of a benefit-cost analysis can also be expressed in the form of the ratio of the present value of benefits to the present value of costs, that is, as the benefit/cost ratio (B/C). This formulation incorporates the same information used in the net present value method, but the present value of benefits is computed separately from the present value of costs and the outcome is expressed as a ratio rather than as a dollar value. Again, if the project selection is not constrained by outside factors, any project showing a benefit/cost ratio greater than 1/1 (unity) would be recommended for approval by the analysis and any project with a benefit/cost ratio less than 1/1 would not be recommended for approval.

Internal rate of return. A third way of expressing the results of a benefit-cost analysis is to calculate the internal rate of return of the project. In this approach, benefits and costs are estimated as usual and are related to the point in time at which they will be realized. Then the net present value equation is solved to determine the discount rate (r) which will result in a net present value of zero for the project. When the internal rate of return method is used, the test employed in deciding whether a project should be accepted or rejected

---

[1] The impact of this and other constraints on benefit-cost analysis will be discussed later in this chapter.

is whether the internal rate of return for that project is greater or less than the rate of return chosen as the criterion for project selection. Once this minimum necessary rate of return has been selected, projects that show an internal rate of return greater than this rate would be approved, and projects that show an internal rate of return lower than this minimum necessary rate would be rejected. The internal rate of return method of presenting the results of benefit-cost analysis focuses attention on the importance of the discount rate. That is, it emphasizes that the discount rate is a critical variable in determining whether projects should be accepted or rejected and it points out that selection of the appropriate discount rate requires calculations and decisions distinct from the estimation of benefits and costs themselves.

Each of these methods of expressing the results of benefit-cost analysis—the net present value method, the benefit/cost ratio method, and the internal rate of return method—utilizes the same basic data and each is a useful way of measuring the profitability of the project. However, certain hazards arise, particularly with respect to the ratio method and to the internal rate of return method. For example, consider what happens when the scale or size of a particular project is increased. So long as the incremental benefits of an expanded project exceed the incremental costs of the expansion, the net present value of the project will rise so that maximizing net present value will ensure that the most profitable scale for the project will have been identified. The same assurance is not available when the project is evaluated in terms of the benefit/cost ratio or the internal rate of return. Increments to the size or scale of the project may be profitable in terms of net present value but nevertheless may lower the benefit/cost ratio or the internal rate of return for the project as a whole. In fact, one may expect that this normally will be the case since, as the project is expanded to the efficient size where marginal benefit is equal to marginal cost, the ratio of benefit to cost and the rate of return on the incremental units will be lower than the ratio or rate of return on inframarginal units. Thus, benefit/cost ratios and internal rates of return can be increased by designing projects of less than optimal size that waste or throw away opportunities for further profitable investment. These problems will be discussed further in connection with constraints in project selection arising from budget limitations or mutually exclusive projects.

The Final Decision

Benefit-cost analysis provides quantified estimates of benefits and costs that can assist the legislature in reaching a final decision as to which proposals should be accepted. The decision, however, remains with the legislators. Benefit-cost analysis supplements the political process, but does not replace it. The supplementary nature of benefit-cost analysis should be emphasized. Legislators may disagree with the judgments and estimates made in the analysis and thus may reject its findings. Moreover, the quantifiable aspects of benefit and cost cannot incorporate all the factors that legitimately go into a final decision. For example, the distribution of benefits and costs among different individuals or sectors of the society is an important element in government decision making, but it is not a factor that can conveniently or reliably be incorporated into benefit-cost calculations. Thus, benefit-cost calculations are said to be *indifferent* to the income distribution consequences of alternative projects.

It may be possible to identify the groups that will enjoy differential benefits from an undertaking and to identify the groups that will be required to pay more of the costs and capture less of the benefits, but it is the elected legislator rather than the technical analyst whose views on the relative merits of one distribution of income over another should prevail. Benefit-cost analysis may report estimated distributional consequences of alternatives, but the task of applying weights or importance to these effects must be left to elected representatives. Projects that appear relatively attractive on pure benefit-cost terms may be rejected in favor of less attractive alternatives because of the distributional aspects of the choice, and there is no ground to fault the elected representatives for this action.

Similarly, elected representatives may introduce policy variables in making their decisions among alternative undertakings; that is, they may support a certain alternative in apparent contradiction to findings of benefit-cost analysis. When this happens, it means that the elected representative has introduced benefit or cost elements which were not used in the analysis or that some difference exists between the decision maker and the analyst in the measurement of benefits and/or costs. There is nothing necessarily wrong with this outcome. Benefit-cost analysis cannot consider all the variables important to the final decision. In short, benefit-cost analysis is a tool in the decision-making process but it is not a replacement for the legislator.

Some of the practical difficulties of relating benefit-cost analysis to actual decision making can be illustrated with the question of whether personnel for the military services should be recruited on a volunteer basis or whether conscription should be used. Benefit-cost analysis clearly indicates that conscription is wasteful of resources because people are compelled to accept military employment when they would, in fact, be much more productive if allowed to remain in the civilian labor force. Conscription permits the military services to employ labor at wage rates well below equilibrium rates prevailing in the private sector. These substandard wage rates not only involve distortion in the allocation of resources between public and private employment, but also encourage wasteful use of labor in the military services and an uneconomic attachment to labor-intensive rather than capital-intensive technologies.

But the elected representative, who must in the end decide between the volunteer and the conscription army, may wish to introduce considerations perhaps not examined by the benefit-cost analyst. He may conclude, for example, that a volunteer or competitive wage system would not be effective in times of actual war and that the transition from peacetime to wartime could be made more effectively if the conscription system operated at all times. The elected representative may also realize that the higher wage rates necessary to supply the volunteer personnel would require that the hidden tax the conscription system imposes on those compelled to supply military service would have to be replaced with explicitly legislated taxes or reductions in programs presently supported by explicit taxes. Because the elected representative wants to be reelected, he may be unwilling either to cut back on other programs or to increase explicitly legislated taxes. He may prefer to continue with the hidden tax the conscription system imposes. These and many other considerations not included in the technical benefit-cost analysis may play a role in the actual decision.

SELECTING THE APPROPRIATE DISCOUNT RATE

Selecting the appropriate discount rate is a complicated matter; different analysts may arrive at different conclusions if they make different assumptions in the course of their work. But the basic logic of discount rate selection is a simple and straightforward exercise in opportunity cost thinking. The discount rate is the opportunity cost of resources, given the existing state of technology and the array of alternative projects in which these resources are demanded. If resources are used in a certain project, they cannot be used in alternative projects. Therefore, the cost of using resources in one project amounts to the productivity (rate of return) these resources would have generated if they had been used in the best alternative. The task of selecting the appropriate discount rate therefore includes discovering the project that is the actual alternative to which the resources would be applied if the proposed project were not undertaken and determining the rate of return the resources would generate in this alternative application.

Consequences of Incorrect Rates

The importance of selecting the correct discount rate can be illustrated by observing the types of biases or distortions of resource use that arise if the wrong rate is applied. Table 6.1 summarizes two types of biases. One of these is the *sector* bias; that is, the misallocation of resources between the public (government) sector of the economy and the private sector of the economy. If the discount rate or internal rate of return used in the selection of public projects is too low (that is, below the rate applied in the private sector), then too many resources will be employed in the public sector and too few in the private sector. If the rate is too low, it means that a less demanding test of productivity is applied to resources used in the public sector than to resources used in the private sector. Because the criterion or threshhold test for resource use in the public sector is lower than in the private sector in this situation, some resources

TABLE 6.1   Sector and Time Bias Resulting from the Use of Incorrect Discount Rates

DISCOUNT RATE ON PUBLIC PROJECTS	SECTOR BIAS	TIME BIAS
Too low	Too many resources used in the public sector relative to the private sector	Too many resources used on long-term projects relative to short-term projects
Too high	Too many resources used in the private sector relative to the public sector	Too many resources used in short-term projects relative to long-term projects

will be expended in public projects in spite of the fact that they would have made a greater contribution to welfare if they had been permitted to remain in private sector employment. In terms of the net present value equation, a low value for the discount rate (r) will increase the net present value of proposed projects because costs ordinarily are incurred early in the time span of the projects, whereas benefits typically are realized later in this time span.

The time bias that arises from use of an incorrect discount rate reflects the fact that this rate works over and over again with each passing year of the project's life. The present value of net benefits realized in the early years of a project's life are not seriously eroded by the discounting process because this process does not have very many years in which to work its effect. But the present value of net benefits realized in later years of the project's life (such as those realized in year n in the net present value equation) are seriously diminished by the operation of the discounting process. Thus, if the discount rate is too high, projects that yield their greatest benefits in the distant future will appear to have a low present value compared to projects that yield their greatest benefits in their early years. Conversely, if the discount rate is too low, the net present value of long-term projects is overstated relative to the net present value of short-term projects, resulting in a selection bias in favor of the long-term projects. Discount rates can be interpreted as showing the *rate of time preference* in the society. A high discount rate means that society places greater value on immediate benefits. A low discount rate reflects a social preference placing greater value on future benefits. Thus, selecting the correct discount rate is an important aspect of deciding which public projects should be undertaken.

If the correct rate of discount is discovered and applied in benefit-cost analysis, neither a sector nor a time bias will be present in the calculations, and benefit-cost analysis can bring about resource allocation consistent with the *equimarginal* principle. The last dollar's worth of resources devoted to public projects will yield the same benefit increment as the last dollar's worth of resources devoted to private sector projects and the last dollar devoted to long-term projects will yield the same benefit as the last dollar devoted to short-term projects. Resource allocation can be "efficient," resulting in the highest level of welfare consistent with the stock of resources available and the distribution of income in the society. The problem, of course, is to discover the "correct" discount rate.

Is the Private Sector Rate "Correct"?

The day to day operations of the private market generate the discount rates applied to private sector decisions. Therefore, discount (interest) rates actually observed in the private market sector of the economy provide a starting point in the search for the correct discount rate to apply in benefit-cost analysis in the public sector. The question is whether any adjustments should be made from the observed market discount rates in determining the rate for public projects. If no adjustments are required, the observed market discount rate could be applied directly to public projects. The observed rate would reveal the rate of return that would be sacrificed when resources are withdrawn from the private sector for use in the public sector. Such a withdrawal of resources would be appropriate only when the rate of return on the public project equaled or exceeded the observed private market rate.[2]

The first fact that would become apparent in seeking to apply the observed private market rate of discount is that there is no single discount rate which applies uniformly in the different portions of the private economy. In response to the request "Will the true discount rate please stand up," several different discount rates would submit that they constitute an equilibrium discount rate in regular day to day use. Some of this diversity in observed market discount rates arises from imperfections in private capital markets, that is, from factors that inhibit the flow of capital supplies from one market to another or from barriers that prevent demanders of capital from gaining access to certain markets supplying capital.

If these imperfections were eliminated, some of the variance in observed rates would disappear, the private market allocation of resources would be better than it actually is, and the benefit-cost analyst might be able to find a single "best" discount rate to apply in his calculations. But the fact is that the analyst must operate in an imperfect world, and his task is complicated by the fact that different rates of return prevail in different portions of the private sector. Therefore, he must determine the particular segments of the private sector from which resources would be withdrawn if the public project were undertaken and then calculate the rates of return resources actually would earn, at the margin, if they were allowed to remain in their private employments. If the public project would utilize resources withdrawn from several different segments of the private market, the analyst must compute the discount rate for the public project as an average of the rates of return in these different segments, weighted according to the quantities of resources withdrawn from each segment.

The individual income tax and the corporation income tax are the major sources of general revenue for the federal government. Therefore, we may illustrate the discount rate estimation process by considering resources withdrawn from private use by individuals and resources withdrawn from use by corporations. The risk-free government bond rate provides a benchmark in the case of individuals, but an adjustment for taxes is required for resources withdrawn from corporate uses.

The Risk-Free Government Bond Rate

Resources commanded by individuals are productive, even when used to generate purely private consumption benefits. Each family or individual is a "do-it-yourself" production enterprise that acquires resources and applies them in the production of satisfaction or benefits for its members. In the search for discount rates, the task is to determine the rate of return generated, at the margin, by resources employed in consumption activities. If resources are taken

---

[2] See William J. Baumol, "On the Discount Rate for Public Projects " in Robert H. Haveman and Julius Margolis (eds.), *Public Expenditures and Policy Analysis* (Chicago: Markham, 1970).

away from individuals through the individual income tax, what amount of benefit is sacrificed per dollar's worth of resource withdrawn? In the private market sector, some evidence on this rate of return is revealed in the rate of interest that prevails for government bonds purchased by private households.

When private households voluntarily purchase government bonds that pay interest at a rate of, say, 6 percent, it means that the alternative uses of these funds are judged by this household to yield a rate of return of less than 6 percent. Since the likelihood of default on these government bonds is nearly nil, the household is not engaged in a risk-taking operation but is simply exchanging current or immediate resource use in favor of resource use at some future time. If the funds to finance the public project were derived exclusively from funds that otherwise would have been put into risk-free government bonds, the discount rate applicable to this project would be the rate of interest paid on these bonds. But it is unreasonable to suppose that all revenues collected through the individual income tax would otherwise have been used to buy government bonds. If not spent for immediate consumption, the money might have been used to purchase securities with higher yield, thus suggesting that the risk-free bond rate would understate the private rate of return on resources. Therefore, the rate of return on risk-free government bonds becomes a minimum rate to use for benefit-cost analysis of public projects. The correct rate presumably lies somewhere above this lower limit rate.

The Adjustment for Taxes

Taxes imposed on production activities in the economy, such as the tax on the net profits of corporations, drive a wedge between the rate of return on resources as measured by prices paid by consumers and the rate of return as measured by the after-tax earnings of the company and credited to the shareholders (owners) in dividends or retained earnings. Since the discount rate in benefit-cost analysis relates to the question of whether resources should be taken from the private sector and used for public projects, the rate of return as measured by the prices consumers pay for products is more appropriate than the rate of return measured by the yields shareholders received from ownership rights in the productive enterprise. If resources were withdrawn and production consequently reduced, the welfare loss would be the benefits sacrificed by giving up the consumption of the product. Thus, the appropriate rate of return in regard to resources withdrawn from the corporate sector is the before-tax rate of return. If the rate of tax on corporation profits is 50 percent, an 8 percent rate of return realized by the owners (stockholders) indicates that a 16 percent rate of return has been realized from the resources employed. In other words, in order to discover the "social" rate of return to be used in estimating benefits and costs for the public project, the realized private rate of return to investors must be divided by $(1 - t)$, where t is the rate of tax imposed. If private investors realize an 8 percent rate of return *after* tax and if the tax rate is 25 percent, the *before*-tax (or social) rate of return would be 10.67 percent, which is 8 percent divided by .75. The tax simply has required that the 10.67 percent return generated by the activity must be shared between the private owners and the government, with an 8 percent return going to the private owners and a 2.67 percent return going to the government. In terms of real resource use, the rate of return is 10.67 percent, and this is the figure that should be used in deciding where the resources may best be employed.

Should Adjustment Be Made for Risk?

Risk means there is some likelihood or probability that a given project may not turn out the way it was planned. Benefits and/or costs may prove to be different than anticipated when the project is undertaken. Thus, the net benefit from the project is subject to some amount of variance. The degree of risk will differ among projects, and judgments about the degree of risk involved in a given undertaking must be made before the project is started. Indeed, these advance judgments are made by private investors when they select the projects or companies in which they will make investments. A *risk premium* will be demanded by investors to persuade them to place their resources in a risky undertaking, that is, investors will insist on some greater yield or average rate of return from risky projects in order to make up for or "cover" the particular instances when the outcome will be disappointing. Some undertakings will pay off more generously than the insisted-upon average yield and other undertakings will pay off less generously than this average. Another way of expressing this situation is to observe that risk or variance in actual rates of return on particular undertakings is an inconvenience or difficulty experienced by investors in risky undertakings. In managing their financial affairs, these investors will have to make adjustments or develop flexibility elsewhere in their portfolios in order to accommodate to the fluctuations in actual returns on their risky investments. Since these adjustments and accommodations are costly, compensation must be realized through the premium rate of return demanded from the risky undertakings. This is why the risk premium is demanded and this is why observed market rates of return display a range of interest or yield rates, with higher rates applying to risk-taking companies and lower rates applying to companies that do not engage in risky operations.

In selecting the discount rate to use in public project benefit-cost analysis, the question is whether these observed risk premiums in the private market should be included in the discount rate used for the public project or whether these risk premiums should be wiped out or erased and the observed rates rolled back to the no-risk level. The answer is that the private risk premiums should *not* be erased or wiped out. Instead, the risk premiums should remain in the rate of return figure used to test the acceptability of public projects that withdraw resources from those sectors of the private economy engaged in risky undertakings. Suppose, for example, that a company in business in the private economy is tooled up to work in relatively risky areas of endeavor and is generating returns at 12 percent. Assuming this to be an equilibrium state of affairs, investors are willing to submit to the variance in profits in this company in exchange for this 12 percent return. Another company may be tooled up for less risky undertakings and generate average returns of 10 percent. This also may be assumed to be an equilibrium state of affairs. Investors in this company are willing to invest at the 10 percent return level.

The two percentage point difference in observed rates of return between these two companies is the risk premium investors require to persuade them to put up with the extra variance in actual returns experienced by the company working in the more risky area. In selecting the rate of discount to use in public projects, resources withdrawn from the first company in this illustration should be credited with an opportunity cost return of 12 percent; resources withdrawn from the less risky company should be credited with an opportunity cost return of 10 percent. The point is that risk taking itself is a useful activity. Enterprises that perform successfully in risky areas are generating genuine benefits to consumers and these consumers are revealing the extent of these benefits by paying prices for the final products which support the rate of return, including the risk premium.

This discussion has centered on the discount rate that should be employed in the equation calculating the net present value of proposed public projects. The proposed public projects themselves may involve differing degrees of risk or variance in expected benefits and costs. This simply means that the estimates made for benefits and costs over the years of the life of the project will not be a single unique figure in each case but will appear as a range of expected values. Several estimates of net present value may be necessary if there is risk that the project may not turn out precisely as expected. For example, a "normal" or best-estimate net present value may be supplemented by estimating a "high" and "low" net present value with estimated probabilities attached to each. Thus, government decision makers can be provided with information on the riskiness of public projects and can make judgments incorporating these considerations.

Time Horizons and Underinvestment

When a private investor decides whether or not to place resources in an investment project, an important element in the decision is the *rate of time preference* of that investor. This is one of the variables influencing the location of the supply curve of resources offered for utilization in investment activities.[3] If the individual investor has a high rate of time preference, it means that he places a relatively higher valuation on immediate consumption or short-term rewards. This frame of mind, or preference ordering, discourages the placing of resources in investment projects, which is to say that it reduces the supply of resources to investment markets (shifting the supply curve to the left) and results in a relatively higher equilibrium rate of return in the market. Conversely, a lower rate

---

[3] Textbooks on economic principles will display a demand curve for investment which reflects the rate of return that can be realized from investment. The supply curve illustrates the willingness of resource owners to place resources in these investment activities. The equilibrium rate of return is the rate at which the quantity of resources demanded is equal to the quantity supplied. This discussion of time horizons focuses on a supply-side aspect of the observed market rate of return on investments.

of time preference by investors increases supply and lowers the equilibrium market rate of return.

The time horizon argument in connection with discount rates for public projects points out that private investors are mortal human beings with limited life expectancies. These mortal investors will place a relatively higher valuation on investment undertakings that will pay off during their own lifetimes and a lesser valuation on longer-term undertakings. Of course, it is not contended that mortal investors have zero interest in projects which will pay off after they are gone, since these people have some interest in the welfare of their descendants. Investments can, of course, be liquidated, although perhaps at some sacrifice. The point simply is that limited life expectancy will have some influence in the direction of increasing the rate of time preference and the equilibrium market rates of return. The argument then is made that society as a whole goes on in spite of the limited tenures of its individual members, so that the rate of time preference generated by the actions of mortal individuals may be higher than that which would be appropriate from the point of view of society as a whole. The implication of this line of argument is that future generations are inadequately represented in private market investment decisions and that government, as a trustee or guardian for future generations, ought to adjust observed market rates of return downward in order to make up for the time horizon bias in individualized market decision making.

In evaluating this line of argument, it will be helpful to recall the earlier discussion of the time and sector biases that arise from utilization of incorrect discount rates. First consider the sector bias. To the extent that there is validity to the time horizon phenomenon, an adjustment of the observed private market rate would lower the rate of return required of public projects and would increase the amount of public investment relative to the amount of private investment activity. The private sector would continue to use the (allegedly too high) discount rate reflecting the time horizon factor, while the public projects would use a lower rate. A type of sector bias would be introduced if such an adjustment in observed market rates were used. If the private sector is making incorrect decisions because of the limited time horizons of investors, a general solution for the problem suggests that government should attempt to correct discount rates in the private markets themselves, perhaps through the use of monetary and fiscal instruments. If monetary and fiscal instruments can offset the time horizon bias in private market decision making, then benefit-cost calculations for public projects could use the same rate as would then exist in the private sector. The problem would be resolved without introducing the sector bias. In other words, using a time horizon correction only for public projects would provide only a partial solution for the time horizon problem and would add a sector bias distorting resource use in the society. The net efficiency gains from such a procedure might be quite small and could be negative.

Now consider the time bias dimension of the limited time horizon of private investors. If limited time horizons result in discount rates that are too high, private markets will direct too many resources into short-term undertakings and too few resources into longer-term undertakings. The rate of growth of the economy will be slowed and the standard of living of future generations will be lower than it would have been if the correct (social) discount rate had been used. Correcting for the time horizon bias through monetary and fiscal measures that lower the rate of discount in both the private and the public sectors would increase the rate of growth of the economy and increase the standard of living of future generations. Now the question is "How large should the correction be?" In the context of resource allocation, an estimate of the time horizon bias could be made and the correction could be specified on that basis. But in this situation, the resource allocation question focuses on the present versus future utilization of resources and raises questions that may be part of the concern of the distribution branch of government as well. Should the welfare of future generations be increased at the expense of the welfare of present generations? Historically, economic progress has meant that the living standard of future generations generally has been higher than that of present generations, so that a discount rate adjustment to correct for a time horizon bias would, in effect, transfer real income from the relatively poor present generation to the relatively rich future generation. Thus, distribution as well as allocation considerations become important in discovering the correct social rate of discount.

In summary, the analysis does not support the introduction of a rate of discount on public projects different from the rate applied to private sector projects. If discount rate adjustments are made in recognition of the time horizon phenomenon, they should be made to the private as well as to the public rates. However, the magnitude of any such general adjustment raises questions that extend beyond allocation considerations alone.

CONSTRAINTS IN PROJECT SELECTION

A *constraint* is a factor or consideration which forces certain proposals to be rejected, that is, it confines or sets limits to the range of acceptable projects. Thus far in the discussion of benefit-cost analysis, the only constraint imposed is the requirement that the rate of return on the proposed project be equal to or greater than the rate of return that would be realized in the alternative use of the resources. Thus, projects could be recommended for approval (a) if the present value of benefits exceeded the present value of costs $(B > C)$, (b) if the ratio of present value benefits to present value costs is greater than one $(B/C > 1)$, or (c) if the internal rate of return on the project exceeded the rate of return on alternative uses of the resources required $(R_i > R_a)$. In actual allocation decisions, additional constraints may be imposed that further confine the range of acceptable projects. When additional constraints are present, care must be exercised in applying the decision criteria outlined above.

Mutual Exclusivity

Mutual exclusivity means that carrying out one project will preclude the possibility of carrying out an alternative project. For example, construction of a dam at a particular site on a river will preclude the construction of a larger or a smaller dam on that same site. Construction of a reservoir for irrigation and flood control purposes may preclude the construction of a facility for recreational purposes, since a variable water level is required for one purpose and a constant water level is required for the other. When projects are mutually exclusive, selection of the alternative that offers the highest ratio of present value benefits to present value costs will *not* necessarily be the best choice. A small-scale project that takes the most profitable potential of the particular site may demonstrate a ratio of benefits to costs considerably greater than the ratio which would emerge if the larger-scale project were undertaken in order to secure the additional benefit potentials of the site.

As long as there is no budget constraint on the total number of dollars that can be spent, these additional or incremental benefits should be sought and the incremental expenditures made so long as the net present value of the incremental effort is positive. This simply says that the present net value of the project will be maximized by adopting the efficient scale or size for the project, which can be realized by carrying the project to the point where marginal benefits and marginal costs (both expressed in present values) are equal. Among mutually exclusive projects, the choice should go to the one with the largest net present value rather than to the one with the highest ratio of benefits to costs. Choosing among mutually exclusive projects on the basis of internal rates of return introduces the same risks of error as choosing on the basis of benefit-cost ratios. The basic test is to choose the project with the highest net present value.

Budget Constraints

A budget constraint means that there is some limit on the amount of money (resources) available for allocation among various competing public investment projects. The total budget available would be exhausted before all projects offering positive net values could be funded. In this situation, an acceptable procedure again is to use the net present value criterion for project selection. Projects may be accepted in descending order according to their net present values until the available budget has been exhausted. The selection process using the ratio of benefits to costs (both in terms of present values) also can be used in the face of budget constraints. Projects may be approved in descending order of their benefit/cost ratios until the available budget has been fully committed.

The method of project selection that compares the internal rate of return in the proposed project with some minimum necessary rate of return is *not* readily applicable in situations involving a budget constraint. The problem is that the internal rate of return on the proposed project has been calculated so as to result in a zero net present value for the project. When a budget constraint exists, a zero net present value is no longer the effective criterion for selection, since a cutoff point in terms of project selection is reached while net present values still are positive. Thus, calculated internal rates of return are not appropriate criteria for project selection when a budget constraint exists unless the internal rate is recalculated so as to yield the positive net present value imposed by the constraint.

It is apparent that the presence of a budget constraint introduces a degree of inefficiency in the allocation of resources between the public and the private sectors of the economy. When the constraint is imposed, some projects offering positive net present values will be foregone and the resources that might have been utilized in these projects will be employed elsewhere, in undertakings that are presumably less productive. In terms of benefit/cost ratios, some tendency will be injected to "cream off" particularly profitable portions of undertakings and thus preclude larger-scale undertakings that would yield net benefits if the constraint were not imposed. These inefficiencies in project selection are costs that must be recognized in connection with any benefits which may arise from the imposition of the budget constraint.

In an aggregate sense, the entire notion of a budget constraint is an anachronism to benefit-cost analysis. If taxpayers are unwilling to provide enough money to fund a project that appears to have a positive net present value, then there is simply a difference between the benefit-cost estimates of the analysts and the benefit-cost estimates of the taxpayer-voters. Both the analysts and the voters might be asked to reexamine their estimates in the hope of resolving their differences. In other words, the notion of an aggregate budget constraint reopens the whole question of voter sovereignty and the political process.

In a more narrow or microeconomic sense, however, budget constraints exist for particular government agencies because administration of a large aggregate budget requires a dividing up of responsibilities among subordinate units. This dividing up leads to budget constraints on particular agencies and to decision making according to criteria referred to as "suboptimizing."

Suboptimization

The essential idea in *suboptimization* is that the total array of decisions to be made is divided up, with separate parts assigned to separate units in the hierarchy of government. Each of these separate and subordinate units in the government is assigned the responsibility for making recommendations for legislation with respect to its component of the total array of matters to be dealt with. Each of the subordinate units is expected to make optimizing recommendations on the subgroup or category of matters assigned to it. The term "suboptimizing" is applied to the efforts of these entities.

The suboptimizing procedure means that benefit-cost analysis typically will be conducted with more constraints than simply the requirement that the rate of return on the public project equal or exceed the rate of return on alternative projects. The budget constraint, which already has been noted, is an example of one such added constraint. Constraints also may exist on the scope or range of alternatives that may be considered. For example, suboptimization may be carried to the point where the amount of money available is fixed and the nature of the output narrowly specified. In this situation, the analysis becomes a study in cost effectiveness, in which the task is simply to obtain the largest amount of the specified output possible with the fixed money available. Operations research is another illustration of a rather extreme degree of suboptimization. In operations research, the task to be accomplished is specified and the job of the analyst is to discover the least-cost method of achieving this outcome.

Lesser degrees of suboptimization reduce the number of constraints imposed and increase the flexibility or number of options available for analysis. Objectives still must be specified, but the specification may be broader than in operations research or cost effectiveness studies. The available methods of accomplishing the objective may be broadened to include a number of component programs which together are viewed as constituting a "system" or coordinated set of efforts directed toward the objective. *Systems analysis* is the study of the various possible groupings that might be set up in the organizational structure of government decision making.

The notion of systems analysis could be applied to the whole process of government decision making. The objective would be to discover a decision-making process that is efficient in the sense of adopting programs consistent with the benefit and cost perceptions of voters. Suboptimization itself would be a technique or production technology applicable to the achievement of this objective. Use of suboptimization increases specificity in the statements of objectives, permits more objective measurement of benefits and costs, and limits the opportunities for the insertion of the researcher's own value judgments in the analysis. But these advantages are gained at the expense of generality and increase the danger that the left hand may not know what the right hand is doing. That is, the work of one unit may be at cross-purposes with the work of another unit or opportunities for coordination may be missed. Thus, some optimal degree of suboptimization can be sought at which the marginal benefits of specificity are equal to the marginal costs in the loss of generality. Technological advances in information systems and data processing suggest that the optimal degree of suboptimization may be shifting through time. Thus, the search for efficiency in government decision making is a continuing task.

SUMMARY

Since resources are scarce, choices must be made among alternatives. Benefit-cost analysis is simply an orderly way of selecting those alternatives that will yield the greatest welfare from available resources. The technique of benefit-cost analysis requires a specification of objectives, and estimates of benefits and costs of alternative ways of realizing these objectives. The timing of benefits and costs is an important dimension of benefit-cost analysis. Selecting the appropriate discount rate requires that the rate of return on public projects be related to the rate of return on resources in the private sector, after appropriate adjustments for taxes have been made. Additional constraints on project selection arise when projects are mutually exclusive or when suboptimization of government decision making imposes a limit on the amount of money that can be spent in a particular area. Effective application of benefit-cost analysis assists legislators in deciding which projects should be undertaken, but it cannot replace the judgment of the legislator, because benefit-cost analysis is subservient to policy considerations and is unable to evaluate the income distribution effects of different projects.

SUGGESTED READINGS

HAVEMAN, ROBERT, and JULIUS MARGOLIS (eds.). *Public Expenditures and Policy Analysis* (Chicago: Markham, 1970). See especially William J. Baumol, "On the Discount Rate for Public Projects."

BRADFORD, DAVID F. "Constraints on Government Investment Opportunities and the Choice of Discount Rate," *American Economic Review*, Dec. 1975, pp. 887–99.

7

The Distribution Function

Distribution means the distribution of income among individuals in the society, that is, the degree of inequality that prevails among individuals in terms of income. The income distribution is consumed collectively in the sense that each member of the society must consume the same configuration of inequality as every other member of the society. Because of this collective consumption aspect of income distribution, income redistribution becomes a responsibility of government. It is a responsibility of government to determine whether individual incomes should be redistributed or changed from what would exist in the absence of government action. In this sense, the distribution function of government might better be termed the "redistribution" function.

The day to day actions of government inherently incorporate some position about the distribution of income. Since each expenditure and each tax proposal carries the possibility of distributional effects, questions of equity or justice are frequently debated and are influential in the outcomes of actual legislation. Each action becomes a brick in the structure that is the income distribution position of the government. But nowhere in the decision-making process is an attempt made to specify the desired degree of inequality, although particular emphasis on this matter arises in connection with the degree of progressivity in tax legislation and with transfer payment proposals in welfare legislation. The point is that even a conclusion that no change in the prevailing distribution was the correct policy would not relieve government of the necessity of becoming involved in distributional questions. Careful analysis of distributional effects is necessary, and choosing among alternative government projects cannot be divorced from distributional questions. Projects with attractive benefit-cost patterns may be rejected because of their impact on the distribution of income. Government cannot be indifferent to income distribution.[1]

THE DESIRED DEGREE OF INEQUALITY

The question of the degree of inequality that ought to prevail can be approached in several ways. One approach commences from a "blank slate" and seeks to discover an ethically desirable distribution of income in terms of maximizing human welfare, catering to human needs, equating rewards with efforts, or working out and implementing a social contract for justice. This approach is unconstrained by the prevailing state of distribution; it is an attempt to work out an ideal social order. The approach adopted in this text starts from the other end of the question and presents an analysis starting from the circumstances prevailing in a market-oriented society. It begins with an examination of interdependent utility functions, analyzing the basis for redistribution based on voluntary action and democratic procedures, and then explores the causes of and remedies for inequality in the context of a market system.

Interdependent Utility Functions

A utility function is a statement of the variables that contribute to the welfare of an individual. For example, suppose that the utility of some individual (U^a) is a function of a number of variables, such as income, wealth, leisure time, the prices of various commodities, and so on. This may be expressed as follows: $U^a = f^a(Y^a, W^a, L^a, P_1, P_2, \ldots)$. As thus stated, this person's utility function is not dependent upon the income, wealth, leisure, or consumption of other persons. That is, the income, wealth, or consumption of another person is not an independent variable in the utility function of individual A. But it is perfectly possible for the income, wealth, or consumption of some other person (Y^b, W^b, C_1^b) to appear as independent variables in the utility function of individual A. When this is the case, the utility function of individual A is said to be interdependent with the income, wealth, or consumption of individual B.

If the relationship is positive, then the welfare of A can be increased by an increase in the income, wealth, or consumption of certain goods by individual B, and individual A would be willing, voluntarily, to make some contribution toward the welfare of B. Private charity is a demonstration of interdependent utility functions on the part of the donor. The donor voluntarily accepts a reduction in his own income or wealth in exchange for an increase in the income, wealth, or consumption of a particular good by the recipient of the transfer and considers himself better off after having made the transfer. If the interdependence is related to general income or wealth, the transfer will take place in the

---

[1] Economists, as individual human beings, also may not be indifferent to the distribution of incomes. But as scholars and scientists, they do attempt to exclude individual value judgments about income distribution. Modern welfare economics is not able to "prove" that one distribution is superior to another because interpersonal comparisons of utility are not acceptable in this analysis. Thus, a scientific benefit-cost analysis may be indifferent to distributional effects even though the decision maker cannot be accorded the comfort of such indifference.

form of money. If the interdependence is related to the consumption of some particular good or service, the transfer will take place in the form of provision of that good or service to B. The form of the transfer is donor's choice, since the transfer is undertaken by him as a means of employing his own resources to promote his own satisfaction or welfare.

The same process of voluntary exchange can be extended to explain the income redistribution activities of government in a democratic society. A person whose welfare function is interdependent (positively) with the income or consumption of others may find that his willingness to participate in such transfers is dependent on the assurance that others will also participate. He may reason, for example, that his own personal efforts toward the redistribution of income will have no appreciable impact on the degree of inequality in the society unless they are matched by some significant number of others in the society. Or, if his efforts would produce a significant change in income distribution, he may resent the idea that nonparticipants would be given a free ride from his personal efforts. Thus, a potential contributor to income redistribution may support legislation that would provide transfers (in either money or goods, depending upon the nature of the interdependence he experiences) and that would finance these transfers with compulsory taxes collected from himself and all others in like circumstances. Thus the machinery of government can be used for income redistribution programs in the same way it can be used to provide other collective services.

If the mechanisms of collective decision making were functioning perfectly (perhaps as illustrated by Wicksell's ideal model), the entire redistribution effort would be carried out inside the bounds of *Pareto optimality*, that is, benefits would be realized and no one would be harmed by the transfers made. The division of the transfers between those carried out in money and those carried out in specific goods or services would be consistent with the nature of the interdependence in utility functions.[2] In short, reasoning on the basis of interdependent utility functions leads to the finding that some amount of redistribution can be expected to take place in a well-functioning democratic political process and that the steps taken will be optimizing in the sense that they will move the distribution after taxes and transfers in the direction desired by the citizens.

Limitations of Pareto Optimality

The problem with the interdependent utility function approach to redistribution lies with the fact that the initiative for the redistributional effort arises inside an existing state of distribution and that the recognized interdependencies themselves are conditioned or influenced by this preexisting distribution. Individual voters who, on the basis of the existing distribution, know that they will be the recipients of transfers may vote on the proposed program of redistribution quite differently than they would have voted in the absence of such knowledge. Those who know they will be net contributors to redistribution may also

[2] An interesting analysis of money transfer payments in the context of interdependent utility functions is presented in Harold M. Hochman and James D. Rodgers, "Pareto Optimal Redistribution," *American Economic Review*, LIX (September 1969), 542–57.

be influenced by this knowledge. In other words, to carry out a program of redistribution subject to the constraints imposed by Pareto optimality automatically accepts the existing state of distribution and permits only changes acceptable in this preexisting state of affairs.

Redistribution in the Democratic Process

Programs of income redistribution therefore pose fundamental problems for political democracies. The democratic process of voting implies adherence to the basic notion of Pareto optimality that voters are expected to vote in favor of and not contrary to their own self-interests. The desired amount of redistribution revealed at any given time is conditioned by the preexisting degree of inequality. But each round of redistribution which is carried out sets up new conditions that may lead successively to new distributions. If the changes are in the "correct" direction and if the citizenry exhibits the requisite degree of patience, an evolutionary process consistent with orderly democratic procedures may emerge. If these conditions are not fulfilled, democratic processes may break down and totalitarian alternatives may be attempted.

In a democratic system, there are more eligible voters with below-average income, that is, the distribution of income is skewed so that the median income is less than the average income. Lower-income citizens have the political power to impose redistributional taxation on the rich that could require them to contribute more than they would voluntarily contribute in terms of interdependent utility functions. Political power could thus break through the bounds of Pareto optimality so that the gains to some would not be confined to the amounts which would impose no real loss on others. Aggressive exercise of majority rule power could lead to substantial equality in incomes after taxes and transfers. Yet it is apparent that this has not happened in the United States.

Part of the explanation for this phenomenon lies in the proposition that "money votes," that is, that command over resources is an important dimension of the political process. Real resources are required to develop an effective political organization, to collect information, and to disseminate it to potential voters. Higher-income groups are better able to finance political campaigns than are lower-income groups; and for those with very low income, lack of access to financing can amount to effective disenfranchisement.

The median voter majority rule model also provides some explanation for the limited extent to which redistributional efforts have been carried in the United States. In this system, the median voter probably is found in the lower-middle income group, and this group has not demonstrated great enthusiasm for large-scale redistributive efforts. It may be that voters in this income range identify more comfortably with persons in income ranges somewhat higher than their own (who may be their employers and the molders of opinion in their society); persons in lower income ranges may be viewed as potential job competitors.[3] It may also be that some voters in the middle income ranges entertain aspirations of rising into higher ranges.

---

[3] It is interesting to note that Hochman and Rodgers, *op. cit.*, found evidence, that actual redistribution programs tend to channel transfer payments not to the very lowest strata of the income distribution but to groups somewhat above this lowest level.

Those who entertain such aspirations may not wish to establish tax systems that would diminish their opportunities for success. The aspirations argument cuts both ways, however, since the other side of that coin is the possibility that misfortune may seriously reduce the individual's income position in the future. In this frame of mind, the person might willingly vote for some degree of redistribution as a hedge against possible misfortune. He may reason that the promise to pay higher taxes in the event that he enjoys high income is well worth the assurance that he will receive transfer assistance if fortune does not smile on him. In a society with considerable income mobility, this reasoning will provide for some degree of redistribution through the political process. The fact that only modest redistributive efforts are observed in the United States may reflect the strength of the Horatio Alger success theme in American culture as well as the individualistic notion that each person can determine his own destiny and must assume responsibility for it. Finally, there may be some social acceptance of the argument that incentives are important in economic and social relations and that the opportunity to become wealthy (or the hazard of being poor) are constructive forces. Although this need not be couched in terms of maximizing real national product (an economist's construct), it may have an impact on votes cast on redistributional questions.

CAUSES OF INEQUALITY

A considerable amount of inequality can be expected to arise from the operation of the market system of production and distribution. In a society characterized by heavy reliance on this market system, this inequality provides the starting point for collective action for income redistribution through political processes. In economic analysis, *marginal revenue product* is the basic construct used to explain the distribution of income in a market system. It will therefore be helpful briefly to review the marginal revenue product model and to examine the elements of this model that have a bearing on the redistribution programs undertaken through collective action.

The Marginal Revenue Product Model

In the marginal revenue product model, resources (labor, capital, land) are owned by private individuals who may sell the services of these resources to employers. The demand for the services of these resources is derived from the demand from consumers for the products resulting from their employment. The derivation of this demand is through the link of productivity, that is, through the contribution the resources make toward the satisfaction of consumers' wants. In competitive markets, employers are intermediaries between consumers and the owners of resources; the remuneration these employers are capable of paying for resource services is limited by the productivity of the resources. The demand curve for resources reflects marginal revenue productivity—that is, the increment or addition to the revenue of the employer arising from the employment of the last or marginal unit of the resource. The supply curve reflects the willingness of resource owners to sell the services of their resources. The equilibrium rates of pay for resources (wages, interest, rent) are determined by the interaction of supply and demand. If competition prevails and there are no imperfections arising from ignorance, immobilities, and so on, rates of pay cannot be maintained either above or below this marginal revenue product level.

In this perfectly competitive model, the income of an individual will be equal to the number of resource service units he sells times the price or rate of pay these resource units command. A person will have a high income if he sells a large quantity of services and if these services command a high rate of pay. Lower measured incomes will be received by those individuals who sell smaller quantities of services or whose services command lower rates of pay. Figure 7.1 illustrates how these factors contribute to determining an individual's income. Services sold multiplied by the rate of pay that they command determine the market income of the individual. The boxes below each component of the model identify factors which influence the distribution of income. Figure 7.1 shows that government may attempt to alter the distribution of income by changing individual capabilities, by influencing market rates of pay, or by direct redistribution or income maintenance programs.

FIGURE 7.1   Sources of Inequality in the Market System

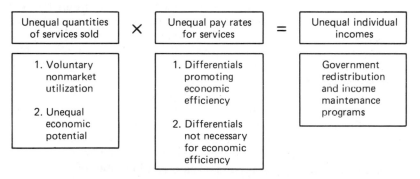

Unequal Sales of Resources

The market distribution of income is influenced by the quantity and quality of resource services sold by an individual. An individual who sells only a small quantity of resource service will have a lower measured income than a person who sells a large quantity, other things (such as the pay rate for the resources) being equal. If an individual owns a sizable stock of resources which would command a high price on the market but chooses to withhold these resources from the market, his measured income will be lower than it would have been if he actually had sold these resources. But his real income will not be lower just because he has chosen to utilize his resource capabilities outside the market system by applying them in some "do it yourself" undertaking. In fact, a reasonable presumption is that the do it yourself undertaking is more productive of real income than the market alternative. Thus *measured income*, that is, income realized through market transactions, understates the level of the person's *real* income. Inequalities in measured income that arise through an individual's choosing to withhold resources from the market are *fictitious* inequalities. Individuals may choose part-time jobs rather than full-time jobs, or reject offers of overtime employment because the nonmarket applications of their resources are more productive in their judgments. College professors may turn down summer teaching opportunities in favor of alternative uses of their time, and it does not matter whether these alternative uses are termed "leisure" or whether they are investments, such as research or additional schooling.

Inequality in measured income arising from the exercise of personal choice is not the type of inequality government redistribution programs seek to reduce or eliminate. But adjustments in measured income inequality to filter out the do it yourself elements are difficult. How many resource units actually are devoted to nonmarket production? Is the choice actually voluntary? What would these resources have received had they been offered on the market? The difficulties of quantifying fictitious elements in measured inequalities of income argue against attempting to incorporate this refinement into income redistribution programs, but some implicit recognition of the problem is shown in the observed reluctance to extend welfare assistance to employable persons and in the efforts to include a work requirement among the conditions for welfare eligibility. Those drawing unemployment benefits, for example, must be registered for work and willing to accept reasonable employment offers.

Income inequalities also arise from differences in economic potential. Individuals are not identical to one another at the moment of conception, when the combination of genes programs a package of characteristics, nor are they identical at birth, nor at any other chosen point at which comparisons are attempted. Each individual is subject to a lifelong series of influences such as nutrition, medical care, environment, educational opportunities, and accidents of good or bad fortune that alter the index of economic potential. Even circumstances clearly external to the individual, such as economic conditions that govern the income-earning potential of certain combinations of characteristics, have a bearing on the degree of inequality which may exist, at any time, among the economic potentials of individuals.

Inequalities arising from differences in economic potential or endowments offer an especially attractive focus for government redistribution activities because they may achieve a more desirable distribution of income and, at the same time, develop valuable human resources. Redistributional programs in this area seek to increase the equality of opportunity by making investments in human capital. Subsidies for medical care and for educational services for people who could not finance them otherwise can increase equality of opportunity and thereby reduce income inequality. Manpower training programs are another example. Aid for Families with Dependent Children (AFDC), one of the largest and fastest-growing elements in the welfare program in the United States, can be classed as a human capital program in which the immediate selection of the nature of the investment is entrusted to the parents or guardians of children who otherwise would lack opportunities to develop their economic potential.

Unequal Pay Rates

The rate of pay that can be commanded by the resources owned by an individual is an important factor influencing the level of that person's income. If the equilibrium rate of pay is zero, the owner of these resources will not be able to secure any income through the market process no matter how many units of these resources he offers. Low pay rates for a person's resource capabilities are likely to mean low income for the individual unless he is able to sell in large quantity.

According to the marginal revenue product model, pay rates are important in the efficient allocation of resources in the economy. Resource prices are signals that assist employers in deciding which products to produce and which method of production to use. Resources that are expensive per unit of final product cannot be employed in the production of the product unless the satisfaction experienced by consumers (revealed in their willingness to pay for the final product) is great enough to pay for their use. Resource prices are also signals to the owners of resources and assist them in allocating their resources among different possible employments. In pursuit of his own self-interest, the resource owner is expected to channel his resources into those employments that offer the highest rates of pay. These are, of course, the employments that result in the greatest satisfactions to consumers of final products.

In the context of perfectly competitive markets, the marginal productivity model paints an attractive picture of efficient resource allocation, and different pay rates for resources are integral components. Attempts to redistribute incomes through the establishment of artificial resource prices will lead to inefficient functioning of markets and are thus high-cost methods of securing altered income distribution. Moreover, the results achieved through artificial resource pricing may be quite small and contrary to the objectives of the redistribution effort. If the artificial price is above the free market equilibrium price, the quantity of the resource actually employed will be less than would have prevailed in the absence of the artificial price and some resource units will be forced into other employment. Those resources able to retain employment at the high artificial price will enjoy higher pay rates and presumably higher incomes, but those forced into other employments will be the least productive units in the class of resources subjected to the artificial rate. Inequality of income within this group will be increased rather than diminished, which may be an outcome contrary to the objectives of the redistribution program. Examples of artificial resource pricing include minimum wage laws and price supports for agricultural products. To the extent that these actions have been undertaken with the objective of securing income redistribution in the direction of greater equality, their outcomes have been disappointing and have imposed real costs in terms of economic inefficiency.

When markets are not competitive, economically inefficient pay-rate inequalities may arise. For example, monopoly conditions in product markets will lead to restrictions in output as monopolists recognize that profits can be increased through such restrictions. Fewer job opportunities will be available to resources suitable to the production of monopoly-produced goods and services, and some of these resources will be forced into alternative (less suitable and

lower paying) employments. Those remaining on the job may be paid according
to marginal revenue productivity (and may even be able to appropriate some
portion of the monopoly profit), but inequality will be increased among resource
owners. Thus, in monopoly circumstances, a pattern of economically inefficient
rate differences may increase inequality in the distribution of incomes. Government programs to combat monopoly can both improve economic efficiency
and alter the distribution of incomes among individuals. The monopoly profits
themselves (which are an economic rent received by those who hold the monopoly position) also introduce income differentials that are not operationally
necessary to the market system. Thus, government programs to combat monopoly can have an impact on the distribution of income in the direction of greater
equality, although income redistribution may not be the prime objective of
such programs.

Noncompetitive conditions in resource (factor) markets have a more
direct impact on the distribution of incomes. For example, an employer who
holds a dominant position in a factor market (a monopsonist) may be led to
pay a wage rate lower than the marginal revenue product of the factors
employed. This is illustrated in Figure 7.2. The average cost for the resource

FIGURE 7.2   Wage Rate and Productivity in a Monop-
sony Factor Market

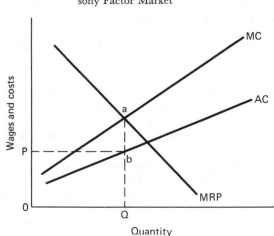

slopes upward to the right because the monopsonistic employer's hiring of the
resource is a significant part of the total market for this resource and expanded
hiring by this employer will bid up the wage rate. The employer will recognize
that the marginal cost curve for this resource lies above the average cost because
the higher pay rate needed to acquire the marginal unit will have to be extended
to the inframarginal units of the resource (assuming that the employer cannot
discriminate by paying different pay rates to different units of the identical
resource). In these circumstances, the equilibrium pay rate will be P and the
quantity hired will be Q, and a gap (ab) will exist between the marginal revenue
product of the resource and the pay rate it receives. The resource will receive
less than its marginal revenue product.

Pay rates that do not match up with marginal revenue productivity have an adverse effect on efficient resource allocation and also exert an influence on the distribution of incomes. Owners of the resources are subjected to "exploitation" and receive lower pay and have lower incomes than would exist in a more competitive factor market. Therefore, actions to improve competitive conditions in factor markets have a distributional as well as an allocational dimension, and conflict need not arise between allocational and distributional objectives. Inequalities arising through exploitation are "unnecessary" insofar as efficient resource allocation is concerned. Corrective action involves increasing the mobility of the factors of production, thereby releasing them from subservience to the wage offers of the dominant employer, and extending the scope of the factor market in which the employer must compete for resources. In terms of Figure 7.2, this extending of the factor market flattens the average cost as viewed by the employer and narrows the gap between wages paid and the marginal revenue product of the resource.

Employment services operated by government and private agencies increase factor mobility and can be beneficial to employers and to employees. Direct subsidies for moving expenses and tax deductibility for these expenses also contribute to increased factor mobility. Discrimination in hiring based on sex or race restricts factor markets and opens the way for exploitation that may produce both economic inefficiency and unnecessary inequality in incomes. Legislation combatting such discrimination can result in greater equality in the distribution of income and, at the same time, improve the operation of the market system.

Several conclusions may be drawn from this discussion of unequal pay rates and the distribution of income. First, careful analysis must be focused on the underlying causes of pay-rate differentials observed in the markets. Some of these differentials are important or "necessary" for efficient allocation of resources and interference with them would obtain redistribution only at a high real cost in lost efficiency. Other observed pay-rate differentials may be unnecessary and in fact contrary to efficient allocation of resources. These arise through imperfections in markets and restrictions on the free mobility of resources. Corrections in these areas can improve both income distribution and allocational efficiency. In general, attempts to redistribute through artificial resource prices do not deal effectively with the underlying causes of either inefficiency or inequality. Instead, corrections must focus on the underlying causes themselves, such as monopoly, immobility, and discrimination.

REMEDIES FOR INEQUALITY

Three areas or arenas of action are available to government for dealing with the unequal incomes which arise from the market process. These were identified in the boxes in Figure 7.1. Government may attack the sources of inequality which lie in different economic potentials. This is an "ex ante" or preventative approach. Government also may attack inequalities that arise through monopoly and discrimination in the functioning of the market itself. The third approach is to deal with the market outcome, through redistribution and income maintenance programs that undertake to alter the distribution of incomes after the markets have determined individual shares. This is an "ex post" or corrective approach. The ex post method operates through a system of taxes and transfers; the test to determine whether a person pays a tax or receives a transfer is simply the amount of that person's income. General assistance programs that require only a means test in order to qualify for a transfer illustrate this approach. Negative income tax systems also focus only on the outcomes of market processes and do not consider the underlying factors contributing to these outcomes.

Choosing Between Ex Ante and Ex Post

Both the ex ante and the ex post approaches are constructive elements in carrying out government's distribution responsibility. The ex ante approach is especially attractive because it seeks to achieve a more desirable distribution of incomes and at the same time to be economically efficient by developing valuable human resources. But this approach requires more resources for administration and implementation than does the ex post approach and it also is subject to certain inherent limitations which mean that it cannot provide a complete remedy for inequality and poverty.

The ex ante approach requires identification of those people who will make good use of government investment in them. This is a substantial administrative task. In addition, the investments themselves (such as medical care and vocational instruction) demand resources. If the programs succeed in directing help to worthwhile recipients who can make constructive use of the investment, a return may be realized through an increase in society's economic potential. This return may meet the extra costs of developing the programs. Because the ex ante redistribution efforts provide incentives for the development of human capital, they have an important advantage over ex post approaches which, because they disregard the extent to which economic potentials are unequal or undeveloped, may result in incentives that actually discourage investments in human capital.

But the limitations of the ex ante approach should not go unnoticed. It is extremely difficult to identify latent individual potential and to develop effective systems for choosing good investments. Facilities for human capital investment for disadvantaged groups are as yet undeveloped, and those that are installed by government may be difficult to evaluate because of the long time period required before results will be known. In addition, investments in economic potential are not equalizing in and of themselves but in fact are nonequalizing among those whose incomes are below the norm set by society. Economically efficient allocation of investments within this group will provide help to those with greater potential for development, that is, for those with both the potential to benefit from the investment and the incentives to apply the financial assistance effectively. Others in the needy group will not receive human capital investment financing and will continue to require ex-post-oriented redistributions.

Thus, the choice between the ex ante and the ex post approaches will not result in a system exclusively dedicated to either of these alternatives. The ex ante method can be employed as long as the additional costs are justified by additions to the economic potential of the society. But the ex post method will still be required for those who have low incomes and who are not able effectively to utilize investments in human capital.

Money Transfers and Transfers in Kind

The choice between money and in kind transfers hinges partly on whether the redistribution effort is of the ex ante or the ex post variety. If the program is of the ex post type, that is, if it is not intended to serve as a subsidy or incentive for investments in human capital, pure money transfers permit the recipient full freedom of choice in expenditure of the funds. This freedom offers him the best chance of maximizing his own welfare according to his own utility function. If the interdependence of utility functions is of a general sort, that is, not related to specific expenditures, the pure money transfer is the most efficient form of redistribution, unless it is presumed that the recipient of the tranfers is not competent to determine his own self-interest. Transfers in goods or services may reflect the paternalistic notion that the recipient is incompetent, or they may indicate that the interdependence of utility function motivating the majority was specifically related to those goods or services. In either case, it is apparent that transfers in kind raise delicate issues about the competence of recipients or about the extent to which majorities should impose life-style restrictions on minorities through the bribery of transfers.

If redistributive programs are of the ex ante investment in human capital variety, a stronger case can be made for transfers in kind or for subsidies conditional upon specified uses of the transfer funds. Money transfers not conditional on any particular expenditure will be invested in the development of economic potential only if the recipient decides that this is the best use of these funds. If the recipient decides that current consumption is more beneficial than investment in economic potential, then the objective of income redistribution through investments in human capital will not be realized. For this reason, there is a tendency for redistributional expenditures designed to operate through human capital investment to take the form of transfers in kind or transfers conditional upon specified expenditure of the transfer funds. Food stamps and rent supplements illustrate transfers conditional on specified uses of the money, as do scholarships in which preference is given to low-income or minority-group applicants. But there is still a problem concerning the choice among alternative human capital investments. Greater latitude in the expenditure of transfers and fewer restrictions of the "in kind" variety will be more efficient to the extent that recipients are able to make sound judgments among alternative opportunities.

SUMMARY

The distribution of income is a dimension of the social order consumed collectively and thus is an appropriate object of concern for government. Government may redistribute incomes in order to alter the degree of inequality prevailing in the society, but the ideal degree of inequality cannot be established by scientific analysis. Interdependent utility functions may prompt individuals to vote in favor of redistribution, but the votes cast in such democratic processes are themselves influenced by the preexisting state of distribution so that the outcome of this process does not necessarily establish an "ideal" degree of inequality.

In a market system, inequality arises from a variety of causes. Remedies for inequality that ignore its causes or that fail to recognize connections between pay-rate differences and the allocation of resources may be ineffective and may damage the efficient operation of market processes. Remedies for inequality that do recognize causes and allocational interrelationships may utilize either direct money transfers or transfers of selected goods or services. The appropriate medium for redistribution depends on the source of the inequality and on the strategy chosen to deal with it.

SUGGESTED READINGS

HOCHMAN, HAROLD M., and J. D. RODGERS. "Pareto Optimal Redistribution," *American Economic Review*, LIX, September 1969, pp. 542–57.

RAWLS, JOHN. *A Theory of Justice* (Cambridge: Harvard University Press, 1971).

THUROW, LESTER C. "The Income Distribution as a Pure Public Good," *Quarterly Journal of Economics*, May 1971, pp. 327–36.

HOCHMAN, HAROLD M., and GEORGE E. PETERSON. *Redistribution Through Public Choice* (New York: Columbia University Press, 1974).

8

Programs
for
Income Redistribution

This chapter surveys explicit government distribution programs. It is important to recognize, however, that *all* activities undertaken by government have an impact on the distribution of real income. This is true for activities that are purely regulatory in character (and which therefore do not involve significant transactions in the fiscal accounts of revenues and expenditures) as well as for programs that actually require the collections and disbursements of funds. Moreover, in the fiscal accounts category itself, distributional considerations are important in most decisions about expenditures and taxation even for programs that aim primarily at other government responsibilities.

A complete examination of the distribution activities of government would therefore be an exercise of great breadth and complexity. Here we will briefly discuss the distributional importance of general taxing and expenditure activities and then focus on government programs that involve explicit transfer payments. These are the programs most commonly recognized as directed toward fulfilling the distribution responsibility. Although they fall far short of reflecting the full distributional features of government activities, an examination of them gives some insight into voter attitudes toward redistribution.

EXPENDITURES AND TAXATION IN GENERAL

In the pure normative model for government finance, income distribution programs would be implemented through tax and transfer payment systems in which taxes would be collected from those whose income was to be reduced and transfer payments would be made to those whose income was to be increased. Transfer payments would be made in money because the collective concern would focus on the distribution of spending power and would be unconcerned with the particular goods and services consumed by persons in the various income categories. Actual practice departs from this pure model because a substantial portion of the distribution activity of government is carried out through expenditures on goods and services that yield different amounts of benefit to people in different income categories in the general population. In some cases, such as food stamps and subsidies for housing, the distributional orientation of the expenditure program is explicitly recognized through eligibility requirements for beneficiaries of the programs. In other instances, such as education, the distributional motivation is generally recognized even though the service is provided to the entire population and no income-related eligibility requirements are used. But the fact is that all expenditure programs have some income distribution dimension and that this dimension probably is given consideration in the legislative process. The distributive aspect may not be the primary consideration when the expenditure is enacted by the legislature and the legislation may not contain specific reference to distribution considerations, but the consequences of these expenditures are nevertheless important in the total picture of income redistribution.

Taxation is also an important part of the distribution program of government. In the pure normative model of government finance, progressive taxation would be a concern of the distribution branch, benefit taxes would be used by the allocation branch, and the stabilization branch would impose its taxes and dispense its transfers according to guidelines from the distribution branch. But, once again, actual practice deviates substantially from the normative model because a general revenue system is used. Collections from a great variety of taxes are pooled into a general fund which then is used to finance a great variety of expenditures. Some taxes, such as the federal individual income tax, clearly incorporate an income distribution consideration in the selection of the tax base and in the setting of tax rates. Others, such as motor fuel taxes, do not include distributional factors in the selection of the base or the establishment of rates. But all taxes have income distribution consequences even though these effects may not be explicitly written into the law or generally recognized as important aspects of the tax. Therefore, careful analysis of the incidence of taxes actually used is necessary to determine the distributional effects of the tax system. The findings of these studies must be combined with similar studies of the distributional effects of expenditures if we are to have a full picture of the government's distribution program.

Tracing the incidence of benefits from government expenditures and the incidence of burdens from taxes is an extremely complicated undertaking and one in which critical assumptions frequently must be made to enable researchers to arrive at conclusions. Because the particular assumptions made have important influences on the findings, there is often disagreement about many aspects of the net effect of taxes and expenditures on the distribution of income. In expenditure programs, for example, the total amount of money appropriated for welfare programs cannot be accepted as a measure of benefits received by low-income clients of the programs because a significant portion of the money is used to pay the people who administer these programs and who are not members of the poverty population. In other words, poverty programs differ from one another in their *target efficiency*. The difficulty of assessing incidence on the tax side of the fiscal accounts is illustrated by the uncertainty that surrounds the question of who bears the burden of the corporation income tax. The tax may be judged to be quite progressive if the incidence is determined to fall on corporate shareholders, but the tax will be judged to be regressive if the incidence is determined to fall on the consumers of products produced and sold by these corporations.

Thus, the distributional consequences of general taxing and spending programs are shrouded in considerable uncertainty. In general, however, it appears that the net effects of government expenditure and taxing programs as presently practiced have the effect of reducing the degree of inequality prevailing in the economy. Moreover, there is substantial agreement that expenditure programs are more powerful in bringing about this net result than taxation programs, which is somewhat ironic since public discussion of redistribution so frequently focuses on the progressivity of tax programs rather than on the progressivity of expenditure programs. Expenditures for education, public health services, and manpower training programs tend to raise the real income of people in lower-income categories proportionately more than they raise the real income of people in higher-income categories. And because of the large volume of expenditures in these areas, they may have a greater redistributional effect than explicit transfer payment programs, even though the latter may have a greater effect per dollar of expenditure. On the other hand, taxation appears to have only a moderate net effect in the direction of greater equality of income, because taxes judged to be progressive, such as the federal individual income tax, are offset to an important degree by taxes judged to be regressive, such as payroll and sales taxes.

THE TRANSFER PAYMENTS APPROACH

We now examine programs that utilize explicit transfer payments. The distinction between the ex ante and the ex post approaches to income distribution (developed in the preceding chapter) can be helpful in understanding the role of explicit transfer payment programs in the general distribution responsibility of government. General expenditure programs, such as those for education, public health, and manpower training, are in the ex ante category because they attempt to alter the economic potential of individuals so that ordinary market processes may produce a more equal distribution of incomes. Transfer payment programs, on the other hand, are in the ex post category, that is, they undertake to adjust the distribution of income which arises out of the market processes but make little attempt to alter the processes themselves or the potentials of individuals to generate income through these processes. It has been pointed out that the ex ante approach alone cannot fulfill the government's responsibility in income distribution, since some members of the population are less able to utilize these programs than others and since efficiency considerations suggest that there are limits to the extension of these programs. Thus, ex post transfer payments systems are a necessary part of government's distribution program.

Many transfer payment programs exist. Some, such as unemployment compensation and social security retirement, disability, and hospital programs, are financed through trust funds maintained by specially ear-marked taxes and thus are insurance-type programs. Other transfer payment programs are financed from general revenues and therefore are more clearly welfare or distribution-oriented operations. An examination of these programs, and of proposals for a negative income tax, suggests that voters in the United States have proceeded in a somewhat reluctant and ambivalent manner in respect to ex post provisions for income redistribution. Individualistic rather than social values have been important in the development of distribution programs and have resulted in a preference for ex ante rather than ex post approaches to income distribution.

SOCIAL SECURITY

Social Security, an income maintenance program, is characterized by a connection between the benefits or transfers received by an individual and the contributions that individual has made to the program. Thus, no need test must be passed in order to receive benefits. Benefits are received as a matter of right based on prior contributions or premium payments. Benefits are received by the nonpoor as well as by the poor, although the payroll tax method of financing excludes the unemployed (and therefore the very poor) from the system.

Social Security Benefits and Taxes

When the social security system was launched, it provided only old age and survivors benefits (OASI). Disability benefits were added in 1956 (when the system became OASDI), and hospital benefits were added in 1966 (completing the present OASDHI system). When hospital benefits were introduced, provision was made through which individuals could voluntarily purchase medical care insurance to supplement the hospital benefits provided under the regular program. This optional additional insurance requires a monthly premium payment by the individual, but the program is subsidized with equal contributions from government general revenues.

Benefits under social security are available only to those who are covered according to the specifications of that law and who therefore have paid taxes into the program. Originally, coverage was required only for employed persons and some employees were excluded, such as government and railroad employees already covered by other insurance programs, agricultural and domestic employees, and self-employed and professional persons. In 1950 coverage was extended to the self-employed and to regularly employed agricultural and domestic workers and in 1965 a further extension brought professional persons into the program. Thus, the social security system now covers practically the entire labor force, except for the unemployed and for employed persons covered by other social insurance programs (although some of these may opt for coverage under social security).

The amount of benefits receivable through social security is determined from a table included in the law which relates the amount of benefit to the average "covered" earnings of the individual. Usually the calculation deals only with years since 1950 and permits the five years of lowest covered earnings to be excluded in computing the average. After the primary insurance amount has been determined from the table, adjustments are made: Additional benefits are given retirees who are married and benefit amounts are reduced if the individual has retired earlier than the specified ages of 65 for men and 62 for women.

Benefit determination is so complex that it is simply impossible for the individual to make his own estimate of the benefits to which he is entitled. Persons wishing to obtain this information must request the Social Security Administration to provide it to them. Part of the complexity arises from the fact that the social security system covers only part of the total earnings of many individuals. When the system started, only the first $3,000 of wages were covered. In subsequent years, the covered level of wages was increased several times; the level reached $16,500 in 1977. Therefore, the amount of covered earnings required for calculation of benefit amounts depends on the year in which the money was earned and upon the amount of earnings covered by the law in that year. Additional complexity in benefit determination arises from the fact that the table used in the law introduces variations in the relationship between the primary benefit and the amount of average covered earnings. These variations result in some progressivity inside the social security system. Benefit amounts are a higher percentage of covered earnings (and tax contributions) for persons with low average covered earnings than they are for persons with higher average covered earnings.

The extent to which the social security system is internally progressive cannot be determined solely from the table used to relate benefits to amounts of average covered earnings. Two persons with the same level of benefit entitlement may have paid different amounts of tax into the system. A person who was unemployed during some of his working years would have paid less tax into the system than one who was regularly employed, but the unemployment need not reduce the average covered earnings if those years were excluded in calculating the average. This would increase the internal progressivity of the system. Similarly, a person who entered the labor force later in life, perhaps because some years were devoted to obtaining a university education, would pay lesser amounts of tax than a person who entered earlier. But the university-trained person could realize a higher income because of his training so that internal progressivity could be reduced rather than raised. When the coverage of the social security system was extended in 1950 and in 1965, particularly advantageous ratios between benefits received and taxes paid were realized by persons entering the program in the latter stages of their working lives.

Rates of tax applicable to covered wages have increased through the years of the social security program. Half of the tax is paid by the employee and half is paid by the employer. At the start of the program, the sum of these taxes amounted to only 2 percent of covered wages. But in 1972 the combined rate amounted to 11.7 percent of covered wages, and further increases were contemplated. Historically, rate increases have tended to correspond with increases in the levels of primary benefits legislated through the years, but the benefits received by an individual are determined on the basis of the table of benefits applicable at the time he is entitled to receive benefits, that is, at and subsequent to retirement. Since increases in the amounts of benefits are extended to all eligible beneficiaries without regard to the tax rates paid by that individual during his working years, increases in benefit rates significantly increase the rate of return on tax payments enjoyed by the current beneficiary group. This also means that people currently paying into the system cannot calculate the rate of return on the money put into the program simply by comparing current tax rates with current benefit levels. The rate of return calculation requires comparison of current tax rates with the benefit levels expected to prevail when the contributing individual becomes eligible to collect benefits.

Benefit calculations have been further complicated by the introduction of automatic adjustments in both benefits and contributions based on changes in the cost of living revealed by the consumer price index. Legislation enacted in 1972 specified that all benefit payments shall be adjusted according to this cost of living index and that the maximum level of wages subject to tax to pay for the system shall also be adjusted on this basis. Thus, adjustments to recognize changes in the cost of living no longer wait upon explicit congressional action but are automatically incorporated into the revenue and expenditure structure.

Incidence of Social Security Taxes

Economic analysis indicates that the burden of social security taxes (both the share paid directly by the worker and the share paid on his behalf by the employer) is on the worker himself. There is little difficulty in recognizing the incidence of the part of the tax paid by the worker himself, which is explicitly withheld from the paycheck. The part of the tax paid by the employer also is borne by the worker, but some knowledge of elementary economics is necessary to recognize this.

Figure 8.1 illustrates demand and supply curves for labor. The demand curve reflects the marginal revenue product of labor and shows the wage rates employers can afford to pay to hire workers. The supply curve shows the wage rates that must be paid by the employer in order to succeed in hiring various possible quantities of labor. The supply curve reflects the willingness of workers to sell their labor services and is drawn to suggest a rather inelastic supply. The employer's share of social security taxes is incorporated into Figure 8.1 by shifting the supply curve upward by the amount of the tax, because the necessity of paying the social security tax becomes part of the cost of employing labor. In the absence of the tax, the equilibrium wage rate is W_1 and the quantity of employment is Q_1. The equilibrium position after the tax has been imposed indicates a wage rate of W_2, of which the worker receives only W_2', which is lower than the marginal revenue product of labor by the amount of the tax. Thus, the employer's share of the social security tax is financed out of the productivity of labor and workers themselves receive lower pay rates than they would have received in the absence of the tax.

Social security taxes will also alter the allocation of resources in the economy. This is because, on an industry by industry basis, both the demand and the supply for labor will exhibit some degree of elasticity. Supply elasticities will differ among industries because workers possess varying degrees of

FIGURE 8.1   Shifting the Employer's Share of Social Security Taxes

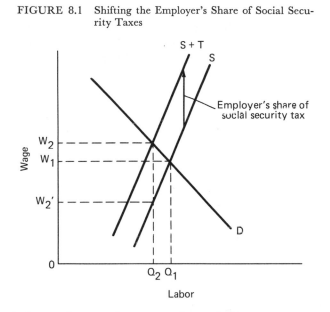

ability to switch to other employments when take-home pay is threatened by the tax. Demand elasticities will differ because it is easier to substitute capital for labor in some industries than in others and because final product demand will be more elastic for some industries than for others. Generally speaking, social security taxes are likely to have a greater impact on industries that are labor-intensive than on industries that are capital-intensive.

The conclusion that wage rates paid will be less than marginal revenue product by the amount of the tax is applicable regardless of the degrees of elasticity or inelasticity of the demand and supply curves illustrated in Figure 8.1. If supply were completely inelastic, the imposition of the tax would cause no reduction in the number of jobs, but wage rates would fall by the full amount of the tax. Supply elasticity modifies this result in that some workers will turn to alternative activities rather than accept the pay reduction. The wage-rate reduction experienced by those remaining employed will be somewhat moderated in this situation. Different demand elasticities also influence the tradeoff between reductions in the number of jobs and the take-home pay rate. Demand elasticity increases the "job loss" effect and also increases the amount by which take-home pay rates fall due to the tax, because capital replaces labor in the production process or because final product customers switch to other commodities rather than pay higher prices for the product.

The Intergeneration Transfer Model

In privately operated insurance systems, the premiums paid by the insured individual provide the funds to operate the insurance company and to finance the benefits that will be paid to the insured or to his estate when the terms of the contract are fulfilled. The premiums paid by the insured are placed in a reserve fund which is invested to earn interest to help finance benefits payable to the insured. If interest rates are accurately predicted and if premium rates are set in accordance with accurate calculations of life expectancies, and so on, the insurance program will be actuarially sound and premium payments from the insured group of persons will finance the benefits payable to that group. When it was launched, the social security system was expected to operate in a similar manner; that is, it was expected that a reserve would be accumulated sufficient to cover the discounted value of the benefits promised to persons who had paid premiums to establish the reserve. Shortly after the social security system was under way, however, it was converted into a pay as you go program under which benefits payable during the current year were financed by social security taxes collected during that same year. The amount of reserve accumulated no longer equaled the discounted value of future benefits payable, but instead was a "contingency reserve" sufficient only to cover relatively short-run fluctuations in the flows of money into the fund from current tax collections and out of the fund to current benefit payments.

The transformation of social security into a pay as you go system meant that it became an *intergeneration transfer* program in which the working population financed benefits paid to contemporary members of the retired or benefit population. Instead of a person paying for his own retirement, the working population pays for the retirement benefits of other persons in exchange for the implicit promise that their retirement benefits, in turn, will be financed by future generations of workers.

In the intergeneration transfer model, the rate of return on premiums paid into the program is not determined by interest earned on funds accumulated in a reserve. Instead, the rate of return is heavily influenced by the size of the benefits package that will be legislated into effect by the time the individual becomes eligible to collect benefits, and this benefit package, in turn, will depend on the future size of the labor force relative to the size of the beneficiary group, the productivity of that labor force, and the level of tax rates imposed. Suppose, for example, that the social security tax rate and the ratio between the working population and the beneficiary population were constant through the years. In this case, increases in the productivity of labor over the years would provide the basis for increases in the benefit package and the rate of return would be equal to the rate of increase in labor productivity. Members of the covered population would continue to share in the fruits of increased productivity even after they had retired from active membership in the labor force. Their living standard relative to other members of society would be maintained throughout their retirement years even though they would no longer be active participants in increased productivity.

The rate of return on money put into the social security system will deviate from the rate of productivity increase if the other determinants of the benefit package (that is, the ratio of working population to the beneficiary group and the rate of tax) are allowed to change. Increases in tax rates can finance richer benefit packages and will convey especially advantageous windfalls to those who are members of the beneficiary group at the time the enrichment takes place. Indeed, very substantial enrichments in the social security program took place during its first forty years and resulted in very attractive rates of return to persons in the beneficiary groups during those years. During these first forty years, the program was immature, that is, the beneficiary group had not reached its full potential. Tax-rate increases were installed with widespread acceptance in exchange for enrichments in the program of benefits.

Variations in the birth rate and the consequent changes in the ratios among various age cohorts in the population can bring substantial changes in the size of the benefit package that can be financed with any given rate of social security tax. The high birth rates of the 1950s and early 1960s followed by the low birth rates of the 1970s (which are of unpredictable duration) have created a situation likely to require a searching reassessment of the social security system in the future. Persons born in the 1950s and 1960s and entering the labor force in the 1970s and 1980s will contribute to a ratio between the working group and the beneficiary group that can support a reasonable benefit package at reasonable tax rates, but the low birth rates of the 1970s will impact on this ratio before the turn of the century. A condition of severe financial stress may arise in the early decades of the twenty-first century. At that time, a relatively small working cohort will be asked to finance retirement benefits for a relatively large retired population.

General Revenue Financing for Social Security

As conceived and operated thus far, the social security program has been financed by contributions paid by covered individuals and their employers. General government revenues have not been used.[1] From the beginning, however, there have been proposals that the system should make use of general revenues in place of or as supplementary to the funds contributed by covered individuals. Under the contributory system, separate accounts are maintained of payments made by or for separate individuals and amounts of benefit are related (although not without some variance) to amounts contributed. Under general revenue financing, separate individual accounting of tax payments would not be necessary and benefits could be determined on some other criteria.

The choice between one approach or the other reflects significantly different conceptions of the nature of the program itself. The contributory approach has its roots in individualistic concepts of insurance in which need alone does not constitute a sufficient ground for the receipt of benefit. Instead, benefits are received because the individual has paid insurance premiums. The amount of benefit is related to the amount of premium paid; persons who pay no premiums receive no benefits. Benefits are legitimized, and become a matter of right or entitlement, because of the premiums paid. The program is not a welfare or an income redistribution program. Indeed, the argument is made that the only reason a compulsory insurance program is necessary at all is that, under a purely voluntary arrangement, some persons would fail to make appropriate advance provision for retirement so that the more prudent members of the society would be forced to either grant transfers to them or permit their prodigal fellow citizens to starve. In this light, social security is compulsory

---

[1] The Medicare extension of social security, introduced in 1965 included some use of general revenues and thus is an exception to this statement.

insurance and is an alternative to direct welfare transfers. It is not a welfare system or a redistribution program at all, but in fact is designed to reduce the need to establish such welfare or income redistribution programs. It is not designed to provide economic security to those whose economic potential is very low, but is designed to require that all who are financially capable of providing their own economic security in fact do so. It is reasonable to presume that the contributory basis of social security was established and has been maintained because the individually financed insurance philosophy is firmly rooted in American political thought.

Proposals for general revenue financing reflect a different and broader concept of social insurance—specifically, accepting government responsibility for income distribution and for the provision of economic security to all members of the society. Individuals who are able but perhaps unwilling to provide their own economic security would, of course, be included in the program as is the case with the existing contributory system, but general revenue financing would also include those unable to provide for their own economic security and would establish benefits on a different basis than amounts contributed. When seen from this broader perspective of social insurance, the contributory social security program is inadequate to the full responsibility of government in the area of income distribution, and certain aspects of the contributory system appear anomalous.

The benefit structure is anomalous because social security benefits under the contributory system are sometimes so small as to leave the individual in poverty. Likewise, the taxes used to finance contributory social security are anomalous because they are regressive elements in the total picture of taxes used to finance government. Contributory social security taxes are flat rate taxes, but they apply only to earnings up to a specified cutoff point and thus are regressive if the frame of reference encompasses the entire range of income (as is appropriate to this broader view of social insurance or income security). High-income persons pay a smaller percentage of their income for social security than do lower-income persons. The fact that the contributory social security system is moderately progressive within its own rate and benefit structure provides very little correction for the regressivity of the taxes used to finance it. As social security contribution tax rates have increased, their regressive impact on the revenue structure of the government has increased.

The point raised by proposals for general revenue financing of social security is *not* that it is *in*appropriate for government to install a compulsory insurance program. Compulsory insurance may indeed reduce the demand for outright tax-transfer programs to the extent that it forces some persons to make provision for retirement who would not otherwise have done so. The point is that a compulsory insurance program alone is not a fulfillment of government responsibility for income redistribution or income maintenance. Other programs, discussed later in this chapter, are required to accomplish these broad responsibilities. There is, however, a distinct possibility that the contributory, compulsory insurance social security program will, in the future, be modified or displaced through the infusion of general revenue funding, in spite of the fact that such financing would constitute a radical change in the nature of the program.

The first step was the alteration of the original social security system into a program of intergeneration transfer. Under this arrangement, benefits were increased and tax rates were kept at acceptably low levels because the ratio of the beneficiary population to the working population was low. This ratio was low because the program was immature in the sense that the beneficiary group had not reached its full potential. As the beneficiary group reached its potential, the birth rate increases of the 1950s and early 1960s extended the interval of relatively low ratios between the beneficiary population and the working population. But the inexorable march of the age cohorts coupled with lengthening life expectancy has set the stage for a significant increase in the beneficiary-worker ratio around the beginning of the twenty-first century, and this higher ratio will require either lowered benefit allowances, higher contributory tax rates, or recourse to alternative financial arrangements such as general revenue funding. Reduced benefit entitlements are not likely to be legislated, especially at a time when the beneficiary group will be large and politically powerful. Large increases in contribution tax rates probably also will be politically unpopular. Thus, general revenue financing may emerge as the most acceptable way of resolving the financial dilemma. Ironically, if these events do come to pass, the transition from compulsory individualistic insurance to broadly conceived social insurance will have taken place by the force of events rather than through conscious or rational political decision.

WELFARE PROGRAMS

Welfare programs differ from insurance because there is no connection between the amount of benefit received by an individual and the amount contributed by that individual into a special trust fund. Welfare funds are financed from general revenues and are genuine transfer payments from one group of individuals in the society to another group, that is, they are part of an income redistribution program.

A bewildering variety of different welfare programs exists in the United States. A brief and simple description of these programs is virtually impossible. It is helpful, however, to recognize certain general characteristics. First, welfare programs in the United States typically are of a categorical nature, which means that need alone, in the sense of having an income level below the poverty line, usually is not a sufficient condition to qualify for benefits. The individual must, in addition, exhibit some specific type of disability, such as age or physical impairment, or be responsible for dependent children. General assistance programs, which dispense aid solely on the basis of need, are of little importance in welfare programs in the United States. The second characteristic is that most welfare programs are combined efforts of both the federal and the state governments. Much of the funding comes from the federal government, but administration is carried out by state government agencies according to the provisions of state legislation (which, however, are substantially determined by federal guidelines established as conditions for the receipt of federal money). Thus, both the generosity of the programs and the extent to which they are financed with federal money differ from state to state. Federal guidelines establish minimum standards for eligibility and benefits, but some states apply less stringent eligibility requirements or pay greater benefits than others. Federal funding differs among the states and includes some attempt to provide more assistance to states with lower financial capacity. The third characteristic of United States welfare programs is that they have developed on an ad hoc or program by program basis and that modifications continue to be made in the various programs.

Supplemental Security Income

Old Age Assistance (OAA), Aid to the Blind (AB), and Aid to the Totally and Permanently Disabled (ATPD) were among the earliest categorical welfare programs, perhaps because these particular disabilities were readily recognizable (as contrasted to deafness or partial disability), were clear contributors to poverty, and thus were able to mobilize enough votes to secure adoption in the political process. Aid to the blind and aid to the permanently and totally disabled were relatively small-scale programs and old age assistance, although initially of substantial magnitude, became considerably less important as larger portions of the aged population became covered by social security insurance. Starting in 1974, these three federal-state programs were combined into a single federally operated program of supplemental security income (SSI), which provides a guaranteed annual income to persons who are 65 or over or blind or totally disabled. Benefits under the SSI program differ among eligible individuals because earnings, other income, and property ownership influence the amount that will be paid in order to guarantee a minimum income. Benefit differences also arise on a state by state basis, since state money may be added to the federal guaranteed income allowance.

Medicaid and AFDC

Medicaid and aid to families with dependent children (AFDC) are more recent additions to the categorical welfare program group and are large and rapidly growing programs. These newer programs exhibit certain characteristics that distinguish them from the older welfare programs. Medicaid relates benefits specifically to the need for medical care and thus is supplementary to other forms of aid, although otherwise it fits the pattern by being a category of disability that achieved a level of political visibility sufficient to collect the necessary votes. Medicaid is distinguished from hospitalization insurance provided under the social security insurance system and from the medical insurance that can be purchased under the Medicare program because it requires a demonstration of need on the part of the recipient and because the program is carried out on a cooperative federal-state basis with substantial funding from federal general revenues and state responsibility for administration and partial funding.

AFDC is distinctive because the tests for qualification under the program include the absence of the father (which is a variable subject to control by the recipient family itself) and also the unemployment of the father (which is a variable related to general economic conditions and thus external to any specific disability of the recipient family itself). AFDC has experienced great difficulty and has been subjected to severe criticism because of the absent-father criterion for qualification for aid, since this requirement provides an incentive for fathers to abandon their families. Moreover, determination of whether or not the father actually has abandoned his family brings objectionable snooping into family life. The criterion that the father be unemployed creates an incentive for fathers to not actively seek employment or to conceal actual employment. Need factors used in determining the amount of benefit create negative incentive effects when the amount of the transfer is reduced on the basis of employment earnings by the recipient individual or family. A benefit formula that reduces transfers dollar for dollar when the recipient receives earned income amounts to a 100 percent tax on the earned income, a rate much higher than that imposed on other employed persons. It can be expected to have significant disincentive effects on employment.

Other Programs

The range of explicit welfare programs presently existing in the United States extends well beyond those specifically mentioned here. Under the heading of "public assistance," federal funds are granted to the states to provide partial financing for a variety of state-administered programs in the areas of health, maternity, and child care services. These programs are financed with various mixtures of federal and state money, with service levels varying from state to state but always equal to or above minimum federal standards. Federal matching funds are provided according to formulas that consider state fiscal capacity, effort, and estimates of needs for the various services.

The food stamp program is a welfare program of substantial magnitude and one that does not employ the federal-state mixture of funding and administration. Funding comes from federal general revenues through appropriations that presently constitute a major portion of the budget for the Department of Agriculture. Eligibility requirements for food stamps differ from those established for other welfare programs; a significant amount of the benefit from this program goes to persons or families who have incomes well above the poverty level and who do not qualify for other welfare programs. The food stamp program, like the federal assumption of responsibility under the supplementary security income program, suggests a trend in the direction of a more exclusively federal responsibility in welfare programs.

Critique of Welfare Program

The list of complaints about the categorical welfare program is long and probably reflects an underlying sentiment that these programs have failed to achieve an alleviation of poverty commensurate with the amount of money put into them. For our purposes, it is useful to separate complaints that relate to specific features of these programs from the more general type of concern, which is critical of the categorical approach itself as an instrument for dealing with government's distribution responsibility. Specific criticisms include objections to the incentive effects that arise when benefit amounts are reduced in recognition of earnings by the recipient, opposition to the high costs of administering complicated eligibility requirements, and frustration because of abuses when eligibility is obtained illegally. Unfortunate side effects arise when fathers are persuaded to abandon their families in order to enable their families to qualify for ADFC and when the enforcement responsibilities of administrators create an adversary relationship between the administrative staff and the client group, rather than the more wholesome and constructive cooperative or supportive relationship. There is also criticism of the specific features of the programs themselves, such as the way benefits are calculated or the requirements for eligibility.

The more general level of criticism is aimed at the categorical approach itself and points out that this approach fails to help those segments of the poverty population that do not fall inside any of the selected target groups. Help is not provided to those whose need for assistance cannot be attributed to any of the governmentally certified disabilities or needs. A person who does not suffer from a governmentally certified disability and who is employed may nevertheless have an income below the poverty line if his economic potential is low. Only a few welfare programs, such as food stamps and general assistance (relief) are helpful to a person in these circumstances. The result is that the "working poor" constitute a segment of the population which tends to be neglected in welfare programs organized along categorical lines. This gap, plus widespread dissatisfaction with specific aspects of the categorical welfare system, provides the basis for reform proposals that existing categorical programs should be supplemented or replaced by an income maintenance program which would offer transfers solely on the basis of need—that is, with a program which would be frankly and forthrightly redistributional in character. The apparent preference for ex ante approaches to income distribution and experience with social security and categorical programs suggest that the American electorate has been reluctant to face the problems of poverty and income distribution on their own terms, that is, in terms relating only to need, without any supporting qualifications of specified disability or previous contributions.

NEGATIVE INCOME TAX

Negative income taxation means that a person whose income is lower than some specified level will receive a check from the government (a *negative* tax), just as a person whose income is above this specified level will make a payment to the government (a *positive* tax). The only condition that would have to be met to qualify for receipt of these transfer payments would be to show that income actually fell below the breakeven level. In its pure form, the negative income tax is a straightforward program of income redistribution that would provide a guaranteed minimum amount of annual spending power to all citizens. It is quite different from insurance-type programs, which relate benefits to prior contributions, and categorical welfare programs, which require some conditions in addition to low income.

The Three Basic Elements

Two of the basic elements in a negative income tax system are (1) the breakeven income level, which is the amount of pretax and pretransfer income which would neither obligate the individual to pay any positive tax nor entitle the individual to receive any negative tax transfer, and (2) the rate of negative tax, which would determine the amount of the transfer an individual would receive if his income was lower than the breakeven level. For example, if the rate of negative tax was 25 percent, the individual would receive a payment from the government equal to 25 percent of the difference between his actual income and the breakeven level of income. If the breakeven level were set at $8,000 and if the rate of negative tax were 25 percent, a person who earned income of $6,000 would receive a check from the government in the amount of $500, which is 25 percent of the difference between $6,000 and $8,000.

It is apparent that the combination of the breakeven level and the rate of negative tax operate to determine the third basic element in this system, namely, the guaranteed minimum income level. In the above illustration, if the individual had received zero income, his transfer from the government would have been $2,000, which would be the guaranteed minimum income level from that combination of the breakeven level and rate of negative tax. In designing a negative income tax system, any two of the three basic elements can be established independently of one another, but when two of the elements have been set, the third will have been determined automatically as a consequence.

The relationships among the three basic elements of negative income taxation can be illustrated with the help of Figure 8.2. The vertical axis of the graph

FIGURE 8.2 Negative Income Tax

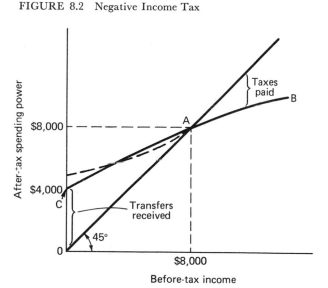

records the after-tax and after-transfer spending power of the individual; the horizontal axis records his before-tax and before-transfer income. The straight line radiating at a 45-degree angle from the origin of the graph depicts the pretax and posttax relationships that would prevail if there were no taxes (either positive or negative) on the individual's income. Posttax spending power would be equal to pretax income at all income levels.

Suppose first that only positive income taxes are imposed and that allowable exemptions and deductions are such that tax must be paid to the government only when income exceeds $8,000. The breakeven point would be $8,000 and the pretax-posttax relationship would follow the line OAB. Taxes paid are illustrated as the gap between the 45-degree line and the line AB. The curve in the line AB suggests that progressive rates are applied in the positive income tax.

Next, suppose that a negative income tax is established with a flat negative tax rate of 50 percent. The individual whose income was less than the breakeven level of $8,000 would receive a check from the government equal to 50 percent of the difference between his before-tax income and the breakeven amount. Under this arrangement, the pretax-posttax relationship line is CA for those individuals entitled to receive the negative tax transfers. The amount of these transfers is illustrated by the distance between the 45-degree line and the CA line. An individual who had zero before-tax income would receive transfers in the amount of $4,000, which would constitute the guaranteed minimum income. This guaranteed minimum income level is the automatic consequence of the initial selection of the $8,000 breakeven level and the flat 50 percent rate of negative tax.

Figure 8.2 reveals that alternative patterns can be developed among the three elements of negative income taxation. For example, given a flat 50 percent rate of negative tax, a higher guaranteed minimum income can be achieved if the breakeven level is moved farther up the 45-degree line. Or, if the $8,000 breakeven level is to be retained with a guaranteed minimum income of more than $4,000, a rate of negative tax higher than 50 percent will be required. Calculations are simple as long as a flat rate is used for the negative tax. For example, the guaranteed minimum income will be equal to the breakeven income multiplied by the tax rate $(Y = BR)$, or the breakeven income will be equal to guaranteed minimum divided by the tax rate $(B = Y/R)$, or the rate of negative tax will be equal to guaranteed minimum income divided by the breakeven income $(R = Y/B)$. Of course, the rate of negative tax could be graduated so that a lower rate would apply to individuals only slightly below the breakeven level and a higher rate would apply to those with very low before-tax incomes. The dotted line in Figure 8.2 illustrates this modification of the program.

Policy Constraints

Each of the basic elements of a negative income tax (the guaranteed minimum, the breakeven point, and the rate of negative tax) is subject to policy constraints, that is, for each of these elements there are policy positions which indicate that certain choices are better than other choices. Constructing a specific negative income tax program therefore produces conflict among different policy objectives, because selecting the preferred position for any two of the elements may mean that the position related to the third element must be sacrificed. Alternatively, a policy-balanced negative income tax requires compromise among objectives.

Let us first consider the policy constraints connected with establishing the guaranteed minimum level of annual income. If the responsibility for the complete elimination of poverty were placed on the negative income tax system, it would be necessary to set the guaranteed minimum at or above the income level determined to be the "poverty line." Complications would arise if the poverty line were set at different levels for different people, related perhaps to differences in the cost of living in rural as compared to urban areas, and so on. If the negative income tax were not charged with the responsibility for the complete elimination of poverty, the guaranteed minimum could be set at lower levels and other programs could make up the difference between negative income transfers and the poverty line.

The policy constraint connected with setting the breakeven income level relates to the total amount of money voters are willing to devote to the tax-transfer program. Moving the breakeven point upward to higher income levels would shift many families out of the tax-paying group and into the transfer-receiving group. Such a move would rapidly increase the rates of tax that would have to be paid by people above the breakeven level because it would have the double-edged effect of simultaneously increasing the number of people in the recipient group and reducing the number of people in the paying group. This can be observed in Figure 8.2 if that graph is interpreted to show only those taxes required for the tax-transfer program. Since the budget for a tax-transfer program should be balanced, sliding point A upward along the 45-degree line would require much higher tax rates on those in the tax-paying group. In Figure 8.2, the line AB would have to be flatter as the breakeven point is moved upward. In the 1972 presidential campaign, candidate McGovern's proposal for an annual "social dividend" of $1,000 per family would, in effect, have moved the breakeven point in the prevailing tax-transfer system upward. Although the social dividend itself would have been reportable for income tax purposes, the program would have required a large flow of tax and transfer payments and a significant increase in tax rates on higher incomes.

The constraint in setting the rate of negative tax relates to work incentives, an area where the level of scientific knowledge is low but political sensitivity high. In Figure 8.2, tax rates are shown (inversely) by the slope of the pretax-posttax relationship line. For example, the 45-degree line illustrates zero tax rates. At the other extreme, a horizontal line would indicate a 100 percent tax rate, that is, a 100 percent tax on all income above the breakeven level and a 100 percent negative tax (transfer) on the gap between the breakeven level and the actual earnings of persons whose pretax earnings were below that level. Complete equality would result from such tax-transfer rates.

Of course, an operational negative income tax would use neither a zero nor a 100 percent tax rate. The problem is to find some intermediate tax rate which will (1) assure an adequate guaranteed minimum income, (2) keep the breakeven level and the expense of the program low enough to be acceptable to the tax-paying group, and (3) not impose unreasonably severe disincentives on the people receiving the transfers. One of the main arguments in favor of negative income taxation is that recipients should always be able to improve their after-tax spending power by accepting income-earning employment.[2] At a 50 percent rate of negative tax, after-tax spending power will increase by 50 cents for each dollar of income earned by a person below the breakeven income level. At a 75 percent rate, after-tax earnings will increase by only 25 cents for each dollar of income earned by people in this group. Thus, the rate of negative tax becomes a critical factor in devising the program.

Graduated negative tax rates can extend the range of options in the prac-

[2] Some existing categorical welfare programs actually impose a 100 percent tax on earnings of people receiving welfare transfers. This situation arises when welfare benefits are reduced dollar for dollar for earnings received. This amounts to a 100 percent tax on earnings. Clearly, the incentive to seek and accept employment will be damaged by such effective tax rates.

tical matter of working out policy compromises among incentive effects, guaranteed minimum income levels, and the breakeven level. The dotted line in Figure 8.2 suggests that rates of negative tax might be set at very high levels (a nearly horizontal pretax-posttax relationship) for very low income groups, which would raise the guaranteed minimum income in exchange for larger disincentive effects for this group. As incomes rise, the dotted line approaches a 45-degree slope, showing lower rates of negative tax for persons in the upper ranges of the transfer-receiving group. These lower tax rates offer greater work incentives for these people in exchange for smaller transfer payments. Graduation of this sort amounts to a kind of redistribution within the group below the breakeven income level. It permits a higher guaranteed minimum income level without expanding the total tax-transfer volume of the program, that is, without raising the breakeven level and thereby requiring larger tax payments from those above that level.

The Family Assistance Plan proposed by the Nixon administration in 1972 contained many features of a negative income tax system, although certain eligibility requirements beyond simply a showing of low income were included. That plan was not adopted, but similar negative income tax features have been enacted as part of the supplemental security income program, in which the amount of federal transfer payments to eligible individuals is determined by formulas that focus on the difference between the income a person received from his own sources and a guaranteed annual income level specified in the legislation. Although the SSI program is a categorical welfare program available only to persons who are over age 65, blind, or disabled, it may be indicative of the way in which the negative income tax idea will find its way into the established transfer payment programs for income distribution. In the SSI program, previously separate categorical programs have been combined into a single program, cooperative federal-state financing has been substantially replaced by full federal financing, and the guaranteed annual income idea has been used to determine the amount of the transfers. Each of these steps is a movement away from the prevailing system for categorical welfare transfers and toward a negative income tax system. Reduced emphasis on categorical eligibility requirements and increased emphasis on the guaranteed annual income dimension of the system could evolve into a general system of negative income taxation. Perhaps this sort of evolutionary approach to welfare reform is to be expected in a democratic based political system.[3]

SUMMARY

Redistribution programs actually in effect in the United States utilize both the *ex ante* approach, through general expenditure and taxation actions that include distributional considerations, and the *ex post* approach, through explicit transfer payment systems. In the *ex ante* efforts at redistribution, expenditures probably accomplish a greater movement toward equality than is

---

[3] Earned income credit features recently installed in the U.S. Individual Income Tax also have features similar to negative income taxation. See Chapter 12.

accomplished through progressive taxation, in spite of the widespread attention paid to the progressivity of taxation. Explicit transfer payment programs exemplify the ex post approach to income distribution and include both contributory insurance systems and systems of transfer payments financed from general revenues. Neither the contributory social insurance system nor the programs of categorical welfare are fully effective arrangements for income maintenance. Contributory insurance does not provide a defense against poverty for those with very low incomes, who contribute little to the program and who qualify for low benefit amounts. Likewise, the categorical welfare programs do not provide a defense against poverty for those who do not exhibit the special characteristics needed to qualify under these programs. Only the general assistance programs provide transfer payments related unambiguously to the objective of income maintenance, and these programs are relatively small. The implication is that voters in the United States have been reluctant to undertake income maintenance programs which are carried out forthrightly through transfer payments and which are based on need alone. The categorical welfare system, in particular, reveals an equivocal or ambiguous state of the public mind on questions of income maintenance.

In its pure form, the negative income tax proposal poses directly the questions of income redistribution and income maintenance, but the pure form of negative income taxation has not generated sufficient support to obtain adoption. Significant features of the negative income tax approach and the concept of a guaranteed annual income have, however, been incorporated into modifications of the categorical welfare programs, particularly in the supplemental security income program launched in 1974. Widespread dissatisfaction with existing welfare programs is likely to bring further changes. A degree of tension between individualistic and social approaches to welfare and income redistribution continues to characterize the implementation of redistribution responsibilities in the United States.

SUGGESTED READINGS

GREEN, CHRISTOPHER. *Negative Taxes and the Poverty Problem* (Washington: The Brookings Institution, 1967).

BRITTAIN, J. A. *The Payroll Tax for Social Security* (Washington: The Brookings Institution, 1972).

SCHILLER, B. *The Economics of Poverty and Discrimination* (Englewood Cliffs, N.J.: Prentice-Hall, 1973).

FELDSTEIN, MARTIN. "Unemployment Compensation: Adverse Incentives and Distributional Anomalies," *National Tax Journal*, June 1974, pp. 231–44.

REYNOLDS, MORGAN, and EUGENE SMOLENSKY, "The Post Fisc Distribution: 1961 and 1970 Compared," *National Tax Journal*, Dec. 1974, pp. 515–30.

BROWNING, EDGAR K. "Tax Reductions Versus Transfers in a Public Choice Model," *Public Finance Quarterly*, Jan. 1976, pp. 77–87.

9

The Stabilization Function

The Employment Act of 1946, which is usually referred to as the full employment act, formally acknowledged the national government's responsibility to engage in stabilization activities. The two decades preceding the adoption of this legislation had seen the economy move from high levels of employment in the 1920s to severe unemployment during the 1930s and back to high levels of employment during the war years of 1941 through 1945. Price levels also had experienced considerable fluctuation, falling during the early 1930s and rising during the war. The adoption of the Employment Act clearly indicated that the public did not want to repeat this experience of economic instability.

The experience of the 1930s and 1940s demonstrated that government actions do have important impacts on the level of economic activity. In the early years of the depression, the contraction of the money supply contributed to the severity of the downward movement. During the war years, increases in the money supply contributed to economic expansion. Taxation and government expenditure were also important influences. Budget deficits were instituted during the 1930s specifically for the purpose of stimulating the economy and the massive deficits of the war years clearly pushed the economy to high levels of activity. Thus, when the Employment Act of 1946 was adopted, the question was not whether the economy, if left to itself, would experience unacceptable levels of unemployment and economic instability. The fact was that the economy would not be left to itself and that government had become such an important element in the economy that it could not abstain from active efforts to achieve high-level employment and economic stability. In other words, the question was not whether government *should* engage in stabilization activity, but rather *how* these stabilization responsibilities should be conceived and implemented.

The Council of Economic Advisors was established by the Employment Act of 1946 and was charged with the job of advising the President in connection with his responsibilities under the act. Members are appointed by the President and participate in the formulation of the government's stabilization policies. They assist in developing the budget submitted by the President to Congress each year, and the report of the council is submitted to Congress and published each year in conjunction with the Economic Report of the President.

Although the Employment Act of 1946 is popularly referred to as the full employment act, it does not commit the government to maintaining full employment—nor does it define full employment. As interpreted and implemented, the stabilization responsibilities of the national government include "high levels" of employment, reasonable stability in both employment and price levels, and an acceptable rate of growth in the nation's economy. This chapter outlines the economic model of the determination of the equilibrium level of aggregate economic activity and shows how government is able to influence the level of employment and the stability of prices. It also considers the policy issues raised by the choice between unemployment and price inflation and describes the monetary and fiscal instruments available for carrying out stabilization policy.

THE EQUILIBRIUM LEVEL OF NATIONAL INCOME

The theory of national income determination is a statement about the factors that determine the equilibrium level of national income and the way in which these factors interact with one another and with other elements in the economy to bring about this equilibrium. Thus, an understanding of the theory of national income determination is an essential part of the tool kit of the Council of Economic Advisors and of others studying the aggregate performance of the economy.

The *equilibrium level* of national income is that level of aggregate economic activity (measured in various ways) toward which the economy is expected to move and at which the economy would stabilize if the forces which determine it were to remain unchanged for a sufficient length of time. It is important to recognize that the equilibrium level is not necessarily a *desired* level of economic activity. In an economy in which institutional factors result in rigidity of prices and interest rates and in which resource mobility is limited, the equilibrium level of national income may involve unacceptable amounts of unemployment or unacceptable rates of inflation. The economist is interested in identifying the equilibrium level of national income because the information will enable him to predict the circumstances that will prevail as the economy approaches equilibrium. Moreover, if the economist is able to identify the factors that determine the equilibrium level of national income, it may then be possible to design ways to alter these factors and thereby to influence the equilibrium level itself.

The Circular Flow Model

Figure 9.1 illustrates the circular flow model of the operation of an economy. The model is constructed around two institutional elements, households,

FIGURE 9.1   The Circular Flow Model

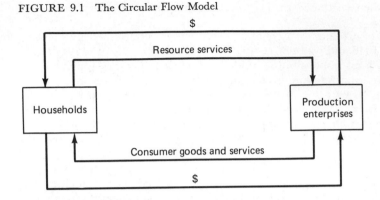

the owners of the resources of the society and the consumers of the goods and services provided in the economy, and production enterprises, which purchase resource services from households, combine them in the production of goods and services, and sell these goods and services to households. In the illustration, the interior (clockwise) path of relationships between the households and the production enterprises denotes the flow of real resource services and of real consumer goods and services. The exterior (counterclockwise) path denotes the flow of money between households and production enterprises as the flows of real services and goods are implemented through market transactions exchanging real goods and services for money. The circular flow of money (the exterior path) is a measure of the value of the goods and services flowing in the interior path. The money obtained by the households from the sale of resource services is the money they use to purchase goods and services from production enterprises. Likewise, the money production enterprises obtain through the sale of goods and services is the money they use to purchase resource services from households. The model suggests that the economy is a continuous flow of goods, services, and money between households and production enterprises.

A measurement of the level of economic activity is provided in this model by recording the amount of money flowing past any selected point in the exterior path during some specified interval of time. Stability in the level of economic activity would be revealed if the amounts recorded did not exhibit severe fluctuations from one time period to another.[1] Full employment is indicated when the flow of economic activity represents the output of all resources used at their capacity. Unemployment exists when the flow of activity is less than the flow that would exist at capacity. Inflation occurs when the flow of expenditures is greater than the flow of real goods and services produced in the economy.

[1] Of course, the circular flow model is an extreme simplification of the real economy. Do it yourself activities do not involve a transaction between the household and a separate production enterprise and therefore generate no money flow that can be recorded to measure the level of economic activity. Thus, national income measured by money flows is not the whole story, and care must be taken in comparing one economy with another and in comparing levels of activity in a given economy in widely separated time periods.

The Components of Aggregate Demand

At the heart of the conventional income determination model is the notion that demand is the mainspring which propels the circular flow and determines the level of employment and prices. The idea is that the level of employment will be determined by the level of demand for the goods and services which can be produced by these resources. Unemployment will exist if aggregate demand is insufficient to require the utilization of all available resources. Full employment will prevail if aggregate demand equals the productive capacity of the resources available. If aggregate demand exceeds the productive capacity of resources measured at current price levels, the excess demand will bid up (that is, "inflate") price levels until the balance is restored.

The critical importance of accurate estimates of aggregate demand suggests the desirability of disaggregating total demand into any subparts or components that exhibit behavior patterns or relationships with other measurable variables which will facilitate accurate estimation. In Figure 9.2, the basic

FIGURE 9.2   Demand Components in the Circular Flow Model

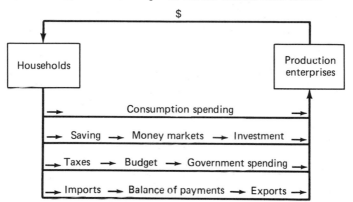

circular flow model is modified by dividing aggregate demand into several components. In addition to the demands from households for consumer goods, it shows that resource services are demanded to produce investment goods, to produce services provided through government, and to produce goods demanded by foreigners. Each of these additional demand components is financed by a diversion of funds from the household consumption stream, and in each case the funds diverted pass through an intermediate agency or market before being returned to the circular flow. For example, the funds for investment are diverted through the act of saving (voluntarily not consuming) and pass through domestic money markets before returning to the circular flow through investment. Funds to finance government services are diverted through taxation and pass through the government budget before returning to the circular flow through government expenditures. Funds to finance purchases by foreigners are diverted from spending for domestically produced goods by purchases of foreign-produced goods (imports) and pass through the international money markets and the balance of payments before returning to the domestic circular flow through exports.

The roles played by the various intermediary agencies, (that is, the domestic money markets, the government budget, and the international money markets) are particularly important to the implementation of the stabilization responsibilities of government. Not only do these intermediary operations provide information useful in the estimation of aggregate demand, but they also offer opportunities for the active implementation of government stabilization measures. In general, the banking system and the money markets are the arena for governmental *monetary* operations, the government budget is the arena for governmental *fiscal* operations, and the international money markets are the arena for government operations on *exchange rates* and the *balance of payments*.

National Income Determination

The national income determination model is illustrated in Figure 9.3. The horizontal axis measures various possible levels of national income and production, that is, the value of goods and services produced and the amount of income earned during an accounting period. The various points along this horizontal axis show the value of goods and services offered for sale (a supply-related concept). By incorporating information about the quantity and productivity of resources, the horizontal axis can also be used as a measure of the level of employment in the economy. The vertical axis measures expenditures on currently produced goods and services (a demand-related concept). The unit of measurement on both axes is dollars and both axes are set to the same scale. Therefore, a line drawn at a 45-degree angle from the origin of the graph connects all points at which the value shown on one axis is equal to the value shown

FIGURE 9.3   National Income Determination I

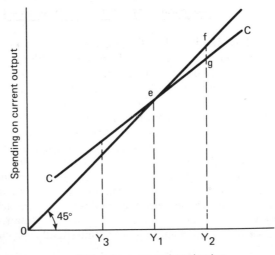

National income and production

on the other axis. Since equilibrium requires that the dollar volume of expenditure must equal the dollar volume of production, the 45-degree line identifies all combinations of expenditures and production which can qualify as potential equilibrium combinations. Any combination of expenditures and production that does not fall on this line is not an equilibrium combination.

The next step in the income determination model is to record on the graph the relationships believed to exist between expenditures and income. To illustrate this, assume for the moment that there is no investment expenditure, no government expenditure or taxation, and that there is no international sector of exports or imports, so that the only component of aggregate demand is consumption expenditure. The *CC* line on the graph represents an estimated relationship between consumption expenditure and income and is the graphic representation of what is known as the *consumption function*, that is, it reflects a finding that consumption expenditure is some function of income, $C = f(Y)$. On the graph, the *CC* line is drawn as a straight line and the functional relationship to income is described in the statement $C = a + bY$. In this equation, the a term shows the level at which the *CC* line intercepts the vertical axis and the b term shows how consumption expenditure changes as income (Y) changes.

The straight-line consumption function illustrated on the graph says that the b term is positive (since the *CC* line slopes upward to the right) and that its value is greater than zero, but less than 1.0. The value of the b term is called the *marginal propensity to consume* and is of great importance in the multiplier concepts to be developed shortly. It means that as income rises, consumption expenditure also rises but by an amount less than the increase in income. By definition, the portion of incremental income not expended for consumption is saved, and it is apparent that the *marginal propensity to save* is $1 - b$. The accurate estimation of the consumption function is extremely important in the application of the income determination model in the government's stabilization program, but income is not the only variable that influences the level of consumption expenditure. A more complete estimation of consumption expenditure would include independent variables such as income in previous time periods, wealth, expectations, inventories of consumer goods, and so on.

If consumption expenditure were the only component in aggregate demand, the equilibrium level of national income and production would be Y_1 in Figure 9.3, as determined by the intersection of the *CC* line and the 45-degree line at point e. At this level of income and production, the entire output of goods and services during the accounting period would be sold and there would be no tendency for production enterprises either to increase or decrease employment and output. Conversely, if employment and output were greater than Y_1, say at Y_2, aggregate demand would be less than output and income by the amount fg, which is the amount of saving at income level Y_2.[2] Production enterprises would respond to this inability to sell all output by reducing employment and output in the next accounting period so that the level of national income and output would move in the direction of Y_1. If employment and out-

---

[2] The 45-degree line is a convenient device that permits horizontally measured volumes of income and production also to be read as the vertical distance between the 45-degree line and the selected point on the horizontal axis.

put were less than Y_1, say Y_3, aggregate demand would exceed output, inventories would be drawn down below desired levels, and enterprises would respond by increasing employment and output in the next accounting period, providing, of course, that the Y_3 was not "full employment" in the economy, that is, provided that additional resources were available to be hired at existing wage rates.

The investment expenditure component in aggregate demand may now be incorporated into the model. The first step in doing this requires the estimation of an *investment function* that is conceptually equivalent to the previously described consumption function. Like a complete consumption function, a complete investment function would include the level of national income among its independent variables, as well as income in previous time periods, profits in previous time periods, inventory levels, expectations about future levels of income and technology, and so on. In practice, the level of national income is considered to be a less reliable basis for predicting investment expenditure than consumption expenditure and more importance is attached to the other independent variables, which are called *exogenous* because their values are determined outside the model built around the relationships between the level of national income and the level of expenditures. Therefore, for simplicity and convenience in the elementary income determination model, investment expenditure is recorded as invariant with the level of national income, that is, as a horizontal line *II* (see Figure 9.4).[3]

Figure 9.4 illustrates a national income determination model in which aggregate demand consists of the sum of consumption expenditure and invest-

FIGURE 9.4   National Income Determination II

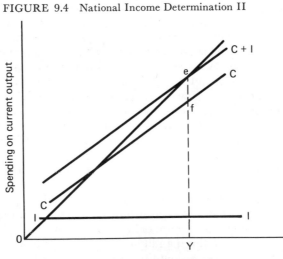

National income and production

[3] Greater realism would be incorporated into the model if investment expenditure were shown as positively related to the level of national income, that is, as an upward sloping *II* line in Figure 9.4. Still greater accuracy in the estimation of investment expenditure would incorporate the acceleration principle, which relates investment expenditure to previous investments and to changes in the levels of consumer demand.

ment expenditure. Aggregate demand is represented by the $C + I$ line, which is determined by vertically adding together the consumption expenditure line CC and the investment expenditure line II. The equilibrium level of national income and production is Y, as determined by the intersection of the aggregate expenditure line $(C + I)$ with the 45-degree line at point e. As in the previous illustration, levels of national income and production other than Y would not be equilibrium levels, and forces would be set in motion that would tend to move the level of economic activity in the direction of the equilibrium level of Y. It can be observed from Figure 9.4 that equilibrium occurs when the volume of investment expenditure is equal to the volume of saving, each of which is represented by the distance ef. The money withdrawn from the circular flow through saving has been returned through investment expenditure so that the volume of flow in the model is stabilized.

A FISCAL APPROACH TO STABILIZATION

Government budget operations affect the income determination model in two distinct ways. Expenditures on currently produced goods and services are a component of aggregate demand and cause the aggregate expenditure line to shift upward. Tax collections, however, reduce disposable income in the private sector of the economy and lead to reductions in the private expenditure components of aggregate demand. It is convenient to analyze the impact of expenditures separately from the impact of taxes.

Suppose that the government expends $10 billion on currently produced goods and services without withdrawing any funds from the private sector to finance these expenditures.[4] In Figure 9.5 (which reproduces the $C + I$ and the CC lines from Figure 9.4), the $10 billion of government expenditure shifts the aggregate expenditure line upward by $10 billion, resulting in the line labeled $C + I + G$. This new aggregate expenditure line intersects the 45-degree line at point d and indicates an equilibrium level of national income at Y'. The new equilibrium level of national income (Y') is higher than the previous equilibrium level by an amount considerably greater than the $10 billion of government expenditure because of the operation of the multiplier process. The income generated by the government expenditure is partially respent in the private sector, leading to still further increases in national income and product.

In Figure 9.5, the total expenditure lines are drawn with a slope of 0.67, meaning that two-thirds of any increment to income is expended to purchase goods and services and that one-third is withdrawn from the circular flow through saving. The multiplier process is illustrated in Table 9.1. The initial $10 billion increment to production and income came from the government expenditure. Two-thirds of this incremental income was allocated by its recipients to expenditures and thereby generated an increment of $6.67 billion to production and income in the second round of the multiplier process. Subsequent rounds of income and expenditure exhibit diminishing increments to

---

[4] In this illustration, it is assumed that the government neither imposes any taxes with which to finance these expenditures nor covers the deficit through the sale of bonds to the private sector of the economy. Instead, the assumption is that the deficit is financed through the creation of $10 billion of new money.

FIGURE 9.5   National Income Determination III

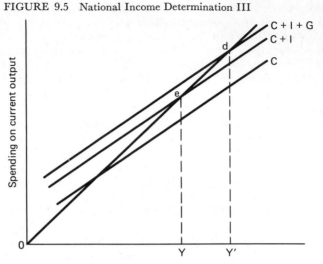

National income and production

TABLE 9.1   The Multiplier Process (billions of dollars)

INCREMENTS TO PRODUCTION AND INCOME (1)	ALLOCATION OF INCREMENTAL INCOME	
	EXPENDITURE (2)	SAVING (3)
$10.00	$6.67	$3.33
6.67	4.44	2.23
4.44	2.96	1.48
2.96	1.98	.98
.	.	.
.	.	.
.	.	.
30.00	20.00	10.00

production and income. The summation of the increments to production and income approaches $30 billion, indicating a multiplier value of 3, that is, that the ultimate change in equilibrium national income will be three times the amount of the initiating shift in total expenditure.

It is apparent that the value of the multiplier depends on the portion of incremental income allocated to new expenditure, that is, it depends on the marginal propensity to consume, which was the b term in the consumption function equation of $C = a + bY$. The value of the multiplier is equal to $1/(1 - b)$ The larger the marginal propensity to consume, the greater the multiplier. It also is apparent that the full impact of increased expenditure on the equilibrium level of national income does not occur instantaneously, since some lags or delays will be experienced in the respending of increments to income. However, Table 9.1 suggests that a large portion of the total impact occurs in the first three or four rounds of income and expenditure which, under the institutional factors presently applicable in the economy, will ordinarily be accomplished within one year of the initial expenditure.

The Taxation Multiplier

Taxation withdraws funds from the private sector of the economy and leads to reductions in the private components of total expenditure. However, private expenditures will be reduced by an amount smaller than the amount of tax collected because some of the money paid in taxes was destined for saving rather than expenditure had the tax not been collected. Once more, the marginal propensity to consume helps to explain what happens. If taxes were increased by $10 billion, consumers would find their spending power reduced by $10 billion in comparison with the situation that would have prevailed if the tax had not been imposed. With spending power (that is, disposable income) reduced by $10 billion, both expenditures and saving will be reduced by the amounts indicated by the marginal propensities to spend and to save, respectively. The reduction in expenditures is the critical element in connection with the multiplier process. In terms of the illustration presented in Table 9.1, this reduction would amount to $6.67 billion, which is the amount shown in the *second* round of the expenditures multiplier process.

Since the *first*-round impact on production and income is absent in the case of the taxation multiplier, the ultimate multiplied effect of the tax in this illustration would be $20 billion, which is smaller than the expenditure multiplier effect by the amount of the government action that initiated the process. Thus, the taxation multiplier is smaller than the expenditure multiplier. If the expenditure multiplier has a value of 3, the tax multiplier will have a value of 2; if the expenditure multiplier has a value of 4, the tax multiplier will have a value of 3, and so on.[5]

The taxation multiplier can also be illustrated graphically, as in Figure 9.6. The before-tax aggregated expenditure line is $C + I + G$, and the before-tax equilibrium level of national income is at Y. If it is assumed that government expenditure (G) and investment expenditure (I) are exogenously determined and thus unaffected by the tax, the impact of the tax will be on consumption expenditure (C), leading to a reduction in consumption expenditure and to a new aggregate expenditure line $(C' + I + G)$. The new aggregate expenditure line is lower than the before-tax aggregate expenditure line by the distance ab, which is the amount by which consumption spending was reduced by the tax, that is, the tax multiplied by the marginal propensity to consume. The amount of the tax itself is shown by the horizontal distance cb, which is to say that the amount of expenditure at point b on the new aggregate expenditure line is the

---

[5] It has been suggested that the marginal propensity to spend need not be the same for reductions in disposable income as it is for increases in disposable income. For example, it may be that people have greater difficulty cutting back on expenditures when their income falls than they have in increasing their expenditures when income rises. This would suggest that the expenditure change resulting from a dollar's increase in income would be greater than the (negative) spending change resulting from a dollar's reduction in income. In this situation, the simple rule of the tax multiplier being smaller than the expenditure multiplier by one unit would no longer hold.

FIGURE 9.6   The Taxation Multiplier

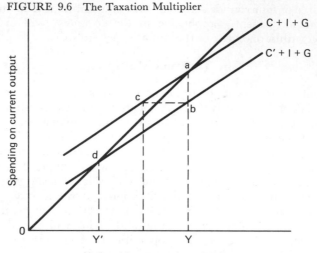

National income and production

same as the amount of expenditure on the old aggregate expenditure line at an income level less than Y by the amount of the tax. In other words, the effect of the tax can be illustrated either as shifting the expenditure function to the right by the amount of the tax or as shifting it downward by an amount equal to the tax multiplied by the marginal propensity to spend.[6] In Figure 9.6, the after-tax equilibrium level of national income is determined by the intersection and the $C' + I + G$ line with the 45-degree line at point d, indicating an equilibrium level of Y'. The equilibrium level of national income has fallen by an amount equal to twice the amount of the tax collected. The tax multiplier has a value of 2 when the marginal propensity to spend has a value of 2/3.

The Balanced Budget Multiplier

The difference between the government expenditure multiplier and the taxation multiplier reveals that a change in government expenditures matched by an equal change in tax collections will not be neutral in its effect on the equilibrium level of national income. An increase in the size of a balanced government budget will have an expansionary effect on the economy; a decrease in the size of a balanced government budget will have a contractionary effect on the economy. For example, if the marginal propensity to consume is equal to 2/3, the expenditure multiplier will have a value of 3 and the taxation multiplier a value of 2, and the combination of the two will leave a net multiplier effect with the value of 1. A $10 billion increase in expenditure matched with a $10 billion increase in taxes will cause the equilibrium level of national

[6] The type of tax illustrated in Figure 9.6 is one that would collect a fixed sum of money without regard to the level of national income. Thus, the new expenditure line is parallel to the old expenditure line, and the marginal propensity to spend is unchanged. It is apparent that a tax in which the amount collected was itself a function of income would both shift the expenditure line and alter its slope, thus complicating the analysis of the tax multiplier.

income to rise by $10 billion. Conversely, a $10 billion reduction in expenditure matched with a $10 billion reduction in taxes will cause the equilibrium level of national income to fall by $10 billion.

This is illustrated graphically in Figure 9.7. The initial level of aggregate demand $(C + I + G)$ intersects the 45-degree line at point a and indicates an equilibrium level of national income at Y. A $10 billion increase in government expenditure would shift this aggregate expenditure line upward by $10 billion to the line labeled $C + I + G'$, which would intersect the 45-degree line at point b and would indicate an equilibrium level of national income at Y'. However, a matching $10 billion increase in taxes would cause the aggregate expenditure line to shift downward by two-thirds of the amount of the tax, if the marginal propensity to spend is equal to two-thirds. This is illustrated by the dashed total expenditure line $(C' + I + G')$, which intersects the 45-degree line at point c and indicates an equilibrium level of national income at Y''. The equilibrium level at Y'' is greater than the original equilibrium level (Y) by $10 billion, that is, by an amount equal to the change in the size of the balanced budget.

FIGURE 9.7   The Balanced Budget Multiplier

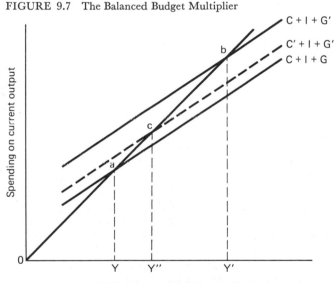

National income and production

A MONETARY APPROACH TO STABILIZATION

The monetary approach to stabilization focuses attention on the importance of the nation's money stock for the behavior of the components of aggregate demand. Whereas the fiscal view emphasizes the role of government expenditures and taxation in shifting the aggregate expenditure function, the monetary approach emphasizes that changes in the stock of money can also lead to shifts in this aggregate expenditure function and to changes in the equilibrium level of national income. The monetary approach is implemented by the Federal Reserve System through several devices available to it—namely,

open market operations, control of the discount rate, and control of the requirements governing the reserves banks must hold. Through these devices, the
Federal Reserve System regulates the reserves available in the banking system
for lending to potential borrowers, and this in turn enables it to influence the
stock of money in the economy, the rate of interest, and the volume of lending.

The Linkage of Money and Aggregate Demand

The linkage between changes in the stock of money and the level of aggregate demand is illustrated in Figure 9.8. The left-hand graph in this figure
illustrates the relationship between the stock of money, shown on the horizontal

FIGURE 9.8   Money Instrument Linkages

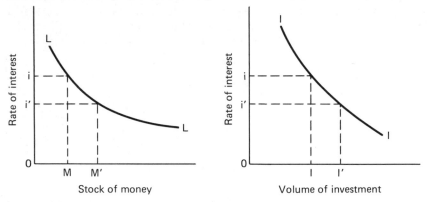

axis, and the rate of interest, shown on the vertical axis. The *LL* curve on this
graph can be interpreted as a demand curve for cash balances and the location
of this curve reflects the *liquidity preference* of the economy. The idea behind this
demand for cash balances curve is that wealth holders have a choice of whether to
hold their wealth in the form of cash balances or in other forms, such as securities, stocks, or bonds. Since cash balances do not earn interest, the cost or price
of holding cash balances is the rate of interest that would have been earned had
the wealth been held in one of the alternative forms. The curve is drawn sloping
downward to the right because higher rates of interest will coax wealth out of
cash balances and into other forms while lower rates of interest will favor the
holding of larger cash balances.

The next fact to recognize is that, at any given moment, the entire stock
of money in the economy is accounted for, either as circulating money to support
the needs of trading activity or as cash balances held throughout the economy.
If the transactions (circulation) demand for money is considered to be fixed by
the current volume of trading activity, increases or decreases in the stock of
money instituted by the Federal Reserve Board *must* be accepted into the cash
balances of the wealth holders of the economy. Suppose, then, that the stock of
money is increased by moving from *M* to *M′* in Figure 9.8. Immediately, more
money is available for cash balances than is desired at the original rate of
interest (*i*). Persons who find themselves in possession of excessive amounts of

cash will seek to correct the situation by using some of the cash for the purchase of securities or other earning assets, thus bidding up the prices of these alternative assets and lowering the rate of interest. The slope of the *LL* function in Figure 9.8 shows the effectiveness of monetary measures in influencing the rate of interest. As shown, increasing the money stock from *M* to *M'* results in a reduction in the rate of interest from *i* to *i'*. If the *LL* curve were very flat, as is the case at very low rates of interest, changes in the stock of money would have little ability to alter the rate of interest. This situation, known as the *liquidity trap*, is believed to have existed at some periods during the depression of the 1930s. However, in reasonably normal circumstances, changes in the stock of money can be expected to alter interest rates.

The right-hand graph in Figure 9.8 illustrates the relationship between the rate of interest (shown on the vertical axis) and the volume of investment (shown on the horizontal axis). The *II* curve on this graph says that larger volumes of investment will be undertaken at low interest rates than at high interest rates. Behind the *II* curve is the notion that a number of investment projects are available at any given time and that some of these projects will generate higher rates of return than others. As interest rates are lowered, a larger portion of these available projects will become profitable (since financing costs are a significant part of the costs of carrying out these projects) and a larger volume of investment will be undertaken. The slope of the *II* curve is another important determinant of the effectiveness of monetary instruments in influencing the volume of investment and thereby influencing the level of aggregate demand in the economy. If many investment projects are available, the *II* curve will exhibit a significant degree of elasticity and changes in the interest rate can exert an important influence on the volume of investment. On the other hand, if the *II* curve is relatively inelastic, interest rates and monetary instruments will be relatively ineffective.

The two graphs in Figure 9.8 indicate that monetary instruments operate through the liquidity preference function and through the investment function in order to have an impact on the level of investment expenditure and aggregate demand in the economy. If the current level of economic activity is lower than the target level established for stabilization policy, expansionary use of the monetary instruments may be able to move the equilibrium level of economic activity up to the target level. Conversely, if the economy is operating above the target level (presumably experiencing excessive inflationary pressures), contractionary application of monetary instruments can help to correct the situation.

The Monetary Approach and Budget Imbalances

Budget deficits and surpluses ordinarily are associated with the fiscal approach to stabilization, but it is appropriate here to recognize that these fiscal instruments overlap significantly with the monetary approach. Monetary considerations actually have a great deal of influence on the stabilization effects of budget deficits or surpluses because the actual impact of the deficits and surpluses cannot be fully understood until the method of financing the deficit or of disposing of the surplus has been determined. If the budget is operated at a deficit, some source of funds must be found to cover this deficit; if the budget is operated with a surplus, some arrangement must be made for disposing of this surplus.

Let us now consider the devices that may be used to cover deficits and to dispose of surpluses. If a deficit exists, the Treasury must sell bonds in order to obtain the funds to cover it, since the Treasury does not print money in the United States financial system. These bonds may be sold either to the Federal Reserve System or to the general public. If a surplus exists in the budget, the funds may either be held as idle balances or used to retire outstanding Treasury bonds. Since retiring outstanding Treasury bonds will reduce the interest costs that must be paid by the Treasury, this method of dealing with the surplus is more attractive to the Treasury than the holding of idle cash balances. Therefore, attention is once again focused on bond transactions by the Treasury and on whether the bonds retired are those held by the Federal Reserve System or by the general public. The impact of budget deficits and surpluses on the equilibrium level of national income will depend on whether bond transactions are carried out with the Federal Reserve System or with the general public.

Bond transactions with the private sector. Treasury bonds sold to the private sector of the economy withdraw funds from the private sector and place these funds in the hands of the government. Thus, if a deficit in the government budget is covered by issuing new Treasury bonds and selling these bonds to persons and businesses in the private sector of the economy, the spending power of the private sector will be reduced and some reduction will follow in the investment or the consumption function components of aggregate expenditure. These reductions in the private expenditure components of aggregate demand will counteract, to some extent, the increase in aggregate expenditure introduced by the initial imbalance between government expenditures and tax collections. That is, the expansionary effect of the budget deficit on the equilibrium level of national income will be reduced when the deficit is covered by bond sales to the private sector.

Whether the expansionary effect is completely canceled depends on how the behavior of the private sector changes as a result of its purchase of the Treasury bonds. If the funds used to purchase the government bonds otherwise would have been held as idle (excess) reserves in the private sector so that no reduction in private spending follows upon the purchase of the bonds, the full expenditures multiplier or tax multiplier effects may follow from the budgetary deficit. Even if the funds used to purchase the government bonds would not otherwise have been idle, the reduction in private expenditure may not completely cancel the expansionary effect of the deficit. Those who purchase government bonds will consider them to be part of their wealth, and the possession of this wealth may persuade them to spend their remaining funds somewhat more freely. In essence, this *wealth effect* suggests that a net expansion will result from a budgetary deficit financed by the sale of government bonds to the private sector. The money received by the government through the bonds sales is, of course, expended and circulated in the economy, whereas the wealth effect of the bonds now held in private portfolios prevents private expenditures from falling by the full amount of the funds received by the government.

Treasury bonds sold to the private sector probably will have a greater impact on investment than on consumption expenditure because the funds used to purchase these bonds are more likely to have been destined for savings and investment than for use in financing consumption. In effect, the Treasury offers its new bonds on the general money market in competition with privately offered securities, increasing the demand for loanable funds and causing interest rates to increase. The rise in interest rates will call forth a greater quantity of loanable funds (sliding upward along the supply curve of loanable funds), but some private investment undertakings will be rendered unprofitable by these higher interest rates, so that private investment will be reduced when the budget deficit is covered by bond sales to the general public. A tradeoff will take place whereby the increased government expenditures made possible by the deficit are countered by a reduction in private investment expenditures. If the government expenditures are of a current consumption variety, the economy will experience a net shift away from investment and toward consumption, and the rate of growth in economic capacity will be reduced.[7]

Disposing of a budget surplus sets up the reverse situation. Government bonds held in private portfolios may be purchased by the government with the surplus budget funds. Once again, the effect is to moderate the effect of the initial budgetary imbalance on the equilibrium level of national income. The purchase of outstanding government bonds injects the surplus funds back into the economy through the intermediary of the money markets, where interest rates can be expected to fall. Lower interest rates will increase the volume of private investment and have a stimulating effect on the equilibrium level of national income and on the rate of growth in private real capital. The wealth effect will be contractionary rather than expansionary. The point, however, is that the contractionary effect of the budget surplus itself will be reduced if the surplus is disposed of through the purchase of outstanding privately held government securities. The full effect of the budget surplus will be realized only if the excess of tax collections over expenditures is not allowed to return to the circular flow at all, as when the surplus is simply held as an idle balance by the Treasury.

Bond transactions with the Federal Reserve System. Budget deficits covered by the sale of Treasury bonds to the Federal Reserve System will have their full expansionary effects on the equilibrium level of national income because this method of covering the deficit requires no withdrawal of funds from the private sector. In fact, this method involves the creation of new money, and the deficit itself becomes simply the mechanism for injecting this new money into the economy. When a bond is purchased by the Federal Reserve System, the amount is recorded as an asset held by the system and the checking balance of the U.S. Treasury is increased by an equal amount. The Treasury draws down its checking balance as the budgeted expenditures are carried out.

[7] The special arrangements made to promote the sale of Series E savings bonds are designed to entice the desired funding away from consumption expenditure rather than out of saving. Series E bonds are not available for purchase or sale on the open market. Payroll savings plans are promoted in order to channel the money into the government bond program before it reaches the household and becomes available for consumption purchases.

Recipients of government checks deposit them in their local banks, and when these checks are cleared, the reserve position of the banking system has been increased by the amount of the deficit. Thus, covering the deficit through bond sales to the Federal Reserve System results in no withdrawal of funds from the private sector, but in fact augments the reserve position of the private banking system and promotes economic expansion through the multiple expansion of bank deposits.

The reverse procedure takes place when a budget surplus occurs and the surplus tax collections are held in idle Treasury balances or used to retire Treasury bonds already held by the Federal Reserve. The reserves of the private banking system have been drawn down as the checks written by taxpayers to pay their taxes have been cleared through the banking system. The Treasury balance in the Federal Reserve System is increased by these tax collections and, to the extent of the surplus, these funds are not returned to circulation. If these funds are used to retire Treasury bonds held by the Federal Reserve System, it is a bookkeeping operation in which the Treasury balance is reduced and the equivalent value of Treasury bonds is canceled.

Coordinating Fiscal and Monetary Approaches

The discussion of Treasury bond transactions shows that effective action requires coordination of the fiscal and the monetary approaches to stabilization, but of course the need for coordination goes much deeper than this, since both approaches attempt to influence aggregate demand and the equilibrium level of national income in various ways. In practice, however, these two approaches are conducted by different agencies in the United States. Responsibility for management of the monetary instruments of stabilization is in the hands of the Board of Governors of the Federal Reserve System, whose members are appointed by the President for long (fourteen-year) terms in an attempt to insulate them from short-run political pressures and to make it difficult for any administration or political party to dominate the Board. The responsibility for the management of the fiscal instruments, on the other hand, is entrusted to Congress and to the executive branch of the government. These branches design tax and expenditure programs and determine whether the budget shall be in deficit or in surplus. If the managers of these different approaches to stabilization share a common target for national income and if their actions are coordinated, an effective program may result. On the other hand, if different targets are established or if specific actions are not coordinated, disappointing results and frustration are likely to ensue.

Consider, for example, the situation in which a budget is formulated by Congress to produce a deficit for the explicit purpose of increasing the equilibrium level of national income. This would reflect an initiative launched through the fiscal instruments of stabilization. But the effectiveness of this initiative would depend on whether or not the monetary instruments, controlled by the Federal Reserve Board of Governors, were manipulated in a supportive manner. If the monetary authorities increase their purchases of government securities and thus cover the deficit through money creation, a substantial increase in the equilibrium level of national income may be achieved. But if the fiscal initiative is met with a restrictive exercise of monetary instruments, the bonds issued to cover the deficit will, in effect, extract spending power from the private sector and thus reduce the expansionary effects of the program. Therefore, the Federal Reserve Board of Governors, through its day to day open market operations and its power to regulate discount rates and the volume of reserves that must be held in the banking system, may choose to support budget initiatives, to counteract them, or to moderate the effects of the budget in varying degrees. In the final analysis, it becomes difficult or impossible to determine whether the fiscal instruments or the monetary instruments should be credited (or blamed) for the outcome.

Even at a conceptual level, it is difficult to establish a clear line of demarcation between fiscal and monetary operations. For example, a neutral monetary position might be defined as one that instituted increases in the stock of money only in step with increases in the real production capacity of the economy. In this situation, it might be possible to determine whether manipulation of the fiscal instruments of the budget would significantly alter the equilibrium level of economic activity. On the other hand, defining a purely neutral operation of fiscal instruments is an especially obscure task. The coercive force of taxation and the semicoercive force of expenditures are pervasive throughout the economy, and government access to money markets is an acceptable financing device for capital projects. Only if a neutral fiscal posture could be identified and adhered to would it be possible to measure stabilization effects clearly attributable to the manipulation of monetary instruments.

In practice, regular communication takes place between the Board of Governors and the Treasury, policy objectives ordinarily are consistent within a reasonable range of tolerance, and fiscal and monetary instruments are manipulated in a supportive relationship. However, the supportive relationship has not always been realized. Monetary instruments were in position of rather complete subservience to fiscal instruments in the several years prior to the "accord" reached in 1951, which reestablished an independent role for monetary instruments.[8] But rather explicit conflict again arose in the latter part of the 1960s. In other words, the Board of Governors of the Federal Reserve System conducts monetary operations according to its judgments about the needs of the economy while Congress and Treasury undertake fiscal initiatives according to their judgments about those needs, so that policy differences can and do arise. Proposals of marriage, which would centralize policy making, are sometimes advanced by one party or another or by outside matchmakers, but no centralization of stabilization authority has yet been established. A desire for orderliness and clear lines of authority motivates the push for union, but caution is signaled by an awareness of the complexity of stabilization operations and by the uncertain state of economic knowledge on the subject. Divided authority, checks and balances, and operational veto powers provide protection against errors.

[8] Prior to the "accord," Federal Reserve policy was to purchase bonds in order to keep interest rates on the national debt low, thus lowering the taxes needed to service the debt. The "accord" changed this policy and permitted the Federal Reserve to place greater emphasis on controlling inflation. The "accord" was an agreement between the Federal Reserve and the Treasury.

STABILIZATION POLICY

The primary objectives of stabilization policy are to maintain high levels of employment and reasonable stability in the general price level. A secondary objective is to ensure that the economy experiences an acceptable rate of economic growth. During the first half of the 1970s, the United States economy experienced both unacceptably high levels of unemployment and unacceptably high rates of inflation. Understandably the stabilization efforts of the government were given "low grades" by the voters. We now examine some of the difficulties encountered in establishing and implementing stabilization policy according to the national income model, and explore explanations for the simultaneous existence of large-scale unemployment and price inflation.

The Unemployment-Inflation Dilemma

The national income model implies that the goals of price stability and high employment can be achieved by measures which adjust the equilibrium level of national income so that it will correspond with some desired level of national income. The implicit assumption is that some level of national income exists which will provide both a level of employment and a degree of price stability sufficient to satisfy public demands in these areas. Let us review this model with special attention to employment and price stability.

In the graphs used to illustrate the model, different points along the horizontal axis correspond with different levels of employment; that is, the level of economic activity and the level of employment increase as the equilibrium level moves farther right on this horizontal dimension. If full employment were the only objective of stabilization policy, setting the desired or target level of national income would be a relatively simple task. An inventory of resources would be made, productivity would be estimated, and these two factors, multiplied together, would identify the full employment level of national income and product. If the general price level would remain unchanged as the economy expanded to the full employment level, there would be no conflict between the objectives of full employment and price stability. Both goals could be achieved simultaneously.

Unfortunately, however, experience indicates that the general price level will actually start to move upward before the economy reaches its full employment level of output. Therefore, selecting the target level for national income confronts policy makers with the dilemma of choosing between higher levels of employment and higher rates of inflation. This unemployment-inflation dilemma is illustrated by Figure 9.9. The horizontal axis records the level of employment in the economy as did the horizontal axes of the graphs used to develop the income determination model. The vertical axis records the rate of inflation in the general price level associated with various possible levels of employment. An extreme case will help to demonstrate the construct. Suppose, for example, that the level of employment could be increased up to the point where all resources were fully employed and that this increase in employment could be accomplished without *any* increase in the general price level, that is,

FIGURE 9.9   The Unemployment–Inflation Dilemma

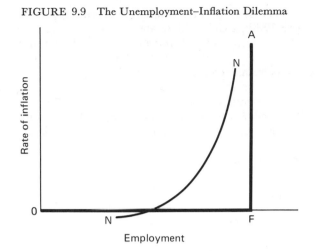

Employment

without any inflation. In this case, the line showing the relationship between employment and inflation would correspond with the horizontal axis (zero inflation rate) of the graph all the way over to the full employment point for the economy, designated as F. At this point, the relationship would become a vertical line, indicating that any attempt to achieve a further increase in employment through further increases in aggregate demand would result only in price inflation. This extreme case is illustrated by the heavy line (0FA) in Figure 9.9. Policy makers would have no difficulty in selecting the desired target level of national income and product if this line represented the actual relationship between employment and inflation. The desired level of national income and product would be that level corresponding with F because this level of national income would achieve both objectives, full employment and price stability.

Unfortunately, the actual relationship does not exhibit the backward L shape illustrated in this extreme case. Instead, experience indicates that as the level of employment increases, the general price level will start to rise before full employment is reached, as illustrated by the curved line *NN*. This curved relationship arises because aggregate demand increases are not likely to be distributed across the economy in a way that matches the availability of unemployed resources; bottlenecks arise in certain areas and price increases in these areas are not likely to be matched by price reductions in other areas. Therefore, the general price level is forced upward. Also, as employment increases, the bargaining strength of resource owners increases, enabling those with especially advantageous bargaining positions to obtain pay increases in excess of productivity, which also pushes up the general price level.

The Phillips Curve

The *Phillips Curve* is pictured in Figure 9.10, which is a modification of Figure 9.9 accomplished by changing the label on the horizontal axis from the level of employment to the rate of *un*employment. This is done because most policy discussion focuses on the rate of unemployment rather than the level of employment.[9] The Phillips Curve illustrated by NN in Figure 9.10 does not offer policy makers the option of selecting a target level for equilibrium national income that possesses the ideal attributes of full employment and zero inflation. Instead, policy makers are confronted with the unpleasant task of choosing among different points on the Phillips Curve, none of which will be acceptable to all segments of the electorate. A low unemployment choice, such as point a, will require acceptance of a high rate of inflation; a low inflation choice, such as point b, will require acceptance of a high rate of unemployment.

FIGURE 9.10   The Phillips Curve

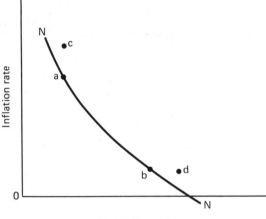

The practical politician can be expected to search for the particular point along the Phillips Curve that will bring enough votes to permit him to establish an operational stabilization policy. But it is conceivable that no such point may exist! If the voting public demands a level of performance in terms of employment and price stability beyond the reach of the stabilization powers of the government (that is, a combination that falls to the left of the Phillips Curve shown in Figure 9.10), incumbent elected officials will be ousted from office at the next election and a new group will be installed to try their hands at what may also turn out to be an impossible task. If no point along the Phillips Curve can command enough support to permit the continuance of the policy it expresses, the stabilization program of government may oscillate among various frustrating possibilities. Either voters must content themselves with solutions lying within the realm of possibility, or the realm of possibility itself must be expanded by better analysis and more effective policy instruments. Clearly, economists must explore the latter course.

[9] This change from an emphasis on the level of employment to an emphasis on the rate of unemployment not only changes the perspective from which stabilization policy is viewed, but also produces a measure that is much more sensitive to changes in the size of the labor force.

Shifting the Phillips Curve

An important question exists about the reliability and stability of the Phillips Curve itself. An economist attempting to locate the Phillips Curve would proceed (as did A. W. Phillips, who developed the concept) by plotting the relationships between the unemployment rate and the inflation rate for a number of different years. He would then use statistical techniques to fit a curve to these observations. If most of the observations were located on or near the fitted curve, he might conclude that he had discovered a significant relationship between inflation and unemployment. If, on the other hand, a poor fit were obtained, that is, if many observations were located some distance from the fitted curve, he might conclude that no useful relationship had been discovered. Between the extremes of a good fit and a poor fit lie various degrees of usefulness for the Phillips curve concept.

Economists and government stabilization officials experienced a great deal of frustration with the Phillips Curve concept in the first half of the 1970s because actual relationships between the rate of inflation and the rate of unemployment turned out not to fall on or even reasonably near the Phillips Curve construct based on historical experience. Instead, actual inflation-unemployment relationships fell well to the right of the curve. A policy aimed at achieving the low unemployment position *a* on the Phillips Curve in Figure 9.10 might turn out to require the much higher inflation rate illustrated at point *c*. Similarly, a policy aimed at achieving the low inflation position *b* on the Phillips Curve might turn out to require the much higher rate of unemployment illustrated at point *d*. Since the actual inflation-unemployment combinations appeared regularly to lie to the right of the original Phillips Curve, the hypothesis was offered that the curve may have shifted to the right from its original position. Clearly, such a shift is undesirable in terms of the goals of low unemployment and price stability.

Cost-Push Inflation

Why might the Phillips Curve shift outward to locations that offer policy makers the unhappy necessity of selecting positions which involve both price inflation and substantial amounts of unemployment? One explanation is that this is a natural short-run phenomenon for an economy which has recently experienced a serious bout with inflation. If the preceding inflation caught important sectors of the economy, such as organized labor, by surprise and forced them to accept reductions in real income because price increases were greater than negotiated wage rate increases, the Phillips Curve might move outward temporarily as these groups insisted on pay-rate increases to make up for the losses suffered in the previous round of inflation. Pay increases would be demanded for increased productivity, for a recovery of past inflation losses, and for protection against anticipated future inflation. Demands of this sort can produce the phenomenon known as *stagflation*, in which prices are rising while unemployment also is rising. The Phillips Curve shift is therefore a hangover from the previous inflation experience.

Explanations for longer-term shifts of the Phillips Curve must look to more fundamental characteristics of the economy and to explanations that involve both micro and macroeconomic factors. Suppose, for example, that powerful sectors of the economy become convinced government policy will not permit unemployment to rise above some specified level for any appreciable period of time; that is, suppose these sectors expect that the government will step in with expansionary monetary and fiscal measures whenever unemployment threatens to exceed this specified level. In this situation, price and wage determination in the economy will turn out to be anticipations of government stabilization measures and the Phillips Curve will be a vertical line at this rate of unemployment. Labor will not have to fear that increased unemployment will follow from demands for increased wages, and management can expect to be able to pass along increased costs of production through price increases to consumers. In this model, the economy stabilizes in real terms in the long run at the level corresponding to some "natural" rate of unemployment (as determined by prevailing degrees of competition and factor mobility), and government stabilization policy becomes simply a matter of determining the rate of inflation. If the government wishes to alter the rate of unemployment, that is, to shift the (vertical) Phillips Curve to the left, it must look to measures that will increase price competition and factor mobility in the economy.

Price Controls and Incomes Policy

Conventional approaches to government stabilization responsibilities, such as those outlined in this chapter, were severely tested in the first half of the 1970s and did not produce results satisfactory to many voters. Although these approaches have not been abandoned and there is hope that more "normal" economic circumstances may again enable their use to yield good results, experiments have been carried out with other methods of obtaining satisfactory relationships between price and unemployment levels. Direct controls on prices and wages were imposed in the United States in 1972 and 1973 in an attempt to deal with the phenomenon of cost-push inflation that was believed to prevail at the time. Incomes policies, which attempt longer-term government regulation of prices and incomes, have been proposed for the United States and have actually been implemented in some economies suffering from similar problems and frustrations, but the results have not yet demonstrated that satisfactory price and employment outcomes can be achieved through these procedures. In short, government stabilization programs that can effectively ensure both price stability and high levels of employment in an economy characterized by significant concentrations of economic power have not yet been discovered.

SUMMARY

Stabilization was explicitly recognized as a responsibility of government in the United States in the Employment Act of 1946, although in practice the government had been engaging in stabilization activities for some years prior to its passage. The standard approach to economic stabilization is based on the idea that the volume of aggregate demand is the key factor determining the level of employment and prices and that, by manipulating the various components of aggregate demand, the government can establish an equilibrium level of national income and production which will satisfy the demand for full employment and price stability.

The manipulation of aggregate demand may be accomplished by using *fiscal* instruments, which are incorporated in the taxation and expenditure programs of government and which place particular importance on whether the budget is balanced, in deficit, or in surplus. It may also be accomplished by using *monetary* instruments, which are implemented through the control of the stock of money exercised by the Board of Governors of the Federal Reserve System. These two approaches are intimately related because each is aimed at regulating the level of aggregate expenditure in the economy. They overlap specifically with respect to the financing of budgetary deficits and the disposal of surpluses. Although coordination of the fiscal and monetary approaches is essential for effective stabilization action, it has not always been achieved because the management of the two approaches is entrusted to different agencies of the government.

The aggregate expenditures model of stabilization indicates that policy makers must identify and establish an equilibrium level of national income which will result in a degree of price stability and a level of unemployment acceptable to the society. The Phillips Curve suggests that a relationship exists between these two objectives of stabilization policy and that this relationship consists of a tradeoff in which success in achieving one of the objectives can be had only at the expense of less success in achieving the other. If officials responsible for stabilization policy can discover an inflation-unemployment combination that is acceptable to the voting public, a firm policy can be established and stabilization accomplished within the limits of the possibilities expressed in the Phillips Curve. If, however, none of the possibilities expressed by the Phillips Curve is acceptable, no stabilization policy will receive the support needed for consistent application. This unsatisfactory situation appeared to prevail during the first half of the 1970s, when both the rate of inflation and the rate of unemployment were unacceptably high and when the economy suffered from faltering rates of economic growth, a combination of circumstances known as *stagflation*.

The unsatisfactory performance of the stabilization responsibility in the first half of the 1970s prompted a reexamination of the Phillips Curve concept and a review of the adequacy of the aggregate demand approach to the task of stabilization. A short-run explanation suggested that the Phillips Curve may have shifted to a less satisfactory location through a cost-push pattern of price increases, as powerful segments of the economy insisted on recovering real income losses suffered in the preceding period of inflation. Long-run explanations, on the other hand, suggested that the Phillips Curve would become a vertical line corresponding with a "natural" unemployment rate determined by the institutional structure, the degree of competition, and the degree of factor mobility prevailing in the economy. According to the vertical construct of the Phillips Curve, stabilization programs operating through the standard expenditures control approaches could influence the rate of inflation in the economy but would be unable, in the long run, effectively to control the level of unemployment. This model suggests that efforts to control the rate of unemployment must be pursued not through the aggregate expenditures approaches, but through approaches which can influence the operational performance of the economic system itself.

SUGGESTED READINGS

MORLEY, SAMUEL A. *The Economics of Inflation* (Hinsdale, Ill.: Dryden Press, 1971).

Economic Report of the President (Washington, D. C.: Government Printing Office). This annual publication includes the report of the Council of Economic Advisors and presents an up-to-date report of stabilization programs.

U.S. Department of Commerce. *Survey of Current Business* (Washington, D.C.: Government Printing Office). This monthly publication provides current information on the level of national income, employment, government expenditures, and so on.

Students may wish to review the appropriate chapters in a standard macroeconomics text for a more complete development of the theory of national income determination and the multiplier process.

10

The National Debt

National debt comes into being as government bonds are sold to cover deficits in the budget. The current total of public debt is therefore the historical total of net government deficits incurred.[1] The size of the debt can be expressed in a number of ways, but unfortunately none of these expressions provides an entirely satisfactory measure of the significance of the debt. For example, it is popular to calculate the amount of the national debt per capita, although this analogy with individual private debt ignores the role of earning capacity as an indicator of ability to carry indebtedness. A more meaningful approach is to express the national debt as a percentage of national income (or GNP), as shown in Table 10.1. This measure recognizes the relevance of income to the ability to carry indebtedness and also reduces somewhat the problems that arise from changes in the value of money over time.

A still more sophisticated approach focuses on the interest costs of servicing the debt and relates this interest cost to national income. In this case, the rates of interest prevailing each year and the term structure of the debt itself become operational in determining the significance of the debt. Both interest rates and term structure can be influenced by government action and are themselves dimensions of government policy. Therefore, interest cost as a percentage of national income is not an unambiguous measure of the importance of the debt. Whatever measure is used, comparisons among different points in time for the United States and comparisons between the United States and other nations

[1] The statistical tables published with the annual *Economic Report of the President* provide a convenient reference for up to date information on the national debt. Information is also available in the *Survey of Current Business* and *The Treasury Bulletin*.

159

TABLE 10.1   National Debt as a Percentage of GNP, Selected Years,
1951 to 1976 (billions of dollars)

YEAR	DEBT	GNP	PER-CENTAGE
1951	$259.4	$330.2	78.6%
1956	276.6	420.7	65.7
1961	296.2	523.3	56.6
1966	329.3	753.0	43.7
1971	397.3	1063.4	37.4
1976	620.4	1692.4	36.7

Source: Computed from *Economic Report of the President, 1976* and *1977.*
Data for 1971 and 1976 exclude notes held by the International
Monetary Fund.

suggest that the national debt, *in itself,* is not a cause for alarm at the present
time. However, it does not follow that the national debt is unimportant.

OWNERSHIP, MARKETABILITY, AND TERM STRUCTURE

Ownership, marketability, and term structure are important considerations in managing the national debt. This section defines these terms and discusses how they are related to the stabilization responsibilities of government.

Ownership

The people and organizations that lend money to the U.S. Treasury by
buying government bonds are the owners of the national debt. It is useful to
divide these owners into three groups and to record the portions of the total
debt held by each group. Table 10.2 provides this information. The largest
portion of the national debt is owned by private investors, including banks,
insurance companies, corporations, private individuals, and state and local
governments (which are classed as private investors because their decision to

TABLE 10.2   Ownership of the National Debt, Selected Years, 1951
to 1976

	PERCENTAGE OF TOTAL DEBT HELD BY		
YEAR	FEDERAL RESERVE BANKS	PRIVATE INVESTORS	GOVERN-MENT ACCOUNTS
1951	9.2%	75.7%	15.2%
1956	9.0	72.5	18.5
1961	9.8	72.5	17.7
1966	13.5	66.6	20.0
1971	16.5	57.6	25.9
1976	15.2	60.7	24.1

Source: Computed from *Economic Report of the President, 1976* and *1977.*
Data for 1971 and 1976 exclude notes held by the International
Monetary Fund.

buy bonds is voluntary and based on ordinary financial management considerations). The privately held portion of the debt has decreased considerably over the past twenty-five years. The second largest portion of the debt is held by government accounts, such as the social security and highway trust funds and the reserves of retirement programs for federal government employees. This portion has increased greatly over the past twenty-five years. The smallest portion of the debt is held by the Federal Reserve banks. These banks acquire government bonds in the process of money creation. They may purchase bonds to help the Treasury to cover a deficit in the budget (as discussed earlier); they also may purchase bonds in open market operations when they are pursuing an expansionary stabilization policy. The portion of the debt held by Federal Reserve banks has also grown over the past quarter century.

The distinctions among these different groups of owners is important because they reflect different types of debt operations and different obligations for debt retirement and the payment of interest. For example, debt held by the Federal Reserve banks is related to stabilization activities and to the creation of money. Money creation and Federal Reserve open market purchases of government bonds are entirely appropriate dimensions of stabilization activity and have already been discussed. However, debt incurred in the process of money creation does not carry the same kind of obligation for repayment as debt incurred in the sale of bonds to private individuals or companies. Even the payment of interest technically is unnecessary in the money-creation activities of government, since the provision of money is explicitly authorized in the Constitution. The Treasury does pay interest on debt securities held by Federal Reserve banks, but the laws that govern these banks require that earnings above a certain percentage of invested capital must be paid over to the Treasury. Thus, some of the interest paid on bonds held by Federal Reserve banks comes back to the Treasury.

The debt owned by private investors represents genuine borrowing by the federal government. This borrowing involves a transaction between the government and an investor who agrees to transfer funds to the government in exchange for the receipt of periodic interest payments and eventual repayment of the sum loaned. Interest payments are necessary to persuade investors to purchase these bonds, and the maturity date, which is part of the conventional bond agreement, obligates the government to repay the principal at some specified date. Genuine borrowing withdraws funds from the private sector of the economy and therefore has effects on the equilibrium level of national income similar in many respects to those of taxation. Taxation, however, is compulsory; genuine borrowing is a voluntary transaction.

Bonds owned by government accounts are not money creation indebtedness because the money used to purchase them has come from taxes collected from the public. But these bonds do not reflect genuine borrowing in the sense of a voluntary transaction between the buyer and the seller. These government accounts are required by law to place their reserves in U.S. Treasury bonds and are not permitted to purchase privately issued securities. Interest is paid by the Treasury to the agencies holding these debt instruments. The rate of interest paid on these special issues is calculated through formulas that reflect average rates paid on other parts of the debt.

Marketable and Nonmarketable Securities

Some U.S. government bonds issues are *marketable*, which means that a person who owns such a bond may sell it to another person for whatever price is mutually agreeable. Therefore, the market value of these bonds can fluctuate depending on the interaction of supply and demand. The Treasury promises to pay regular periodic interest of a specified amount (usually expressed as a percentage of the face value of the bond) and to repay the principal sum (face amount) of the bond on its maturity date. The actual yield or rate of return the owner receives on these bonds, therefore, depends on their current market price. Since the dollar amount of periodic interest is fixed, the market value of the bonds will move in the opposite direction from changes in interest rates prevailing in the economy. For example, if prevailing interest rates rise, the market price of the bonds will fall until the actual yield on the bond corresponds with prevailing interest rates.

Nonmarketable bonds are also issued. United States savings bonds are the most familiar example of nonmarketable U.S. government bonds. These bonds are not bought and sold in transactions between private persons. Instead, a person who wishes to liquidate his holding of nonmarketable government bonds must sell (redeem) the bonds back to the U.S. Treasury. A schedule of redemption values is part of the bond agreement and determines the yield or rate of return the owner obtains. The face value of the bond is its redemption value upon maturity. The schedule of prematurity redemption values is graduated so that the effective yield or rate of return increases the longer the bond is held.

Nonmarketable bonds are designed to take money out of circulation in the private sector of the economy. Special efforts are made to sell savings bonds when stabilization policy is attempting to forestall inflation by withdrawing money from circulation. Inflation itself, of course, will erode the real value of these (as well as other) bonds. Therefore, if holders of these nonmarketable bonds anticipate inflation, they will redeem their bonds in order to avoid suffering a loss in real value. Redemptions increase the amount of circulating money and add to the inflationary pressure in the economy. This self-fulfilling prophecy pattern might be changed if purchasing power bonds were issued instead of the conventional U.S. savings bond. The redemption value of a purchasing power bond would be indexed to some measure of the general price level so that inflation would no longer erode real value. This would reduce the tendency of bondholders to redeem their bonds in anticipation of inflation and would increase the effectiveness of bond sales as a device to prevent inflation.

Term Structure

The *term* of a debt instrument is the length of time that must elapse before the obligation matures and the principal sum of the loan must be repaid. The Treasury issues a variety of different debt instruments, some with short-term maturities of a few months and some with long-term maturities of twenty or thirty years. At the short end of the term structure are Treasury *bills*, which mature 90 or 180 days from the date of issue. Treasury bills are sold on a discount basis according to competitive bidding, which means that the rate of interest actually paid on each issue is determined only after the issue has been sold. Because the time period is short, the risk incurred by buyers is low; interest rates on Treasury bills therefore are typically the lowest in the family of government debt instruments. Treasury *notes* are intermediate-term debt instruments and have maturities of from one to five years. Interest rates on Treasury notes ordinarily will be somewhat higher than those on Treasury bills because the longer time before maturity exposes the buyer to greater risk. Part of the Treasury strategy in issuing different types of debt instruments is to accommodate the needs of different groups of potential bond buyers and thus to secure the desired funds at the lowest possible rates of interest. For example, tax anticipation notes are sold to persons and businesses to provide a convenient way for these buyers to earn interest on funds they wish to set aside for the payment of future tax obligations. The long end of the term spectrum consists of Treasury *bonds*, which carry maturities of up to thirty years into the future. Typically, these bonds require the highest rate of interest in the family of government debt instruments.

The term structure of the debt shows the amount of debt outstanding, classified according to the time remaining before maturity. This term structure changes from time to time as some bonds mature and are retired and other bonds are issued. Table 10.3 shows the average length of time before maturity for the marketable portion of the national debt in selected years over the past

TABLE 10.3   Average Maturity Length of the Marketable Interest-bearing Public Debt, Selected Years, 1951 to 1976

END OF YEAR	YEARS	MONTHS
1951	6	7
1956	5	4
1961	4	6
1966	4	11
1971	3	6
1976	2	6

Source: Economic Report of the President, 1976 and 1977.

quarter century. The average length of the outstanding marketable debt was shorter at the end of 1976 than at any time in the preceding twenty-five years, which is an important observation in connection with the task of debt management and the "moneyness" of the debt, both of which will be examined below. On maturity day, of course, the term of a particular bond is zero. If this bond is retired with money obtained from the sale of a new bond, the refunding operation will lengthen the term of the total debt, but the amount of lengthening will depend on the term of the new debt instrument. If the term of the new instrument is shorter than the average for the total debt, then the average length of the total debt will be shortened by the refunding, and vice versa. It is apparent that refunding operations have tended to shorten the average maturity of the debt in recent years.

All the debt instruments described carry specified maturity dates and all require the payment of interest to the lender. But it is possible to finance deficits with instruments that do not pay any interest or with instruments that do not carry any maturity date. For example, deficits could be covered through the direct printing of money itself, which carries no maturity date and pays no interest to the holder. This has been done on occasion by the Treasury. It would also be possible to finance deficits or refund maturing securities through the sale of *consols*, debt instruments that promise to pay a specified amount of periodic interest but have no maturity date. The amount of money that could be raised through the sale of a consol would depend on the rate of interest prevailing in the economy at the time of the sale. That is, the amount the buyer would pay for the consol would equal the present value of the stream of future interest payments promised by the Treasury. Once the consol had been sold, the Treasury would have no obligation to retire it on any maturity date. The only obligation would be to continue to pay the promised periodic interest as long as the consol was outstanding. If the Treasury wished to reduce its obligations to pay periodic interest, it would have to buy back the consol through the general money markets, paying the price determined by the interaction of supply and demand at that time. The interest costs of debt financing through consols would be higher than for financing with securities carrying a specified maturity date, but the absence of a maturity date would give the Treasury greater flexibility in timing its entries into the money markets.

REFUNDING AND DEBT MANAGEMENT POLICY

Obtaining the money needed to retire maturing debt instruments by selling new debt instruments is called *refunding*. It simply replaces an old series of debt instruments with a new series and leaves the total amount outstanding unchanged. Refunding, or "rolling over," the debt is a regular and more or less routine operation of the Treasury and means that particular issues of debt are not necessarily connected with particular government expenditures. It also means that the maturing, or potential maturing, of particular debt issues is not the occasion for taxation designed to retire outstanding debt.

Debt management includes the tasks of refunding maturing issues, issuing securities to finance budget deficits, and retiring debt securities if a surplus arises in the budget. A debt management policy establishes the criteria or guiding principles for the management of the national debt. For example, debt management policy might be to minimize the housekeeping chore of refunding. This policy would instruct debt managers to issue long-term rather than short-term obligations, since this would mean relatively infrequent entries into money markets to roll over maturing debt instruments. Consols would provide the ultimate reduction in necessary refunding operations because they carry no maturity date. But the policy of minimizing obligatory refunding conflicts with an alternative management policy of minimizing the interest cost of carrying the debt. This conflict arises because long-term debt instruments typically require higher interest rates than short-term instruments.

A policy of minimizing the interest cost instructs debt managers to select for new issues the type of instrument that will commit the Treasury to the lowest interest charges. This minimum interest policy generally favors the use of short-term rather than long-term instruments. The issuance of money itself (green-backs) would be the ultimate in interest minimization. However, interest rates fluctuate over time, so that situations may arise in which the sale of long-term securities would be consistent with a policy of interest minimization. Ordinarily, interest rates are lower in recession periods and higher during prosperous (and potentially inflationary) times. Therefore, rates on long-term securities in recession periods may be lower than rates on short-term securities in prosperous times. Interest minimization suggests issuing long-term securities in recession periods and short-term securities in periods of prosperity. But in this situation, a policy of minimizing interest cost may conflict with still another possible objective, that of supporting efforts to stabilize the level of economic activity.

Moneyness and Stabilization

The *moneyness* of the national debt refers to the ease with which the owners of debt instruments can convert this wealth into spendable money. For example, short-term debt (such as Treasury bills) is sometimes called *near money* because only a short waiting period is necessary before the instrument matures and can be redeemed for cash. Conversely, debt instruments that are far away from maturity are less liquid because a longer waiting time must elapse before the Treasury is required to retire the bond and pay cash to its owner. Consols are the ultimate of nonliquidity, since the Treasury is under no obligation to return the borrowed money to the private sector. Nonmarketable securities such as savings bonds are relatively liquid or near-money components of the debt because of the guaranteed redemption schedule incorporated in the obligation.

The liquidity or moneyness of the national debt provides a connection between debt management and the stabilization responsibility of government and means that stabilization is a third possible policy guideline. The basic idea is that greater liquidity or moneyness of wealth holdings is an expansionary or stimulative factor for the level of activity in the economy and thus is desirable from a stabilization point of view when the economy is performing below the target level of equilibrium national income. Conversely, less liquidity or money-ness of wealth holdings is desirable when the economy is facing the threat of inflation. For example, suppose that inflationary pressures exist in the economy. Holders of debt instruments denominated in fixed dollar amounts, realizing that inflation will erode the real purchasing power of wealth held in these forms, will attempt to liquidate these instruments in order to place their wealth in forms less vulnerable to inflation damage. If the debt instruments held are short term or near to maturity, only a short wait would be required to carry out this conversion. Thus, short-term outstanding debt can be converted into actual spendable money quickly. When this liquidated debt enters the stream of spending, the money stock is increased, increasing the danger of inflation and the anti-inflation task of the monetary and fiscal instruments of stabilization policy. Short-term debt is said to "overhang" the money markets and to increase the hazard that inflation, once recognized as imminent, will become a reality. In other words, when it is relatively easy for debt holders to liquidate their wealth, the money stock circulating in the economy is subject to fluctuations that magnify changes taking place and increase the demands on the monetary instruments of stabilization policy.

Debt management policy supportive of economic stabilization indicates that the term structure should be lengthened when the objective is to combat inflation. Maturing obligations would be refunded into new obligations of a longer term, reducing the moneyness of the debt and protecting the money stock from increases arising from the liquidation of debt. Conversely, when stabilization policy is expansionary, maturing debt issues would be refunded into shorter, more liquid instruments, thus increasing the availability of funds to finance new investment opportunities should they become available. The interest rate ramifications of this supportive policy require the sale of long-term debt instruments during inflationary times when interest rates are high and of short-term debt instruments during recession periods when interest rates typically are low. Thus, the stabilization policy of debt management conflicts with the policy of minimizing interest costs. Conversely, a debt management policy of keeping interest costs low favors selling long-term debt instruments during periods of recession and avoiding long-term commitments during periods of prosperity and potential inflation. This strategy is directly contrary to the supportive stabilization policy. Thus, a conflict exists between the policy alternatives of supporting stabilization policy and minimizing the interest cost of carrying the debt. Historically, Treasury debt management policy has favored low interest rather than stabilization support. In the recent period of unusually high interest rates, a further complication arose because upper limits on interest rates were imposed by law, and these limits required additional shortening of the structure of the debt.

THE BURDEN OF THE NATIONAL DEBT

Debt burden is a fairly simple concept if the debt is continually refunded or rolled over so that no arrangements need to be made for its eventual retirement. In this situation, the primary burden consists of the taxes collected to pay the interest costs of carrying the debt. Even this notion of burden is tempered by the fact that the money collected from taxpayers is paid over as interest to those who own debt securities and who generally are members of the same society. National income accounts, in fact, list debt interest as a transfer payment. However, tax payments are compulsory whereas the receipt of interest is a consequence of a voluntary transaction, and this difference means that interest costs are genuine burdens. Voluntary bond purchases do not burden the bond purchaser in a financial sense nor does the receipt of interest under the terms of the contract necessarily measure benefit to the bondholder. Tax payments, on the other hand, force taxpayers to forego alternative uses of their money and therefore impose a burden.

It is apparent, however, that analysis of the burden of a debt already in existence overlooks considerations relevant to a benefit-cost analysis of debt financing. To get a complete picture, we must examine the entire debt-financing package, including the initial borrowing, the payment of interest, and the eventual retirement or refunding of obligations. In respect to the national debt, orderly analysis also requires a distinction between debt incurred in the process of money creation and debt incurred through genuine borrowing from the private sector.

Money Creation Indebtedness

Table 10.4 presents a life cycle summary of the borrowing-interest-repayment aspects of public debt incurred in the process of money creation. The analysis examines each phase in the life cycle for indications of gain or loss in real living standards. If stabilization policy is well conceived and well executed, money creation debt is incurred when the target level of national income is greater than the prevailing equilibrium level. This suggests that unemployment exists in the economy and that the money created through the debt operation will remove resources from the unemployment lines and place them in activities in which they will produce goods and services and thereby contribute to higher real living standards.

TABLE 10.4   Life Cycle Analysis of Debt Burden

PHASE OF CYCLE	BORROWING FROM FEDERAL RESERVE BANKS	BORROWING FROM PRIVATE INVESTORS
1. Incurring debt	No burden if the stabilization policy is correct	No current burden in voluntary transactions; no current taxation
2. Interest payments	Taxpayer burden moderated by return of some Federal Reserve earnings	Taxpayer burden
3. Retiring debt	Taxpayer burden if taxation is used to retire debt	Taxpayer burden

In the ideal case of a backward L-shaped Phillips Curve, no inflation effect would follow from this money creation so that no members of the society would find their real living standards eroded. Idle resources would be constructively employed without harm being done to other members of the society. No burden would arise since the opportunity cost of the otherwise unemployed resources would be zero. On the other hand, burden would arise from money creation if stabilization policy were poorly conceived or poorly executed, resulting in inflation. Inflation forces some people to accept a lower standard of living and also can disrupt the efficient functioning of the economy and thus produce real burdens. However, in the perspective of an examination of the burden of national debt, such burdens should be attributed to decisions taken in stabilization policy and implementation and not to the use of debt instruments themselves. Direct money creation would produce similar effects even if the device of debt creation were not used.

Interest is paid on debt instruments issued for money creation, and some burden can be attributed to the compulsory exactions involved in the taxation required to pay this interest. If debt instruments had not been used, this burden would not be present. The interest paid on bonds held by the Federal Reserve banks helps to finance the operation of these institutions, but the law requires that income above a certain level received by these banks must be turned over to the U.S. Treasury. Thus, even the interest burden arising from the use of debt instruments in the money creation process is not a serious problem.

Debt held by the Federal Reserve System could be retired when stabilization policy called for contracting the economy; that is, when the prevailing equilibrium level of national income was above the target level. Taxes could be imposed to provide the funds to retire this debt and these taxes would impose burdens on taxpayers. The tax burdens, however, are attributable to the means chosen to combat inflation and are not necessarily connected to the retirement of debt held by the Federal Reserve. The tax money could be held as idle Treasury balances and the debt left intact. Alternatively, the fight against inflation might have been conducted by bond sales to private investors (that is, through genuine borrowing), so that no tax burdens would be imposed. This summary suggests that the burden aspects of debt instruments used in connection with stabilization policy are largely confined to tax burdens required for the payment of interest on debt issued in this process. Although technically unnecessary, the amount of this burden need not be substantial.

Genuine Borrowing

Genuine borrowing means that bonds are sold to private purchasers in voluntary transactions in exchange for interest payments and the return of the principal sum upon maturity of the debt instrument. The life cycle picture of this type of borrowing is also shown in Table 10.4. Several circumstances justify genuine borrowing by government. In the microeconomic sense, government may utilize genuine borrowing to finance the construction of capital projects which, once constructed, will generate a stream of benefits continuing for some time into the future. The argument is that the present generation of taxpayers should not be *compelled* to forego current benefits in order to provide capital items which will yield benefits only to some future generation of taxpayers. Both equity and efficiency suggest that the taxpayer group (or generation) which enjoys the benefits of public projects should also be the taxpayer group (or generation) required to bear the costs of providing those benefits. Thus, projects not beneficial to present taxpayers should not be financed by taxes imposed on those taxpayers. Bond sales are therefore more appropriate than current taxation in the financing of construction costs.

The fundamental difference between bond and tax financing is that bond sales are voluntary exchanges, whereas taxation is a compulsory payment. The voluntary bond purchaser relinquishes current command over resources in exchange for the promise of future command over resources. The terms of trade in the exchange are revealed in the rate of interest mutually acceptable to seller and buyer. Since the purchaser is not obligated to buy the bond unless the rate of interest is sufficient to compensate him for any hardships imposed, there is no net burden on bond buyers when genuine borrowing takes place. Since no current taxes are collected, there is no burden on the current generation of taxpayers, although a commitment has been undertaken that may require higher taxes from future generations of taxpayers.

If full employment prevails in the economy, the case for genuine borrowing to finance long-term projects is especially strong since idle resources are not available for employment in the project and public demand for resources therefore must be accompanied by a reduction in private demand if inflation is to be avoided. If unemployment exists, money creation is called for and genuine borrowing need not be used to finance capital projects, although this should not permit those who make allocation decisions to avoid the question of whether the idle resources might be better employed in the private sector. In inflationary periods, genuine borrowing may be used as an instrument of stabilization policy. However, the question is whether a campaign against inflation can properly be supported as a project yielding benefits to future generations rather than to the current generation. Inflation erodes current wealth held in forms denominated in fixed money amounts. Therefore, the current generation is the primary beneficiary of successful anti-inflation efforts. Since genuine borrowing establishes commitments for future taxpayers, it is less appropriate than taxation in conducting anti-inflation programs.

Once the borrowing operation has been carried out, the government is obligated for the payment of interest and for the repayment of principal according to the terms of the bond sale transaction. These are the second and third phases in the life cycle model. Although no burden arose in phase 1 because no compulsory transactions were carried out, phases 2 and 3 are different because commitments have been made which require that some actions be taken in the servicing of the outstanding indebtedness. Thus, burden (in the sense of obligatory transactions) arises in these phases of the life cycle. Taxes may be collected to pay interest due on outstanding debt or to retire debt when bonds reach maturity. These taxes are compulsory payments requiring the taxpaying segments of society to transfer resources to the bondholding segments to fulfill the promises made when the bonds were sold. If the bonds were sold initially to finance the construction of capital goods, tax payments to meet interest costs and to amortize (repay) the initial sum loaned should extend throughout the beneficial life of the capital item, matching the benefits enjoyed by the taxpayers through these years.

In summary, the analysis suggests that genuine borrowing is a device through which the costs (in the sense of compulsory transfers of command over resources) can be shifted through time and therefore among different generation groups of taxpayers. Its appropriateness is apparent when a time gap exists between the date when resources must be expended in the production of services and the date when the beneficial services themselves are enjoyed. Genuine debt financing does impose a burden on future generations of taxpayers, but whether the complete picture of borrowing, paying interest, and finally retiring this debt imposes a net burden on future generations depends upon the amount of benefit these generations obtain from the project financed through the debt process. It is apparent that the temporal burden-shifting capability of debt financing can be abused if bonds are sold to finance current operating expenditures. Inevitably, delicate issues arise when present-generation legislators face decisions involving benefits and costs to be realized by future generations. Debt financing is simply an instrument applicable to that dimension of public choice.

DEBT RETIREMENT AND MONETIZATION

Should the government undertake a policy of retiring or substantially reducing the size of the national debt? The answer depends on the consequences of such a policy on the standard of living in the society. Once again, it is helpful to distinguish between debt held by the Federal Reserve banks and debt owned by private investors. The case for retiring debt held by the Federal Reserve banks is weak because this debt is an instrument for stabilization and provides the raw materials for open market operations of monetary control. Retiring this debt through taxation would reduce the stock of money and lead to economic contraction or price deflation. Of course, Federal Reserve debt could be retired with Treasury-issued greenbacks, thus replacing one institutuional arrangement for monetary control with another.

The case for retiring privately held public debt is more interesting. For example, this debt might be retired through taxation, that is, a budget surplus, generated by increased tax collections, could be used to retire outstanding debt instruments. To the extent that the taxes withdrew funds that otherwise would have been used for consumption expenditures, this method of debt retirement would reallocate resources out of consumption, lower the rate of interest in the money markets, and channel resources into investment. A higher level of investment and a more rapid rate of growth in productive capacity could result, provided that the procedure did not cause recession and unemployment. The present generation of taxpayers would have been compelled to finance the debt reduction and the subsidy to the future, and there is little basis for contending that present taxpayers are ethically obligated to do either of these things. Much of the present public debt was incurred in wartime. There is little basis for contending that the present generation of taxpayers has a unique obligation to retire this indebtedness any more than do future generations. Likewise, it is difficult to make a persuasive case for a forced investment in economic growth for the benefit of future, perhaps more affluent, generations.

Monetization is another device that could be used to retire outstanding indebtedness. In a crude sense, monetization means that money would be printed and used to retire debt or, following the procedures actually used, debt held by the Federal Reserve System would be increased in order to finance the retirement of debt held outside the System (which is simply open market purchasing of government securities). Debt monetization would be inflationary if carried out in the context of a fully employed economy because nonspendable bonds would be replaced by spendable cash. However, in an economy experiencing real growth in productive capacity, some increases in the money stock may be appropriate to prevent unemployment and to maintain stability in price levels. In this growth situation, debt held outside the Federal Reserve System could be retired through the process of monetization without producing inflation. The question is whether the fruits of real growth should be channeled toward the investment money markets through debt retirement or toward current consumption through tax reduction or increases in government expenditures.

In practice, significant retirement of the public debt is not seriously contemplated. The institutional structure of the financial markets (for example, banks and insurance companies) has developed a great reliance on the availability of securities essentially free of default risk. However, the interest component in the annual government budget is large and involves a continuing and substantial transfer from taxpayers to bondholders.

SUMMARY

The national debt, expressed as a percentage of gross national product, has diminished over the past twenty-five years. This suggests that the size of the debt itself is not a serious problem. Management of this debt, however, does influence the stability of the economy and may influence the allocation of resources between consumption and investment. Conflicts exist among several policy guidelines that could be established to govern the management of the debt. Specifically, a conflict exists between the policy of managing the debt to minimize the interest carrying costs and management aimed at economic stabilization. In the stabilization-oriented policy, debt management regulates the liquidity or moneyness of outstanding debt in order to support monetary and fiscal measures of economic stabilization.

The distinction between debt owned by the Federal Reserve banks and debt owned by private investors is useful in considering the burden of the national debt. The burden of debt financing arises through the taxes collected to pay the interest cost of carrying the debt. Relatively little direct burden arises in respect to debt held by the Federal Reserve banks, and even this burden could be eliminated if different institutional arrangements were made for the administration of monetary instruments of stabilization. The inflation burdens of money creation financing, however, can be serious. Borrowing from private investors is a mechanism for shifting the cost of government expenditures to later generations of taxpayers so that the burden of tax financing can be imposed on the generation of taxpayers enjoying the benefits of the expenditure. Although the retirement of privately held government debt is not an established policy, this debt could be retired through monetization as economic growth indicated a need for increases in the stock of money.

SUGGESTED READINGS

BUCHANAN, JAMES M. *Public Principles of Public Debt* (Homewood, Ill.: Irwin, 1958).

FERGUSON, J. M. (ed.). *Public Debt and Future Generations* (Chapel Hill: University of North Carolina Press, 1964).

I I

Individual Income Taxation: What Is Income?

The individual income tax is the dominant revenue producer for the United States government. In fiscal 1976, the individual income tax generated approximately 43 percent of the total budget receipts of the federal government.[1] Therefore, it is appropriate to give careful consideration to the definition of income used in establishing this tax base, to the exemptions and deductions allowed to taxpayers, to the rates of tax imposed, and to the economic effects of this tax.

The federal individual income tax is imposed under the authority of the Sixteenth Amendment to the Constitution, adopted in 1913, which authorizes the federal government to collect taxes on income from whatever source derived and without regard to "apportionment." Apportionment was important because the court had ruled, in 1896, that income taxes actually were direct taxes on individuals, with the amount of the tax determined on the basis of income, and were therefore subject to the constitutional requirement that direct taxes imposed by the federal government must be apportioned among the states on the basis of population. This meant that the government would have to collect twice as much money from a state with 10 million people as from a state with 5 million people. Since per capita income levels in some states are higher than in others, neither a flat rate tax nor a graduated rate tax measured by income and collected by the federal government would be constitutional. In effect, federal direct taxes would have to be poll taxes collected uniformly throughout the country. The Sixteenth Amendment, by removing the appor-

[1] *The Economic Report of the President, 1977*, Table B–68, p. 267.

tionment constraint, cleared the way for modern federal individual income taxation.

CONCEPTS OF INCOME

If a tax is to be imposed on income, it is important that some concept of income be elaborated as a reference point in evaluating actual or proposed provisions in income tax legislation. Certainly it is not sufficient simply to accept the Internal Revenue Service definition of income. The possession of some concept of income can also be helpful in ensuring that actual income tax provisions will have some internal consistency which will prevent variations due to administrative caprice or special pleading. Several concepts of income have achieved legitimacy in economic literature. The actual taxation of income in the United States does not conform entirely to any of these concepts, but they are useful references in the analysis of income taxation.

The Consumption Concept

The *consumption* concept of income asserts that a person's real standard of living is, in fact, the income of that person. If a person consumes many resources for his own personal and private satisfaction, that person is said to have a high standard of living or income. A person who consumes fewer resources for his personal satisfaction is said to have a lower standard of living or income. According to this concept of income, the manner in which consumption is financed is not relevant. If two persons expended identical amounts on personal consumption they would be credited with the same level of income, even though one of them may have financed his consumption by going into debt while the other financed his consumption through current earnings, gifts or inheritances, or by drawing on past accumulations of savings. The amount of a person's earnings would be irrelevant to the measurement of income, as would the amount of funds under his control from whatever source. Savings would not be included as income, nor would expenditures the individual might make to acquire ownership rights to property. Even though the individual may possess and exercise command over resources, those resources not used for personal consumption continue to possess their economic potential and no real income has been realized.

The consumption concept of income is not easily faulted on philosophical grounds. In fact, the concept goes straight to the heart of the proposition that human welfare and satisfaction constitute the genuine end products of economic activity. The concept does incorporate the implicit assumption that different individuals are equally efficient in realizing satisfaction or happiness from the acts of consumption. The accuracy of this assumption may be questioned, but such questioning goes well beyond the matter of taxation.

The consumption concept of income also possesses certain attractions on pragmatic or public policy grounds. For example, consumption can be looked upon as taking resources from the social "stockpile" for the purpose of personal enjoyment. If this taking were made the basis for taxation, a result would be a greater conservation of resources for future enjoyment or for utilization in further production. Thus, this concept would produce incentives directly opposite from those generated by income concepts that levy taxes on activities which put resources into the social stockpile. Taxation on the basis of the consumption concept would mount powerful forces in favor of saving, investing, economic growth, and environmental conservation.

A genuine application of the consumption concept probably would require the use of a *general expenditures* tax, which would differ in many ways from both income and sales taxation as presently practiced. The general expenditures tax would require the preparation of an annual return similar in many respects to the present income tax return, but would report total consumption expenditure rather than total earnings. Personal deductions and exemptions could be allowed, and rates could be graduated to make the effective rate of tax progressive on total consumption expenditure. The expenditures tax would differ from the present income tax because saving would not be subject to tax. It would differ from conventional sales taxes because it would cover a much wider range of consumption spending than the typical sales tax and because exemptions, deductions, and graduated rates could be used.[2]

The Production Flow Concept

The *production flow* concept of income comes closer to matching the definition of income actually used in individual income taxation in the United States. This concept can be explained in terms of a fundamental rule used in income taxation—namely, the *compensation* rule. When an individual receives something of value (usually money), the question is asked whether or not this receipt was compensation for a service rendered, either by the individual himself or by property owned by that individual. If the answer is "yes," the receipt is classified as income and must be reported for tax purposes. The rationale is that when a service has been rendered, production has taken place and income has been generated. Conversely, if the answer to the compensation question is "no," the rationale is that no production has taken place, and consequently that no income could have been generated. In this case, the receipt itself would be considered a transfer of wealth from one person to another and would not be taxable as income. Scholarships, gifts, and inheritances are not counted as income in United States income taxation.

Capital gains would not be counted as income under a strict application of the production flow concept. Suppose, for example, that a person purchases a share of stock for $100 and that, while he owns this stock, the prospects for future income for the company increase so that the market value of the stock increases. This increase in the value of the stock is a capital gain, but this gain arises from an anticipation of future production and income and not from any production taking place during the current accounting period. Thus, the production flow concept would suggest that this capital gain is not income and should not be taxed. Since the gain was not the result of current production, no

---

[2] Students interested in further exploration of the theory and application of the consumption concept of income and expenditures taxation may consult Irving Fisher, *Constructive Income Taxation* (New York: Harper & Row, 1942), and Nicholas Kaldor, *An Expenditures Tax* (London: Allen and Unwin, 1955).

current income was generated and no tax should be collected. It makes no difference whether or not the gain is "realized" through an actual sale of the stock; in neither case would the gain properly be considered income.[3]

In fact, federal income tax rules do consider at least a portion of capital gains to be income for tax purposes. Precisely what part is counted as income is not important at this point; what is important is that the decision to tax capital gains (even in part) implies that the production flow concept of income may be somehow unsatisfactory. If capital gains were excluded from taxation, complaints surely would be raised that the tax was unfair because it treated unequals as if they were equal. That is, the person who experienced a capital gain would be treated in the same way as another person who did not experience a capital gain. If the receipt of capital gains introduces distinctions among taxpayers that are generally perceived as relevant to the payment of taxes, then the production flow concept leaves out something that is felt to be important. A more inclusive concept of income is desired.

The Accretion to Wealth Concept

According to the *accretion to wealth* concept, an individual's income consists of the change in his net worth during the accounting period plus the amount spent on consumption during this period. Thus, it extends the consumption-is-income view by adding net worth change to the annual accounting of consumption. The accretion view says, in effect, that if net worth at the end of the period is greater than net worth at the start of the period, income has been received, or something has taken place relevant to the ability to pay taxes. Reductions in net worth would mean that income would be smaller than the total amount of consumption. Income could be zero if all consumption spending were financed out of net worth. Negative incomes could be reported if the decline in net worth exceeded the amount of consumption expenditure. Thus, the accretion concept is broader than either the consumption or the production concepts of income and, unlike the consumption view, which would generate incentives for saving, the accretion view is indifferent to the manner in which funds are expended.

The implementation of a tax on the basis of the accretion concept would require an annual report of consumption expenditure similar to that required for implementation of the consumption concept. All receipts would have to be accounted for, with deductions permitted for funds expended for nonconsumption purposes. In addition, the accretion approach would require the submission of an annual net worth statement. Capital gains and losses would be accounted annually, without regard to whether the gains or losses were realized through actual sales transactions. Administration and compliance undoubtedly would be complicated by the necessity of evaluating assets in the absence of actual market transactions.

The accretion to wealth concept of income is attractive because it is neutral so far as the various sources and possible dispositions of income are concerned. This neutrality means that an accretion-based tax would introduce rela-

---

[3] Stock value increases that arise from retained earnings generated during the accounting period are a different matter and would be considered income under the production flow concept.

tively little distortion into the economic decisions of the taxpayer. In contrast, each of the alternative concepts biases individual decisions rather explicitly. Consumption taxes favor saving; production taxes may harm work incentives. The accretion concept also gets high marks because it is a broad measure of ability to pay and takes into account most of the factors considered relevant to taxation. Thus, it is a broadly inclusive basis for determining both horizontal and vertical equity.

ADJUSTED GROSS INCOME

The federal individual income tax does not reflect a consistent application of any of the income concepts outlined above, although it corresponds in general terms with the production flow approach. Scholars themselves are not in agreement about the correct concept of income, but the actual definition developed in the Internal Revenue Code involves more than simply a conceptual approach to what constitutes income for tax purposes. Some receipts that conceptually would be considered income are excluded because it is not administratively feasible to obtain an unambiguous reporting of the amounts involved. Practical administration suggests that reported amounts should be established through transactions which can be verified in the auditing process. Policy considerations are also apparent in the definition of income actually used in income taxation. Certain receipts which clearly would be included as income at the conceptual level and for which accurate reporting could be obtained are excluded on the basis of policy positions that single out certain types of activities for special treatment. Therefore, an understanding of the definition of income actually used in the federal income tax, which is an amount referred to as *adjusted gross income*, requires a review of specific provisions of the income tax law.

It is convenient to organize an analysis of the definition of income in tax law as a "subtraction" game, that is, to begin with a hypothetical listing of all of an individual's receipts during the income accounting period and to proceed by subtracting from this total those receipts which do not become part of adjusted gross income according to the law. This is not the procedure used in the actual preparation of a tax return, for some receipts need not be reported at all. However, starting with a hypothetical listing of all receipts has the advantage of completeness and reveals the particularly subtle type of "subtraction" that takes place when amounts need not be reported.

Receipts That Are Not Income

Two basic rules are applied in identifying receipts that can be excluded from the tax return because they are not considered to be income to the recipient. These are the *net income* rule and the *compensation* rule. The United States individual income tax is collected on the basis of net rather than gross income. This means that total receipts may be reduced by subtracting the costs of producing goods and services sold for the purpose of generating net income. These subtractions are called *business deductions*. The adjusted gross income of individual taxpayers includes only the net proceeds of activities undertaken for the purpose of profit.

The basic question in determining business deductions is whether these outlays are "ordinary and necessary" expenses of generating income. Wages paid, raw materials costs, and depreciation of plant and equipment illustrate ordinary and necessary expenses of generating income. The income tax law itself, however, may have an important influence in determining which business expenditures are in fact ordinary and necessary. This circular reasoning phenomenon arises in a competitive business environment because any expenditure, once it is allowed as deductible to one firm, will soon become ordinary and necessary for all the firms in that industry. The firm first granted the deduction will be more profitable and a more threatening competitor because of the deduction and other firms will be forced to emulate the practices of the first firm if they wish to survive in the industry. For example, lavish expenditures by salesmen in entertaining potential customers may be ordinary and necessary business expenses when the tax law permits them to be deducted, but these expenditures might not have become ordinary and necessary had the tax law denied their deductibility.

Problems also arise in determining whether or not an individual is actually engaged in business for profit and in segregating expenditures made in business-related ventures from those made for private consumption purposes. "Hobby farms" are a classic illustration of the problem. A person with taxable income from other sources may also engage in farming and contend that this activity is undertaken for the purpose of generating net income. But "purpose" is extremely difficult to establish in some instances. In the hobby farm situation, agricultural or animal husbandry activities may in fact be undertaken for pleasure rather than for profit, and if they result in operating losses rather than in profits, the losses may be deducted from other income with the result that the government, in effect, shares the costs of the individual's hobby or consumption activity. The extent to which the government shares the costs of the hobby farm or similar activities depends on the tax bracket in which the taxpayer finds himself, so that hobby farms are more tempting to high-income than to low-income taxpayers.

The compensation rule was outlined earlier in explaining the production flow concept of income. The rule states that receipts which are compensation for services rendered shall be treated as income to the recipient while other receipts, that is, those not in compensation for services rendered, shall not be treated as income. Receipts of gifts or inheritances clearly are excluded from income by the compensation rule and become merely transfers of wealth among individuals. These are neither taxable to the recipient nor deductible to the person from whom the funds were received. Once again, administrative problems can arise in determining whether particular receipts are compensation for services rendered. Scholarships that require no qualifying services from the recipient are not income for tax purposes, although assistantships, which require that the recipient perform certain services, are taxable income. Prizes won by contestants on television quiz shows are taxable as income because the contestant performed a service related to receiving the prize. Lottery and gambling winnings are income, as are tips and gratuities received by providers of personal services.

Receipts Without a Transaction

Compensation for services may be realized even if no transaction takes place between separate individuals. The concept of a receipt without a transaction is subtle yet important, because receipts of this sort are *not* subject to income tax although the amounts involved are substantial and their exclusion has important effects on the economy. In common terminology, do it yourself activities illustrate the phenomenon of receipts without a transaction. A person may grow food for family consumption, construct furniture in the basement, build additions to his home, or perform his own auto maintenance all without subjecting himself to income tax.

Housekeeping services provided by a member of the family are a leading example of income without a transaction. These services could command significant compensation in the market, yet the real income generated is not subject to taxation because no transaction takes place. The exclusion of this income from taxation is a subsidy to do it yourself housekeeping and probably has been a factor in confining women to domestic servitude. If the homemaker chooses to take wage employment instead of serving the household directly, the earnings from the wage job are subject to taxation. In this situation, deductions are allowed for expenditures made to hire replacement household help, and the earnings of the replacement are taxable. This deduction for household help when both spouses are employed tempers the restrictive effects on job choice inherent in the exclusion of the do it yourself income, but the remaining effect undoubtedly is substantial.

The net rental value of owner-occupied homes provides another illustration of a receipt not subjected to taxation because no transaction takes place. The homeowner is a do it yourself landlord. If the provision of housing were carried out through a market landlord-tenant transaction, the net rental income of the landlord (rental receipts minus the costs of the facilities rented) would be subject to income tax. Therefore, the exclusion from income taxation of the net rental value of owner-occupied homes injects a bias in favor of home ownership. It sometimes is contended that the heavy property tax responsibilities homeowners bear offset their income tax advantages, but tenant-occupied dwellings also carry property tax liabilities which are included in the rent paid by the tenant.

Many other examples of the receipts without a transaction phenomenon could be cited. Most durable goods items generate net income streams that escape income taxation when the consumer is also the owner. As a practical matter, the reason for excluding receipts without a transaction from income taxation is the great difficulty of trying accurately to measure the amount of such income. Market transactions provide an impersonal and reasonably unambiguous measure of the value received, and this is an essential ingredient in practical income taxation. In the absence of market transactions, estimates of value would have to be used and these probably would be difficult to establish (except perhaps in the case of the net rental value of owner-occupied housing, where established markets often exist for reasonably comparable properties). There is also the likelihood that many do it yourself activities, in fact, are leisure activities and have not been undertaken primarily for the purpose of gaining income. There is little sentiment in favor of taxing leisure activity. But the fact remains that the exclusion of receipts without a transaction probably introduces some distortion in the allocation of resources and that this distortion probably is in the direction of reducing the efficiency of resource use. For example, if tax considerations prompt a successful lawyer to take time off to paint his own home rather than stay on the job and earn money to hire a painter, it is probable that inefficient resource use has occurred.

Nonmoney Receipts

The fact that a receipt is in goods or services rather than in money does not prevent it from being potentially taxable. If the receipt is a compensation for services rendered and is not qualified for exclusion on some other ground, it must be reported by the taxpayer at its *fair market value*. At first glance, the fair market value rule seems reasonable enough. However, a closer examination suggests that this may constitute excessive taxation for some people, at least in comparison with those who receive their compensation in money. Money is worth more than any specific good of equal market value. The difference is the value of the *choice* the possession of money provides to the individual. Had the individual received the market value of the good in money instead of in the physical form of the good, he might have chosen to purchase a different item that to him was more valuable. Thus, the requirement that income "in kind" be reported at its fair market value can lead to differential treatment among individuals (unequals being treated as if they were equal) and result in some overstatement of income.

Fringe Benefits

Fringe benefits are nonmoney receipts employees receive from employers that are not reportable as income by the employee. Thus, the treatment of fringe benefits violates the rule that nonmoney receipts must be reported at fair market value. In fact, the fringe benefit exceptions to the nonmoney income rule are considerably more important than the rule itself. Enormous amounts of employee benefits regularly are excused from income taxation under the fringe benefit rubric. Employees receive life insurance, health and accident insurance, retirement annuities, and many other benefits. These constitute an important part of the compensation package negotiated between employers and employees. Most of these benefits are excused from income taxation.

The preferential treatment for fringe benefits has its origin in the difficulty of distinguishing between compensation to the employee for services rendered to the employer and the working conditions or facilities provided by the employer. For example, when an employer provides well-lighted, well-ventilated, and otherwise pleasant working conditions for employees, it is unlikely that this would be considered compensation for services rendered by the employees. Convenient toilet facilities are not fringe benefits. They are working conditions. But the idea of working conditions need not stop here. The employer may find that the provision of cafeteria services, parking facilities, and in-plant medical services reduces working time lost, facilitates the scheduling of work shifts, and so on. Employees may benefit from these facilities even though they are installed primarily for the convenience of the employer and for the purpose of increasing the profitability of the business. But the convenience of the employer idea need not stop here either. For example, it may benefit the employer to have all employees equipped with certain safety clothing, and it may be more convenient for the employer to provide these items directly rather than to require that the employee acquire them for himself. Even housing may be provided to some employees (such as hospital interns) whose continuous ready availability is important to the employer.

A breakthrough in the evolution of the fringe benefit idea came when tax-exempt status (on the employee's tax return) was given to employer contributions to insurance programs in which employees were beneficiaries. The Social Security Act required employer contributions to the trust fund established to provide retirement benefits to employees. The amount of the employer's contribution was related to the amount of pay received by the employee, but the employee did not have the option of accepting direct pay in place of the employer's social security retirement contribution. Participation in the retirement program became a condition of employment, and the employer's contribution was not considered compensation for purposes of income tax. With the pattern thus established, the extension of similar treatment to other employer-financed fringe benefit programs was a relatively small step.

The main point about the tax treatment of fringe benefits is that these nonmoney receipts are compensation for services and would have been taxable had it not been for the particular form in which the compensation was made. The preferential tax treatment of fringe benefits has been a strong force in the great expansion of this type of compensation. The fringe benefit package has become an important part of all labor-management contract negotiations, and the exclusion of fringe benefits from taxation has caused a major erosion of the tax base. The result has been higher rates of tax on the remaining taxable income.

Resource allocation is undoubtedly altered by the exclusion of fringe benefits from taxation, since people probably buy different things through the fringe benefit route than they would have had their compensation been paid in cash. But the alternative of actually requiring the reporting of fringe benefits for tax purposes would pose difficult administrative problems. Evaluation would be difficult in some situations, such as when an employee's entitlement to retirement benefits is conditional on some specified term of service with the employer which, of course, cannot be determined at the time the employer's contribution to the retirement fund is made.

Tax-Sheltered Retirement Programs

Tax-sheltered retirement programs for self-employed persons are a natural outgrowth of the treatment given to retirement programs financed by employers. Clearly, equal treatment of equals requires that the advantages provided for one group should not be denied to another group. Thus, the tax laws include provisions that excuse from current taxation amounts (up to a limit) an individual sets aside for his own retirement.

Tax-sheltered retirement programs provide only a postponement of tax rather than an outright exclusion. When the individual retires and begins to collect the benefits from his retirement program (ordinarily in monthly annuity payments), the payments will become subject to taxation. But the postponement of tax is of considerable benefit to the taxpayer. He will undoubtedly find himself in a lower bracket after retirement, so that the postponement has moved income out of higher brackets and into lower ones. Also, the amount of money the individual can put into the retirement fund in the first place is greater because the tax collector has not extracted money before the investment was made. This means that more money will be at work earning interest before retirement and that the final proceeds of the retirement program will be greater.

To some extent, a similar sheltering of interest income takes place even in life insurance contracts for which the premium payments are not tax sheltered. As the individual pays regular premiums to the insurance company, the company invests the funds, interest is earned, and the cash value of the individual's policy increases. But the cash value increase is not income for tax purposes. When a life insurance policy matures (at the death of the insured), none of the proceeds is taxable as income. The components of life insurance proceeds include (a) a return of the insured's own money paid as premiums and on which income tax has already been collected, (b) the interest earned on these funds during the time the policy was in force, and (c) perhaps some pure insurance amount if the individual died sooner than normal life expectancy would have indicated. The difficulty of untangling the various components in the life insurance proceeds package is a strong administrative reason for the exclusion of the interest component. It also results in some favoritism: the individual who buys pure term insurance and chooses to carry out his own savings program finds that program subject to normal income taxation.

Privileged Sources of Income

Some income sources have all the earmarks of taxability but nevertheless are not subjected to income tax. That is, these receipts are compensation for services rendered, they are received in cash, and there are no strong administrative considerations that might argue against their taxation. Income from these sources is excluded on grounds of public policy rather than on grounds of administrative necessity.

Interest on state and local bonds. Interest received on bonds issued by state or local governments is not subject to income tax. This exclusion reflects a federal government policy of assisting state and local governments in their financial operations. It originated in the belief that it would be unconstitutional for one sovereign government to tax an instrumentality of another sovereign government. This *immunities doctrine* arose out of the ruling of the Supreme Court in the famous case of *McCulloch* v. *Maryland* (1819), which dealt with an attempt by Maryland to tax banking operations conducted by the federal government.

The argument was advanced that "the power to tax is the power to destroy" and that therefore the instrumentalities of one sovereign government should be immune from taxation by another sovereign government. Bond interest, along with the salaries of government employees, thus was excused from taxation by another sovereign government.

The immunities doctrine was respected by the federal and the state governments for over one hundred years. In 1938, however, the Supreme Court held that the salaries of state and local government employees were subject to the federal income tax. The argument was that the immunities doctrine did not prevent taxation by another sovereign government so long as the tax itself was a general one imposed on all incomes of a certain type and did not single out a specific source for punitive taxation. Federal income tax was collected on salaries of state and local government employees, but taxability was not extended to interest paid on state and local bonds, even though this exclusion no longer rested on the immunities argument. The continued exclusion of state and local bond interest from federal income taxation therefore became an expression of policy rather than a requirement for constitutionality.

The exclusion of bond interest from federal income taxation gives state and local governments a subsidy because it enables these governments to sell bonds at lower rates of interest than would be necessary if the interest were taxable. The effectiveness of the subsidy depends upon the tax rate that would be imposed if the interest were not excluded, and this tax rate, in turn, depends on the tax rate bracket of the purchaser of the bonds. For example, the tax saving conveyed by the exclusion is greater for bond purchasers in the 50 percent marginal tax bracket than it is for bond purchasers in the 20 percent bracket. This results in a *class price* for state and local government bonds. For a bond with a given maturity value paying a given dollar amount of periodic interest, the amount willingly paid by a high-bracket taxpayer to purchase it will be greater than the amount willingly paid by a low-bracket taxpayer. Therefore, most state and local government bonds are held by persons in the upper income tax brackets.

Criticism of the exclusion of state and local bond interest from federal income taxation focuses on the fact that it reduces the progressivity of the income tax itself (with some high-income persons paying little tax because of their utilization of this tax avoidance device) and on the contention that the interest exclusion is an inefficient way to convey a subsidy to state and local governments. The inefficient subsidy argument suggests that some of the government tax loss arising from the exclusion goes to the individuals who purchase the bonds rather than to the governments that sell them. Specifically, if the volume of state and local bonds issued is so great as to fill up the purchasing inclinations of the highest-bracket taxpayer group, then somewhat higher interest rates (lower purchase prices) will have to be offered in order to make the bonds attractive to persons in somewhat lower brackets. Since these higher yields will be enjoyed by the top-bracket purchasers as well, some fraction of the federal subsidy is captured by the top-bracket bond purchasers rather than by the bond-issuing governments.

Concern over this situation has led to proposals for the replacement of the exclusion of interest with some more direct assistance to state and local debt financing. Since the revenue loss to the federal treasury resulting from the exclusion probably exceeds the subsidy realized by the issuing governments, a direct subsidy could accomplish the desired objective at lower cost and without the erosion of income tax progressivity inherent in the present system. However, state and local officials have been reluctant to support such reform, perhaps out of concern that reform would eventually lead to elimination of the subsidy itself.

Exclusion of dividends received. Another type of income excluded from income tax because of its source is the first $100 of dividends an individual receives from domestic corporations. There is no question that these receipts are income. The rationale for granting the exclusion is that the simultaneous existence of a tax on individual income (including dividends) and a tax on the corporate net income out of which the dividends are paid is double taxation. Although uncertainty about the actual incidence of the corporation tax raises some doubt about the extent of the actual double taxation, some double taxation of corporate dividends probably does happen and the exclusion of $100 of these dividends from the individual income tax provides some correction. However, the $100 limit is arbitrary. To the extent that dividends are subjected to double taxation, the extra burden presumably extends to all dividends received by an individual and not merely to the first $100. In this sense, a more reasonable approach might be to exclude a fraction of all dividend income from individual income tax, with the fraction determined according to the supposed extent of the double tax element. At one time, the dividend exclusion was accompanied by a credit against individual income tax liability calculated at 4 percent of the dividends received in excess of the excluded portion.

Capital Gains and Losses

Capital gains or losses arise when the value of assets changes during the time they are held by an individual or company. Under an accretion to wealth approach to income taxation, capital gains and losses would be reported for tax purposes as they accrued and would be subject to full taxation. In the federal income tax, however, capital gains and losses are reported only when they are "realized" through a sales transaction. A *capital gain* in realized when an asset is sold for an amount greater than its tax value or "basis" as carried on the tax records of the taxpayer. The tax value or basis is the amount at which the asset was valued when originally acquired, reduced by the amount of any tax deductions claimed on the asset (such as for depreciation) during the time it was owned by the taxpayer. When the sale price exceeds this basis, a capital gain is realized. If the sale price is less than this basis, a capital loss is realized.

Special treatment is accorded capital gains realized on assets owned by the taxpayer for one year or longer. These are called long-term capital gains to distinguish them from short-term capital gains, which arise when assets have been held for less than one year. In preparing his tax return, the taxpayer must bring together all his long-term gains and losses and determine his net long-term gain or loss. He also must bring together all his short-term gains or losses. Special treatment is allowed on the amount by which net long-term gains exceed net short-term losses.[4] The special treatment consists of the option of (a) claiming a deduction equal to half the net long-term capital gain or (b) making a separate calculation of the tax liability on net long-term capital gains at the tax rate of 25 percent on the first $50,000 of long-term gain. The effect of these options is that net long-term capital gains are taxable at one-half the tax rate applied at the margin on ordinary income of the taxpayer, and often at a rate of only 25 percent. If the taxpayer realizes a net long-term capital loss for the year, the loss is deductible against other income up to a limit, with the provision that unused capital loss deductions may be carried over for deduction in other tax accounting periods.

Preferential treatment. The treatment given capital gains is one of the most controversial aspects of the federal income tax. It is apparent that taxation at half ordinary income marginal rates or at a preferential rate of 25 percent is a powerful incentive device, especially for taxpayers in the higher income brackets who have both the means to engage in capital asset operations and the tax incentives to do so. Preferential treatment of capital gains encourages investments in growth industry projects and thus may stimulate investment and economic growth, but it also provides a temptation to discover devices that can convert ordinary income into capital gains. Examples of the latter include undistributed profits and stock option plans. The progressivity of the income tax is severely moderated by the preferential treatment of capital gains, which has become the dominant tax avoidance route for high-income taxpayers.

The realization rule. In analyzing the preferential treatment of capital gains, it is convenient to separate the consequences of the realization requirement from the more general question of whether capital gains should or should not be subjected to taxation. Many of the problems and some of the arguments for preferential treatment arise from the requirement that gains and losses be reported only when they are realized. Administrative necessity (or convenience) is the argument that supports the realization requirement, since an annual reporting of gains and losses as they accrue would involve sometimes debatable estimates of value. But realizations may be manipulated for tax purposes, and it is not obvious that annual accounting of accrued gains and losses should be ruled out as administratively infeasible. Many assets, such as securities which are regularly traded in established markets, are continuously evaluated with an accuracy that would be adequate for tax purposes.

Several arguments for preferential treatment of capital gains arise directly from the realization rule, because gains that have been accruing over a number of years may be subjected to taxation in the single year of realization. Under a

---

[4] This method of calculation helps to explain why securities transactions that take place toward the end of the tax year may be motivated by tax considerations. Net long-term capital gains receive preferential treatment. On the other hand, capital losses may be set off against other income that would be taxed in full if they are realized in a tax year in which the taxpayer has no capital gain. Thus, taxes may be reduced if realizations are timed to separate gains from losses.

progressively graduated rate structure, taxation in one year of gains that have accrued over several years will penalize receipts from this source, since a portion of the gain may be subjected to rates of tax which would not have been experienced had the tax been imposed year by year as the gain accrued. If gains were taxable as they accrue, this problem would not exist, but in a system with both graduated rates and the realization rule, some allowance for the problem is appropriate. However, an effective averaging system for irregular income would be a more appropriate correction than the granting of preferential rates, since irregularity of income is not unique to capital gain recipients.

Inflation is also cited as an argument for preferential treatment of gains that have accrued over a number of years. If the gain has arisen purely as result of a fall in the value of money (inflation), then no real increase in wealth has taken place. The realization procedure focuses attention on the inflation problem but, once again, it should be recognized that other sources of income, such as wages, profits, interest, and rent, are also influenced by inflation. Inflation relief for capital gains through preferential tax rates violates horizontal neutrality unless similar relief is extended to other forms of income.

An especially controversial aspect of the realization process existed prior to 1977 in connection with property transferred by gift or bequest. Unrealized capital gains were forgiven for tax purposes when these transfers took place, since they were not an occasion for realization of gains. The tax value or basis of the asset in the hands of the new owner was the market value at the time of the transfer, but the difference between the current market value and the tax value or basis in the hands of the old owner was excused entirely from income tax.

The Tax Revision Act of 1976 changed this by requiring that the basis of property received by gift or bequest shall be the old owner's cost or the value of the property on December 31, 1976, whichever is greater. Thus, capital gains accruing after that date will not escape income tax. However, the death or gift transfer does not constitute realization. Therefore, income tax on the gain is not taxable to the old owner and will become taxable to the new owner only when a regular realization takes place. Thus, capital gains tax can be postponed and perhaps moved into a lower tax bracket by these transfers.

Nonparallel treatment of capital losses. The nonparallel treatment of capital losses as compared to capital gains is also related to the realization procedure. Net long-term capital losses are deductible against other income only up to the limit of $3,000 in a single tax year, with unused capital losses carried over for deduction in other tax years. This constraint is imposed because the timing of loss realizations can be manipulated by the taxpayer in order to coincide with tax years in which other income would face unusually high marginal tax rates. The requirement that capital losses be spread over several years reduces the temptation to manipulate loss realizations for the purpose of reducing tax on ordinary income, but the result is a nonparallel treatment of capital gains and losses. If the realization rule were abandoned in favor of annual taxation on the basis of accrued gains and losses, the argument for such nonparallel treatment would no longer be persuasive. The existance of nonparallel treatment injects a bias into the economy that may discourage risk taking.

Should capital gains be taxed as income? Aside from the complications that arise because of the realization rule, the basic question of whether or not capital gains ought to be taxed as income focuses attention, once again, on the concept of income appropriate for taxation. Capital gains would not constitute income according to the consumption concept. Under the production flow concept, capital gains would be income only to the extent that they arose through the retention of earnings generated during the tax accounting period. On the other hand, full taxation of capital gains and full allowance for capital losses would be appropriate under the accretion to wealth concept of income.

SUMMARY

This chapter has reviewed three abstract concepts of income and defined the components of *adjusted gross income* as utilized in the federal individual income tax. The approach to adjusted gross income was through a subtraction game: from a hypothetical listing of all receipts during a tax year were subtracted those portions of these receipts not considered income for tax purposes or excluded because of policy considerations. However, the subtraction game is not over when adjusted gross income has been established. Tax is not levied directly on adjusted gross income, but instead is levied on net income subject to tax, which is the amount remaining after personal deductions and exemptions have been allowed. The subtraction game will be continued in the next chapter, which examines personal deductions, personal exemptions, and the rates of tax imposed on net income subject to tax.

SUGGESTED READINGS

SIMONS, HENRY C. *Personal Income Taxation* (Chicago: The University of Chicago Press, 1938).

SIMONS, HENRY C. *Federal Tax Reform* (Chicago: The University of Chicago Press, 1950).

KALDOR, NICHOLAS. *An Expenditure Tax* (London: Allen and Unwin, 1955).

BREAK, GEORGE F., and JOSEPH A. PECHMAN. *Federal Tax Reform: The Impossible Dream?* (Washington, D.C.: The Brookings Institution, 1975).

GOODE, RICHARD. *The Individual Income Tax* (Washington, D.C.: The Brookings Institution, 1976).

PECHMAN, JOSEPH A. *Federal Tax Policy* (Washington, D.C.: The Brookings Institution, 1977).

12

Individual Income Taxation: Deductions, Exemptions, and Tax Rates

Tax liabilities could be based directly on adjusted gross income if government tax policy determined that it would be desirable to do so. In other words, there is nothing inherent in the idea of income taxation itself which requires that any personal deductions or personal exemptions must be allowed. The subtractions allowed from adjusted gross income are of a distinctly different character from those necessary for the determination of adjusted gross income itself. Subtractions from total receipts such as those for the ordinary and necessary expenses of generating income are essential as long as the term "income" is taken to mean net income, which is the accepted meaning of the term. But subtractions permitted after adjusted gross income has been determined are expressions of a policy that certain portions of adjusted gross income *should* be relieved from tax. *Personal deductions* relieve income from taxation because such relief is believed to relate taxation more appropriately to ability to pay or because it is government policy to favor certain types of personal expenditure. *Personal exemptions* simply establish that a certain amount of income shall be subjected to a zero tax rate, that is, that some amount of income shall be free of tax.

PERSONAL DEDUCTIONS

The taxpayer may itemize allowable personal deductions under several classifications, such as medical expenses, contributions, interest, taxes, and casualty losses. These categories of personal deductions will be discussed below. As an alternative to itemization, the taxpayer may choose (subject to some limi-

187

tations) to claim the standard deduction, which is calculated as a percentage of adjusted gross income or as a minimum standard deduction amount. The standard deduction will be discussed after the several categories of itemized deductions have been examined.

Certain of the allowable personal deductions are best understood as refinements of ability to pay, that is, the allowance of these deductions is believed to improve the equity or fairness of the allocation of tax responsibilities among taxpayers. Other allowable personal deductions arise from policy decisions to favor or subsidize certain types of personal expenditures. Still other allowable personal deductions are difficult to rationalize under either the ability to pay or the public policy subsidy point of view, so that their inclusion in the list of allowable personal deductions can be questioned.

Medical Expenses

If an individual incurs medical expenses during a tax year, it seems reasonable to conclude that his ability to pay taxes is reduced, on this account, in comparison to an individual with equal adjusted gross income who was not faced with similar expenses. On the basis of this reasoning, the medical expense deduction is a refinement of ability to pay for tax purposes. Since most persons will incur some medical expense under normal circumstances during a tax year, the ability to pay refinement requires only that "extraordinary" medical expenses be recognized for tax deduction. Consequently, deduction is permitted only to the extent that medical expenditures exceed 3 percent of the adjusted gross income of the individual. Expenditures for medicines and drugs are also classed as medical expenditures. Since most individuals will make some expenditures for medicines and drugs during the tax period, only "extraordinary" expenditures on these items justify deduction. For medicine and drugs, only amounts exceeding 1 percent of adjusted gross income can be counted in the calculation.

The medical expense deduction is firmly rooted in the ability to pay philosophy of taxation. Nevertheless, some controversy exists about certain aspects of the allowance. Since the recognition of medical expenses takes the form of a deduction rather than a direct credit against tax liability, the tax saving per dollar of deductible medical expense is greater for the high-bracket taxpayer than for the low-bracket taxpayer. The deduction approach is used on the grounds that the recognition of medical expenses is a refinement of ability to pay rather than an attempt to reimburse the individual for a portion of the expense incurred. The tax credit approach would provide a workable alternative if the rationale were that the government wished to provide a direct subsidy for medical care and medicines. Even as it is applied, the medical expense deduction can be described as a kind of "back-door" health insurance system, for, in this way, a significant portion of medical bills are paid by the government. A direct health insurance system, however, probably would permit a more generous allowance to low-income than to high-income people, which would be the reverse of the effect of the existing system.

Medical expense deductions are allowed only to the extent that these expenditures are not covered by insurance. However, the premiums paid to purchase health and hospital insurance coverage are includable in the itemization of medical expenditures, and half of the premium payment is not subject to the 3 percent of adjusted gross income limitation.

Casualty Losses

Theft, lost items, damages from fire and wind, automobile accidents, and similar casualties can reduce an individual's ability to pay taxes to the extent that these losses are not compensated through insurance claims. If an individual experiences casualty losses during the tax year, a deduction may be claimed for the amount of such losses not compensated by insurance.

As a refinement of ability to pay, the deduction for casualty losses is similar to that for medical expense, since the individual experiencing such losses clearly has a lesser tax-paying ability than one with equal adjusted gross income who did not experience an equivalent loss. The chief criticism of the casualty loss deduction is that no deduction is permitted for the premiums paid to carry insurance against such losses. In effect, the tax system encourages individuals not to carry casualty insurance since deduction is allowed for uninsured losses, but no allowance is permitted for the insurance premiums. Precedent exists for the deductibility of insurance premiums, since premiums for health insurance are allowable as part of the medical expense deduction.

Charitable Contributions

An individual who contributes to his church or to other recognized charitable organizations may deduct the full amount of these contributions up to a limit determined as a percentage of his adjusted gross income. A contribution must be distinguished from a gift, however. If the recipient of the transfer is not a recognized charitable, religious, or educational organization, the transfer is termed a gift and no deduction is permitted. Gifts are, in fact, subject to a separate tax imposed upon the donor.

The deductibility of charitable contributions is an expression of public policy; it is not a refinement of ability to pay. Contributions are voluntary and the contributor presumably enjoys some satisfaction from having put his funds to charitable uses. The public policy basis for the deduction of charitable contributions contends that there are collective consumption aspects to the goods and services provided by religious, educational, and philanthropic organizations and that the government has chosen to assist in the financing of these activities through the vehicle of the personal deduction rather than through direct budgetary expenditures. That is, they are tax expenditures rather than expenditures made through normal appropriations legislation.

The conclusion that the allowance for charitable contributions is a subsidy program rather than a refinement of ability to pay raises an interesting question about the appropriateness of the deductions approach as compared to the alternative approach of granting a tax credit for charitable contributions. The deductions approach is appropriate when the objective is a refinement of ability to pay, since tax liabilities and the progressivity of the tax should be based on ability to pay after the adjustments necessary to measure this ability have been made. But it is not obvious that tax expenditures (subsidies for particular personal expenditures) should be handled through the deduction method.

The deduction method means that the tax saving or subsidy per dollar of contribution is greater for high-bracket taxpayers than it is for low-bracket taxpayers, that is, that the net cost of supporting charitable operations (the total contribution minus the tax saving) per dollar of contribution is higher for low-bracket taxpayers than it is for high-bracket taxpayers. This injects a *regressive* element into the financing of charitable services when these services are viewed as financed through tax expenditures. The funding of charities is likely to depend heavily upon higher-income persons in any event, but the deduction method tends to increase the role of high incomes in the funding and control of charities. If the favored educational, philanthropic, and religious organizations are, in fact, providing goods and services of a collective nature, a broadening of public participation would appear appropriate. A tax credit approach, which would permit a portion of the contribution to be subtracted directly from actual tax liability, merits consideration as a device for subsidizing charitable contributions.

It is appropriate to recognize that the subsidy involved in charitable deductions (or credits) is a subsidy to the educational, philanthropic, or religious activities themselves rather than a subsidy to the taxpayer. If these tax expenditures are legitimate, they presumably pass the test of being collectively demanded services and would qualify for direct budgetary support if the deduction or credit method were not employed. From this point of view, the tax saving to the contributing individual only partially reimburses him for the contribution made to finance collective services. His net contribution (total contribution minus tax saving) is a voluntary contribution that finances services consumed collectively by the entire community.

As a practical matter, it is difficult to determine the extent to which particular organizations in fact are providers of genuine collective services. What criteria should be employed in determining whether a particular organization qualifies as an appropriate recipient of tax expenditures? Many organizations combine the provision of collective services ("good works") with services of private benefit to their own members ("good times"), and an acceptable dividing line between approved organizations and those not approved is difficult to identify and maintain. Also, the deductibility of contributions to religious organizations approaches a violation of the church-state separation doctrine. Although it operates to help established religion in general rather than any particular sect, it does favor established or organized religion as distinguished from an individual's private religion or atheism as a religion.

The Deduction for Taxes

General taxes paid to state and local governments are deductible in determining an individual's net income subject to tax. An attempt to determine whether this personal deduction is a refinement of ability to pay or whether it is a public policy subsidy intended to assist the financing of state and local collective services poses subtle and difficult questions. On ability to pay grounds, it can be contended that an individual's ability to pay federal taxes arises only after he has complied with the compulsory obligations imposed on him by his state and local governments (and likewise that his ability to pay state and local taxes arises only after he has met the demands of the federal government). However, the individual has some power through political processes to influence the amount of local taxes he is required to pay. Therefore, these payments are in some degree voluntary, which distinguishes them from the medical expense and casualty loss deductions as refinements of ability to pay. Moreover, in a well-functioning state or local community, it is expected that benefits are received from government services to match the tax costs borne by the citizen. From this benefit-received viewpoint, state and local payments have no more claim for deduction than would a claim for the deduction of expenses for food, clothing, or shelter. In fact, special property assessments imposed by local governments for the construction of streets and gutters are recognized as benefit-received taxes and are not allowed as a deduction in determining the federal tax base. Gasoline taxes also carry a strong benefit-received relation but are deductible in the federal income tax.

Public policy is perhaps a more persuasive rationale for the deduction of taxes than ability to pay. The deductibility of state and local taxes reduces the net burden of these taxes and assists state and local financing. If assistance is the objective, an allowance for state and local taxes is not unreasonable. Once again, the question arises of whether a deduction or a tax credit is the more appropriate device to employ for this sort of tax expenditure. The deduction approach provides a greater tax saving per dollar of state and local tax paid for high-bracket taxpayers than for low-bracket taxpayers and thus reduces the progressivity of the federal tax and, indirectly, the progressivity of state and local taxes.

Of course, state and local governments may respond by increasing the progressivity of their taxes compared to the progressivity that might prevail in the absence of the deduction for these taxes on the federal return, although there is no way to determine the extent to which this may actually take place. The whole question of the appropriate degree of progressivity hinges on whether taxes are viewed as related to benefits received or whether they are instruments for the redistribution of income. If redistributive taxation is seen as a responsibility of the federal government and if state and local taxes are accepted as indicators of benefits received from services rendered by these governments, there would appear to be little justification for permitting higher-income citizens to receive state and local services at a lower tax price than is effectively charged, per dollar of benefit received, to lower-income citizens. This line of reasoning supports a tax credit method of subsidizing state and local governments rather than the deduction method of tax expenditure.

Property taxes are an important part of the local taxes that are deductible on the federal tax return, and it sometimes is contended that this deduction introduces favoritism for homeowners and penalizes those who rent residential property. However, the deduction of property taxes is also allowed (as a business deduction) to the landlord, thus reducing the cost of providing rental property. In a competitive housing market, the cost reductions occasioned by the deductibility of property taxes would be passed along to the tenant in the form of lower rent charges. The federal income tax may indeed discriminate between homeowners and renters, but the deduction for property taxes paid is not the root of the problem. The root source of the discrimination lies in the failure to tax the implicit net rental income of owner-occupied housing. However, the property tax deduction does contribute to difficulties connected with the standard deduction, which will be discussed shortly.

Deductions for Interest Paid

If an individual itemizes personal deductions, he may claim a deduction of the full amount of interest paid during the tax year. It is important to note that the deduction applies to all interest paid,[1] and not merely to interest paid as an expense in income-generating activities, which are deductible under the business expense category. Interest on home mortages, on bank loans, and on installment credit illustrate the various consumption aspects of the interest deduction.

An adequate rationale for the deductiblility of interest paid on consumption loans is not readily apparent. At first glance one might suppose the deduction to be some adjunct to the ability to pay rationale for progressive taxation. If a person's income is so low that he is forced to incur debt, one might argue that some allowance is justified in terms of ability to pay. But if a person's income is very low, the interest deduction is of no use since there may be no net tax liability in any case and no advantage arises from the deduction. It is also relevant to recognize that the bulk. of the interest payments in the United States are made by persons with middle-range incomes rather than by persons with low incomes, perhaps because the higher income carries with it the credit rating which makes it possible to negotiate the loan. Equity notions are strained still further when it is recalled that the *imputed* (that is, income without exchange) income which accrues to the owner of durable goods such as owner-occupied residences is not subjected to income tax.

An alternative rationale for the interest deduction may be that it is intended to be an encouragement for debt-financed expenditures. When a person undertakes to finance a consumption expenditure with borrowed funds, he is making a decision about the time pattern of his consumption. He is choosing to increase his consumption now and to repay the debt at a later date through reductions in his consumption expenditure at that time. Perhaps the person expects that his income will be greater at the future date so that the reduction in consumption required to repay the debt and to pay the interest will be less burdensome than would the present foregoing of consumption. Similarly, the person may judge that his want for the consumption item is greater now than it will be at some future date so that the benefits received through the advancement of the date of consumption is sufficient to justify payment of the necessary interest. Thus, if the interest paid deduction is seen as an expression of a public policy incentive program, it would appear to be a policy favoring the advancement of consumption.

Neither the ability to pay nor the incentive-subsidy rationale provides

---

[1] Interest paid on money borrowed to purchase tax-exempt securities is not deductible.

strong support for the deductibility of interest expenditures. Interest expenses clearly should be deductible when incurred to finance undertakings that will generate taxable income. These are ordinary business expense deductions. But when the interest expenditure is not related to the generation of taxable income, there is little justification for allowing its deduction for income tax purposes.

Mortgage interest on owner-occupied residences accounts for a major portion of the interest deduction claims. The interest deduction itself is not responsible for discrimination between homeowners and tenants, since the interest cost of providing rented property is also deductible as a business expense for the landlord. But the deductibility of mortgage interest combined with the exclusion of the net rental value of owner-occupied homes does permit owner-tenant discrimination.

THE STANDARD DEDUCTION

The taxpayer has the option of claiming personal deductions in an itemized manner as outlined above or of claiming a *standard deduction* in an amount equal to 16 percent of adjusted gross income up to limit of 2400 on a return for a single individual or 2800 on a joint return. Provision is also made for a *minimum standard deduction* of $1700 on a return for a single individual and $2100 on a joint return. In effect, the minimum standard deduction permits a deduction of more than 16 percent of adjusted gross income and is particularly relevant to low-income persons.

Since the standard deduction is available as an option, it is expected that the taxpayer will utilize this provision only if it will provide a larger deduction than would be provided by itemizing. If itemized deductions exceed 16 percent of adjusted gross income, or if they exceed the maximum dollar allowances, then deductions will be itemized, since that approach will minimize the tax liability.

The standard deduction was established when personal exemptions were lowered and the individual income tax became a mass tax with the advent of World War II. Its intent was to simplify the reporting and auditing aspects of income tax compliance and administration in order to accommodate the greatly increased number of returns filed. Unfortunately, the advantages were obtained in exchange for sacrifices in equity, specifically in the sense that equity requires the unequal treatment of taxpayers who are unequal to one another in some respect considered relevant to tax obligations.

Nonneutrality of the Standard Deduction

Among taxpayers who utilize the standard deduction, differences in medical expenditures, casualty losses, contributions, taxes, and interest payments have no impact on the final tax obligation. That is, if the sum total of these allowable deductions does not add up to 16 percent of adjusted gross income or to the minimum standard deduction, they are ignored for tax purposes, presumably on the ground that the refinements in tax liabilities which would result from specific consideration of these differences would not be worth the administrative and compliance costs of recognizing them. From the point of view of the taxpayer who utilizes the standard deduction, the government is providing no recognition for any extraordinary medical expenses incurred or for payments of state and local taxes and interest, and is providing no incentive in regard to his charitable contributions.

A particularly disturbing aspect of this nonneutrality situation becomes apparent when attention is focused on the factors that help to determine whether or not an individual will itemize deductions. Home ownership probably is one of the most important factors influencing this choice. An individual who owns his own residence is in a position to claim itemized deductions for property taxes paid and for the interest paid on the home mortgage. These two items alone may approach or exceed the amount available under the standard deduction, so that itemization clearly will be the preferred choice. With the standard deduction equivalent either wholly or partially achieved through property taxes and interest payments, the taxpayer is in a position to claim the additional allowances for extraordinary medical expenses, casualty losses, contributions, other taxes, other interest, and the miscellaneous deductions allowed for other expenditures. Thus, the ability to pay refinements and the incentives to favored items of private expenditure are more likely to be available to the homeowner than to the person who occupies rented property. A pattern thereby arises in the incidence of the nonneutrality consequences of the standard deduction. People who reside in rented properties are more likely to experience nonneutral tax treatment than are people who own their own residences. A similar pattern may arise between large and small families if extraordinary medical expenditures are significantly related to family size.

The point is that the nonneutrality aspects of the standard deduction arise from the lumping together of several distinct deductible items and from making tax consequences hinge on the sum total of these items. Less nonneutrality would arise if each allowable class of deduction were treated separately, which would mean the abandonment of the standard deduction.

Fiscal Illusion

Taxpayers select the standard deduction because their tax liability will be lower than it would be if they itemized. However, this tax saving is partly a fiscal illusion. The difference between the amount of the standard deduction and the amount that would have been deductible through itemization is an erosion of the tax base, that is, the aggregate base for income taxation is less than it would be if the standard deduction were not allowed. This reduced tax base requires an increase in tax rates, assuming that a given total amount of revenue is to be collected from the income tax, and these higher tax rates recapture for the government some of the tax the person feels he is saving through the use of the standard deduction. The fiscal illusion experienced by the person who selects the standard deduction is not complete, however. This is because the higher tax rates necessitated by the tax-base erosion are imposed on all taxpayers, not only on those who select the standard deduction. Some of the tax saving users of the standard deduction believe they are receiving is canceled by the higher tax rates imposed on them. But some saving does accrue to them. The actual tax saving experienced by those who select the standard deduction is being funded by the increased taxes paid by those who file itemized returns.

An Alternative Approach

Convenience in compliance and administration are the chief advantages of the standard deduction. However, the procedures presently followed in allowing deductions for extraordinary medical expenditures suggest an interesting alternative that could achieve equivalent convenience advantages without the unfortunate side effects that accompany the standard deduction. Under this alternative, each of the several categories of personal deductions (medical expense, casualty losses, contributions, taxes, interest) would be calculated separately and would be allowable separately, but for each of them deductibility would be allowed only to the extent that expenditures exceeded some threshold determined as a percentage of adjusted gross income. The thresholds themselves could be set high enough so that only taxpayers who made extraordinary expenditures in a given category would find it desirable to itemize their expenditures, and their itemization would relate only to that category of expenditure.

For most taxpayers, a rather rough or approximate calculation would be sufficient to determine whether detailed itemization in any given category would be required. Many returns probably would be submitted without any itemization at all. Itemizations submitted would relate only to one or a few categories of expenditure, which would limit the amount of administrative attention required. A particularly attractive feature of this alternative would be the elimination of the nonneutralities that presently arise due to the lumping together of allowable deductions in determining whether or not to select the standard deduction. It is this lumping together that drives the wedge between homeowners and nonhomeowners in gaining recognition for their other allowable deductions.

Demise of the Standard Deduction?

The Tax Reform Act of 1976 set the *minimum* standard deduction at $1700 for single returns and at $2100 for joint returns. The *maximum* standard deduction was set at $2400 for single returns and at $2800 for joint returns. Thus, there was a range of only $700 on each type of return within which calculation of the standard deduction at 16 percent of adjusted gross income had any influence on the amount deductible. The character of the standard deduction itself changes significantly as the gap between the minimum allowable amount and the maximim allowable amount is narrowed. As the minimum and maximum amounts approach one another, the deduction increasingly assumes the character of an extra personal exemption for taxpayers who do not itemize deductions. This extra personal exemption makes no allowance for the number of dependent children in the household. The relatively narrow gap between maximum and minimum standard deductions reduces the influence of income size in determining the amount of the deduction and provides further support for the proposition, offered earlier, that the equity argument that unequals should be treated unequally is not served by the standard deduction. If the standard deduction increasingly assumes the character of an extra personal exemption, voters may cease to associate the standard deduction with the itemized personal deductions and the standard deduction may be eliminated as a step in the calculation of net income subject to tax.

PERSONAL EXEMPTIONS

The deduction of personal exemptions is the last step in the subtraction game in reporting income subject to tax. The exemption is a specified deductible amount for the taxpayer, the spouse, and each dependent. Additional exemptions are allowed for blindness of the taxpayer or spouse and for taxpayers or spouses over age 65. Various criteria are applied to determine which persons are eligible to be claimed as dependents. In general, the taxpayer must provide over half of the dependent's support during the tax year and the dependent may not be claimed as an exemption on any other tax return. There is an exception to the latter, however. Dependents who are full-time students may file their own tax returns and claim themselves as exemptions without preventing their parents from claiming them as dependents on their returns.

Rationale for Exemptions

In respect to the taxpayer and spouse, an ability to pay rationale clearly supports some allowable exemption. The exemption allowances for the taxpayer and spouse amount to a zero tax rate bracket and simply assert that no ability to pay tax exists until income (after other deductions) exceeds the specified exemption amount. It is suggested that the personal exemption amount ought to correspond with the amount of money needed to maintain some minimum standard of living. Prior to World War II, however, the dollar amount of the personal exemption was considerably higher than it is today, although the dollar figure for subsistence was considerably lower. The exemption was lowered to $500 at the start of World War II, was increased to $600 shortly after the war, and remained at that level for over twenty years in spite of great increases in the cost of living. The decision about the size of the exemption for taxpayers and spouses is a decision about the size of the zero tax rate bracket and is considered in connection with the degree of progressivity desired in the tax rate structure.

The rationale for the exemption allowance for dependents raises questions that are not encountered in respect to exemptions for taxpayer and spouse. The question is whether the exemption is a refinement in ability to pay or whether it is a subsidy to taxpayers with dependents. The ability to pay rationale implies that the taxpayer's responsibility for the support of the dependent is a fact of life beyond the control of the taxpayer. In this context, the responsibility for the support of the dependent reduces the taxpayer's ability to contribute to the financing of collective services and the exemption allowance recognizes this reduction in ability to pay. On the other hand, the subsidy rationale for the exemption allowance for dependents implies that the taxpayer does have some choice in determining the number of dependents for whom he is responsible. In this view, the exemption conveys a subsidy to those taxpayers who have chosen to undertake responsibility for the support of dependents. The granting of the exemption is an expression of a public policy designed to encourage taxpayers to assume financial responsibility for dependents. Since most dependents are children, this view holds that the exemption for dependents is a subsidy favoring the propagation of children.

The Tax Credit Alternative

Tax allowance for exemptions could be provided through a direct credit against tax liability rather than as a deduction in determining the tax base. The argument in favor of the credit system is a familiar one. Advocates point out that, under the credit system, the tax saving would be the same over all tax brackets and contend that such an arrangement would be more consistent with conventional notions of need and of ability to pay.

Ability to pay is cited by those favoring a change to the credit system and by those favoring continuation of the existing system of deductions. Therefore, a careful review of ability to pay logic is necessary to understand the issue. Those favoring continuation of the existing (deduction) approach view the personal exemption as an initial bracket in the graduated system of tax brackets. This first bracket carries a zero tax rate; these initial "subsistence" amounts have no ability to pay tax. The ability to pay tax arises only with income received above the levels of this initial bracket. When a baby is born into a family with higher income, the amount of income required for the subsistence of the family (the zero rate bracket amount) increases and the amount of income that has tax-paying ability decreases. Tax savings come off the top bracket, as is appropriate when a reduction in tax-paying ability has taken place. When the child ceases to be a dependent, tax-paying ability will increase and tax liabilities will increase, again at the top bracket end of the income column, as appropriate in a graduated tax system based on increasing ability to pay.[2]

The distinction between refinements in ability to pay, which are appropriately recognized through deductions, and tax expenditures designed to favor or subsidize certain dispositions of private funds, which are appropriately recognized through tax credits, has been apparent throughout the entire discussion of personal deductions and exemptions. The point is that the nature or purpose of each particular adjustment must be recognized in order to determine whether the deduction approach or the tax credit approach is appropriate. In the evolution of the federal income tax, the deduction approach generally has been employed and has been applied in some situations in which a tax credit would appear to have been a better choice. Perhaps the distinction between credits and deductions has not been adequately recognized in the development of the income tax.

TAX RATE STRUCTURE

Net income subject to tax is the amount that remains after the subtraction game has been played. It is the bottom line figure after allowances have been made for all exclusions, deductions, and exemptions. Using this figure, the

---

[2] Gerard M. Brannon and Elliott R. Morss, "The Tax Allowance for Dependents: Deductions Versus Credits," *National Tax Journal*, XXVI, 4 (December 1973), 599–610.

taxpayer refers to the appropriate tax rate schedule in order to determine the amount of tax liability.[3]

The Bracket System

The graduation of tax rates in the federal income tax is accomplished through the use of a system of brackets; that is, the individual's net taxable income is divided into layers and each succeeding layer of income in subjected to a higher tax rate. For example, for 1976 taxable income the initial bracket rate for a single individual was 14 percent and applied to net taxable income up to $500, the second bracket rate was 15 percent and applied to net taxable income from $501 to $1,000, etc. Higher rates are applied to higher brackets or layers of income up to the top rate of 70 percent, which applies to all net taxable income in excess of $100,000 for a single taxpayer. For taxpayers whose income does not exceed $20,000, the law provides a set of tax tables in which tax liabilities are precalculated. Thus, after the subtraction game has been completed and net taxable income has been determined, taxpayers in this income range simply consult the tax tables to discover the amount of tax payable. Taxpayers with net taxable income greater than $20,000 must calculate the amount of tax themselves, using the appropriate tax rate schedule.

The *marginal tax rate* is the rate which applies to the highest bracket or layer of income reached by the taxpayer. This marginal tax rate is important in connection with the incentive or disincentive effects of income taxation on the behavior of the individual. It determines the amount by which the individual's tax will increase if his income increases and the amount by which his tax will decrease if income decreases. High marginal tax rates may discourage people from seeking overtime work or positions which combine higher pay with greater responsibilities. They also may encourage people to develop tax avoidance opportunities to lower the amount of net income subject to tax.

The rate of tax imposed on an individual's income also can be examined from the perspective of the *average tax rate*, which is computed by dividing total tax liability by total net income subject to tax. The average tax rate is a more appropriate indicator of tax burden than the marginal tax rate, and the relation between changes in the average rate and changes in the size of net income subject to tax is a measure of the degree of progressivity in the rate structure of the income tax. The average rate is lower than the marginal rate when the graduation of rates is upward or progressive. The rate structure of the U.S. individual income tax is graduated upward, but the graduation is uneven and moderates considerably as income levels increase. Brackets are narrow at the lower end of the scale and a one-percentage-point increase in marginal rate occurs every $500, whereas brackets are $10,000 wide for taxable incomes

[3] The U.S. individual income tax is a "global" type of income tax in which income from all sources is lumped together and taxed according to a single rate schedule. This global approach to income taxation is contrasted to a "schedular" approach in which different rate schedules are used for income from different sources. Even the U.S. individual income tax has a schedular nature in the special case of long-term net capital gains, and in the earned income allowances which will be examined later. It is apparent that the global approach is better suited to a graduated or progressive tax on individuals.

between $50,000 and $100,000, with only a two-percentage-point increase in marginal rate between brackets. Graduation ceases on income above $100,000.

The *effective* tax rate is still another concept used to express the progressivity of the individual income tax. In computing the effective tax rate, the total tax liability is divided by some measure of income that is more inclusive than net income subject to tax. For example, an effective tax rate may be calculated by dividing tax liability by adjusted gross income if the purpose is to incorporate the effects of personal deductions and exemptions in the degree of progressivity of the system. Of course, the base used in computing effective tax rates is somewhat controversial. For example, including personal exemptions in the base would appear reasonable if these amounts are viewed as the first (zero rate) bracket of tax, but inclusion of deductions that are refinements of the ability to pay base (such as medical expenditures) may bring more confusion than enlightenment about the progressivity of the tax.

A still more inclusive approach to computing an effective tax rate would use a base figure even larger than adjusted gross income by including the deductions allowed for long-term capital gains and the excluded amounts of state and local bond interest income. It is apparent that calculation of effective tax rates involves questions about the proper definition of income itself. Effective rate calculations that include in the base all exemptions, deductions, and excluded capital gain and interest receipts suggest that the income tax is less progressive than it would appear to be on the basis of the average tax rate, since deductions and exclusions are proportionately of greater importance for high incomes.

Several problems arise because the rate structure of the income tax is graduated upward. Because larger aggregations of net taxable income pay a higher average rate of tax than do smaller aggregations of income, a lower total tax liability can be achieved if a single large income can be split among several separate tax returns or spread over several different tax years. The advantages of splitting or spreading income are inherent in a progressively graduated system of tax rates. Attention therefore must be given to the definition of the tax-paying unit and to provisions permitting the averaging or spreading of income over different tax years.

The Taxpaying Unit

The definition of the taxpaying unit is important when rate schedules are graduated. If the same rate schedule were required for married couples filing jointly as for single individuals, the married couple would face a serious disadvantage if each of them had taxable income. The average rate of tax on their combined income would be higher than the average rate that would apply if their incomes were reported separately. Because of this type of problem, four different tax rate schedules are included in the U.S. individual income tax law. One of these is for single individuals, a second is for married couples who file a joint return, a third is for married couples who file separate returns, and a fourth is for a head of household, that is, for a person who has family support responsibilities but who has no spouse with whom a joint return might be filed. The rate schedule for married couples filing jointly provides a correction for the tax rate effect of reporting two incomes on the same return. The head of household schedule occupies an intermediate position in terms of average tax rates between the single individual and the married couple filing jointly.

Some historical background is helpful in understanding the problem in defining the tax-paying unit in a progressively graduated individual income tax. In the United States, income and property rights are established under state rather than under federal law and some states (generally those with some Spanish law traditions) are community property states in which legal title to income and property is divided equally between spouses. Thus, married couples in these states can enjoy the advantages of splitting income even if separate individual returns are filed. To correct this situation, in 1948 the joint return was authorized for married couples. This joint return provided full splitting of income for all married couples regardless of the state of residence. But this solution gave a large tax advantage to married couples over single persons, who could not obtain the advantages of income splitting. In 1969, a new rate schedule for single persons partially relieved their disadvantage. To prevent married couples in community property states from using this new schedule, a special schedule was prescribed for married couples filing separate returns.

Although the multiple rate schedule system adopted in 1969 reduced the inequities that had prevailed prior to that time, horizontal equity problems still exist. Married couples still have some advantages over single taxpayers, and establishing fully parallel treatment among married couples themselves is complicated by the exclusion of income without a transaction, such as that generated by the housewife. Consider two married couples, each with $20,000 of taxable income. In one case, each of the spouses is employed outside the home and thereby contributes to the taxable income. In the other case, the entire taxable income is earned by one of the spouses and the other spouse devotes full time to the generation of income without a transaction, which is excluded from taxation. In real terms, these two couples are not equal in income or ability to pay tax. The couple in which both are employed outside the home has less ability to pay than the other couple. Some relief may be achieved by permitting deductions for expenses incurred to hire housekeeping help, but it is not clear that this relief results in fully equal treatment between the two households.

Fluctuating Incomes and Averaging

Incomes that fluctuate over time experience a higher average rate of tax than do incomes that are stable over time, other things being equal. This non-neutrality for fluctuating income arises from the same lumping or bunching problem discussed in relation to the tax-paying unit and splitting, although in this case the problem is related to the irregularity of income flow rather than to the definition of the tax-paying unit. The accounting period is now the problem. Professional athletes and entertainers may find their highest income concentrated into a few years. Those in occupations experiencing cyclical fluctuations, such as entrepreneurs, have fluctuating incomes. Speculative activities may result in irregular income, and professions that require an extensive period of training, such as medicine, tend to concentrate earnings in a relatively short span of years.

The solution to the irregular or fluctuating income problem lies with some form of averaging. Some relief is presently available. Special treatment is allowed for that portion of income in a given year that exceeds 120 percent of the average income over the preceding four years. The excess is termed *average-able* income, and the tax on this averageable income is calculated to be five times the tax that would be due on one-fifth of it, a procedure which removes a portion of the averageable income from the higher marginal tax rates that otherwise would apply. This somewhat complex formula is administratively feasible since it requires only information available on already filed tax returns and does not require a recalculation of the tax paid in prior years. Its workability is enhanced (although its equity is compromised) by the fact that averaging is carried out only when current income is unusually high. Averaging is not permitted in cases where current income is unusually low by the standards of previous income levels.

A more comprehensive system of averaging would increase the number of years over which averaging calculations might be carried out and would recognize unusually low as well as unusually high income years. But such extensions would increase the administrative and compliance costs of the system and would raise especially difficult questions when the rates of tax or the definition of income itself change over time due to new legislation. The record shows that both income definitions and tax rates are changed occasionally, so that an averaging system which required recalculation of taxes previously paid would be a complicated matter. Comprehensive averaging schemes must confront the "on and off" problems that arise when individuals enter and leave the labor force. In general, it appears that a complete solution to the fluctuating income problem would encounter substantial administrative and compliance problems. Compromise solutions designed to relieve the most severe cases of unequal treatment may be the most that can be expected.

Special Rates

The procedure which lumps together income from all sources into a single figure for "net income subject to tax" means that the U.S. individual income tax is a "global" type of income tax rather than a "schedular" type of income tax, which would use different tax rate schedules for income from different sources. Under a pure "global" income tax, the amount of tax that an individual would pay would depend on the amount of income received and would not depend on the sources of that income. Although the U.S. individual income tax is basically a "global" tax, it does depart from this approach in some important instances. For example, it already has been noted that interest received from state and local bonds is excluded in the calculation of adjusted gross income (and thus is subjected to a zero tax rate) and that a special deduction is allowed for net long-term capital gains which results in an effective tax rate on these gains equal to only half of the rate imposed on ordinary income. These are examples of income source distinctions which are made in calculating income subject to tax. But there are also some situations in which income from certain sources receives special attention in the rate structure itself.

Two special rate structures have the effect of placing upper limits on the rate of tax which will be applied to income from certain sources. One of these relates to net long-term capital gains and the other relates to "earned" income, that is, to income from wages, salaries, and professions. The alternative method for taxing net long-term capital gains sets a tax rate of 25 percent on the first $50,000 of net long-term capital gains. This alternative calculation is advantageous for taxpayers who otherwise would have to pay tax on one-half of net long-term capital gains at marginal rates above 50 percent. The special rate structure for earned income specifies that the marginal tax rate shall not exceed 50 percent on income from these sources. These special rate arrangements limit the applicability of marginal tax rates in excess of 50 percent and suggest that the congress has been concerned about the incentive effects of high marginal tax rates on work, on risk taking, and on the search for tax avoidance devices.

The *minimum tax* special rate arrangement approaches the tax rate situation from the opposite direction; that is, it sets minimum tax rates rather than maximum tax rates. The minimum tax focuses on certain exclusions and deductions in the normal income calculation (such as the exclusion of state and local bond interest and the deduction of half of net long-term capital gains) which are sometimes regarded as tax "loopholes." After the taxpayer has determined his tax in the normal way, the various "preference" exclusions and deductions which have been claimed are added up and an additional tax is assessed.

The *earned income credit*, which was introduced into the tax law in 1975, is another special tax rate arrangement and is one that is especially interesting because it incorporates several features similar to negative income tax proposals. The earned income credit allows a credit against tax liability equal to 10 percent of earned income up to $4,000 (that is, a maximum credit of $400) with this credit then reduced by 10 percent of the amount by which adjusted gross income exceeds $4,000. Thus, the credit completely disappears for taxpayers with income of $8,000 or more. This earned income credit, therefore, is a special tax advantage for low income persons whose income is mainly from earned sources. The feature which imparts a negative income tax flavor to the earned income credit is that cash payments will be made to the taxpayer for the amount by which the credit exceeds income tax otherwise payable. The earned income credit is a rather weak negative income tax because the rate is low (10 percent) and because it is available only to persons with earned income, but it could be the start of more powerful negative income tax procedures.

TAX COMPLIANCE AND WITHHOLDING

Tax law places the responsibility for filing a return of income on the individual, that is, the individual is obligated to file a tax return if the amount of his income is such as to result in a positive tax liability. This means that a return must be filed if income exceeds the amount of allowable personal exemptions plus the minimum standard deduction. An individual must also file a return in order to claim any refund of tax due if income tax withheld or paid on the basis of estimated income exceeds the amount of actual tax liability. Thus, the income tax is based on self-reporting of income and the burden of proof falls upon the individual.

The Internal Revenue Service performs audits of returns filed, and the taxpayer is obligated to provide supporting evidence of the accuracy of his return if called upon to do so. Penalties may be imposed for failure to comply with the requirements of the tax. These penalties take the form of additions to the tax, interest on tax liabilities not paid when due, and criminal penalties of fine and/or imprisonment if it is established in court that noncompliance was motivated by intent to defraud the government. It is important to note the distinction between tax *avoidance*, which is the adjustment of an individual's affairs within the provisions of the law in order to minimize liability, and tax *evasion*, which is a violation of the law through incorrect reporting of income, deductions, or liability for the purpose of reducing liability.

Tax avoidance is perfectly legal; indeed, it is reasonable to conclude that it is a purpose of the law that individuals should avail themselves of all permissible exclusions, deductions, and exemptions. However, it is apparent that compliance with the complex requirements of the income tax is not a simple matter and that costs of compliance are substantial. Many taxpayers find that the obligation to comply with the intricate requirements of the tax forces them to purchase professional assistance in the preparation of their returns. Although the amount paid to purchase such professional assistance is deductible in computing net income subject to tax, it is unfortunate that the law has become so complicated as to require such expenditures from ordinary taxpayers. A law that cannot be understood by those required to follow it breeds frustration and distrust. Simplification of the income tax probably would strengthen the support given it by the public.

Withholding and current payment of estimated tax were instituted during World War II, shortly after the tax became a mass tax through the lowering of personal exemption allowances and the rapid increase in tax rates and liabilities. Employers are required to withhold income tax from the paychecks of employees, to forward these withheld monies to the Internal Revenue Service, and to provide the employee with a report of the amount withheld shortly after the close of the tax year. Withholding is not required on interest or dividends or other income payments, but those who make these payments are required to submit an information return to the Internal Revenue Service (with a copy to the taxpayer) showing the amount of the payments. These information returns are used in the auditing process to verify the accuracy of the return filed by the taxpayer. It is apparent, however, that the enormous number of returns and supporting information filed with the Internal Revenue Service make it impossible (with present technology) for the IRS to audit thoroughly each return filed. Computers, however, have greatly increased the capability of the auditing process.

Withholding results in a high level of income reporting compliance for those sources of income subject to it. It has been proposed that the withholding procedure be extended to other sources of income, such as dividends and interest, where reporting compliance may be less complete, thus improving the horizontal equity of income tax enforcement. Tax delinquency is also reduced by the withholding procedure, since the taxpayer ordinarily does not face the necessity of remitting a substantial sum of money to the Internal Revenue Service when the actual return is submitted. In fact, as the withholding system actually operates, many taxpayers have no net tax due with the final return and instead are entitled to a refund of amounts withheld in excess of actual tax liability. Thus, for many taxpayers, the withholding system collects more tax than actually is due and provides a strong incentive for prompt filing of the final return. However, no interest is paid on amounts refunded even though these funds have been available for government use for an average period of more than half a year.

The withholding system speeds the responsiveness of the tax system to changes in tax rates or the definition of taxable income, which is of obvious importance in carrying out the stabilization responsibilities of the federal government. If stabilization measures indicate a reduction in the equilibrium level of national income through increased tax collections, the impact of the change will be felt by wage and salary recipients within a few weeks as withholding rates are increased and net take-home pay is consequently reduced. Conversely, reductions in withholding rates can quickly place increased spending power in the hands of wage and salary recipients.

SUMMARY

This chapter has outlined the deductions from adjusted gross income permitted in calculating net income subject to tax. Certain personal deductions, such as those for extraordinary medical expenses and for casualty losses, are refinements of ability to pay and are designed to improve the horizontal and vertical equity of the tax. Others, such as the deduction for charitable contributions, are "tax expenditures" or subsidies designed to influence the taxpayer's allocation of his own resources. Tax deductions are appropriate when the objective is a refinement of ability to pay, but tax credits, which permit the taxpayer to subtract some amount directly from his tax liability, may be more appropriate when the objective is to subsidize certain types of private expenditure.

Taxpayers may choose to use the standard deduction instead of a detailed itemization of specifically authorized personal deductions. The standard deduction is calculated directly from adjusted gross income (or according to specified dollar amounts in the case of the minimum standard deduction) and thus provides no explicit recognition of specific items in the list of allowable deductions. Therefore the standard deduction fails to recognize relevant differences among taxpayers who choose this deduction. To some extent, the tax saving gained from the use of the standard deduction is a fiscal illusion.

Personal exemptions for the taxpayer and spouse provide a zero tax rate bracket in the income tax and suggest that income up to this amount has no ability to pay tax. More complicated questions arise in connection with exemptions for dependent children, which may be regarded either as refinements of ability to pay or as subsidies to encourage the rearing of children. If the latter rationale is accepted, tax credits would be more appropriate than the present deduction approach.

Tax rates are graduated according to a bracket system, which introduces a distinction between the marginal and the average rate of tax. Marginal rates are important in regard to the incentive effects of the tax, whereas average rates measure tax burden and the degree of progressivity. The graduated tax rate structure means that the average rate of tax on large aggregations of income is higher than the average rate on small aggregations. Consequently, definition of the tax-paying unit and special arrangements for incomes that fluctuate over time are important questions in a progressive tax system. Current tax law approaches the tax-paying unit question through the use of several different rate schedules and moderates the impact of taxes on fluctuating income through a system of averaging. Compliance with the income tax is facilitated through the use of a withholding system.

SUGGESTED READINGS

WHITE, M., and A. WHITE. "Horizontal Inequality in the Federal Income Tax Treatment of Homeowners and Tenants," *National Tax Journal*, XVIII, 3 (September 1965).

AARON, H. "Income Taxes and Housing," *American Economic Review*, LX, 5 (December, 1970).

ROLPH, E. "Discriminating Effects of the Income Tax Treatment of Owner-Occupants," *National Tax Journal*, XXVI, 3 (September 1973).

FREEMAN, R. "Tax Relief for the Homeowner?" *National Tax Journal*, XXVI, 3 (September 1973).

MAXWELL, J. "Income Tax Discrimination Against the Renter," *National Tax Journal*, XXVI, 3 (September 1973).

BRANNON, GERARD M., and ELLIOTT R. MORSS. "The Tax Allowances for Dependents: Deductions Versus Credits," *National Tax Journal*, XXVI, 4 (December 1973).

POGUE, THOMAS F. "Deductions vs. Credits: A Comment," *National Tax Journal* XXVII, 4 (December 1974).

FELDSTEIN, MARTIN. "The Income Tax and Charitable Contributions: Part I—Aggregate and Distributional Effects," *National Tax Journal*, XXVIII, 1 (March 1975).

OBERHOFER, TOM. "The Redistributive Effect of the Federal Income Tax," *National Tax Journal*, XXVIII, 1 (March 1975).

FELDSTEIN, MARTIN. "The Income Tax and Charitable Contributions: Part II—The Impact on Religious, Educational, and other Organizations," *National Tax Journal*, XXVIII, 2 (June 1975).

GOTTSCHALK, PETER. "Deductions Versus Credits Revisited," *National Tax Journal*, XXIX, 2 (June 1976).

AARON, HENRY J. (ed). *Inflation and the Income Tax* (Washington, D.C.: The Brookings Institution, 1976).

I3

Economic Effects
of Income Taxation

Taxes generate economic effects when they alter the operation of the economy. If the economy would operate in the same way (for example, produce the same set of goods and services, use the same technological processes, generate the same distribution of income, experience the same rate of growth) whether or not the tax were imposed, the tax would have no economic effect. It is apparent, of course, that every tax, whether it is an income tax, a consumption tax, a wealth tax, or a tax on some particular product or activity, will have some effect.

This extremely broad definition of economic effects is correct, but it is so general that it is not much use in dealing with actual problems or issues. What is needed is a working definition. This chapter will focus on the effects of income taxes by making the somewhat unrealistic assumption that changes in the income tax can be made while other things, such as the size and composition of the government's budget, remain unchanged. Of course, if we assume that the size and composition of the government's budget remain unchanged, a change in income taxation would require change in some other source of financing to compensate for increases or decreases in revenue from the income tax. These compensating changes, in turn, would trigger their own sets of economic effects. For convenience and simplicity, however, we will simply ignore the effects that would arise from these compensating changes in government finance or assume that they could be carried out with financing arrangements that would produce no economic effects at all. In other words, we will explore the effects of income taxation against a background of alternative financing methods that have no effect. This procedure is called a *differential analysis* of income tax effects.

The assumption that the size and composition of the government's budget remain unchanged while the revenue sources used to finance this budget are changed contradicts the model of government finance presented in Chapter 3. According to that model, changes in the methods of finance will lead to changes in the size and/or composition of the budget. Nevertheless, the differential approach can be helpful and can contribute to rational and informed decision making in government finance. The knowledge that different taxes produce different effects can give voters and legislators a more complete understanding of the consequences of alternatives available to them.

In this chapter the effects of income taxation will be examined in terms of *partial equilibrium analysis* rather than in terms of general equilibrium analysis. This is another limitation or narrowing of the frame of reference. Eor example, it is easy to recognize that economic effects experienced by one industry or group of people can have repercussions on other industries or groups of people. If high-income people spend their money on different things than low-income people, then a tax on high-income people that reduces their spending may lead to unemployment or lower wages for the people whose resources are especially suited to providing the things high-income groups buy. These second-round effects may lead to third-round effects, and so on.

A full or complete picture of economic effects would require *general equilibrium analysis*, in which the initial tax change was introduced into an economy in general equilibrium and in which the effects of this tax change included all the differences between the starting equilibrium and the new general equilibrium that would eventually be established. Partial equilibrium analysis considers only the first-round effects of the tax change and ignores all the second-round and subsequent effects. It is therefore an incomplete picture of the effects of the tax. The relative simplicity of partial analysis justifies its use in an introductory examination of the economic effects of taxes, but the cautionary note that it does not present a complete picture of economic effects is appropriate.

A NOTE ON INDIFFERENCE CURVES

Indifference curve analysis is useful in gaining an understanding of the economic effects of income taxation. Therefore, a brief review of this analytical technique is appropriate before proceeding.[1]

Figure 13.1 illustrates typical indifference curves in elementary economic analysis. First note that the axes of the graph show quantities of different goods or services which may be obtained by the individual whose indifference curves are being illustrated. The vertical axis shows quantities of good Y and the horizontal axis shows quantities of good X. Thus, each point in the field of the graph represents a particular combination of quantities of the two goods. The indifference curve on the graph (I_2) consists of a series of these points or different combinations of the two goods and the idea behind the indifference curve is

---

[1] A standard text on economic principles may be consulted for a more complete exposition of indifference curve analysis.

FIGURE 13.1   Indifference Curves

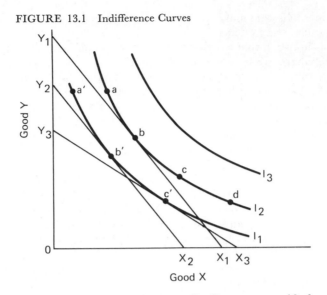

that the individual feels himself to be as well off at any specified point of this curve as he would be at any other point on this curve. In other words, he is *indifferent* in his preferences among different combinations shown on this curve. Figure 13.1 illustrates four points on indifference curve I_2 (points *a*, *b*, *c*, and *d*). The individual feels that his total welfare from the combination of the two goods is the same whether he obtains combination *a*, *b*, *c*, or *d*, or any other combination represented by a point on this curve.

Now note that the indifference curve has a generally negative slope and is drawn convex toward the origin of the graph. The economic principle behind this construction is the law of diminishing marginal utility. The slope of the indifference curve shows the rate at which the individual is willing to give up units of one of the goods in order to obtain more units of the other good. For example, if we start at point *c* and move to point *b*, the individual is giving up units of good X and is obtaining more units of good Y. The rate at which the exchange is made is approximately equal to one unit of X being sacrificed in exchange for one added unit of Y. But as we continue to move along the indifference curve, proceeding now from point *b* to point *a*, we observe that the individual is insisting on greater increments of good Y before he will be persuaded to sacrifice a unit of good X. In other words, the marginal utility of good Y is decreasing as the individual obtains more of it and the marginal utility of good X is increasing as he obtains less of it. Thus, the law of diminishing marginal utility suggests why indifference curves have negative slopes and are drawn convex to the origin of the graph.

Figure 13.1 presents a "family" of indifference curves, providing a more complete picture of preferences of the individual. Each of the curves (I_1, I_2, and I_3) is constructed according to the basic model outlined above, but curve I_2 illustrates a higher level of well-being from the two goods than is shown by curve I_1, and curve I_3 shows a higher level of well-being than curve I_2. This arrangement may be illustrated by comparing point *a* on curve I_2 with point

a' on curve I_1. The individual has the same amount of good Y at both a and a', but he has less of good X at a' than he had at a. Therefore, if X is an economic *good* and not an economic *bad*, the combination at a' shows a lower level of welfare for the individual than the combination at a. If we now apply the logic of indifference curves, it follows that *any* point on I_2 will be preferred to *any* point on I_1. Also, so long as the goods retain their qualities as economic goods rather than economic bads, indifference curves will neither touch nor intersect one another.

The combination of the two goods the individual actually chooses will depend on his preferences, as represented by the indifference curves, on the prices of the two goods, and on the amount of money he allocates for the purchase of these goods. The prices of the two goods and the size of the individual's budget are represented by a budget line, such as line Y_1X_1 in Figure 13.1. If the individual allocated all of his budget to the purchase of good Y, he could acquire OY_1 units of this good. If he devoted all of his budget to the purchase of good X, he could purchase OX_1 of that good. If the prices of the goods are not affected by his purchasing, he can select any combination of X and Y shown along the budget line Y_1X_1. Assuming that the individual tries to reach the highest possible indifference curve, given the size of his budget and the prices of the goods, he would select the combination shown at b in Figure 13.1.

Changes in the size of the individual's budget and changes in the prices of the goods can be illustrated by relocations of the budget line. For example, suppose that a tax which is neutral in respect to the relative prices of the two goods (e.g., a poll tax) is collected from the individual. The individual's spending power will be reduced by the tax money paid and a new budget line can be drawn parallel to the original budget line but located closer to the origin of the graph, such as budget line Y_2X_2. With this smaller budget, the individual will select point b' on indifference curve I_1. The changes in the purchases of X and Y that would result from this shrinking of the budget are called *income* effects, since the relative prices of the two goods have remained the same as they were in the initial situation.

Now let us consider the effects of changing the relative prices of the two goods. Suppose that the tax collected from the individual not only reduced his real income from indifference level I_2 to indifference level I_1 but also resulted in a change in the relative prices of good X and good Y. The effect of the change in relative prices is illustrated by the budget line Y_3X_3, which indicates that the price of Y has increased relative to the price of X. In response to this change in relative prices, the individual would move along indifference curve I_1 from point b' to point c'. This change is called the *substitution* effect because it arose from the change of relative prices between the two goods. The individual's real income is the same at c' as at b' (since these points are on the same indifference curve) but a change in the individual's behavior has been produced by the change in relative prices.

Two observations can be made about substitution effects and income effects. The first is that substitution effects will regularly alter resource allocation in favor of the good which has fallen in relative price and against the good which has increased in relative price. This is because indifference curves are convex toward the origin of the graph. For example, along a given indifference curve, the tangency point for a flatter budget line will always be farther to the right than the tangency point for a steeper budget line. The second observation is that income effects on the allocation between the two goods depend on the way indifference curves are arranged with respect to one another. The chosen amount of a particular good may either increase or decrease if the real income of a person is reduced by taxation. We are not able to determine the direction of the income effect on a good unless we know the pattern or arrangement of the individual's indifference curves. In other words, to predict an income effect, we would need to know how an individual would adjust his expenditures if he were faced with the necessity of accepting a reduction in his real income. Since different individuals may have different ways of making this adjustment, generalizations about income effects are risky.

INCOME TAX EFFECTS

The basic model for analyzing the economic effects of income taxation is presented in Figure 13.2. The vertical axis of this graph is labeled "money income" and represents the income from a person's resources (for example, time) devoted to activities that give rise to money income. As the analysis progresses, these will be the activities that give rise to the kind of income which will be taxable. The horizontal axis is labeled "nonmoney income" and represents the income from a person's resources for (example, time) devoted to the kind of do it yourself activities that do not give rise to money income and that, in this analysis, will not be subject to taxation. The individual is free to allocate his available resources between these two types of activities, but this allocation is limited by the total amount of resource he possesses and by the terms of trade or rate at which he can exchange one type of income for the other.

These constraints on the individual's allocation are illustrated by the straight lines drawn between one axis and the other. For example, if the indi-

FIGURE 13.2   Income Tax Economic Effects

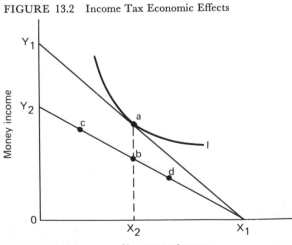

Nonmoney income

vidual devoted all his resources to nonmoney income activities, he would be able to have quantity OX_1 of this type of income. On the other hand, if he were to devote all his resources to money income activities, he would have quantity OY_1 of this type of income. The slope of the line connecting X_1 and Y_1 reveals the terms of trade or the rate at which nonmoney income can be converted into money income. This is essentially a money wage rate. The steeper this line, the more the terms of trade favor money income activities, that is, the wage rate is higher.

If the individual makes full use of his resources, as we assume he does, he may select any point along this X_1Y_1 line when he makes his allocation between money and nonmoney income activities. The point actually selected depends on the preferences of the individual. If he happens especially to enjoy those things money can buy, he will choose some point in the upper left range of this pos-sibilities line, that is, he will allocate a large portion of his resources to money income activities and relatively little to nonmoney income activities. On the other hand, if his preferences run more toward the satisfactions he can derive from nonmoney income activities, he will select a point nearer the lower right end of the line. The nature of these preferences is indicated by indifference curve *I*. When the possibilities or alternatives are those shown along X_1Y_1, this individual will select the combination of money income and nonmoney income identified at point *a*. The allocation of the individual's resources can be read along the horizontal axis. When point *a* is selected, OX_2 of the individual's resources is devoted to nonmoney income activities and the remainder, X_2X_1, is devoted to money income activities.

Now suppose that a proportional tax is imposed on money income and no tax is imposed on nonmoney income. The amount of after-tax money income the individual can realize by devoting his resources to these activities is reduced compared to what it was before. The possibilities line becomes Y_2X_1. The alloca-tion between the alternative kinds of activities now must be made along the new possibilities line, and any change in the allocation becomes an economic effect of the tax. If the new allocation were made at point *c* in Figure 13.2, the effect of the tax would have been to reduce the amount of the individual's resource devoted to nonmoney income activities and to increase the amount devoted to money income activities. The tax would be said to have increased incentives to apply resources to money income activities. But the new allocation need not be at point *c*. The new allocation could be at point *b*, indicating that the tax had not caused a change in the allocation of resources to money income activities, since point *b* corresponds with the same allocation (X_2) as had prevailed before the tax. Or the allocation might be at point *d*, indicating that the tax has reduced incentives to devote resources to money income activities.

We are not able to determine, *a priori*, what the actual effect of this income tax will be, that is, we cannot say whether the new situation will find the indi-vidual at point *b*, at point *c*, or at point *d*. We know that the individual will be on some lower indifference curve (since the size and composition of the budget are unchanged even though this person is paying more tax), but we do not know whether this lower curve will be tangent to X_1Y_2 at *b*, *c*, *d*, or some other point. Since the tax has reduced the take-home wage rate for the individual (as shown by the flatter slope of line X_1Y_2), we can be sure that the *substitution* effect of the tax has tended to increase the portion of the person's resources devoted to nonmoney income activity and to reduce the portion of his resources devoted to money income activity. But we cannot be sure about what the *income* effect did to the person's allocation of resources between money and nonmoney income activities. The conventional view is that, when the tax collector takes some money away from a person, that person may respond by working harder and longer in order to make up for his loss of spending power. This kind of response would tend to counteract the adverse work or money income activity consequences of the substitution effect and, if this income effect were strong enough, the net effect of the tax could be an increase in the portion of resources devoted to money income activities. In other words, the substitution effect makes it less worthwhile for a person to give up an hour of nonmoney income activity because the tax has reduced the amount of money take-home pay that can be gotten from it. The person will devote less time to earning money. But the tax payment takes money away from the individual (the income effect) and this may lead him to put more time into money income activity in order to regain some of the lost purchasing power. We cannot be certain about the net effect of these two forces.

Research which has been conducted in an effort to discover the actual net incentive effects of income taxation has failed to demonstrate that income taxation either increases or decreases the activities generating taxable income. In these studies, difficulties are encountered in maintaining a control group of persons who are otherwise similar to the group facing the tax but who are not themselves subjected to the tax. But the distinction between income and substitution effects is not a futile exercise in economic theorizing just because it fails to resolve the question of the net economic effect of income taxation on the choice between taxable and nontaxable activities. An understanding of these effects is useful in further analysis of income taxation.

Excess Burden

Excess burden means that the tax lowers total real income. In a basic sense, excess burden suggests that the behavioral responses to the tax result in a less efficient functioning of the economy. It is a subtle concept and requires careful analysis and expression. The burden part of the term indicates that the private sector of the economy must relinquish some command over resources so that these resources may be utilized in the provision of collective goods and services. But the collective goods and services presumably are beneficial to the society so that, in a well-functioning government, the basic burden of taxation should be compensated (or more than compensated) by the benefits received from these services. Private real income is reduced in exchange for increased collective real income and no net burden need arise. The idea of *excess* burden suggests that the reduction in private real income is greater than necessary, that is, that the provision of collective services could have been provided at a lower real cost in reduced private real income. The amount of excess burden is the amount of the unnecessary reduction in private real income.

Excess burden is illustrated in Figure 13.3. This figure reproduces Figure 13.2, but adds some additional information. Let us assume that, when the

FIGURE 13.3   Excess Burden of Taxation

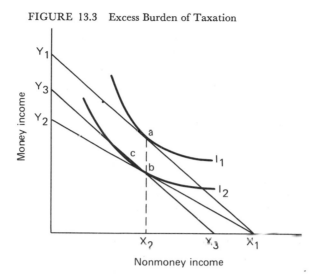

Nonmoney income

income tax is imposed, the individual selects point *b* on the new possibilities line which arises because of the tax. Selecting point *b* indicates that the allocation between money and nonmoney income activities is the same after the tax as it was before, that is, that the income effect and the substitution effect have canceled each other, leaving no net effect on the individual's allocation. Now let us suppose that a lump sum or poll tax is imposed to replace the income tax and that the amount of tax collected through this poll tax is the same as the amount which had been collected through the income tax. With the poll tax, the amount of tax payable does not depend on the allocation the individual makes among alternative activities; he must pay the same amount of tax regardless of how he divides his resources between money and nonmoney income activities. Therefore, the terms of trade or slope of the possibilities line with a poll tax will be the same as the slope of the possibilities line that existed before any tax was imposed, that is, its slope will be the same as line $X_1 Y_1$. In Figure 13.3, the possibilities line under the poll tax is line $X_3 Y_3$. It is parallel to the original possibilities line and it lies below that line by the amount of money collected from the taxpayer. This amount of money is illustrated by the distance between points *a* and *b*. This is the amount of money that had been collected through the income tax and now will be collected through the poll tax.

Will the individual alter his allocation of resources when the income tax is replaced with the poll tax? The answer is yes. This can be seen in Figure 13.3. When the individual selected point *b* after the income tax was imposed, this indicated that one of his indifference curves was tangent to the line $X_1 Y_2$ at that point. Since indifference curves are convex to the origin of the graph, it follows that the poll tax possibilities line will lie above this indifference curve (I_2) for some distance to the left of point *b*. This is true because the possibilities line $X_3 Y_3$ (the poll tax line) is steeper than the possibilities line $X_1 Y_2$ (the income tax line). Therefore, when the income tax is replaced with an equal yield poll tax, the individual will adjust his allocation to some point, such as *c*, because point *c* will lie on a higher indifference curve than I_2. In other words, the individual will enjoy a higher real income (that is, less burden) if the tax is collected through a lump sum poll tax than if the tax were collected through the income tax.

The excess burden is the difference in real income under the lump sum tax, which imposed no discrimination among alternative activities through altered terms of trade, and real income under the income tax, which did impose some discrimination among alternative activities. The idea is that an individual will be able to use his resources to best advantage and gain the highest possible real income from them if he is free to allocate his resources without constraints other than those imposed by market situations. Since the poll tax imposes only income effects and does not impose substitution effects, it is the substitution effect of the income tax that alters the terms of trade among alternatives from what they would be in the market, imposes extra constraints on the individual's allocation of his resources, reduces real income, and imposes an excess burden. The policy thrust of the excess burden argument is that taxes should be devised so as to be neutral in terms of the individual's choice among alternative ways of allocating resources. In this sense, neutrality seeks the elimination of substitution effects and seeks to support the provision of collective services through taxes that produce only income effects, which are regarded as neutral and as producing no excess burden.

The concept of excess burden can be a useful tool for improving the instruments of taxation, but great care must be used in applying the concept. Excess burden is like sin: it is easy to be against it, but it is sometimes difficult to recognize in the real world. For example, alterations in the terms of trade arising from taxation may be imposed when markets themselves are not efficient or neutral. Actual market prices may not be reflections of perfect competition. Likewise, collective services provided by government may not be neutral as among alternative allocations of private resources. Thus, the condemnation of substitution effects implicit in the excess burden argument may not hold in an uncertain real world since distortions arising from taxation may counteract distortions arising from other sources and actually result in higher real income than would otherwise have prevailed.

Even the supposed neutrality of the income effect loses much of its force when the frame of reference shifts from the realm of economic theory to the realm of government tax policy. Those who propound economic theory may be unwilling to certify one distribution of income as being better than another, but those who make social policy cannot retreat to this noncommittal point of view. Income effects change the allocation of resources if different people demand different things. These facts of life must be accepted as relevant to the development and evaluation of tax instruments. If social policy and tax instruments are to be formulated intelligently, both income and substitution effects must be recognized.

NONNEUTRALITIES OF INCOME TAXATION

Income taxation typically is given a high ranking as a relatively desirable tax instrument because a very large portion of available activities falls in the taxable category and because relatively few available activities fall in the non-taxable category, that is, because income taxation is more "general" than are most alternative taxes. This generality of income taxation means that it is relatively difficult or unattractive to avoid income taxes by switching to nontaxable activities, thereby generating economic effects. Nevertheless, some switching from taxable to nontaxable activities does follow from the imposition of an income tax, so that the tax does generate economic effects. It is appropriate to examine some of these effects.

Saving and Consuming

In the language of economics, saving means *not consuming*, that is, the alternatives available to the individual with command over resources are simply whether or not to use these resources for current consumption. If the individual chooses in favor of consumption, no income tax is payable on the satisfaction or enjoyment realized from this consumption, even though consumption means a higher current standard of living than does nonconsumption. On the other hand, if the individual chooses in favor of saving, income tax will be payable on the interest received if the wealth accumulated through the saving is placed in interest-earning assets. Consuming becomes an activity on the nontaxable axis of the economic effects graph, postponing consumption in exchange for interest becomes an activity on the taxable axis of the graph. Thus, income taxation, if interest is included in the tax base, alters the terms of trade between consuming and saving, and the predicted substitution effect is a reduction in saving relative to consuming. The substitution effect of income taxation on saving is adverse when this tax is compared to a lump sum tax in which the amount of tax is unrelated to the choice between consuming and saving. Of course, the effects are markedly different from those of a consumption tax, which does not tax interest or income saved.

Whether or not the nonneutrality toward saving is inherent to income taxation depends on the concept of income upon which the tax is based. If a tax were constructed according to the "consumption is income" philosophy, saving would be exempt and consumption would be taxed, which would reverse the present approach. According to the production-flow philosophy, the present system of income taxation amounts to a double taxation of saving, since the amounts saved are taxed once when earned and then again when these funds are used to generate interest. Another way of saying this is to state that funds which are saved are taxed once when received and that the present value of the saving is reduced further because taxation of interest shrinks the stream of future income, which determines present value. Of course, the double tax argument is not persuasive under the accretion to wealth concept of income, since the receipt of interest is a contribution to the wealth of the recipient just as the original receipt of the funds which were saved contributed to this wealth. Some substitution effect adverse to saving is inherent in the accretion to wealth approach to taxation.

The *income* effect of taxation will be adverse to saving if saving is a "luxury" type of activity, that is, if it is the type of activity which displays an income elasticity greater than 1.0. For example, if both consumption and saving exhibited income elasticities of 1.0, then a 10 percent reduction in income would produce a 10 percent reduction in both consumption and saving and no discrimination against saving would be evident. If, however, the income elasticity for saving is greater than 1.0 (and the income elasticity for consuming is therefore less than 1.0), a 10 percent reduction in income will reduce saving by more than 10 percent and will reduce consuming by less than 10 percent. The income effect of taxation would discriminate against saving.

This would be true under a lump sum tax, it would be true to a greater extent under a proportional income tax, and true to a still greater extent under a progressive income tax. Each step in the sequence from lump sum to proportionality to graduated tax rates increases tax progressivity, since the average rate of tax on higher-income persons is increasingly greater relative to the average rate on lower-income persons as each step in this sequence is taken. If the propensity to save is directly related to income size, the progressive graduation of tax rates impacts on saving through both the income and the substitution effects. Marginal tax rates are the cutting edge for the substitution effect, since it is the marginal tax rate that alters the terms of trade (the slope of the possibilities line) at the margin, where decisions are made between saving and consuming. In progressively graduated systems of tax rates, both the marginal and the average rate rise as income advances, so that both income and substitution effects are stronger at high-income than at low-income levels.

In the United States individual income tax, the actual force of the disincentive for saving is moderated considerably by special features that work in the direction of favoring saving relative to consumption. The favorable income tax treatment accorded to capital gains is the leading illustration of an income tax special feature favorable to saving, although the exclusion of interest on state and local government bonds also operates to produce this result. Capital gains may be obtained by abstaining from consumption (that is, by saving) so that resources can be invested in activities which will be productive of capital gains. Thus the favorable treatment of capital gains encourages saving, and this favorable treatment is especially attractive to high-bracket taxpayers who have the means to save and for whom the difference in tax rates between ordinary income and capital gains is greatest.

Because the income tax contains forces that operate to encourage saving and also contains forces that operate to discourage saving, it is extremely difficult to estimate the net effect of the tax on saving. However, an understanding of the forces at work in income taxation is useful for the implementation of government policy. For example, a policy in favor of increasing the rate of saving could be implemented by reducing the progressiveness of the tax (assuming that saving exhibits an income elasticity greater than 1.0), or it could be implemented by offering still more favorable treatment to capital gains and to other saving-related features of the tax law. If the propensity to save is higher at high-income levels than at low-income levels, the second option would also have the effect of lowering progressivity. The choice among implementation approaches is further complicated by the likelihood that the special treatments approach (such as those for capital gains and bond interest) would introduce still other distortions into the economy. In any event, it appears that a conflict exists between the objective of increasing the rate of saving and that of using progressive taxation as an instrument for the redistribution of income.

Occupational Choice (LABOR VS. LEISURE DECISION)

The basic model of the economic effects of taxation can be applied to occupational choice questions in much the same way as it can be applied to the choice between consuming and saving. In each case, the question relates to an individual's allocation of resources. For occupational choice matters, the resources are the time and talents of the individual. Occupations differ from one another in the composition of the package of rewards they offer to the individual. The part of the package which is "compensation for services rendered" and which ordinarily is paid in money is subject to income tax, whereas the other part of the package, which includes working conditions, amenities, fringe benefits, and so on is not subject to income tax. To the extent that the alternative occupations differ in the mix of taxable and nontaxable components in the reward package, income taxation is not neutral among them.

Substitution effects of income taxation are favorable to occupations that offer a relatively large nontaxable component in the reward package and are adverse to occupations that offer a relatively large taxable component in this package. For example, college professors enjoy working conditions sheltered from the rigors of direct exposure to weather and the risks of physical injury. They also are accorded some degree of social status related to their occupational choice. None of these rewards is subjected to income taxation. On the other hand, construction workers face working conditions ordinarily regarded as less comfortable or attractive, and the pay received in these occupations includes some amount in compensation for these aspects of the work. This extra compensation is taxable. Similarly, persons engaged in occupations that subject them to hazards of physical injury find that they must pay higher premiums for health, accident, and life insurance than do persons in comparatively "safe" occupations. Therefore, hazardous occupations must pay higher money wages in order to attract workers (who either use the money to buy insurance or assume the risk of accident personally), and these higher wages are subject to income tax.

The difference in insurance costs between hazardous and nonhazardous occupations is a measure of the potential substitution effects of income taxation. Of course, this potential income tax effect can be avoided by providing fringe benefit status for insurance against these hazards. Money wages can be reduced in exchange for fringe benefit insurance coverage, thus removing the income tax bias. But the income tax effect cannot be avoided so conveniently when differences in the reward package mix arise from such factors as social status, pleasantness of the work routine, the amenities of life in the area where the work is performed, and so on. In competitive markets among occupations these differences appear as differences in taxable money wage rates, and income taxation will produce substitution effects favorable to occupations with attractive working conditions and adverse to occupations with unattractive working conditions. Substitution effect analysis suggests that an economy with income taxation probably will have relatively more college professors and lawyers and relatively fewer garbage collectors than an economy without it. However, the income effects of taxation may operate to counteract substitution effects on occupational choice. If the society is such that access to the "good things in life" generally requires money, then income effects may prompt people to sacrifice working conditions, amenities, and status in favor of occupations that provide greater amounts of money. The net outcome of combined income and substitution effects cannot be determined at the theoretical level.

Once again, progressivity adds a special dimension to the effects of income taxation. Both marginal rates, which trigger substitution effects, and average rates, which trigger income effects, are relatively low for low-income persons, so that occupational choice effects at these income levels may be small. Moreover, the range of occupational alternatives available to persons with smaller endowments of economic potential may be quite restricted and subject to institutional constraints on hours per day, vacation time, and so on, which leave little flexibility for response to income tax pressures. Higher-income groups, on the other hand, are likely to have a wider range of occupational options and these options themselves may incorporate less institutional rigidity, so that these groups are in a position to respond to inducements presented by income taxation. With progressive taxation, both average and marginal rates are higher for these higher-income groups, so that the inducements themselves will be relatively strong. Thus, the model suggests that occupational choice effects may be greater among high-income groups than among low-income groups. But the motivational factors also may differ among income groups. Power, status, prestige, or a sense of responsibility or achievement, which are elements of the nontaxable component in the reward package, may be strong motivational factors in higher-income ranges and may therefore dilute the effects of income taxation of occupational choice.

Risk Taking

Risk taking is a dimension of occupational choice in which the problem relates to the uncertainty or variability that surrounds the rewards which may be realized from alternative undertakings. A risky undertaking is one in which the return is subject to great variance due to forces beyond the control of the individual. Enthusiasm for success must be tempered by the realization of the possibility of failure and the consequent necessity of making provision to deal with failure. Since provision for failure is costly, a higher average rate of return must be demanded of risky undertakings than is demanded of undertakings free from risk.

The substitution effects of taxation on risk taking depend on whether the tax alters the terms of trade or relative rates of return between taking risks and not taking risks, and this in turn depends on whether the tax offers an offset for failure equivalent to the tax that would be payable in the event of success. If no loss offset were allowed, that is, if no deduction of losses against other income were allowed and no tax rebate were allowed for a negative income position, the tax collector would be playing a game of "heads we win, tails you lose," and the terms of trade clearly would be altered against risk taking. The expected gains from risk taking would be reduced relative to the gains from nonrisky undertakings. Substitution effects would result in less risk taking.

If a complete loss offset is allowed, a different situation arises because the government in effect is agreeing to share both gains and losses with the individual. The amount of risk assumed by the individual from a given undertaking actually is reduced—that is, both the possible gain and the possible loss from the undertaking are reduced. Given the individual's inclination to assume a given amount of risk in exchange for a given return, the response will be to *increase* the volume of risk-taking activity until he has regained his preferred net balance between risk assumed and return expected. Thus, full loss offsetting puts the government into the risk-taking business along with the private individual and increases the aggregate amount of risk taking in the economy.

The income effects of taxation on risk taking are especially obscure. Will a reduction in real income persuade a person to be more inclined to assume risk, that is, to sacrifice comfort and security in order to obtain a higher rate of return, or will a reduction in real income persuade an individual to be less inclined toward risk because losses would force retrenchment of expenditures in areas considered to be necessities rather than luxuries? There is no unambiguous resolution of this question at the theoretical level nor has empirical research succeeded in providing an answer. In a normative sense, it is suggested that higher-income persons ought to be in a better position to assume risk than low-income persons, but this is not the same as a positive finding that this is actually the case.

Progressive taxation adds still further complexity to the problem of determining the economic effects on risk taking. Under progressively graduated marginal tax rates, even full deduction for losses will not put the government into an equal partnership with the individual. This is because successful ventures will put the taxpayer into a higher tax bracket, whereas unsuccessful ventures (losses) will put the taxpayer into a lower tax rate bracket, so that deduction of losses provides tax relief at the lower rate imposed in that bracket. In other words, the government will not share equivalently in both gains and losses, so that some substitution effect adverse to risk will be imparted to the terms of trade or rate of return for risk taking. The government is still a partner to some degree, which contributes to greater aggregate risk taking in the economy, but substitution effects adverse to risk taking are present and operate to reduce aggregate risk taking. The net effect of these opposing tendencies is not apparent.

Even the special features of the tax law do not consistently operate either in favor or in opposition to risk. The preferential treatment of capital gains probably encourages risk because capital gains will be realized through risky undertakings, but there are restrictions on the deductibility of capital losses and these moderate the incentives for risk taking. Preferential depletion allowances and accelerated depreciation reduce the costs of undertaking risky ventures, but these allowances are also available for ventures that are not especially risky. On the other hand, the exclusion from taxation of interest on state and local government bonds, which are not risky investments, is a special feature that encourages nonrisky rather than risky undertakings. The complexity of the question and the lack of knowledge about the strength of the various effects set in motion by the income tax suggest that no firm conclusions can be offered on the overall impact of income taxation on risk taking.

Erosion of the Tax Base

Erosion of the tax base is a dynamic concept which suggests that the operation of the tax itself may, through time, reduce its generality and lead to a reduction in its desirability rating from the point of view of economic analysis. In other words, erosion of the tax base raises the question of the effect of the tax upon itself.

The analysis of tax-base erosion involves dynamic interactions between the level of tax rates and the willingness of the legislature to enact modifications in the tax base. The level of tax rates is important because high tax rates generate stronger incentives for tax avoidance than do lower rates. High marginal tax rates are especially important because these are the rates that determine the tax savings which can be realized by successful tax avoidance. When marginal rates are high, sizable expenditures will be made in the search for ways to avoid tax through modified behavior or through efforts to influence the legislature to change the tax law itself. If these efforts to persuade the legislature to modify the tax base succeed, erosion will have taken place and the income tax will have become less general.

Once launched, the erosion process can be circular or self-reinforcing because the eroded tax base will require higher tax rates to generate a given amount of revenue than would have been required if the erosion had not occurred. The higher tax rates and the reduced generality of the tax set the stage for another round in the erosion process and suggest that, in the future, the legislature will be even less able to resist requests for tax concessions. Once the erosion process has begun, it may be very difficult to stop. Of course, the circular or self-reinforcing process conceivably could operate in the opposite direction, increasing the generality of the tax and reducing tax rates, but thus far efforts to close loopholes in the tax law have not succeeded in reversing the movement toward less generality, although they may have slowed the erosion process to some extent.

The tax base erosion process is closely related to the attractiveness of using alterations in the definition of income or changes in deductions as devices for generating desired economic effects. The income tax enters into decision-making calculations throughout the economy and when tax rates are significant, alterations in the definition of taxable income can produce large and quickly implementable economic effects. Since tax reductions and preferences are politically more attractive than increases or penalties, using the income tax for short-run policy purposes probably involves a bias toward erosion of the tax base rather than toward greater generality.

It is conceivable that the erosion process could be carried to the point where the loss of generality in the tax results in general disillusionment or dissatisfaction with the tax itself. Should the tax cease to be regarded as a fair means of raising needed revenue, it probably no longer could serve as the primary revenue source for government finance. From the perspective of economics, this would be an unfortunate state of affairs, because the generality, neutrality, and directness of a more or less pure income tax are attractive for government finance in a market economy. Concern about the erosion of the tax base directs attention back to the importance of the concepts of income that underlie income taxation. General agreement about what constitutes income for tax purposes is therefore an important aspect of government finance.

SUMMARY

This chapter examined the economic effects of income taxation in the context of partial equilibrium analysis and with the technique of differential incidence analysis, which assumes that the size and composition of the expenditures budget are fixed while different tax devices are employed to finance these expenditures. The basic model used in the analysis identified *substitution effects*, which arise from the alteration of the terms of trade or relative rewards from alternative activities, and *income effects*, which reduce spending power but leave the terms of trade among alternative activities unchanged. Since substitution and income effects may sometimes operate in opposite directions to one another, theoretical analysis is often unable to offer an unambiguous picture of net economic effects from income taxation. The concept of *excess burden* was outlined, suggesting that taxation may inject inefficiencies into the operation of the economy.

Economic effects arise when taxation is applied in a nonneutral manner among alternative activities. The economic effects model was applied specifically to the alternatives of saving and consuming, to occupational choice, and to risk taking. Erosion of the tax base was characterized as an effect of the tax upon itself and upon its stability as a continuing major source of government revenue. The circular or self-reinforcing nature of the erosion process emphasized the importance of developing and maintaining a generally accepted concept of income for tax purposes.

SUGGESTED READINGS

FELDSTEIN, MARTIN A. "The Effect of Taxation on Risk Taking," *Journal of Political Economy*, September–October 1969.

FROMM, GARY (ed.). *Tax Incentives and Capital Spending* (Washington, D.C.: The Brookings Institution, 1971).

BREAK, GEORGE F. "Federal Tax Policy and the Private Saving Ratio," *National Tax Journal*, XXVI, 3 (September, 1973).

EISNER, ROBERT. "Tax Incentives for Investment," *National Tax Journal*, XXVI, 3 (September, 1973).

ROLPH, EARL R. "Discriminating Effects of the Income Tax Treatment of Owner-Occupants," *National Tax Journal*, XXVI, 3 (September, 1973).

SURREY, STANLEY S. *Pathways to Tax Reform* (Cambridge: Harvard University Press, 1973).

BREAK, G. F., and J. A. PECHMAN. *Federal Tax Reform: The Impossible Dream?* (Washington, D.C.: The Brookings Institution, 1975).

RICHARD D. HOBBET (Special Symposium Editor). "Federal Taxation and Charitable Organization," *Law and Contemporary Problems*, 39, 4 (Autumn, 1975).

RICHARD GOODE. *The Individual Income Tax* (revised edition) (Washington, D.C.: The Brookings Institution, 1976).

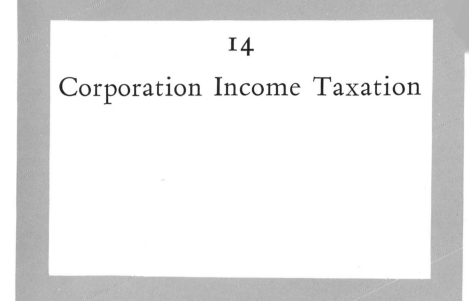

14

Corporation Income Taxation

Corporation income tax is imposed on the net profits of businesses organized in the corporate form. The tax rate is 20 percent on the first $25,000 of corporate net profit, 22 percent on the second $25,000, and 48 percent on profits in excess of $50,000. Since the bulk of corporate income tax payments are made by corporations whose profits greatly exceed the $50,000 level, in effect, the tax rate approximates a flat 48 percent on corporate profits. It is apparent that taxation at these rates is an important factor in business decision making and that a great deal of attention is focused on the provisions of the law dealing with the definition of taxable profits. Corporate expenditures that qualify for deduction in the computation of taxes are only about half as expensive as expenditures that do not qualify for such deduction. Tax law provisions have a powerful influence on corporate behavior, and corporations in turn are extremely interested in any proposed modifications in this law.

The government is concerned with the corporation income tax for a variety of reasons. The revenue collected through this tax is substantial, ranking third (behind individual income taxes and social insurance contributions) in budget receipt sources and amounting to about 15 percent of budget receipts for fiscal 1978.[1] Corporate income tax revenues are especially sensitive to fluctuations in the level of economic activity, making the tax an important instrument in the implementation of stabilization policy. Finally, the tax is a powerful device for the regulation of corporate behavior itself, since the high rate of tax acts as a lever to ensure that corporations will respond to any modifications

[1] *Economic Report of the President, 1977,* Table B–68, p. 267.

the law. State governments also impose taxes on corporate net income, but the rates are much lower than those utilized by the federal government. State governments are less reliant on corporate income tax revenues than the federal government.

THE RATIONALE FOR TAXING CORPORATE PROFITS

The corporation net income tax is a firmly established component in the institutions of government finance. However, this tax does not derive persuasive justification from the conventional tax philosophies of benefits received or ability to pay. Moreover, economic analysis of the effects of the tax generally suggest that it is more harmful than beneficial to the efficient functioning of the economy. The corporation income tax is an institutional "fact of life" that has emerged out of social and political attitudes toward the corporation and out of the very uncertainty which surrounds its incidence and effects.

The Benefits-Received Case

It is apparent that corporations receive valuable benefits from services rendered by government. Many of these services, however, are available to all business enterprises, whether or not they are organized as corporations. Government services to business could provide a case for general business taxation, but it does not provide a case for the taxing of corporate profits and the nontaxing of profits from partnerships or individual proprietorships as such.

Some government services are specifically related to corporations, that is, the corporate form of organization provides certain advantages to firms using this arrangement which are not enjoyed by noncorporate firms. The corporation can incur debt in its own name and the liability of shareholders for these obligations is limited to the amount these shareholdders have invested in the company. Considerable financial advantage is realized through this arrangement. Other advantages include the perpetual life of the corporate entity so that it is not forced into reorganization upon the death or withdrawal of any of the participants. Also, the corporate form sets up a system for the separation of ownership from day-to-day management decisions, which may convey advantages in the operation of the enterprise.

But the fact that advantages are conveyed by the use of the corporate form of doing business is not a sufficient justification for the existing level of taxation imposed on corporate profits. Two problems arise. First, the benefit-received principle justifies the collection of a tax or a charge only to the extent necessary to cover the costs incurred by the government in providing the services that generate the benefits. The public sector costs of providing the advantages of incorporation appear to be very small in comparison to the vast amounts of revenue collected through the corporation income tax. The issuance of the charter and the supervision of the corporation's activities are not expensive operations; fees charged for the issuance of charters could be used to cover these costs. Certainly a tax rate of 48 percent on net profits appears to be excessive in relation to the cost of providing the benefits of incorporation. The second problem is that net income itself is probably a poor measure of the amount of benefit received from these government services. For example, the benefits of limited liability may be greater for corporations that experience losses than for those that realize profits. It can be argued that large corporations receive more benefit from incorporation than small corporations and that the cost of providing the service is greater for large corporations than small corporations, but these are arguments for a tax related to asset size rather than to net profits.

The Ability to Pay Case

The ability to pay philosophy of taxation suggests that persons with high incomes should pay more for the financing of government activities than persons with low incomes. Since the ability to pay philosophy relates to real persons rather than to fictitious legal persons such as corporations, its application requires that the corporate entity itself be set aside and a search undertaken to discover the real persons who bear the actual incidence or burden of the tax on corporate profits. Economists have had little success in tracing the actual incidence of corporate income taxation, but the groups that may bear this burden include the shareholders of the corporation if the tax is not shifted, the purchasers of the products sold by the corporation if the tax is shifted forward, or the employees and suppliers of materials if the tax is shifted backward. Since there is little reason to suppose that the customers, the employees, or the suppliers of materials to corporations have especially high incomes compared to the general population, the thrust of the ability to pay case for corporate income taxation rests on the proposition that the incidence of the tax is on the shareholders and that shareholders constitute a high-income group on whom it is appropriate to impose the corporate tax in addition to the individual or personal income tax.

The entire line of reasoning is tenuous at best. The proposition that the incidence of the tax is on shareholders can be contested, and although shareholders generally are higher-income persons, this is not uniformly the case. Some shareholders are not high-income persons, and beneficiaries of pension funds or insurance plans that invest in corporate shares include many persons of low to moderate income. The imposition of a uniform tax rate on persons of different incomes violates the norm of vertical equity. Horizontal equity is violated when persons at a given income level who own corporate shares are taxed differently from persons at the same income level who receive their income from other sources. At best, the corporate income tax is a crude and imperfect instrument for ability to pay taxation of individuals.

A stronger ability to pay case can be made for corporation income taxation if ability to pay is related to different sources of income rather than to the amount of income received by different individuals. Income from capital may have a greater ability to pay, dollar for dollar, than income from labor services, and the corporate income tax does impose a tax on capital income that is not imposed on labor income. Although income source distinction is not the conventional interpretation of the ability to pay philosophy of taxation, the concept is not without merit and may provide the strongest philosophical foundation for corporation income taxation.

Separate Entity Arguments

The separate entity point of view rejects the notion that the corporation is merely a representative of the interests of the shareholders. Corporations hold property and incur debt as separate entities, and management control is effectively separated from the ownership. Moreover, corporations dominate the economic landscape of the United States economy. According to the separate entity point of view, these facts of life suggest that the corporation as such is the object of taxation.

Conventional ability to pay approaches to taxation, which have been developed in the context of the taxation of individual persons, are not readily applicable to the taxation of corporations as separate entities. It seems apparent that the dollar amount of corporate net income is not a reliable guide to ability to pay because corporations differ greatly from one another in size and in capital structure. For example, a $100,000 profit earned by a large corporation probably is not equivalent, in ability to pay terms, to a $100,000 profit earned by a small corporation. For the large corporation, this profit may reflect a very low rate of return on capital and suggest that the corporation is in serious economic trouble. The same amount of profit for a small corporation may reflect a high rate of return on capital and a considerable ability to pay tax. In other words, the rate of return on capital may be a more appropriate guide to ability to pay taxation than simply the dollar amount of corporate profit, which provides the tax base under the existing system. Certainly to collect the same amount of tax from each corporation in this illustration, without regard to differences in size or rate of return, makes little sense in terms of taxation according to ability to pay.

Taxation of the corporate entity can be a powerful device through which government may undertake to regulate the behavior or character of corporations. In this approach, the nature of the tax would depend on the objectives of the regulatory program. For example, corporate size might be regulated by the application of progressive rate structures to assets. If the regulatory objective were to influence the allocation of profits between the payment of dividends to shareholders and the retention of profits for reinvestment, differences in tax liability could be made dependent on the allocation actually made. Deductibility of dividends paid would increase the proportion of profits distributed as dividends and convert the tax into one on undistributed profits. Conversely, deductibility of retained earnings would promote corporate reinvestment of profits. However, none of these features is present in the existing corporation income tax system.[2]

[2] Cooperatives and mutual companies, such as mutual insurance companies, illustrate some of the difficulties in attempting to tax the corporation as a separate entity. Customers and shareholders are the same people. These enterprises themselves do not generate profits as separate entities but instead distribute patronage dividends or attempt to sell at lower prices so that no net profit remains with the enterprise. Cooperatives and mutual companies contend that patronage dividends are not profits to the company but are simply reductions in the price of goods sold. Patrons themselves contend that receipt of these dividends is not income to them, since all they have done is purchase items at bargain prices. At one time it was possible for cooperatives to accumulate investment funds free of either corporate or individual tax by declaring patronage dividends which were not actually paid to patrons but were only allocated to the

The accounting procedures used in the determination of net income are important regulatory devices. Accelerated depreciation allowances and investment credits have been used extensively to regulate the volume of business investment. Deductibility of various expenditures, such as expenditures for exploration, research, and development, provide a powerful stimulus to these dimensions of business activity and can be viewed as reflecting a regulatory purpose. But the general use of taxation for regulatory purposes extends the argument beyond the question of whether corporations as such, as distinguished from other forms of business organization, should be singled out for separate treatment. Depreciation, investment credits, and the deductibility of certain expenditures are matters of concern to all businesses, whether corporate or noncorporate. The corporation income tax means that these regulatory instruments affect corporations more directly than they affect noncorporate enterprises, but the devices themselves are not specifically related to the corporation as a distinct type of business organization, and a direct relation to the corporation itself is required to provide a foundation for the separate taxation of corporations.

Revenue Yield and Political Appeal

None of the arguments noted above (benefits received, ability to pay, and regulation of corporate enterprise) provides a plausible explanation for the reliance placed on corporation income taxation by the federal government. Each argument contains some elements of validity, but in each case, closer examination fails to provide a sufficient justification for the extent or manner in which corporate profits actually are subjected to taxation. Perhaps the most plausible explanation for the importance of the tax lies in its demonstrated ability to generate sizable revenues for the government, in the uncertainty that surrounds the final incidence of the tax, and in the widely held notion that heavy taxation of corporate incomes somehow is a companion or necessary supplement to the heavy taxation of individual incomes. Although the analogy between individual and corporate income taxation is a false one, its political appeal seems substantial. Even uncertainty about the final incidence of the tax may be an advantage, in a political context, if each voter believes that the final incidence of the tax is on someone else. Shareholders may support the tax in the belief that its burden is shifted to consumers, whereas consumers may support the tax in the belief that the burden is on shareholders. This uncertainty about the actual incidence of the tax raises a particularly troublesome concern for economists interested in public sector decision making. Because of its indirect and more or less hidden character, the tax provides very little guidance to legislators in determining the types of expenditures desired by voters. Economic analysis also suggests that the tax may be detrimental to investment and to the efficient functioning of the economy.

---

patron's account on the books of the cooperative. Similar separate entity problems arise for personal holding companies, where the corporation is set up for the purpose of reinvesting on behalf of its shareholders, whose individual tax rates are higher than the corporation tax rate. Provisions of the law now limit this use of the corporation as a shield from high individual income tax rates.

INCIDENCE AND EFFECTS

The actual incidence of the corporation income tax is one of the most controversial subjects in the economics of government finance. Part of the problem arises from the complexity of the tax itself. The tax is not general because only income from capital is taxed; income from labor services is not taxed. Moreover, it is not directly a tax on all capital income, since only the return on equity capital invested in corporate enterprises is taxed. Nor is the tax a simple excise on a specified product, since corporations produce a great variety of different products, each of which faces different demand conditions and different competitive relationships among producers. This diversity in the competitive situations confronting firms subject to the tax is another part of the problem of analyzing its incidence and effects. Diversity of market structures, in turn, raises questions about the objectives that guide corporate decision making. The notion of profit maximization, which is a fundamental element in orthodox economic analysis, may not be applicable to corporations that hold monopolistic market positions when the interests of management may be effectively separated from the interests of shareholders.

The analysis that follows begins with the assumption that corporations operate in competitive markets. This assumption is then discarded in order to consider monopoly situations and various management objectives other than profit maximization.

Competition—A Tax on Capital

Under the conditions of the competitive model, corporations do not, in the long run, generate any extra or monopoly profits. All factors of production employed by the corporation, including labor services, management services, and the services of capital, receive compensation based on their marginal revenue productivity. These payments absorb all the revenues obtained from the sale of products. The net profits of the corporation constitute the return to equity capital (shareholder investments) used by the corporation; since the corporate income tax is based on these net profits, the tax is a levy on the equity capital of corporations. Since net profits are the residual after all other corporate obligations have been met, the imposition of a corporate net income tax reduces the size of the residual available to shareholders, reducing their return and the value of their investment in the corporation. In the short-run situation, the incidence of the tax clearly is on the shareholders of the corporation at the time the tax is instituted. They cannot escape the burden by selling their shares to someone else because the reduction in the return on shares will simultaneously reduce their market value. By definition, the real capital held by the corporation cannot be reduced in the short run, and therefore no economic effects occur in this time period.

Economic effects and a somewhat different distribution of incidence will arise in the long run, when the owners of capital resources are able to include the expectation of the tax itself (its *announcement effect*) in their investment decisions. Owners of capital resources will not place their funds in corporate equity shares unless the rate of return on these shares is equivalent to the rate of return that can be obtained from alternative uses of these funds. In the long run (that is, after the tax has been announced and resource owners have adjusted their behavior accordingly), the corporation income tax will result in a reallocation of capital between corporate (taxable) and noncorporate (nontaxable) invest-ments, producing economic effects and a wider distribution of the incidence of the tax. The nature of these long-run adjustments is illustrated in Figure 14.1.

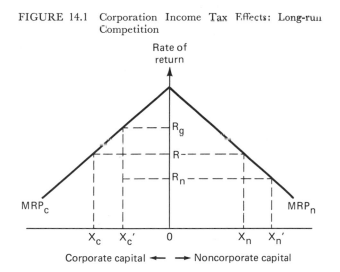

FIGURE 14.1   Corporation Income Tax Effects: Long-run Competition

In this figure, the stock of capital and its allocation between corporate and noncorporate enterprises are displayed along the horizontal axis. Capital employed by corporations is shown by OX_c and capital in noncorporate employ-ments is shown by OX_n, and the total stock of capital is the distance X_cX_n. The vertical dimension of Figure 14.1 shows the marginal revenue productivity and the rate of return on capital. The sloping line on the left side of the figure illustrates declining marginal revenue productivity of capital employed by corporations; the sloping line on the right side illustrates declining marginal revenue productivity of capital in noncorporate employments.[3] If no corpora-tion net income tax were imposed, the available stock of capital, X_cX_n, would be allocated between corporate and noncorporate employments so as to equalize the rate of return obtained in each sector, as shown at R. Capital would be allocated efficiently, since the marginal revenue product of capital would be the same in each sector.

The corporation net income tax drives a wedge between the gross rate of return on capital earned by the corporation and the net rate of return that can be paid to corporate shareholders. It is no longer possible for the corporation to employ OX_c amount of capital, generating a pretax rate of return of OR, and

[3] In the figure, the marginal revenue product curves are drawn as symetrical and as meeting at a common point above point 0 on the horizontal axis. This construction is not essential to the model or necessarily reflective of actual circumstances. All that the model requires is that the marginal revenue product of capital diminishes in each sector as additional amounts of capital are employed in that sector.

pay dividends to shareholders large enough to yield an after-tax rate of return competitive with returns available in alternative noncorporate investments. In order to attract equity capital, corporations must increase their pretax rate of return on capital, and this can be accomplished only by reducing the amount of capital employed, thereby moving up the marginal revenue product curve to higher rate of return levels.

As this process of adjustment is carried out, capital is released from corporate employment and transferred to noncorporate employments, causing the rate of return to capital in noncorporate employments to fall as the increase in noncorporate capital causes the rate of return to move down along the noncorporate MRP curve. The new equilibrium is reached when enough capital has been transferred to raise the pretax rate of return in the corporate sector to R_g, which permits an after-tax rate of return to shareholders of R_n, which is equal to the rate of return obtained on capital employed in the noncorporate sector of the economy. In Figure 14.1, the amount of capital shown as $X_c X_c'$ has been transferred out of the corporate sector and placed in the noncorporate sector, where it appears as $X_n X_n'$.

Several conclusions are apparent from the competitive model illustrated in Figure 14.1. First, the incidence of the corporation net income tax is experienced by capital in noncorporate employments as well as by capital employed by corporations. The rate of return enjoyed by capital resource owners has fallen from R to R_n whether their capital is employed in the corporate or in the noncorporate sector. Second, capital is less efficiently allocated than it was in the absence of the tax on corporate net income. This can be seen in Figure 14.1 by observing that the capital which was transferred out of the corporate sector $(X_c X_c')$ generated a higher level of marginal revenue product than the capital added to the noncorporate sector $(X_n X_n')$. The corporate sector employs less capital than is warranted by technological conditions and the noncorporate sector employs more capital than is warranted. The tax imposes an "excess burden" on the economy because total production is less as a result of the inefficient allocation of capital resources.

Still other economic effects can be expected to follow from the tax, although these are not directly shown in Figure 14.1. For example, the total amount of capital may be diminished if the reduction in the rate of return to capital (from R to R_n) results in a reduction in aggregate saving and capital formation. In this respect, the rate of growth in economic capacity may be slowed by the tax. Finally, a variety of excise effects may follow from the tax. The output of products utilizing a particularly large amount of capital or produced primarily in the corporate sector may be reduced and experience price increases to consumers. Conversely, the tax may favor products produced by labor-intensive technologies or produced primarily through the noncorporate sector of the economy.

The economic effects of the corporation income tax according to the competitive model, and especially the excess burden dimension of these effects, constitute a severe economic condemnation of the corporation net income tax. The policy implication of this model is that the corporation income tax should be abolished in the interest of eliminating the excess burden and the impediments to economic growth it generates. According to this line of reasoning, the tax would be replaced by the individual income tax or integrated with the individual income tax, which provides a clearer model of incidence and fewer impediments to efficiency and economic growth.

Profit-Maximizing Monopoly

The tax on corporate net income is a tax on equity capital for a corporation holding a monopoly position, just as the tax is a levy on equity capital for corporations that do not hold a monopoly position. The difference between the monopoly and the competitive situation is that the return to equity capital in monopoly includes an economic rent or monopoly profit component that is not present in the returns of a competitive firm.

The conventional graphs presented in Figure 14.2 illustrate the distinction. The firm at the left is a corporation operating in a competitive market, that is, its average revenue does not change as its output changes, since this firm is unable to influence the price of the product. At price OP and output OQ, the firm is in long-run equilibrium and no extra or monopoly profits are earned, that is, it is generating a return to equity capital just equal to the normal return to capital in the economy. These returns to equity capital are costs to the corporation, since it would be unable to attract this capital if these returns were not generated. A tax on returns to equity capital would increase the costs of operating the enterprise. That is, the normal returns to capital would still have to be paid, and in addition, a tax would have to be paid to the government. The consequence of the tax is illustrated by the upward shifting of the average and marginal costs of doing business shown as the AC' and MC' curves on the graph. The tax will make it impossible for the firm to cover its average costs (including tax) as long as the price remains at OP, and economic adjustments will have to be made. The firm may be forced to cease operation as a corporation. Production of the product may be taken over by noncorporate enterprises

FIGURE 14.2   Corporation Income Tax on Firms

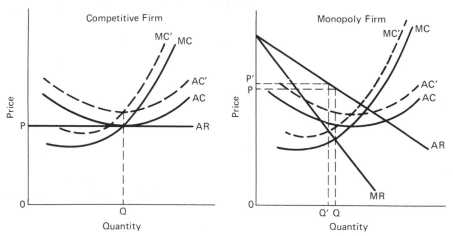

or enterprises using less capital-intensive methods. The point is that, in the competitive model, the tax on equity capital will force the industry to undergo the package of economic effects outlined in the competitive model.

The monopoly model is illustrated on the right-hand side of Figure 14.2. The average and marginal cost curves are the same as for the competitive corporation, but the average revenue curve slopes downward to the right, reflecting the fact that the output of this firm will influence the price of the product. Because of its ability to influence price, output decisions are based on the marginal revenue curve and the profit-maximizing output of OQ is set at the intersection of marginal revenue and marginal cost. At this output, price is OP and extra or monopoly profits are earned in excess of average costs. A corporate net income tax on the returns to equity capital from this corporation will increase the average and marginal costs of doing business just as it did for the competitive corporation, since the portion of earnings that constitute necessary or normal returns to equity capital are included in the base of the tax.

These higher average and marginal costs of doing business (shown by the AC' and MC' curves) will lead to some reduction in output and some increase in product price as shown by output OQ' and price OP' in Figure 14.2. In other words, the portion of the tax based on normal or necessary returns to equity capital will produce excise effects in the monopoly case just as they did in the competitive case.[4] But the main point is that the portion of the tax based on the extra or monopoly returns will not produce these effects. The monopoly or extra profit is an economic rent arising from the possession of a strategically advantageous market position. The corporate income tax will capture a portion of this monopoly rent for the government, but the portion that remains in the hands of the private owners still offers a better return than could be obtained by placing funds elsewhere in the economy. Thus, to the extent that the corporation income tax is imposed on pure monopoly rents, it does not produce economic effects.

It seems likely that some part of the popular acceptance of corporation income taxation arises from the notion that monopoly rents constitute a large portion of the net income of corporations. Certainly a major portion of the revenue collected through the corporation income tax comes from large companies that hold dominant positions in the markets for many products. But the degree of monopoly power differs among corporations, and since a single corporation may produce a variety of products, its monopoly position in one division of its activities may differ greatly from its monopoly position in other divisions. Thus, it is not possible to arrive at any firm conclusion on the extent to which the corporation income tax is a tax on monopoly rents and the extent to which it is a tax on normal returns. Moreover, the analysis of the economic effects of the corporation income tax on monopolistic enterprises hinges on the assumption that the behavior of these companies and their responses to the tax are

---

[4] The model suggests that these effects may be somewhat less severe in the monopoly case because adjustments are determined according to the marginal revenue curve rather than according to the average revenue curve. Since the marginal revenue curve is steeper than the average revenue curve, a given upward movement of marginal cost leads to a smaller quantity adjustment along the marginal revenue curve.

based on the motive of maximizing profits. A vast array of possible economic effects of the tax arises if the assumption of profit maximization is set aside.

Nonmaximization of Profits

Firms that operate in competitive markets are forced by circumstances to make decisions in the light of profit maximization. But firms that operate in noncompetitive (monopolistic) markets may permit other objectives to influence price and output decisions. Since the incidence and effects of the corporation income tax depend on the responses that follow from the tax, the objectives which direct these responses become factors that may influence corporation income tax incidence and effects.

Oligopoly and price leadership. Oligopoly is a type of market structure in which the supply of a product is controlled by a relatively small number of firms. Each firm in the oligopoly market provides a large enough portion of total supply so that a change in its output would have an effect on price, but each is constrained in its price and output policy by concern about the response the rival members of the oligopoly might make to any change. A firm might attempt to increase its profit by lowering price and gaining a larger share of the total product market, but this effort would be frustrated if rival firms also lower price. Likewise, an attempt to increase profit by increasing price encounters the danger of a loss of a substantial share of this market if other firms do not follow suit with equivalent price increases.

Price rigidity and failure to maximize industry profits are likely outcomes of this situation unless some coordinating mechanism is developed to free the firms from uncertainty about the behavior of rival members of the oligopoly. A leadership role by one of the firms provides such a coordinating mechanism if it is understood that actions initiated by the leader will be followed by the other firms. But leadership is a delicate operation, since it implicitly involves rationing of profits and market shares. The establishment of a corporation income tax or a change in its rates or accounting requirements will affect all the firms in the oligopoly simultaneously and may provide the occasion for parallel responses by all firms in increasing price. In other words, the corporation tax may itself be a coordinating instrument that will enable the firms to set aside their concerns about the response of rivals and move simultaneously to a position of greater profits. Profits may increase more than enough to cover the tax increase, so that net profit and the return to equity capital may be greater after the tax than before, and the tax will have been shifted forward to consumers through higher prices. Moreover, using the tax as the occasion for industry-wide price adjustments can provide a smokescreen or protection against possible antitrust charges of having made agreements in restraint of trade. The tax increase provides a kind of legitimacy for both the price increases and the parallel action in establishing these increases.

Sales maximizing and satisficing. In the large modern corporation, company policy may be effectively controlled by management, subject only to the constraint that profits are maintained at a level satisfactory to the shareholders. This is not to say the shareholders prefer smaller profits to larger profits. Satisfactory profits are not as good as maximum profits from the point of view of the shareholder, and shareholders presumably want management to maximize profits. The point is that, in the large and complex corporation, shareholders probably are not able to determine whether the profits actually realized are the result of policies directed at profit maximization. So long as profits are maintained at levels high enough to prevent widespread discontent among shareholders, management may be able to pursue goals other than profit maximization. The profit goal is one of *satisficing*, and objectives other than the earning of maximum profits may be pursued, subject only to the constraint that some minimum level of profit must be maintained.

The "not for profit" goals of corporate management may include economic power, political influence, social service, harmonious relations between management and labor, comfortable working conditions, and sales maximization. The goal of sales maximization is especially attractive because it may enhance both the power and the size of the business bureaucracy. When a sales maximization goal is pursued, output and sales may exceed the levels dictated by profit maximization. Both product price and the level of profits are lower than they would be if output were set according to the goal of maximum profit. The sales maximization objective can be pursued as long as the profits actually realized are satisfactory to the shareholders. But the imposition of a corporate income tax on a company that has pursued the sales maximization goal will reduce after-tax profits and may cause them to fall below the level acceptable to shareholders. In this situation, tax forces the company to move closer to the profit-maximizing level of output in order to restore profits to an acceptable level. Output will be reduced and prices will rise as a result of the tax, which will have been shifted forward to consumers and backward to material and labor suppliers.

Financial Structure, Wasteful Spending, and Mergers

A complete catalog of possible economic effects of the corporation income tax would be lengthy, complicated, and speculative. Several specific economic effects, however, merit brief mention.

Financial structure. The corporation income tax may influence the balance or mix between equity financing and debt financing of corporate activities by favoring the use of debt instruments (for example, bonds) rather than the use of equity instruments (for example, shares). This distortion of the financial structure of corporate enterprise arises because interest paid on debt instruments is deductible in calculating the base of the tax, whereas dividends paid on equity instruments are not deductible. That is, dividends are part of the tax base; interest payments are not part of the tax base. The difference between debt and equity financing is significant because bondholders have stronger claims upon the corporation and because the corporation has less flexibility in meeting these obligations. Interest payments and the repayment of borrowed funds are contractual obligations of the company, and inability to meet these obligations can force the corporation into reorganization or bankruptcy. Equity shares, on the other hand, do not impose equivalent obligations on the company. Dividend rates can be raised or lowered according to the fortunes or financial plans of the company, and there is no obligation for the repayment of amounts invested.

The corporate income tax bias in favor of debt instruments, therefore, may discourage the undertaking of risky ventures by corporations and promote a more cautious economic posture. Moreover, a distortion of corporate financial structure in favor of heavier reliance on debt instruments may increase the vulnerability of the corporate sector during recessions in aggregate economic activity. Business failures may be more frequent during recessions than they would be if greater reliance were placed on equity financing. A destabilizing element may be injected into the aggregate performance of the economy itself.

Wasteful spending. With the marginal rate of tax on corporate net income at 48 percent, the federal government in effect absorbs almost half of the cost of expenditures that qualify for deduction in calculating net income. Deductible items can be purchased for "52 cent dollars" by the corporation, and this differential may lead to wasteful spending. Activities may be undertaken that would not have been undertaken in the absence of especially advantageous deductions for certain types of expenditures. The point is that deductibility becomes an important consideration in corporate decision making when the tax rates are at the 48 percent level. The tax law rather than purely economic considerations may determine the actions taken.

Because the character of business operations differs from one industry to another, the tax law can introduce pervasive distortions into the operation of the economy. The deductibility of research and development expenditures promotes this type of activity, just as the deductibility of advertising expenditures promotes advertising and the deductibility of expense account allowances and entertainment expenditures promotes these activities. Rapid depreciation deductibility and investment credits are particularly helpful to capital-intensive and growing industries. Percentage depletion allowances for the extraction of petroleum and minerals are perhaps the most widely recognized instance in which tax law provisions influence the operation of the economy. The impact of tax law provisions on the activities and profitability of corporations means that political activity and lobbying to influence the law become important dimensions of corporate enterprise. The process is self-reinforcing, leading to an ever-increasing mixture of economic and political considerations in the activities of corporations.

Loss carryover mergers. A corporation that experiences a net operating loss may carry the loss deduction back to the two preceding tax years, recalculating these taxes and regaining some of the tax paid, and may carry losses forward to apply against net profits earned in the following five tax years. This averaging arrangement is necessary to avoid tax discrimination against firms with fluctuating incomes, and as noted earlier, the willingness of the government to share in losses as well as profits increases the willingness of corporations to undertake risky ventures. The availability of loss carryover deductions may also result in mergers or acquisitions that would not have taken place in the absence of the carryover provision. The opportunity to carry loss deductions forward to future tax years is valuable only if profits can be earned in these future years. If the corporation that has experienced losses has little prospect for profitable future operations, the loss carry-forward provision will have little value unless the firm is sold to or merged with a corporation that does anticipate profits. The carrying forward of past losses becomes a corporate asset that can be realized only through merger or sale to another corporation. Because mergers or acquisitions that would not otherwise have occurred may take place, tax considerations will again have influenced the structure of the economy.

Empirical Evidence

The models outlined above suggest that the incidence and effects of the corporation income tax depend on the degree of competition or monopoly which exists in the corporate environment and on whether corporate responses to the tax reflect profit maximizing or other objectives. Empirical evidence therefore is required in order to determine the actual incidence and effects of the tax. A considerable amount of research has been devoted to the question, but the findings to date are inconclusive. If the incidence of the tax is on capital, as suggested by the competitive profit-maximizing model, the net return to equity capital would fall with increases in the rate of the corporation income tax, other things remaining unchanged.

Since the corporate income tax rate was 12.5 percent in the 1920s and rose to 52 percent during World War II, this time period was analyzed to explore the incidence and effects of the tax. The findings showed that the net return to equity capital did *not* decline as the tax rate was increased, suggesting that the tax was being shifted forward in higher prices to consumers or backward in lower returns to material suppliers. These findings support the monopoly and nonmaximizing models of the incidence of the tax. However, the time period between the 1920s and the post-World War II period was one of great economic change and turbulence and the increase in the rate of the corporate income tax was not the only factor that may have influenced the net return to capital. For example, technological progress could increase the before-tax rate of return to capital and permit after-tax returns to be maintained even after the payment of increased tax liabilities. Models that incorporate measures of technological progress suggest that this factor can "explain" the stability of after-tax rates of return. Thus, the view that the tax is a levy on capital is not necessarily contradicted by the evidence of this time period. The question of the actual incidence and effects of the corporate income tax remains unresolved by economic analysis.

RESTRUCTURING CORPORATE INCOME TAXATION

Proposals for major restructuring of corporate income taxation are perennial topics of discussion in government finance. The tax is not popular among economists because it lacks a firm philosophical foundation and because the effects of the tax, although shrouded in considerable uncertainty, are widely believed to be detrimental to economic efficiency and growth. Restructuring is too mild a term to describe some proposals, which advocate abolition of the tax by "integrating" it with the individual income tax. Proposals that are almost as extreme would narrow the tax to one on undistributed corporate profits. Other proposals would broaden the tax base to one on value added by both corporate and noncorporate enterprises.

Integration with Individual Income Taxation

The proposal that the corporate net income tax should be integrated with the individual income tax is a euphemistic way of advocating that the corporate tax should be abolished and that the net income of corporations should be reported, in full, on the individual tax returns filed by shareholders. If this integration were carried out, income earned through the ownership of shares in corporate enterprises would be taxed in the same way as income derived from any other source. Dividend income would not be double taxed, as it is now, through the imposition of both the corporate tax before the dividend is distributed and the individual income tax after the dividend is received by the shareholder. Corporate income not distributed as dividends, that is, the undistributed profits of corporations, would not be subject to a corporation income tax but would be taxable to the individual at rates applicable to the individual and in the accounting period coinciding with the earning of the income by the corporation.

With integration, the total net income of the corporation would be allocated among shareholders according to their respective interests in the corporation and the amount of this allocated share would be reported both to the shareholder and to the government. This is parallel to the procedure presently required of partnerships. It would not mean that the corporation would be required actually to distribute all profits as dividends to shareholders. The corporation could retain profits for reinvestment, but the income reported by shareholders and the tax liability of shareholders would not be altered by the corporation's decision on the amount of dividend to be declared. If the corporation tax were integrated with the individual tax, some vestige of the corporate tax might remain if withholding was required on shareholder earnings as is presently required for employee earnings. The amount withheld and forwarded to the government by the corporation would, of course, be reported to the shareholder along with the report of his share of corporate income and would be applicable as a credit against the individual's tax liability. The withholding system would be particularly appropriate if corporations continued to retain shareholder earnings for reinvestment by the company.

Undistributed Profits Tax

The corporation income tax would be converted into a tax on undistributed corporate profits if dividend payments were permitted to be deducted in determining the base for the tax. Dividends paid then would receive the same treatment as interest paid on bonded indebtedness, which would eliminate the discrimination between equity and debt financing, and dividends no longer would be subjected to taxation at both the corporate and the individual levels.

The corporation tax would no longer be purely a tax on equity capital, and a strong incentive would be generated to secure equity financing by direct solicitation in the stock market rather than through the practice of retaining net income. Whether shareholders would prefer the corporation to declare dividends or to retain earnings would depend on the rate of tax imposed on undistributed profits, on the marginal tax rate applicable to the individual shareholder, and on the treatment given to the capital gains generated by the retained earnings. Shareholders facing high marginal tax rates would favor retention rather than distribution of corporate income, but shareholders in lower brackets would prefer profits to be distributed as dividends.

It is apparent that an undistributed profits tax would not achieve the kind of neutrality between corporate and noncorporate business and between different sources of income that would be realized by the complete integration (abolition) of the corporate tax. Instead, a kind of tradeoff would be established between income distributed in dividends and income retained by the corporation. Income retained would be subjected to the special tax on undistributed profits, but would be excused from current taxation under the individual income tax (although it might be subject to taxation as capital gain when shares are exchanged). On the other hand, income distributed as dividends would be subject to current taxation as individual income, but would not be subject to the special tax on undistributed profits. A complicated set of considerations would be injected into securities markets relating to the individual tax situations of investors and to the dividend policies of corporations. Moreover, the system would mean that earnings retained by noncorporate enterprises would be treated in the opposite way to earnings retained by corporations. That is, earnings reinvested by noncorporate businesses would be subject to the individual rates but not to the special undistributed profits tax.

Excess Profits Tax

During World War II and the Korean conflict in the early 1950s, the regular corporation income tax was supplemented by the addition of a special tax on excess profits. When individual income tax rates are increased and sacrifices are required of many elements in society, corporations are also called upon to carry an extra share of responsibility for government finance. An excess profits tax, however, is not simply an increase in the corporation income tax rate, nor is it simply the addition of an additional tax rate bracket to higher amounts of corporate profit as ordinarily defined. Instead, the excess profits tax imposes an extra or supplementary tax on that portion of corporate income defined to be *excess* profit. The implication is that corporations which experience significant increases in profit during the emergency period are profiting from the emergency itself (profiteering) and should be required to contribute a substantial portion of these excess profits to the public treasury. The reasoning is persuasive enough to suggest that excess profits taxes may again be imposed if future emergency situations arise which require sacrifices and tax increases throughout the society.

The special problem of excess profits taxation is to devise a way to distinguish excess profits from normal or reasonable profits. The obvious way to do this is to examine the profit experience of the company during a recent and presumably "normal" time period and to define excess profits to be those that significantly exceed these normal base period profits. This approach is disarmingly simple, but subject to great complexity in application to actual cases. A time period which is "normal" for some companies will not have been "normal" for other companies. New companies established in response to the emergency conditions will have no historical records through which normal returns can be estimated, and even established companies probably will have made new investments and altered their operations in response to the demands and opportunities of the emergency. In this context, the question of identifying excess profits requires a finding about the rate of return on capital which is normal. This, in turn, focuses attention on the valuation of capital and on differences in the degree of risk associated with emergency-related operations. Both capital evaluation and estimation of risk are exceedingly difficult and uncertain in emergency periods.

The effects of excess profits taxation are also unclear. Production incentives may be motivated by patriotic considerations so that direct disincentive effects of the extra tax may not be as severe as would be expected in more normal times, but the exceedingly high marginal tax rates that arise from the combination of both the regular corporate tax and the excess profits tax can lead to ill-considered and wasteful spending on items which qualify as deductible in determining the tax base.

Value Added Tax

The value added tax, which is widely used in European countries, has also been proposed for use in the United States. It is sometimes suggested that value added taxation could replace corporation income taxation. The replacement of the corporation income tax with a value added tax would mean the introduction of an entirely new and different tax. The type of value added tax most frequently suggested is equivalent to a sales tax on consumption purchases. Therefore, replacement of the corporate income tax with a value added tax would amount to the entry of the federal government into the sales tax field and to a radical restructuring of the revenue sources of the federal government. In the public mind, value added taxation may be linked with corporation income taxation because both are collected from business enterprises rather than directly from individuals, but this linkage is essentially spurious. They are different taxes and should be recognized as such.

The value added tax is well named because its base consists of the increment or increase in value imparted to materials as they are handled or processed by a business enterprise. The base of the tax consists of the difference between the amount received by the company from the sale of its output and the amounts paid by the company in acquiring the materials used in producing the product. This difference between sales receipts and materials costs is *value added* and arises from labor services employed by the company and from the services of land and capital owned by the company.

There are three different varieties of value added tax. The GNP type of value added tax would allow no deduction for capital equipment used in production. Since the materials used in producing capital equipment would be taxed and since the value added when the equipment itself was used in further production would also be taxed, this type of value added tax would discriminate against the use of capital in production processes and would invite inefficient use of technology. A second variety, called the income type, would allow a deduction for depreciation of capital equipment so that the tax would be on net, rather than gross, value added. This type would not discriminate against the use of capital, but as an income tax it is considered inferior to individual taxation because the value added tax does not relate the amount of tax to the amount of income received by different individuals in a way that permits the use of deductions or rate graduation related to individual circumstances. The third variety is called the consumption type because it would permit the immediate deduction of amounts paid in the acquisition of capital equipment (rather than the periodic deduction of depreciation). The consumption type of value added tax is equivalent to a sales tax on consumption goods. At each stage of the production process, the tax paid by the company is shifted forward to the next stage, and the sum total of tax is finally paid by the purchaser of the product, since there is no further or subsequent purchaser to whom the tax can be shifted.[5]

It is apparent that replacement of the corporation income tax with a consumption type of value added tax is more than a restructuring of corporate taxation. Like the integration approach, it would abolish separate taxation of corporate income and replace the lost revenue with revenue from a different tax. With the integration approach, the replacement would be individual income tax revenues; under the value added alternative, it would be a type of sales tax. On the other hand, undistributed profits taxation and excess profits taxation would continue to single out the corporation as a separate and distinct taxable entity. Regulatory rather than revenue objectives would characterize corporate taxation under the latter approaches.

SUMMARY

The corporation income tax provides large amounts of revenue for the federal government and is a firmly established component of the tax structure in spite of the fact that the tax is difficult to rationalize under either the benefit-received or the ability to pay philosophies of taxation. Its continued importance is supported by the revenue it produces, by the regulatory opportunities it provides, and by an analogy in the public mind between the taxation of individual incomes and the taxation of corporate income.

Economic analysis generally suggests that the corporate income tax gener-

---

[5] The incidence model can be carried further by suggesting that consumers, who pay higher prices because of the consumption tax, may be able to demand and receive wage increases as a result of the tax on consumption. However, this sequence suggests that the tax produces a general inflation of prices throughout the economy and requires that monetary and fiscal actions of the government be such as to permit this inflation to take place. The questions raised are broader than those related to value added taxation as such.

ates effects detrimental to economic efficiency and economic growth, but this analysis is clouded by uncertainty about the objectives that direct corporate decisions and by the diversity that prevails within the corporate sector. In a competitive framework, the tax is clearly a burden on equity capital, but in noncompetitive situations or when goals other than profit maximization are effective, the tax may be shifted forward to consumers or backward to suppliers of resources. The tax also injects distortions into capital structures and may encourage wasteful spending.

Awareness of the inefficiencies generated by the corporate income tax leads to proposals for abolition or restructuring of the tax. Integrating the corporate tax with the individual tax would abolish the corporate tax and replace the lost revenue with increases in individual income tax revenues. Proposals to replace the corporate tax with a value added tax also amount to an abolition of the tax as it presently exists and its replacement with a tax likely to be equivalent to a sales tax. An undistributed profits tax would modify the corporate tax by restricting its base only to earnings not distributed as dividends to shareholders. During emergency periods, the corporate tax may be modified by superimposing an additional tax on profits found to be excessive in relation to profits earned in more normal periods.

A tax system designed by economists probably would not make use of the corporation income tax as it now exists. But the tax system has not been designed by economists; instead, the corporation income tax has risen to prominence through the interaction of many social, political, and economic considerations. Once established as a social-political-economic institution, it is unlikely to undergo significant modification unless changes take place in underlying attitudes toward the corporation.

SUGGESTED READINGS

HARBERGER, ARNOLD. "The Incidence of the Corporation Income Tax," *Journal of Political Economy*, June 1962.

KRZYZANIAK, M., and R. MUSGRAVE. *The Shifting of the Corporation Income Tax* (Baltimore: John Hopkins University Press, 1963).

HARBERGER, A. C. and M. J. BAILEY (EDS.). *The Taxation of Income from Capital* (Washington, D.C.: The Brookings Institution, 1969).

MIESZKOWSKI, P. "Tax Incidence Theory," *Journal of Economic Literature*, December 1969.

SIEGFRIED, JOHN J., "Effective Average U.S. Corporation Income Tax Rates," *National Tax Journal* XXVII, 2 (June 1974).

National Tax Association and Tax Institute of America Symposium. "The Taxation of Income from Corporate Shareholding," *National Tax Journal*, XXVIII, 3 (September 1975).

15

Commodity Taxation

Commodity taxation means that certain commodities or activities are singled out for special taxation, that is, a tax is imposed on some commodities or activities but not on other commodities or activities. Commodity taxes are essentially selective or discriminatory and thus should be distinguished from general or broad-based taxes, such as income or general sales taxes. Motor fuels, alcoholic beverages, tobacco products, airline tickets, and telephone service are among the commodities subjected to special taxation by the federal government. Gambling is also subjected to special taxation. Some commodity taxes are known as *excise* taxes, meaning that they are imposed on the manufacturing of the commodity; others are referred to as *selective sales* taxes, meaning that the tax is imposed on the sale or purchase of the commodity. The commodity tax category also includes customs duties (tariffs), which are imposed on imported items.

Before the advent of income taxation, the federal government relied heavily on revenue collected from customs duties. Now commodity taxation is a relatively minor source of revenue. Excise taxes and customs duties account for less than 10 percent of federal budget receipts. (State governments, however, rely heavily on selective commodity taxation.) Except for gasoline and motor vehicle taxes, revenue raising often is not the main purpose of selective commodity taxation. Instead, federal use of these taxes typically reflects a decision to intervene in market processes and to influence the allocation of resources; that is, it is essentially taxation for nonfiscal purposes. Taxes on gambling, for example, are designed to provide help in the enforcement of other laws dealing with gambling as an illegal activity. Consumption of alcohol and tobacco is not illegal, but the imposition of selective taxes on them suggests a "sumptuary" objective of discouraging their use.

It would be wrong, however, to conclude that the only application of selective commodity taxation is to try to persuade people to stop consuming things or engaging in activities which allegedly are bad for them. These taxes also may be used in an effort to conserve resources; indeed, many selective taxes have been imposed as emergency measures when particular resources were in short supply. Taxes on utility services, telephone calls, and airline tickets arose in emergency periods when facilities providing these services were especially scarce. In this situation, the taxes were used as rationing instruments. In the current energy crisis, special taxes on petroleum and other energy sources may be employed to limit consumption. Finally, selective taxation may be used to correct for faulty operation of the market processes themselves. Special taxes on activities that pollute the environment illustrate this corrective application of selective commodity taxation when markets may fail to take account of pollution costs imposed by certain activities. Corrective excises are in the nature of charges on the users of environmental services, and as such may promote more efficient use of these services.

Thus, commodity taxation is an instrument of government finance that can be used to accomplish many different purposes. These taxes can be used to raise revenue, to influence individual behavior, to ration selected commodities during emergency periods, or to improve the functioning of markets in their task of allocating resources. In each of these applications, the effectiveness and the costs of commodity taxation hinge on relationships revealed through economic analysis.

INCIDENCE AND EFFECTS

The economic analysis of the incidence and effects of commodity taxation is a simple and straightforward application of elementary economic principles and has been a standard feature of government finance economics for a long time. Moreover, the application of this analysis is not limited to taxes explicitly labeled excise taxes or taxes on selected commodities. Excise tax effects are triggered by taxes on inputs as well as by taxes on outputs, since a tax on an input will result in a higher cost of providing a product and have an excise effect similar to a tax on the product itself. For example, the corporation income tax has been characterized as a tax on capital that generates excise effects by modifying the way that capital is employed in the production of different products. Payroll taxes for social security or unemployment compensation are taxes on labor inputs that generate excise effects. Property taxes on equipment and inventories also produce excise effects. Therefore, the economic analysis of the incidence and effects of excise taxes is part of the analysis of most tax instruments.

The analysis begins with the simple supply and demand illustration in Figure 15.1 and with the proposition that the tax can be viewed as an increase in the cost of producing the commodity subjected to tax. Certainly, taxes on inputs are seen by producers as increases in the costs of production, and taxes on the product itself, since they are collected initially from the firm, are treated

FIGURE 15.1   Shifting and Effect of a Commodity
             Tax

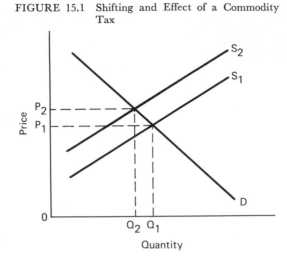

Quantity

in the same way. It is as if the government had become a factor in the production process and requires payment, just as payment is required for labor and raw materials. Since costs of production are a basic ingredient underlying the supply curve for commodities, the increase in costs introduced by the tax will cause the supply curve to move upward by the amount of the tax, that is, from S_1 to S_2 in Figure 15.1

The producers of the products subjected to taxation will, of course, wish to shift the tax forward to the purchasers of the commodity through higher prices. But it is quite likely that a complete forward shift of the tax will not be possible. The quantity of the commodity consumers will purchase at any specified price is shown by the demand curve for that commodity, and, in the conventional analysis of commodity taxation, this demand curve is *not* shifted as a result of the imposition of the tax. The demand curve for a commodity reflects the utility or satisfaction purchasers expect to realize from it, the amount of purchasing power that purchasers command, and the prices of other goods or services that might be purchased. Since none of these aspects of demand is altered by the imposition of the tax, no shift in the demand curve will take place. Attempts to shift the tax forward to consumers will have to be carried out subject to the constraints imposed by the existing demand curve. When the demand curve exhibits some elasticity, as illustrated in Figure 15.1, sellers will find that price increases to recover amounts paid in tax will cause consumers to purchase a smaller quantity of the commodity, as shown by the decrease in the quantity sold from Q_1 to Q_2. Thus, only part of the burden or incidence of the tax is shifted forward to consumers, through the price increase from P_1 to P_2, and the tax has produced an economic effect on the allocation of resources through the reduction in the quantity produced and sold. The reduction in the quantity produced may cause some of the incidence of the tax to be shifted backward to resource owners through lower wages or lower input prices.

It is apparent that the incidence of commodity taxes and their effects on the allocation of resources are strongly influenced by the elasticity of demand

and supply for the commodity. Let us first examine the role of demand elasticity and then explore, in somewhat greater detail, the importance of supply elasticity and the market structure of the industry producing the commodity.

The Elasticity of Demand

The importance of the elasticity of demand for the taxed commodity is illustrated in Figure 15.2, which shows two demand curves, one of which (D_i) is completely inelastic and one of which (D_e) exhibits some degree of price elasticity. In the extreme case in which demand is completely inelastic, the price of the commodity would rise by the full amount of the tax (from OP to OP_i) and the quantity purchased would be the same as before the tax was imposed (OQ). The entire incidence of the tax would be shifted forward to consumers and there would be no direct economic effects on the allocation of resources. The tax would fail completely in its sumptuary or rationing purposes. Of course, customers would spend more money on the commodity than they spent on it before the tax was imposed, so that some indirect effects could arise through reductions in saving or reductions in expenditures for other commodities customers previously had purchased. If demand exhibits some elasticity, as illustrated by demand curve D_e, a smaller portion of the tax will be shifted forward to consumers and a reduction in the quantity purchased takes place. Less revenue will be collected by the government but there will be direct effects on the allocation of resources, and the possibility arises that some of the incidence of the tax will be shifted backward to the resources used in producing the product. If the coefficient of elasticity is numerically greater than -1.0, consumers will spend less money for the commodity after the tax than they had spent for it previously and increased spending might be directed to other products, where resource owners might become indirect beneficiaries of the tax.

The main point that emerges from this analysis of the importance of demand elasticity on the incidence and effects of commodity taxes is that a tradeoff

FIGURE 15.2   Demand Elasticity and Tax Shifting

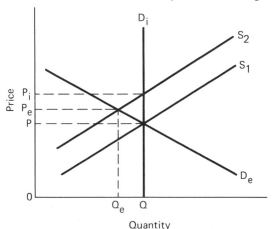

or conflict exists between the objectives of raising revenue and generating economic effects. If demand for the taxed commodity is relatively inelastic, significant amounts of revenue may be collected by the government, but only minor economic effects and little backward shifting will take place. In general, the commodities actually taxed by the federal government (and by the states as well) appear to face rather inelastic demand. It is reasonable to conclude that they have had little effect on the allocation of resources in the economy. Tobacco taxes probably have done little to reduce smoking and alcoholic beverage taxes probably have done little to reduce drinking. Likewise, taxes on airline tickets and telephone calls probably have had little effect. Perhaps they are token gestures to those voters who desire sumptuary legislation. A political hypothesis can be suggested for the apparent legislative preference for taxation of commodities with inelastic demand. Legislatures may be subject to more political pressure from producer-oriented groups than from consumer-oriented groups. Since less backward shifting and resource reallocation will arise when demand is inelastic, producer groups may be less sensitive to taxes on these commodities and may exert less pressure on legislators.

A welfare or equity case for commodity taxation can be made if the commodities selected for taxation are considered luxury or nonessential items and if they also exhibit demand that is price inelastic. Of course, price inelasticity does not mean that the commodity is a luxury good and not all luxury goods are price inelastic, but if the combination does exist, then a tax on that commodity will have its incidence on consumers of the good and will tap the consumer surplus that they enjoy from the good. If the consumers of this good also happen to be those in higher-income categories (that is, if the good has an income elasticity coefficient greater than $+1.0$), the tax can result in some redistribution of income. However, many commodities presently subjected to commodity taxation probably do not satisfy these conditions.

SUPPLY RESPONSE: COMPETITIVE MODEL

Supply conditions in the industry producing the commodity subjected to tax have important influences on the economic effects of the tax and on whether the incidence of the tax is shifted backward to the owners of resources used in the production processes. The competitive or noncompetitive nature of the industry is important in this analysis, as is the time period allowed for the effects to be realized. It is convenient to begin with a description of the response process in a competitive industry.

Short-Run Response

Figures 15.3(a) and (b) illustrate market supply and demand conditions for a commodity and the cost conditions confronting a firm in the industry that produces the commodity. A pretax long-run equilibrium situation is illustrated by the P_1Q_1 relationships on each graph. In this situation, the quantity demanded is equal to the quantity supplied and the firm is receiving normal profits. The imposition of a tax on the commodity or on an input used in produc-

FIGURE 15.3 Short-run Tax Shifting

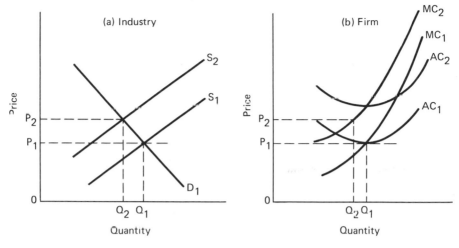

ing it causes both the average cost curve and the marginal cost curve of the firm to shift upward by the amount of the tax. If sales continue to be made at price P_1, it is apparent that losses will be incurred.

The supply curve in part (a) is the (horizontal) summation of the marginal cost curves of the firms in the industry. Since the marginal cost for each firm has shifted upward by the amount of the tax, the industry supply curve is also shifted upward by this amount, as illustrated by S_2. In the short-run adjustment to the tax, the equilibrium conditions become $P_2 Q_2$. Each firm must accept price P_2 and adjust its output to Q_2 as shown in Figure 15.3(b). Each firm is doing the best it can in the circumstances, since price is equal to after-tax marginal cost, but losses are being incurred, since price P_2 is less than after-tax average cost. Some forward shifting has taken place, since some of the tax is being paid by consumers through the higher price, and some resources have lost employment. However, some of the tax has not been shifted and is being absorbed by the firms themselves. Further adjustments and tax shifting will take place in the process of reaching a long-run equilibrium, which will not be attained until the firms in the industry are no longer incurring losses.

Price P_2 prevailing in the short run covers the variable costs of production including the tax, but it is not sufficient to cover some fixed or overhead costs of being in business. Some firms continue in business in the short run simply because this is the least expensive way of recovering their investment in fixed equipment, that is, equipment inventories are being liquidated by being used up in production. When the process is completed, equipment will not be replaced and an exodus of capital from the industry will take place. The point is that the losses being incurred by the firms in the short run are subsidizing a certain amount of output of the commodity, so that the full effect of the tax will not be felt in this time period. The sumptuary, rationing, and corrective objectives of the tax will not be fully realized in the short-run time period.

Long-Run Response

A new long-run equilibrium situation evolves when the subsidization via losses and the liquidation of excess equipment has been completed. The full range of consequences of the tax can now be examined. In this analysis, the industry supply curve is no longer determined by short-run marginal costs such as those illustrated in Figure 15.3(b), which typically slope upward to the right because of the production constraints imposed by fixed stocks of capital equipment. Instead, long-run supply curves reflect long-run marginal costs, which may be constant, decreasing, or increasing, depending on the responses of technology and resource prices to long-run changes in the level of output.

The constant cost case. The constant cost case is illustrated in Figure 15.4, where the long-run supply curve is horizontal, indicating that unit costs of production are not altered by changes in the volume of output in the industry. This situation exists when there are no technological economies or diseconomies of scale and when the resources used in the industry are not specialized. Because the resource inputs are not specialized, they will be able to move out of the taxed industry and into other employments with no reduction in productivity or compensation (wage) rates. Thus, no backward shift of the tax will take place; all of the tax will be shifted forward to consumers. The tax causes the supply curve to shift upward by the full amount of the tax, the price to consumers rises by this amount, and there is some reduction in the quantity produced and sold depending on the elasticity of demand for the commodity. The economic effects of the tax are determined by the elasticity of demand for the commodity. The only tax-induced burdens on resource owners are the short-run costs of transferring from the taxed industry to alternative employment.

The long-run constant cost case can be reconciled with the short-run illustrations in Figure 15.3 by recognizing that the exodus of resources from the

FIGURE 15.4   Tax Shifting in a Constant Cost Industry

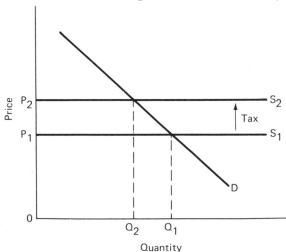

industry results in no change in the technology and resource-price factors reflected in the location of the before-tax marginal and average cost curves. Therefore, in order for the firm to survive in the industry, the product price must rise by the full amount of the tax so that the output of the surviving firms can return to Q_1 and the firms can again enjoy normal profits by covering both the resource costs and the tax cost.

The increasing cost case. The increasing cost case is illustrated in Figure 15.5, where the long-run supply curve slopes upward to the right, indicating that the unit costs of production rise as output increases and fall as output decreases. This situation exists when the resources used are specialized or particularly suited to the tasks required by the industry. If output were to expand, progressively less suitable resources would be called into service and unit costs of production would increase. Conversely, when output is decreased as a result of a commodity tax, the least suitable resources are released from employment and average costs of production decrease, thus absorbing some of the effects of the tax. Backward shifting of the tax takes place because the owners of resources would not be able to find equally remunerative employment in other industries if they lost their jobs in the taxed industry. This is because of their specialized nature, that is, their special talents are less productive in industries other than the one subjected to tax.

FIGURE 15.5   Tax Shifting in an Increasing Cost Industry

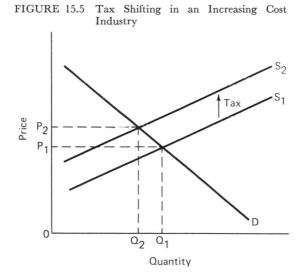

Faced with the prospect of lower wages in alternative occupations, resource owners will consent to a reduction in their pay rates in order to remain in the taxed industry. When this happens, the marginal and average resource costs (that is, the costs exclusive of the tax) will fall as a result of the tax. The price increase needed to establish the new long-run equilibrium will be less than the amount of the tax. The reduction in output (that is, the economic effect) will be less than in the constant cost case (assuming identical demand curves), and some of the incidence of the tax will be shifted backward to resources that now accept lower pay. This backward shift includes both resources that remain in the taxed industry and accept lower pay and resources that migrate to other industries and receive lower pay than they enjoyed before.

The decreasing cost case. Decreasing cost industries are also conceivable. Figure 15.6 illustrates long-run tax shifting in this situation. As the industry long-run supply curve is moved upward by the amount of the tax, price increases by more than the amount of the tax. A substantial reduction in output may take place if the demand for the product is sufficiently elastic. Substantial shifting may take place, both forward and backward.

FIGURE 15.6   Tax   Shifting   in   a   Decreasing   Cost
Industry

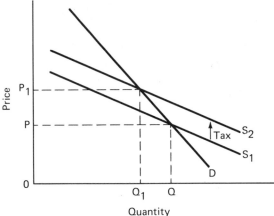

Decreasing cost situations suggest the presence of external economies of scale that arise because of the size of the industry itself. For example, special railroad cars for the shipping of automobiles may be feasible if the industry is large but not if the industry is small. If these specially designed railroad cars reduce the cost of providing automobiles, they illustrate an economy of scale external to the individual firms in the automobile industry—that is, they provide economies of scale which arise from the size of the industry rather than from the size of the firms in that industry. If a tax on automobiles caused the industry to shrink so that these external economies were no longer available, the price of automobiles to the final consumer could rise by more than the amount of the tax. Some excess burden would have arisen because of the tax. If the industry is a monopoly (that is, if the industry consists of only one firm), a decreasing cost situation can arise from internal economies of scale (from technological mass production economies). In this case, a tax on the product that caused a reduction in the volume of output could make some of the mass production technologies infeasible and thus also lead to an excess burden from the tax.

If the resources used in the industry are relatively specialized and therefore confront the likelihood of lower pay rates in alternative employments, backward shifting will take place as these resources accept lower pay, either as a concession to remaining in the industry or as a consequence of moving elsewhere. This phenomenon would moderate the long-run decreasing cost character of the industry and the excess burden aspects of a tax on that industry.

SUPPLY RESPONSE: NONCOMPETITIVE MODELS

Commodity taxes imposed on products of noncompetitive industries are analyzed with essentially the same procedure used for analysis in competitive industries, that is, the tax increases the cost of providing the commodity so that output volume and price may be altered. However, the incidence and effects of the tax may be modified by the noncompetitive structure of the industry producing the product. Specifically, the presence of a cushion of extra profits in monopoly and the phenomenon of price leadership in oligopolistic industries may either reduce or increase the effects of the tax.

Monopoly

Figure 15.7 illustrates demand and cost circumstances confronting a monopoly firm. The short-run marginal and average cost curves are essentially the same as those confronting any other producer. The crucial distinction between a monopoly and a competitive firm is that the monopoly recognizes that the demand for its output is not perfectly elastic. That is, it recognizes that a change in its volume of output will bring a change in the price of the commodity. The monopoly firm is not a "price taker," as was the competitive firm that provided a portion of the total industry output so small that it had no perceptible impact on price. The average revenue curve for the monopoly is equivalent to the industry demand curve and thus is not infinitely elastic.

FIGURE 15.7 Commodity Tax Shifting: Monopoly Case

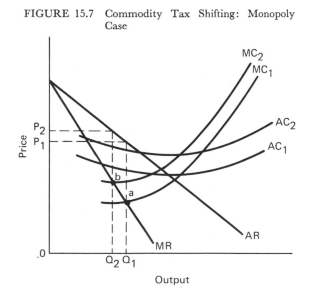

Because the average revenue curve is not infinitely elastic, marginal revenue (the change in total revenue arising from a change in the quantity sold) will be less than average revenue, since the price reduction necessary to sell the last unit of output must also be granted to purchasers who previously had paid a higher price. In contrast to the competitive model, the marginal revenue curve does not coincide with the average revenue curve. It is a distinctive and important feature of monopoly decision making.

A tax on the output of a monopoly will bring about an upward shift in average and marginal costs. In Figure 15.7, AC_2 and MC_2 are higher than AC_1 and MC_1 by the amount of the tax. When the tax is imposed, the profit-maximizing output, as indicated by the intersection of marginal revenue and marginal cost, is reduced as the intersection of MC and MR moves upward and to the left along the MR curve, from point a to point b in Figure 15.7. The tax will cause the profit-maximizing output to fall from Q_1 to Q_2 and the price of the commodity to rise from P_1 to P_2. Some part of the tax is shifted forward to consumers. The reduction in output lowers the demand for resources used in production and raises the possibility for backward shifting of the tax. If the resources used by the industry are somewhat specialized, the reduction in demand for them will lead to lower rates of pay to resource owners, which will moderate the upward shift in the cost curves and lessen the output reduction and price increase brought about by the tax.

The mechanics of the shifting model for monopoly are the same as in the model for the competitive situation except for the fact that adjustments to the tax are determined by movements along the marginal revenue curve, which is steeper than the equivalent segment of the average revenue or industry demand curve. The tax leads to a smaller adjustment in the monopoly case, assuming that the demand curve for the commodity is the same in each situation. The "undershifting" in the monopoly model is related to the possible presence of a cushion of extra profits for the monopoly. Monopolies will operate where demand has elasticity numerically greater than -1.0. Therefore, a price increase will bring a reduction in the total amount of money expended by consumers in the purchase of the commodity. After remission of the tax to the government, less revenue will be realized by the monopoly. Monopoly profits will decrease if factor markets do not permit an equivalent reduction in input prices. Thus, part of the tax will be absorbed by a reduction in the profits of the monopoly. The industry itself shrinks and the value of a monopoly position in that industry is smaller because of the tax.

Oligopoly

In the oligopoly case, the industry supply is provided by a relatively small number of firms that are rivals for shares in the market. Each firm is large enough, relative to industry supply, so that its output can influence market price. In the absence of agreements and without established patterns of action among the firms, oligopoly can lead to price rigidity and to a failure to maximize industry profits. Each firm may be reluctant to reduce output and increase price because it fears that rivals may maintain the old price and capture a larger share of the market. Similarly, firms may hesitate to increase output and reduce price, since rivals might respond with similar measures, thus triggering a price war and damaging the profits of all the firms.

If a commodity tax is imposed on an industry that is not maximizing profits, the tax itself may invite parallel actions by all the oligopolists. Uncertainty about the behavior of rivals still exists, but it may be less than in other circumstances. Since all the firms simultaneously experience an increase in costs, a mutual response of reducing output and increasing price may result from the tax, so that forward and backward shifting will take place in generally the same manner as in the monopoly case. In fact, the adjustment arising from the tax may be larger than could be accounted for on the basis of the tax itself. If the oligopoly has been unable to realize a profit-maximizing price and output position prior to the tax, the adjustment to the tax may provide an opportunity to correct this situation. Overshifting or overadjustment may take place. The size of the price and output change actually necessitated by the tax may be difficult to determine, especially for outsiders, so that the tax may provide a screen behind which the firms can act to restore maximum industry profits. Moreover, the price increase following the imposition of the tax may not damage the public image of the industry or raise questions about possible collusion or monopoly practices by the firms.

The oligopoly case probably is more important than either the competitive or the monopoly case in the United States because a substantial portion of total manufacturing is carried out in market situations characterized by varying degrees of oligopoly. Moreover, the problems associated with the taxation of commodities produced by oligopolistic industries are considerably more serious than simply the uncertainty about the amount of supply response that will be brought about by the tax. It is quite clear that the *direction* of the response will be a reduction in the quantity produced. The problem is that oligopolies and monopolies, even in the absence of a commodity tax, will be producing less than the allocationally efficient quantity of the product, since profit maximization in these industries involves selection of an output volume less than that indicated by an equality between marginal cost and marginal benefit as shown by the demand curve for the product. Thus, a tax on the product produced by a monopoly or oligopoly will *increase* the extent to which the product is underproduced, at least in comparison with the ideal allocative conditions that would prevail in a perfectly competitive economy.

If the resources forced out of the oligopoly or monopoly industry by the tax are reemployed in industries that are more perfectly competitive, resource misallocation is increased by both the reduction in oligopoly or monopoly output and the increase in the output of the competitive industries. It is apparent, however, that this line of reasoning soon encounters the problems that arise for taxation efficiency in an imperfect world. That is, if most of the economy is characterized by oligopoly and very little of it is perfectly competitive, it is no longer obvious that a tax on a commodity produced by an oligopolistic industry necessarily reduces overall economic efficiency because of different industrial structures. It is conceivable that a system of commodity taxes could be devised to reduce allocational inefficiencies arising from different market structures. Since commodities produced by noncompetitive industries will be underproduced compared to those produced by competitive industries, allocative efficiency might be improved if a tax were imposed on the commodity produced under competitive conditions and if a subsidy were provided to the commodities produced in the noncompetitive sector. However, such a system would require a great deal of information about demand elasticities and market structures and would invite a great deal of lobbying in the legislative process. Prudence suggests that legislatures should decide not to enter into this realm of tax policy.

EXCESS BURDEN AND CORRECTIVE TAXATION

Commodity taxes generate economic effects and influence the allocation of resources by altering the relative prices among commodities. The price of the commodity subjected to tax rises relative to the prices of other commodities, consumers purchase less of the taxed commodity, a smaller portion of the society's resources are used in producing the taxed commodity, and a larger portion of these resources is devoted to producing other things. If an optimal allocation of resources prevailed before the selective commodity tax was imposed, the tax will distort this allocation and result in an excess burden and a reduction in total welfare. If an optimal allocation did not prevail prior to the tax, corrective commodity taxation may be able to improve resource allocation and increase total welfare.

Excess Burden

In Figure 15.8, D is the demand for the commodity, S is the supply curve for the commodity (assuming constant costs), and an equilibrium condition exists at a, with consumers purchasing quantity OQ_1 at price OP_1. If we assume that the demand and supply curves are accurate representations of benefits and costs (that is, that there are no external effects from the production or consumption of this commodity and the industry is competitive), this equilibrium represents an efficient allocation of resources to this commodity. Consumers are enjoying a consumer surplus represented by the triangle area P_1ab, which is

FIGURE 15.8   Excess Burden of Commodity Taxation

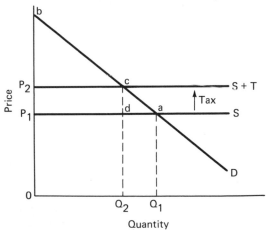

part of the total benefit or welfare derived from this commodity. If a tax imposed on this commodity changes the supply curve to $S + T$, the new equilibrium will be at c, with price at OP_2 and quantity at OQ_2.

We may identify the excess burden by examining what has happened to the consumer surplus that existed before the tax. The portion represented by the triangle P_2cb is still enjoyed by consumers, the portion represented by the rectangle P_1dcP_2 has been captured by the government through tax revenue collected, and the portion represented by the triangle acd is a dead loss, since it is neither retained by consumers nor captured by government. This triangle acd is the excess burden of the tax that has arisen because the tax has driven a wedge between the price paid by the consumer and the actual opportunity costs of the resources used in producing the commodity, as illustrated by the original supply curve. Price is no longer equal to real marginal cost, consumer choice has been distorted, and the taxed commodity is underproduced compared to other commodities. Of course, government revenue can be expended to finance the provision of collective services or to subsidize consumption of other commodities, but these expenditures may not be sufficient to recover the welfare loss from the excess burden of the commodity tax.

Corrective Commodity Taxes

The idea of corrective commodity taxation is illustrated by reversing the reasoning applied above to Figure 15.8, that is, if the original supply curve, S, is *not* an accurate representation of the true net costs of providing the commodity, then a tax on the commodity (or a subsidy to it) that moves this curve to a more accurate representation of true net cost can improve resource allocation and increase total welfare. The prevailing supply curve may be inaccurate in terms of true costs if the industry providing the commodity engages in monopoly pricing, since price will then be in excess of marginal cost. As previously noted, this suggests that a system of corrective taxes might be devised on the basis of differing market structures. However, a much more promising role for corrective commodity taxation arises in connection with supply curves that are inaccurate because they fail to take into account externalities generated by the production or consumption of the commodity. If external effects are positive, that is, if benefits accrue to persons who are not parties to the market transaction, a subsidy (negative tax) could be granted to the commodity. If external effects are negative, imposing costs on persons not party to the market transaction, a corrective tax on the commodity can improve resource allocation and total welfare.

The case of pollution. Corrective commodity taxes are particularly appropriate to deal with negative externalities associated with pollution. For example, automobile operation may generate air pollution that is a cost to the people who must breathe the polluted air. The use of certain fuels for heating or manufacturing may also generate this type of negative externality. Jet aircraft engines may produce noise pollution. The point is that negative externalities are costs associated with the production or consumption of certain commodities but not recognized in the market transaction between the seller and the purchaser of these commodities. As long as these negative externalities are unrecognized, the cost of the commodity is understated, price is too low, and an excessive quantity of the commodity is produced and consumed.

In effect, the consumers of these products are being subsidized by the people who are forced to endure the negative externalities. A corrective excise is a tax imposed on the commodity responsible for the negative externality or, preferably, on the specific attribute responsible for it. The tax forces the buyers and sellers of the commodity to recognize the costs imposed on other people. The tax causes the supply curve to shift upward by some amount related to the negative externalities, the price of the commodity to the buyers is increased, quantity diminishes, and a more efficient allocation of resources is achieved. Thus, economic analysis suggests that corrective excises can improve the allocation of resources. The case for corrective excises is much stronger than the crude sumptuary case for excise taxation.

Applying the theory. Although the theory of corrective excise taxation is simple and straightforward, efficient and effective application is extremely complicated. First, the magnitude or severity of the negative externality must be measured. Then its source must be identified, and finally a tax instrument that can be applied to the source must be devised. Each of these steps is difficult. Pollution damage may arise from a combination of factors rather than from the effects of a single factor. A great deal of research effort has been devoted to identifying, measuring, and tracing negative externalities, but our knowledge is far from complete. Of course, it is unreasonable to expect that corrective action will be postponed until perfect knowledge of the problem is achieved, but actions instituted on the basis of incomplete information may do more harm than good.

Effective use of the corrective excise tax remedy requires that the tax be imposed in a way that avoids the frustration and ineffectiveness which will result if the demand for the taxed item is inelastic. This means that reasonably good substitutes or alternatives must exist for the commodity or input subjected to tax. For example, a tax on gasoline may be an ineffective way to reduce the pollution costs of automobile operation if no attractive substitutes for automobile transportation are available, so that demand for gasoline is inelastic. On the other hand, if the source of pollution can be traced to some component of gasoline, such as a lead additive, a tax on this component may be able to generate a significant economic effect because a reasonably attractive alternative or substitute, such as unleaded gasoline, is available. The demand for leaded gasoline may be relatively elastic. Similarly, a tax on jet airplanes would be quite ineffective in reducing the noise pollution, whereas a tax graduated according to the volume of engine noise could be effective in bringing about the use of quieter engines. The point here is that effective use of corrective excises requires the discovery of taxable items that are responsible for the external damages and for which reasonable substitutes exist or can be developed.

The problem of introducing corrective excises is political as well as technological. Effective corrective excises will cause economic losses to those people whose present occupations are tied to the taxed items. At the same time, these corrective excises will open opportunities for new jobs and high profits for those who can provide acceptable substitutes for the taxed commodity or input. Vested interests in existing occupations and processes can be expected to mount opposition to truly effective corrective excise taxation. At the same time, however, groups that will be able to profit through the expanded use of the untaxed alternatives may support the proposed tax. Corrective excises mobilize the energy and ingenuity of profit seekers in the search for nontaxed alternatives.

Advantages of excises. As corrective devices, excise taxes are preferred over the cruder and less flexible instruments of direct regulation or prohibition because the rate of tax can be adjusted upward or downward until the desired amount of economic effect has been realized. Consumers are also able to adjust their behavior more efficiently to the new situation. The argument here is that the "correct" adjustment for negative externalities ordinarily does not require the complete elimination of products or processes. In respect to environmental pollution, for example, it is important to recognize that natural processes themselves may possess a certain recycling capability. Flowing streams can rid themselves of some potential pollutants and chemical processes can break down certain waste materials without disrupting ecological systems. Therefore, prohibition of potentially polluting activities may be unnecessary and actually would be wasteful of the recycling resource. The proper level of corrective excise tax will permit some consumers to continue to use the taxed commodity. In this sense, the excise tax becomes a device for rationing or allocating the permissible level of consumption among different consumers. Following the logic of the price system, the permitted amount of output will be purchased by those consumers for whom marginal benefits are greatest. Thus, the corrective excise can satisfy the aggregate or macro requirement of securing the correct total amount of the product and the allocative or micro requirement of directing this output to those consumers most benefited by it.

MOTOR FUELS TAX

The federal government collects excise taxes on motor fuels, automobile tires, and other automotive commodities. These taxes are different from the other federal excises. They are not sumptuary levies nor rationing devices nor efforts to correct for externalities not recorded in market transactions. The federal excises on motor fuels and on automotive equipment are devices through which the federal government collects money from highway users to pay for highway services. The problem is that more direct methods of collecting payments from highway users, such as the use of toll roads, would be too expensive to use on most highways. The solution is to levy the tax, or user charge, on the purchase of commodities related to highway use. The money collected from highway user excises is placed in the Highway Trust Fund and expended for the construction and maintenance of the federal highway system.

Motor fuels taxes are used much more extensively by state governments than by the federal government, and a more detailed discussion of these taxes and of highway finance in general will be found in Part III. Only a few observations are offered at this point. Primarily, the problem is that the consumption of motor fuel is not a perfect proxy for highway use. The purchase of gasoline does not provide information about which sections of highway will be used by the motorist and since the cost of providing highway service differs according to the type and location of the highway, the tax is deficient both in terms of an equitable distribution of payments and in terms of directing the payments to the appropriate sections of highway. In this sense, it is appropriate that the major utilization of highway user taxes is at the state level, where a somewhat closer (although still seriously imperfect) connection between payments and benefits received is possible.

If extra motor fuels or automotive excises are imposed as conservation measures during an energy crisis or as measures to control pollution, it is important that such taxes be clearly distinguished from the conventional highway user levies. For example, the revenue collected from such regulatory taxes should not be placed in the Highway Trust Fund and employed for the construction and maintenance of highways. Such an application of these funds would operate to counteract the regulatory objectives of the taxes. However, regulatory motor fuel taxes will have an impact on Highway Trust Fund revenues if they actually result in a reduction in the quantity of motor fuel consumed. Less money would flow into these trust funds and smaller expenditures would be made for highway construction and maintenance.

SUMMARY

Commodity taxation is selective taxation, that is, certain commodities are singled out for special taxation. They yield a relatively small portion of federal revenue, but are of greater importance at the state level. They may be employed to raise revenue or to produce some intended economic effect, such as limiting the consumption of certain commodities.

Tracing the incidence and effects of commodity taxation is an exercise in conventional economic analysis. The analysis suggests that these taxes can be viewed as increasing the costs of providing the commodity, thereby altering the market supply curve for the commodity subjected to tax. The tax may be shifted forward to consumers through higher prices or backward to producers through reductions in the quantity of the commodity produced and sold. The balance between forward shifting on the one hand and backward shifting and economic effects on the other depends on the elasticities of demand and supply for the taxed commodity. If demand for the taxed commodity is quite inelastic, as appears to be the case for most commodities currently subjected to commodity taxation, most of the incidence will be borne by consumers and the economic effects of the tax will be relatively minor.

Selective commodity taxes alter resource allocation by inserting a wedge between the price paid by consumers and the resource costs of production faced by the producers of the commodity. If resource allocation is efficient before the tax is imposed, the tax will result in an excess burden and a reduction in total welfare. If pretax resource allocation is not efficient, corrective commodity taxes may be employed to move the economy to a higher level of total welfare.

Corrective commodity taxes are especially attractive as instruments to use in attempting to correct for misallocation arising from the negative externalities associated with pollution, provided that the sources of negative externalities can be identified and that taxes can be imposed on commodities or inputs for which reasonably close substitutes are available.

Taxes on motor fuels and other commodities related to highway use occupy a distinctive place in the catalog of commodity taxes because they are essentially user charges designed to collect from highway users the funds needed to construct and maintain highways.

SUGGESTED READINGS

Coase, R. H. "The Problem of Social Cost," *Journal of Law and Economics*, October 1960.

Freeman, A. M., R. H. Haveman, and A. V. Kneese. *The Economics of Environmental Policy* (New York: Wiley, 1973).

Buchanan, James M., and Gordon Tullock. "Polluters' Profits and Political Responses: Direct Controls Versus Taxes," *American Economic Review*, 65, 1 (March 1975).

Dorfman, Nancy F., and Arthur Snow. "Who will Pay for Pollution Control?—The Distribution by Income of the Burden of the National Environmental Protection Program, 1972–1980," *National Tax Journal*, XXVIII, 1 (March 1975).

16

Federal Estate
and Gift Taxation

Transfers of wealth which take place at the death of the owner and transfers which are gifts between living persons are "gratuitous" transfers, which means that they are not transactions involving compensation for services rendered by the person receiving the wealth. Thus, these receipts are not taxable income to the recipient under the production flow concept generally applied in income taxation. Taxes on gift and death transfers are collected from the maker of the gift or from the estate of the deceased and not from the recipient of the gratuitous transfer.[1]

A brief discussion of the history and rationale for gratuitous transfer taxation will be helpful in understanding why taxes are collected on these transfers. The taxation of death transfers has a very long history. In the middle ages, property rights were bestowed by the sovereign and would revert to the sovereign upon the death of the individual to whom the rights had been granted. Death transfer taxation arose when, in exchange for a fee or a tax, the sovereign would permit the holder of property rights to himself determine the person to whom the rights would pass on the death of the current holder. Gift taxes, on the other hand, are of more recent origin. Since transfer by gift is an alternative to transfer at death, gift transfers could be a convenient way for the holder of

---

[1] Many state governments collect inheritance taxes, which also are taxes on gratuitous transfers. Although inheritance taxes are determined according to the amounts received by various beneficiaries, they are not income taxes because they take no account of the other receipts of these beneficiaries. Inheritance taxes and other types of death transfer taxes collected by state governments will be discussed later.

property to arrange for the avoidance of death transfer taxes unless the gift transfers also were subjected to tax.

THE RATIONALE FOR ESTATE AND GIFT TAXATION

Tax philosophy offers several arguments in support of death transfer taxation. One of these, called the *trusteeship* principle, comes remarkably close to the notion that the sovereign is entitled to determine to whom property shall pass upon the death of the current holder. According to the trusteeship argument, the person who has amassed wealth has evidenced a certain special competence in the management of resources and thereby has qualified as a constructive "trustee" to preside over the management of the wealth of the society. In order to ensure competent management of society's wealth, government refrains from taxation during the lifetime of the trustee, but upon the death of the trustee, a settling of accounts is called for in the form of the death transfer tax. The trusteeship view is rather vague about what constitutes good wealth management or just what sort of settlement is appropriate upon the death of the trustee.

The notion that the government has refrained from taxation during the life of the individual and that the death tax is a kind of settling of accounts suggests another rationale for death taxation. This position holds that income from property has a greater ability to pay tax than does income from labor services, so that capital income should be subjected to higher tax rates than labor income. In this view, taxation of wealth at death makes up for the failure to apply special taxes to capital income during life. This case is a bit tenuous, however, since the wealth transferred at death may have been accumulated from many sources and may not accurately reflect the capital income of the deceased.

Another argument for death transfer taxation is that these taxes can equalize the distribution of wealth in the society. Wealth is indeed very unequally distributed in the United States and the progressively graduated tax rates used in the estate and gift tax can effectively break up large concentrations of wealth. However, a genuine effort to use death transfer taxation to equalize wealth holdings would suggest that rates of tax might be related to the wealth position of the beneficiary rather than to the size of the estate of the deceased. Neither estate taxes nor inheritance taxes graduate tax rates in this way.

Estate and gift taxation has not been a large producer of revenue for the federal government. Although the volume of wealth transferred each year is large, most of these transfers escape taxation because substantial exemptions and deductions are allowed. Most of the revenue actually collected comes from the few very large estates transferred each year. Increased revenues would require a lowering of the exemptions and deductions presently permitted and an increase in rates on small to moderate sized estates. But changes in tax rates or in the definition of the tax base are particularly difficult to legislate, partly because the revenues that could be gained from such changes are modest but especially because many vested interests have developed around the rates and provisions presently in effect. Taxes play a prominent role in estate planning, and the plans of many people have been established on the basis of these rules of the game.

THE UNIFIED ESTATE AND GIFT TAX

The Tax Revision Act of 1976 instituted a major change in gratuitous transfer taxation in the United States. Prior to this legislation, two separate taxes had been imposed, one of gift transfers and one on the estate of a person at the time of his or her death. Each of these separate taxes had its own rate structure and its own set of deductions and exemptions. The Tax Revision Act unified these two taxes by establishing a single rate schedule applicable to all gratuitous transfers (previously gift tax rates had been lower than rates on transfers at death), by treating transfers made at death through the estate of the deceased as additions to the accumulated total of transfers made as gifts, and by replacing exemption allowances with a single unified credit against the tax. Thus, the two separate taxes were unified into a single gratuitous transfer tax.

The Tax Base

The total value of all transfers by gift or bequest made by an individual is subject to tax under the unified estate and gift tax except for certain transfers that are deductible in calculating the tax base. Gifts of up to $3,000 given to any recipient during one year are deductible. Thus, relatively small gifts are not counted in determining the tax base and a person can give away an unlimited amount in any year without incurring tax liability if he or she is willing to spread the largesse among a sufficiently large number of recipients. Gifts to the same recipient can be made year after year without incurring any tax liability if the amount of the gift each year is less than $3,000.

Gifts to recognized charitable organizations are fully deductible and gifts to the spouse of the person making the gift are deductible within certain limits. The deduction for gifts to the spouse of the donor is called the *marital deduction*. Under the marital deduction, the first $100,000 of accumulated taxable gifts to the spouse (that is, amounts in excess of $3,000 annually) is fully deductible, the next $100,000 is fully taxable, and a 50 percent deduction is allowed for taxable gifts to the spouse in excess of the accumulated total of $200,000.

A tax return is filed for each year in which taxable gifts are made and the taxable gifts made in that accounting period are added to the taxable gifts made in previous accounting periods and the total tax on all gifts up through the current period is determined from the schedule of tax rates. The tax on gifts made in previous years is subtracted from this total and the difference is the tax payable for the current accounting period. Thus, there is no advantage in spreading gifts through time except for the deductibility of gifts of less than $3,000 to individual recipients each year.

When an individual dies, an estate tax return is filed listing the total value of property owned at the time of death.[2] The final expenses of the deceased and any debts outstanding are deducted from this total. As with gift transfers, trans-

---

[2] Among the various properties that may be included in the estate, particular interest attaches to the proceeds of insurance on the life of the deceased. In most cases, life insurance proceeds will be included in the value of the estate. If, at the time of death, the deceased person held certain "incidents of ownership," such as the power to alter beneficiaries, this fact will be sufficient to require the proceeds of the insurance to be included in the value of the estate.

fers made at death to the surviving spouse and to recognized charitable organizations may be deductible in arriving at the tax base.

The marital deduction. Under the estate portion of the unified tax, bequests to the surviving spouse are deductible up to a limit of $250,000 or one half of the estate, whichever is larger. Bequests to the spouse of amounts in excess of these limits are part of the net base for the tax. This provision recognizes that the surviving spouse frequently will be of approximately the same age as the deceased, so that without the deduction the family wealth could be subjected to estate taxation twice in a reasonably short period of time. The marital deduction means that this part of the estate will escape taxation in the first instance but will become subject to tax when the surviving spouse dies. It also means that the effective progressivity of the estate tax is considerably reduced because the deduction removes transfers from the higher brackets of the rate structure. If this wealth becomes taxable on the death of the surviving spouse, the rates applied will be those at the lower end of the rate structure since a new return will be filed when the spouse dies.

Charitable deductions. The value of property that passes at death to recognized charities also is deductible in computing the base for the tax. This deduction introduces a strong encouragement for charitable bequests, especially from large estates. If the estate is large, the marital deduction can provide adequate tax-free provision for the surviving spouse, but since rates of tax on the remaining part may be high, the reductions attainable through charitable bequests may be substantial. The logic of charitable deductions in the estate and gift tax is similar to the rationale for charitable deductions in the income tax. In other words, it constitutes a kind of tax expenditure designed to encourage private financing of institutions that presumably are providing collective services. Some of the criticism directed at the income tax deductibility of charitable contributions is also applicable to the estate and gift tax deduction. Charitable activities are likely to be dependent on contributions from wealthy persons in any event, and the allowance of tax deduction for these contributions increases the influence of wealthy persons over the activities of these organizations.

The deductibility of charitable bequests can also be used to avoid the fragmentation of economic power that otherwise might arise as a result of the tax. Tax liabilities must be paid in cash. Therefore, a sizable amount of cash would be required to settle tax liabilities for a large estate. In order to acquire this cash, the estate might be forced to sell (liquidate) substantial holdings of property or securities. This liquidation could break up the concentrations of wealth that wield economic power. But if large blocks of property or securities are bequeathed to designated charitable organizations, this breaking up need not occur, although the economic power henceforth would be in the hands of the charity. This application of the charitable deduction in estate and gift taxation helps to explain the origins of some of the major charitable foundations.

Tax Rates and Credits

The tax rates under the Unified Estate and Gift Tax start at 18 percent on the first $10,000 of taxable transfers and range upward through a number of brackets to a rate of 70 percent on taxable transfers in excess of $5,000,000. As noted, these rates are applied to the accumulated total of taxable gratuitous transfers for an individual. The Tax Revision Act of 1976 abolished the old system of allowing a personal exemption as a deduction from the tax base and instituted, instead, a system of tax credits. For 1977, this credit was $30,000, equivalent to a deduction of $120,000 and meaning that actual tax payments would commence in the 30 percent bracket of the rate schedule. The Act, which became effective on January 1, 1977, scheduled annual increases in the amount of the unified credit up to $47,000, for 1981 and thereafter. According to the unified rate schedule, this credit of $47,000 will be equivalent to a deduction of $175,625 of taxable transfers. Thus, the new system substantially increased the amount of personal exemption from that allowed under the previous system, but instituted a common rate schedule for gift and death transfers, thereby eliminating some of the opportunities for tax avoidance which previously existed for people who could divide their gratuitous transfers between gifts and bequests and take advantage of the lower end of two separate rate schedules.[3]

In addition to the unified credit, credit also is allowed (up to a limit) for death transfer taxes paid to state governments under their estate or inheritance taxes. These credits will be examined later in connection with state taxation of gratuitous transfers.

ECONOMIC EFFECTS

The fact that a tax does not generate a great amount of revenue does not mean that it may not produce important economic effects. In fact, the implication is precisely the reverse. If tax rates are high but escape from these rates is available through allowable deductions, economic effects arise through the utilization of deductions and other devices that minimize taxes.

Financing of Charities

It seems likely that the major effect of death and gift taxation is the stimulation these taxes provide for gifts and bequests to charities. Educational and philanthropic organizations rely heavily on gifts and bequests that presumably are increased significantly by the deductibility of contributions from income taxation and the deductibility of charitable bequests from estate and gift taxation. The power and influence of nonprofit organizations has increased greatly in the United States, and tax deductions permitted for funds transferred to these organizations undoubtedly has contributed to this growth.

Fragmentation of Wealth Holdings

Death and gift taxation may result in some fragmentation or breaking up of large concentrations of privately held wealth, but this fragmentation effect

---

[3] The new law requires that tax paid on gifts made in the three years before death must be included in calculating the tax base for the estate portion of the tax. This is called "grossing-up" and is designed to reduce the incentive to make gifts "in contemplation of death" in order to remove the tax paid from the base for calculating the tax payable on death transfers.

requires careful examination. It is true that the gift tax, with its annual deduction, encourages the dispensation of many small gifts rather than a few large ones and it also is true that the cash required to pay estate taxes may require the liquidation of property and security holdings and thus reduce wealth concentrations. Two considerations, however, qualify the conclusion that these taxes reduce concentrations. First, as already noted, charitable gifts and bequests may be used to avoid taxes and the consequent requirements for liquidity. Bequests and gifts of large fortunes to a single foundation can maintain the concentration of economic power and may even operate to increase concentration if these foundations receive gratuitous transfers from several different estates and continue to accumulate them over time. Thus, the deductibility of contributions and charitable bequests may actually operate to increase the concentration of economic power in the economy rather than to diminish it. The power wielded by religious and charitable organizations is great and continues to grow.

The second qualification that must be recognized in judging the fragmentation effects of gratuitous transfer taxes is that these taxes take no account of the wealth position of the recipients of the transfers. Even though the tax collector may take a bite out of gifts and bequests, little reduction in the concentration of wealth in the society will take place if these recipients themselves are already large wealth holders. The institution of private property sets up a situation in which an initial amount of wealth provides the seed from which greater amounts of wealth may grow. Whereas the nonwealthy person has only two hands with which to expand his economic status, the wealthy person has three hands, that is, his left hand, his right hand, and his bank account. The bank account mobilizes the potentials of compound interest and provides a powerful force for greater wealth concentrations. Gratuitous transfer taxes can cut back the growing plant of wealth accumulation and restrain the wealth accumulation effect, but these taxes will not necessarily mean that wealth concentration will be diminished over time.

Work Incentives and Saving

Presumably, the desire to be able to transfer wealth to the next generation or to other worthy recipients is an element in the work incentives of individuals. The intrusion of taxation on these transfers reduces the number of dollars of net transfer an individual will be able to provide from any given amount of work effort. This reduction in the rate of return or reward for work (a substitution effect) may reduce the amount of work done. But the disincentive effect may be counterbalanced by an income effect tending to generate incentives for greater work. That is, if the individual entertains a target of being able to transfer some specified net amount, the intrusion of the tax collector may motivate the individual to exert even more effort in order to meet his goal even after the tax has been paid. Thus, the income effect and the substitution effect tend to counterbalance each other and may leave a rather minor net effect on work incentives. Moreover, the whole set of calculations may have little to do with work incentives if people keep thoughts of death and death taxes out of mind.

Gratuitous transfer taxation may have a greater effect on the choice between saving and consuming. Consuming is an alternative to saving, and not a particularly unpleasant alternative. If taxation reduces the rewards from saving by eroding the amounts that may be transferred to others by gift or by bequest, it seems likely that saving will be reduced relative to consumption. However, this antisaving effect may not be especially strong. Charitable bequests are deductible and can purchase a kind of immortality for an individual without the intrusion of the tax collector, and of course there are rewards from saving that are not related to the transfer of wealth to others.

Trusts and Estate Planning

Prior to the Tax Revision Act of 1976, *generation skipping* trusts provided a widely used way to minimize tax on death transfers. Under the generation skipping procedure, wealth would not be left to the children of the deceased but instead would be left to the grandchildren or great grandchildren under terms of a trust which entitled the intervening generations of descendants to receive the income from the property, such as rents, royalties, dividends, and interest. These trust arrangements meant that the intervening generations did not have legal title to the property itself so that the value of the property would not be part of their estates when they died. Thus, several interventions of the tax collector could be avoided by the generation skipping trust. Although trust arrangements of this sort may be quite appropriate in many situations, the argument was made that the attractiveness of these trusts as devices for tax avoidance caused them to be used in some situations where other arrangements might have been preferable on more genuine economic grounds. Although life estate trustees could be given wide latitude in managing the wealth, tax considerations introduced constraints or limitations not otherwise desirable.

The Tax Revision Act of 1976 substantially eliminated the generation skipping trust as a tax avoidance device by imposing a tax on "termination of interests" held by the intervening generations so that wealth passing through successive generations of trust holders now is taxable as if gifts had been made between one generation and the next. But the generation skipping trust certainly was not the only way that estate planning assistance could help to reduce taxes and a large amount of legal talent and energy continues to be devoted to helping people plan for the management and eventual transfer of their wealth. When tax rates are high and the tax law is complicated, sizable fees for this type of legal assistance can be justified. With lower rates and less complicated laws, some of this talent would be employed in other ways. The Tax Revision Act of 1976, by instituting sweeping changes in the law, will prompt many people to review their estate plans.

GRATUITOUS TRANSFER TAX ALTERNATIVES

The Tax Revision Act of 1976 replaced the separate taxes on gifts and estates with a unified *successions* tax having single tax rate schedule and exemption credit for all transfers made by an individual. But the tax liability still is on the initiator of the transfers and rates still are determined according to the amount of these transfers. An alternative approach would impose the tax on the recipient rather than on the initiator of these transfers.

The essential difference between imposing the tax on the recipient rather than on the initiator of gratuitous transfers relates to the tax rates that would be imposed. Under the existing system, in which the tax is imposed on the initiator of transfers, the economic status of the recipient plays no part in determining tax rates. It does not matter whether the recipient is wealthy or poor or has received other gratuitous transfers. But these differences in economic position can be incorporated into the tax system if the tax is imposed on the recipient. Thus, ability to pay factors can be related to living persons and efforts to use the tax to control the concentration of wealth in the society can be more successful. Since the effective burden of transfer taxes is on recipients rather than on initiators, there is implicit good sense in relating these taxes to the circumstances of recipients.

Treating Gratuitous Transfers as Income

Gratuitous transfers could be treated as part of the income of the recipient. This would be consistent with the accretion to wealth concept of income, which is indifferent among the various sources of income. A person who received a gift or a bequest would find either his net worth or his consumption increased and would be subject to income tax on this accretion to wealth. There would be no separate tax on death or gift transfers as such. The rate of tax would depend on the economic situation of the recipient, with a higher rate of tax collected on transfers to high-income recipients. Principles of vertical equity would be applied through progressive tax rates of the income tax, and these rates would operate to restrain the accumulation of concentrations of wealth.

Certain problems would arise, however, if gratuitous transfers were treated as income. For example, if the accretion to wealth concept were applied consistently to both the initiator and the recipient of these transfers, a gift made by a living person would reduce his net worth and lower his income tax. If the initiator of the transfer was in a higher tax bracket than the recipient, a clear incentive would arise to use gift transfers as a way to reduce total tax liability. Problems also would arise in the treatment of transfers among members of a given family. Transfers among members of a single family unit probably would be exempted from tax, but difficulties would arise in defining the limits of the family unit. Should adult children be considered part of the family unit?

Another problem in the integration of gratuitous transfers into the income tax arises because these transfers are likely to be infrequent or irregular for any given recipient and because the amounts involved may be relatively large. If an adequate averaging system is not provided in the income tax, the progressive rate structure of the tax will place higher effective rates on gratuitous transfers than on other receipts and will tax large transfers at a higher rate than would have applied had the same total amount been transferred in a series of smaller amounts. As a matter of tax policy it could be argued that gratuitous transfers have a greater ability to pay than other receipts because they are unearned, but the horizontal equity problem of discrimination between large transfers and a series of smaller transfers might require a separate averaging procedure for gratuitous transfers.

An Accessions Tax

The difficulties that would arise in integrating gratuitous transfers into the income tax suggest that a separate tax on gratuitous transfers might be appropriate, even though it is imposed on the recipient rather than on the initiator. An *accessions* tax imposes liability on the recipient of transfers. The base for the tax consists of the total of such transfers received by an individual from all donors. A continuing record of gratuitous receipts would be maintained by the taxpayer, and the transfers received in a given accounting period would be added to transfers previously received in determining the tax base. Tax would be calculated according to the cumulative total of transfers received, and credit against the tax would be granted for tax paid in previous years. If tax rate changes were legislated during the lifetime of the individual, the credit for taxes previously paid could be adjusted consistent with the new schedule of rates. Exemptions could be allowed for small transfers, and a system of exemptions could be provided based on the relationship between the recipient and the initiator of the transfer.

The cumulative nature of the accessions tax base avoids the problem of discrimination between large and small transfers. A progressively graduated rate structure could mount incentives for the dispersion rather than the concentration of wealth holdings. The fragmentation effect could be increased if rate structures incorporated information about the wealth of the recipient before the transfer was received, although this modification would complicate the tax calculation. Incentives would still exist for the use of trust devices (such as the skip-a-generation trust) to avoid the accessions tax. Incentives of this sort (which operate to reduce options in the management of wealth and in the mobility of capital) appear to be inherent in any type of tax on the transfer of property.

SUMMARY

Federal estate and gift taxes are taxes on gratuitous transfers and are imposed on the initiator rather than on the recipient of these transfers. These taxes are rationalized as efforts to promote a greater equality in the distribution of wealth and as special taxes reflecting a greater ability to pay for capital income than for labor income. Relatively little revenue is generated because generous exemptions and deductions are allowed. Particular interest attaches to deductions for death transfers to the surviving spouse and to deductions for amounts given to recognized charities. Perhaps the major economic effect of these taxes is the encouragement given to gratuitous transfers to organized charities. The deductibility of charitable transfers can be used to avoid the breaking up of wealth concentrations that otherwise might be required in order to obtain cash for the payment of taxes. The concentration of wealth and power in the hands of charitable organizations probably is increased by these deductions. The effect of these taxes on work incentives is probably small and only slightly greater effects may arise in favor of consumption as an alternative to saving. But the tax generates considerable stimulation for the formation of trust arrangements that may limit flexibility in the management or mobility of capital.

The profession of estate planning is closely related to gift and death tax provisions. The plans made in response to tax considerations mount strong forces in opposition to changes in tax laws relating to gratuitous transfers. Nevertheless, major changes in federal gift and estate taxation were made in the Tax Revision Act of 1976, which unified the previously separate taxes by establishing a single rate schedule and a single system of personal exemption credits. A strong case can be made that gratuitous transfer taxes should be related to the economic situation of the recipient rather than to the economic situation of the initiator. Gift and estate taxes could be abolished in favor of counting gratuitous transfers as income to the recipient. Alternatively, an *accessions* tax on the accumulated transfers received by an individual might be substituted for existing gratuitous transfer taxes.

SUGGESTED READING

National Tax Association and Tax Institute of America Seminar. "Federal Tax Reform," *National Tax Journal*, XXVI, 3 (September 1973). See pp. 439–71 for several papers on estate and gift taxation.

III

State Governments

Part III examines the financing of state governments in the United States. The first chapter in this part, "The Economics of Multilevel Government," is especially important because it presents an economic model for the allocation of functions in a multilevel system of governments. Thus, Chapter 17 actually is an introduction both to the material on state governments and to that on local governments, which is the subject of Part IV. The model emphasizes that there may be a geographic dimension or pattern to the benefits derived from collective services. This geographic dimension, in turn, provides a basis for deciding whether the provision of a given collective service can best be entrusted to the national government, to state governments, or to local governments. It is a model for fiscal federalism and is especially relevant for the United States because the United States employs a multilevel system of governments, and because changing circumstances require a continuing evaluation of the appropriate allocation of functions among the different units of government.

The examination of state government financing begins with a general overview of budget expenditures and receipts (Chapter 18), which reveals that considerable diversity exists among the states in their financial operations. Chapters 19 through 22 examine the major internal revenue sources for state government. Chapter 23 considers the special problems of highway financing.

17

The Economics
of Multilevel Government

The concept of collective consumption was developed in Chapter 2, where it was shown that efficient provision of goods and services consumed collectively requires the use of government instruments for measuring demand and for financing the delivery of these services. These instruments were examined in some detail in Chapter 3, which explored the relationships between financial instruments and decision making in democratic political processes. A system of multilevel governments adds an additional dimension to the mechanism for allocating resources to the provision of collectively consumed goods and services. Can a multilevel system of governments do a better job of resource allocation than a single unitary government? A case for a multilevel system of governments exists if it can be shown that such a system improves the allocation of resources for collective consumption.

ALLOCATING FUNCTIONS
IN A MULTIGOVERNMENT SYSTEM

The very notion of collective consumption suggests that some number of individuals are joined together and constitute a group because they consume some good or service mutually or collectively. In the case of a pure collective good, the entire output of the good is consumed equally by all members of this group. For nonpure or quasi-collective goods, some portion of the total output of the good is consumed equally by all members of the group. The question is whether the individuals who constitute the group or collectivity can be identified, that is, whether the individuals who collectively consume some specified

273

good or service can be distinguished from those who are not joined in the collective consumption of that good or service. If this distinction can be made in some reasonable and workable way, then it is useful for the group of individuals to organize themselves into a collective decision-making unit and to equip themselves with the instruments of collective action necessary to enable them to provide the good or service. That is, there is reason for the establishment of a "government."

The Geography of Benefits

Let us begin by considering a group of individuals who reside on the shores of a lake. These individuals are collectively consuming certain services provided by the lake, such as its scenic beauty or its attractiveness for swimming and boating. None of these shore dwellers can consume a different lake than the one consumed by the others, and if congestion is not present in the use of the lake, consumption by one does not diminish the consumption of another. Therefore, certain services provided by the lake fit the definition of collectively consumed services. There would appear to be good reason for the establishment of some government whose citizens would be the shore dwellers around the lake. Let us refer to this community as Laketon.

The Laketon illustration provides an easily visualized picture of a local collective good or service, just as national defense provided a ready picture of a national collective good or service. But care must be taken in understanding the distinction between the national and the local dimensions. Each citizen of the nation must accept ("consume") the same national defense system, but this also is true of the lake at Laketon, that is, each citizen of the *nation* must accept ("consume") the same collective features of this lake. The difference between the two lies in the concentration or dispersal of the *benefits* from this collective consumption.

Figure 17.1 illustrates patterns of benefit dispersal, one for national defense (a) and the other for Laketon Lake (b). Benefit perception is an individual

FIGURE 17.1   Dispersal of Benefits from Collective Consumption

(a) National defense

(b) Laketon Lake

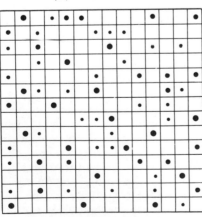
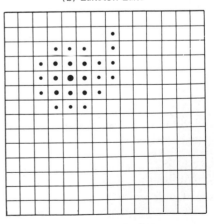

matter. On these charts, the size of each dot represents the *amount* of benefit perceived by an individual. Imagine that individuals are distributed uniformly over the area of each illustration so that the absence of a dot in a box indicates an individual who perceives no benefit from the collective service in question. The picture of benefit perceptions from national defense shows a random scattering of benefits among the people of the nation. Some perceive more benefit than others, but there is no geographic pattern in the distribution of these benefits. The benefit distribution for Laketon Lake, however, reveals a definite geographic pattern. The largest benefits are clustered immediately around the lake and smaller benefits are experienced by people who reside farther away from the lake. Most individuals in the nation are so little affected by the services of Laketon Lake that involving them in decision-making about the lake would be completely unjustified considering the benefits and costs of such involvement. But the people residing near the lake are affected to such an extent that they would be quite willing to undertake the responsibilities of citizenship in connection with the lake.

If similar charts were constructed depicting patterns of benefit perceptions from other collectively consumed services, some would reveal local concentrations perhaps approaching that for Laketon Lake. These could be characterized as local collective services appropriately administered at local government levels. Others, such as the monetary system, would reveal no such localized concentration and would, like defense, be characterized as national collective services appropriately administered at the national government level.

Let us now consider a cross-sectional view of the geographic pattern of benefit perceptions. Let us retain Laketon Lake as one of the collective services to be examined, but let us consider the school of the Laketon community as another illustration. Figure 17.2 provides a cross-section picture of perceived benefits from Laketon Lake (a) and from the collective services provided by the Laketon school (b). In these figures, the horizontal dimension represents the distance from the location at which the service is rendered—the distances from ground zero, so to speak. The vertical dimension represents the amount of benefit from this service perceived by individuals residing at various distances from the place where the service is performed. In Figure 17.2(a), the pattern of benefit is well defined and limited to a small geographical area. Technological considerations suggest reasons for this. The time required to travel to and from the

FIGURE 17.2   Cross-section Views of Pattern of Benefit

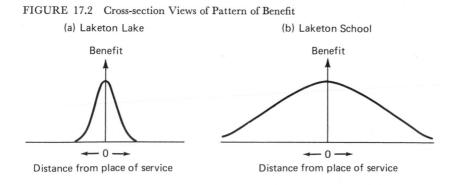

(a) Laketon Lake   (b) Laketon School

lake strongly influences the geographic pattern of benefit from it. The geographic extent of the jurisdiction that would find it feasible to interest itself in this lake is rather precisely defined and is limited to a small area. Beyond a certain distance, people have very little interest in the service it provides and would be unwilling to devote energy or resources to managing it.

Figure 17.2(b) illustrates a cross-section picture of the collective benefits of the services of the Laketon school. The level of perceived benefit diminishes more gradually as the distance from the site of service increases, and persons residing some distance away feel themselves to be significantly affected by the service rendered by the school. Among the factors influencing this benefit pattern is the mobility of persons, especially those persons educated in the school. If the people educated in the Laketon school, for example, lived out their lives in Laketon and were not involved in decisions affecting people who live elsewhere, and if other people rarely had occasion to associate with the society of Laketon, the collective benefit profile for the Laketon school would be much the same as the benefit profile for Laketon Lake. But this is not the case. As mobility of persons increases and as Laketon residents vote on state and national questions, the benefit pattern from the Laketon school extends to wider geographic ranges. People residing some distance from the school may find it worthwhile to seek some voice in its affairs.

THE CORRESPONDENCE PRINCIPLE

The question now posed is that of determining the appropriate jurisdictional boundaries for the governments that will be responsible for the provision of collective services. In the context of the illustration in Figure 17.2, we are asking at what distance from ground zero the boundary line will be established. We may begin by elaborating a concept known as the *correspondence principle*, which, if perfectly achieved, would mean that the people who participate in the government and who are subject to its jurisdiction are the same people who are joined together in enjoying the benefits and in incurring the costs of the collectively consumed services provided through that government. But we must be sure that we understand the full meaning of the correspondence principle. If correspondence is fully achieved, no benefit or cost from the collective service is not recognized because the consumer is not a member of the collectivity; that is, there are no external or spillover effects triggered by the actions of the government. In other words, full realization of the correspondence principle requires that people who are not citizens of the decision-making jurisdiction are not affected in any significant way by the actions taken by that government.

The concept of perfect correspondence is a benchmark or ideal situation for decision making about the provision of collectively consumed goods and services. If perfect correspondence is achieved, all the costs and all the benefits from proposed services can be recognized in the legislative process, and economically efficient decisions conceivably can be reached about the quantity of the service that should be provided. Conversely, inefficient quantities of the service may be chosen if perfect correspondence is not achieved—that is, if some of the benefits or some of the costs are not recognized in the decision-making procedure. If some benefits are not recognized, an inefficiently small output of the service will be selected. If some costs are not recognized, an inefficiently large output of the service will be selected. Thus, the model for collective decision making suggests that it is desirable to locate jurisdictional boundaries so that they correspond, as nearly as possible, with the boundaries of the beneficial consumption of the collective services provided. As a practical matter, of course, there are many reasons why perfect correspondence will not be achieved and why spillovers of benefit or cost must be faced in a system of multiple governments. Some noncorrespondence can be explained by examining the costs of extending or contracting jurisdictional boundaries. Other noncorrespondence situations arise from institutional and historical factors.

The Costs of Extending Jurisdictional Boundaries

If the costs of extending jurisdictional boundaries to include greater areas and greater numbers of people were zero, then an efficient solution to the boundary question would suggest that the jurisdiction should extend to the very limit of the geographic area of perceived benefits. And because different collective services have different benefit areas, this would mean that there would be a separate jurisdiction for each collectively consumed service. On the other hand, if the cost of extending jurisdictional areas is positive, then the appropriate boundary of the local jurisdiction will be smaller than the full geographic area of perceived benefits.

This concept is illustrated in Figure 17.3, which reproduces the benefit profile for the Laketon school and which adds the line *CC*, which represents the costs of extending the jurisdictional boundary to include additional people in the governing group. The line *CC* actually is a marginal cost line, since it illustrates the cost of extending the boundary to include one additional citizen. If the marginal cost of extending the boundary is positive, as shown in Figure 17.3, it follows that at some distance from the place where the service is delivered, the cost of including additional people in the governing unit will become greater than the benefit realized by those people. For people residing outside the *AA* area in Figure 17.3, the costs of citizenship are greater than the benefits they derive from the services rendered by the collectivity. Since their willingness to contribute to the support of the government is limited to the benefits

FIGURE 17.3   Locating Jurisdictional Boundaries

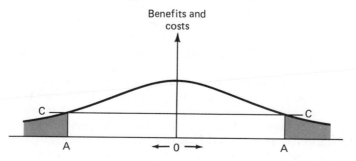

which they receive from this government, the people outside the *AA* area will be unwilling to be annexed into the Laketon school jurisdiction. The jurisdictional boundary will be established to include only the *AA* area. The shaded areas under the benefit curve and outside the *AA* area illustrate spillovers or external benefits enjoyed by outsiders.

The cost of extending the jurisdictional boundary may also be positive from the point of view of people inside the *AA* area who are already citizens of the collectivity. As noted in Chapter 3, collective action in a democratic system requires the achievement of some degree of agreement among the members of the collectivity, and the larger the number of persons who must be brought into agreement, the higher will be the negotiating costs of searching for satisfactory terms and conditions. Thus, under any given set of decision-making rules, negotiating costs argue against the expansion of the jurisdiction for a given collective service even if the expanded jurisdiction would encompass a greater number of beneficiaries and taxpayers. If the cost of including additional persons in the decision-making process is positive, some limit on the efficient size of the collectivity will exist. Negotiating costs bias the jurisdictional question in favor of smaller jurisdictions; they increase the amount of spillover benefit members of the community are willing to tolerate. Another way of looking at the same outcome is to note that small populations may find it feasible to incur the negotiating costs of working out agreement on more questions of collective concern than would a jurisdiction with a larger population. Local people can maintain closer control by limiting the size of the jurisdiction.

The *risk of losing* cost noted in connection with the establishment of decision-making rules also favors relatively small jurisdictions. Each individual recognizes that his own view at times may not prevail in the decision-making process and that he may suffer some welfare loss from being required to pay for services he does not want or from being unable to obtain services for which he would willingly pay. The risk of losing cost operates in favor of small jurisdictions because migration is easier should the individual face too many adverse decision possibilities. Moreover, because small jurisdictions lower the cost of migration, more migration will take place into and out of these jurisdictions, with the result that small jurisdictions will possess a more homogeneous citizenry (in terms of tastes and preferences) than large jurisdictions. Thus, the substantive differences between the majority and minority positions on particular questions can be expected to be relatively small because of the homogeneity of the population. Both the risk of losing and the consequences of losing (the odds and the stakes) will be smaller in the smaller jurisdiction.

As we noted in Chapter 3, negotiating costs and risk of losing costs are related to one another through the decision-making rules accepted by the citizens of the collectivity. If unanimous consent were required (individual veto power), the risk of losing would be zero, but the negotiating costs would be very great. The whole context within which this tradeoff is resolved is related to the degree of homogeneity prevailing in the community itself. Indian tribes could operate with unanimous consent rule because culture and bonds of tradition introduced homogeneity and because the number of persons in each tribe was small. Difficulties arose with decisions in larger and less homogeneous groups.

Limits on Jurisdictional Smallness

Thus far, the examination of the jurisdictional boundary question has led to conclusions that boundaries will be established so as to incorporate areas smaller than the whole area of beneficial collective consumption. Spillovers of benefit are likely to exist. Other considerations can lead to the opposite result, that is, to boundaries that extend beyond the geographic area of collective benefit from particular services. These considerations include recognition that there are overhead costs of maintaining the agencies through which governments operate and that there are advantages in establishing governments responsible for several services simultaneously, that is, for governments that are multiprogrammatic.

The idea that there are overhead costs in maintaining a government establishment is straightforward and readily understandable. Administrative entities require real resources for their maintenance; spreading these costs over a larger range of services and a larger number of citizens can reduce the average costs. If a separate jurisdiction existed for each of the many collective services consumed by an individual, citizens would find the election process very complicated, with different sets of candidates competing for office in the various governments in which the individual would be a constituent. Information costs to the voting citizen would be increased. If the individual had a grievance or wished to express his position on a public matter, he might encounter some difficulty in locating the appropriate official. Some incentive to expand a government jurisdiction, both geographically and programmatically, can arise.

Multiprogrammatic jurisdictions also offer advantages in addition to simply spreading the overhead cost of government. The special advantages of a multiprogrammatic jurisdiction arise from recognizing that choices must be made *among* collective services themselves as well as between collective services on the one hand and private services on the other. If each collective service were provided by a different jurisdiction, direct confrontation and debate between alternatives would be awkward and inefficient. For example, choices between police expenditures and school expenditures may, in contemporary systems, be inefficiently debated because hearings have to be conducted before different groups of decision makers. City government proposals may be opposed because citizens are hard pressed by school taxes, or school proposals may go down to defeat in an expression of taxpayer opposition to the generally high level of property taxes. The point is that multiprogrammatic jurisdictions may offer efficiency advantages in the deliberative process itself.

There are, however, some disadvantages to the multiprogrammatic jurisdiction. These arise from the reduction in the homogeneity of the population when a number of programs are operated by the same government. Some citizens may have no interest in some of the programs being carried out. This increases the negotiating and risk of losing costs for citizens. However, the disadvantage is one of degree rather than of kind. Even the perfect correspondence model incorporated differences in the amount of benefit perceived by different citizens from the program carried out by their government. Although all citizens presumably received some benefit in the perfect correspondence system, the benefit to some was greater than the benefit to others. In the multiprogrammatic jurisdiction, the range of benefit differential is merely extended to include some who receive no benefit at all. The degree of internal disharmony is increased somewhat, but the point is that some amount of disharmony cost may be acceptable in exchange for the overhead cost reduction and decision-making advantages of the multiprogrammatic arrangement.

Other Boundary and Spillover Factors

As a practical matter, many factors influence the location of jurisdictional boundaries and the nature and magnitude of spillovers. For example, the illustration of the Laketon school was carried out in terms of the *collectively* consumed services of this school, but most of the services of the school are *private* rather than collective. That is, they are consumed individually by the students who are educated rather than by the community at large. These private benefits of the services of the school are likely to be a dominating consideration in locating the actual boundary of the school district. The student attendance area of the school and jurisdictional boundaries relating to the governance of the school undoubtedly will correspond, with little consideration given to the collective benefits generated. School district boundaries frequently do not coincide with the boundaries of other government units, and the substantial collective spillovers from the activities of local school districts give rise to important state government involvement.

Another factor that results in noncorrespondence between jurisdictional boundaries and the areas of collective benefit is that once boundary lines are established, changes are very difficult to make because of vested interests which quite naturally develop in connection with the existing boundary. Alteration of established boundaries between sovereign governments is almost impossible to bring about peacefully, but the areas affected by the services provided by these governments may change as changes take place in technologies and life styles. An examination of experience with local jurisdictional boundaries provides an interesting perspective on the model of local government functional allocations.

Transportation and communication technologies, for example, have produced important changes in the geographic areas of benefit from locally provided collective services. Several generations ago, these changes led to increased concentrations of people in cities. The number of different services consumed collectively increased and the responsibilities of these local governments expanded. Later, as transportation and communication technologies led to dispersals of population and to larger geographic areas of collective consumption, municipal boundaries expanded and efforts were made to establish metropolitan governments. But many of the difficulties and problems of local governments reflect the difficulty of adjusting jurisdictional boundaries to the ever-changing areas of collective effects. Many jurisdictional boundaries and functional assignments today appear as "accidents of history" or at least as having been established in response to circumstances that no longer exist. Institutional arrangements have great staying power because of interests vested in the status quo and because change itself would impose real costs. But if boundary changes or effective arrangements for intergovernment relations cannot keep pace with the forces that alter the benefit areas from collective services, local governments may become increasingly ineffective in satisfying citizen demands for those services.

Types of Noncorrespondence

The analysis of the location of jurisdictional boundaries has shown that the boundaries of actual local governments will not correspond precisely with the boundaries of the areas of collective benefit from the services provided by these governments. Certainly, this conclusion is consistent with observations about real world jurisdictional boundaries. Rarely do actual boundaries correspond perfectly with the areas of benefit from the collective services. It will be helpful, however, to summarize by pointing out that two distinct types of noncorrespondence have been identified. These two types of noncorrespondence may be labeled type I and type II and are illustrated in Figure 17.4.

FIGURE 17.4   Types of Noncorrespondence

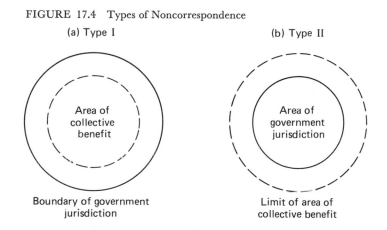

(a) Type I

(b) Type II

Boundary of government jurisdiction

Limit of area of collective benefit

In each of these figures, the dotted circle represents the area of beneficial consumption from collective service and the solid line circle represents the government jurisdiction responsible for the provision of this service. Figure 17.4(a) illustrates type I, in which the area of government jurisdiction extends beyond the area of beneficial collective consumption. This situation may arise through spreading the overhead costs of government and through attempts to obtain the decision-making benefits of multiprogrammatic organization. Little further attention need be paid to this type of noncorrespondence, since the problems associated with it are simply those of devising an internal revenue system that can accurately measure consumer demand for collective services when some of the citizens are not benefited by some of the services rendered by the government.

Type II, illustrated in Figure 17.4(b), shows that the area of beneficial consumption of collective service extends beyond the jurisdictional authority of the government responsible for the provision of the service. There are beneficiaries or potential beneficiaries of the service rendered by this government who are not represented in the decision-making processes. In this situation, resources may be misallocated unless some means is found to provide representation for these excluded groups. Providing a means for representing these external beneficiaries requires institutions for intergovernment relations, such as programs of grants-in-aid through which the external beneficiaries can gain an effective voice in influencing the output of the service in question.

The Marginal Rule, Again

The marginal rule was outlined in Chapter 2 in connection with the provision of nonpure or quasi-collective goods or services. In that situation, part of the benefit from a particular good or service was enjoyed privately and part was enjoyed collectively. The marginal rule suggested that private finance could be relied upon to provide some quantity of the nonpure good and that government finance would not be called upon to make any payment in recognition of the collective benefits that arose as by-products in the process of satisfying private demand. In a sense, collective consumption would be permitted to enjoy a free ride. Under the marginal rule, governmental financing would be appropriate only if collective demands were not satisfied through the by-product or free-ride procedure. If, at the margin of private provision, collective demands remained unsatisfied, then government financing could be introduced to the extent necessary to meet collective demands.

A similar rule may be applicable to situations in which services rendered by one jurisdiction spill over to affect citizens of other jurisdictions. In the illustration of the benefit profile from collective services rendered by the Laketon school, external benefits or spillovers accrued to persons residing outside the Laketon school district. The level of these benefits was not great enough to justify annexing these external beneficiaries into the Laketon school government. They were not contributing to financing this government and were obtaining a free ride. But the question remains whether the level of these collective services is satisfactory for these outside beneficiaries.

If the level of collective service being enjoyed by these outside beneficiaries is satisfactory, that is, if their demand for collective service is met as a by-product of the services rendered by the citizens of Laketon, the marginal rule suggests that there is no need for these external beneficiaries to be involved in the activities of the Laketon government. Indeed, in many instances, it seems likely that the type and quality of collective service demanded by external beneficiaries will be the same as the type and quality demanded by the citizens of the local service-rendering jurisdiction, so that the marginal rule, rather regularly, would eliminate the necessity for explicit action due to benefit spillovers. External interests in collective service are not likely to remain unsatisfied at the margin of local provision unless important geographic differences prevail in preferences or in the ability to finance collective services. Thus, benefit spillovers frequently may provide no ground for intergovernment transactions if the marginal rule is followed.

But other situations may require some intergovernment transactions. If the collective service demands of persons outside the jurisdiction are not satisfied as by-products of the local government's actions, a case arises for an intergovernment transaction. The unsatisfied outsiders may be willing to make a payment to the Laketon school in exchange for some influence in the decision making for the school. This involvement may be less than complete citizenship, but will provide some representation to the outsiders. Intergovernment grants-in-aid illustrate this type of involvement. Of course, if the external effects generated by the Laketon school are negative, that is, if they harm outsiders, it is apparent that some intergovernment actions may be required.

The marginal rule is not a necessary part of the model of functional allocation based on geographic profiles of benefits from collective consumption. Other approaches to joint responsibility could be applied. The marginal rule is a policy guideline that incorporates some preference for local or small unit responsibility for the provision of collective services in a multilevel system of governments, just as it reveals a preference for private provision, as distinct from collective provision, of partly collective services.

THE PURE THEORY OF LOCAL EXPENDITURE

If we recognize that certain collective services have distinctly localized benefit areas, and if we assume that external effects are either nonexistent or adequately provided for through a system of intergovernment transactions, we may now examine the *pure theory* of local government expenditure, which develops a model of how resources may be efficiently allocated in a system of governments.

Local Governments as Competing Firms

In this model, local governments are viewed as analogous to firms that supply collective services. A variety of services or combinations of services are offered by these different firms.[1] For example, some communities offer the amenities of quiet living and others offer the attractions of more urbanized living. Some offer features related to the presence of some natural or locational characteristic, such as a beach or a lake, a congenial climate, or proximity of mountains. Others may establish a distinction through their own initiatives, perhaps by the development of cultural attractions, educational services, or special emphasis on transportation, sanitation, and so on. These service packages distinguish the different communities and are offered to people in a market for local collective services. The people, in turn, purchase their preferred package of collective services by establishing residence in the community of their choice. This process of revealing individual preferences for different local collective services by choosing among alternative communities is called "voting with your feet." If a person discovers a community that offers a package of services more to his liking or obtainable at lower price than that prevailing in his present community, he can move to the community that offers the better or more economical satisfaction of his wants for local collective service.

[1] Charles M. Tiebout, "A Pure Theory of Local Expenditures," *Journal of Political Economy*, October 1956, pp. 416–24.

Local Government Efficiency

If the variety of alternative communities is large, if knowledge about these different service packages is readily available, and if the cost of voting with your feet is not prohibitive, the model of communities as competing firms has a number of implications about the efficiency of local governments. For example, each local government will attempt to keep the tax price of its services as low as possible consistent with the costs of producing the services and will attempt to finance these services with internal revenue systems that are as equitable as possible. The communities that offer attractive service-tax packages will attract population, and the quantity of these desired service-tax arrangements will increase. Conversely, communities offering relatively unattractive service-tax packages will lose population and the quantity of these less desired combinations will decrease. The outmigration from communities is especially important because the migrating group is likely to include those who may have been exploited by the majority in the community and thus required to help finance services that mainly benefited others. The exodus leaves a community that is more homogeneous in its preferences and that must finance its services through payments received from actual beneficiaries. Voting with your feet thus reduces the opportunity for majority-group exploitation of minority groups and exerts pressure toward the establishment of benefit-related financing measures.

The model also suggests that some limit will exist for the expansion of the communities offering attractive service-tax packages and that this size limit will have production efficiency characteristics. For example, if the services rendered by these attractive characteristics require the utilization of some fixed inputs (such as given locational characteristics), average costs of service may decline as the community expands, thus providing an extra incentive to immigration. The presence of a fixed input, however, also determines that average costs of service would start to increase if population grew beyond some technically efficient optimum. For example, congestion would arise if the fixed input were overutilized by the expanded population. Thus, the model again suggests an analogy with the conventional cost patterns of the firm or business; that is, that average costs of providing output will exhibit a U-shaped pattern such as that illustrated in Figure 17.5. In this illustration, average costs of service will decline for output (population) expansion from 0 to N, as fixed factors become more fully utilized and as overhead costs are spread over a larger number of consumers. Expansion beyond N encounters rising average costs as congestion arises in the utilization of the fixed resource. The rising average cost beyond N would require higher tax rates by the community, and these additional taxes would reduce its attractiveness to potential newcomers.

Policy Implications and Constraints

The key idea in this model of local government expenditures is the recognition that people can express their preferences for collective services by voting with their feet as well as by the conventional method of voting at the ballot box. The distinctive characteristic of collective services is, after all, uniformity in consumption. Each member of the collectivity must consume the same collec-

FIGURE 17.5 Community Size and Average Costs of Service

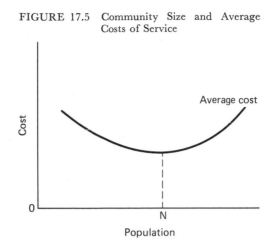

Population

tive services and pay taxes under the same rules as every other member of the collectivity. As long as decisions are made by less than unanimous consent, there is the definite likelihood that some citizens will have a smaller net advantage from their citizenship than will others. In a unitary government system there is little recourse for a citizen who finds himself regularly in a minority position in collective decisions, except through vote trades and the formation of political coalitions. The pure theory of local expenditure suggests, on the other hand, that arrangements which offer a wide variety of local government alternatives give the individual an additional way of expressing his preferences. In turn, this additional means of preference revelation implies that resources can be more efficiently allocated in a system of local governments than in a unitary government and provides the basic theoretical argument in favor of allocating service responsibility to the smallest unit of government capable of supplying this service efficiently. The question of just how small such government may be was explored in the earlier portion of this chapter.

The availability of migration exerts pressures for each community (a) to adopt revenue systems that accord with the benefit perceptions of its citizens and (b) to carry out its provision of services at a technologically efficient level. Potential migration stimulates governments to manage their operations in a nonwasteful manner and to adopt any new technology that promises to reduce costs. The city manager is comparable to the manager of a business firm who is under pressure from owners and the customers to generate output at the least possible cost. The factors that limit or constrain the ability of individuals to change their affiliation from one jurisdiction to another limit the extent to which voting with your feet can realize efficiency advantages in a multigovernment system. Moving from one community to another is an expensive undertaking and a considerable amount of misallocation (from the viewpoint of a given citizen) by the present community may be absorbed by an individual before he takes the drastic step of parting company with his friends and neighbors and establishing a new place of residence. There are risks in making the move, since full information about the new community may be expensive to obtain or obtainable only by actually living there. Glowing anticipation may turn to bitter disappointment after the move has been made. Thus the cost of moving and the cost of information clearly are important constraints on the effectiveness of the system.

Certain groups of individuals may be more severely constrained under the system than others. Low-income families, for example, are much more likely to find the cost of voting with their feet to be beyond their means than are more affluent families and thus may more frequently find themselves in a minority and potentially exploited group. Similarly, if an individual happens to have a set of preferences shared by only a few other people, it is likely that no community will cater specifically to his pattern of preferences. Some second-best choice of community becomes unavoidable for him.

The model implies a policy in favor of a multigovernment rather than a unitary government system. It also supports measures to increase the availability of information about the expenditure-tax packages of different local governments, and measures that reduce the costs of moving from one community to another.

SUMMARY

This chapter has developed a model of *fiscal federalism*, that is, a model which suggests how responsibility for providing collective services may be allocated among different jurisdictions in a multigovernment system. The basic ingredient in this model is the proposition that geographic concentrations may exist in the pattern of benefits generated by collective services. If such concentrations exist, the *correspondence principle* suggests that the boundaries of government jurisdictions should match the boundaries of benefit, that is, that the people who benefit from services should be the same people who make decisions about and pay for these services.

The correspondence principle will not be fully realized in practice for a variety of reasons. If there are positive costs associated with extending jurisdictional boundaries to include wider areas and more people, then efficiency logic indicates that the boundaries established will permit some benefits to spill over to persons who are not included in the jurisdiction. No great concern need arise about these spillover benefits if the outside beneficiaries find that their interest in these services is adequately served through the by-product route. However, the marginal rule suggests that some explicit intergovernment transactions will be desirable if collective service demands are not met through the by-product system or if external effects are harmful to the outsiders.

Some circumstances suggest that government boundaries actually may extend farther than the area of benefit from some services rendered. This is also a deviation from perfect correspondence. Spreading overhead costs and achieving the advantages of multiprogrammatic decision making can lead to this type of *noncorrespondence*. The problems that arise because of this type of noncorrespondence are internal to the jurisdiction and do not require intergovernmental arrangements.

The model of government organization and functional allocations based on geographic benefit areas leads to a pure theory of local government expenditure which suggests that a multigovernment system can be efficient, both technologically in delivering services at least cost and economically in catering to individual demands for collective services.

SUGGESTED READINGS

TIEBOUT, CHARLES M. "A Pure Theory of Local Expenditures," *Journal of Political Economy*, October 1956, pp. 416–24.

OLSON, MANCUR. "The Principle of 'Fiscal Equivalence': The Division of Responsibilities Among Different Levels of Government," *American Economic Review*, 59, 2 (May 1969), pp. 479–87.

LITVACK, JAMES M., and WALLACE E. OATES. "Group Size and the Output of Public Goods: Theory and Application to State–Local Finance in the United States," *Public Finance*, 25, 1 (1970), pp. 42–58.

OATES, WALLACE E. *Fiscal Federalism* (New York: Harcourt Brace Jovanovich, 1972), Chap. 2.

MILLER, STEPHEN M., and WILLIAM K. TABB. "A New Look at the Pure Theory of Local Expenditures," *National Tax Journal*, XXVI, 2 (June 1973).

ARONSON, J. RICHARD, and ELI SCHWARTZ. "Financing Public Goods and the Distribution of Population in a System of Local Governments," *National Tax Journal*, XXVI, 2 (June 1973).

GIERTZ, J. FRED. "Decentralization at the State and Local Level: An Empirical Analysis," *National Tax Journal*, XXIX, 2 (June 1976).

18

An Overview
of State Government Finance

The boundary lines between the states are among the least obvious features of the American landscape. Sometimes they are identified with a river crossing, but typically the boundary merely is a line on a political map with no physical counterpart on the land itself other than, perhaps, a cluster of gasoline stations or a sign conveying the welcome of the state governor and the admonition to drive safely. From a contemporary point of view, state boundaries appear as historical accidents: Chicago might have been in Wisconsin rather than in Illinois had events evolved in only a slightly different way; West Virginia and Virginia might still be one. But boundaries are not easy to change; once established, they become facts of life of the federal system.

The purpose of this chapter is to provide an overview of the fiscal affairs of the fifty states of the United States and to illustrate both the similarities and the differences among them. The similarities arise in part because states are sovereign governments and therefore have broad powers to tax and to regulate. Most states employ a wide range of roughly similar taxes. Another common characteristic shared by the states is that all of them are bound by the laws passed by the federal government. Federal government legislation requires that certain activities be performed, establishes minimum standards, and dispenses large amounts of grant-in-aid money. Differences among the states arise from a variety of geographic, economic, social, and historical factors. Each state presents its own more or less distinctive package of geographic, economic, social, and institutional characteristics. Since state boundaries constitute no significant barrier to the conduct of economic activity or to the migration of population, changing circumstances in the national society and economy affect different states in different ways. Interstate differences in population, income, urbanization, and so on, become subjects for scholarly examination in efforts to determine the variables that influence state revenues and expenditures.

STATE GOVERNMENT EXPENDITURES

State governments are primarily financers of education, highways, and public welfare. These three categories account for approximately 70 percent of state government expenditures, with lesser amounts divided among a great variety of services, such as health, hospitals, and natural resources. But a comprehensible picture of state expenditures is difficult to obtain for several reasons. A significant portion of the money expended through state budgets originates with the federal government and is transmitted to the states for expenditure on programs which, for the most part, are rather precisely specified by the federal government. Therefore, state expenditures may not be fully funded by revenues collected inside the state and the states do not have full authority to determine the character of these expenditures. The importance of federal money in state government finance will be explored further later in this chapter.

A second complicating factor arises because state expenditures may be administered either directly through state agencies or indirectly through grants of money to local governments which then have immediate responsibility for expenditure. The sharing of financing responsibility between the state government and its local governments differs from one function to another inside each state. For example, the sharing of responsibility for education usually is different from the sharing of responsibility for highways. There are also differences among the states in the manner in which responsibilities are shared in respect to specific functions. State responsibility for education may be greater in some states than in others. Because of this diversity in the sharing of responsibilities, the statistical comparisons given below will use the combined state plus local per capita expenditures for each of the functions and the discussion will indicate, in a general way, how responsibilities are divided between the state and its local governments.

Expenditures for Education

In 1974–75, combined state and local direct expenditure for education averaged $412.24 per capita, but the range among the states was substantial. Educational expenditures were $854.89 per capita in Alaska, whereas these expenditures were $289.01 in the state that spent least.[1]

The factors associated with interstate variations in per capita education expenditures have been examined by several scholars. Not surprisingly, a relatively high level of per capita education spending is associated with relatively high levels of per capita income, and the relationship appears to hold whether the focus is on local schools or on higher education. But income is not the only factor that appears to influence education spending. Sparseness of population (that is, a low population per square mile) is also associated with greater levels

---

[1] U.S. Bureau of the Census, *Governmental Finances in 1974–1975*, GF75, No. 5 (Washington: Government Printing Office, 1976), Table 22, p. 63.

of per capita educational expenditure, both for local schools and for higher education. For local schools alone (as distinguished from higher education), there is some suggestion that the distribution of income may be important. The association appears to be negative between per capita spending for local schools and the percentage of families in low-income categories. That is, communities with a larger portion of families in low-income groups may spend less (per capita) on public education than do communities with a smaller low-income family component, even after allowance has been made for differences in the average level of per capita income.

Other variables that have been examined in attempts to explain interstate variations in education (and other) expenditures include urbanization, population increase, two-party competition, average levels of educational attainment, the yield of a representative tax system, state aid, and federal aid. Some of these variables add explanatory power to the efforts to account for interstate variations, but the sum total results generally are able to account for only some 60 percent of the total observed variation in per capita educational expenditure. Still other factors may be important. For example, private schools are substitutes for public schools, and private educational institutions are more important in some parts of the country than in others. If private schools are relatively important in a given state, a relatively low per capita figure for public education spending need not indicate inadequate public school funding on a per pupil basis. Also, many of the less densely populated states developed after strong encouragement for public education came from the federal government through land grants for public schools under Northwest Territory ordinances after 1785 and under the Morrill Act of 1862.[2] The relatively lesser importance of private schools in these states may be as important as sparseness of population in explaining their larger amounts of public spending per capita for education.

Educational financing is organized differently in some states than in others. Hawaii presents an extreme instance of centralization of educational responsibility at the state level of government. The state provides almost 100 percent of the combined state and local expenditure for education. Moreover, Hawaii's educational spending is carried on directly by the state government rather than through the use of grants to local governments. Although Hawaii is unique among the states, many state governments assume substantial financial responsibility for education. Even in states where local finance is most important, state government funding is substantial.

State aids or educational grants are the usual instruments for the implementation of state government financing of local schools. Slightly more than half of total state expenditure for education is dispensed through these intergovernment devices. Typically, state education aid formulas provide a basic amount per pupil enrolled in local public schools, with adjustments in the per pupil amount designed to compensate, at least in part, for differences in local financing ability as measured by taxable local property values. In some instances, additional adjustments are provided to recognize differences in local fiscal "effort" as revealed by the rates of tax that local citizens have imposed on themselves to finance education. Through the use of intergovernment trans-

2 Rivlin, Alice M., *The Role of the Federal Government in Financing Higher Education* (Washington, D.C.: The Brookings Institution, 1961), Ch. 2.

fers, states are able to assume major financial responsibility for local schools while leaving operational details in the hands of local and school district authorities. Direct state educational spending, on the other hand, is channeled primarily to institutions of higher education.

Expenditures for Highways

Highway spending is an important part of total state expenditure, although it is of considerably less magnitude than spending for education. In 1974–75, combined state and local expenditure for highways amounted to $105.70 per capita.[3] Intergovernment funding of highway expenditure through state aids to local governments is of relatively little importance in many states. On a national average, about one dollar of every five dollars of state government highways expenditure was channeled through intergovernment transfers, and in many states this portion was zero or almost zero. But state intergovernment spending for highways is important in some states.

Alaska led all other states by a wide margin in the number of dollars of state and local highway spending per capita in 1974–75. Alaska's expenditures of $415.47 per capita were some four times the national average. In other states, per capita amounts sometimes were one-third below the national average. Per capita highway expenditures differ among the states for a variety of reasons, and, of course, data that include capital outlays can fluctuate from year to year as construction programs are begun or completed. Low population density and "wide open spaces" undoubtedly have something to do with per capita highway spending, but other variables may also affect it. Considering all fifty states, population density has rather limited explanatory power. Much more importance attaches to the level of personal income and the portion of the state's population residing in urban areas. Income is positively related to per capita highway spending; that is, the higher the income, the greater the per capita spending on highways. Urbanization is inversely related to highway spending so that more highly urbanized states spend less, per capita, on highways than do less urbanized states.

Federal highway aid clearly plays an important role in state and local highway expenditure. When federal aid is included in the estimating equation, it becomes the main determinant of variations in highway spending; the apparent importance of income and urbanization diminish greatly. There is some question, however, about whether federal aid can be included as an independent variable along with such other variables as per capita income. Federal highway aids typically utilize a matching system, which means that a state able to spend a large amount of its own money on highways can thereby qualify for more federal money. Thus, if federal highway aid is closely related to such internal factors as personal income, its dominant position as a determinant of highway spending may be more apparent than real.

Expenditures for Public Welfare

There are vast differences in per capita state and local welfare spending among the states. The states that spent the most per capita in 1974–75 expended

---

[3] *Governmental Finances in 1974–75*, Table 22, p. 63.

sums almost twice the national average of $127.58 and five or six times the per capita amounts spent in states at the low end of the list.[4] Welfare expenditures are typically carried out through a variety of categorical aid programs. The amounts expended through these programs reflect the generosity of the programs themselves, the conditions that must be met in order to qualify for aid, and the number of persons who actually apply for and meet these conditions for aid. The latter two factors clearly are interrelated and appear to be important determinants of the per capita welfare expenditure differences among the states. Among the variables ordinarily used to explain interstate variations in welfare spending, urbanization appears to carry some explanatory power, suggesting that the dependent populations typically reached by existing welfare programs are associated with urban dwelling places. Interstate variations in per capita welfare spending thus appear to reflect the need for and the access to existing welfare programs as well as the generosity of the programs themselves.

Federal government transfers are extremely important in welfare spending in all states, and a substantial portion of the funds expended by states and localities originates with the federal government. When federal aid is included in the calculations seeking to explain interstate variations in welfare spending, the total explanatory power is greatly increased, the apparent importance of urbanization recedes markedly, and differences in per capita income among the states becomes the second most important determinant (after federal aid) of variations. States with relatively high per capita income levels may be able to qualify for more federal aid through the maintenance of more generous welfare programs, but it also seems plausible that states differ in the range of income inequality they encompass within their borders and that high per capita income may be associated with a dependent population of considerable relative importance.

States differ greatly from the one another in the manner in which welfare expenditures are administered. In many states, substantially all welfare expenditure originates at the state government level (although much of the money comes to the state from the federal government), and in no state does local funding amount to much more than one-third of total state and local expenditure. But great differences appear in the choice between direct spending by the state itself and the alternative of indirect expenditure through grants from the state to local units of government. In some states, practically all combined state and local welfare spending is done directly by the state. In other states, welfare spending is implemented through intergovernment transfers to local units of government. In New York, where per capita welfare spending level was among the highest in the nation, direct state spending was of relatively little importance; most state welfare expenditure was carried out through grants to localities.[5]

Events in the past several years strongly suggest that major changes are likely to take place in the nature and organization of welfare expenditures in

---

[4] *Ibid.*, Table 22, p. 64.

[5] U.S. Bureau of the Census, *State Government Finances in 1975*, Series GF–75, No. 3 (Washington: Government Printing Office, 1976), Table 4, p. 12.

the United States. Income distribution clearly is a responsibility of the federal government rather than of the states and localities, and basic decisions to alter the prevailing welfare system must originate at the federal level. In the late 1960s, federal initiatives in welfare and medicare programs placed great strains on state finances. Court decisions outlawing residency requirements for qualification under state welfare programs forced a recognition that varying benefit and eligibility levels among the states could not be maintained. Thus, the stage is set for a major revamping of the welfare system in the nation. When a new system is established, state and local financing patterns will undergo major alteration.

Per Capita Spending for All Functions

The foregoing discussions of education, highway, and welfare spending suggest that great variations may also exist among the states in total spending. This indeed is the case. In 1974–75, direct state and local spending per capita averaged $1,076.73 in the United States. Per capita spending ranged up to levels some two and one half times this national average in some states and down to levels some 25 percent below the national average in others.[6]

When all functional categories of expenditure are lumped together, the most important determinants of per capita state and local expenditure are the amount of federal aid received and the level of personal income in the state. Each of these variables is positively associated with the level of per capita spending, so that states with high personal income levels tend not only to spend more per capita on state and local government services, but also tend to receive larger amounts per capita from the federal government. However, care must be taken in interpreting these data on interstate differences. In general terms, a relatively high level of per capita expenditure on a given function suggests relatively high levels of quality or quantity for the service provided. But the number of citizens in need of a particular service and the cost per unit of providing this service are not the same in all areas of the country.

It is quite possible that high per capita expenditure levels may, in some instances, merely reflect cost differentials and reveal little about the quality or quantity of service actually rendered. Similarly, if the number of citizens in need of a given service is especially large, even very high levels of per capita expenditure may fail to provide service levels per beneficiary equivalent to those available to people in other areas that spend considerably smaller sums per capita. Finally, it should be noted that there may be regional differences in the preferences of citizens for various types of government services, or in the social and political institutions that have arisen to provide these services. For example, if a substantial number of citizens in a given state prefer private education to public education, it does not follow that education is underfinanced just because state and local budgets reveal relatively low per capita expenditures for education. In a federal system, when different governments provide different levels or combinations of service, the individual has some opportunity to choose the community that offers the package most congenial to his own preference

[6] *Governmental Finances in 1974–75,* Table 22, p. 62.

system. Rationalizations such as this can readily be overdrawn or misapplied. Nevertheless, there is virtue in diversity as well as in uniformity.

STATE REVENUE SOURCES

A wide-ranging use of the tax power is characteristic of state governments in the United States. Many different taxing instruments are used; no single instrument achieves a dominance approaching that of the property tax for local government or the individual income tax for the federal government. General sales taxes and individual income taxes are the most important revenue instruments utilized by the states, but neither of these generates revenues amounting to 20 percent of the total general revenues of the states. In 1975 only three revenue instruments (general sales taxes, individual income taxes, and motor fuel taxes) generated revenues exceeding 5 percent of total general revenue of the states in the nation.[7] Table 18.1 displays the revenue instruments used by the states and shows the percentage of total state general revenue realized from each in 1975.

Major Internal Sources

General sales taxes and individual income taxes are the major internal revenue sources for state governments in the United States. In 1975, these two sources combined to provide almost one-third of state general revenues. In terms of national averages, general sales taxes raised $116.66 per capita in 1975 and individual income taxes raised $88.60 per capita, but a considerable range existed among the states in their reliance on these basic sources of internal revenue. In that year, every state made use of one or the other of these sources, but five states did not use the general sales tax and six states recorded zero per capita collections from individual income taxes. At the top end of the spectrum, general sales tax revenues were $332.05 per capita in Hawaii and $245.89 per capita in Washington. Individual income tax revenues were $247.09 per capita in Alaska and $237.65 in Delaware.

At one time, general sales taxes and individual income taxes were widely considered as alternatives in the structuring of revenue sources for individual states. Income taxation was first in the field following Wisconsin's establishment of the tax in 1911. General sales taxes became widespread during the depression years of the 1930s, and for some years thereafter it was popular to characterize certain states as "income tax states" and other states as "sales tax states." After World War II, the adoption of "new" revenue sources proceeded at a much slower pace than that experienced during the emergency periods of the 1930s. Some states adopted sales taxes during this period, but the greatly increased level of income taxation imposed by the federal government discouraged the extension of state income taxation. During the decade of the 1960s, however, increased public service demands brought new "emergency" situations to many states and the pace of new tax adoptions increased. Both general sales taxes and individual income taxes appeared among these new adoptions, with the

[7] *State Government Finances in 1975*, Table 1, p. 7.

TABLE 18.1   Sources of State General Revenues, 1975

SOURCE	PERCENTAGE OF GENERAL REVENUE	
Major internal sources		
General sales taxes	18.4%	
Individual income taxes	14.0	32.4%
Minor internal sources		
Alcoholic beverage taxes	1.5	
Tobacco product taxes	2.4	
Corporation income taxes	4.9	
Property taxes	1.1	
Death and gift taxes	1.1	
Nonhighway license fees[a]	1.7	
Miscellaneous selective sales taxes[b]	3.8	
Other miscellaneous taxes[c]	1.6	18.1
Highway user sources		
Motor fuel taxes	6.1	
Motor vehicle licenses	2.7	
Motor vehicle operator licenses	.2	
Highway tolls and charges	.7	9.7
Current charges and miscellaneous sources		
Education	4.3	
Hospitals	1.3	
Other current charges[d]	1.4	
Miscellaneous general revenue	4.6	11.6
Intergovernment revenues		
Federal government	26.9	
Local governments	1.2	28.1
		100.0

[a] Includes licenses for corporations, alcoholic beverages, hunting and fishing.
[b] Includes taxes on insurance, utilities, parimutuels.
[c] Includes severance taxes and documentary taxes.
[d] Includes charges relating to natural resources and miscellaneous commercial activities.

Source: U.S. Bureau of the Census, State Government Finances in 1975, *Series G–75, No. 3 (Washington, D.C.: Government Printing Office, 1976), Table 1 (detail may not add to total because of rounding).*

result that it became increasingly unusual for a state to fail to utilize *both* revenue instruments. Unless revenue demands slacken, it can be predicted that the trend of the 1960s will continue until most, if not all, of the states will utilize both general sales taxes and individual income taxes.

Minor Internal Sources

The rather bewildering array of minor internal revenue sources used by the states are of relatively little importance individually but combine to channel sizable amounts of revenue into general state funds. Some of these revenue sources occasionally are characterized as "nuisance taxes." Others are imposed at such low rates or on such obscure or infrequent transactions as to fall below the threshhold of tax consciousness of the ordinary citizen. From the point of view of the state legislator, however, these revenue sources are quite attractive precisely because of their low political visibility. Many states have balanced budget requirements in their constitutions or are subject to severely limited borrowing powers, so that each session of the legislature is confronted with the necessity of adjusting either expenditures or revenues or both in order to come within these limitations. On the revenue side, frequent (and probably minor) changes in the rates or bases of the highly visible sales or income taxes are expensive in terms of compliance costs imposed on taxpayers and the political costs to legislators. Thus, the opportunity to bring the budget into balance through adjustments in the minor and relatively invisible revenue sources is a notable convenience directly to the legislators and indirectly to the general citizenry of the state.

Most of the states employ the full array of specific sources noted in the "minor source" category in Table 18.1 and only rarely does any one of them constitute a source of great importance to a state. Certain exceptions may be noted, however, in regard to severance taxes (included among "miscellaneous other taxes") and corporation income taxes. Severance taxes are applied to the extraction of petroleum and mineral deposits and are of considerable importance in those states where such activity is substantial. Similarly, the rather high rating for corporation income taxes (4.9 percent of aggregate general revenue as shown in Table 18.1) arises from heavy use of this tax in certain states.

Charges for Services

An important part of state general revenues comes from charges collected from persons who purchase services provided by the state. Highways are the most prominent illustration of this semicommercial type of government activity. When motorists and commercial enterprises purchase motor fuels and pay the state tax levied on these purchases, they are purchasing the opportunity to use the road system constructed and maintained by the state. The same reasoning applies to the collection of charges for driver and vehicle licenses. In the aggregate, highway user charges (including motor fuels taxes, operator licenses, vehicle licenses, and toll road charges) accounted for almost 10 percent of state general revenues in 1975. Motor fuel taxes provide the major portion of highway user charges and are imposed in all states. Per capita collections in 1975 reached a high of $54.77 in Wyoming; the national average was $38.87.

Charges for educational and hospital services are in the same category as charges for highway services, although these are of much less financial importance. Tuition charges at state institutions of higher education are the main source of educational service charge revenues. Although "charge for service" collections are classed as general revenues, the common practice is to channel or earmark these revenues for expenditure in providing the service associated with the payment itself. Almost all highway expenditure is financed by highway user charges and federal funds specifically restricted to highway use, but this is not the case for education and hospital expenditure, which receive appropriated general revenues in addition to the use charges.

Intergovernment Revenues

Intergovernment revenues are an extremely important part of the revenues received by the states. Most of these funds come from the federal government and must be expended according to the conditions set forth by that government. Federal funds for public welfare purposes were the major component in intergovernment revenues in 1975, followed by those for education and highways.

Intergovernment revenue from the federal government averaged $170.18 per capita in 1975. The state receiving the greatest per capita amount of federal revenue received $666.36. The state that received the least received $107.42. Most federal funds are distributed through categorical grants with different terms and conditions applying to the different categories. Therefore, the amount received by a state reflects the extent to which the state met federally established qualifications in a number of areas.

REVENUE CAPACITY AND EFFORT

States differ from one another in their ability to finance collective services. They also differ in the effort they make to finance them. These differences would be of little general interest if the levels of service provided and the rates of tax imposed affected only the residents of the jurisdiction providing the service and imposing the tax. According to the pure theory of local expenditure, people can vote with their feet if service levels or tax rates are unsatisfactory.

Many of the goods and services provided by state and local governments, however, generate effects that extend beyond the boundaries of the government actually supplying the service. Consequently, citizens of the other jurisdictions (that is, of the nation and the other states) desire assurance that these goods and services are provided in quantities and qualities which reach certain minimum levels of adequacy. Both capacity and effort therefore become relevant in determining the distribution of intergovernment revenues. In general, the amount of intergovernment aid transferred to a state or locality is related inversely to its capacity and directly to its effort. Thus, the measurement of capacity and effort becomes important in the process of deciding about intergovernment revenues.

Neither revenue capacity nor effort lends itself to absolute measurement. In an absolute sense, revenue capacity is limited only by the total income and total wealth (including borrowing power) located in the area or owned by the residents of the area and by the willingness of these people to permit this income and wealth to be taken by government. Clearly, absolute notions of capacity have little application in the analysis of normal government operations. Effort lends itself even less to an absolute measurement, since no independent unit of effort exists. Therefore, both capacity and effort are measured in relative terms —that is, the capacity and effort of given states or areas are expressed in terms of comparisons with the revenue potential and performance of other states or areas. In the measurement process, *capacity* is the more fundamental concept that requires formulation and quantification. Once agreement is reached on revenue capacity, an index of effort is established by comparing actual revenues with the amount of revenue estimated to be capacity.

Personal Income as a Capacity Criterion

The concept of personal income has been developed for use in the system of national income accounting. *Personal income* reports the amount of money received by persons and available to them for disposition in consumption, saving, or the payment of personal income taxes. Estimates of personal income are published regularly by the Department of Commerce for the nation as a whole and for the states and standard metropolitan statistical areas. The availability of the personal income statistic on a state and area basis largely accounts for its widespread use as a basis for the estimation of revenue capacity. A number of federal grant programs specify that personal income shall be used in determining the distribution of aid funds. Such specifications imply that personal income is a useful guide to the revenue capacity of the recipient governments.

If personal income is the only criterion used, the calculation of revenue capacity and effort is simple. The state or area with the largest per capita personal income is credited with the greatest capacity, the state or area with the lowest per capita personal income has the lowest capacity, and relative capacity can be expressed by dividing the per capita personal income of each state or area by the national average. Effort measures can be calculated with equal ease. For each state or area, actual government revenues (less federal grants) are expressed as a percentage of personal income and compared to the national average to determine an index of relative effort.

The main weakness of personal income as a criterion for estimating state or local revenue capacity is that it ignores many institutional factors which actually influence the ability of states and localities to raise government revenues from internal sources. Direct taxation of income yields less than 20 percent of state general revenues.[8] Most states rely heavily on other taxes, and for these other taxes, revenue capacity may not be directly or consistently related to personal income. In areas with substantial tourist activity, for example, sales taxes may be collected from nonresidents to a degree quite disproportionate to the in-state personal income generated by the tourist activity. For local governments, property tax capacity may be quite out of line with capacity as indicated by personal income. If property is owned by nonresidents, a substantial property tax revenue capacity would not be revealed by personal income statistics, since the income from the property will be recorded in the state of residence of the owner. Moreover, certain activities, such as agriculture, exhibit a rather high property to income ratio, so that capacity rated on the basis of income would yield a lower amount of revenue than would capacity rated on the basis of property taxation. The property to income ratio may also distort capacity measures in the opposite direction. Service activities may involve a low property to income ratio, so that an income-based capacity measure would over-

---

[8] Even income taxes do not reach all income levels at equivalent rates. Very low incomes, for example, ordinarily are exempted or taxed at low rates. Ability to pay enthusiasts are quick to point out that revenue capacity may be some function of the distribution of income as well as of the level of per capita income.

state the actual revenue capacity in a system relying heavily on property taxation.

Personal income is a widely accepted basis for measuring tax-paying capacity for individuals and families, but when the revenue capacity of a government unit is being examined, personal income ceases to be an entirely adequate measuring rod. The probability of divergence between the revenue capacity of the government and the personal income of its residents increases when smaller units of government are considered. Therefore, a capacity measure more directly relevant to governments themselves is needed.

The Average Financing System Capacity Criterion

The *average financing system* is a method of estimating state and local revenue capacity that recognizes the institutional "facts of life" governing revenue raising by states and localities.[9] In the average financing system approach, a separate capacity estimate is made for each of the numerous revenue-raising devices ordinarily employed by state and local governments. Estimates are based on the experiences of states and localities actually using each instrument. For example, the estimated revenue capability of property taxes is based on the market values of taxable properties; sales tax capability is based on the volume of sales transactions; income tax capability is based on income levels; and so on. For each state and area, estimates are developed of the "base" available for each of the revenue devices commonly used by state and local governments in the nation.

Revenue capacity for each instrument is estimated by multiplying the available base by an average rate of tax, which is computed on the basis of national totals. For example, the average rate for the property tax is determined by dividing total property tax collections throughout the country by the estimated total property tax base throughout the country; the average sales tax rate is determined by dividing total actual sales tax collections by the total available sales tax base in the nation; and so on. When these "average" rates are applied to the estimated bases available in a given state or locality, the result is an estimate of the amount of revenue this state or locality would collect if it made use of all the standard revenue-raising devices and if it utilized each of these devices at a rate average for the nation. That is, an estimate of total revenue capacity is developed on the basis of an average financing system.[10] Relative revenue effort is estimated by comparing actual revenues with capacity revenues. Effort measures can be estimated for separate components of the revenue system as well as for the total revenue system of each state or area.

[9] Advisory Commission on Intergovernmental Relations, *Measuring the Fiscal Capacity and Effort of State and Local Areas*, M–58 (Washington, D.C.: Government Printing Office, 1971).

[10] This method may overstate revenue capacity for the nation as a whole if the size of one tax base is affected by a tax imposed on another tax base. However, defenders of the ACIR method contend that its purpose is to develop measures of relative revenue capacity rather than estimates of aggregate capacity revenue production. See John S. Akin, "Fiscal Capacity and the Estimation Method of the Advisory Commission on Intergovernmental Relations," *National Tax Journal*, XXVI, 2 (June 1973) and Allen D. Manvel, "Tax Capacity Versus Tax Performance: A Comment," *ibid.*

VARIATIONS IN CAPACITY AND EFFORT

The ACIR study of fiscal capacity and effort was based on the fiscal year 1966–67 and a comprehensive updating of this information has not been made. Therefore, specific information about variations in capacity and effort now is seriously out of date. Nevertheless, certain general findings probably are still valid and useful in analyzing fiscal capacity and effort.

Capacity Variations

The average financing system showed rather large differences among the states in per capita revenue capacity. If that system had been in effect in 1966–67, per capita revenues in one state would have been 69 percent above the national average but 35 percent below the national average in another state. On a regional basis, the study suggested that western states generally had high per capita revenue capacities relative to the national average, whereas southern states had generally low per capita revenue capacities compared to the national average.

The average financing system method of estimating revenue capacity produced findings that differed markedly from those developed on the basis of personal income statistics. For twenty-four states in 1966–67, per capita revenue capacity estimated on the basis of an average financing system differed by 10 percent or more from capacity as suggested by personal income. In general, the personal-income estimating method resulted in lower revenue capacity estimates in those states and areas where mining, tourism, and agriculture were prominent in the economy. As we noted, the presence of an important tourist industry can provide sales tax revenue capacity that is not tied to the level of personal income in the taxing jurisdiction. Severance and special property taxes lend extra revenue capacity to states and areas encompassing important mining activities, and the prominent role of property taxation provides agricultural states and areas with revenue-raising capabilities differing from those estimated on the basis of personal income.

On the other hand, revenue capacities based on personal income were higher than those based on an average revenue system in urban areas and in areas that had experienced a less than average rate of population growth. Property taxation was important in influencing revenue capacities in each of these circumstances. Service trades are more important in the economies of urban areas and typically involve a lower ratio of taxable property to income than is the case for commercial, manufacturing, or agricultural activities. Also, property tax potential from residential housing may be low relative to income in urban areas, where multifamily dwellings are more common, and in areas experiencing a relatively low population growth rate, since residential structures may be somewhat older and of lower market value than in areas experiencing a more vigorous growth in population.

Effort Variations

The 1966–67 study showed less variation among the states in revenue effort than in revenue capacity, according to estimates made through the average financing system. Nevertheless, effort differences were of considerable magnitude. One state showed revenue effort 26 percent above the national average, whereas another showed revenue effort 23 percent below the national average.[11] However, the Advisory Commission study revealed little evidence of regional effort patterns or of patterns related to revenue capacity. When states were divided into groups displaying generally similar measures of per capita revenue capacity, it was discovered that rather sizable variations in effort existed within each of the groups. Thus, it appeared that the states with relatively low capacity did not consistently try harder in the sense of exhibiting a higher effort; nor did states with relatively high revenue capacity necessarily exert less effort in the provision of government services. Some evidence suggested, however, that less urbanized areas combined relatively low capacity and effort, perhaps because the demand for some services ordinarily provided by urban governments was not present.

Interesting relationships were suggested between state governments and their subordinate local governments. In general, a high effort on the part of the state government appeared to be associated with a relatively low effort on the part of local governments in the state, and vice versa. This balancing relationship between the states and their local governments is not implausible, since the allocation of functional responsibilities is not the same in all states. Certain tasks are financed at the state level in some states and at the local level in other states. It did appear, however, that state governments performed a leadership role in respect to combined state and local fiscal effort. This leadership role was implied by the finding that the state government typically exhibited greater effort than its subordinate jurisdictions in those states which, in total, exhibited above-average effort. Conversely, it was rare that a state would exhibit above-average overall effort when the state government lagged behind its subordinate jurisdictions. Thus, the state government appeared to lead the way in those states where combined state and local effort was above average.

CAPACITY AND EFFORT PROFILES

According to the average financing system, the revenue capacity of a state or area is a package concept, that is, the capabilities of many specific revenue instruments are added together to reveal total capacity. By examining the components of the revenue package for the different states, the study revealed that states would differ significantly from one another in the percentage of total revenue that they would collect from different sources. Income taxes, for example, would produce a much larger portion of total revenue in some states than they would in other states if the average financing system actually were in effect. Sales taxes would be more important in some states than in others and similar findings applied to property taxes and to revenues from various nontax sources. One of the most striking findings of the study was the importance of these nontax revenue sources and their variation in importance among the states. The finding that revenue capacity profiles differ significantly among

---

[11] Local area statistics can be expected to show wider ranges of variation in both capacity and effort than are shown for states, since local areas are less subject to the averaging process inherent in the use of statewide totals.

the states is important. For example, an effort by the national government to encourage greater use of income taxation or to discourage the use of property taxation would be eagerly received in some states but vigorously opposed in others.

The average financing system also is able to calculate measures of effort for each revenue source in a government financing package, and effort profiles can be developed which reveal which sources are overworked compared to the national average and which are underworked. This information can be useful to state and local legislators in considering changes in revenue structure, but it does not mean that states or localities necessarily should adjust their revenue instruments to bring them into conformity with national averages. Differences may continue to exist if legislatures in the various states conclude that their own, perhaps rather unique, revenue structure is preferable to that implied by the national average.

CRITIQUE OF THE AVERAGE FINANCING SYSTEM

Should state and local legislatures attempt to bring the revenue system in their respective jurisdictions into conformity with the national average system? Should the federal government adopt measures that encourage states and localities to revise their revenue systems in this direction? The objective of the Advisory Commission study of fiscal capacity and effort was to provide guidance in the distribution of federal intergovernment revenues. It did not explicitly suggest that the national average system was or was not desirable in itself or that efforts should be undertaken to establish the average system in the states and localities of the nation. Nevertheless, if the average financing system were used as a guide in the distribution of federal intergovernment revenues, an implicit judgment would have been made endorsing the desirability of the patterns incorporated in that system. States and localities would be encouraged to match their systems to the national average, thus reducing the diversity and experimental character of state and local finance throughout the nation. In the extreme, the argument could be made that the average financing system would tend to impose the "dead hand of the past" and to discourage the adaptation of state and local revenue systems to new technologies and new circumstances.

Supporters of the average financing system approach are not without counterarguments to the charge that the system is inherently conservative. They point out that it is not essential that the weights given to the various components of the financial system be those arising out of present practice. By altering the weights (average tax rates) applied to the separate components, or by adding presently unused revenue devices, an entirely different model could be devised and pretested for its impacts on the various states and localities through the techniques employed in the average financing system procedure. For example, if it were proposed that income taxes should play a greater role in state and local financing, the model could be developed with higher income tax rates and lower rates for other components of the system, and the differential impacts of the change among the states and localities could be estimated.

Whether the model uses existing practices as a guideline or whether it introduces variations from existing practice, it could be argued that the very concept of an average financing system poses a threat to the autonomy and diversity so cherished in a federal system. Such a criticism, however, focuses on the tool or instrument rather than on the substance of such a threat. If intergovernment revenues are prominent in state and local revenue systems, and if population and business mobility across state lines becomes ever more readily accomplished, diversity and autonomy inevitably are threatened.

SUMMARY

An overview of state government finances reveals that the states have much in common and yet exhibit a great deal of diversity. Education, highways, and welfare dominate state government activities in all states, although the levels of per capita expenditure differ in each of these areas. With few exceptions, the same basic revenue-collecting instruments are used in all states, but variations exist in the amounts of revenue collected from these instruments and in the degrees of reliance placed on one instrument or another. Intergovernment revenue from the federal government is important for all states, but again, wide differences exist in per capita amounts received.

Differences in per capita income among the states explain some of the observed variation in expenditures in each of the major areas of state activity; other variables, such as urbanization or the sparseness of population, add explanatory power for some expenditure areas. Federal aid is positively associated with the level of expenditure in most categories, but since most federal transfers are tied to particular programs and are distributed according to formulas reflecting need or particular federal objectives, its explanatory power must be explored on a program by program basis. Since state boundaries raise no significant barriers to the flow of commerce or to the migration of population, changing circumstances in the nation result in continually shifting patterns of differences among the states.

States generate revenues from a great variety of sources. General sales taxes and individual income taxes are the major internal sources of revenue, but these are supplemented by many other taxes that are unimportant individually but that combine to provide a significant part of state internal revenue. It is noteworthy also that states are engaged in several proprietary or semicommercial activities, such as higher education and highway services, which provide significant amounts of revenue from charges collected from those who directly utilize these services. Intergovernment revenues, primarily from the federal government, are of great and growing importance in the financial structure of state governments.

States also differ in their capacity to finance collective services and in the effort that they make toward financing them. Because these differences are used in the distribution of intergovernmental money, measures of state capacity and effort are important. Traditionally, revenue capacity has been measured on the basis of per capita personal income. However, per capita personal income may not accurately measure relative capacity among the states because many of the revenue instruments actually used are not based directly on personal income. The average financing system approach provides an alternative way of measuring differences in capacity and effort. This system measures capacity separately for each of the major revenue instruments used by state and local governments. For each of these instruments, revenue potential is estimated on the basis of tax rates actually used throughout the country. The average financing system not only provides estimates of overall revenue capacity and effort, but also provides information about the potentially most productive revenue sources for different states and regions. Profiles in revenue capacity and effort can be useful to state and local legislatures when they consider modifications in the revenue instruments used in their jurisdictions.

The average financing system is inherently conservative when tax bases and tax rates actually in use are used in preparing estimates of capacity and effort. But this system could be used to pretest tax systems other than the one revealed in existing national averages.

SUGGESTED READINGS

BAHL, R. "Studies on Determinants of Public Expenditures: A Review," in S. Mushkin and J. Cotton, *Sharing Federal Funds for State and Local Needs: Grants-in-Aid and PPBS Systems* (New York: Praeger Publishers, 1969).

Advisory Commission on Intergovernmental Relations. *Measuring the Fiscal Capacity and Effort of State and Local Areas* (Washington D.C.: Government Printing Office, 1971).

AKIN, JOHN S. "Fiscal Capacity and the Estimation Method of the Advisory Commission on Intergovernmental Relations," *National Tax Journal*, XXVI, 2 (June 1973).

MANVEL, ALLEN D. "Tax Capacity Versus Tax Performance: A Comment," *National Tax Journal*, XXVI, 2 (June, 1973).

HOGAN, TIMOTHY D., and ROBERT B. SHELTON. "Interstate Tax Exportation and States' Fiscal Structures," *National Tax Journal*, XXVI, 4 (December 1973), pp. 553–64.

ROTHENBERG, LEON. "A New Look in State Finances: Tax Reductions and Restructured Tax Systems," *National Tax Journal* XXVII, 2 (June 1974).

The U.S. Department of Commerce (Bureau of the Census) publications on government finance cited in this chapter appear annually and should be consulted for up-to-date information.

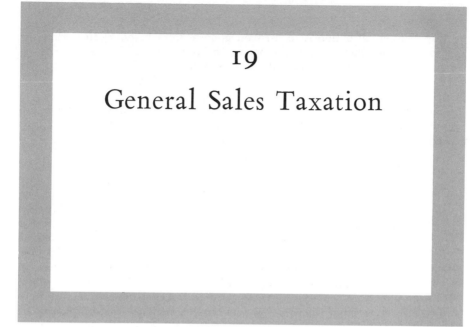

19

General Sales Taxation

What is a sales tax? Broadly speaking, it is a tax imposed on a transaction; the base of the tax is the price paid for the good or service exchanged. Since a great many different types of transactions take place in an advanced economy, the concept of sales taxes can include many different types of taxes. Motor fuel taxes are sales taxes, as are taxes on tobacco products and alcoholic beverages. However, when people talk about "the sales tax" in ordinary conversation, they are referring to a particular type of sales tax, namely, the *general retail* sales tax. The term "general" suggests that the tax has a broad base in the sense that transactions involving many different commodities are subjected to it, in contrast to "selective" sales taxes that single out specified commodities (such as motor fuel, alcoholic beverages, or tobacco products). The term "retail" suggests that only those transactions in which the commodity is transferred to its final consumer will be subjected to tax.

Sales taxes are of great importance in the revenue systems of state governments in the United States. If general and selective sales taxes are lumped together, they account for more than half of the total amount collected in taxes by state governments. Total sales tax collections are divided about evenly between general and selective sales taxes. General sales and gross receipts taxes were imposed in forty-five states in 1975. The typical rate of tax was 3 or 4 percent, but rates ranged from 2 percent to 7 percent in that year.[1]

The major selective sales taxes will be examined in subsequent chapters.

[1] U.S. Bureau of the Census, *State Tax Collections in 1976*, GF–76, No. 1 (Washington, D.C.: Government Printing Office, 1977), Table 8, p. 12.

In this chapter, attention is focused on general sales taxes. Even within the general category, however, a number of variations exist. For example, most general sales taxes are imposed only on transactions at the retail level, but the tax can be imposed on transactions earlier in the production and distribution process. Multistage sales taxes also can be imposed, which means that several transactions in the production and distribution process may be taxed. An examination of these types of general sales taxes is appropriate, since different consequences flow from the various approaches.

TYPES OF GENERAL SALES TAXES

Retail Sales Taxes

The retail sales tax is the most widely used type of general sales tax in the United States. The base is the price paid by the consumer, and the rate is ordinarily expressed as a percentage of this price. The tax is of the single-stage variety; only the sales of goods and services to the final consumer are subject to the tax. One of the basic problems in retail sales taxation lies in distinguishing retail from nonretail transactions. In the United States, two general rules have evolved for determining whether a particular transaction is taxable as a retail sale. One is called the *ingredients* rule; the other is the *direct use* rule. According to the ingredients rule, if the item exchanged is to become an ingredient in or component of some item that itself will be sold, the sale of the ingredient is not a retail transaction and is therefore not subject to the tax. The reasoning is that the value of the ingredient will be included in the value of the item of which it later becomes a part and that it will be taxed when the subsequent product is sold for consumption.

The direct use rule is more generous in permitting transactions to be exempted from sales tax, although its goal is also to restrict the application of the tax to the final consumption sale. According to the direct use rule, a transaction is exempt from the tax if the item exchanged is to be used directly in the production of some product for eventual resale. Several examples will illustrate the difference between these two rules. Fuels or electricity used in production processes ordinarily would not be considered ingredients of the final products and thus would be taxed under the ingredient rule, but exempted under the direct use rule. Similarly, fertilizers used in agriculture, machinery used in manufacturing, or display equipment used in merchandising would not qualify for exemption under an ingredients rule, but would qualify under a direct use rule. The ingredient rule and the direct use rule are general guidelines. In practice, retail sales tax laws contain listings of specific transactions that are taxable or exempt, and no two sales tax laws are exactly alike in their coverage.

A consumption tax philosophy of retail sales taxation would suggest that all retail transactions should be taxed and that all transactions not at retail should be excluded from the tax base. But state retail sales tax practice does not achieve this goal.[2] Including nonretail transactions in retail sales taxation injects an inequality into the effective rate of tax imposed on different items of

[2] Daniel C. Morgan, Jr., *Retail Sales Taxation* (Madison: The University of Wisconsin Press, 1964).

consumption. When nonretail transactions are included in the tax base, the tax collected becomes part of the financial costs to subsequent producers and will be included in the price charged to the consumer of the end product. When the end product is again taxed, multiple taxation has taken place. Moreover, when the tax on the end product is determined as a percentage of its price, the initial tax becomes part of the base of the later tax, so that there is a tax on a tax, a phenomenon referred to as *cumulation*. Because of differences in technologics of production and distribution, some commodities may experience more cumulation than others. This type of discrimination among commodities tends to distort consumption purchases and the allocation of resources.

Considerable complexity in retail sales tax legislation and administration arises from efforts to distinguish between retail and nonretail transactions. The nature of the product will not always reveal whether the exchange is retail or nonretail. Are light bulbs retail goods or production goods? What about typewriters, paper, electric power, or fuel? It is clear that the tax administrator must know something about the activities engaged in by the purchasers of goods and services if these taxes are to retain a purely retail character.

Nonretail Sales Taxes

Sales taxes may be imposed at the manufacturing or wholesaling stages of production rather than at the final consumption sale. From the administrative point of view, there are certain advantages to this procedure, since the number of manufacturers or wholesalers is considerably smaller than the number of retailers. Collection and auditing are easier. But there are some serious shortcomings to sales taxation at the manufacturing or wholesaling levels. It is difficult, and perhaps impossible, to determine whether the items taxed are to be used for consumption or whether they are investment goods destined for use in the production process. Consequently, manufacturing sales taxcs are likely to tax investment as well as consumption items. When the tax is imposed on an investment item (that is, on an item used in further production), the cumulation phenomenon of a tax on a tax will arise if a subsequent transaction is also subject to the sales tax.

In an economic sense, the distinction between manufacturing, wholesaling, and retailing is arbitrary. Each of the various stages in the preparation of goods for consumers contributes some value to the final product. The proportion of value added at each stage need not be the same for different products. If the fabricating (manufacturing) stages contribute most to the value of product A but relatively little to the value of product B, then a manufacturer's tax will bear more heavily on product A than on product B. Since it is expected that the manufacturer's tax will be passed forward to the consumer in higher prices, the tax will lead to a distortion of resource allocation quite apart from possibilities of cumulation. The production of services provides an extreme illustration of this problem. Is the doctor, lawyer, barber, or auto mechanic to be considered a manufacturer and subject to the tax? In general, discrimination between tangible goods on the one hand and services on the other can be expected to be even more serious with manufacturers' sales taxes than ordinary retail sales taxes.

Nonretail sales taxes may also give rise to a phenomenon called *tax pyramiding*, which arises when businesses determine sales prices according to a percentage markup of costs. If a sales tax has been collected at some prior stage in the production or distribution process, the base for the percentage markup is increased and the price to the consumer may increase by an amount greater than the amount of the tax originally collected. The significance of pyramiding, or the markup on the tax, depends on the competitive nature of the market in which the wholesaling or retailing businesses operate. If competition is vigorous, the markup on the tax will not be sustainable except to the extent that it increases the real costs of doing business, and this real cost increase may be limited largely to the financing costs of carrying inventories that have acquired a higher price due to the previous tax.

Competition on an interstate basis adds an additional problem. If the manufacturers or wholesalers in the taxing state must compete with manufacturers or wholesalers in nontaxing states, the tax will damage the profit position of firms subjected to the tax. Interstate competition is likely to be more important at manufacturing and wholesaling levels than at the retail level. This may help to explain the relatively minor use of nonretail sales taxes at the state level in the United States. Nonretail taxes are most effective when the state holds some strategic advantage in interstate competition. In some instances, manufacturers' taxes are imposed on specific products (so that they are not general sales taxes). These are attempts by the state to collect tax revenues through burdens exported to consumers in other states.[3]

Multistage Sales Taxes

The general sales taxes discussed in the previous sections were single-stage taxes, that is, they were imposed at only one stage in the process of converting raw materials into final consumption goods. Multistage sales taxes tax each exchange that takes place in the process. Several varieties of multistage taxes exist, such as transaction taxes, turnover taxes, gross receipts taxes, and gross income taxes. These taxes are collected from firms, and the tax base is their total receipts from sales. The gross income tax label sometimes generates confusion because it uses the word "income," but these taxes are, in fact, sales taxes and should be clearly distinguished from taxes levied on net rather than gross income.

The chief advantage of turnover or gross receipts taxes is that sizable amounts of tax revenue can be generated at very low tax rates. Since each item finally sold to consumers ordinarily passes through several prior transactions, turnover or gross receipts tax rates need to be only a fraction of retail sales tax rates to generate the equivalent revenue. The very low rates disguise the true significance of the tax; most of it is hidden in the final price paid by the consumer, so that he may be unaware of the amount actually paid. No attempt is made to separate retail from nonretail transactions, which makes for administrative convenience.

---

[3] This exporting of tax burdens is quite appropriate if the tax is viewed as a payment for services rendered by the taxing state. The benefits of these services may also be passed on to the consumers of the product.

The disadvantages of turnover or gross receipts taxes involve the cumulation and pyramiding phenomena mentioned earlier. Discrimination is introduced against goods that pass through many transactions compared to those handled by only a few firms in the process between raw materials and final consumption. Cumulation is clearly present in these taxes, since the taxes collected in the earlier stages of the production process become part of the base in the determination of subsequent levies. Thus, a commodity that passes through several firms in the production and distribution process is subjected to multiple taxation and to pyramiding as well, if competitive conditions permit. It is apparent that considerable encouragement is provided for the vertical integration of production and distribution processes. If a firm is able to combine within a single business entity all the stages from raw material extraction through final retailing, only the tax at the final sale will be payable and the firm will enjoy a competitive advantage over nonintegrated firms.

The Value Added Tax

The value added tax is a multistage tax that avoids multiple taxation and cumulation and the consequent discrimination among products. The value added tax is collected from each firm that handles goods between the raw material stage and the final consumption sale. The base of the tax, however, is limited to the value added to the product by each firm. This is accomplished by permitting each firm to deduct from its gross receipts the amounts paid to other firms also subject to the tax.[4] Through this procedure, the tax base of each firm is limited to the contributions to value arising from the resources owned by the firm itself and from the labor services employed by that firm.

There are three varieties of value added tax, namely, the *GNP type*, which allows no deduction for capital used in the production process, the *income type*, which allows depreciation of capital equipment to be deducted in calculating the tax base, and the *consumption type*, which permits the immediate deduction of capital equipment purchases. The consumption type is equivalent to a general retail sales tax, since investment items are not taxed. The expectation is that the tax paid by each firm will be passed forward so that the tax burden will come to rest with the retail purchaser of consumption goods.

In 1975, Michigan replaced its corporation income tax and several other business taxes with a consumption type value added tax imposed on noncorporate as well as corporate businesses. The motive for this change was to improve the state's competitive position in attracting capital investment, since the consumption type value added tax, unlike the corporation income tax, does not impose tax on capital. The value added tax might also permit the state to export some of the tax to consumers residing in other states, although this possibility will be severely limited if instate producers face vigorous competition from producers located in other states. In fact, the value added tax could place instate producers at a competitive disadvantage compared to outstate producers even in respect to the home state market. If both a consumption type value

---

[4] An alternative administrative arrangement calculates the tax on total receipts but permits the firm to claim a tax credit for taxes paid by previous handlers of the item or its components.

added tax and a general retail sales tax are imposed in a state (as is the case in Michigan), the cumulation problem will arise, since the value added tax will be part of the price paid by consumers and therefore a part of the tax base for the general retail sales tax.

SALES TAX OMISSIONS AND EXEMPTIONS

The notion of a general sales tax suggests that all items of consumption should be taxed equally, but sales taxation in the United States fails to realize this ideal. Saving probably is the most prominent item not included in the base of sales taxation, but the nontaxability of saving is the major distinction between sales and income taxation, so that a failure to tax saving can hardly be cited as failure to achieve generality in the sales tax. Certain consumption purchases, however, are ordinarily not included in sales taxation and therefore can be characterized as omissions or exemptions.

The Omission of Services

Consumption purchase of services, as distinguished from purchases of tangible goods, typically are not taxed by general sales taxes in the United States. Since services are as much a type of consumption as tangible goods, their omission is an important gap in the coverage of typical sales taxes. Resource allocation is altered in a way that favors the purchase of services and discriminates against the purchase of tangible goods. People whose preferences are more in the direction of services than the average enjoy differentially favorable treatment. Part of the view that sales taxes are regressive is based on the belief that higher-income families devote a larger portion of their expenditures to services than do low-income families.

The omission of services from sales taxation may reflect a legislative preoccupation with tangible goods as distinguished from services. However, administrative considerations also tend to focus sales taxation on tangible goods rather than on services. The collection of sales taxes on services is more difficult than the collection of these taxes on exchanges of tangible items. Sellers of services frequently are small enterprises rather than large and long-established firms. Prices may exhibit considerable variation and may be negotiated for individual transactions. Records maintained by sellers of services may be less complete or reliable than those maintained by sellers of tangible goods. Moreover, sales taxation of services may be confused with a tax on the income of the person rendering the service.

Exemptions of Food and Medicine

Medicine and food frequently are exempted from sales taxation. The exemption of food from sales taxation is a major decision, since the resulting revenue losses are substantial. The food exemption ordinarily is defended as a device which will reduce the regressivity of general sales taxation, since food expenditures account for a larger fraction of the income of low-income families than of high-income families. The food exemption also introduces a distinction between large and small families, since a large family will have a larger food budget than a small family, other things being equal. In this way, the food exemption serves an objective similar to a personal exemption in income taxation. With food exempted, however, the sales tax is considerably less general than it would be with food subject to the tax. Administrative problems also arise in establishing distinctions between food items and nonfood items. Should soft drinks be considered food? Are vitamins food?

The exemption of medicines is less significant, from a revenue point of view, than the exemption of food. It can be contended that illness reduces ability to pay and that an exemption for medicine is a gesture in recognition of this factor. More realistically, perhaps, the exemption arises in a sense of compassion for the sick. Once again, the exemption gives rise to administrative problems in distinguishing medical from nonmedical commodities.

Exemption of Previously Taxed Items

Items are sometimes exempted from sales taxation on the ground that they are subjected to some other tax imposed by the state government. Motor fuels provide the most common example of this practice. Whether an item can properly be exempted from a general sales tax on the ground that it has already been taxed under different legislation depends on the purpose for which the other tax is imposed. Ordinarily, the other tax is a selective levy designed to raise funds for a specified purpose (such as motor fuel taxes to finance highways) or to implement a legislative intent to impose a special tax on a selected type of consumption. Under these circumstances, there is no reason for exempting the item from the general sales tax unless the legislature has changed its position about its desire to impose a special tax on selected consumption items.

The exemption of motor fuels from general sales taxation is an especially questionable practice, since motor fuel taxes are special-purpose, benefit-related taxes with revenues earmarked for the construction and maintenance of highways. Motor fuel taxes are the motorist's method of paying for the consumption of highway services, and there would appear to be little reason why this type of consumption spending should be exempt from general sales taxation. Moreover, the base for the general sales tax on motor fuel purchased for highway use could include not only the price paid for the fuel itself, but also the price paid for the highway service, as expressed in the motor fuel tax.

SALES TAX ADMINISTRATION

Sales taxes ordinarily are thought to be relatively easy to administer. The cost of administration per dollar of revenue compares favorably with other taxes imposed at the state level. However, certain problems in sales tax administration can increase administrative and compliance costs or reduce the quality of administration. The separation of taxable from nontaxable transactions causes difficulty. Limiting the tax to retail transactions (or to the particular transactions specified in the tax legislation) is one dimension of this problem; the presence of specific exemptions adds a further dimension. For state sales taxation, an additional difficulty arises because of interstate commerce, since persons residing in a sales tax state may make consumption purchases either in person or by mail from sellers in nonsales tax states.

Use Taxes

In order for a state to impose a tax on a transaction, it must have jurisdiction in the location where the transaction takes place. A transaction that takes place outside the boundaries of the state cannot be made subject to the tax. The *use tax* has been developed in an effort to close this avoidance route. A use tax is imposed on the use of the commodity rather than on the purchase transaction. If the commodity is used in the taxing state, it may be subjected to the use tax even though purchased outside the state.

Use taxes ordinarily are imposed at the same rates as those for the companion sales tax, and sales tax paid may be credited against the use tax liability. Thus, commodities on which the sales tax has been paid are not taxed additionally by the use tax, but commodities on which sales tax has not been paid do have a use tax liability. Enforcement is the chief problem for the use tax. It is difficult for the state tax administration to detect instances in which taxable items have been purchased outside the state and used inside the state. As a practical matter, use tax collection is largely confined to the taxation of automobiles purchased outside the state, since the taxing state can detect taxable situations at the time the automobile is registered.

Mail order transactions pose some difficulty for sales or use taxation. Effective enforcement requires that the tax be collected and forwarded by the seller. If the mail order seller maintains a place of business in the taxing state, the state may require the collection of the use tax as a condition of being permitted to carry on business activity in the state. When the seller maintains no place of business in the taxing state, the legal basis for requiring the mail order seller to collect the tax is weaker, but judicial opinions have moved in the direction of obligating the seller for the collection and forwarding of the tax.

Underreporting and Audits

Effective enforcement of sales taxes requires that merchants maintain a reliable account of the amount of their taxable sales. Difficulties arise when the firm is engaged in selling both taxable and nontaxable items, since a separate tabulation of these categories must be maintained. Not all firms maintain reliable records, so that audits by the tax administration are necessary. Small firms pose particular difficulties, since the cost of auditing is high relative to the amount of tax involved and recordkeeping may be of poorer quality.

A considerable compliance cost arises in separating taxable from nontaxable transactions and keeping appropriate sales tax records. Compensation for these costs is provided in many states either through a discount on the tax collections remitted to the state or through a bracket system of tax rates that produces an effective tax rate on transactions higher than the rate collected from the firm on the basis of its total taxable sales. A bracket system is necessary for convenience in any event, since collection of fractional portions of one cent is not possible unless a system of tokens is used, which further increases administration costs. Bracket systems typically impose effective rates above the general statutory rate, especially for smaller transactions.

SALES TAXES AND HORIZONTAL NEUTRALITY

Equal treatment of equals, a basic part of the generally accepted canon of equity or fairness, is called horizontal equity. Establishing the criteria by which to determine whether different individuals are equal for tax purposes is the fundamental challenge in formulating the tax base. A general sales tax that taxed all consumption expenditure and exempted all nonconsumption spending would be horizontally neutral if consumption were accepted as a criteria for tax responsibility. Conversely, sales taxes would be nonneutral to the extent that they failed to tax all consumption spending or actually did tax spending which was not for consumption.

Sales taxes actually imposed in the United States do not cover all items of consumption spending and thus open the possibility of horizontal nonneutrality. Some consumption items, especially services, ordinarily are not included in the sales tax base. Conversely, some items not intended entirely for current consumption, such as major appliances, autos, and construction, are taxed on the full market price at the time of purchase and may be subjected to a second tax if resold during their useful lives. In some situations, sales taxes are imposed on items used in production processes in which the end product is again subject to sales tax, so that these products bear a relatively greater sales tax than do other products. Each of these aspects of sales tax practice may and presumably does lead to horizontal nonneutrality. Individuals whose tastes favor consumption of items exempted from sales taxes will experience lesser tax than those whose tastes favor products subject to tax. Individuals whose preferences run to products subjected to multiple sales taxation experience an above-average tax liability. If individual taste patterns are considered irrelevant to tax responsibility, then horizontal nonneutrality results from current sales tax practice.

Family size is one factor that has a particularly pronounced impact on sales tax liabilities. Large families are likely to spend a greater portion of their receipts on consumption than are small families, other things being equal. Thus, sales taxes work in the opposite direction from the personal exemption allowances generally permitted in income taxation. If personal exemption allowances are considered an important ingredient in ability to pay, sales taxes can be labeled "perverse" in this regard.[5]

How should family size be treated in determining tax liabilities? Should the tax-paying unit be the family or should each separate individual constitute a separate unit? Should the dependency status of the individual, particularly that of minor children, be recognized in determining the equal or unequal status of individuals as taxpayers? One viewpoint suggests that rearing children is the same as a choice in consumption on the part of parents or guardians. According to this view, no income tax exemptions are required for equitable treatment and the positive sales tax relation between tax payments and family size is not perverse. If the rearing of children is treated as a consumption choice, tax exemptions for children appear as a policy decision granting a subsidy for population growth.

[5] Reed R. Hansen, "An Empirical Analysis of the Retail Sales Tax with Policy Recommendations," *National Tax Journal*, March 1962.

In summary, sales taxes are criticized as being "perverse, capricious, and uncertain" in terms of horizontal neutrality. Their perversity relates to their alleged regressivity on income and their failure to provide exemptions for children. Their capriciousness relates to the differential tax liabilities that arise from variations in individual preferences among consumption items. Their uncertainty relates to the multiple taxation that arises when both production inputs and final outputs are taxed and to the inability of tax-shifting analysis to reveal the final incidence of these multiple tax elements.

SUMMARY

Sales taxes are taxes on transactions. Since many different types of transactions take place, there are many possible varieties of sales taxation. *Selective* sales taxes are imposed on particular commodities; *general* sales taxes are imposed on broadly defined categories of transactions. State governments in the United States use both selective and general sales taxes, and revenues from these sources are important in state government revenue structures.

The most common variety of general sales tax used in the United States is imposed on transactions at the retail level. However, sales taxes may be imposed at manufacturing or wholesaling levels, although taxation at these earlier stages results in distortion of resource allocation through different *cumulation* or *pyramiding* effects among commodities. Multistage sales taxes levy tax at several different stages in the production and distribution processes. Except for the *value added tax*, these multistage taxes also distort resource allocation by favoring certain commodities over others. Most retail sales taxes in the United States probably collect some tax from nonretail transactions, since the distinction between retail and nonretail transactions is sometimes difficult to establish.

The philosophical foundation for sales taxation is that consumption is an appropriate basis for taxation. Thus, the ideal sales tax would cover all items of consumption. This ideal is not achieved in practice because services typically are exempt from tax and because food and medicines are frequently exempted in an effort to make the tax less regressive. These exemptions reduce the revenue yield of a sales tax and increase the difficulties of administration. Administrative difficulties also arise in connection with interstate transactions, where *use taxes* are imposed rather than sales taxes.

Criticism of general sales taxes typically focuses on their alleged regressivity in respect to income. However, this criticism presumes that income, rather than consumption, ought to be the basis for taxation. Sales taxes also are criticized for horizontal inequity. Some of this criticism also reveals an implicit preference for income taxation. However, horizontal inequities also arise from exemptions or exclusions of some consumption items. In these situations, relative prices and resource allocation are altered by the tax. Thus, both efficiency and horizontal equity considerations suggest that sales tax reform proposals should be in the direction of broadening the coverage of consumption purchases and of reducing the imposition of taxes on investment goods. The burden of proof that resource allocation or ability to pay considerations justify deviations from generality falls on proposals for specific exemptions of consumption items.

SUGGESTED READINGS

MORGAN, DANIEL C. *Retail Sales Taxation* (Madison: University of Wisconsin Press, 1964).

DUE, JOHN F. *State and Local Sales Taxation* (Chicago: Public Administration Service, 1971).

DUE, JOHN F. "Evaluation of the Effectiveness of State Sales Tax Administration," *National Tax Journal*, XXVII, 2 (June 1974).

VARS, R. CHARLES, JR. "Equity Trade-offs in Sales Taxation", *National Tax Journal*, XXVII, 4 (December 1974).

DAVIES, DAVID G. and DAVID E. BLACK. "Equity Effects of Including Housing Services in a Sales Tax Base," *National Tax Journal*, XXVIII, 1 (March 1975).

GHAZANFAR, S. M., "Equity Effects and Revenue Potential of Sales Taxation of Services: Some Empirical Findings," *Public Finance Quarterly*, 3, 2 (April 1975), pp. 163–90.

BRINNER, ROGER E., and CHARLES T. CLOTFELTER. "An Economic Appraisal of State Lotteries," *National Tax Journal*, XXVIII, 4 (December 1975) pp. 395–404.

20

State Individual
Income Taxes

Individual income taxation is a long-established practice at the state government level. Wisconsin established its income tax in 1911, before the current federal individual income tax. Hawaii had adopted an individual income tax in 1901. But the track record of state individual income taxation has been uneven. Sixteen states adopted individual income taxes during the decade of the 1930s, probably in response to the financial stresses facing state governments during those depression years, but individual income tax collections are very sensitive to changes in the level of incomes, so that the depression years were not ideal for income taxation.

The revenue potential for individual income taxation improved greatly with the prosperity that came with World War II. But state governments were slow in availing themselves of this increased potential. One of the reasons was the great increase in federal government individual income tax collections that began with the rate increases and exemption reductions at the onset of the war. It was contended that the federal government had preempted individual income taxation. States also had other revenue sources to rely upon in the postwar period.General sales taxes were adopted by a number of states and proved to be powerful revenue producers.

State utilization of income taxation increased sharply during the 1960s and 1970s. Revenue requirements mounted steadily, resistance to increases in the rates of other taxes was encountered, and the federal government reduced income tax rates and increased exemptions and deductions. Individual income taxes were imposed by forty-four states and provided 24.0 percent of total state tax collections in 1976. Per capita collections in 1976 were $100.30.[1]

PROS AND CONS OF STATE INCOME TAXATION

Table 20.1 presents an outline of certain advantages and disadvantages of individual income taxation by states. At one time, consideration of these advantages and disadvantages was used to determine whether states should adopt an income tax or some other revenue source. This question has been resolved, since most states do now utilize this tax. But the *extent* to which states should rely on income taxation is still an important question.

TABLE 20.1 Advantages and Disadvantages of State Individual Income Taxation

	ADVANTAGES	*DISADVANTAGES*
Merit considerations	Little tax shifting	Incentives
	Adjustment to individual circumstances	Migration
Revenue considerations	Response to growth	Instability
Coexistence with federal individual income tax	Cooperative administration	Preemption
		Fiscal policy
		Redistribution

Merit Considerations

The leading merit argument in favor of individual income taxation emphasizes the unshiftable nature of the tax. Because it is relatively difficult for the individual who pays the tax to transfer the burden or incidence to someone else, legislators can allocate the responsibilities for government finance with reasonable assurance that their intentions will be realized in practice. Thus individual income taxes differ from taxes that are less broadly based and less directly related to the individual. With these taxes, shifting may take place and the ultimate burden may fall on persons who were not the intended bearers of the tax.

Income taxation also permits more precise adjustment in individual tax liabilities than is possible with other tax bases. With income taxation, rates may be graduated by the size of the individual's income according to legislative notions about ability to pay. Likewise, exemptions may be provided to reflect the view that income below a specified annual amount should be subjected to a zero tax rate. Each of these refinements permits the legislature to allocate tax liabilities more explicitly. Moreover, the taxpayer himself can be reasonably well informed about the amount of tax he is required to pay and about how this amount is determined. A well-informed electorate is considered important in a democratic decision-making process.

[1] U.S. Bureau of the Census, *State Tax Collections in 1976*, GF-76, No. 1 (Washington, D.C.: Government Printing Office, 1977), Tables 1 and 2, pp. 5, 7.

Counterarguments to the proposition that income taxation is especially meritorious note the incentive effects which may follow from the taxation of individual incomes. In a general sense, it is contended that income taxes are penalties on success and tend to stifle work incentives. This position can support opposition to income taxation at the national as well as at the state level. Incentive effects, however, may be especially important considerations at the state level, since both people and business activities have some options about whether to locate in one state or in another. If income taxation is greater in one state than in another, location decisions may be distorted by the tax consideration. The basic question is whether location decisions are more sensitive to income taxation than to other types of taxation, and the thrust of the merit case suggests that this is indeed true. Higher-income groups may be more sensitive to income taxation than lower-income groups, and the higher-income individuals may be precisely the ones who command location options, either because they are in positions to make business decisions or because the ability to employ highly paid executive talent is considered important to business enterprises.

Revenue Considerations

Income taxes have a greater income elasticity of revenue yield than most other taxes. This means that income tax revenues are more responsive to changes in income levels. The equation yielding the measure of income elasticity of revenue yield is the following:

$$\frac{\text{percentage change in revenue yield}}{\text{percentage change in income}} = \text{income elasticity of revenue yield}$$

Experience suggests that state individual income taxes exhibit income elasticity coefficients ranging between 1.5 and 2.0. This means, for example, that if income rises by 10 percent, income tax collections will rise by 15 to 20 percent. Conversely, if incomes fall by 10 percent, income tax collections will fall by 15 to 20 percent.

This response pattern arises because of the presence of personal exemptions (zero tax rates) and is increased to whatever extent progressive tax rates are applied to taxable income above the exemption level. When incomes rise, a smaller portion is subject to the zero tax rate through the operation of personal exemptions. If rate structures are progressive, income increases push taxpayers into ever-higher tax brackets, further increasing the effective rate of tax on total income. Sales taxes and property taxes, which have neither personal exemptions nor graduated rates, respond roughly in proportion to income changes; some taxes, such as those on cigarettes, respond less than proportionately to income changes.

Revenue responsiveness is an advantage of individual income taxation if attention is focused on long-term growth trends in the level of incomes. Rising incomes will generate more than proportionate increases in state revenues, and if demand for government services increases more than proportionately with income, these rising tax collections may be precisely what is needed. Cost considerations may also justify higher tax collections and effective rates as incomes rise. Here, the argument is that governments are heavily engaged in providing personal services which are labor-intensive and which appear to benefit little from technological change or increases in the amount of capital per worker. But government must compete with the private sector to obtain labor services. Therefore, as incomes advance in the private sector due to technological change and increases in capital per worker, the price of labor and the unit costs of government services will rise.[2] In summary, the argument is that increasing effective rates of taxation is justified both because both the demand for government services and the unit costs of providing these services increase as income advances. The built-in revenue responsiveness of income taxation, it is contended, can automatically keep pace with these changes in the economy.

Revenue responsiveness is a disadvantage if attention is focused on short-term (business cycle) fluctuations in income. A dynamic model of fiscal decision making suggests that fluctuating revenues may lead to stair-step increases in the amount of government expenditures. When revenues increase, expenditures may increase as legislatures avail themselves of the opportunity to fund programs that have been "waiting in the wings." No increase in tax rates is needed to finance these new programs when the revenue under the old rates rises because of generally prosperous conditions. When prosperity wanes and tax collections decline, a crisis arises in state government finances. Program expenditures must be reduced or tax rates increased, or some tradeoff between rate increases and expenditure reductions must be discovered. Legislators are under great pressure during these crisis periods, and both expenditure reductions and tax rate increases are likely to be enacted. Experience suggests that new taxes or rate increases in old taxes are typically adopted in these crisis periods. The new taxes or higher rates on old taxes set the stage for a further extension of expenditures in the next period of prosperity, when revenues once again are abundant. Thus, revenue sources that produce fluctuating flows of collections may lead to a stair-step increase in the level of expenditures. The recurring crisis model is a disadvantage of revenue sources that fluctuate over the business cycle if the tests imposed on proposed expenditures are more severe in some years than in other years.

Once adopted, many state expenditure programs require relatively constant flows of funds over the years, and some programs require funding that actually fluctuates inversely with the level of prosperity. Educational expenditures, for example, must continue whether the economy is prosperous or not, whereas welfare programs, assistance, and unemployment requirements usually are greater in bad times than in good times. States typically have limited debt finance capabilities, and attempts to establish reserve funds during prosperous periods to be drawn on during periods of recession have met with little success. Thus, the relatively greater sensitivity of income tax revenues to changes in economic conditions poses serious short-run problems in state government finance, even if the tax is considered desirable in the long run.

[2] William J. Baumol, "Macroeconomics of Unbalanced Growth," *American Economic Review*, LVII, 3 (June 1967), 415–26.

Coexistence with the Federal Income Tax

Most state income taxes are patterned closely after the model provided by the federal individual income tax. The definition of income developed by the Internal Revenue Service applies, with only minor modifications, to the reporting of income for state tax purposes. Thus, most taxpayers find that filing a state income tax return is a relatively simple matter after the federal return has been completed, since adjusted gross income can be transferred from the federal return to the state return and only a few further calculations are needed to arrive at the amount of tax due the state. Thus, coexistence of the two taxes brings compliance cost savings to citizens that would not be possible if completely different taxes were used by the different levels of government. Administration is also facilitated by the coexistence of both state and federal income taxation. Auditing reports can be exchanged between the two levels of government and an error discovered by a federal auditor will soon bring a call from the state tax administration for a parallel adjustment in the state return, and vice versa. Coexistence benefits both compliance and administration.

Perhaps the most effective (political) argument against the coexistence of both federal and state income taxation is the federal preemption view noted earlier, which contends that the federal government makes such heavy use of income taxation that there is little opportunity for state taxation without raising the combined tax to intolerable levels. A more sophisticated position suggests that income taxation ought to be *reserved* for the federal government because it is especially suited to serve the fiscal policy and income distributional functions that are the responsibility of the federal government and that cannot be effectively carried out at the state level. Adjustments in individual income tax rates, deductions, exemptions, and the definition of taxable income itself may be accepted as appropriate instruments for carrying out these national government responsibilities.

The argument for reserving the income tax for the federal government suggests that the federal government might be unable or reluctant to make needed adjustments in the tax because of concern about the impact these changes might have on state revenues. The extent of the impact of federal changes on state income tax revenues would depend, of course, on the nature of the federal change and on the manner in which state tax requirements were patterned on the federal tax. If state tax liabilities were based directly on federal tax liabilities, the impact would be direct. If states used only the federal adjusted gross income entry, changes in federal rates, personal exemptions, and personal deductions would have little direct effect on state revenues. Changes in the definition of taxable income, such as alterations in depreciation allowances, would directly alter state revenues, but the impact would differ among the states, depending on the economic base in the individual state.

CHARACTERISTICS OF STATE INCOME TAXES

The person completing a state income tax return ordinarily begins with adjusted gross income as reported on the federal return and proceeds to make any adjustments required by differences in the definition of income. The adjustment process is illustrated by the treatment of interest earned on government bonds. The federal government does not tax interest earned on state and local government bonds, but does tax interest earned on federal government securities. State income taxes reciprocate by excluding interest earned on federal bonds and (in most cases) by including interest earned on state and local government bonds. Thus, the state income taxpayer must adjust the adjusted gross income shown on his federal return by subtracting interest earned on federal securities and perhaps by adding interest earned on state and local securities.

Income adjustment calculations may also be required for such matters as sick pay, social security benefits, allowances for retirement income, armed services pay, capital gains, gains or losses on the sale of a residence, and so on, depending on the particular state tax under consideration. These differences may arise either because the state has charted its own course somewhat independently of federal practice or because the state has not brought its law up to date to incorporate more recent changes in federal practice. In general, however, a trend in the direction of conformity with federal income definition is evident.

Greater departure from federal practice occurs in respect to personal deductions and exemptions. Some states follow the federal model of allowing itemized personal deductions or a standard deduction. A few states calculate their tax directly from the federal tax liability, thus incorporating federal tax rate schedules as well as federal allowances for personal deductions. But some states ignore the refinements involved in personal deduction allowances and base their taxes on federal adjusted gross income with only a few adjustments. Simplicity probably is the main reason for this procedure. For allowances that are essentially policy-related subsidies for certain types of expenditures (such as the deduction for charitable contributions), it seems reasonable that the federal subsidy granted through the much higher federal tax rates may be sufficient to generate the desired response so that state deductions are not necessary.[3] However, failure to permit deductions for those items related to ability to pay (such as extraordinary medical expenses) may mean that state income taxes are less well tuned to ability to pay. Exemptions for the taxpayers and their dependents typically are more generous on state returns than on the federal return, and some states grant exemption allowances as direct credits against net tax liability rather than as deductions in determining the tax base. This credit system means that the tax saving per exemption is the same for all taxpayers, without regard to income level. Rates of tax are much lower on state returns than on the federal return. Some states impose a flat, ungraduated tax rate, but most employ a graduated structure. Graduation of rates usually ceases at relatively low income levels compared to the federal system, but the allowance of generous personal exemptions means that state income taxes often are quite progressive, at least up to moderate income levels.

---

[3] Some states allow deductions or credits for contributions to educational institutions in the state.

Jurisdiction

States claim jurisdiction to tax income both on the basis of the *domicile* of the recipient of the income and on the basis of the *situs* of the income itself, that is, on the basis of where the income was earned. It is apparent, therefore, that a person domiciled in one state and earning income in another state could be subjected to double taxation on his interstate income unless some agreement is reached among the states for the relief of taxpayers who find themselves in this situation.

Reciprocity provisions in a state income tax law provide one approach to overlapping or double-tax situations. For example, the income tax law of state A may simply provide that residents of state B who earn taxable income in state A shall be treated in the same manner as has been established by state B for residents of state A who find themselves in equivalent circumstances. This procedure does not guarantee that double taxation will be prevented, but it does provide an incentive for other states to give some attention to the problem. Agreements among individual states may be negotiated to specify formulas to be used to allocate income and tax responsibilities between the two states.

The widespread use of withholding as a means of collecting income taxes on wage and salary income favors the adoption of a credit to resident system for relieving double taxation of interstate incomes. Under this system, the state of domicile permits the taxpayer to claim a credit for income taxes paid to other states.

Deductibility of Federal Income Tax

Some states permit taxpayers to deduct federal income taxes paid in determining the amount of their income subject to taxation by the state. This allowance is of considerable significance, both for the amount of revenue collected by the state tax and for the degree of progressivity of the tax imposed by the state. The revenue loss is substantial, since federal taxes are high and deductibility significantly reduces the base for the state tax. The impact on the progressivity of the state tax is also significant, because the deduction is larger for high-income than for low-income taxpayers and because it "comes off the top" of an individual's income, where marginal state tax rates are highest.

Deductibility of federal tax paid is not required on any constitutional ground, such as the sovereignty of one government from taxation by another government, as is sometimes argued in relation to the taxability of interest on government bonds. Also, since the federal government permits the deduction of state income taxes paid, deductibility on the state return is not necessary to ensure that the combination of the two taxes will not lead to marginal rates in excess of 100 percent. Deductibility on either tax return can provide this assurance.

Although the question of whether the state tax base should be computed before or after an allowance for federal tax is becoming moot in practice, it does raise an interesting question about the proper basis for state income taxation in a federal system. If federal payments are seen as payments for benefits received from federal government services, there is little case for allowing these taxes to be deducted on state income tax returns. Payments for government services would be treated in the same way as payments for other consumption services, and no deductions would be needed unless a policy decision had been made to subsidize these services. In fact, the federal income tax provisions allowing the deduction of state taxes paid and exempting from tax interest on state and local bonds are best understood as expressions of a decision in favor of providing some assistance to state and local government financing. But if the federal income tax is seen as a device for income redistribution, the case in favor of the deductibility of federal taxes on state returns is much stronger. Here it can be argued that the federal tax has brought about a distribution of after-tax income generally in accordance with accepted notions of distributional equity and that state income taxation, if it is to be justified on ability to pay grounds, should begin only after the federal tax has been taken into account.

Property and Sales Tax Credits

States can use the income tax as a convenient vehicle for allowing credits or rebates on property taxes or sales taxes. Since income tax returns report the amount of income received and the number of dependents claimed, they provide the information and also the occasion for adjusting the burden of these other taxes. Sales tax credits are determined according to the number of personal exemptions listed on the income tax return. The credit per dependent is established either on the basis of the sales tax paid for food purchases or on the basis of total consumption taxes paid. A direct cash rebate is paid to those whose income tax liability is less than the amount of the credit allowed. People who otherwise would not be required to file any income tax return may find it necessary to file in order to receive their rebate. The income tax credit method of reducing the regressivity of sales taxation is much less costly to the state than the alternative approach of exempting all food purchases from the sales tax, since the amount of the credit need not equal the total amount of sales tax paid on food purchases.[4]

Credits or rebates for property tax relief require the individual to report information on the amount of property tax or rent paid. The amount of credit or rebate is usually determined by the extent to which property tax, or the property tax component in rent paid, exceeds some specified percentage of the individual's income. That is, the rebates are designed as *circuit breakers* to prevent the property tax from taking an excessively large portion of the individual's income. This type of property tax relief also moderates the effect of property tax rate differentials among communities and thus is related to the larger problem of interjurisdictional fiscal disparities. The amount of the rebate will depend on the income of the individual, the value of the property he occupies, and the tax rate imposed under the local property tax. Thus, substantial rebates may go to people who are not in low-income categories.

The credit and rebate system illustrates an advantage enjoyed by a state that uses the full slate of standard internal revenue sources, since the income

[4] J. A. Papke and T. G. Shahen, "Optimal Consumption Base Taxes: The Equity Effects of Tax Credits," *National Tax Journal*, XXV, 3 (September 1972).

tax can become an instrument through which undesired features of other taxes can be moderated. The income tax credit or rebate system is an especially attractive device for property tax relief because it permits relief without reducing the property tax base and thus the revenue capacity of local governments, which depend heavily on this tax. The alternative procedure of legislating statewide property tax exemptions would reduce the revenue potential of local governments and impose difficult administrative problems.

INCREASED UTILIZATION OF INCOME TAXATION

Individual income taxation was introduced as a state government internal revenue source before any significant use was made of general sales taxes or motor fuels taxes. But for many years individual income taxes remained a relatively minor source of revenue as sales and motor fuels taxes rose to prominence in the revenue systems of most of the states. This laggard performance of income taxation is partly attributable to the heavy use that the federal government made of income taxation during and after World War II. During the 1950s and into the decade of the 1960s, a number of proposals were advanced by which the federal government would have provided special incentives for states to adopt individual income taxes or to increase their reliance on this revenue source. Some of these proposals suggested that greater federal grants in aid should go to states that used income taxation than to states that did not. Other proposals suggested that taxpayers should be given special credits against their federal income tax liabilities for income taxes paid to state governments. Some of the proposals for revenue-sharing formulas would have provided more money to income tax states than to other states.

None of these proposals gathered enough political support to be adopted by Congress. The basic argument against federal government favoritism toward state income taxation was that the federal government should not interfere with a state's choice in selecting its own instruments of internal revenue. Political sentiment may favor income taxation in some states and be opposed in other states, and these differences may be legitimate reflections of the diversity to be served by a federal or multigovernment system. Moreover, income taxation has greater revenue potential in some states than in others, and this factor too may account for differential reliance on this revenue source.

In the late 1960s and early 1970s, fiscal necessity accomplished what the advocates of federal encouragement of state income taxation had failed to accomplish in the preceding decade. Increased demands for public expenditure forced state governments to seek additional sources of internal revenue, and the introduction of income taxation proved, in many cases, to be more attractive than increased rates on already established sales taxes. Thus, sales tax rates tended to stabilize, and the needed extra revenue was obtained through the adoption of individual income taxes. As more and more states found themselves using both general sales taxes and individual income taxes, interstate competition, which previously had operated to discourage the adoption of income taxation, lost much of its force. Income taxation crossed a threshold of general acceptability. State individual income tax revenues probably will continue to grow in relative importance as more states adopt this revenue source and as income tax rates rise to achieve some equilibrium with revenues generated through general sales taxes.

SUMMARY

State individual income taxation exhibited an uneven track record between the time it was introduced in 1911 until it became a generally accepted component in state revenue systems in the 1970s. Individual income taxation provides state governments with an instrument that can adjust tax liabilities to income levels and to individual family circumstances. These burden adjustment capabilities can also be used to moderate the regressive characteristics of other state taxes, such as sales and property taxes. Other advantages of individual income taxation include its responsiveness to economic growth and the opportunity to share administrative responsibilities with the federal government, since most state individual income taxes are modeled closely after the pattern established in the federal income tax.

There are, however, certain disadvantages associated with individual income taxation at the state level. Interstate migration may be more sensitive to income taxation than to other forms of taxation, so that states may be unwilling to establish rates that are much higher or much more progressive than those prevailing in nearby states. Instability of income tax revenues may be the most serious disadvantage of income taxation at the state level. Business cycle fluctuations affecting the national economy will result in fluctuations in income tax revenue, and states may encounter difficulty in adjusting to these fluctuations, since the debt-financing capability of most state governments is limited.

State individual income taxes typically employ the same definition of income as that established for the federal income tax and some also follow the federal example in allowing personal deductions and exemptions. But personal exemptions usually are larger in state income taxes and rates of tax much lower. Special arrangements are needed for persons who reside in one state and earn income in another state.

SUGGESTED READINGS

ROTHENBERG, LEON. "A New Look in State Finances: Tax Reductions and Restructured Tax Systems," *National Tax Journal*, XXVII, 2 (June 1974).

Advisory Commission on Intergovernmental Relations. *Federal-State-Local Finances: Significant Features of Fiscal Federalism*, (Washington, D. C.: Government Printing Office, 1974).

State Inheritance, Estate, and Gift Taxes

Death and gift taxes are not important revenue producers for state governments in the United States. In 1976, these taxes provided only 1.7 percent of state tax collections, and the amount collected averaged only $7.07 per capita. Yet every state except Nevada obtained some revenue from these sources.[1] Inheritance and estate taxes are imposed on gratuitous transfers that take effect at death; gift taxes are imposed on transfers between living persons. Only fifteen states impose tax on gift transfers. The relatively little interest that states have shown for taxing gifts is easy to understand. The gift tax is designed primarily to discourage people from attempting to avoid death transfer taxes by giving away wealth prior to death. Since the federal government already imposes a tax on gift transfers and since federal rates are higher than state rates, the federal tax is a stronger deterrent and it is unnecessary for state governments to enter the field.

ESTATE AND INHERITANCE TAXES

Two basic approaches are used in the taxation of death transfers. One utilizes what is called an *inheritance* tax and the other utilizes an *estate* tax. The estate tax is the simpler of the two approaches because the base of the tax is the entire lump sum of the value of the property of the deceased at the time of death. Deductions are allowed for amounts bequeathed to charities and for amounts

[1] U.S. Bureau of the Census, *State Tax Collections in 1976*, GF–76, No. 1 (Washington, D.C.: Government Printing Office, 1977), Tables 1, 3, pp. 5, 7.

left to the surviving spouse. Rates imposed on the net amount subject to tax ordinarily are progressive. The estate tax approach is used by the federal government and by eleven states, although it is the exclusive form of death transfer tax in only two states.

The inheritance tax is a more complicated levy. In determining the tax, consideration is given to the division of the estate among various classes of beneficiaries. The exemptions allowed and the rates imposed are dependent upon the relationship of the beneficiary to the deceased person. As a general rule, exemptions are largest and rates lowest on amounts bequeathed to the surviving spouse. Exemptions shrink and rates increase as the degree of relationship extends to more distant relatives, and the smallest exemptions and the highest rates apply to bequests to unrelated persons. Rates may be progressive within these various classes of beneficiaries, and since the total tax is affected by the manner in which the estate is divided, the system offers some encouragement to fragmentation. Thirty-six states impose inheritance taxes, although in only two of these is it the only form of death transfer tax.

FEDERAL CREDIT FOR STATE DEATH TRANSFER TAXES

State governments had established themselves in the death transfer tax field before the federal government established its death tax in 1916. These taxes were considerably more important in state tax systems then than they are today, since such major revenue producers as sales and income taxes had not yet been developed. Therefore, the federal entry into this area was criticized as an encroachment on a preserve of the states. It also was pointed out that property rights derive from state rather than from federal law. But the states' opposition to the new federal tax was weakened by some serious new problems. As the mobility of persons from state to state increased, some states began to compete with others to encourage wealthy persons to establish residence. The idea was that then business would be stimulated and other taxes, such as property, sales, and income taxes, would yield more revenue. Elimination of a state death tax would be one way to attract precisely the type of in-migration desired by these states. Florida enacted a constitutional prohibition against death transfer taxation, Nevada followed suit, and California considered a similar arrangement. It was feared that this type of competition would mean the end of significant death transfer taxation at the state level.

In an effort to reduce interstate competition in death transfer taxation, a credit provision was enacted into the federal estate tax law in 1926. Death transfer tax payments made to state governments could be credited against the federal estate tax liability up to a limit of 80 percent of the federal liability. Under this arrangement, reductions in state death transfer taxes would not lead to reductions in the total tax payable by the estate, and interstate competition would be effectively eliminated. In fact, these crediting provisions encouraged states to adopt and maintain death transfer taxes, since the choice was whether the money would flow into the state or into the federal treasury. By adopting the tax, the state could be sure the money would stay in the state.

The Pickup Tax

The *pickup* tax is a death transfer tax explicitly designed to enable the state government to collect enough revenue to secure the entire available credit against the federal estate tax. In five states, it is the only type of death transfer tax imposed, and the rate of tax is simply 80 percent of the 1926 federal tax. Other states use the pickup tax as a backup for other state death taxes to make sure that the federal credit is fully utilized. In fact, only five states do not employ a pickup tax. Table 21.1 illustrates the extraordinary complexity of state death tax systems, which include inheritance, estate, and pickup taxes in various combinations.

TABLE 21.1   Types of State Death Taxes

TYPE OF TAX	STATES
Pickup tax only	5
Estate tax only	2
Estate tax and pickup tax	7
Inheritance tax only	2
Inheritance tax and pickup tax	32
Inheritance, estate, and pickup tax	2
No tax	1

Source: Advisory Commission on Intergovernmental Relations, State-Local Finances: 1972 (Washington, D.C.: Government Printing Office, 1972), Table 113, p. 274.

Since 1926, federal estate tax rates have been increased several times, but the credit arrangement has not been changed to allow for these increases. That is, the upper limit on the amount of state tax that may be credited against federal tax is still based on the rates which existed in 1926. As a result, the maximum credit is now equal to approximately 10 percent of the federal liability, rather than the 80 percent available when the system was started. Today, state death tax collections typically exceed the amounts that can be claimed as credit against the federal tax, except for those states which use only the pickup tax. Competition among the states is not entirely eliminated.

PROBLEMS AND PROPOSALS

An indictment of state death transfer taxation would include the following specific charges. First, these taxes yield relatively little revenue on the average for state governments, and the revenue that is generated tends to be quite unstable from year to year. Since exemptions and deductions are substantial, only relatively wealthy individuals are subject to significant tax liabilities, and the number of such individuals who die in a given state in a given year is subject to great variation. Second, state death transfer taxation is unnecessarily complicated by the great variety of taxing instruments employed by the different states. The complexity revealed by the tabulation of tax approaches used in the various states suggests some truth to the cynic's comment that these taxes have been devised "of the lawyers, by the lawyers, and for the lawyers." It seems apparent that administrative and compliance costs could be reduced by the establishment of some degree of uniformity among the states. Third, problems sometimes arise in determining which state has jurisdiction to tax in particular death transfer situations. It is not uncommon for wealthy persons to maintain residences in more than one state. When this is the case, states may disagree as to which location constitutes the individual's residence for tax purposes. The states are legally sovereign, so that each may insist on its right to tax the wealth transfer and double (or multiple) taxation may result.

The search for remedies for the problems of state death transfer taxation has been a long one, but there is now considerable agreement on what reforms are needed and on the use of the federal credit instrument to make changes attractive to state legislatures. The complexity could be reduced if the states could agree to employ the same type of death transfer tax. The estate tax format is the leading candidate as the favored instrument for death transfer taxation, since the federal government already uses this type of tax.[2] Administrative and compliance costs would be reduced, since administration could be conducted in cooperation with the federal government. Moreover, the estate tax is potentially a better revenue producer than the inheritance tax, since fragmentation of the estate will not reduce tax liabilities as it does under the inheritance tax approach. States probably could be persuaded to adopt the estate tax as their sole death tax instrument if the federal credit were allowed only for state taxes paid through estate taxes. Of course, this strategy would be an invasion of state sovereignty.

Increases in state death transfer tax revenue and reductions in the instability of these revenues could be accomplished by reducing exemption and deduction allowances so that the tax would have a broader base. The number of small to moderate estates transferred in a given year is substantial and variations from year to year are modest, so that even rather low rates of tax on these estates could generate significant amounts of revenue. Again, the federal credit system could be used to bring about this modification in state death transfer taxation. The Advisory Commission on Intergovernmental Relations has suggested that a two-bracket system of federal credits could be adopted, with more generous crediting arrangements provided in respect to small or modest sized estates.[3] In this way, the national government would become primarily responsible for the taxation of death transfers for large estates (where wealth distribution may be the prime concern and where state taxation would mean unstable revenues), and state governments would be primarily responsible for taxation of small to moderate sized estates (where revenue potential is significant and year to year fluctuations less).

The problem of conflicting jurisdictional claims by different states in regard to specific estates is more difficult to resolve unless the national government is willing to impose a uniform set of rules. But if states were to become primarily interested in the taxation only of small to moderate estates, jurisdictional issues would recede to the background. Less would be at stake in any individual

[2] The restructuring of federal estate and gift taxation in the Tax Revision Act of 1976 may raise complicated problems in coordinating federal and state death taxation.

[3] Advisory Commission on Intergovernmental Relations, *Tax Overlapping in the United States, 1964* (Washington D.C.: Government Printing Office, 1964) p. 159.

case, and small to moderate estate holders are less likely to have maintained residences in more than one state.

Despite the awareness of both problems and solutions, death transfer tax reform is extremely slow in coming to pass. Part of the explanation may lie in its rather low visibility, which may have caused reform to be continually postponed in deference to more pressing legislative concerns. Most people are not immediately (if ever) affected by death transfer taxation, and it generates little revenue.

Vested interest in the status quo can also explain reluctance to reform the tax. If an individual has purchased professional estate planning advice and organized his affairs so as to minimize the impact of death transfer taxes, he would indeed have grounds to complain if frequent and substantial changes were made in tax laws. Property dispositions motivated at least in part by tax considerations often are not reversible, so that changing the rules in the middle of the game raises both ethical and efficiency questions.

Finally, the rationale for death transfer taxation at the state level is somewhat tenuous. The benefit-received rationale can be used to suggest that the accumulation of wealth and the opportunity to transfer this wealth have been facilitated by the general system of laws and property rights prevailing in the society. But the value of such benefits is extremely difficult to assess, and a strong case can be made that taxes levied under this principle should be limited to fees or charges to cover the government costs associated with these benefits. Moreover, the state that exercises jurisdiction to tax the transfer may not be the state in which the wealth was accumulated.

The ability to pay rationale is more persuasive, since the tax can be utilized to redistribute wealth and bring about somewhat greater equality of opportunity, but these are functions of the national government. Realistically, the ability to pay approach should focus on the beneficiaries of gratuitous transfers. It sometimes is proposed that gratuitous transfer taxes might be merged into the federal income tax structure (with some allowances for transfers within the immediate family), so that gratuitous transfer receipts would be considered together with other receipts which contribute to the recipient individual's ability to pay. This approach, of course, would place death transfer tax responsibility with the national government rather than with the state governments.

SUMMARY

Every state except Nevada derives some revenue from death or gift taxes, but collections provided only 1.7 percent of state tax collections in 1976. Only fifteen states impose tax on gift transfers. Three basic types of death transfer tax are used at the state level: *estate* taxes, which are based on the total wealth of the deceased; *inheritance* taxes; which are based on the separate amounts received by individual beneficiaries; and *pickup* taxes, which are designed to ensure that state collections are sufficient to utilize the full credit available against federal estate tax liabilities. The federal crediting arrangement was adopted in 1926 to prevent competition among the states from eliminating death taxation from state revenue systems. However, increases in federal estate tax rates enacted since 1926 have not been incorporated into the system, so that credits available today are limited to about 10 percent of the federal death tax liability.

Proposed reforms of state death taxation are aimed at reducing the administrative and compliance costs of these taxes and increasing their revenue potential for state governments. Administration and compliance costs would be reduced if states adopted uniform death tax procedures modeled on the estate tax form and following federal definitions. Greater revenue would be obtained if states focused on moderate estates and reduced exemption allowances so that their death taxes would collect revenue from the relatively large number of moderate estates transferred each year. This step would also mean that revenues would be relatively stable from year to year. Reform proposals have been advocated for a long time, but few changes have actually taken place. Federal pressure, through differential availability of the credit against federal tax, probably would be necessary to persuade the states to install greater uniformity in death tax laws, but reform appears to carry a low priority. Jurisdictional disputes also complicate the administration of state death taxes.

SUGGESTED READINGS

MERZ, PAUL E., and DAVID L. HANON. "Reforming State Taxation of Wealth Transfers at Death in Missouri," *National Tax Journal*, XXVII, 4 (December 1974).

See also suggested readings for Chapter 16.

22

State Corporation
Income Taxation

Corporation net income taxes were imposed by forty-six states in 1976 and provided 8.1 percent of state tax collections in that year, an average of $33.93 per capita. But corporation net income taxes are much more important in some states than in other states. Three states (California, New York, and Pennsylvania) accounted for over 40 percent of total state corporation income tax collections in 1976. Because corporate net income tends to fluctuate markedly over the business cycle, the revenue collected from a corporation net income tax will also fluctuate. This revenue instability helps to explain why corporation income taxes pay a relatively minor role in most state revenue structures.[1]

State corporation net income taxes generally are patterned after the federal model, except for the requirement that income must be allocated among the states in which the corporation does business. Tax rates are much lower for state taxes than for the federal tax. The most common practice is to use a flat (ungraduated) tax rate ranging from 4 percent to around 8 percent of net income. A few states employ a two-bracket system of graduation, and some graduate tax rates through a number of income size brackets. These graduated rate systems are designed to provide tax relief for small corporations, since the top bracket rate is reached at very low income levels.

The arguments advanced in favor of state taxation of corporation net income are similar to those used to support the federal tax and probably reflect the commonly held notion that corporation incomes ought to be taxed if per-

[1] U.S. Bureau of the Census, *State Tax Collections in 1976*, GF–76, No. 1 (Washington, D.C.: Government Printing Office, 1977), Tables 1, 3, pp. 5, 7.

sonal or individual incomes are taxed. State corporation income taxes may also be supported by the argument that they enable the taxing state to export some of the tax burden to purchasers of corporation products who live in other states. But the tax-exporting argument is difficult to sustain. If the rate of tax imposed by the state is the same as the rates imposed by other states, the analysis can follow the model discussed in connection with the federal corporation income tax. The incidence is on the owners of capital, and excise effects are related to the importance of capital in the production of different commodities and the attractiveness of different locations in producing these goods.

But if the state imposes a tax rate higher than those imposed by other states, it will be difficult to export the burden either to consumers in other states, who may purchase from suppliers located in other states, or to the owners of capital, who may choose to invest their resources in states with lower tax rates. Thus, it is likely that the part of the tax which arises from above-average tax rates will mainly trigger excise effects that will reduce the amount of capital investment in the state with those rates. Some of the burden of the extra tax may fall on labor in the taxing state if job opportunities are diminished by the exodus of capital. In the long run, the incidence of the extra tax is likely to appear in lower valuations for resources with fixed location in the state.

ALLOCATING INTERSTATE INCOME

Legally, a state can tax only that portion of a corporation's income which can reasonably be attributed to operations carried out within the jurisdiction of the taxing state. To attempt to tax income other than that reasonably allocated to the taxing state would bring the charge that corporate property was being taken without "due process of law." Consequently, each state that imposes a corporation net income tax uses some formula to determine the portion of the income of interstate corporations which can reasonably be subjected to taxation.

The three factors ordinarily used in income allocation formulas are property, payroll, and sales. For example, if a corporation had 40 percent of its property, 30 percent of its payroll, and 20 percent of its sales in a given state, that state might claim jurisdiction to tax 30 percent of the total net income of the corporation (if each of the three factors were given equal weight in the allocation formula). But some states do not use these factors, and even when they are used, different weighting patterns are employed. Each state tends to select the factors and the weighting pattern most advantageous to itself, within the rather loosely defined meaning of a reasonable allocation. States that, on balance, are net importers of corporate products will tend to place extra weight on the sales factor, whereas states that are exporters of corporate products will place extra weight on the origin factors of property and payroll. The revenue gains obtained from this type of formula manipulation probably are not large enough to justify the additional costs that arise. States that export large amounts of corporate production also tend to import large amounts and states that export small amounts of corporate production also tend to import small amounts. Therefore, formula manipulation results in little net advantage in state revenues. The costs of formula manipulation fall mainly on the corporations themselves, since they must attempt to comply with the laws of many states.

Overapportionment

So long as each state selects an allocation formula favorable to itself, interstate corporations can expect that the sum total subjected to state corporation income tax will add up to more than 100 percent of actual net income. This is called *overapportionment*. Overapportionment implies overtaxation, but it is not correct to presume that overapportionment necessarily means that the corporation is burdened by excessive taxation. Under the benefit-received rationale, overtaxation would arise if the amount of tax paid exceeded the benefits received from services rendered by the governments of the states collecting. tax from the corporation. Thus, the amount of benefit and the rates of tax must be considered along with the size of the income base before it is proper to conclude that overtaxation has taken place. If states tax more than 100 percent of the corporation's income, but do so at tax rates that are compensatingly low, no net overtaxation has occurred.

Origin of Production Formula

An *origin of production* formula for interstate allocation of corporation income would use the property and the payroll factors, but would eliminate sales from the formula. This approach is based on the view that the justification for state taxation arises through benefits received from government services and that property and payroll factors are much more likely to correlate with these services than is the sales factor. The protection of property is an important government service, as are services related to employment, such as government-operated employment services and educational and training facilities. Any state services associated with the destination of sales, it is contended, would be adequately recognized by the property factor for sales outlet facilities or by the payroll factor for sales personnel.

The cost of complying with state corporation income tax laws would be reduced if allocation formulas were simplified through the elimination of the sales factor. For many corporations, property and payroll operations may be limited to relatively few states, whereas sales may take place in a great many states. So long as the sales factor remains in allocation formulas, corporations must maintain records sufficient to enable them to comply with the laws of many states. Elimination·of this factor could reduce the number of laws whose requirements must be met and thus ease the compliance task for corporations. Estimates suggest that the revenue consequences of eliminating the sales factor would be minor for most states and that the gains from simplified administration and compliance could mean that no state would experience a net revenue loss from the change.[2]

[2] Elliott Morss, "An Evaluation of the Report on State Taxation," *National Tax Journal*, XVIII, 3 (September 1965).

ENFORCEMENT AND COMPLIANCE

Neither vigorous enforcement nor diligent compliance characterizes state taxation of corporate net income. From the enforcement point of view, a problem exists because information for auditing the return filed by a corporation must come from the corporation itself. A penetrating audit would require the services of highly skilled personnel, whose salaries could not be justified in terms of the additional revenues that might be collected. Corporations also confront a dilemma in determining the expenses that can be justified in order to comply with the corporation income tax laws in the (perhaps many) states in which they do business. Full and detailed compliance would require the services of many skilled and expensive legal and accounting personnel, since state laws and allocation formulas differ. And since the limitations of state audits are recognized, both corporate officials and state tax administrators know there are limits to the amounts that can be expended on compliance and enforcement. Therefore, both administration and compliance are carried on at a somewhat superficial level in many states, and there is little prospect for change unless a greater degree of uniformity can be established in the terms and requirements of the corporate income tax laws.

INTERSTATE COMPETITION

The location of corporate activity can be expected to show some sensitivity to corporate income taxation, whether the tax is thought to be shifted forward to consumers or a tax on equity capital financing. If the tax is shifted forward in higher prices for products, the company may find itself at a competitive disadvantage. States that enjoy uniquely advantageous circumstances for corporate activity may be able to export some tax incidence through the corporation income tax, but few states enjoy locational advantages great enough to eliminate the possibility that aggressive income taxation might drive corporate facilities to locate in other states. The same general conclusions follow if the tax is seen as a levy on equity financing. Financial markets are nationwide, so if a state's corporation tax results in a lower net rate of return to the company than could be realized elsewhere, the tendency again will be for the corporation to seek an alternative location. In the long run, the fact of interstate competition for industrial locations is likely to discourage large interstate differences in corporate income tax rates and to impose subtle pressures in the direction of keeping effective rates relatively low.

In 1975 Michigan replaced its corporation net income tax with a value added tax applicable to unincorporated businesses as well as to corporations. Interstate competition for industrial locations played an important part in bringing about this change in tax instruments. The switch to the value added tax broadened the tax base considerably, both because unincorporated business must now pay tax and because the value added base includes noncapital inputs (such as labor) as well as capital inputs. Thus, a given amount of revenue can be obtained with a lower tax rate than would be needed if only corporate net income were taxed, and the lower tax rate on capital inputs can provide an advantage in interstate competition for capital investments. Labor and other noncapital inputs may bear a larger share of the burden of a value added tax than they would of a corporation net income tax, but greater capital investment may increase the demand for these factors and thus compensate for the heavier tax.

SUMMARY

Corporation net income taxes are imposed in most states, but on the average, these taxes make only a modest contribution to state revenues. A few states with a relatively high concentration of corporate activity account for the bulk of the total state collections from this tax. Interstate competition and the instability of revenues from corporate net income taxes explain why most states place little reliance on this revenue source. State corporation income tax administration and compliance are complicated by the necessity of allocating corporate income among the states so that each state taxes only that portion of net income which reasonably falls within its jurisdiction. Administration and compliance are especially complicated by the presence of a sales factor in these allocation formulas. The sales factor could be eliminated under an origin philosophy of interstate allocation, and it appears that this simplification would not result in major changes in the amounts collected in individual states. The combination of relatively low rates and relatively complicated reporting requirements means that both enforcement and compliance may be somewhat superficial in many instances.

The competitive model for the incidence of corporation income taxes (which was outlined in Chapter 14) is especially applicable to state corporate income taxation because corporations in one state ordinarily must compete with corporations located in other states. States that impose a rate of tax higher than those existing in other states probably cannot expect that the burden of this extra tax will be shifted to consumers in other states or to shareholders. Therefore, much of the burden of above-average rates may be shifted backward to labor and suppliers of materials in the taxing state itself. Interstate competition means that state corporation income tax rates will be relatively low and quite uniform among the states.

SUGGESTED READINGS

Morss, Elliott. "An Evaluation of the Report on State Taxation," *National Tax Journal*, XVIII, 3 (September 1965).

Clark, Owen L. "The Taxation of Income from Corporate Shareholding: State and Local View," *National Tax Journal*, XXVIII, 3 (September 1975).

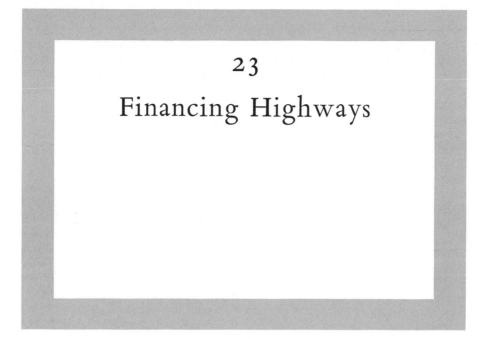

23

Financing Highways

State and local governments are the primary direct suppliers of highway services in the United States. In 1974–75, about 62 percent of direct highway expenditure was carried out by state governments, about 36 percent was carried out by local governments, and less than 2 percent was carried out by the federal government. But the federal government is important in the financing of highway services. About one-fourth of the funding for highways comes from the federal government, although most of this money is dispensed through transfers to state and local governments. State governments also transfer substantial amounts of highway money to their local governments, which are then responsible for the direct expenditure of these funds.[1] The funds for highway finance originate with motor fuel taxes, excises on vehicles, license fees, operators' permits, and tolls.

This chapter examines three dimensions of the economics of highway finance: (a) Should people who do not use highways be obligated to help pay for them? (b) How should the costs of providing highway services be divided among people who actually use highways? (c) Should money collected from highway users be diverted to help finance other government services?

USER AND NONUSER FINANCING

Highway users include motorists who consume highway services for pleasure as an item of personal consumption. Traveling salesmen, bus lines, and

[1] U.S. Bureau of the Census, *Governmental Finances in 1974–75*, GF–75, No. 5 (Washington, D.C.: Government Printing Office, 1976), Table 6, p. 20.

trucking companies use highway services as inputs for their business activities. Those who use highway services as business inputs are agents for the ultimate consumers of the products of their business enterprises and are expected to pass the costs of highway use forward in the price of the products. Therefore, most people in the society are highway users even if they do not personally operate a vehicle on the highways. When a person buys groceries, he is indirectly a user of highway services; some demand for highway service is derived from the demand for groceries. Thus, the highway user category is broad and inclusive.

In addition, highways also provide external or collective services, such as the contribution to national security provided by an effective road transportation system or the promotion of economic development and social integration. These collective components of highway service are consumed by all members of the society, whether they are highway users or not. They are part of the nonuser component of highway service. Of course, not all external or nonuser elements of highway service are consumed collectively. For example, a person who owns land near an interchange for a newly constructed interstate highway is an external beneficiary, since the market value of his land is likely to increase even though his use of the highway is not different from that of other persons.

The distinction between user and nonuser beneficiaries from highway service permits us to employ the model developed earlier to illustrate efficient production and financing of collective services. In Figure 23.1, BB represents the marginal benefits accruing to users of highways and AA represents the marginal benefits accruing to nonusers. Since the total demand for highway services should recognize benefits received by users and by nonusers, the total demand for highway service is illustrated in Figure 23.1 by the line BCD, which is the vertical summation of the benefits of users and nonusers. The allocationally efficient quantity of highway service is that at which the total marginal benefit $(AA + BB)$ is equal to the marginal cost of providing highway service.

The Nonuser Share

Whether nonusers should make any payment to finance highways depends on whether they experience any positive marginal benefit when the efficient quantity of highway service is being provided. This is an application of the marginal rule explained earlier. In Figure 23.1(a), the allocationally efficient quantity of highway service is Q_1. Financing for these services should come in part from users, who would pay a unit price of P_u equal to their marginal benefit from the service, and in part from nonuser beneficiaries, who would pay a unit price of P_n, equal to their marginal benefit at this level of highway service production.

The appropriateness of nonuser financing of highway services is illustrated by further examination of Figure 23.1(a). Suppose a nonuser share was not imposed and the entire marginal cost of highway service was imposed on users of the service in the form of a unit price equal to P_t. At this price, the quantity of service demanded would be Q_2. In this situation, however, the benefits of an additional unit of highway service would be greater than its cost and the additional unit should be provided. Payments made by nonuser beneficiaries would lower the unit price required of the users of highway services and bring about an increase in the quantity of the service, from which the nonusers as well as the users would benefit.

In Figure 23.1(b), the user demand for highway services (*BB*) has increased substantially, while the nonuser benefits (*AA*) have remained unchanged. At the allocationally efficient quantity of highway service, Q_3, the marginal benefit to nonusers is zero. Any payment by nonusers that would lower the unit price to users would be inappropriate, since a lower unit price to users would result in marginal units of service for which costs exceed benefits. Resources would be misallocated, with too much being applied to highway service and too little being applied elsewhere in the economy.[2]

FIGURE 23.1   User and Nonuser Financing of Highway Service

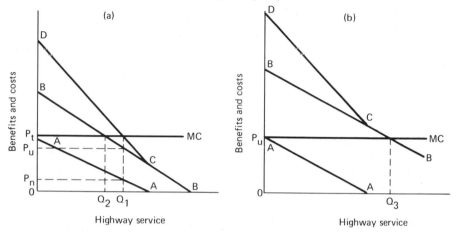

The implication of this analysis is that the appropriateness of a nonuser contribution to highway finance depends in part on the level of demand for highway services by *users*. If user demand is substantial, as appears to be the case for many roads in the United States, nonuser and collective benefits from highway services are inframarginal and can be provided as by-products from the provision of service demanded by users. Consumer surpluses and economic rents are generated, but these are not appropriate sources of finance for highway purposes, although they might be appropriate subjects for taxation for general revenue purposes if economic rents taxation were adopted by the society. In less developed economies, where user demand for highway services may be low, nonuser or general fund financing for highways may be appropriate.

Nonuser Payments for Specific Roads

The practical application of the model provided in Figure 23.1 must be in terms of specific roadways rather than in general terms of all highway services. Even in the United States, a nonuser contribution for less-traveled

---

[2] Milton Z. Kafoglis, "Highway Policy and External Economies," *National Tax Journal,* XVI, 1 (March 1963), 68 80.

roads, such as rural farm-to-market roads or residential streets, may be appropriate. Merchants in a farming community may be willing to devote some general fund revenue to road maintenance if this will persuade more farm people to patronize their stores. Property owners may be willing to help finance roads so that fire trucks and ambulances can arrive quickly in emergency situations. In each of these illustrations, property values are increased by expansions of highway services. Special property tax assessments are a familiar illustration of road financing based on the property value consequences of highway use.

PRICING SERVICES TO HIGHWAY USERS

The major portion of highway service consumption is similar to that of the services of a public utility. The service is consumed privately by individuals who may choose to consume differing amounts. If effective and reasonably economical exclusion devices are available, resource allocation theory suggests that a unit price should be established for highway services and that each consumer should be free to consume as much or as little of the service as he chooses, so long as he is willing and able to pay the price of the services he does consume. Money spent to purchase highway service would be a reliable measure of demand, and payments would be made by consumers enjoying the benefits of the services provided. But effective and economical exclusion devices are not available for the services rendered by most highway systems. Instead of direct pricing of highway services, proxy measures of consumption, such as motor fuels consumption, must be used. The pricing problem is made doubly difficult by the fact that there are as many different varieties of highway service as there are different types of vehicles using the road. In addition, the correct price may be different for one type of vehicle than for another. Toll roads illustrate a direct application of the price system for highway finance; gasoline taxes illustrate an indirect or proxy system.

Toll Roads

The toll road is familiar to American motorists. High wire fences, barricades, and toll booths are exclusion devices that prevent a vehicle operator from utilizing the service of the road unless a toll or user price is paid. His willingness to pay this price demonstrates that his marginal benefit from the service is at least equal to the amount of the toll. It is an example of direct market pricing of highway service. The toll road system for highway finance is efficient when the volume of traffic is great enough to justify the costs of maintaining and operating the exclusion devices.

Weighing stations along main highways are also toll road installations. These facilities are expensive to maintain and operate, but they are less expensive than a complete toll road system. The vehicles that must use these stations are heavy trucks, which are recognizable on sight by the personnel operating the station. When the volume of truck traffic is great and the toll charges high enough, the weighing station system is economically feasible. But these arrangements are not complete toll road systems. Access to these roads is not restricted and requirements that heavy trucks refrain from using alternate routes are hard to enforce.

The toll road method of highway finance is not feasible for most roads given the existing state of technology for exclusion devices. But advances in that technology may greatly increase the attractiveness of this approach, especially for heavily traveled commuter routes in and around major cities. Electronic "taxi meters" in vehicles could be activated by transmitters or reflectors installed in roadways so that heavily traveled roads could become toll facilities without expensive collection systems, limited access points, and delays in traffic flow. The meters could be read periodically and tolls collected along with licensing or inspection fees. With even more advanced technology, the meters would be unnecessary. Laser beam equipment installed along the highways could read the license numbers of passing vehicles and compute toll charges. Then a monthly statement could be sent to the owner of the vehicle. An especially attractive feature of these exotic systems is that toll charges could differ from one time of day to another, so that higher tolls could be charged at peak load hours. The importance of this feature will be examined further when the costs of providing highway services are considered.

The Motor Fuel Tax

The motor fuel tax is a proxy for user pricing of highway services, and the gasoline pump is a toll station that can be maintained at much lower cost than toll stations located on the roadways themselves. The presumption is that the number of gallons of gasoline purchased measures the amount of highway service consumed. The station operator collects the toll and transmits the money to the state government, which spends it to finance the delivery of highway services.

Although some relationship exists between the amount of gasoline purchased and the amount of highway service consumed, the motor fuel tax is clearly an imperfect measure. In general terms, the amount of gasoline purchased is positively related to the number of miles traveled and to the weight, speed, and size of the vehicle, which are useful indices of highway consumption. But the imperfections in this proxy measure are important. Certainly the performance of a poorly tuned or improperly functioning engine bears little relation to the consumption of highway service. The main difficulty with the motor fuel proxy is that the purchase of fuel provides those who must decide on the distribution of maintenance funds with little or no information about which sections of the road system are actually used by the consumer. In practice, motor fuel tax revenues are distributed among state highways, county roads, and city streets on the basis of formulas developed in the legislature that may reflect political considerations quite as much as they reflect the demands of consumers. Motor fuel purchased for nonhighway uses, such as fuel for airplanes and farm equipment, generally is exempt from the motor fuel tax, but it is difficult to ensure that fuels purchased under these exemptions do not, in some instances, actually come into use on highways.

THE COSTS OF HIGHWAY SERVICES

The public utility model for pricing services to highway users requires that the price charged be equal to the marginal cost of providing the service—

that is, resources will be efficiently allocated when price is equal to marginal cost for each user of the service. The pricing of highway services is greatly complicated by the fact that many different types of vehicles use the highways, and the cost of providing service depends on the type of vehicle involved. For example, the cost of providing highway service for a heavy truck is greater than the cost for an ordinary passenger car because the weight of the truck requires that the roadbed be thicker and stronger. The size of the vehicle is also important. A wide vehicle requires a wider roadway than a narrow vehicle and long vehicles occupy more road space than do short vehicles. Vehicle speed is another factor that influences costs: curves must be more moderate or more steeply banked for fast vehicles. On the other hand, slow vehicles may require longer straight stretches of highway in order to allow safe passing zones. Since all vehicles must use the same road system, allocating costs among different users is difficult.

Figure 23.2 illustrates an *incremental cost* method of assigning highway costs to different categories of highway users. The area labeled "basic costs" reflects those features of the road system utilized in common by all users. These basic costs include the acquisition of the right of way, the grading and surfacing necessary for the least demanding type of service, the minimum necessary control and maintenance operations, and so on. The other areas show different varieties of incremental costs, that is, additional costs required because of types of usage not common to all users. One group of incremental costs arises because certain vehicles are heavier or larger than others and therefore require that the road be stronger or wider than the road that could be constructed with basic cost financing. A second group arises because of peak load requirements during rush hour traffic periods. Extra lanes of traffic may be demanded and additional control and maintenance operations may be necessary during these times. The task is to allocate the various costs to the vehicles that make the expenditures necessary.

FIGURE 23.2   Basic and Incremental Costs of Highways

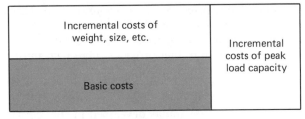

Allocating Basic Costs

The basic costs of highways are analogous to the fixed or overhead costs of the firm in standard economic analysis. They are *joint costs* in respect to the various vehicles served by the highways. The problem in financing is to determine a way to allocate these joint costs among the different highway users. There is no clearly correct way, but it is reasonable to conclude that all highway users should bear some portion of these costs; that is, that no class of vehicles should be given a free ride at the expense of other classes of vehicles. A reasonable presumption is that joint costs might be allocated among vehicles on the basis of miles traveled, with assessments calculated from periodic checks of odometer readings. If such direct assessments are technically or administratively infeasible, motor fuel taxes provide a second best method of financing these costs. Of course, fuel consumption is an imperfect indicator of miles traveled. Heavy vehicles that travel fewer miles per gallon of fuel will thus pay more than their share of basic costs, but this excess payment may be carried over and applied as an adjustment in incremental cost payments required from these vehicles.

The problems of the motor fuel tax as a financing method for basic costs are not limited to its imperfection as an indicator of miles traveled. The basic costs of highways differ greatly from one segment of the road system to another. Construction costs are much greater in mountainous regions than on level terrain. The costs of land acquisition for rights of way are much greater in densely populated areas than they are in sparsely populated areas, and so on. Since a gallon of fuel pumped into a vehicle can be used as readily on a high-cost segment of road as on a low-cost segment, motor fuel taxes cannot accurately take account of differences in highway basic costs. Nevertheless, the motor fuel tax may be the best instrument presently available for financing basic costs.

Fees charged for motor vehicle registration and for operator licenses are not calculated on the basis of miles traveled and therefore should not be used to finance the construction or maintenance of highway services. Motor vehicle registration provides a service to vehicle owners because it helps police trace stolen vehicles and identify vehicles exceeding speed limits, violating parking regulations, and so on. Registration fees should help finance the costs of providing services of this sort. Operator licenses provide similar types of services, and the fees charged for these licenses should be set accordingly. Thus, purely regulatory services should be distinguished from services related to highway usage. The collection of regulatory fees, such as those for vehicle registration and driver licenses, may provide a convenient occasion for the collection of other taxes or user prices, but the fees themselves should be distinguished from other charges collected at the same time.

Incremental Costs: Size, Weight

The incremental cost approach suggests that extra costs incurred because of a certain type of use or service should be charged to the vehicle demanding that service. Heavy trucks, for example, hasten the breakup of paved surfaces or require a much thicker paving base than do ordinary passenger vehicles. The added costs of repair or of initially providing the needed strength should be charged to vehicles on the basis of weight. The size of the vehicle is another factor in incremental pricing, since wide-load vehicles require wider roadways than do vehicles of normal width. Under incremental cost pricing, the extra cost of roadway widening beyond the requirements for normal vehicles would be charged against the wider vehicles.

License fees can differentiate among vehicles on the basis of size and can be applied on an incremental cost basis, but some factor that can also reflect weight and distance traveled is needed for an accurate measure of incremental costs. Weight-distance (ton-mile) taxes can be collected in conjunction with the payment of license fees, although accurate determination of weight and mileage may require the operation of expensive inspection stations.

Incremental Cost: Peak Load Users

Highway service provided at one time of day is not the same commodity as highway service provided at another time of day; a roadway adequate to meet demand during normal traffic hours may be quite inadequate during rush or peak load hours. If the road capacity must accommodate the volume of demand at peak load times, the incremental cost of providing this additional capacity should be assessed against the vehicles demanding service during these times. Financing the incremental cost of the additional capacity from motor fuel revenues would be unfair to normal (non-peak load) highway users and would fail to provide information about the true level of peak load demand. Moreover, the failure to apply differential pricing for peak load highway users loses the opportunity to introduce incentives for these users to adjust their schedules to avoid peak times. A better measure of peak load demand would be available if special tolls were charged to peak load highway users, and a better allocation of funds could be made among alternative sections of roadway. Plans for investment in special peak load facilities would be analogous to business investment planning, with the expected revenues from the special tolls providing the funding for the new construction. Of course, peak load tolls require collection instruments capable of establishing different prices for different times of day for a given section of roadway.

DIVERSIONS OF HIGHWAY USER FUNDS

A *diversion* of highway user funds occurs whenever money collected from users is expended for some purpose other than the financing of highway services. Over the years, highway interests have fought vigorously and successfully against such diversions. Recently, however, arguments in favor of diversion have strengthened. Extra gasoline taxes have been proposed to conserve the supply of petroleum or to reduce air pollution by encouraging people to drive less and to drive smaller automobiles. Therefore, it is likely that future revenues from highway users may not be used exclusively for the construction and maintenance of highways.

Paying All the Costs

The first step in examining the matter of diversions is to recognize the distinction between (a) diverting highway funds and (b) requiring highway users to pay the full costs of their use of highways. The operation of motor vehicles generates many costs which are external in the sense that market transactions provide no means whereby those who suffer the burdens of them can either be compensated for their welfare loss or put a stop to the activities responsible for these costs. Noise and air pollution are examples of such external costs of motor vehicle operation, as are physical injury hazards created by traffic conditions.

The economist's recommendation concerning external costs is that they should somehow be *internalized*, either through the regulatory process of prohibiting the activity which gives rise to the negative externality (for example, by prohibiting the operation of internal combustion engines without emission control systems) or by imposing a tax or charge on such activities. If the regulatory approach is adopted, there is no public revenue collected and no apparent diversion of highway user funds, although the money cost of highway use is increased and the external cost eliminated. If the tax or user charge approach is used, some public revenues will be generated to the extent that some motorists find it more economical to pay the tax than to desist from the activity. Of course any revenues actually collected from a pollution tax should not be expended to finance highway services as ordinarily conceived, but in fact should be used to correct the damage done or to compensate the injured parties. These uses of funds would not constitute diversions of highway money but instead would ensure that highway users pay the full costs of the services they consume.

In terms of economic efficiency, the pollution tax approach is preferred to the outright prohibition of activities giving rise to potential negative external effects. This preference arises from the realization that the resource costs of equipping vehicles with emission and noise prevention systems is significant, given the existing technology, and that the benefit gained from the reduction of pollution depends on such factors as when, where, and for how long the vehicle is in operation. The cost of emission control equipment will exceed the benefits from it for vehicles operated infrequently or at times or in places where the natural environment is capable of recycling the emissions without damage to any ecological system.

The pollution tax approach to the internalization of externalities leads, once again, to an appreciation of the welfare gains that could be realized through the development of better exclusion devices. Taxi-meter technology (a kind of built-in toll collection system) might incorporate the emission characteristics of the vehicle itself along with information about how much, where, and when the vehicle was operated. Such a system could lead, in turn, to an awareness by the vehicle operator of the full costs imposed by operation of the vehicle and provide money incentives to desist from operations that generate negative externalities. The old adage that an ounce of prevention is worth a pound of cure has great relevance in the matter of negative externalities, where ex post corrections or compensations are difficult if not impossible.

Highway Congestion and Rationing

In noncongestion situations, the entry of an additional vehicle onto a given section of highway during a given time period causes no significant interference with the use of that roadway by other vehicles; that is, the average time and nervous tension costs of operating a vehicle on this road at this time are not changed by the presence of the additional vehicle. Average cost of vehicle operation is constant, and the marginal cost arising from the presence of the additional vehicle is the same as the average cost to all vehicles.

Congestion arises when the presence of an additional vehicle results in a slowdown of all vehicles attempting to use the road, thus causing average time and nervous tension costs for all vehicle operators to increase. This increase in the average cost which arises because of the presence of the additional vehicle means that the marginal cost of the additional vehicle is greater than the average cost per vehicle. In Figure 23.3, the horizontal axis records the number of vehicles utilizing a section of roadway per unit of time and the vertical axis records the cost of traversing this section of roadway, measured perhaps in the time required to complete the journey. No congestion is experienced so long as the demand for the services of this section of roadway is such that the number of vehicles attempting to use it is less than Q_1. Over the range of usage between 0 and Q_1, average cost and marginal cost are equal. No congestion is experienced at the nonrush-hour demand of D_1.

FIGURE 23.3   Highway Congestion

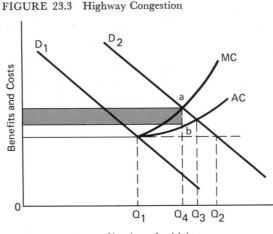

Number of vehicles

During rush hours, the demand for the services of the roadway is D_2, and the quantity of service demanded would be Q_2 if no congestion were present. However, congestion does exist, as shown by the rising average cost per vehicle for quantities to the right of Q_1, and some potential users are persuaded by these higher costs to desist from using this road at this time. Therefore, congestion costs themselves discourage some usage, and the actual number of vehicles attempting to use the road at this time will be Q_3, as indicated by the intersection of D_2 with the average cost curve. The operator of the marginal vehicle has concluded that the benefit of using the road at this time is at least equal to the cost *he* must incur to use it, which is the average cost per vehicle on the road at this time.

Each vehicle in excess of quantity Q_1, however, is imposing external costs on all other vehicles on the road, as illustrated by the increases in average cost that arise due to the presence of these additional vehicles. Although each additional vehicle must itself incur only the average cost of using the road, the full cost of its presence (the marginal cost) must also include the external costs imposed on all the other vehicles. It is apparent, therefore, that quantity Q_3 is *not* an efficient level of utilization for this roadway, since the marginal cost resulting from the presence of the added vehicle is in excess of the marginal benefit to the additional vehicle, as shown by the demand curve D_2. Congestion costs alone do not efficiently allocate the service capability of the roadway.

The efficient level of utilization of the road illustrated in Figure 23.3 is quantity Q_4, at which the marginal benefit to the additional vehicle is equal to the marginal cost of its presence. A toll equal to the difference between average cost and marginal cost (interval *ab* in Figure 23.3) is needed to bring about this efficient level of utilization. The toll will reduce the quantity demanded from Q_3 to Q_4, as some vehicle operators are forced to recognize that the marginal cost of their presence on the roadway at this demand period is greater than the marginal benefit they will derive from using the road at this time. Some congestion will prevail even at Q_4, but the existing highway facility will at least be efficiently utilized.

The revenue collected from the toll is shown as the shaded area in Figure 23.3, which is the toll per vehicle, *ab*, times the number of vehicles using the roadway. William Vickery has suggested that "a system of congestion-based tolls is a beautiful way to levy taxes" and that they offer "not only a marvelous solution to the traffic problem but a solution to the financial problem of a great many cities as well," implying that these revenues could be diverted from highway uses to general revenue purposes.[3] The point is that tolls necessary to allocate efficiently the services of *existing* roadways are distinguishable from tolls established under an incremental cost philosophy for the construction of new or expanded highway facilities and may legitimately be used for nonhighway financing. Of course, the argument should not be extended to the point of suggesting that inadequate roadways are desirable because they provide a means of financing other services. That would be an especially unpleasant type of exploitation of highway users. If peak load demand, as evidenced by willingness to pay toll charges, is great enough to justify the construction of additional facilities, then investments in these additional facilities should be undertaken. But during the interval when congestion cannot be relieved, congestion tolls may be diverted to other expenditure areas.

Highway User Funds for Mass Transit

Should highway user funds subsidize mass transit services? Benefit-received logic suggests that the answer to this question hinges on whether services rendered by the mass transit system convey benefits to highway users and whether these external benefits exist at the margin of mass transit service financed by mass transit users themselves.

Figure 23.4, illustrates a situation in which highway users might subsidize mass transit services. It is the same as Figure 23.1, which considered the relations between highway users and nonusers. In Figure 23.4, the horizontal axis measures mass transit services and the vertical axis measures benefits and costs

[3] William S. Vickery, "The Economics of Congestion Control in Urban Transportation," in Frank C. Emerson (ed.), *The Economics of Environmental Problems* (Michigan Business Papers, No. 58, Division of Research, Graduate School of Business Administration, The University of Michigan, Ann Arbor, 1973), p. 69.

FIGURE 23.4   Highway User Subsidies for Mass
              Transit

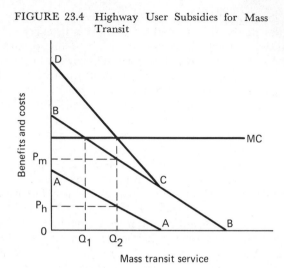

Mass transit service

of these services. The *AA* line illustrates benefits realized by highway users that
result from utilization (by others) of mass transit service. Patronage of the mass
transit service, for example, may reduce the demand for highway service and
result in a reduction in highway congestion, which will lower the cost of highway
usage and thereby benefit highway users. The marginal benefit from mass
transit service to mass transit patrons themselves is *BB*, and if the price of use
were set to equal its marginal cost, the quantity would be Q_1. At this volume,
highway users would realize benefits from an expansion of mass transit patronage and would be willing to permit some highway user funds to be diverted to
reduce fares on the mass transit system. An equilibrium situation exists at
quantity Q_2, with mass transit patrons paying a price of P_m and highway users
paying a subsidy equal to P_h per unit of mass transit service.

The model illustrated in Figure 23.4 suggests that reduction in highway
congestion costs is the basis for highway user subsidy to mass transit and assumes
that transferring patronage from the highways to the mass transit system is the
lowest-cost means of relieving highway congestion. Highway users who do not
suffer from the congestion costs reduced by the mass transit system would be
unwilling, as highway users, to contribute to the subsidy for mass transit.

SUMMARY

Highway finance is an important dimension of state government activity.
A basic insight into the economic model for highway finance comes from the
realization that highways are a public utility type of operation, not unlike water
or electric power. Nonusers of highway services may be called upon to help
finance highways if they enjoy positive marginal benefits at the limit of service
financed by users. In the United States, however, where user demand is great,
this situation is likely to exist only for city streets and lightly traveled sections of

roadway. For reasonably well-traveled roads, the public utility model suggests that highway users themselves should finance the highways.

Financing highways with charges collected from users would be a simple application of market system economics if effective and economical exclusion devices existed. The willingness and ability to pay established prices for highway service would measure the demand for this service and would direct resources to the provision of those roads most demanded by users. Toll roads illustrate this type of market solution, but the exclusion devices required are too expensive to be feasible for most roads. The motor fuel tax, collected at the gasoline pump, is an economical exclusion device; motorists pay for highway services when they pay this tax. But motor fuel consumption is an imperfect measure of highway service consumed and provides little information to help in allocating funds among different sections of highway.

The costs of providing highway service depend, in part, on the type of vehicle using the road. An efficient pricing system should recognize cost differences in setting user prices for different types of vehicles. The incremental cost approach suggests that basic highway costs, which provide services to all vehicle types, might be allocated among all vehicles according to mileage traveled. Incremental or additional costs incurred to serve particular types of vehicles should be collected from these particular vehicle types. Because motor fuel taxes alone probably cannot meet the requirements of the incremental cost approach, other levies, such as license fees or weight-distance taxes, may be necessary.

Money collected from highway users should be expended on providing highway services. A burden of proof is required for proposals that highway user money be diverted to other uses. However, highway users should not be permitted to impose external costs on other people, as in the case of air or noise pollution. Pollution taxes imposed on highway users simply require users to pay all the costs of their highway use. Diversion of highway user money may be justified if highway users enjoy positive marginal benefits from other services, such as mass transit. Diversion may also be justified if taxes are collected in the process of controlling congestion on highways.

SUGGESTED READINGS

KAFOGLIS, MILTON Z. "Highway Policy and External Economies," *National Tax Journal*, XVI, 1 (March 1963), 68–80.

ROTH, GABRIEL. *Paying for Roads: The Economics of Traffic Congestion* (Baltimore: Penguin Books, Inc., 1967).

VICKREY, WILLIAM. "Externalities in Public Facility Use: The Case of Highway Accidents," in J. Margolis (Ed.), *The Analysis of Public Output* (New York: National Bureau of Economic Research, 1970), pp. 317–38.

VICKREY, WILLIAM. "Responsive Pricing of Public Utility Services," *Bell Journal of Economics and Management Service* (Spring 1971).

RENSHAW, EDWARD F. "A Note on Mass Transit Subsidies " *National Tax Journal*, XXVI, 4 (December 1973), pp. 639–44.

MILLER, EDWARD. "The Economics of Matching Grants: The ABC Highway Program," *National Tax Journal*, XXVII, 2 (June 1974).

IV

Local Governments

Local government is especially interesting to students of government finance. From a theoretical point of view, local government jurisdictions are small and heterogeneous, so that the model of "voting with your feet" developed in Chapter 17 is especially applicable. It is the level of government closest to the individual and the one in which he can actively and effectively participate with relatively little difficulty. The participatory aspect of local government is heightened by the widespread use of property taxation, which itemizes tax rates and liabilities on a function by function basis so that the taxpayer can readily identify the services financed with his payments.

Local government is also the focus of several widely recognized problem areas in government finance. The financial difficulties of central cities and of metropolitan areas are well known and are tied to the institutional arrangements of public finance. Elementary and secondary education is an important responsibility of local governments, and major issues surround such questions as whether property tax financing for education operates to deprive students of their rights to equal opportunity.

Local government finance has been subjected to major stresses in recent decades as demands for education and welfare services have grown and as population and industry have relocated from central cities to suburban and rural areas. The key role of property taxation in these matters has prompted states and their local governments to explore alternative revenue sources, such as user charges, local sales or income taxes, and increased intergovernment revenues from higher levels of government.

Chapter 24 provides a brief overview of local government expenditures and revenues. Chapters 25, 26, and 27 examine the procedures, problems, and proposed reforms for property taxation. Chapter 28 reviews user charge, income tax, and sales tax opportunities; Chapter 29 presents a model for state grants-in-aid to local governments; and Chapter 30 considers the role of debt financing.

24

An Overview
of Local Governments

There were 78,218 units of local government in the United States in 1972, according to the U.S. Bureau of the Census.[1] Many of these units overlap one another so that the individual citizen finds himself affiliated with several of them. A convenient way to discover the units of government with which a citizen is affiliated is to examine the local property tax statement. It will ordinarily reveal that the citizen is affiliated with a school district, with a county government, and with either a municipal or a township government, depending on whether his residence is located inside or outside a city or village. In addition, many citizens will find they are affiliated with one or more special districts that provide services financed with taxes in addition to those levied by other local governments. Even the property tax statement may fail to identify all local governments if some of them do not use the property tax in their financing.

Table 24.1 shows the number of the various types of local governments in the United States in 1972 and the changes that took place during the preceding five-year period. The magnitude of the change in the numbers of local governments is impressive. For example, 6,001 school districts disappeared as separate government units between 1967 and 1972, while 2,621 new special districts and 469 new municipalities were added. Five counties and 114 townships ceased to exist as separate governments during this period. Impressive as these numbers are, the birth and death of local government units is nothing new in

[1] U.S. Bureau of the Census, *Census of Governments, 1972*, Vol. I, "Governmental Organization" (Washington, D.C.: Government Printing Office, 1973), Table 1, p. 23.

TABLE 24.1   Local Governments in the United States 1972, and
the Change Between 1967 and 1972

TYPE	1972	CHANGE
School districts	15,781	−6,001
Counties	3,044	− 5
Municipalities	18,517	469
Townships	16,991	− 144
Special districts	23,885	2,621
Total	78,218	−3,030

Source: U.S. Bureau of the Census, Census of Governments, 1972, Vol. I,
"Governmental Organizations" (Washington, D.C.: Government Printing
Office, 1973), Table 1, p. 23.

the United States, and the changes between 1967 and 1972 were continuations
of trends evident for some time. During the twenty years from 1952 to 1972,
the number of school districts was continuously decreasing from the 67,355 that
existed in 1952. The increase in the number of special districts and municipalities was also continuous over this same span of years. In fact, all these trends
were evident long before 1952.

A detailed examination of the forces behind these rearrangements of local
governments would be a complicated undertaking, but even casual observation
suggests that reductions in the number of people living in rural areas, improvements in transportation and communication, and relocations of population
had much to do with these changes. Many of the school districts that were
discontinued were in rural areas. Declining populations and improved bus
transportation meant that many of these could be consolidated or merged with
existing districts in more populated areas. The increase in the number of municipalities can be traced to the establishment of suburban communities made
attractive by the availability of convenient automobile transportation. The
increased number of special districts suggests a more complicated picture.
Many of these special districts are transportation authorities directly concerned with planning and coordinating transportation services in metropolitan
areas. Others are concerned with the provision of water, sewer, and other utility
services in these areas. In rural areas, special districts deal with planning, water
supply, and soil conservation.

The impressive changes in the numbers of the various types of local
governments give an initial impression that a good deal of flexibility exists at
the local level of government in the United States. This in turn can be judged
a desirable characteristic of local government if it means that these units are
able to respond effectively to changing times. But a more penetrating examination suggests that a lack of flexibility may be an important problem in the local
government area. Central cities sometimes find themselves hemmed in by a
ring of suburban communities that serve as tax shelters for more affluent citizens
and enable these citizens to enjoy the availability of the central city and some
of its services while escaping the obligation to help to pay for them. Thus, the
metropolitan area, which may in fact be a single entity in terms of economic
and social affairs, is fragmented in terms of government responsibilities in such

a way as to render none of the existing governments capable of dealing effectively with situations that confront the area as a whole. In this context, the special district becomes an escape valve that permits some degree of coordination in those services. Thus, the proliferation of special districts, while itself an evidence of flexibility, also suggests that severe problems of inflexibility may exist among the conventional and geographically separate governments.

Chapter 17 offered a model for the allocation of functions in a multigovernment system. The proliferation of special districts illustrates one aspect of this model. Spillovers of benefits or costs are common among local governments, especially in metropolitan areas. These spillovers generate a demand for the relocation of jurisdictional boundaries. The formation of a special district is a boundary relocation limited to some specific government responsibility. Through these special districts, jurisdictional boundaries are brought into better correspondence with the geographical dimensions of benefit from the service. But special districts also illustrate other aspects of the model of local government outlined in Chapter 17. When special districts abound, citizens may find that the complicated organization of local government makes it difficult to be well informed and to vote effectively.

EXPENDITURE AND REVENUE

The magnitude of local government expenditure is impressive. Table 24.2 shows the amounts of direct general expenditures by local governments in the United States for fiscal years that ended between July 1, 1974, and June 30, 1975. General expenditures do not include utility, liquor store, and insurance trust expenditures but do include all other regular or standard spending by government units. The term "direct" denotes that the data do not include expenditures made through grants to other units of government. Local governments do not dispense large grants to other governments, but are the recipients of large amounts of intergovernment revenue. The expenditures listed in Table 24.2 are attributed to the government that received intergovernment money and actually administered the spending. Direct general spending by local governments was greater than the equivalent figure for state governments

TABLE 24.2   Local Government Direct General Expenditure, 1974–75 (millions of dollars)

EXPENDITURE	AMOUNT
Education	$64,956
Public welfare	9,733
Health and hospitals	9,878
Highways	8,270
Police	7,073
Interest on general debt	5,511
Other	37,727
Total	143,148

Source: U.S. Bureau of the Census, Governmental Finances in 1974–75, GF–75 No. 5 (Washington, D.C.: Government Printing Office, 1976), Table 7, p. 21.

(which was $86.3 billion in 1974–75) and also greater than the direct general expenditure of the national government net of spending for national defense and international relations.

Education is the dominant type of expenditure made by local governments, and it is not surprising that school districts are the largest spenders when local direct general expenditures are classified by type of government unit, as is shown in Table 24.3. What this table really shows is that school districts,

TABLE 24.3   Direct Local General Expenditure, by Type of Government, 1974–75 (millions of dollars)

TYPE	AMOUNT
School districts	$52,230
Municipalities	47,963
Counties	30,903
Townships	4,918
Special districts	7,134
Total	143,148

Source: U.S. Bureau of the Census, Governmental Finances in 1974–75, GF–75, No. 5 (*Washington, D.C.: Government Printing Office, 1976*), Table 16, p. 28.

municipalities, and counties are the main spending units of local government in the United States and that a relatively small amount of direct general expenditure is made by townships and special districts. School districts are not general governments, however. They spend only for educational services. Municipalities, counties, and townships are general governments and spend money to finance a wide variety of services, including some expenditures for education.

Table 24.4 shows the sources of the money that finances local government expenditure. Intergovernment revenues are extremely important to all types of local government and provide almost half the funding for counties and school districts. Most intergovernment money comes from the state rather than from

TABLE 24.4   Sources of General Revenue of Local Governments in 1974–75, by Type of Government, as Percentage of Total General Revenue

TYPE	INTER-GOVERN-MENT REVENUE	OWN SOURCES		TOTAL
		PROPERTY TAX	OTHER	
Counties	45%	31%	24%	100%
Municipalities	39	26	35	100
Townships	30	56	14	100
School districts	50	42	8	100
Special districts	37	12	51	100
All local government	42	34	24	100

Source: Computed from U.S. Bureau of the Census, Governmental Finances in 1974–75, GF–75, No. 5 (*Washington, D.C.: Government Printing Office, 1976*), Table 16, p. 28.

the federal government, but special districts are an exception and receive more from the federal government than from the state. "Own source" revenues are dominated by the property tax in school districts and townships, but special districts and municipalities derive less money from property taxation than they do from other internal sources. Both derive sizable amounts of revenue from charges collected from purchasers of services provided by these governments: that is, many of their activities are of a semicommercial or public utility nature. Municipalities are also able to administer sales and income taxes, which generate significant revenue for larger cities.

MUNICIPAL GOVERNMENT FINANCES

Municipal government finances merit special attention in an overview of local government expenditures and revenues. Municipalities are general governments and provide a wide variety of services, which distinguishes them from school and special districts. Also, they are natural focal points of economic activity: that is, they have been established and have grown in certain locations because of economic advantages associated with these locations. This distinguishes them from counties and townships, which owe their existence to the surveyor's rod and transit. Municipalities are open economies, with jurisdiction over rather limited geographic areas. They are continually engaged in somewhat competitive relationships with other municipalities and other government units in nearby areas.

An impression of the diversity of municipal government expenditures is provided in Table 24.5, which lists selected expenditure items and notes the percentage of total general expenditure attributed to each in 1974–75. Aside from expenditures for education, which present a special situation,[2] the only separately classified item to exceed 10 percent of total general expenditure was police protection. City expenditure budgets contain many different items, and

TABLE 24.5   Importance of Selected Items of City Government General Expenditures, 1974–75

ITEM	*PER-CENTAGE*
Education	14.7%
Police	10.8
Public welfare	7.9
Highways	7.9
Fire protection	5.9
Sewerage	7.0
Hospitals	5.6

Source: U.S. Bureau of the Census, City Government Finances in 1974–75, *GF–75, No. 4 (Washington, D.C.: Government Printing Office, 1976), Table 1, p. 5.*

[2] A few major cities, including New York City, finance their public schools through the regular city budget rather than through separate school districts.

no single category of expenditure can be held responsible for the total size of the budget.

Some especially interesting insights about city government finances emerge when selected items of revenue and expenditure are examined in relation to the population size of the city, as in Table 24.6. When these revenue and expenditure data are expressed in per capita amounts, it becomes clear that important differences exist between large, medium size, and small cities. The general impression is that the middle-sized cities (those with populations from 50,000 to 500,000) are not very different from one another in per capita amounts for various revenues and expenditures, but that cities with populations above the half-million mark show significantly larger per capita amounts in most categories of revenue and expenditure.

TABLE 24.6   Per Capita Amounts of Selected City Finance Items, by Population Size Groups, 1974–75 (rounded to nearest dollar)

	POPULATION SIZE						
ITEM	1,000,000 OR MORE	500,000 TO 999,999	300,000 TO 499,999	200,000 TO 299,999	100,000 TO 199,999	50,000 TO 99,999	LESS THAN 50,000
Expenditures							
Total general expenditure	$844	$532	$414	$395	$341	$296	$194
Highways	26	36	26	31	28	30	27
Public welfare	163	46	4	16	7	3	1
Hospitals	79	31	10	11	9	11	8
Health	23	17	8	6	4	2	1
Police protection	73	58	48	40	38	33	25
Revenues							
Intergovernment revenue	438	217	156	154	119	91	63
Property taxes	198	121	91	96	111	101	57
General sales taxes	56	29	20	17	17	17	10
Selective sales taxes	35	22	17	20	11	7	10
Current charges	64	55	56	46	40	67	29

Source: U.S. Bureau of the Census, City Government Finances in 1974–75, *GF–75, No. 4 (Washington, D.C.: Government Printing Office, 1976), Table 4, p. 8.*

The most dramatic instances of high per capita expenditures for the large cities are in the categories of public welfare and hospitals. It is not surprising that large cities also show large per capita amounts for intergovernment revenues, since these revenues are important contributors to the financing of these services. Most of the expenditure categories, however, show higher per capita amounts for the large cities than for the moderate sized cities, and as might be expected, a parallel pattern is apparent in categories of internal revenue sources. The data support the hypothesis that population density increases the quantity of collective consumption. Services that are not demanded at all in sparsely populated areas or that, if demanded, are supplied privately in those areas, appear to become responsibilities of government in densely populated or urbanized areas. It also is possible that the unit costs of providing collective services is greater in large cities than it is in moderate or small cities. Cost differences of this nature would mean that the greater per capita expenditure amounts in large cities overstate the differences between these cities and smaller cities in the actual amounts of collective consumption.

The 1970 census reported that 132 million persons resided in organized municipal areas. Forty-six percent of this total resided in the smallest category of city listed in Table 24.6, that is, they lived in cities with populations of less than 50,000. At the other extreme, 23 percent of this total lived in cities with populations of a half-million or more; the remaining 31 percent lived in the moderate sized cities with populations of between 50,000 and 500,000. Thus, all three general groups are important in the total picture of local government finance in the United States.[3]

SUMMARY

Local governments in the United States include counties, townships, municipalities, school districts, and special districts. Each citizen is likely to be affiliated with several units of local government because these governments are not geographically distinct from one another. Counties, townships, and municipalities are general-purpose governments, whereas school districts and special districts are governments with responsibilities limited to the provision of certain specified services. A degree of flexibility in the organization of local government enables this level of government to respond to changes in the geography of benefits and the costs of the services they provide. Population movements and improved transportation have resulted in a reduction in the number of school districts, but have led to increases in the number of municipalities and special districts. The proliferation of special districts illustrates both the advantages and the problems of a multilevel system of governments.

Direct general spending by local governments is greater than the equivalent figure for state governments or for the federal government if spending for national defense and international relations are subtracted from the latter. Spending for education is the dominant category of local government expenditure. Intergovernment revenue, primarily from state governments, provides an important part of the financing for the services provided by local governments, but internal sources, such as the property tax, are also important. School districts and townships are especially reliant on property taxation for revenue derived from their own internal sources. Municipalities and special districts, on the other hand, are able to generate internal revenues from a wide variety of sources. Fees and charges for services rendered are important for each of these types of local government. Municipalities also can obtain revenue from income or sales taxes.

[3] U.S. Bureau of the Census, *City Government Finances in 1973–74*, GF-74, No. 4 (Washington, D.C.: Government Printing Office, 1975), Table 3, p. 9.

Municipal government finance is especially interesting because of the wide range of services provided and because of the relationships that appear to exist between the size of the city and per capita amounts of revenue and expenditures. Large cities spend considerably more per capita than do medium and small cities, which suggests that the demand for collective services is greater in large cities. The relatively high per capita spending in large cities is especially evident in spending for public welfare, hospitals, health, and police protection.

SUGGESTED READING

National Tax Association–Tax Institute of America Symposium. "Urban Fiscal Problems," *National Tax Journal*, XXIX, 3 (September 1976).

The Bureau of the Census publications cited in this chapter appear annually and may be consulted for up-to-date information on local government finance.

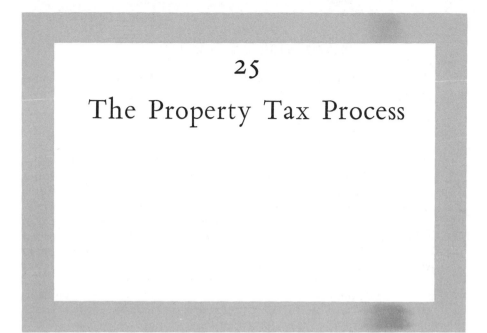

25

The Property Tax Process

The property tax is the basic source of internally generated revenue for local governments in the United States, despite the importance of intergovernment revenues to most governments and of local sales or income tax revenues to some. These other revenues come with strings attached or in insufficient amounts or are simply unavailable because of taxing restrictions imposed by state governments. To the extent that local governments wish to be autonomous and make their own spending decisions, most must turn to the property tax as the major source of revenue.

Over the years, the property tax has repeatedly confounded the predictions of those who concluded that it had reached its limits of revenue capability. Yet the property tax is not a bottomless well; in fact, the limits of the property tax make themselves known through restrictions on the quantity and quality of public services that can actually be rendered by local governments. Because the property tax is well understood and highly responsive to the sentiments of the public, local governments operate under conditions of accountability and restraint unmatched at either the state or the federal levels in the United States.

This chapter outlines the basic procedures generally used in local property taxation and examines the crucially important process of assessment. Subsequent chapters will consider exemptions, modifications of the basic taxing process, and the economic effects of property taxation.

THE BASIC PROCEDURE

The basic property taxing process is quite simple. The sequence of actions that leads to the determination of tax liabilities and the collection of tax revenues is traced in the following steps.

Step 1: What Is Taxable?

State laws specify the types of property that are taxable and the types that are exempt. Local governments do not have control over this important aspect of the process, and some critics contend that state legislators sometimes grant property tax exemptions without adequate consideration of the consequences for the fiscal capability of local governments. State legislation also specifies how properties shall be evaluated for purposes of taxation. As a general rule, the *tax value* of property is defined as the price at which the property would ordinarily be exchanged in a sale between a willing buyer and a willing seller. In some states, tax value is set at some percentage (for example, 50 percent) of the price at which property would exchange, and in a few instances, a classification system is established under which tax value is set at a different percentage of market value for some types of properties than for others.

Step 2: How Much Revenue Will Be Collected?

The amount of revenue to be collected through the property tax is called the property tax *levy*. The levy is determined through the budget deliberations of local government authorities. The various agencies and departments of local government prepare budget requests. These requests are examined and evaluated by the elected officials of the local government, public hearings are held, and a decision is reached on the size of the property tax levy for the coming fiscal year.

Step 3: What Is the Size of the Local Tax Base?

The sum total of the tax values of properties in the local jurisdiction constitutes the property tax base for that jurisdiction. In order to determine the size of the tax base, an *assessment* must be made of the tax value of each parcel of taxable property in the jurisdiction. Clearly, the assessment process is extremely important if the property tax is to be regarded as equitable. After the assessment has been carried out, property owners are notified of the valuation placed on their property and are provided an opportunity to appeal for an adjustment of the assessment before a group of local officials designated as a Board of Review. In addition to the adjustment that may be made by the Board of Review, another adjustment may be necessary through the process of *equalization*, which seeks to ensure that properties in different taxing jurisdictions are actually assessed at the same percentage of market values. In practice, this adjustment is implemented through an *equalization factor* applied to each parcel.

Step 4: What Is the Property Tax Rate?

The property tax rate is determined by dividing the tax lavy of the jurisdiction by the tax base of the jurisdiction. Typically, the property tax rate is expressed in terms of *mils* (or *millage*). A mil is equivalent to a rate of 1/10th of a percent, that is, $1 of tax liability for each $1,000 of tax value. For example, a 20 mil tax rate on full market value would mean that a property assessed at a value of $10,000 would have a tax liability of $200. The property tax is a *flat rate* tax, meaning that the same rate is applied to the tax value of all properties in the jurisdiction, no matter what their value.

It is especially worthwhile to note that the property tax rate is set *after* the government has determined how much money it will spend and that the rate is set so as to yield the amount actually budgeted, no more and no less. This is notably different from the procedure for sales or income taxes, where the rate is predetermined and the amount of money to be collected, rather than the rate of tax, becomes the operational variable. Not only does this property tax procedure heighten citizen interest in the process of budget making, it also increases citizen sensitivity to the granting of exemptions, since an exemption granted to property A must, as a direct consequence, result in a higher tax rate and a higher tax payment from properties B and C.

Step 5: Collecting the Property Tax

After the rate has been determined, statements are prepared for each parcel of property and mailed to the owners of these properties, often with the addition of a collection fee equal to one or two percent of the tax liability. If the tax is not paid by the due date indicated on the statement, penalty charges and interest may be added, usually on a monthly basis, until such time as the tax is paid. If the tax remains unpaid after a legally specified period of time, delinquency proceedings will be undertaken that can lead to a *tax sale* of the property itself. The proceeds of the sale are used to pay government claims for taxes, penalties, and interest due. The delinquency and tax sale procedure illustrates that property taxes are obligations of the property itself rather than obligations of the person who happens to hold title to the property.

ASSESSMENT OF PROPERTY VALUES

Accurate assessment of property value is indispensable to the equitable operation of the property taxing process. Properties of equal value must appear on the tax rolls with equal assessments and properties with different values must appear on these rolls with assessments that correctly reflect these different values. It is the responsibility of the assessing officer to maintain the tax rolls, which list all the taxable properties in the district and record the valuations placed on these properties for tax purposes.

Underassessment and the Assessment Ratio

Statutes typically require that assessment be at full market value or at some specified fraction of full market value, but underassessment is widespread in practice. It is not difficult to understand why this situation prevails. From the point of view of an individual property owner, who ordinarily is not aware of the assessments placed on properties other than his own, a high assessment means a high property tax bill and a low assessment means a low property tax bill.[1] Therefore, if assessments actually were made at 100 percent of market value, a sizable number of property owners would be likely to challenge the assessment, thus increasing the workload and the general unpleasantness of the assessor's task. By routinely making assessments at lower values than those specified in the statutes, the number of challenges can be reduced and the work of the assessor is easier. In fact, when underassessment is practiced, property owners may feel that they are paying less than their share of taxes and that a challenge would reveal the underassessment and result in an increase in tax. Thus, underassessment shields the assessor from a number of taxpayer complaints and helps the process to operate more smoothly, albeit at the expense of some instances of undetected inaccuracy in assessed valuations.

Although underassessment is generally practiced, it does not follow necessarily that property taxes are unfairly divided as a result. It does mean, however, that the property owner must examine the accuracy of the assessment of his property in reference to the *assessment ratio* rather than the actual market value of the property. The assessment ratio is a fraction or percentage determined by dividing the assessed value by the market value of the property in question. For example, a property with an assessed value of $4,000 and a market value of $10,000 has an assessment ratio of 40 percent. In order to determine whether his property is paying its fair share in tax, the owner must compare the assessment ratio for his property with the ratio applied to the other properties in the jurisdiction. His property is fairly assessed if its ratio is the same as the average ratio prevailing in the district. An error in assessment has occurred if the ratio for an individual property is either above or below the ratio for the district.

Sources of Assessment Error

The basic source of error in the assessment process is the difficulty and complexity of the assessment task itself. Properties differ greatly from one another and these differences are difficult to detect and evaluate, even by well-trained and experienced assessors. In many jurisdictions, however, the assessment task is entrusted to a part-time employee who has received little or no training for the job and who may be elected to the position rather than selected on the basis of qualifying examinations. Assessment errors can be reduced if the job is placed in the hands of a full-time, well-trained person. But many tax jurisdictions are small and the assessment job is not big enough to justify the

---

[1] Of course, this perception of the relation between the assessment and the amount of tax liability is not necessarily accurate. If all properties are assessed at high values, the tax rate or millage needed to obtain budgeted funds will be low, and vice versa, so that the level of assessment need not alter the amount of the tax payment.

expense of employing a full-time assessor. Consolidation of assessment districts, at least up to the level where full-time competent assessors can be employed, can improve assessments.

Another source of error lies in the not uncommon practice of copying the assessments from the previous year. This can happen when the assessor is relatively untrained (or underpaid) or when the security of his position is doubtful. Copying old assessment lists leads to a predictable pattern in the errors. When property values are rising, underassessment becomes progressively more severe. Newly constructed properties, or properties that have been subjected to reassessment for some reason, are likely to be overassessed relative to the other properties. A common complaint is that newly constructed properties tend to be overassessed in the property tax system.

Another pattern of assessment error can be attributed to "average consciousness" on the part of poorly trained personnel. Guidebooks or manuals for the assessor may list typical or average values for different types of properties. The assessor may tend to cluster his assessments around these average values. High-value properties then tend to be underassessed relative to low-value properties, leading to a regressive pattern of assessments within classifications. Another viewpoint suggests that the assessor may be a person of relatively modest means who may be unfamiliar with the true values for exceptionally high- or low-value properties. Again, the result may be regressivity among properties. Moreover, if high-value properties are owned by individuals who are prominent or politically powerful in the jurisdiction, the assessor may be tempted to moderate his assessment of these properties.

The assessor must discover taxable property before he can evaluate it, and certain types of property are easier to discover than others. For example, real estate (land and buildings) is relatively easy to discover; personal properties such as farm livestock and machinery, business equipment and inventories, household goods, and intangible properties such as stock, bonds, and mortgages may be difficult to discover. Household goods and intangible properties have been exempted from property tax in many jurisdictions, partly because of the difficulty of discovering these items and partly because of more basic objections to their being taxed as property. The enumeration and evaluation of household goods is complicated and time-consuming, and assessors are sensitive to complaints about snooping into private circumstances. The taxation of intangibles constitutes a kind of double taxation, since both the physical property and the intangible rights to it would be taxed.

Business inventories are taxable in most jurisdictions, but problems can contribute to inequity among different taxpayers. Depending on the nature of the business, inventories may be large or small relative to the volume of final sales. It can be argued that commodities handled by businesses that maintain large inventories relative to final sales are subjected to greater taxation than those handled by businesses that maintain relatively small inventories. Problems also arise when the size of business inventory is subject to considerable variation during the different seasons of the year, since merchants have a tax incentive to manipulate inventories (or move them out of the tax district) to have as small an amount as possible at the time of the assessment. To cope with the problem of fluctuating inventories, assessments may be made at several different times during the year, with the tax based on the average inventory. Since the administrative costs of this procedure would be great, inventory reporting may be entrusted to the merchants themselves, enforced through audits that make use of sales figures adjusted through the application of standard ratios of inventory to sales appropriate to different types of businesses.

The Board of Review

If a property owner believes that his property has been incorrectly assessed, he must initiate a claim for adjustment by bringing his case to the Board of Review, which is a locally appointed body that hears challenges to assessed valuations. The Board of Review will consider appeals only during a limited period of time after assessment notices have been distributed, and it is the responsibility of the property owner to present his request for adjustment during this period. Failure to initiate a challenge during the specified time period operates to prevent any subsequent claim for adjustment.

In considering whether to appeal his assessment to the Board of Review, the property owner should begin by discovering what the average assessment ratio is in the jurisdiction and should supplement his case, if possible, by citing assessments applied to other properties which he alleges are equivalent in market value to his own. The importance of submitting a well-documented case is reinforced by recognition that the Board of Review may be reluctant to grant adjustments, since relief granted to one taxpayer constitutes an invitation to other property owners to seek similar relief. If assessments are shown to have been faulty in a significant number of cases, the data on which to base adjustments become suspect and a general reassessment may be required. If this happens, the local government may negotiate a contract with an appraisal firm (ordinarily from outside the jurisdiction) to make a general reassessment of all properties in the jurisdiction. Expenses are incurred and many complications arise because of the delays involved.

Measuring the Quality of Assessment

The quality of assessment can be measured through the use of a statistical device known as a _coefficient of dispersion_. First, a sales survey is made of market values revealed by actual transactions between willing buyers and sellers in the district during a recent period of time. For each property in the survey, an assessment ratio is determined by dividing assessed value by sale value. Next, the average assessment percentage for all the properties in the survey is determined by dividing the total assessed value by the total market value. The deviation of each individual percentage from the average percentage is computed; these individual percentage point deviations are added together (ignoring plus or minus signs); and the total percentage point deviation is divided by the number of properties to determine the average percentage point deviation. Finally, the average percentage point deviation is divided by the average assessment percentage (ratio) to determine the coefficient of dispersion. The following example illustrates the procedure, assuming only three properties in the survey.

	PROP-ERTY A	PROP-ERTY B	PROP-ERTY C	Total
Assessed value	$10,000	$15,000	$20,000	$45,000
Market value	$15,000	$30,000	$45,000	$90,000
Assessment ratio	67%	50%	44%	50%
Deviations (in percentage points)	17	0	6	23
Average deviation (23/3)				7.67
Coefficient of dispersion (7.67/.50)				15.3

In this example, property A is seriously overassessed and would pay a tax 34 percent greater than it should, since 67 is 34 percent more than 50 percent. Property B is correctly assessed and is paying its fair share of the property tax. Property C is underassessed; its tax is 12 percent below its fair share. The coefficient of dispersion does not reveal how many or which properties are incorrectly assessed, nor are there any established criteria to indicate when a coefficient of dispersion is so high as to be unacceptable. The 15.3 coefficient shown in the example is lower than those achieved in many jurisdictions in the United States. It is clear, however, that assessment which results in liabilities incorrect on the average by 15.3 percent reflects a rather low standard of fairness among properties. Internal inequities in property taxation are among the major complaints about this tax.

Equalization of Assessments

Fairness of property tax assessment is achieved *within* an assessment district when all properties in that district have been assessed at the same percentage of their true market value. It makes no real difference whether the assessment ratio that actually prevails is 40, 50, or 100 percent. But the average assessment ratio of the district does make a difference when property tax revenues from several assessment districts are combined to finance some common undertaking (such as a school district) or when funds from a higher level of government are distributed to local districts on the basis of local property values (as with state school aid programs). Because these interdistrict money transfers are common practice, it becomes necessary to ensure that the average assessment ratios in the different districts are equal to one another. *Equalization* is the procedure which adjusts the average assessment ratios of local districts so that they are brought into conformity with one another. It is important to note that equalization adjusts only the average assessment ratio and does nothing to correct inequities between one property and another inside any single assessment district.

The basic step in equalization is a study of prices paid in property exchanges that have taken place in the district during a recent time period. The values revealed in the study are compared to the assessment made by the local assessor, and the average assessment ratio for the district is determined. An *equalization factor* is then determined that will bring the average assessment ratio of the district into line with the average ratios in other districts or with the ratio specified in state legislation. For example, suppose the sales study reveals that assessments in a given district are at 40 percent of market value while the standard to be applied throughout the state is 50 percent of market value. An equalization factor of 1.25 would be determined, and the assessed value of each parcel in the district would be multiplied by this factor to bring tax values into conformity with the state standard. If similar procedures are applied in other districts, the average tax value in all districts would be at the standard 50 percent level.

The importance of the equalization procedure may be seen through a brief summary of several forces that may encourage local assessors to make assessments at something other than the generally prescribed ratio. The school district example has already been noted. If the same school millage is to apply to the several assessment areas in the school district, local assessors may be tempted to underassess and thus reduce the payment required from their area. If all the assessment areas engage in this strategy, a situation known as *competitive underassessment* exists, and equalization is important to maintain order in the taxing process. Another temptation to competitive underassessment arises when state-to-local aid formulas include an ability factor based on property valuations. Underassessment can increase the local area's entitlement under such a formula.

Some situations encourage local assessors to overvalue properties. Property tax rate ceilings sometimes are established by state laws. By increasing the assessment ratio, the local assessor can permit more revenue to be collected from a given rate, and the effect of the rate ceiling can be avoided. Similarly, state laws or credit rating systems may relate the amount of borrowing that can be undertaken by the locality to the value of taxable property in that locality. By increasing the assessment ratio, the local assessor can alter the impact of these arrangements.

Still another force may persuade the local assessor to raise or lower the average assessment ratio: a situation in which property tax exemptions, such as homestead exemptions, are expressed in terms of certain dollar amounts of valuation. If an exemption exists for, say, the first $5,000 of tax value, a low assessment ratio will increase the real impact of the exemption, whereas a high assessment ratio will decrease the real impact of the exemption. That is, a larger fraction of total value will be exempted with a low assessment ratio.

Finally, it should be noted that equalization can ease the task of the individual property owner considering whether or not to seek an adjustment before the Board of Review. When the equalization factor has been applied to his assessment, he is in a better position to determine the actual assessment ratio in his area and whether or not his property has been overassessed. Of course, equalization does not automatically correct for faulty individual assessments inside a district, but it may indirectly improve the quality of these assessments by facilitating the calculations of both the individual taxpayer and the Board of Review.

STRENGTHS AND WEAKNESSES

The basic property taxing process is simple and well understood by most citizens. The inherent difficulty and the consequent inaccuracy of the assessment process is clearly a weakness of the property tax, but the fact remains that most citizens are well informed about how much they must pay, why they must pay, and what the money will be used for. Moreover, the total millage or tax rate imposed on property is usually printed on the tax statement and broken down into its several components, so that the property owner can determine the amount being paid for the support of specific activities carried out by the government. As a result, the property tax promotes the development of a vigilant group of citizens who subject government decisions to careful examination and who actively participate in the decision-making process. In the context of participatory democracy, these features are strong arguments in support of property taxation.

But the weaknesses and deficiencies of the property tax also are significant. With the passage of time, property values have become increasingly less adequate measures of ability to pay, and with the proliferation of services rendered by local governments, the connection between the value of property and the benefits of public services has become weaker and weaker. Criticism of the property taxes focuses on the narrowness of the tax base in relation to ability to pay and benefits received (a problem that has increased in severity as more and more property types have been exempted from the tax), and on the economic effects of the tax, which are seen as distorting both the allocation of resources and the location of economic activity, and generally as contributing to the complex of problems confronting central cities and their relations to surrounding areas.

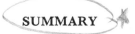

SUMMARY

The basic property taxing process is simple and straightforward. The amount of money to be collected (the *levy*) is determined when the local budget is adopted. The tax base is determined by local assessors in accordance with state rules governing the taxability and tax value of property. The rate of tax is calculated by dividing the levy by the tax base. The tax obligation is on the property itself, rather than on the person who owns the property, and the collection procedure may culminate in the sale of the property in order to fulfill the tax obligation.

Accurate *assessment* of property values is fundamental to fairness in property taxation, but this is a complicated and difficult task. Property owners may appeal to the local Board of Review for correction of assessment errors. The *coefficient of dispersion* measures the quality of the work done by the assessor. Underassessment, which is a common practice in property taxation, does not necessarily lead to inequity among properties, but it does make it more difficult for the property owner to decide whether to appeal to the Board of Review. Underassessment can result in unfair distribution of state aid money among localities and to unfair allocations of financial responsibilities when several assessing districts contribute to the support of some common undertaking. *Equalization* is carried out in order to ensure that the same assessment ratio is applied in each district.

Several features of the property tax process promote active citizen participation in government decision making. The relative simplicity of the process means that most taxpayers can calculate the amount of their own contribution to the support of the various services provided by local government. It is especially significant that the tax rate (*millage*) is determined *after* the budget or levy has been established. This means that citizens realize that active participation in the budget process can lead directly to changes in the tax rate and the amount of their tax liabilities. The weaknesses of the property tax, on the other hand, lie in the probability that property values and tax liabilities may not be well correlated either with ability to pay or with benefits received from services rendered by local government.

SUGGESTED READINGS

LINDHOLM, RICHARD W. (ed.). *Property Taxation USA*, (Madison: University of Wisconsin Press, 1969). In this volume, see especially: Arthur D. Lynn, Jr., "Property Tax Development: Selected Historical Perspectives"; John Shannon, "Conflict between State Assessment Law and Local Assessment Practice"; and Paul E. Alyea, "Property Tax Inducements to Attract Industry."

U.S. Department of Commerce, Bureau of the Census. "Taxable Property Values and Assessment-Sales Price Ratios—Assessment-Sales Price Ratios and Tax Rates," *1972 Census of Governments*, Vol. 2, Part 2, (Washington, D.C.: Government Printing Office, 1973).

ENGLE, ROBERT F. "De Facto Discrimination in Residential Assessments: Boston," *National Tax Journal*, XVIII (December 1975), pp. 445–51.

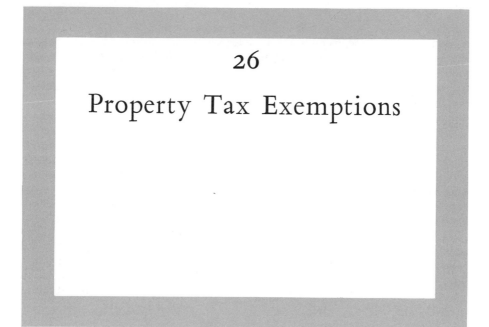

26

Property Tax Exemptions

State legislation specifies the types of property that shall be subject to taxation and those that shall be exempt. Sometimes these specifications are set forth in the constitution of the state. Thus, although property tax rates are set at the local level, decisions about which properties shall be exempt and which shall be taxable are made at the state level. Exemptions are important because they have a lot to do with the amount of revenue that can be generated by the tax, with its economic effects, and with the equity or fairness of the allocation of liabilities. But there also is a dynamic dimension to the question of property tax exemptions. Progressive erosion of the tax base may take place if exemptions or favorable treatments are extended to more and more types of property. Erosion of the tax base is a kind of nibbling at the fringes of the tax through a process in which each exemption granted provides an argument in favor of further exemption, since, at the margin, each advocate of exemption can point out that little distinction can be made between the exemption previously granted and the one he now seeks.

Tax base erosion is not unique to the property tax (the income tax apparently experiences the same phenomenon), but it has a particularly sharp cutting edge because of several features unique to property taxation. Because property tax rates are set *after* the levy has been determined, exemptions have a direct impact on nonexempt properties through higher rates. The result is an increase in the incentive for these other properties also to seek special advantages. Because local governments are open economies, rate differences stimulate competitive pressures for property tax exemptions. Also, there is a separation between the level of government that grants exemptions and the level that suffers the revenue consequences of these exemptions. State legislators may grant politically attractive exemptions without necessarily unbalancing the budget of the state government. If the erosion process is carried too far, the tax itself may fall into disrepute as capricious, inequitable, or excessively subject to political manipulation by narrow interest groups. The property tax, like the income tax, may be in danger of being undermined.

Basic provisions governing property taxation sometimes specify that the tax shall be both "universal" and "uniform." These are expressions of what might constitute an ideal system. Universality suggests that all types of property should be subjected to tax, but a truly universal property tax has never been achieved in practice, and in fact it is difficult to contemplate what such a tax would be like. Early property taxes in New England included a person's earning potential, or "faculty," in the property tax base, so that the tax included assessment of human capital and thus was first cousin to income taxation. The uniformity provision requires that the same rate of tax shall be applied to all taxable property and precludes the possibility of using variable tax rates. The combination of universality and uniformity gives property taxation an "all or nothing" flavor and focuses attention on exemptions and the definition of property.

EXEMPTIONS FOR ADMINISTRATIVE CONVENIENCE

Assessment is a crucial and expensive step in the taxing process, and for some types of property, the cost of assessment (both political and pecuniary) may exceed the revenues that can be obtained. Moreover, if the assessment task is especially difficult or onerous, the result may be halfhearted, piecemeal, or based on a "what the traffic will bear" philosophy. The tax may become grossly inequitable or a tax on the honesty or candor of the taxpayer. *Household personal property* is exempted from tax in most jurisdictions on the grounds that it is difficult to locate and evaluate, that little revenue is actually realized, and that many citizens object to the invasion of privacy. *Intangible personal property*, such as stocks, bonds, and mortgages, is generally exempted from tax because it can easily be concealed from the assessor and because taxation would involve a kind of double taxation, since both the item itself and the intangible ownership rights in the property would be taxed. Another instance of an exemption based on administrative considerations arises in the case of automobiles, which are sometimes exempted from the general property tax on the ground that the annual license fee may include a quasi-property tax element through the use of such value-related variables as weight, model, and age of the vehicle.

As a practical matter, no serious objection can be raised to exemptions based on genuine administrative difficulties, although the seriousness of omissions that arise from this factor should not be underrated. The exemption of automobiles from property taxation is particularly difficult to defend. Human capital ("faculty") is no longer taxed as property, but investments in human capital are of major importance in the modern economy, and the omission of this type of wealth from taxation does impart a kind of inequity to the operation of the tax.

EXEMPTIONS BASED ON PUBLIC POLICY

The exemptions that generate the most controversy and that most directly involve the problem of erosion of the tax base are those based on a political conclusion that certain activities or property uses should be encouraged because there is a significant collective good component in the production generated by these uses. Two important questions are raised by exemptions granted on this basis, which in effect grant a subsidy to specified uses: (1) Is there, in fact, a collective good component in the output of the favored use that justifies the amount of the subsidy conveyed by the exemption? If errors are made in this calculation, resource allocation will be distorted. (2) What group of taxpayers should pay the increased taxes needed to finance the subsidy? Property tax exemption means that the subsidy is paid by properties that have not been granted exemptions. The incidence or burden of such subsidies is decidedly different from that which would arise if the subsidy were financed through income or sales taxes.

Exemptions for Government Property

Government-owned properties are exempt from local property taxes. Historically, the base for this exemption has been the view that it would be a breach of sovereignty for the nation or a state to permit its instrumentalities to be subject to taxation by another government. Of course, it would seem to make little sense for a local government to subject its own properties to its own taxation. But the amount of government-owned property has increased steadily and significantly over the years, so that these exemptions imply a great loss of potential revenue, especially in urban areas. Moreover, government properties require and receive many local services, such as fire and police protection, so that a strong case exists for some payments to local governments from these properties. Payments *in lieu of taxes* sometimes are made to compensate local governments for the costs of services rendered to tax-exempt government properties.

The question of whether government properties should be subject to local taxation in the same manner as other local properties points up an especially interesting dimension of the collective good case for property tax exemption. It can hardly be argued that government properties do not produce collective goods, but the exemption question cannot be resolved with this conclusion alone. If the collective good output of the government property accrues primarily to the benefit of the local population, exemption would be quite acceptable, since the local rate increase that follows from the exemption could be viewed as a means of paying for the benefits received from the exempt property. But if the property provides collective goods that generate benefits which accrue to the nation as a whole or to a substantial region beyond that of the local government itself, there would seem little reason why local properties should be called upon to finance these benefits to outsiders. A counterargument exists, however. The location of government facilities in a community may trigger multiplier effects that increase employment, business activity, and property values throughout the community. These effects may be capitalized into higher real estate values in the community, which may offset or prevent the higher property tax rates that otherwise might be the result of the exemption.

Exemptions for Religion and Philanthropy

The exemption of properties used for religious and philanthropic purposes has become increasingly controversial as property tax rates have increased and the demands for local government services have expanded, since properties of great value are exempted on these grounds. The problem is compounded by the fact that these exempted properties tend to be concentrated in more urban areas, where fiscal pressures are especially great.

The basic case for exemption is that these properties are employed in the production of collective goods, and the implication is that government itself would be called upon to provide these collective goods and services if private agencies were not willing and able to do so. Thus, the granting of exemption reflects the view that private management of the provision of these collective goods and services is preferable and also the view that property tax exemption is an effective and equitable means of securing the provision of collective goods without the direct intervention of government.

Quite apart from the question of the appropriateness of the subsidies themselves and of using the property tax exemption as the means of providing them, a number of practical difficulties arise in the implementation of exemptions for religious and philanthropic properties. Religious and philanthropic organizations may engage in a variety of activities, only some of which generate collective goods. Drawing the line between property uses that justify exemption and those that do not is an exceedingly difficult and delicate task. If a specific parcel of property is used exclusively for a specific purpose, a decision can be made and exemption can be granted or denied on that basis. Churches, for example, sometimes voluntarily pay taxes on the parsonage or residence of the minister while at the same time accepting exempt status for the church building itself. But when a parcel of property is put to a variety of uses, as is often the case, the operation of the property tax requires that it be either completely exempted or fully taxed, depending on the type of use which predominates. Many civic and fraternal organizations serve the private enjoyments of their members ("good times") and also engage in "good works," but the proportion that must go to good works, and the definition of good works, are difficult questions to resolve.

Exemption of properties used for religious purposes is an especially sensitive area in view of the prohibition in the U.S. Constitution of laws relating to the establishment of religion. Exemption requires some enactments or judicial determinations separating those activities that constitute religion from those that do not. Organized religion is a beneficiary of the exemption, although an individual's private religion might qualify as education or philanthropy. Atheists may complain that their more organized competition is provided with a special advantage through the exemption.

A side effect of exemption that is becoming recognized as a difficult problem is the encouragement it offers for land speculation. Property taxes are an important cost to a person or group interested in holding land in the expectation that it may be sold at high prices at some future time. By reducing these costs, property tax exemption poses a temptation for religious and philanthropic organizations to think in terms of land value speculation, even when the current use of the land is clearly in the collective good category. The fact that such organizations also are exempt from income tax on capital gains compounds the temptation. A resolution of the problem is extremely difficult, however, because of the near impossibility of separating speculative use from current physical use of the property.

Exemptions for Business

It has become common practice for local governments to attempt to encourage business or industrial activities to locate within their jurisdictions by granting favorable property tax treatment to these enterprises. Business inducement exemptions may be accomplished extralegally through "understandings" that significant underassessment will be practiced for the properties involved or permitted under authority of state laws allowing this practice. Alternatively, business inducements may be provided through favorable lease terms for government-owned commercial or industrial facilities.

Legally, the problem of business inducement exemptions involves the use of public or government funds for private purposes. In order to avoid the illegality of diverting public funds to private purposes, some evidence must be submitted that securing the location of the business or industry in the community would serve a public purpose. Additional employment opportunity to the local population is often used to show public purpose; economic development and industrial diversification are also considered as a public interest. Landowners are likely to benefit from successful economic development through an increase in land values. Providers of labor services who are located in the community at the time the development takes place may also benefit from the increased demand for their services, although this benefit may be of temporary duration since an additional labor supply may migrate to the community if rewards are attractive.

There are important limitations and hazards involved in the use of business inducement exemptions. Property taxes are not the only cost confronted by the potential business entrant, and variations in taxes may not significantly influence the location decision. If the business does move in after the exemption has been granted, it may not be clear whether the tax reduction was the operational variable or whether the business would have come anyway, so that the community may have sacrificed tax revenues to no net advantage. If the tax reduction was the operationally significant variable, the community may have subjected itself to a continuing threat that the business may move away if the exemption is removed or if some other community makes a still more attractive offer. Loss of an existing business ordinarily creates more hardship to the community than failure to obtain the business in the first place, so that tax-attracted businesses hold a trump card and can subject the community to a kind of economic blackmail. Moreover, tax differences are most likely to be location-determining variables in choices between a given community and its immediately surrounding suburbs, since nontax costs are more likely to be similar between these locations than between these locations and more distant sites. Business inducement exemptions thus become a part of the complex of problems relating to the city and its suburbs.

The collective service case for property tax exemption becomes especially tenuous if the advantage realized by one community is matched by the hardship suffered by another. Clearly, competition among communities through property tax exemptions for business is an open invitation to erosion of the property tax base. Vigorous competition may result in very little actual relocation of business and may simply reduce effective property tax rates for those businesses especially sensitive to these inducements.

Benefit-cost analysis provides a strikingly different perspective on intercommunity competition for business through the granting of property tax exemptions. Recall that the theory of efficient taxation and decision making indicates that the tax price charged to a particular taxpayer should be equal to the marginal benefit that the taxpayer enjoys from collective services and also equal to the marginal cost of providing these collective services. The eagerness of communities to attract businesses implies that tax prices may be above the marginal cost of providing collective services to these businesses, and the eagerness of business to respond to offers of tax concessions implies that tax prices (at normal rates) are above their marginal valuation of collective services. In other words, normal tax rates (tax prices) may not be efficient in terms of the model. The interest both in offering and in accepting tax concessions suggests that the normal tax rate does not provide an equilibrium solution. Competition for business location can be a constructive phenomenon if it provides a move toward a new and more efficient equilibrium. Of course, care must be taken by the community in offering business inducement exemptions. Some businesses may impose costs on the community that exceed the tax revenue which would be realized from their presence, so that a business inducement exemption would be both counterproductive in terms of resource allocation efficiency and financially unwise for the community. Exemption is a kind of forced investment imposed on the general property taxpayers of the community, and some such investments may be nonprofitable.

Exemptions and Rebates for Housing

The impact of property taxation on housing has been recognized for a long time. As property tax rates increase (partly due to the exemption of other properties), the demand for tax relief for housing also increases. One form of property tax relief designed to aid residential housing is the *homestead exemption*. In original homestead exemption laws, a homestead was a residential property occupied by its owner. Supporters of these laws contended that home ownership was a desirable characteristic for the community, since homeowners were alleged to take better care of property, thus maintaining property values throughout the community. As might be expected, the chief objection to the homestead exemption arose because the tax burden lifted from the favored (homeowning) groups was absorbed by other properties, such as nonresidential properties and residential properties occupied by tenants. Assuming that the total tax levy remained the same, a reduction in the tax base through exemptions granted to homeowners meant that the tax rate would be higher, thus increasing the liability of properties not granted the exemption. Even if it were agreed that the exemption effectively encouraged home ownership and that this in turn resulted in community betterment, it was doubtful that the cost of these improvements should be borne disproportionately by tenant-occupied housing and the nonresidential segments of the tax base. Moreover, if tenants as a group have lower incomes than homeowners, there was a serious question of vertical equity involved in these homestead exemptions.

In more modern homestead exemption laws, the ownership requirement has been eliminated and the exemptions have covered all residential properties. This eliminates many of the equity objections to the older versions of the homestead exemption concept, although the exemptions still operate to increase tax rates on nonresidential properties.

More selective forms of property tax exemption for housing are those granted to specified groups in the population, such as veterans, the aged, or low-income families. In contrast to the community betterment theme, these selective exemptions suggest that the beneficiary groups are, for some reason, entitled to special assistance. An exemption for veterans, for example, may be a kind of deferred compensation for military service; exemption for low-income families may be a means of income redistribution; and exemption for the elderly may be a recognition that inflation and rising tax rates impose especially difficult burdens on people with fixed incomes. As in the case of homestead exemptions, the chief objection to these systems is simply that nonexempt properties are singled out to bear a disproportionate share of the cost of the benefits granted to the favored groups. Moreover, since the state legislatures grant the exemptions, the charge is made that state legislators are granting subsidies paid not out of state-collected funds, but out of funds that otherwise would go to local governments. As a matter of both equity and efficiency, it is contended that direct subsidies to aid selected groups would be preferable and that the funds to support these subsidies should be raised through general taxes applicable to the entire population.

In recent years, states have responded to demands for property tax relief for housing by providing credits against state income tax liabilities. The amount of credit is determined by formulas that include the income level of the taxpayer and the amount of property tax paid, either directly or as a part of rent payments. Cash payments are made to those whose income tax liability is less than the amount of the property tax credit. Thus, both owner-occupied and tenant-occupied properties receive some relief, although in some cases, the relief is available only to selected groups, such as the elderly. The income tax credit procedure has the advantage of offering property tax relief without triggering erosion of the local property tax base and without placing a disproportionate burden on properties not eligible for relief.

PARTIAL EXEMPTIONS AND VARIABLE TAX RATES

Uniformity provisions in property taxation, which require that all properties shall be subjected to the same tax rate, have proved to be uncomfortable in some situations and may have encouraged erosion of the tax base, since "all or nothing" exemption decisions may create net subsidies or inequities that antagonize other property owners and encourage them to seek equivalent treatment. Partial exemption systems or variable tax rate systems may, it is contended, lessen the erosion-encouraging aspect of the all or nothing approach and produce a more equitable and stable system. Classified property taxation, use value taxation, and variable tax rates based on public services actually received are attempts to develop more or less general systems for increased flexibility in property taxation.

Classified Property Taxes

Under a *classified* property tax system, legislative action specifies that the tax value for some classes or types of properties shall be a different percentage of market value than it is for other classes of properties. For example, mineral lands or deposits may carry a tax value equal to 100 percent of their market value; urban real estate may carry a tax value of 60 percent of market value; rural real estate may have a tax value of 40 percent of market value; urban personal properties may have a tax value of 30 percent of market value, and rural personal properties may have a tax value of 20 percent of market value. The effect of differential tax values is to impose different effective rates on the different classes of property when all are subjected to the same nominal rate on tax value.

A number of considerations are submitted to justify the deviations from uniformity involved in classified property tax systems. One of these relates to a property to income ratio. For example, supporters of this view observe that generally lower incomes prevail among farmers and suggest that properties related to agricultural activity should therefore be taxed at lower rates. In one sense, this view reveals a preference for income taxation rather than property taxation. But there is a basic fallacy in the property to income ratio argument. The income-generating capacity of property is what determines its market value. That is, the amount people are willing to pay to acquire the property provides a good indication of the present value of the anticipated stream of future net income from the property. In a reasonably competitive situation, market values will arrange themselves in such a way as to equalize the rates of return on market value. Differential tax treatment is not needed to bring tax liabilities into line with the income-generating capacity of the property. Moreover, differential property taxation would alter anticipated net (after-tax) income and would be capitalized into property values. Thus, differential property taxation would alter the allocation of resources by channeling greater amounts into the favored areas. In effect, the introduction of differential taxation would bring windfall gains or losses to the present owners of properties that experience a change in effective tax rates.

A more defensible case for classified property taxation lies in the benefit-received or cost-benefit approach to taxation. Government services may yield greater benefits to some property types than to others, and where such differences can be identified, an economic case can be made for differential treatment. If the tax rate exceeds the marginal benefits received by certain property types, some adjustment may be appropriate. One such adjustment would be to reduce tax rates to a level matching the level of marginal benefit. If differential taxation devices that match differential benefits can be fashioned, a more efficient allocation of resources would be the result.

Experience with classified property tax systems has led to recommendations against extension of the device. The complaint has been that the legal tax values become political footballs and that the outcomes of the political process are more likely to reflect tax exploitation by powerful coalitions than differences in benefit from collective services. However, this line of argument, which casts doubt on the ability of the political process to devise an efficient tax system, is an oversimplification of the problem. Decision making about taxes and the supply of collective services is inherently political. The root of the problem is the extent to which legislatures should be permitted to exercise discretion in setting tax rates and the extent to which they should be bound or constrained by general rules, such as the rule of uniformity in property taxation. If a classified property tax system would lead only to tax exploitation by powerful coalitions, then discretion should not be permitted and the legislature should be constrained by simple and general rules. The choice between discretion and rules is pervasive in the political process and the best balance depends on the issues involved and on the quality of the legislature itself.

Variable Property Tax Rates

Variable property taxes deviate from the traditional uniformity criteria by subjecting different properties to different rates. They are first cousins to classified property taxes, but the difference is that the rate of tax, rather than the tax value, is the device for differential treatment. Assessment and the determination of tax values are carried out in the usual way, but the millage or tax rate imposed on properties is variable depending on whether or not the property actually receives the full complement of services provided by the local government. Variable property taxes are less subject to political manipulation than classified property taxes because more explicit criteria are used in determining when different rates will be imposed. Certain types of government services, such as fire protection, police protection, street lighting, and sanitation servies, are rather clearly related to property values. When such services are financed through property taxes, a strong case can be made that those properties which do not receive the service should be exempted from that part of the total millage levied to finance the service. A system of direct user charges might provide an even better solution to the problems that arise when properties receive different amounts of service, but if a user charge system is not applied, a system of variable property tax rates can improve both the equity and the efficiency of property taxation.

A particularly attractive application of the variable property tax system arises in metropolitan areas when annexations to the central city are attempted or accomplished before the full range of city services can be extended to the annexed area. Residents of an area will stoutly resist annexation if it will result in an immediate increase in tax liabilities but in delayed or problematical receipt of increased services. Thus, variable property taxation could moderate some of the difficulties that arise in attempts to expand jurisdictions and coordinate government programs in metropolitan areas.

Use Value Assessment

Use value assessments determine the tax value of property according to the use currently being made of the property. Market value assessments, on the other hand, consider alternative uses and, in fact, evaluate the property according to its value in its most profitable use, regardless of the use currently being made. Consequently, a use value assessment will be either equal to or lower than the market value assessment for any given property. A change from a market value to a use value system will mean a reduction in tax for those properties not presently in their most profitable uses, as determined by ordinary market forces. It is apparent that a general change to a use value assessment system would be a radical departure from existing property tax procedures and that it would eliminate the pressure that property taxation exerts in forcing properties into their most profitable uses in the market system.

A complete conversion to a use value system has seldom been advocated, but strong pressures have been mobilized to apply the system to land used for agriculture. Several states do in fact assess land used for agriculture on the basis of its agricultural value. In these states, land used for agricultural purposes is valued according to the discounted or capitalized value of future net incomes from agricultural use or according to the price that would be paid in an exchange in which the land would continue to be used for agriculture for a long period of time.

Use value assessment for agricultural land usually is advocated for the fringes of growing urban areas, where land values may rise markedly as possibilities for profitable urban or industrial uses appear. The increased tax liabilities that follow upon the increased market values put pressure on farm operators, whose money income from agriculture may not be sufficient to permit them to pay the taxes. Farmers complain that the taxes force them off the land. A change to a use value system removes the pressure and permits farming operations to continue longer than otherwise.

Supporters of agricultural value assessment observe that idle land exists on the fringes of growing urban areas and suggest that use value assessment for land in agricultural use would encourage the continued cultivation of this land up to the time it is actually converted to a different use. Of course "idle" urban fringe land is ordinarily being used for speculation, so that use value taxation permits the farmer to engage in this speculation while continuing an agricultural occupation, or encourages the speculator to become a farmer in order to reduce the costs of holding the land.

Opponents of the agricultural use value assessment submit that its effect is to retard or postpone the development of land into more productive uses by increasing the holding power of land speculators. Whether this retarding effect would constrain the development of urban sprawl or whether it would lead to leapfrog development is debatable. Opponents also point out that a workable definition of agricultural use is difficult to establish and that the minimum agricultural use permitted by the law is likely to become the common practice in fringe areas where land speculation is a dominant consideration. How many head of livestock must be grazed per acre of land in order for the land to be deemed as being in agricultural use? The quality of the land and the type of livestock become legislative and legal questions.

The inability of a genuine farmer to support increased tax payments while continuing in agriculture is a liquidity problem rather than a problem of ability to pay. If market values have increased, the wealth position of the farmer has improved, but the gain is in the form of higher land value rather than in the form of money with which to pay the taxes. The liquidity problem could be met through borrowing, using the higher land values as collateral, but interest costs would be incurred. One variation on the agricultural use value system suggests that tax liabilities be computed both on the market value and on the agricultural use value basis, but that the payment of the difference in tax liability be postponed until the property is actually converted to non-agricultural use. At the time of this conversion, the postponed tax liability plus accumulated interest on the postponed liabilities would be payable.

The postponement version of the agricultural use value system carries with it some interesting side effects in respect to urban expansion and to the financial affairs of local government. As has been noted, the tax postponement strengthens the hand of the speculator-farmer and could delay development or lead to leapfrog patterns of development. But the longer the postponement operates for a given property and the greater the difference between use and market value, the greater becomes the interest of the public treasury in the actual conversion of the land to a nonagricultural use. The disquieting aspects of this prospect have led to limitations on the number of years of back-tax differential that would become payable on conversion. A three-year rollback limit significantly reduces the difference between postponement systems and outright use value assessment systems. Some state systems also include provisions aimed at insuring that the benefits of use value assessment are reserved for genuine farmers and do not accrue to persons who are primarily speculators in land values. These provisions require that a person obtain some stated portion of his income from agriculture in order to qualify for agricultural use value assessment and taxation.

SUMMARY

Decisions that determine the types of property which shall be taxable and the types which shall be exempt are made at the state government level, even though the tax is administered at the local level and provides the basic source of local internal revenue. Property tax rates differ from one locality to another, but inside each local jurisdiction, a uniform rate is applied to all taxable property (except in the relatively few jurisdictions where variable property tax systems are permitted). Therefore, exemption from the property tax historically has been the procedure used to provide relief. Erosion of the property tax base occurs if the granting of one exemption leads to the granting of other exemptions. Exemptions granted to certain types of property lead to higher rates on the remaining taxable property and increase the pressure for more exemptions.

Some exemptions are granted because administration of the tax would be difficult and because little revenue could be collected. The exemption of household personal property illustrates this situation. Other exemptions are based on a legislative (public policy) conclusion that collective services are being provided by properties devoted to certain uses and that these uses may be encouraged through exemption from the property tax. Government-owned properties and properties devoted to religious or philanthropic uses are exempted on this basis. Exemptions granted to encourage business and industry to locate in a community are based on the conclusion that economic diversification and expanded employment opportunities serve a public purpose and therefore may be promoted through property tax exemptions. Residential housing is an important part of the tax base in most communities, and demands for tax relief have resulted in the enactment of rebate systems through which a portion of the property tax paid is returned to the taxpayer, either through credits against state income taxes or as direct cash rebates. Property tax rebate systems do not erode the local tax base because the money to finance the rebates comes from the state treasury. Thus, rebates or crediting systems should be distinguished from exemptions.

Classified property taxes, variable property taxes, and use value assessment systems are departures from the traditional uniformity criterion in property taxation. Each of these systems permits the effective rate of tax on some types of property to be different from the effective rate on other types of property. Classified property taxes accomplish this result by specifying different tax values for different types of property. Variable property taxes permit different millage or tax rates to be applied to different types of property. Use value assessment, which is permitted for agricultural property in some states, permits property to be assessed for tax purposes on the basis of its actual current use rather than on the basis of its market value in an unrestricted sale.

SUGGESTED READINGS

PETERSON, GEORGE E. (ed.). *Property Tax Reform* (Washington, D.C.: The Urban Institute, 1973).

U.S. Department of Commerce, Bureau of the Census. "Taxable Property Values and Assessment-Sales Price Ratios—Taxable and Other Property Values," in *1972 Census of Governments*, Vol. 2, Part I (Washington, D.C,: Government Printing Office, 1973).

BENDICK, MARC, JR. "Designing Circuit Breaker Property Tax Relief," *National Tax Journal*, XXVII (March 1974), pp. 19–29.

27

Property Tax Incidence, Effects, and Reform

Property taxation is employed by thousands of units of government throughout the United States, and the tax generates substantial amounts of revenue year after year. Obviously, it is important to have some idea about how the incidence of this tax is distributed among different groups of people and about how this tax produces economic effects on the allocation of resources in the economy. Analysis of the incidence and effects of property taxation is complicated by the fact that the rates of tax and the definitions of the tax base differ among the jurisdictions using the tax. It is convenient, however, to begin with the modern general model of property tax incidence.

INCIDENCE

The modern analysis of the incidence of the property tax is similar to the analysis presented earlier of the incidence of the corporation income tax. That is, the property tax is viewed as a tax on particular types of capital which is diffused, through the operations of the markets for capital, until it becomes a tax on all capital. In Figure 27.1, the amount of capital existing in the economy is shown on the horizontal axis and is allocated between those types subject to tax and those not subject to tax. If no tax were imposed, the rate of return to capital would be OR and the existing stock of capital would be allocated so that amount OC_n would be in nontaxed uses and the amount OC_t would be in potentially taxable uses. When a tax is imposed on the uses of capital shown on the left side of Figure 27.1, the owners of these types of property will find their after-tax rate of return to be lower than that which could be realized in

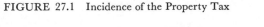

FIGURE 27.1   Incidence of the Property Tax

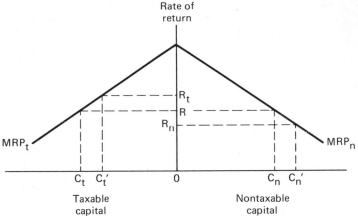

the nontaxed uses of capital. They will proceed to withdraw capital from the taxed uses and to transfer it to the nontaxed uses. As these changes take place, the amount of capital in taxed uses decreases and the before-tax rate of return to capital in these uses increases along the marginal revenue product curve for these uses of capital. Simultaneously, the inflow of capital into the nontaxed uses causes the rate of return for these types of capital to fall. Assuming that the total amount of capital remains unchanged, an equilibrium is reached when the before-tax rate of return to taxed capital (R_t) exceeds the rate of return to nontaxed capital (R_n) by an amount reflecting the tax. After-tax rates of return are equal as between taxable and nontaxable uses of capital and the net burden of the tax, as shown by the decline in the rate of return from R to R_n, is shared by all owners of capital, without regard to whether their capital is in taxable or nontaxable form.

   So long as it is assumed that the total amount of capital is not altered by the tax, the conclusion from this analysis is that the property tax, as a tax on capital, imposes a burden on all owners of capital and that the tax probably is progressive in terms of income, since capital ownership is significantly concentrated in the higher-income groups of the population. The analysis also suggests that an excess burden arises from the fact that the tax discriminates against certain uses of capital. The excess burden, or resource misallocation effects of the tax, arises because the tax causes marginal units of capital to be removed from taxable uses yielding a relatively high before-tax rate of return and transferred to nontaxed uses yielding lower rates of return. Thus, the stock of capital is allocated less efficiently among alternative uses after the tax than it would have been in the absence of the tax.

EXCISE EFFECTS

   In the general model of the incidence of the property tax, the rate of tax is an average of the rates actually imposed by the different jurisdictions using the tax. The distinction between taxable and nontaxable property is a generalization that ignores variations in the definition of the tax base and in assessment practices among different types of property and in different taxing jurisdictions. These generalizations give the model elegance and simplicity and focus attention on broad findings about the incidence of the tax and its effects on economic efficiency. But from the point of view of local government decision makers, a model that uses only an average effective tax rate fails to come to grips with problems which arise when the tax rate in a particular jurisdiction is different from the rates prevailing in other jurisdictions that are alternative locations for economic activity. Likewise, from the point of view of particular consumer groups, a model that deals only in general terms about differences between taxable and nontaxable properties does not provide help in understanding the consequences of taxing specific types of property more heavily than other types of property; that is, it does not provide an analysis of the excise effects of property taxation.

Why Excise Effects Exist

Excise effects arise when taxes discriminate among different commodities and cause the prices of some commodities to rise relative to the prices of other commodities. These changes in relative price will result in changes in resource allocation. In the context of a tax levied at the local level, these allocation effects have both a locational dimension as between one jurisdiction and another and a functional dimension as among different commodities. For example, if housing is taxed more heavily in one jurisdiction than another, not only will housing resources tend to migrate to lower taxed areas, but the mix between housing and other consumption goods inside the community will be distorted. Excise effects can also have an impact on the incidence of the property tax on different groups in the economy. For example, if a particular type of property generally subjected to above-average tax rates happens to be an important input in the production of a commodity consumed mainly by low-income people whose demand for it is inelastic, then the excise effect of the tax will introduce an element of regressivity into the incidence of the tax. If low-income people tend to occupy housing in central city areas where tax rates are above average, the excise effects of the tax may be regressive on income.

The analysis of the excise effects of property taxation is an exercise in microeconomics. The first step is to determine whether the effective rate of tax on a particular type of property is higher or lower than the effective rates prevailing elsewhere in the market area. The second step is to recognize that the tax is an element in the cost of producing commodities using this type of property and to shift the supply curve of these commodities according to the change in cost brought about by the above- or below-average effective rate of tax. This shift in supply is examined in connection with the demand for the commodity to determine the changed price and quantity that arise because of the tax. This model can be demonstrated with an analysis of the effects of property taxation on housing, which constitutes a major portion of the property tax base in the United States.

Effects on Housing

Figure 27.2 represents demand and supply for housing, with the P_1Q_1 situation illustrating an equilibrium price-quantity relationship in the absence of a tax or at a tax rate average for the area. The imposition of a tax or of a tax rate that is above average is shown as shifting the supply curve to the left, since the necessity of paying the tax is an increase in the cost of providing any given quantity of housing. Reading horizontally from the price axis of the graph, the tax can be seen as having the effect of reducing the amount of housing that will be offered on the market at any given price. The demand curve in Figure 27.2 is shown to be unchanged by the tax, since this demand for housing is a reflection of the tastes of consumers, income, and the prices of alternative consumption goods, none of which is altered by the tax. The result of the tax and of the consequent shift in supply is a reduction in the quantity of housing actually provided and an increase in its price; that is, the after-tax situation is shown as a new equilibrium price-quantity relation, P_2Q_2.

FIGURE 27.2   The Effect of Taxation on Housing

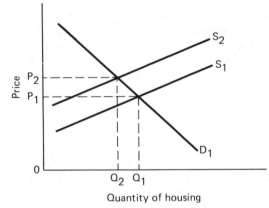

Quantity of housing

Figure 27.2 suggests that the magnitude of the effect of the taxation on housing depends on the amount of tax imposed and on the elasticities of the demand for and supply of housing. It has been estimated that property taxes in the United States are sometimes equivalent to a 25 percent tax on housing expenditures, a level of taxation much higher than that imposed on most other consumption items, with the possible exception of selectively taxed items like gasoline, alcoholic beverages, and tobacco products.[1] It seems reasonable to suppose that the property tax on housing is significantly higher than on most other commodities and can produce significant excise effects if demand and supply curves have some degree of elasticity.

Let us trace the sequence of events that can be expected to follow from an increase in the rate of property tax on housing. First, the owners of existing

[1] Dick Netzer, *Economics of the Property Tax* (Washington, D.C.: The Brookings Institution, 1966), p. 74.

structures find that the necessity of paying the added tax reduces the net income from their investments. An attempt will surely be made to restore the lost profit by increasing rents charged to the occupiers of the structures. But housing is not the only item in the household budget, and reallocations within this budget certainly are possible. An increase in the relative price of housing will encourage economizing on the quantity of housing consumed by reducing the number of rooms or floor space per person and/or through a switch to a lower quality of housing. The quantity and/or quality of housing consumed will fall if the relative price of housing occupancy (rent) increases. In other words, building owners will discover (and undoubtedly already knew) that increases in rent will be followed by rising vacancy rates within the existing stock of housing. Vacant structures earn no rent at all. Therefore, owners will recognize that an increase in rents can be accomplished effectively (and the tax increase shifted) only as the stock of housing structures diminishes. This, then, is the route that must be followed. New construction will be curtailed, and repair and maintenance expenditures will be reduced. As the housing stock shrinks, rents will increase on the remaining structures. When the new equilibrium is reached, rent will have increased (although not by the full amount of the tax due to the elasticity of demand for housing) and the stock of housing will be smaller than before the tax increase.[2]

The excise effects of high property taxes on housing will be especially apparent through their impact on housing quality. In Figure 27.2, the horizontal dimension combined both quantitative and qualitative aspects of the housing stock. At the new equilibrium, both the quantity and the quality of housing presumably will be lower than in the initial situation. During the transitional period between the two equilibrium situations, quality will be deteriorating in the jurisdiction imposing high tax rates, since the liquidation of existing housing investments is begun by decisions not to invest in maintenance and repair. The existing investment is liquidated through direct consumption of the capital stock itself. Housing which is in the process of being removed from the market is simply "used up" through continued occupancy without benefit of repair and maintenance.

A lowering of housing quality is a readily predictable feature of the transition from a pretax to a posttax equilibrium. Several years may be required to complete the adjustment to a given tax increase, and the period is likely to be characterized by frequent and valid complaints from housing occupiers that landlords are failing to live up to their commitments for maintenance and repair. More vigorous enforcement of housing codes will be demanded by occupiers of housing but resisted by owners, who wish to keep the properties occupied as long as possible in order to realize as much as possible in the liquidation process. Since the adjustment process may require several years, repeated tax rate increases can extend adjustment over an agonizingly long period of time and can give the impression of chronic deterioration of housing quality.

---

[2] Some backward shifting may also take place in this process of adjustment to the increase. Demand for resources by the construction industry will fall as the stock of housing is reduced and as the demand for repair, maintenance, and replacement becomes smaller for the reduced housing stock.

Property Taxation and New Construction

The excise effects of high property taxes are illustrated in a particularly striking way in connection with new construction in central city areas, where property tax rates frequently are higher than in surrounding areas. Since property taxes are collected each year on the basis of the value of the property in that year, the construction of a new facility creates tax obligations that will continue to be payable throughout its useful life. The discounted value of the future tax obligations becomes an important factor in determining the profitability of the new construction. If a new structure is expected to have a useful life of sixty years and the discount rate is 5 percent, each 10 mils (1 percent) of property tax rate is equivalent to a 19 percent excise tax on new construction.[3] Since it seems likely that central city property tax rates frequently exceed those in surrounding areas by 10 mils or more, the excise effects of property taxation can erect significant barriers to the reconstruction of central city areas.

The time pattern of property tax obligations is important in the argument that these taxes prevent new construction. Taxes that fall due during the early years in the life of a structure are powerful contributors to excise effects for two reasons. First, if tax rates are assumed constant over time, higher tax bills will come during the early years because the value of the structure will be greatest during this time. Second, the discounting or capitalization process magnifies the present value equivalent of early-year tax obligations in comparison with obligations that will fall due in later years. That is, a dollar of tax obligation due twenty or thirty years in the future will have considerably less impact on present value than a dollar of tax obligation due in the near future. For these reasons, subsidy programs that offer limited term (five- or ten-year) tax abatements or exemptions are especially effective in reducing the disincentives to new construction.

Property taxation can also operate to discourage new construction through a mismatching of benefits and costs in the local government's revenue and expenditure operations. This mismatching arises because revenues are positively related to the value of properties while government expenditures tend to be inversely related. Newly constructed facilities are likely to have relatively high tax values and consequently will pay substantial amounts of property tax, whereas older or deteriorated facilities are likely to have relatively low values and pay smaller amounts of tax. But government expenditures to provide police, fire, and sanitation services will probably be greater for the older, deteriorated, and low-value properties, since newer structures are likely to be built with more fireproof materials and to be equipped with modern sanitation, security, and fire protection devices. Therefore, through a mismatching of benefits and costs in the government budget operation, new construction may in effect be required to subsidize the less valuable portions of the community tax base. This subsidy effect will discourage the construction of new facilities and will permit low-value or deteriorated facilities to continue in use longer than would otherwise be the case.

---

[3] M. Mason Gaffney, "Property Taxes and the Frequency of Urban Renewal," *Proceedings of the 57th National Tax Conference* (National Tax Association, September 14–17, 1964), pp. 272–85.

LOCATION EFFECTS

The excise effects of property taxation have a geographical or location dimension when rates on particular types of property are different in one jurisdiction than in another. If rate differences exist, investors will prefer to locate properties in low-tax rather than in high-tax areas, and a cumulative set of forces may be set in motion that can greatly increase fiscal disparities among different government units. As more and more taxable property is located in the low-tax areas, rates may fall still further; as taxable property leaves high-tax areas, rates in those areas may be forced higher and higher.

The fiscal plight of central cities illustrates one set of circumstances that can trigger the location effects of differential property tax rates. If low-income families are concentrated in central cities and if the presence of these families requires increased local expenditures for health and welfare services, property taxes in these locations may rise to levels greater than those prevailing in surrounding areas. In response, owners of taxable properties will decide to relocate their property investments in the surrounding areas, where expenditure requirements and tax rates are lower. As these migrations take place, central cities must raise property taxes still higher, reduce the levels of service provided, or turn to the national government for assistance. Substantial fiscal disparities can thus arise between the central city and the surrounding areas.[4]

But property tax enclaves or tax havens can arise even in the absence of initial differences in tax rates between neighboring jurisdictions. Even if rates and expenditures per capita initially are equal between two jurisdictions, it is evident that tax advantages can be realized by owners of high-value properties if they can group themselves together in one of the jurisdictions, thereby creating an area that can enjoy a high value of taxable property per capita. A given level of per capita expenditure can therefore be financed with lower tax rates in the enclave than would be required to finance the equivalent level of government services in the jurisdiction with a low value of property per capita. Moreover, once the tax rate differential has been established, the advantageous rate and/or government service level operates in a cumulative way to attract still further installations of high-value properties, adding further force to the location effect of the property tax and widening fiscal disparities among jurisdictions. Tax enclaves built around high-value residential or industrial properties are familiar features of the metropolitan fiscal landscape. In the tax enclaves, per capita levels of government expenditure are high and tax rates are low, whereas in the disadvantaged jurisdictions the opposite situation prevails: low per capita levels of public service combined with high property tax rates.[5]

Interjurisdictional disparities arising from the locational effects of property taxation pose both equity and efficiency problems for a system of local governments. Equity problems arise because the enclave system inherently

[4] Stephen M. Miller and William K. Tabb, "A New Look at the Theory of Local Expenditures," *National Tax Journal*, XXVI, 2 (June 1973).

[5] The enclave problem may be encountered in income taxation as well as in property taxation. A local income tax used to finance local provision of public service encourages the concentration of high incomes in selected jurisdictions, since a given level of public service per capita can be provided with a lower income tax rate by these jurisdictions.

involves segregation of high-income and low-income people, with the high-income group tending to enjoy higher levels of government service and relatively lower tax rates while the low-income people face lower levels of government service at relatively high tax rates. Wealthy jurisdictions, for example, may be able to provide high levels of educational expenditure per pupil at relatively low tax rates. Low-income jurisdictions provide lower levels of education expenditure per pupil even though they impose relatively high tax rates. Efficiency problems arise because location decisions for residential, commercial, and industrial activities will be influenced by jurisdictional boundaries and the institutions of government finance rather than by purely economic considerations of resource availability.

On both equity and efficiency grounds, the problems of interjurisdictional disparities arising from the location effects of local government finance constitute one of the most serious difficulties facing a federal system of government organization. Most solutions offered involve some departure from pure local decision making on government expenditures and revenues. For example, a rather simplistic solution to the disparities problem proposes that separate local jurisdictions (in a metropolitan area) might be consolidated into a single larger jurisdiction. Although this approach would reduce disparities, it would sacrifice the advantages a local system of governments can offer in catering to differences in preferences for collective services.

Another proposed solution to the problem is that certain types of property which are especially sensitive to the attractions of the tax enclave (such as industrial property) might be removed entirely from the local tax base and administered from the state level, so that tax rates would be the same regardless of the location. This approach, however, would require a companion program of state government grants back to local jurisdictions that would have to recognize, in some degree at least, that the location of industrial facilities can place increased government service requirements on the local jurisdictions in which the facilities are located. Still more broadly conceived solutions to the fiscal disparities problem propose that a special system of grants-in-aid from the state to local governments should be established under which the amount of state aid would be determined according to a power equalizing formula guaranteeing to each local jurisdiction a given amount of revenue per capita for each mil of property tax rate imposed by the local government. The power equalizing system will be examined in greater detail in Chapter 29.

PROPERTY TAX REFORM

Property tax reform proposals can be grouped into (a) those proposing improvement in the administration of the tax, (b) those proposing reduced reliance on the tax by local government, and (c) those proposing differential treatment of land and improvements. This grouping does not suggest, however, that these are alternative approaches. Rather, the suggestion is that reform of the property tax might proceed on all three fronts simultaneously.

Administrative Reform

Improvement in the assessment process is the focus of administrative reform proposals. Perhaps the basic step in improving the assessment of property is to ensure that each assessment district is large enough to justify the employment of at least one full-time assessor. This is because the assessment of property requires particular skills and training. Achieving assessment districts large enough to justify the employment of full-time personnel means that small districts, established when transportation was slower and property more homogeneous, must be combined into fewer larger districts. Local resistance is sometimes encountered when the merging of assessment districts is attempted, but considerable progress has been made over the past several decades.

Another reform relating to assessment personnel is to make the position a civil service post rather than an elective office, as it is in many jurisdictions. It seems apparent that elected assessors can be subject to reelection pressures that might interfere with the performance of their duties. Utilization of qualifying examinations and some protection against arbitrary removal from the position could be expected to improve the quality of assessment.

The equalization process and extensive use of sales survey procedures to verify assessments are reforms introduced some time ago. Further improvements in the equalization process may be possible. One would be the use of separate equalization factors for different types or classifications of property. For example, a given assessment ratio for a district could arise through general low assessment of residential or agricultural property combined with a generally higher assessment ratio for commercial and industrial property. If a single equalization factor is used based on the overall assessment ratio for the district, inequities among different property types would persist. Separate sales sample surveys for different property types could reveal differential patterns of this sort, and a separate equalization factor for each property type could be applied. Inequities between individual properties within a given property classification would not be corrected by this process, but the general quality of assessment fairness could be improved.

Considerable improvement in property tax administration has been achieved in the decades since World War II, and coefficients of dispersion calculated by the Census Bureau have moved downward during this time. Although further improvement appears to be possible, the inherent difficulty of the assessment task suggests that the property tax will continue to achieve something less than complete equity.

Reduced Reliance

Some problems associated with the property tax arise because the tax is used to finance services that might better be financed through some other revenue source. If the property tax were relieved of the responsibility for financing certain expenditures, some of the problems would be reduced or eliminated. In this sense, reduced reliance on property taxation can be viewed as a means of reforming the tax.

A leading example of reform through reduced reliance is the proposal that expenditures for welfare and income maintenance programs should be financed not through property taxes, but primarily by the federal government with revenues generated through the federal individual income tax. It is generally agreed that local governments are ill suited to sustain either ambitious redistribution programs or markedly progressive tax systems, since they have little ability to insulate themselves from the migration of people and businesses across jurisdictional boundaries. Removal of welfare-related property tax levies would reduce the level of property taxation, especially in central cities, where these expenditures are now concentrated, and would thereby moderate the rate differentials between cities and their surrounding areas. These rate differentials promote the formation of enclaves and set in motion cumulative forces generating fiscal disparities among local jurisdictions.

A second group of expenditures that might be removed from the property tax levy are those which could be financed by direct user charges on the consumers of the service. Local governments provide a number of public-utility type services such as water supply, sewage treatment, fire protection, recreational and entertainment facilities, parking, and certain traffic and transportation facilities. These are essentially private goods and services, and the consumers of these services could be charged if reasonably accurate measurement could be made of the marginal costs of providing the service and if exclusion devices that permit collection of the charge could be developed.

The introduction of charges for services that many people have come to consider "free" or that citizens have already paid for through their property taxes can expect to encounter voter opposition. But if the user charges finance operating costs and remaining amortization of capital costs that would otherwise be chargeable to property taxes, property owners should expect to benefit from the switch and would probably outnumber those who directly utilize the service and would therefore be faced with payment of the user charge. A very important feature of the user charge method, if properly devised, is that it can provide a means of determining the true demand for the service, discourage wasteful consumption, and lead to improved allocation of scarce resources. Also, some of the "free ride" aspects of the enclave phenomenon would be eliminated by the expanded utilization of user charges. Admission fees for parks and recreational areas and locally imposed gate charges for airline passengers illustrate recent expansions of the user charge system.

Land Value Taxation

The economic effects of taxation of land values are very different from the economic effects of taxing the value of improvements or other reproducible goods. The reason for the difference is that the quantity of land in any given location or area is fixed. In other words, the supply of land will not be changed by the imposition of a tax. Likewise, the physical productivity of land will not be changed by a tax on land value; that is, an acre of land that produced 100 bushels of grain before the tax will also produce 100 bushels after the tax has been imposed. If we assume that the tax will not alter the demand for the product of the land (for grain), then the demand for the use of the land (its marginal revenue product) will not be changed by the tax. Since neither the supply of land nor the demand for the use of land will be altered by the tax, the equilibrium price for land *use* (rent) will not be changed and no change in resource allocation will result. What will happen is that the net return to the landowner will be reduced by the tax. His wealth position will be reduced because the value of land *ownership* will be reduced by the tax. The person who owns the land at the time the tax is initiated suffers a burden that he cannot shift either to the user of the land or to a subsequent purchaser. In a sense, government becomes part owner of the land along with the private owner, and the two owners share in the proceeds of the rental income.

Land value taxation occupies a special position in public finance economics because of its neutrality in respect to land use. Property tax reform advocates have long proposed that more reliance should be placed on land taxes and less on taxing reproducible properties, such as buildings and improvements. Reformers in the tradition of Henry George continue to advocate this restructuring of property taxation.[6] Equity arguments are also submitted: land values arise from the development of the community or neighborhood *around* a given parcel of land rather than from inputs traceable to the landowners themselves. When land values increase, the landowner's gains are called *unearned increments* and are thought of as especially suitable objects for taxation.

The case for differentially heavy taxation of land values is strong on grounds of economic efficiency, but serious equity problems arise in launching such a system. Even though land values may include unearned increments, the present owners of land (especially those who have purchased recently) may not be the same people who have enjoyed these unearned increments. Land values reflect the present value of the anticipated stream of future net income, so that the initiation of a new tax would amount to changing the rules in the middle of the game and would therefore raise difficult ethical questions. Of course, this dilemma confronts every proposal for tax reform. Some more or less arbitrary redistribution of wealth inevitably accompanies fundamental tax reform. Given an established set of tax institutions, reformers confront the puzzle expressed in the advice that if we want to get to there, we should not start from here.[7]

An Agenda for Reform

Aside from administrative improvements, two approaches to property tax reform have been noted in this chapter. One of these was reduced reliance on property taxation through the transfer of some funding responsibilities to other revenue sources. The other was increased reliance on land taxation as a local revenue source free from adverse economic effects. These two approaches, considered in combination, suggest an agenda for property tax reform under which reductions in the property tax levy realized through transfer of funding responsibilities would be applied exclusively to the reduction of tax rates imposed on improvements, with the tax rate applicable to land remaining frozen at present levels. The rate reductions on improvements (buildings, and so on) would realize some of the resource allocation advantages already noted, while the "freeze" on land value millage would prevent the reductions in property tax levies from conveying any windfall or unearned increment gains to current landowners such as would result from the capitalization of a rate reduc-

---

[6] Henry George, (1839–1897) was the author of *Progress and Poverty* (New York: Robert Schalkenbach Foundation, 1931) and founder of the single-tax movement in the United States.

[7] Martin Feldstein, "Compensation in Tax Reform," *National Tax Journal*, XXIX, 2 (June 1976).

tion into the price of land. The trend in property tax rates has been upward for many years. Thus it is reasonable to suppose that present market prices of land have incorporated an expectation of continued increases in tax rate. If the tide of tax rate changes could be reversed, there would appear to be little foundation for an argument that freezing land value tax rates at present levels would operate to exploit existing landowners.

A second and more radical part of a program to introduce differential treatment between land and improvements taxation would be the enactment of a *land value increment* tax. This tax would be separate from and in addition to the existing basic property tax on land value. Figure 27.3 illustrates the nature

FIGURE 27.3   Land Value Increment Tax Base

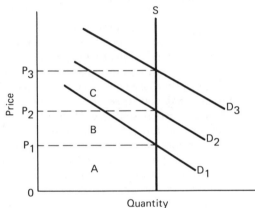

of a land value increment tax. The horizontal axis of this figure shows the supply of land locations (or sites) in a taxing jurisdiction and the vertical axis shows the price or ownership value of these locations. The supply of locations is shown as fixed, while three different demand curves each reflect demand for locations at different points in time. In the initial time period, demand is D_1, and the price is P_1. The community is growing, so that demand for locations in the second time period is D_2 and the price is P_2, and so on for the third time period.

If the land value increment tax were enacted during time period 1, the base price for the calculation of incremental values would be P_1 and the aggregate base value of property would be shown as area A. As demand increases and land values rise, a positive base for the increment tax appears. In period 2, this amounts to area B. As demand increases in period 3, the base for the increment tax grows to include both areas B and C. The land value increment tax would be imposed annually and based on the total increment to land value that had taken place since the date used to establish the base value. In essence, the tax would be a straight application of the traditional case for differential heavy taxation of land value, modified by the recognition that people who had purchased land prior to the enactment of the tax should not be taxed on increments anticipated at that time.

The land value increment tax would make the local treasury a partial claimant to land value gains accruing as a result of community growth, but would not take from current landowners any elements of those gains anticipated at the initiation of the tax program and therefore already built into base land values. Rates could be established to capture for the local treasury a substantial portion of land value increments. A 100 percent (confiscatory) rate might appear undesirable, since land value speculation and the stimulus to development which flows from the quest for capital gains in land are legitimate manifestations of the market process and facilitate reallocation of land resources in changing times. Even-handed treatment suggests that in areas where demand for locations is falling and market values of land are declining, the increment tax should be allowed to operate in reverse, entitling the landowner to a credit against the standard property tax on the land.

A specific, rather than a general, application of land value increment taxation exists when public expenditures are made to finance undertakings that have the effect of increasing land location values in certain areas. If these undertakings are successful, the increment tax collects revenue from the benefited properties and is an excellent example of benefit-received taxation. Since the tax would be paid only if and when the beneficial effects of the expenditures become apparent, properties would be protected from having to finance projects that did not actually benefit them. In contrast, present procedures, such as special assessments for street paving, collect the tax before the beneficial character of the project and the particular distribution of the benefits are known and before the ability to pay the tax has been realized. The incremental land value tax can have particular applicability in situations in which the distribution of benefits from an improvement cannot be determined in advance with sufficient accuracy to justify advance payments.

SUMMARY

The property tax is imposed on certain types of capital assets. However, because capital investments are mobile as between taxed and nontaxed varieties, the final incidence of the tax is shared by all owners of capital through a reduction in the rate of return to capital brought about by the tax. According to this model, the incidence of the tax probably is progressive in terms of income because capital ownership is concentrated in higher-income groups, and an excess burden arises because the tax discriminates among different types of property. In the general model, the tax rate is the average of the different tax rates imposed on different types of taxable property. In practice, however, effective property tax rates vary not only among different types of taxable properties but also among the different government jurisdictions using the tax. These variations in effective tax rates produce excise effects that have both a functional and a location dimension.

The functional type of excise effect is illustrated by the taxation of housing. If housing is taxed more heavily than other types of property, the supply of housing will be reduced and its price will rise, thus altering the allocation of resources. There may also be income-distribution effects if housing consumption is a larger part of the budget of low-income than of high-income families, or if low-income families happen to reside in areas where property taxes on housing are especially high. The location type of excise effect arises when rates are higher in certain jurisdictions than in others. As property investments are relocated in response to these rate differences, fiscal disparities arise among local jurisdictions and pose serious equity and efficiency problems for multi-government fiscal systems. Even in the absence of initial property tax rate differences, property tax enclaves or tax havens that result in fiscal disparities among jurisdictions may be created.

Property tax reform proposals suggest that administration of the tax could be improved, that reliance on property taxation could be reduced by transfer-ring responsibility for welfare services to the national government, and that land might be taxed differently than improvements. The taxation of land value is distinguished from the taxation of reproducible properties because, since the supply of land is fixed, the tax will not reduce supply or alter the allocation of land among different uses.

SUGGESTED READINGS

MIESZKOWSKI, PETER. "The Property Tax: An Excise Tax or a Property Tax?" *Journal of Public Economics*, April 1972.

NETZER, DICK. "The Incidence of the Property Tax Revisited," *National Tax Journal*, XXVI, 4 (December 1973).

CHURCH, ALBERT M., "Capitalization of the Effective Property Tax Rate on Single Family Residences," *National Tax Journal*, XXVII (March 1974), pp. 113–23.

AARON, HENRY J. *Who Pays the Property Tax?* (Washington, D.C.: The Brookings Institution, 1975).

HAMILTON, BRUCE W. "Capitalization of Intrajurisdictional Differences in Local Tax Prices," *American Economic Review*, 66, 5 (December 1976), pp. 743–53.

28

Local User Charges, Income Taxes, and Sales Taxes

Local governments obtain a substantial portion of their general revenues from sources other than grants-in-aid and property taxes. In 1974–75, these other sources divided roughly as follows: 10 percent from current charges, such as those charged for educational, hospital, and sewage services; 5 percent from local sales and income taxes; 5 percent from miscellaneous sources such as interest earnings, special assessments, and sales of property; and additional minor amounts from taxes on public utilities, alcoholic beverages, tobacco products, motor fuels, and so on.[1]

Local governments continually search for alternatives to the property tax, but the search is not simply a matter of trying to obtain property tax relief. Time and again, the property tax has confounded those who predicted that it had reached its limit. The problem is that when a community relies almost exclusively on property taxes for internal revenue, the costs of proposed spending programs will be calculated in terms of the impact and effects of the property tax, and property owners will oppose bond issues and proposals for local spending if they conclude that the benefits to them of the proposed services are less than the tax they would have to pay to finance them. But service proposals that fail to be approved with the property tax might secure approval if alternative or supplementary internal revenue sources were available. The task is to discover revenue sources that can broaden the base of support for community services by providing a better connection between taxes paid and benefits received.

[1] U.S. Bureau of the Census, *Governmental Finances in 1974–75*, GF–75, No. 5 (Washington, D.C.: Government Printing Office, 1976), Table 4, p. 18.

FEES, CHARGES, AND MISCELLANEOUS REVENUES

Fees, charges, and miscellaneous revenues are surprisingly important to local governments in the United States, partly because the provision of semicommercial services directly to consumers is more important at the local than at the state or federal levels of government. Hospital charges, education charges, sewage charges, and charges related to housing and transportation are the major revenue producers in the fee and charge category, although other services, such as parks, recreation, and natural resources, provide some revenue. Miscellaneous general revenues include money collected from special assessments, sales of property, and interest earned on funds held by local governments. Special assessments typically are used to finance construction of street improvements; property sales and interest earnings arise from the routine function of managing public funds and properties. In fiscal 1974–75, fees, charges, and miscellaneous revenues provided about 15 percent of local general revenues, which was about 45 percent as much as came from the general property tax.

The Rationale for Fees and Charges

The basic rationale for fees and charges is that private, divisible benefits arise from some of the services provided by government and that the private consumers who enjoy these services should pay for them. In other words, many local government services are analogous to public utility services, for which consumers are charged a price for services. This does not mean, of course, that the public utility analogy necessarily applies to the entire output of these government-provided services. Many local services provide collective benefits, in which all citizens share equally, along with private benefits consumed separately by individual members of the community. For example, schools, hospitals, parks, transportation facilities, and sanitation services provide collective benefits by enhancing the quality of life in the community and by their general availability to all citizens. General fund financing is appropriate for these collective components in the benefit stream. But persons who make direct use of these services by entering the schools, hospitals, parks, transportation facilities, and so on realize direct private benefits in addition to the general collective benefits provided by the service. Fees and charges collected from these direct consumers may finance this component of the benefit stream. General taxpayers need not subsidize these direct beneficiaries unless the subsidy is accepted as an element of public policy.

Public finance theory provides ample foundation for dividing the benefit stream from semicommercial services between their collectively and privately consumed components and for collecting user charges from the private beneficiaries. Mixed financing (that is, partly private and partly public) is quite appropriate for these quasi-collective services, and the marginal rule could be applied to determine the portion to be financed from each source. In practice, of course, the division between collective and private benefit is difficult to establish. Taxpayers may resent the idea that they should pay a charge for using a service they feel they have already paid for. However, the economic case for fees and charges is very strong both because they provide a means of measuring the demand for the service and because they can operate to prevent wasteful consumption of the service. For example, if a service that provides significant private benefits is offered at zero price, it is likely that private consumption will expand to the point where marginal benefit also approaches zero. If there are positive marginal costs in providing this service, satisfying this zero price demand can become a serious drain on local resources unless some type of rationing is practiced. On the other hand, a fee or charge set at a level approximating the marginal cost of providing the private benefit components of the service will limit consumption to a level consistent with an efficient allocation of resources and will collect revenue from those enjoying the benefits of the service.

User Charges and Ability to Pay

Paying a fee or user charge requires an ability as well as a willingness to pay, and persons with low income may lack the necessary financial ability. If the collective consumption dimension of the benefit from a service, such as park and recreation services, requires widespread utilization throughout the community, user charge financing may be rejected as not compatible with the collective objectives of the program. This can be a perfectly legitimate basis for deciding to fund the program through general revenues rather than through user charges. But opposition to charging fees for the use of government-provided services sometimes arises from egalitarian or redistributional considerations. That is, it is sometimes proposed that private service benefits should be financed from general revenues as a means of redistributing real income among members of the community. However, caution should be exercised in considering this argument, because dispensing private benefit services at zero price or at prices significantly below marginal costs can have undesirable consequences and is an inefficient way to redistribute income. If the quantity of the service demanded at low or zero prices exceeds the quantity the general taxpayers are willing to finance, some form of nonprice rationing, such as long waiting lines, low quality, bureaucratic red tape, or favoritism, will be introduced. The consequence of these procedures, in turn, may be an association in the public mind of government services, low quality, and a predominantly low-income clientele—an association with socially divisive potential.

Underpricing of private benefit services is an inefficient way to redistribute income because the assistance conveyed by the underpriced service may be enjoyed by many people who would not be classified as low income and thereby entitled to assistance. Moreover, many people who might be classified as low income and thereby entitled to assistance may fail to realize any help from the subsidy if their patterns of consumption do not include utilization of the underpriced service. In other words, income redistribution through the underpricing of private benefit services has a low target efficiency rating. Direct money transfers are a more efficient method, but programs of this kind are generally recognized to be a responsibility of the national government rather than of local governments.

Two considerations suggest that local governments may make greater use of user pricing in the future than they have made in the past. First, if local government tax rates rise and if local citizens thus become more concerned with efficiency in local government decision making, user charges may be adopted because of their allocation efficiency qualities. Second, if the national government expands its income redistribution and maintenance programs through systems such as the negative income tax, which dispenses direct money transfers, local governments may find it more acceptable to employ user charges for the financing of private benefit services.

User Charge Efficiency and Financial Adequacy

The economic test for allocational efficiency in user charges is clear and unambiguous. It is that the user charge should equal the cost of providing the marginal unit of output, since, at this price, the benefit realized by the consumer of the marginal unit equals the benefits which could have been realized from using the resources in the best alternative. No reallocation would increase total benefits. But there is no guarantee that marginal cost pricing will generate enough revenue to cover all the costs of providing the service. If the average costs of providing a service are falling over the range of output relevant to the level of demand (as illustrated in Figure 28.1), marginal costs will be less than

FIGURE 28.1   User Charges in Decreasing Cost Operations

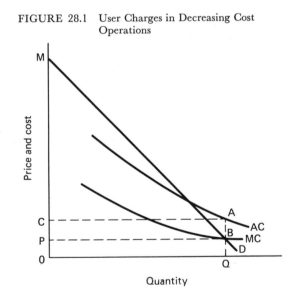

average costs, since it is the lower cost of the marginal units that pulls the average cost downward. A user charge price set at the level of marginal cost (OP) will therefore fail to generate enough revenue to cover total cost ($OCAQ$), and the operation will run at a deficit unless some supplementary source of revenue can be found. This situation is frequently encountered in mass transit services in which fixed costs, including equipment costs and driver time, are large relative to direct operating costs.

If the general taxpayers of the community feel that the service is providing collective benefits along with the private benefits enjoyed by the direct users, general fund revenues may be provided to help cover the deficit, but there is no guarantee that this supplementary source of financing will be sufficient to erase the entire deficit. Thus, it may be necessary to find some additional source of financing from the patrons of the service itself. From an economic efficiency point of view, the problem is to devise a way to collect this additional payment that would not, at the same time, have the effect of discouraging the marginal patron from making use of the service. In other words, efficiency requires a two-price system in which one price is the standard marginal cost price per unit of the service consumed and the other price is some charge that taps the *consumer surplus* being received by the inframarginal consumers of the service. In Figure 28.1, the consumer surplus is illustrated by the triangular area *PMB*. There has been little success in devising ways to collect the consumer surplus part of this two-price system, but several examples illustrate the type of approach that may be used and some of the problems involved.

Private clubs may use initiation fees that are necessary preconditions for the consumption of the services provided by the club but that do not excuse the member from the obligation also to pay a user charge based on marginal cost for the actual consumption of services. These initiation fees may be designed to cover the fixed or capital costs of the services provided and may be assessed at different rates to different members based on some index, such as income, which is thought to be related to the amount of consumer surplus enjoyed. Parking lots may attempt to cover capital costs by selling window stickers that are required for admission to the lot but do not excuse the user from the regular charge for parking. Sewer services involve high fixed costs and relatively low operating costs, so that a two-price system is indicated and actually used. A hookup charge covers capital costs and a regular user charge covers operating costs. Another way to tap consumer surplus is to ask patrons to make voluntary contributions in addition to the regular charge for the service. These voluntary contributions presumably will come out of consumer surplus, although the voluntary approach obviously encounters the free rider problem, since the contribution is not a precondition for the consumption of the service.

Price discrimination among different units of the service consumed by an individual is frequently used as a means of tapping consumer surplus. The supplier of the service operates as a discriminating monopolist and establishes a rate structure for the sale of the service. A higher price is charged for inframarginal units of the service than for the marginal unit of the service. Electric, water, gas, and sewer utilities typically employ this type of rate structure, which requires some information about elasticity of demand in order to establish the appropriate rates for inframarginal units of the service. Price discrimination may also be practiced among different classes of consumers if there is reason to believe that consumer surplus is larger for some classes than for others. Park and recreational facilities may offer season tickets at relatively low prices and charge higher prices for individual admissions on the assumption that occasional users have relatively inelastic demand curves and therefore a larger consumer surplus.

LOCAL SALES AND INCOME TAXES

Income and sales taxes are broad-based taxes, since most people in a community become taxpayers under them in the ordinary course of day-to-day living. Therefore, it is not surprising that local governments look with interest on the possibility of imposing these taxes when they are hard pressed for revenue or when the property tax generates widespread dissatisfaction. For many local governments, however, the imposition of local sales or income taxes is not possible, since the state has not as yet granted them authority to impose these taxes. Even when the taxing authority is available, local voters may choose not to employ these taxes if they believe the taxes will simply mean an increase in their total bill or if they fear the taxes will place the community at a disadvantage in attracting residential, commercial, or industrial investment.

The Decision to Grant Local Tax Powers

Since local governments may impose only those taxes permitted by the state, the first step in establishing income or sales taxes at the local level is the enactment of appropriate state legislation. At first glance, it might seem that there could be little objection to the request that local citizens be granted the authority to tax themselves as they see fit in order to finance local expenditures. It is not this simple. For one thing, not all localities will be equally well served by the opportunity to impose sales or income taxes. Urban centers are in a better position to administer and collect significant revenues from these taxes than are small communities or rural areas. Commercial centers will benefit more from sales taxes than will rural areas, and wealthy communities will benefit more from income taxation than communities with many low-income families. Thus, local government authority to impose sales or income taxes can increase disparities in taxing capacity among localities in the state. The state legislature must also consider the relationships that will exist between the sales and/or income taxes imposed by local governments and the sales and/or income taxes imposed by the state itself. Administrative and compliance considerations clearly suggest that the definition of the tax base should be the same for local as for state taxes. Of course, if it happens that the state is not presently using the particular tax in question, the granting of local authority may seriously modify the options available to the state should it decide, at some future time, to make use of the tax. Finally, there is the alternative that the state might increase tax rates on its own income or sales tax and share the additional revenue with its subordinate units of government on the basis of the origin of the funds or through some grant-in-aid formula. All these factors merit attention in the decision to grant local taxing powers.

Experience has been an important teacher in the matter of granting authority for local governments to impose sales or income taxes. Pennsylvania's early move in this area, which permitted localities to tax anything that the state might but was not in fact taxing, led to an exceedingly diverse and complicated tax situation. Both administrative and compliance costs were greatly increased by differences between one locality and another in the definition of the tax base. The example has not been followed by other states. Instead, it appears preferable that localities be required to use the same tax base definition as is used in the comparable state income or sales tax, or if the state is not using a comparable tax, that the enabling legislation specifically define the tax base that must be used by any locality which decides to impose the tax. Local governments would have only the choice of whether or not to adopt the state-prescribed tax, and all local taxes imposed under this authority would have identical provisions. The *supplementation* approach, commonly used for local sales taxes, provides the clearest illustration of state-local coordination. Under this approach, the locality is authorized to add its own sales tax rate on top of the rate imposed by the state, administration is carried out by the state, and revenues collected from the locally imposed supplementary rate are returned to the locality after deduction of some amount to cover costs of administration.

State coordination of local income taxation is illustrated by Michigan's uniform city income tax law, which was adopted in 1964, before the state itself imposed an income tax. The Michigan law established a uniform tax base definition, which allowed personal exemptions and required the taxation of dividends, interest, and rent as well as wages and salaries, and also specified the crediting arrangement to be used between a city and its suburbs in taxing the income of commuters. Under the Michigan rules, the individual who resides in the taxing jurisdiction is taxed at a rate of 1 percent on his entire net taxable income, from whatever source derived, while a person working in an income-taxing jurisdiction but residing elsewhere is taxed at a rate of 1/2 percent on the income earned in the taxing jurisdiction. If the jurisdiction in which the commuter resides also imposes the local income tax (at the state-prescribed rate of 1 percent of total net taxable income), the jurisdiction of residence is required to allow credit for the tax paid to the jurisdiction in which the income was earned. Thus, a person who lives in one taxing jurisdiction but earns income in another pays the same total tax as a noncommuter. The tax is divided between the city of residence and the city in which he works in a manner specified by state legislation. Since the jurisdiction of residence is required to allow credit for income taxes paid to the jurisdiction in which income is earned, suburbs are not stimulated to enact income taxes in self-defense when the central city enacts the tax.[2]

The Decision to Adopt Local Taxes

After the state has authorized local governments to impose sales or income taxes, the local governments must decide whether they actually wish to do so. Local governments must consider the costs of administering the new tax, the additional revenue that would be generated from it, and the effect the new tax might have on relations between the local government and surrounding jurisdictions, which might or might not also impose the new tax.

Relationships with surrounding jurisdictions. Local governments sometimes decide to impose a sales or income tax in order to collect revenue from

[2] Michigan legislation has permitted Detroit to levy income tax at higher rates than 1 percent. For further discussion of the Michigan system, see Advisory Commission on Intergovernmental Relations, *Federal-State Coordination of Personal Income Taxes* (Washington, D.C.: Government Printing Office, 1965), p. 73.

nonresidents who, it is alleged, are enjoying the benefits of services provided by the city without paying for them. Residents of outlying areas may use city park and recreational facilities; commuters use city streets, traffic control, and police services.[3] But there are counterarguments to the contention that nonresidents do not pay for the services they receive, and there also is concern that the local tax might trigger relocations of residential, commercial, and industrial investments between the taxing jurisdiction and surrounding areas. The small size of most local jurisdictions means that is it relatively inexpensive for both people and business to move from one jurisdiction to another. For example, as transportation facilities have improved, downtown shopping areas have faced increasingly vigorous competition from shopping centers located in outlying areas.

Therefore, the central city may hesitate to enact a local sales tax, even when the authority is available, unless the outlying areas adopt a similar tax. A tax differential between the city and the outlying areas could persuade city residents to patronize the out-of-town merchants. Downtown merchants, faced with nontaxed competition, will either lose customers or be forced to absorb the tax in order to retain their customers. In either case, the profitability of local business will decline and some of these businesses themselves will move to the outlying areas, reducing the property tax base of the central city. Thus, a tradeoff exists between sales and property tax revenues, and it is quite possible that the city would have more difficulties with the sales tax than without it. Certainly, people with vested interests in existing central city property values would oppose adoption of the local sales tax. The analysis also suggests that nonresidents who are benefiting from city street and police services may actually be helping to pay for these services through the increased property values (and property tax base) that arise because of their patronage.

Local income taxes raise similar problems. Since the legal jurisdiction of a city to tax the income of a nonresident is limited to that portion of the non-resident's income earned in the city (the site of the income rather than the domi-cile of the taxpayer), city income taxes are essentially payroll taxes insofar as they relate to nonresidents. If a tax differential exists between the city and surrounding areas, the payroll tax will increase the cost of hiring labor for city employers, and if industrial locations are available in nontaxing suburbs, the payroll tax will create an incentive for outmigration similar to that attri-buted to local sales taxation in the previous analysis. For these reasons, local governments may hesitate to adopt a local income tax even when the authority is available.

More sophisticated local income taxes, such as those adopted under the Michigan system outlined earlier, may be less troublesome for city-suburb relations than the traditional local income taxes, which limit the tax base to wages only and frequently allow no personal exemptions. By including interest, dividends, and rents in the tax base, along with wages and salaries, these more sophisticated local income taxes may hold some attraction for suburban com-munities as well as central cities as a means of obtaining revenue, especially

[3] Woo Sik Kee, "City-Suburban Differentials in Local Government Fiscal Effort," *National Tax Journal*, June 1968.

if an arrangement can be made to have the tax administered through the state government. If both the central city and its suburbs adopt income taxes with identical features and rates, the entire metropolitan area may be able to supplement its tax sources without unduly disturbing economic relations among the different government units.

Costs of administration. Dollars and cents calculations of costs and revenues are important in the decision to adopt either a local sales tax or a local income tax. For a variety of reasons, the tax rates for local sales or income taxes are likely to be relatively low, but the costs of administration will not be lower just because the rate is low. Thus, the portion of collections absorbed in the cost of administering the tax is likely to be relatively high for local taxes, and the ratio is likely to become increasingly unfavorable as the size of the taxing jurisdiction diminishes. Moreover, at low tax rates, efforts to reduce administrative costs may take the form of uneven or poor enforcement, since the tax department may choose not to incur the costs of auditing and investigating more complicated tax returns. Centralized administration by the state, either through the supplementation approach or through contracts based on uniform local taxes throughout the state, is clearly desirable for widespread local use of these taxes.

Revenue instability. Another problem confronted by local governments in deciding whether to adopt a local income or sales tax is the relatively unstable revenue stream generated by these taxes compared to the reliable yield of property taxation. The revenue yield of both sales and income taxes can be expected to respond to changes in income and economic activity in the community. For sales taxes, studies generally suggest a yield elasticity in relation to income in the vicinity of 1.0. This means that a 1 percent fall or rise in incomes will lead to an equivalent 1 percent fall or rise in the money collected from the tax. Income taxes will have a somewhat larger elasticity coefficient, even if a flat rate of tax is imposed, because personal exemptions ordinarily are allowed and the elasticity coefficient will be even larger if tax rates are graduated. Of course, property tax revenues will also exhibit some income elasticity of yield, but the procedures used in property taxation adjust the tax rate annually to provide whatever amount of revenue the community decides to collect. These annual rate adjustments are not part of income or sales tax procedures, so that the latter will provide surplus revenues in some periods and inadequate revenues in other periods. As long as property taxation remains the major source for local internal revenue, property tax rates can serve as a balancing device for fluctuations in income or sales tax revenues. Nevertheless, income or sales taxation will require that local governments learn how to live with less stable revenue sources.

Local Selective Sales Taxes

A selective sales tax is one that taxes only the sale of certain specified commodities, such as cigarettes, alcoholic beverages, gasoline, and utility services. Selective sales taxes have a long history at the local as well as at the state and federal levels of government, and the items subjected to selective taxation at the local level are usually selected from those similarly taxed by higher levels of government. Since the public is accustomed to selective taxation of such items as tobacco, alcoholic beverages, and gasoline, local governments occasionally use them as sources of small amounts of extra revenue. Administration cost is the chief obstacle. Except in rather large cities, administrative costs for selective sales taxes may be prohibitive unless the tax can be administered as a supplement to a tax employed by the state. In some instances, a state selective sales tax may be converted into what is technically a local sales tax through a crediting arrangement between the state and its local governments. For example, a state cigarette tax may be imposed with a provision that businesses remitting the tax may credit against their remittance the amounts collected under a locally imposed sales tax on the item. Local governments invariably will take advantage of the credit arrangement and impose the indicated local tax, since administration is handled by a state agency.

On a national average, more than half of local selective sales tax revenues come from taxes on public utility services. The administrative convenience of taxing public utility services sales is apparent. Ordinarily there is a single seller for each service in the local area and demand is quite inelastic to the minor cost added by the tax. The distinction between the price of the service and the tax is subtle, since the utility is usually either an agency of the government itself or subject to regulations of price and service.

SUMMARY

Local user charges, income taxes, sales taxes, and miscellaneous internal revenues combine to provide more than $1 of every $5 of local general revenue. Although they do provide some property tax relief, these taxes are also attractive as devices to broaden the financing base for community services. In the case of user charges, they provide a direct relationship between taxes paid and benefits received from the semicommercial or public utility type of services offered by many local governments.

The rationale for user charges is a simple application of the economics of benefit-received taxation and public utility pricing. These charges can be used to finance the private benefit component of services provided by government, can help to measure the demand for these services, and can help prevent wasteful consumption. Two problems arise in connection with user charge financing. First, it may violate ability to pay or equity norms for government finance if the consumers of the services generally are low-income families. Second, if average costs of providing the service decrease as the quantity of the service is increased, marginal cost will be less than average cost, and prices or user charges set to equal marginal cost will not provide enough money to cover all the costs of the service. Additional sources of finance will have to be found, either out of general revenues or through special charges or contributions that seek to tap consumer surpluses.

Local governments may impose income or sales taxes if they are authorized to do so by their state government. Both the decision to authorize local governments to use these taxes and the decision by the local governments to exercise the option can pose difficult questions. In authorizing local income or sales taxes, states must consider the relationship between such local levies and state taxes on income or sales. In deciding whether to impose these taxes, local governments must consider the costs of administration, the possible instability of the revenue obtained, and the impact these taxes may have on the location of economic activity in the taxing jurisdiction and in the immediately surrounding areas.

SUGGESTED READINGS

DUE, JOHN F. *State and Local Sales Taxes* (Chicago: Public Administration Service, 1971).

Advisory Commission on Intergovernmental Relations. *Local Revenue Diversification; Income, Sales Taxes, and User Charges* (Washington, D. C.: Government Printing Office, 1974).

STOCKER, FREDERICK D. "Diversification of the Local Revenue System: Income and Sales Taxes, User Charges, Federal Grants," *National Tax Journal,* XXIX (September 1976), pp. 313–22.

29

State Grants
to Local Governments

In 1974–75, 38 percent of state government general expenditures were transfers of money to local units of government. Sixty percent of this intergovernment or "indirect" expenditure was for education, 16 percent was for public welfare, and 6 percent was for highways. Smaller amounts were granted for health and hospitals, police protection, prisons, natural resources, housing, urban renewal, airports, water transportation, and so on. Intergovernment expenditures accounted for 58 percent of all state general expenditure for education, 32 percent of spending for public welfare, and about 18 percent of spending for highways. Clearly, a substantial portion of state activity in these areas is carried out through the mechanism of grants to other governments.

The importance of state grants can also be viewed through the eyes of local governments, which are the recipients of most state intergovernment expenditure. State intergovernment expenditure for education was equal to about 48 percent of total local government expenditure for this function in 1974–75. State intergovernmental spending amounted to 39 percent of total local spending for highways and to 80 percent of local spending for public welfare. In a sense, state and local governments are about equal partners in the financing of education and highways, whereas intergovernment money dominates the local spending scene in public welfare.[1] Transactions of these magnitudes indicate the importance of exploring the economic foundations for grants-in-aid.

[1] U.S. Bureau of the Census, *Governmental Finances in 1974–75*, GF–75, No. 5 (Washington, D.C.: Government Printing Office, 1976), Table 6, p. 20.

CONDITIONAL GRANTS AND EXTERNALITIES

Most state intergovernment spending is conditional, that is, the money must be expended by the recipient governments in a manner specified by the state. Only a small portion of state intergovernment expenditure is dispensed with no strings attached. The economic foundation for conditional grants lies in the observation that services rendered by local governments may generate benefits which spill over and thereby contribute to the well-being of people who are not citizens and taxpayers of the local jurisdiction. Economic analysis, as outlined in Chapter 17, suggests that when interjurisdictional benefit spillovers occur, less than optimal amounts of the service will be produced. External beneficiaries will not be represented in the local demand for the service and local taxpayers will not vote funds to finance the provision of services that do not generate benefits for themselves. Moreover, benefits that spill into the local jurisdiction from services rendered by other jurisdictions do not provide a compensating adjustment, but in fact contribute to a further underprovision of the service, since local taxpayers view these spillins simply as replacing services they otherwise would have to finance themselves.

In Figure 29.1, the horizontal axis records the quantity of a service provided and the vertical axis records the benefits and costs associated with that service. The benefits received by the local citizens are represented by *BB* and the marginal cost of providing the service is *MC*. If only local benefits and costs are represented in the decision-making process, the quantity of the service will be *ON*, as identified by the intersection of *MC* and *BB* at *e*. The benefits realized by outsiders will be ignored in this calculation and too small a quantity of the service will be produced. Aggregate marginal benefit, including both benefits to local residents and benefits to outsiders, is shown as *BCD*. If benefits enjoyed by both residents and outsiders were represented in the output decision, the quantity provided would be *OM*, as identified by the intersection of *MC* and *BCD* at *f*.

A conditional grant-in-aid provides a means for giving the external beneficiaries an effective voice in the local decision about how much of the service to

FIGURE 29.1   Interjurisdictional Spillovers

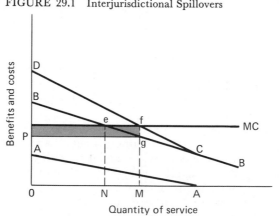

produce. In Figure 29.1, a conditional grant-in-aid equal to the external marginal benefit at the appropriate level of output times the number of units of output (the shaded area) would, in effect, lower the out of pocket price of the service to local taxpayers to OP and lead local decision makers to produce quantity OM of the service, as indicated by the equality between local marginal benefit and local out of pocket price at point g. The condition attached that the grant money be expended for a specified service is the way the outsiders ensure that their interests will be served by the flow of intergovernment transfers.

Tax Exporting

Tax exporting is the reverse of the exporting or spillover of service benefits. When taxes are exported, that is, when the burden of local taxes is shifted to people in other jurisdictions, local tax prices are reduced and the locally chosen service outputs are increased to quantities greater than would have been provided if local taxpayers had been required to bear the entire burden. Tax exporting is similar to the receipt of an unrestricted grant-in-aid and will lead to an excessive output of local services; that is, outside taxpayers are subsidizing local services. When specific revenue sources are tied to specific expenditure programs, the impact of tax exporting can be analyzed on a program by program basis, but when expenditures are financed out of a general fund, tax exporting can result in overproduction of all services financed through the general fund.

Grants-in-Aid as Unit Subsidies

The externalities model suggests that conditional grants are subsidies to the local provision of a service and that the amount of the subsidy should be determined by the amount of external or spillover benefit at the margin of provision of the service. If the external benefit per unit of the service is constant or invariant with the quantity of the service provided by the local jurisdiction (a horizontal AA line in Figure 29.1), the grant should be a fixed amount per unit of the service. But if the external marginal benefit diminishes as the quantity of the service is increased (as illustrated by the downward sloping AA line in Figure 29.1 and the convergence of BC and DC), the amount of the grant per unit of the service also should diminish and become zero if the amount of the service provided locally is so great that external marginal benefit becomes zero. In Figure 29.1, the unit subsidy of fg is approximately equivalent to a 20 percent matching ratio at the level of output of OM. But this 20 percent matching grant system would *not* be correct if a different relationship existed between local and external benefits.

The externalities model suggests that it is extremely difficult to devise an allocationally efficient system of matching grants. If the spillover ratio is a function of the quantity of service provided and if matching grants are set up with variable ratios designed to recognize changes in spillover ratios, it could happen that a local jurisdiction that provided a large quantity of the service would receive a smaller grant, per unit of the service, and perhaps even a smaller total grant, than a jurisdiction that provided a small amount of the service. The point is that the basic unit subsidy nature of the conditional grant should not be forgotten just because these grants may be formulated in terms of matching ratios rather than unit subsidies. If external marginal benefits diminish as quantity increases, variable matching ratios may be appropriate. If such variable ratios are not used, a bias may arise in favor of localities that have a high demand for the service and are wealthy enough to afford a high local budget for the service. For example, suppose the matching grant system were used to subsidize local provision of education services. Some school districts may attach great importance to the education of their children and extend the quantity of education into marginal services from which the spillover benefits may be perceived (by the outsiders) to be minor. A uniform matching ratio system would provide an unwarranted subsidy to these services. The costs of providing education services may also be different in some jurisdictions than in others. Lower marginal cost also could lead to extended provision of service by local decision makers, and a uniform matching ratio again might result in an unwarranted amount of subsidy if external marginal benefit diminishes as output increases.

Open-Ended and Closed Grants

According to the model, intergovernment grants or unit subsidies should continue to be available to the local jurisdiction so long as external benefits are generated at the margin of service output, that is, the grants should be open-ended. The amount of the subsidy may diminish, but it would not be cut off abruptly or fall to zero for output exceeding some predetermined quantity. In practice, however, most conditional grant systems are closed, which means that increases in the amount of local service beyond some specified quantity will not qualify the locality to receive any additional grant funds in spite of the fact that these additional units of service may generate external benefits which would justify a subsidy under the allocationally efficient model. The closed grant system is a departure from the prescription of the pure model of allocational efficiency, but this departure may be defended by at least two lines of argument. First, limiting the subsidy to basic or foundation quantities of the service may prevent some of the unwarranted subsidy consequences that otherwise might result from the use of a uniform matching ratio system. Second, the closed approach can reflect a policy decision by state legislators in allocating scarce funds available for the grant program. That is, given a limited total amount of grant money available, the legislature may simply choose to distribute these funds preferentially so as to give extra incentives or subsidies to localities providing smaller amounts of the service.

CONDITIONAL GRANTS AND LOCAL AUTONOMY

Unit subsidies or matching grants may cause localities to allocate their own money differently. Local spokesmen sometimes complain that the state conditional grant is a bribe which causes local money to be diverted from services highly valued in the locality into services less highly valued. They contend that local autonomy is subverted by the grant system.

Since conditional grants are unit subsidies favoring specified services, they change the local out of pocket price tag on these favored services and can operate to reallocate local funds, depending on the local decision makers' sensitivity to relative prices. In Figure 29.2, the horizontal axis represents quantities of a selected service (X) and the vertical axis represents quantities of alternative services (Y) that might be selected by local decision makers. Budget line AB identifies the combinations available given the local budget and the relative price of the selected service in comparison to other services.[2] The combination of services actually selected depends on the preferences of the decision makers, and given the preferences incorporated in indifference curve I_1, the decision would be to provide quantity ON of the selected service. Budget line AC illustrates the relative prices of services after the unit subsidy or matching grant is made available to encourage increased local output of the favored service. This line is flatter than line AB because the unit subsidy has lowered the relative price of the favored service. With the conditional grant available, the choice will be to produce quantity OM of the service, as identified by the tangency of indifference curve I_2 with budget line AC.

FIGURE 29.2   Conditional Grants-in-Aid

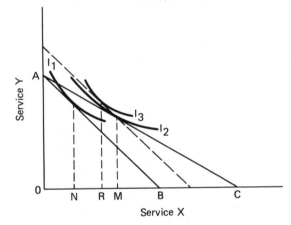

The pattern of indifference curves in Figure 29.2 shows that the local decision makers are very responsive to the change in relative prices instituted by the conditional grant and that their response has indeed channeled additional local money into expenditure for the favored service. Suppose that the budget line AB in Figure 29.2 represents a unit price of $1 for the favored service X, $1 for the alternative service Y, and a total budget of $120, so that OA and OB represent 120 units of each of the alternative services. Let ON be equal to 30 units of service X so that, without the grant, $30 would be expended on service X and $90 would be expended on service Y. The new budget line AC incorporates a grant of 40 cents per unit of service X so that the local out of pocket price of service X becomes 60 cents, while the local out of pocket price of service Y remains at $1. In this new relative price situation, the decision is to purchase 75 units (OM) of service X for a total local expenditure of $45. The

[2] See Chapter 13 for a discussion of budget lines and indifference curves.

"bribe" of the grant has caused local decision makers to purchase 75 units of service X at a local out of pocket price of 60 cents each. Thus, $15 of local money has been diverted from other purchases.

Income and Substitution Effects

The change in the quantity purchased reflects both the substitution effect of the change in relative price and also the income effect of the reduction in the price of the favored commodity. The income effect of a conditional grant can alter local expenditure patterns, since a locality with more money to spend may buy different things than it would if it had less money to spend, but this type of "distortion" should hardly raise serious local objections. In Figure 29.2, the locality is purchasing 75 units of the service and is receiving a unit subsidy of 40 cents per unit, which amounts to $30 of additional funds. Had this additional $30 been received as an unconditional grant, a new budget line would have existed, parallel to line *AB* but representing a total budget of $150 (illustrated by the dashed budget line in Figure 29.2). The dashed budget line, which includes the unconditional grant of $30, would permit the locality to reach an indifference curve such as I_3. With this solution, the choice would be for an amount of service X (*OR*) that is more than was originally chosen (*ON*), but less than the amount which would have been chosen (*OM*) if the grant had been specifically tied to service X. Thus, the distortion effect of the conditional nature of the grant is the difference between *OR* and *OM*, that is, it is the amount *RM*.

Price Elasticity of Local Demand

The outcome shown in Figure 29.2 depended on the location of the indifference curves that influence the local decision makers, or in an alternative presentation, on the price elasticity of local demand for the service favored by a conditional grant-in-aid. A conventional demand curve formulation is illustrated in Figure 29.3 and shows, on demand curve D_1, that a reduction in the

FIGURE 29.3   Price Elasticity of Demand

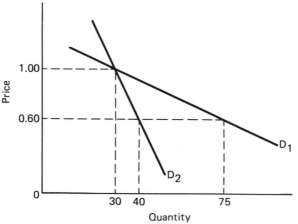

local price of the service from $1 per unit to 60 cents per unit has increased the quantity demanded from 30 units to 75 units and has increased local expenditure from $30 to $45. It is apparent that, over this range of price, local demand for the service is price elastic. Had the local demand been less price responsive, as illustrated by demand D_2, the outcome and the distortion situation would have been quite different. With the inelastic demand curve, D_2, the reduction in the price of the service would lead to an increase in the quantity demanded from 30 units to 40 units and local fund expenditure would fall from $30 to $24, so that the conditional grant program would actually lead to a diversion of local money away from the aided service and into other locally demanded programs, which could include tax reduction.

Stimulation Effects and Local Autonomy

The conditional grant-in-aid mechanism alters the relative price signals that influence local decision makers, but it leaves local autonomy otherwise intact. The stimulation effect of unit subsidies will be great for localities with demands for the service that are price elastic, but small for those localities with demand that is price inelastic. Local autonomy remains a significant force modified only by the obligation to recognize the interests (backed with money) of external beneficiaries of the service.

The role of local autonomy indicates that a state which utilizes unit subsidy grants based solely on external marginal benefit considerations cannot expect to elicit uniform responses from different localities, nor can it expect to achieve a uniform statewide level of service output by this method. In practice, states do not rely solely on unit subsidy conditional grants to influence quantities of services provided. Since states are sovereign and localities are not, states can set mandatory service requirements and directly supersede local autonomy. From this point of view, conditional grants are relatively moderate instruments that do not supersede local autonomy, but instead work through local autonomy to achieve the objectives of the state legislature.

UNCONDITIONAL GRANTS AND FISCAL DISPARITIES

Unconditional grants provide funds that have no strings attached. That is, the recipient government may expend the grant funds in any way it chooses, including tax reduction if the choice is to maintain existing services and use the grant money to replace local taxes that had previously been required.

Tax Prices and Horizontal Nonneutrality

The case for unconditional grants rests on the finding that fiscal disparities among local jurisdictions result in the tax price of a given collective service being greater in some jurisdictions than in others and on the policy conclusion that this type of discrimination is undesirable. Suppose that the resource cost of a standard quality of education per pupil per year is $1,000 and is the same in all localities in the state. A community with a property tax base of $50,000 per pupil could finance the standard education program at a 20 mil

(2 percent) tax rate or tax price, whereas a less affluent community with a tax base of only $25,000 per pupil would have to pay a tax price or rate of 40 mils (4 percent) in order to purchase the same service for each of its pupils. The tax price difference reflects the fact that a given expenditure requires a higher rate of tax in the less affluent community than it does in the more affluent community.

The concept of a tax price involves a careful examination of what is meant by the price of public services. The meaning of the term can be clarified by an illustration. Consider two families, each with equal wealth, with family A residing in the more affluent community and family B residing in the less affluent community. If each family has taxable property valued at $20,000. Family A will pay $400 in taxes for education and family B will pay $800 in taxes for education if the amount of education provided per pupil is the same in each community. Thus, the price per unit of education is twice as great for family B as for family A.

The consequences of this price discrimination are apparent. The community that enjoys the lower tax price will probably purchase a greater amount of education (and other public services), other things equal, than the community that faces the higher tax price. In many situations, families in less affluent communities pay more for education and receive less than do equivalent families in more affluent communities. One of the public policy questions raised by this situation is whether the wealth or poverty of one's community is an acceptable basis for the violation of accepted notions of horizontal neutrality in the pricing of public services. Another consequence is the incentive these horizontal nonneutralities introduce for migration among communities.

Tax Price Differences and Migration

Tax price differences provide incentives for families to select a community offering the services they desire at the lowest tax price. Residents of nonaffluent communities have an incentive to move to more affluent communities where tax prices are lower. This is similar to the type of migration contemplated in the pure theory of local expenditures outlined in Chapter 17, although the pure theory suggests that these movements result from differences in preferences and in real costs of providing services, rather than from differences which arise from the institutions of public finance and unequal distributions of income. If there were no barriers to migration, those communities enjoying tax price advantages would increase in population through migration from less affluent communities. If the new residents were less affluent than the original residents, this migration could dissipate the tax price advantage and result in an equilibrium in which no tax price differentials remained. As a practical matter, however, barriers to mobility that prevent this solution to the fiscal disparities problem exist or are contrived. Low income itself is a barrier to migration, since low income constrains the ability of a family to search for the best community and limits the ability of the family to finance the cost of the move even if the best community is discovered. Contrived barriers arise when zoning ordinances, building codes, and other devices are used to discourage the entry of less affluent families. Thus, it is unlikely that migration can wipe out tax price differences arising because of fiscal disparities among communities.

Power Equalizer Grants

Power equalizer grants eliminate tax price differences that would otherwise exist between affluent and less affluent communities; that is, they result in a situation in which a given rate of taxation yields the same amount of revenue per capita in each jurisdiction regardless of the size of the tax base in the jurisdiction. In a sense, the state itself becomes a taxpayer in each local jurisdiction. The base for computing the state's "tax liability" (the power equalizing grant) is the deficiency of the locality's own tax base below that established as the standard throughout the state. For example, suppose that the state legislature has determined that the standard base for local finance shall be $50,000 of taxable property per capita. If community A actually does possess a tax base of $50,000 per capita, no power equalizing grant will be received from the state, and the community can impose whatever tax rate it chooses and expend the revenue derived from its tax. If it imposed a 30 mil (3 percent) tax rate, it would collect $1,500 per capita. If community B has a tax base of only $25,000 per capita, a 30 mil tax rate would generate $750 per capita from local taxpayers, but a power equalizing grant would be received in the amount of an additional $750 per capita, which is determined by multiplying the tax base "deficiency" ($25,000) by the local tax rate of 30 mils.

The advantages of the power equalizing grant are these: (1) Local taxpayers are put on an even footing throughout the state in terms of the amount of public revenue that can be generated from each mil or percent tax rate they choose to impose on themselves. (2) Each local jurisdiction is free to set its own tax rate according to its own willingness to tax itself. (3) The expenditure of funds is not restricted by any conditions attached to the grant. A community that chose to tax itself heavily for local services would receive a larger grant than a community that chose to impose a low tax rate on its own citizens. Migration incentives based on different tax prices for public services would be eliminated and the size of local budgets would reflect local willingness to pay for services and local real resource costs of providing them.

Equalizing Up and Equalizing Down

If the standard tax base were set equal to that prevailing in the most affluent community in the state, the fiscal power of all other jurisdictions would be "equalized up" to this level and substantial amounts of state revenue would be required to finance the power equalizer grant system. The more affluent communities would be reluctant to support the program, since their citizens would, along with others, pay the general state taxes needed to finance the grants but would receive no power equalizing grant under the pure form of the program. A lesser financial strain on state revenues would be required if the standard base were set at some lower level, but even greater difficulties would then arise in determining the treatment to be accorded those localities whose tax bases exceeded the standard. Under this "equalizing down" procedure, revenues per mil in excess of the standard amount would have to be given up by the affluent communities and paid into the grant-in-aid fund for disbursement to the less affluent communities.

It is apparent that setting the standard base for a power equalizing system of unconditional grants imposes severe political strains on the legislature, with equalizing up being financially out of reach and equalizing down politically unattainable. A partial or compromise solution might take the form of guaranteed minimum revenue per mil of local tax rate. That is, the state would become a taxpayer in less affluent localities, and more affluent communities would receive no unconditional grant, but would not be required to relinquish any of their own tax collections. This compromise would not fully equalize taxing power and would not fully eliminate horizontal nonneutralities.

GRANTS-IN-AID FOR EDUCATION

A substantial portion of the money expended by local school districts comes through grants from state governments, and the manner in which these grants are determined and distributed has become one of the most controversial issues in modern government finance. Controversy exists about the nature of government's responsibility in education finance and also about the level of government that can carry out this responsibility.

Most existing grant-in-aid programs for education are based on the view that government's responsibility is limited to ensuring that all persons in the jurisdiction are provided with a basic "foundation" education program. According to this view, the foundation education program should provide each person with enough education service so that he or she will be able to function adequately in society. Responsibility is lodged with the state governments and, except in Hawaii, state departments of education undertake to carry out their responsibilities through a system of local school districts. The local districts retain discretion over certain portions of the program but are obligated to provide the foundation portion as specified by the state. Grants-in-aid are dispensed to the local districts through complicated formulas based primarily on the number of pupils enrolled in the district and which incorporate adjustments in the basic per pupil grant designed to reflect both the size of the tax base or fiscal capacity of the local district and the local tax rate imposed for education. Further complications arise by attempts to introduce need factors for districts that face unusual educational problems and incentive factors to encourage improvements in the education program. Some equalization of education spending per pupil is accomplished through these programs (although large disparities remain), but there is disagreement about whether foundation programs actually provide services adequate to equip people to function effectively in modern society.

From the point of view of the economics of a federal system, a rationale for the prevailing foundation program system of grants-in-aid arises from an analysis of the spillovers that occur from the locality providing education service. If the quality or quantity of education service provided in a locality is lower than that provided in other jurisdictions, these other jurisdictions will suffer negative spillover effects when persons educated in the low quality-quantity district migrate to other communities and lower the average education level of their populations. On the other hand, positive spillovers arise when those educated in high quality-quantity districts migrate into communities with lower education levels. The foundation program philosophy for grants-in-aid provides only a partial correction for these spillover effects. By establishing a minimum quality-quantity level for education, the approach provides a correction for the most serious negative spillover situations, but it accomplishes little equalization or correction for spillovers in respect to quality-quantity levels above the minimum standard.

In 1971, courts in California (*Serrano* v. *Priest*), in Taxes (*Rodriguez* v. *San Antonio Independent School District*), and in other states found that public school financing systems violated the Fourteenth Amendment to the U.S. Constitution because these systems permitted the quality of education received by a person to be a function of the wealth of the school district in which that person lived. In other words, discrimination in education service among students was found to exist as a result of fiscal disparities and different tax prices for education among school districts. Discrimination based on these factors was found to be unconstitutional because it denied students equal protection under the laws. These court rulings found that state foundation grant systems did not provide sufficient correction for the inequalities arising from fiscal disparities and implied that government is legally responsible to do more than provide a partial correction for spillover effects or guarantee only a minimum standard level of education service for each student. In 1973, the United States Supreme Court, holding that education was not among the rights guaranteed by the Fourteenth Amendment, reversed the Texas court's ruling in the Rodriguez case and nullified the legal force of actions based on the Fourteenth Amendment to the U.S. Constitution. However, legal actions based on state constitutions may still lead to court rulings that will require major restructuring of state education financing systems.

If a state undertakes a major restructuring of its system of education finance, the role that can be played by grants-in-aid from the state government to local school districts will depend on the goals or objectives adopted to guide the restructuring. If the goal is simply to eliminate the discrimination that arises from unequal tax prices caused by unequal fiscal capacities among local districts, the power equalizing system of grants-in-aid could be used so that a given tax rate would result in the same amount of spending power per pupil in every local school district. This approach would eliminate tax price differences among school districts but would leave each district free to decide for itself the actual tax rate to impose (although some minimum level of education expenditure per pupil might still be required by state law). Of course, the power equalizing system would not lead to an equal amount of education expenditure per pupil throughout the state if some districts chose to tax themselves more heavily for education than other districts. In fact, it is reasonable to expect that relatively affluent school districts would be able to afford a higher tax rate than less affluent districts, so that actual education expenditure per pupil would continue to be a function of the wealth of the district in which the pupil lived.

A policy goal or legal requirement to provide equal education expenditure for all students throughout the state probably would require the centralization of education responsibility at the state government level. If property taxation were used to finance education, statewide uniform tax rates would probably be required, and if local district organization were continued, these districts probably would be funded by disbursements from the state department of education. Enormous changes would take place in the allocation of responsibilities between state and local governments and in the institutions of state and local government finance. Although the Supreme Court reversal of the Rodriguez ruling has shifted the legal focus to the level of individual states and has decreased the pressure for major restructuring of education finance systems, the basic issues have not been resolved. Education finance is an area in which major change can be expected.

SUMMARY

Through the system of grants-in-aid, state and local governments are joined in a kind of partnership for the financing of certain collective services. State governments are sovereign, however, and local governments are not, so that the terms of the partnership arrangement are established by the state. A large portion of state government expenditure is carried out indirectly through grants to local governments, and a substantial portion of local expenditure is financed with grants from the state.

Two types of grant relationships have been identified. Conditional grants require the recipient government to expend the grant funds according to specifications determined by the state government. The economic foundation for conditional grants arises because locally provided services that generate benefits which spill over to residents of other jurisdictions will be underproduced if local communities are required to finance these services entirely through their own tax collections. In effect, the conditional grant-in-aid is a device through which the external beneficiaries can have a voice in determining the quantity of such services. The grant is a subsidy for the provision of the selected service and the amount of the subsidy should, according to the model, be equal to amount of external benefit at the margin of production.

From the viewpoint of recipient local governments, conditional grants lower the out of pocket tax price of the service favored by the grant. The local response to the grant depends on the sensitivity of local decision makers to these reductions in tax price. Thus, conditional grants do not eliminate local autonomy in expenditure decisions, although they do alter the circumstances influencing these decisions. If the local demand for the service is price elastic, grants will be effective in stimulating increased output of the service and some local revenue may be diverted to the favored service from other uses. If local demand is price inelastic, grants will have relatively little stimulation effect and localities may actually reduce the amount of their own money devoted to the favored service.

The second type of grant is the unconditional grant, which may be expended in any way chosen by the recipient government. The economic case for unconditional grants arises from tax price differences and consequent horizontal nonneutralities resulting from unequal per capita tax bases among communities. Power equalizing unconditional grants can correct tax price differences, but difficulties arise in establishing a power equalizing system when fiscal disparities are great.

Grants-in-aid play a major role in the existing system of financing for public education, but recent legal proceedings have suggested that the existing system, relying upon local property taxation and state foundation grant-in-aid programs, may be unconstitutional because the local property tax operates to make the amount of education received by a person a function of the wealth of the district in which he lives. Although the Supreme Court, in reversing the Rodriguez case, held that education was not among the rights guaranteed by the Fourteenth Amendment, major restructuring of education finance may come about through court rulings based on state constitutions or through legislative action prescribing new objectives and procedures. Power equalizing grants could eliminate tax price differences among local school districts, but these grants would not necessarily result in equal expenditure per pupil in all districts. A policy objective of ensuring equal per pupil education expenditure throughout the state would probably require uniform statewide rates for property taxes used for education finance and elimination or major restructuring of the grant-in-aid system for school districts.

SUGGESTED READINGS

THUROW, LESTER C. "The Theory of Grants in Aid, *National Tax Journal*, XIX, 4 (December 1966), pp. 373–77.

SMITH, DAVID L. "The Response of State and Local Governments to Federal Grants," *National Tax Journal*, XXI, 3 (September 1968), pp. 349–57.

WEICHER, JOHN C. "Aid, Expenditures, and Local Government Structure," *National Tax Journal*, XXV, 4 (December 1972), pp. 573–84.

REISCHAUER, ROBERT D. and ROBERT W. HARTMAN. *Reforming School Finance* (Washington, D.C.: The Brookings Institution, 1973).

BOWMAN, JOHN H. "Tax Exportability, Intergovernmental Aid, and School Finance Reform," *National Tax Journal*, XXVII, 2 (June 1974), pp. 163–74.

FELDSTEIN, MARTIN S. "Wealth Neutrality and Local Choice in Public Education," *American Economic Review*, 65, 1 (March 1975), pp. 75–89.

LADD, HELEN F. "State-Wide Taxation of Commercial and Industrial Property for Education," *National Tax Journal*, XXIX, 2 (June 1976), pp. 143–54.

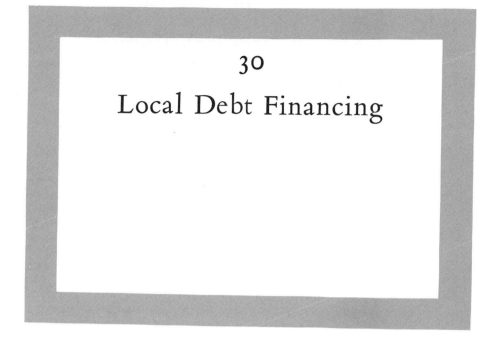

30

Local Debt Financing

Properly speaking, debt financing should not be called a revenue source for local governments. When a local government sells a bond, it is simply borrowing money in exchange for an obligation that the money will be repaid to the lender at some future time and that the lender will be compensated by the payment of interest throughout the period of the loan. In conventional local borrowing, the loan is secured by the taxing power of the local government, so that taxation is the actual revenue source.

An important distinction should be recognized between borrowing by local or state government and borrowing by the national government. The national government has the power to create money, and bond sales by the national government may be the mechanism through which newly created money is made available for federal expenditures. A bond initiated by the U.S. Treasury may be sold to the Federal Reserve System in exchange for a credit entry in the checking account of the Treasury. Thus, new money becomes a source of revenue for federal government expenditures and the bond is simply an instrument in the creation of money. Local and state governments, however, do not possess the power to create money. Bond financing by these governments is a genuine borrower-lender transaction and involves no net revenue gain to the borrowing government. Lenders make already existing purchasing power available to the local government and will be willing to do so only when the terms of the loan (the interest receivable and the assurance of timely repayment of principal) appear advantageous in relation to alternative uses that might be made of funds. Local borrowing faces a market test that subjects it to constraints quite different from those confronting the national government.

THE ROLE OF LOCAL DEBT FINANCE

Local governments ordinarily issue debt (sell bonds) for the purpose of financing the construction of capital facilities expected to have rather long useful lives, such as public buildings, schools, streets, sewer lines, waste treatment facilities, and so on. Bond financing permits the taxes needed to pay for these facilities to be spread over the useful life of the facility. The fairness of this procedure is clear. Taxpayers who currently reside in the city should not be compelled to pay the whole cost of a facility that will be utilized by people who move into the city at some later time during the useful life of the facility. People who move into a city after the facility is constructed should expect to pay their share of the costs of the services from which they obtain benefits. Bond financing permits a pay as you use procedure, which is accepted as more equitable than a pay as you build procedure that would impose all the costs on those residing in the city at the time of construction.

There is a counterargument to the proposition that debt financing is necessary in order to spread the financing responsibility of capital projects equitably over different "generations" of local taxpayers. This argument notes that people moving into a community consider present and anticipated levels of taxation when deciding on the amount they are willing to pay to acquire property there. If there is outstanding bonded indebtedness that will raise the level of taxation required in future years, they will be willing to pay less to purchase property than they would if local capital facilities are paid for and no indebtedness exists. Therefore, the argument is that even a pay as you build approach to capital financing (that is, tax finance rather than debt finance) would not be damaging to current residents who subsequently move out of the community, since they would recover their municipal investment through the higher price they would receive when they sold their local property. The force of this counterargument hinges on the degree of perfection that exists in the property market and particularly on the extent to which prospective buyers inform themselves about anticipated levels of taxation. If present residents doubt that the property market will operate so as to enable them to recover their investments in pay as you build financing, the bond finance route is likely to be chosen.

As a practical matter, there are other reasons for the popularity of pay as you use over pay as you build. In small communities, capital construction activity will not proceed at uniform rates through time. The fluctuating tax bills that this would produce under a pay as you build approach would be inconvenient for taxpayers. Also, the tax exemption of interest paid on local bonds permits the government to borrow at lower rates of interest than individuals who might have to borrow to meet especially high annual tax bills.

Serial Bonds and Sinking Funds

Bond financing imposes two types of payment obligations on the borrowing unit: the interest payment (or rental charge) for the use of the borrowed funds and the repayment of the principal sum itself. Equity requires that each of these payment obligations should be distributed fairly over the useful life of the facility financed by the borrowing. One method of accomplishing this objective is through the use of a *sinking fund*. Under this arrangement, taxes collected annually are levied at a rate sufficient to pay annually accruing interest charges plus an additional amount to be placed into the sinking fund to be used to repay the principal amount of the loan when the bonds mature. The sinking fund grows through the annual tax payments and through interest earnings from investment of the fund. If tax payments and interest earnings have been accurately predicted, the sinking fund provides the means of repaying the principal when the bond matures.

The sinking fund approach has frequently proved unfortunate for local governments. Fund management is a highly technical specialty, and local officials sometimes fail to place the money in secure investments or to earn satisfactory interest on the money. Moreover, a relatively large sinking fund is an ever-present temptation to "raiding" by transferring the funds to other uses in the local government. Consequently, the *serial bond* approach to loan repayment has largely replaced the sinking fund method. Under this approach, the public facility is financed by bonds with differing maturity dates, with the maturities distributed over the life of the facility in such a way that the amount outstanding roughly keeps pace with the depreciating value of the facility itself. No sinking fund is required and the amount of indebtedness (along with interest charges) diminishes with the passage of time. The diminishing interest charge compensates for the interest that might have been earned on a sinking fund and automatically avoids the management problems associated with sinking funds.

Revolving Funds

When financing is spread over a twenty- or thirty-year period, aggregate interest payments constitute a substantial part of the cost of the project. It is sometimes suggested that local governments might save money through the establishment of a revolving capital improvements fund that could be used instead of debt finance. The critical step in this procedure is the establishment of the fund itself. In order to get the system started, taxpayers must contribute something more than would be required under a bond finance system. Once established, the revolving fund is maintained by current tax payments, which match current disbursements from the fund so that borrowing and the payment of interest are not needed. The flaw in the case is that the funds paid to start the system would have generated income to the taxpayers had they not been paid to the government to set up the revolving fund. These foregone private earnings are the real cost of the revolving fund system, and it is not at all clear that these costs would be any less than the interest costs involved in conventional borrowing. In fact, the exemption from federal income tax of the interest on state and local bonds supports the view that bond financing will actually impose lower real costs on the local citizens than the revolving fund.

Revenue Bonds

In conventional bond financing, the payment of interest and the repayment of principal is secured (or guaranteed) by the "full faith and credit" of the borrowing government. This means that the full taxing powers of the local government are committed to meeting these payments when they fall due. Revenue bonds, on the other hand, do not carry the full faith and credit commitment of the issuing government and are sometimes referred to as "nonguaranteed" debt instruments. Revenue bonds are secured by a claim on the revenues to be collected through fees, rents, or charges imposed on the users of the facility financed through the sale of the bonds. Since these fees, rents, and charges are less reliable or certain than the general taxing powers of government, buyers of revenue bonds assume a greater risk than do buyers of "full faith and credit" bonds. The interest rate charged on revenue bonds consequently is higher.

The basic case for financing through revenue bonds is the same as that outlined for conventional bond financing. When individual beneficiaries of a project can be identified and when these beneficiaries can be charged a fee for their use of the facility, there is no reason why the general body of taxpayers should be obligated in the financial transaction. The issuance of revenue bonds to finance the construction of toll roads and bridges illustrates a use of this device that is generally accepted as both proper and feasible.

Because revenue bonds do not pledge the full faith and credit of government for the payment of interest and principal, these bonds have been held to be exempted from debt limitations imposed on states and localities through constitutional provisions or legislative enactments. This opens the way for a utilization of revenue bond financing as a device for the circumvention of debt limits. For example, if a state or locality is prevented from incurring debt by some legal limitation, a quasi-public corporation may be set up with the authority to issue revenue bonds, to construct public buildings (such as schools), and to lease them to the government or school district under rental terms that effectively commit the government to payments sufficient to pay the interest and principal on the bonds. The obligation of the government or school district is not much different than would have been the case under full faith and credit financing, but the debt limit has been circumvented at the expense of higher interest charges on the revenue bonds.

Even more heated controversy has arisen when quasi-governmental corporations have used revenue bonds to finance construction of commercial or industrial facilities which are then leased to private business firms under terms designed to attract these enterprises to the local community. The interest costs on these industrial development bonds may be significantly lower than the firm could have obtained on the private money markets, both because the bonds are those of a semi-public agency and because the interest on these bonds may be exempted from federal taxation as instruments of state or local governments. In effect, the benefits of tax exemption and public borrowing power are passed on to the private firm as an inducement for the firm to locate in the community making the best offer, and the tax exemption costs are borne by the federal government. The use of the tax exemption privilege as an inducement to industrial location is criticized on two counts. First, firms that take advantage of the opportunity may locate in places other than those which are most efficient in terms of general resource allocation considerations. Second, the tax exemption privilege is conceived as a subsidy from the federal government to aid state and local governments in the financing of public projects. It sometimes is questioned whether the securing of industry by the locality is the type of public project contemplated by Congress. As of 1969, limits were placed on the size of industrial projects for which industrial aid bond financing could qualify for federal tax exemption, but these limits do not prevent the effective use of this device for many firms and localities.

The difficulty with the use of revenue bonds to finance facilities leased to private businesses is the tenuous or uncertain nature of the collective benefits that may be provided by the facility. If rather clear-cut collective benefits are generated, there need be no objection to the use of public borrowing power and income tax exemption of interest to promote the construction of these facilities. For example, revenue bonds could be sold to finance the construction of pollution control facilities that could be leased to private firms at rental charges sufficient to pay the interest and amortize the principal on these bonds. Since the reduction of pollution is an accepted objective of public policy and conveys collective benefits, the subsidy provided by revenue bond financing and federal income tax exemption of interest paid can be quite acceptable and effective. Revenue bond financing of pollution control facilities is, of course, a subsidy for the construction of these facilities. Other approaches to pollution control, such as pollution taxes, can still be used. The combination of pollution taxes plus the availability of revenue bond financing for the construction of pollution control facilities can be an effective package, since the pollution tax will mount a powerful stimulus for businesses to interest themselves in pollution-reducing investments and the revenue bond system will provide the local government with an opportunity to introduce local collective concerns into the investment decision. The net private costs of pollution reduction would still be borne by the consumers of the products involved, as is consistent with the view that rights to an unpolluted environment reside with the public in general.

DEBT LIMITS

Prohibitions on debt financing or limitations on the amount of debt that may be undertaken are of long standing both for states and local governments in the United States. The basic reason for the existence of these limitations is that both states and local governments can and have defaulted on their debt obligations. When this happens, the credit ratings of other government units are likely to suffer in a kind of spillover reaction to the unfortunate experience of the defaulting units. Overextension in debt creation may arise from a spirit of boosterism, which in its enthusiasm for community growth overestimates the capability of the locality to meet future commitments. It also is argued that a type of irresponsibility may affect certain groups of local citizens, either because they feel themselves not to be taxpayers under the conventional property tax or because they anticipate that they may move out of the community and away from the repayment responsibility at some future time. Each of these attitudes may be somewhat unrealistic, since tenants pay property taxes as part of their rent and since high indebtedness may be capitalized into property values, depressing the amount that a person might realize on the sale of his property when he leaves the community. Whatever the reason, the notion that localities must be restrained in their borrowing by something more than normal market forces is widely held and firmly embedded in state constitutions and legislative enactments.

Most local government debt limitations are related to the valuation of the taxable property in the jurisdiction and have the further constraint that borrowings beyond a modest amount must be approved by voters in a referendum. But experience has demonstrated that these debt limits frequently can be circumvented if the desire for a project is sufficiently strong. Revenue bond financing has already been noted as one means of circumventing the limitations on conventional debt.

Another means lies in the creation of special districts that can incur debt which is not counted in the debt of the conventional governments overlapping the special district. When government units, each with a separate debt limit, overlap one another, citizens residing in the area of overlap can find themselves in a position of having debt obligations greatly in excess of those contemplated in the debt limitation statutes.

A generally acceptable solution to the problem of local debt limitation has not been discovered. The existing situation, in which rather specific limitations are imposed and yet are circumvented, is not a happy one. Contrivances designed to circumvent limits tend to confuse or obscure the true indebtedness and financial soundness of local governments and invite mistakes and errors in judgment. On the other hand, specifically defined and rigorously enforced limits on indebtedness probably would not be capable of incorporating all the variables that are important in the debt finance decision. New or growing communities may have greater need and justification for debt finance than others. Likewise, some projects offer much more promising assurances of repayment than do others.

The diminishing reliance of local governments on property taxation adds still another dimension to the confusion of considerations relating to local debt limits. Income or sales taxation may add to the financial capability of governments to carry indebtedness. At the same time, since these taxes bring revenues that fluctuate more than do property tax revenues, the need for debt finance may be increased. Moreover, both income and sales taxes may be capitalized into property values in the community, so that debt limits based on property valuations alone can misrepresent the ability to service debt.

If it is concluded that debt limits tied to property values are inappropriate, alternative types of debt limitations might be provided. For example, since the ability to service and repay debt obligations is related to the amount of money the locality collects from a variety of tax sources, constraints on debt finance might be formulated as some maximum fraction of average annual local tax collections that could be applied to debt servicing. Another approach to debt limitation recognizes the usefulness of the analyses made by private lenders in evaluating the productivity of projects and in determining the credit rating of the borrowing unit. In this approach, borrowing constraint might take the form of prohibiting bond issues that require interest rates which exceed some multiple of the prime rate of interest in the general money market.

INCOME TAX EXEMPTION OF LOCAL BOND INTEREST

The interest received from state and local bonds is exempt from the federal income tax. Since marginal rates of tax under this income tax rise to substantial levels, this exemption is of great importance to people in higher tax rate brackets. For example, a taxpayer in the 50 percent marginal rate bracket will find that the take-home yield on a state or local bond with an interest rate of 4 percent equivalent to the take-home yield on a taxable corporate bond paying interest at an 8 percent rate. The exemption permits state and local governments to borrow at considerably lower costs than would be the case if the bonds were taxable and makes these securities especially attractive to high-income investors. A strong alliance of self-interest is established between state and local governments and high-income investors.

The history of the exemption of state and local bond interest from federal income taxation was outlined in Chapter 11. Originally, the exemption arose as part of the immunities doctrine, which held that the states, as sovereign governments, could not be taxed by another government, such as the federal government. The power to tax, it was said, was the power to destroy and thus contrary to the notion of sovereignty. Bonds, as instrumentalities of state governments, were exempt from federal taxation, as were the salaries of the officials and employees of these governments. The immunities doctrine held sway for a considerable period of time, but it no longer provides the basis for the exemption of interest on state and local bonds. When the salaries of state and local employees and officials were made subject to the federal income tax, the decision made it clear that a general tax, such as the federal income tax, could tax state or local instrumentalities in the same way it taxed equivalent private instruments without violating the sovereignty of these governments. Since this decision, the continuation of the exemption for the interest on state and local bonds has been at the discretion of congress and the exemption has been allowed to continue as a means through which the federal government can assist state and local governments.

The tax exemption feature of state and local bonds is of substantial help to capital financing for these governments, and is jealously guarded by them. However, there is no question but that the exemption gives rise to undesirable by-products. A listing of these undesirable aspects constitutes a powerful criticism of this method of aiding state and local governments. The tax exemption creates what can be termed a "class price" for these securities, since the value of the exemption is greater for persons in high income-tax brackets than it is for persons in lower income-tax brackets. In effect, the tax exemption means that moderate and low income persons will not be owners of state and local securities. By the same token, the exemption erodes the progressivity of the federal income tax, since most tax-exempt interest is received by high-bracket taxpayers or by taxpayers who would be in high brackets were it not for this means of tax avoidance. Moreover, the exemption is an inefficient method of aiding state and local governments, since the amount of aid actually received by these governments is less than the tax loss to the federal treasury, the difference being captured by high-bracket owners of these securities.

From the point of view of economic efficiency, a particularly strong objection to the exemption of state and local bond interest arises from the realization that the subsidy is directed primarily to capital projects undertaken rather than to current service expenditures. Local governments must allocate their resources between current service activities and long-term capital undertakings, and the subsidy to bond interest introduces a bias in favor of the long-term projects. Since it is not apparent that long-term undertakings are more important than current services or that the subsidy corrects for a bias that otherwise would operate against long-term projects, it is reasonable to suggest that the interest exemption may be inefficient because it distorts local decisions.

Proposals have been made that the tax exemption might be replaced with some more direct type of subsidy to state and local governments. For example, assuming that the favoritism to capital financing is continued, state and local bonds might be made subject to federal income tax, and the federal government might reimburse the locality for some portion of the interest costs of these bond issues. Another proposal suggests that the federal government might establish a lending agency which would purchase state and local bond issues. However, proposals for change have not fared well in Congress. State and local governments actively oppose major changes in the system, perhaps in the fear that the alternatives would be less secure than the existing arrangement and that they perhaps might be more subject to federal government interference. Nor is the federal government especially interested in making any major change. The federal concern would be primarily the reform of the income tax that would be accomplished by the removal of the interest exclusion. But the interest exclusion could not be eliminated for bonds which are already outstanding, so that the immediate consequence of the reform would be increased complexity of the income tax return, since distinctions would have to be made between bonds issued before the exclusion was removed and bonds issued after that date.

SUMMARY

Local debt financing must be distinguished from federal debt financing because federal debt may be simply a device for money creation, which is an operation not available to state and local governments. Local debt finance is genuine borrowing. Local bonds can be sold only on terms that are acceptable to lenders; that is, local bonds must compete with other securities in the general money markets.

Bond sales provide a perfectly legitimate means of financing the construction of capital facilities that will provide a stream of benefits extending into future time periods and benefiting future generations of taxpayers. Debt finance permits the future taxpayers to pay for the services they enjoy and thus is a useful device in ensuring intergeneration equity in a benefit-received framework for public finance. Serial bonds, with maturities timed to match depreciation of the value of the facility financed, typically are used in local government debt financing. Serial bonds are preferable to sinking funds, which increase the financial management tasks of local officials, and also are preferred to revolving fund systems, which impose a special burden on the generation of taxpayers required to initiate the fund. Revenue bonds pledge the revenues from a specific facility as the basis for the payment of interest and the amortization of principal, whereas general obligation bonds pledge the taxing power of the issuing government.

State governments typically impose limits on the amount of indebtedness that can be incurred by their local governments. These limits are defended as appropriate because localities (and some states) have defaulted on their debt obligations. But debt limits are also the source of some difficulties in local finance. Debt limits may be circumvented through assessment ratio changes or by establishing special districts or agencies with the authority to incur debt. Property valuations typically provide the basis for determining debt limitations, but alternative calculations merit consideration.

Interest received from state and local bonds is exempted from federal income taxation as a means of providing a subsidy to local and state government finance. This method of subsidy erodes the progressivity of the federal income tax, is an inefficient way to subsidize local government, and may lead to inefficient decisions by local governments. Although alternative subsidizing procedures are available, local governments usually oppose abandonment of the existing system.

SUGGESTED READINGS

U.S. House of Representatives, Committee on Ways and Means. *General Tax Reform*—Panel Discussion before the Committee on Ways and Means, House of Representatives 93rd Congress, 1st Session, Part 8, "An Alternative to Tax Exempt State and Local Bonds," February 23, 1973.

GALPIN, HARVEY, and GEORGE E. PETERSON. "The Equity Effects of a Taxable Municipal Bond Subsidy," *National Tax Journal*, XXVI, 4 (December 1973), pp. 611–24.

MORRIS, FRANK E. "The Taxable Bond Option," *National Tax Journal*, XXIX, 3 (September 1976), pp. 356–59.

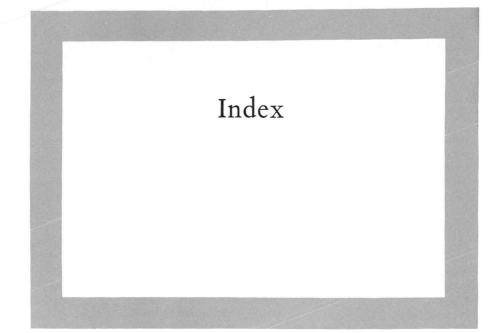

Index